THE MORE, THE BETTER!
독해 실력은 투자한 시간과 노력에 비례한다!

Reading comprehension

편입빈출유형 핵심지문 300

해독제
Vol.2

김영편입
컨텐츠평가연구소
편저

편입영어 기출문제 최신 출제 경향 완벽 반영
실전에 가장 가까운 예상문제들로 구성
단문부터 중·장문까지 다양한 독해지문 수록
수준에 맞는 단계별 독해 학습 가능

문제편

다양한 길이
**난이도별
독해지문!**

기출문제 토대
**실전대비
예상문제!**

다양한 배경지식
**분야별
독해지문!**

김영편입 컨텐츠평가연구소

김영편입 컨텐츠평가연구소는 편입 시험의 다양한 문제 유형과 난이도를 분석하여 수험생에게 올바른 학습 방향을 제시해 줄 목적으로 설립된 메가스터디의 부설 기관입니다. 수십 년간 시행되어 온 대학별 편입 시험을 심층 분석하여 실전에 가까운 컨텐츠를 개발하고 있으며, 김영편입의 우수한 교수진과 축적된 컨텐츠를 기반으로 다양한 교재를 출판하고 있습니다.

주요 집필 교재

「편머리 기본편 시리즈(문법, 어휘, 논리, 독해)」, 「편머리 심화편 시리즈(문법, 어휘, 논리, 독해)」, 「편머리 실전편 시리즈(문법, 논리, 독해)」, 「편머리 FINAL 실전모의고사」, 「편머리 편입영어 기출문제」, 「MVP STARTER」, 「MVP Vol.1, 2」 등

해독제 Vol.2

인쇄 2022년 4월 15일 **발행** 2022년 4월 29일

편저자 김영편입 컨텐츠평가연구소

제작총괄 안진영 **제작진행** 김형석 **연구개발** 안진영, 신종규, 김진희, 김형석
디자인 서제호, 서진희, 조아현 **판매영업** 조재훈, 김승규, 권기원

발행처 ㈜아이비김영 **등록번호** 제 22-3190호
주소 (06728) 서울시 서초구 서운로 32, 5층 (서초동, 우진빌딩)
전화 (대표전화)1661-7022 (컨텐츠평가연구소)02-3476-0331 **팩스** 02-3456-8073

ⓒ ㈜아이비김영
이 책은 저작권법에 따라 보호받는 저작물이므로 무단전재와 무단복제를 금지하며, 책 내용의 전부 또는 일부를 이용하려면 반드시 저작권자의 서면동의를 받아야 합니다.

ISBN 978-89-6512-153-4 (13740)

정가 30,000원

잘못된 책은 바꿔드립니다.

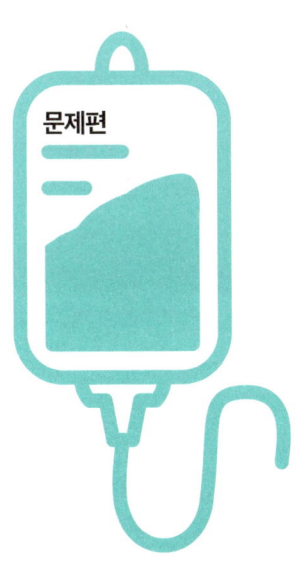

문제편

THE MORE, THE BETTER!
독해 실력은 투자한 시간과 노력에 비례한다!

편입빈출유형 핵심지문 300

해독제
Vol.2

김영편입
컨텐츠평가연구소
편저

김영편입

PREFACE

"해독(解讀)"에는 "어려운 문구나 문장 따위를 읽고 이해하거나 해석하다."는 의미가 담겨 있습니다. 『해독제(解讀題)』는 "해독"의 이런 사전적인 의미를 바탕으로, 편입을 준비하는 수험생들이 독해지문을 이해하고, 문제를 푸는 데 도움이 되도록 기획된 책입니다.

"어떤 사람에게는 약이 되는 것이 다른 사람에게는 독이 된다."는 말이 있습니다. 처음부터 의욕만 앞선 채 어려운 독해지문으로 공부를 시작하게 되면, 이루고자 했던 목표와 관계없이 학습 의욕을 잃게 될 수 있습니다. 따라서 자신의 수준에 맞춰 쉬운 지문에서 어려운 지문으로 점차 난이도를 높여 학습하는 것이 효과적입니다. 『해독제 Vol.1, 2』는 단문부터 중·장문까지 독해 문제를 단계적으로 학습할 수 있도록 구성된 책입니다.

『해독제』는 『해독제 Vol.1, 2』의 두 권으로 이루어진 책으로, 최신 편입영어 출제 경향을 토대로 실전에 가장 가까운 예상문제들로 구성된 독해 문제집입니다. 또한 『해독제』는 『편머리 독해』와 연계해 학습이 가능하도록 기획되었습니다. 따라서 『편머리 독해 기본편, 심화편』을 통해 기출문제의 출제 경향 및 난이도를 확인한 다음, 『해독제 Vol.1, 2』를 통해 실전 예상문제를 풀어봄으로써 편입 독해 시험에 완벽 대비할 수 있도록 했습니다.

『해독제 Vol.1』은 초·중급 난이도 300지문, 『해독제 Vol.2』는 중·고급 난이도 300지문을 각각 수록하여 다양한 길이의 독해지문을 순차적으로 학습할 수 있도록 했습니다. 또한 인문, 사회, 자연, 과학 등의 다양한 분야의 독해지문을 수록해 폭넓은 배경지식을 습득할 수 있도록 했습니다.

독해 실력은 다양한 분야의 좋은 글을 많이 읽고, 여러 문제 유형을 풀이하면서 향상될 수 있습니다. 총 600지문으로 구성된 『해독제 Vol.1, 2』를 통해 여러분의 독해 실력이 크게 향상되기를 기원합니다.

김영편입 컨텐츠평가연구소

CONTENTS

PASSAGE 001~010 ········· 8
PASSAGE 011~020 ········· 18
PASSAGE 021~030 ········· 28
PASSAGE 031~040 ········· 38
PASSAGE 041~050 ········· 48

PASSAGE 051~060 ········· 60
PASSAGE 061~070 ········· 70
PASSAGE 071~080 ········· 80
PASSAGE 081~090 ········· 90
PASSAGE 091~100 ········· 100

PASSAGE 101~110 ········· 112
PASSAGE 111~120 ········· 122
PASSAGE 121~130 ········· 132
PASSAGE 131~140 ········· 142
PASSAGE 141~150 ········· 153

PASSAGE 151~160 ········· 168
PASSAGE 161~170 ········· 182
PASSAGE 171~180 ········· 196
PASSAGE 181~190 ········· 209
PASSAGE 191~200 ········· 221

PASSAGE 201~210 ········· 236
PASSAGE 211~220 ········· 251
PASSAGE 221~230 ········· 270
PASSAGE 231~240 ········· 288
PASSAGE 241~250 ········· 308

PASSAGE 251~260 ········· 330
PASSAGE 261~270 ········· 350
PASSAGE 271~280 ········· 370
PASSAGE 281~290 ········· 390
PASSAGE 291~300 ········· 410

PASSAGE

001
050

The fewer restrictions there are on the advertising of legal services, the more lawyers there are who advertise their services, and the lawyers who advertise a specific service usually charge less for that service than lawyers who do not advertise. Therefore, if the state removes any of its current restrictions, such as the one against advertisements that do not specify fee arrangements, overall consumer legal costs will be lower than if the state retains its current restrictions.

01 If the statements above are true, which of the following must be true?

(A) Some lawyers who now advertise will charge more for specific services if they do not have to specify fee arrangements in the advertisements.
(B) More consumers will use legal services if there are fewer restrictions on the advertising of legal services.
(C) If the restriction against advertisements that do not specify fee arrangements is removed, more lawyers will advertise their services.
(D) If more lawyers advertise lower prices for specific services, some lawyers who do not advertise will also charge less than they currently charge for those services.

Solitude quietly eliminates all sorts of traits that were a part of you — among others, the desire to pose, to impress people as being something you would like to have them think you are even when you aren't. Some men I know are able to pose even in solitude; had they servants who help them dress, they no doubt would be heroes to them. But I find it the hardest kind of work myself, and as I am lazy I have stopped trying. _____ is so tiresome and profitless that you gradually give it up and at last forget how to act at all. For you become more interested in making the acquaintance of yourself as you really are. It is gratifying, for example, to discover that you prefer to be clean rather than dirty even when there is no one but God to care which you are. Clothes, you learn, with something of a shock, have for you no interest whatsoever. You learn to regard dress merely as covering, a precaution. For its color and its cut you care nothing.

01 Which of the following best fits into the blank?
    (A) To act without an audience
    (B) To try dressing yourself
    (C) To have someone else help you dress
    (D) To make others like you
    (E) To act in public

02 In solitude, you learn to think highly of the _____ of clothes only.
    (A) style   (B) size
    (C) utility   (D) color
    (E) cleanness

All the arts depend on preposterous fiction, but the theatre is the most preposterous of all. Imagine asking us to believe that we are in Venice in the sixteenth Century, and that Mr. Billington is a Moor, and that he is about to stifle the much admired Miss Huckaby with a pillow; and imagine trying to make us believe that people ever talked in blank verse — more than that: that people were ever so marvelously articulate. The theatre is a lily that inexplicably arises from a jungle of weedy falsities. Yet it is precisely from the tension produced by all this absurdity that it is able to create such poetry, power, enchantment and truth.

01 The title below that best expressed the ideas of this passage is _____.
(A) The Preposterousness of Fiction
(B) The Imaginative Power of the Drama
(C) The Effects of Power Acting
(D) Producing Theatrical Tension

02 The author's attitude toward dramatic situations that are not true to life is one of _____.
(A) appreciation   (B) indignation
(C) disapproval   (D) indifference

03 Which statement best illustrates the author's meaning when he says, "The theatre is a lily that inexplicably arises from a jungle of weedy falsities."?
(A) The theatre is the flower among the arts.
(B) The theatre helps to raise public taste to a higher level.
(C) The theatre can create an illusion of truth from improbable situations.
(D) The theatre has overcome the unsavory reputation of earlier periods.

I was exploring the far side of the island on the third day. I was also observing myself, an animal covering his territory. It was very quiet, even still. Suddenly a thunderous sound in the leaves and there was a grouse, frozen in fear, three feet from my face. I wasn't sure whether I looked as scared; I certainly had been deeply frightened. The stillness had become noise, and since I was alone on the island, my fantasies at that instant were elaborate. But I unfroze and the grouse did not. The myth of man, the primitive hunter, began to unfold as I reached for stick. But before any action, <u>another myth</u> took hold and there was no taking of life. The basic need of hunger; the basic force of life. I can't forget that encounter.

01 From the passage, we can most safely conclude that the _____.
    (A) grouse flew away
    (B) grouse was an easy prey
    (C) writer disliked the grouse
    (D) writer was familiar with the island

02 The phrase <u>another myth</u> refers to _____.
    (A) a need for action
    (B) a respect for primitive customs
    (C) the powerlessness of animals
    (D) a respect for living things

03 By the end of this episode, the writer feels that he has _____.
    (A) created a new myth
    (B) grown in perception
    (C) learned how to survive
    (D) become a creature of fantasy

The welfare state says that we are not to be a nation of independent people, but a nation of clients whose lives are controlled by bureaucrats, dispensing taxpayers' money according to the vision of the anointed. This is not a new idea, however much advocates of the welfare state proclaim "change." Most of the history of the human race has been of ordinary people having their lives controlled and their destiny decided by some elite. It has taken centuries of struggle and bloodshed to get out from under the thumb of those who acted as if they had been born "booted and spurred, to ride mankind." Now we are heading backward, toward a world where people's fates are not in their own hands but in the hands of some puffed-up political "leaders."

01 Which of the following is NOT true according to the author of this passage?
(A) Ordinary people have fought for centuries to gain independence from the privileged few.
(B) The welfare state is trying to augment its control over people in the name of the welfare of people.
(C) Mankind has long had states where the governing few sway the lives and futures of the governed many.
(D) The welfare state should see its people as the beneficiaries of its welfare work and interfere with every aspect of their lives.

02 Which of the following does the underlined part refer to?
(A) clients
(B) advocates of the welfare state
(C) ordinary people
(D) some elite

The man divided against himself looks for excitement and distraction. He loves strong passions not for sound reasons but because for the moment they take him outside himself and prevent the painful necessity of thought. Any passion is to him a form of intoxication, and since he cannot conceive of fundamental happiness, all relief from pain appears to him solely possible in the form of intoxication. This, however, is the symptom of a deep-seated malady. Where there is no such malady, the greatest happiness comes with the most complete possession of one's faculties. It is in the moments when the mind is most active and the fewest things are forgotten that the most intense joys are experienced.

01 What is the main topic of this passage?
(A) who looks for excitement
(B) what is wrong with strong passion
(C) why people seek intoxication
(D) where the greatest happiness comes

02 Which of the following cannot be inferred from the passage?
(A) Passion tends to degenerate as its intensity grows.
(B) A man whose self is divided indulges in momentary pleasures.
(C) A man with a divided self is apt to fall into escapism.
(D) Forgetting hardships in real life does not contribute to happiness.

So began my unexpectedly intimate encounter with one of the world's most overrun tourist destinations. The last traces of daylight were disappearing as I heard the heavy gate clank shut behind me. Insects and birds chirped loudly. Inca stone walls plunged headlong towards the dizzyingly deep gorge of the Urubamba River, hundreds of meters below. Knife-edged green mountains rose up on all sides, their peaks obscured by a dense layer of cottony clouds turned bluish-grey by the vanishing sun. Before me, great stone steps descended through a trapezoidal door into the complex of temples, houses, terraces and fountains that the Incas built about half a millennium ago. The moon was now almost directly overhead, casting enough light to walk by, moving in and out of the clouds, and there I was, completely alone in the ruins of Machu Picchu.

01 What is the tone of the passage?
(A) sentimental
(B) descriptive
(C) hyperbolic
(D) meditative

02 Which of the following cannot be inferred about 'the ruins of Machu Picchu' from the passage?
(A) Extremely many people are visiting them for sightseeing.
(B) It was around dusk when the author came across them.
(C) They were built in the late 15th or early 16th century.
(D) They are very beautiful and easily accessible.

There is the man who has a genuine grievance, founded upon actual fact, but who generalizes in the light of his experience and arrives at the conclusion that his own misfortune affords the key to the universe; he discovers, let us say, some scandal about the Secret Service which it is to the interest of the Government to keep dark. He can obtain hardly any publicity for his discovery, and the most apparently high-minded men refuse to lift a finger to remedy the evil which fills him with indignation. So far the facts are as he says they are. But his _____ have made such an impression upon him that he believes all powerful men to be occupied wholly and solely in covering up the crimes to which they owe their power.

01 Choose the one that best fills in the blank.
(A) misdeeds
(B) derelictions
(C) endeavors
(D) rebuffs

02 What is the author's purpose in the passage?
(A) to stress that one's personal experience is the key to the whole truth
(B) to point out that it is wrong to generalize from one's own experience alone
(C) to persuade people to protest the government concealing its crimes
(D) to explain how negative emotions can lead people to wrong conclusions

The differences I focus on are certainly common, but there are exceptions. Generally speaking, about 10 percent of women will relate more to being from Mars than from Venus. This is often simply a result of being born with higher testosterone levels than most other women. Even when this is the case, these women still have all the female hormones for pregnancy and childbirth. For these women, this book is often a revelation that helps them identify their feminine needs and gives them more support and permission to nurture their female side. As we explore these differences together, keep in mind I am not describing how women and men should be. _____.

01 Which of the following best fits into the blank?
(A) Gender differences show up the most after getting involved in an intimate relationship, having children together, or when we are under a lot of stress
(B) Certainly there are many problems in relationship that have nothing to do with understanding the opposite sex
(C) I am simply pointing out how and why men and women commonly misunderstand each other when and if these differences show up
(D) This book does not address or provide solutions to all the different kinds of relationship issues

02 According to the passage, which of the following statements is NOT true?
(A) All of women do not come from Venus.
(B) Even with higher male hormones women cannot rebut their fertility.
(C) This book helps manly women find out their own identity and its worth.
(D) This book leads to fight stereotyping what he or she should be.

One should expect the sense of shame to be blurred where socialization of the young becomes ineffectual, and social cohesion is weakened. In this country at present the inability of adults to socialize their young has made it possible for juveniles to act on their impulses and ①_____. The result has been a youth culture flauntingly shameless. The disconcerting thing is that loss of shame is not confined to juveniles. The adult majority is not ashamed of its cowardice and negligence. We have become a shameless society. Our intellectual mentors strive to infect us with a sense of guilt — about the poor, pollution — and frown on shame as reactionary and repressive. But whether or not a sense of guilt will make us a better people, the loss of shame threatens our survival as a civilized society. For most of the acts we are ashamed of are not punishable by law, and civilized living depends upon the observance of unenforceable rules. One also has the feeling that shame is ②_____ than guilt. There is more fear in guilt than in shame, and animals know fear.

01 Which of the following pairs fits best in the blanks ① and ②?
(A) become a victim of crimes — more powerful
(B) materialize their fantasies — more uniquely human
(C) disembody their souls — more logically coherent
(D) become invulnerable to morals — more fearful

Everyone knows someone who always follows bad advice. According to researchers, they could be born that way. A new paper in *The Journal of Neuroscience* details how genetic variations can predict whether people will act in a way others suggest, even if their experience proves they should not. People use two parts of their brain for this kind of reasoning: the prefrontal cortex manages received advice, whereas the striatum, located deeper in the brain, processes experience. Depending on genes, the striatum will cave more easily to what the prefrontal cortex is telling it. The study provides a window into something called confirmation bias — in which acquired beliefs tend to be resistant to new information — and might explain everything from political attitudes to a passion for astrology.

01 Choose the best title of the following passages.
(A) Genetic Variation Linked to Sensitivity
(B) The Method of Dealing with Confirmation Bias
(C) The Modification of Prefrontal Cortex
(D) Reasoning behind a Thought Process
(E) Genes Playing Crucial Roles in People's Behavior

012

All the basic purposes of communication — the sharing of human experience — are being steadily subordinated to the drive to sell. The old kind of newspaper proprietor, who wanted control so that he could propagate his opinions, has, in general, been replaced by a kind of proprietor who says he is not interested in opinions but simply in selling as many papers as he can. What was once a means to some larger policy has become in most cases the policy itself. The organization of communications is then not for use, but for profit, and we have passed the stage in which there has to be any pretense that things are otherwise.

01 위 글의 밑줄 친 otherwise의 구체적인 내용을 고르시오.
(A) not what they seem to be
(B) not for profit, but for use
(C) that we have not passed the stage
(D) not producing as many papers possible

02 위 글의 내용에 부합하는 진술을 고르시오.
(A) Making good papers will profit proprietors nothing.
(B) Proprietors selling many papers aim only to share human experience.
(C) The papers had no meaning at all unless they did their best to sell.
(D) The new kind of proprietor has come to mistake the means for the end.

It is unlikely that many of us will be famous, or even remembered. But no less important than the brilliant few that lead a nation or a literature to fresh achievements, are the unknown many whose patient efforts keep the world from running backward; who guard and maintain the ancient values, even if they do not conquer new; whose inconspicuous triumph it is to pass on what they inherited from their fathers, unimpaired and undiminished, to their sons. Enough, for almost all of us, if we can hand on the torch, and not let it down; content to win the affection, if possible, of a few who know us, and to be forgotten when they in their turn have vanished.

01 Which of the following sentences do you think most adequately expresses the main point of the passage?
(A) We must learn from the experiences of other people.
(B) Great men alone cannot keep up a high level of civilization.
(C) What the future world will be like is really impossible to foresee.
(D) Consistency in thought and conduct is prized among the highest virtues.

The four Galilean satellites of Jupiter probably experienced early, intense bombardment. Thus, the very ancient surface of Callisto remains scarred by impact craters. The younger, more varied surface of Ganymede reveals distinct light and dark areas, the light areas featuring networks of intersecting grooves and ridges, probably resulting from later iceflows. The impact sites of Europa have been almost completely erased, apparently by water outflowing from the interior and instantly forming vast, frozen seas. Satellite photographs of Io, the closest of the four to Jupiter, were revelatory. They showed a landscape dominated by volcanoes, many erupting, making Io the most tectonically active object in that solar system. Io is engulfed by tides stemming from a titanic contest between the other three Galilean moons and Jupiter.

01 According to the passage, which of the following is probably NOT true of the surface of Io?
(A) It is characterized by intense tectonic activity.
(B) Its volcanos have resulted from powerful tides.
(C) It is younger than the surface of Callisto.
(D) It is distinguished by many impact craters.

02 It can be inferred that the geologic features found in the light areas of Ganymede were probably formed _____.
(A) subsequent to the features found in the dark areas
(B) in an earlier period than those in the dark areas
(C) at roughly the same time as the features found in the dark areas
(D) by the satellite's volcanic activity

There is a special kind of writing style that speaks to a woman's spirit and makes her soul rejoice. It can be difficult to find such a book, but when found it is a real treasure. In the novel, *The Secret Life of Bees*, by Sue Monk Kidd, I found myself laughing and crying along with the characters. I felt deeply connected to the women in the novel and was sad to see my new friends go when the story came to an end. Sue Monk Kidd truly breathed life into this book, in a way that takes tremendous talent. I find myself longing for a sequel, just so I can see what my beloved characters are up to now! If you are a woman, you are almost guaranteed to love this book! The writing style is distinctly feminine and beautiful. I thought to myself, "It is about time I read something from a powerful female perspective." <u>For me, reading this book came as naturally as breathing.</u>

01 Which is where you are most likely to see this passage?
(A) The opinion section of a medical magazine
(B) The review section of a magazine
(C) The first chapter of the book on bees' life
(D) A reader's letter to the author, Sue Monk Kidd

02 Which is closest in meaning to the underlined expression "<u>For me, reading this book came as naturally as breathing</u>"?
(A) I was forced to read this book.
(B) Reading this book was recommended to me.
(C) I could not breathe without reading this book.
(D) Reading this book was effortless for me.

That light is the source of color was first demonstrated in 1666 by Isaac Newton, who passed a beam of sunlight through a glass prism, producing the rainbow of hues of the visible spectrum. This phenomenon was observed before Newton, but it had always been related to latent color that was believed to exist in the glass of the prism. Newton, however, took the simple experiment a step further. He passed his miniature rainbow through a second prism, which reconstituted the original white beam of light. His conclusion was revolutionary: _____.

01 What made Isaac Newton come to a revolutionary conclusion?
   (A) a series of persistent researches
   (B) an elaborately controlled experiment
   (C) educated guess and logical reasoning
   (D) incessant discussions with his colleagues
   (E) a simple but fruitful extra experiment

02 Which of the following is the best for the blank?
   (A) color is concealed in the glass prism
   (B) color is in light, not in the glass
   (C) light is mostly white and invisible
   (D) color exists in our minds, not in objects
   (E) original light is refracted in the glass prism

The solution for slavery was not its abolition, at least that was not a total solution, because new forms of slavery were invented under another name. The factory workers who toiled in poisonous air from sunrise till sunset and never saw daylight except on Sundays, obeying in silence, probably led even worse lives than many ancient slaves. And today, all those who prefer to do what they are told rather than think for themselves and _____ the responsibility — one-third of Britons, according to a poll, say that is what they prefer — are the spiritual heirs of the voluntary slaves of Russia. It is important to remember that it is tiring, and trying, being free; and in times of exhaustion affection for freedom has always waned, whatever lip-service might be paid to it.

01 Choose the one which does NOT fit in the blank.
(A) take
(B) assume
(C) put on
(D) shoulder

02 Which of the following is NOT inferred or stated in the passage?
(A) There were people who voluntarily became slaves.
(B) Slavery is not just a matter of physical condition.
(C) Paying lip-service to freedom, none of us want it.
(D) Some modern people are leading worse lives than the ancient slaves.

The symphony orchestra, which grew in size and dimension throughout the nineteenth century as musical technology added more and more complex instruments and as composers eagerly sought to experiment with the new sounds, has become a model of human society at its most ideal. It requires every musician to pull together for one common purpose. No one sound can be any more important than another. The melody is no more beautiful than the harmony and rhythm which support it. The lifetime achievements of each player are as nothing if the whole entity does not create an experience for the listener that is intense, focused, and charged with electricity. At the same time, the ultimate product is a testimony to the <u>genius</u> of the individual. _____.

01 Which of the following is the most suitable sentence for the blank?
(A) A successful symphony orchestra consists of geniuses
(B) If one tone is flat, the entire enterprise collapses
(C) Minor mistakes made by individual musicians are undetectable in concerts
(D) The performance of the individual musician is negligible

02 The underlined word "<u>genius</u>" is closest in meaning to _____.
(A) talent   (B) violence
(C) imitation   (D) courage

The local education authorities in England have recently issued a "prescribed" list of books that are approved for reading in schools by children aged between 5 and 11. A furor has arisen among many parents because an author named Sherry Blanchet, very popular with children, has been omitted from the list. When asked to comment on the omission, the head of the committee who was responsible for preparing the list of books said that the books of Ms. Blanchet have been omitted because "we thought they are of an inferior quality and do not sufficiently stimulate the children's intellectual ability and not because they contain characters which are stereotypes or may show racial prejudice."

01 Which of the following statements can be inferred from the above passage?
   (A) Children and parents are very angry that they will not be reading Sherry Blanchet in school once this decision is implemented.
   (B) The parents' view is that Ms. Blanchet's books might have been left off the list because some of her characters were racist.
   (C) Ms. Blanchet was popular with children and parents because she included stereotype characters in her books.
   (D) If the parents had been consulted, Sherry Blanchet's books would have been omitted.

Stop thinking of it as exercise. That separates it from life, which is counter-productive. No wonder you still don't have those abs of steel you're aiming for! Better to think of being more active. This subtle shift in mind-set appears to be more conducive to long-term health and weight loss. Russell Pate, PhD, a professor of exercise science at the University of South Carolina, compared two people, one who was sedentary (but active most of the day), and one who exercised for 60 minutes daily (but who was not very active). The sedentary person expended 10 percent more energy than the exerciser. So if you're constantly feeling as if you don't have time to get to the gym or to work out, make the world your gym. Do errands on foot, or open the garage door by hand rather than remote. <u>Active is the new fit</u>.

01 Choose the one that is most relevant to the underlined "<u>Active is the new fit.</u>"
(A) Separate exercise from your life.
(B) Have the abs of steel.
(C) Do sedentary work.
(D) Make the world your gym.

02 What is the main idea of the passage?
(A) Doing nothing but think of exercise separates it from life.
(B) We should work out not to build muscle but to keep healthy.
(C) Being active in daily life is better than doing regular exercise.
(D) We should do everything by hand, not by machine, for health.

Seize the very first possible opportunity to act on every resolution you make, and on every emotional prompting you may experience in the direction of the habits you aspire to gain. To make a resolve and not to keep it is of little value. So by all means keep every resolution you make, for you not only profit by the resolution, but it furnishes you with an exercise that causes the brain cells and physiological correlatives to form the habit of adjusting themselves to carry out resolutions. A tendency to act becomes effectively ingrained in us in proportion to the uninterrupted frequency with which the actions actually occur, and the brain 'grows' to their use. When a resolve or a fine glow of feeling is allowed to evaporate without bearing fruit, it is worse than a chance lost.

01 Why should we keep whatever resolutions we make?
   (A) Because it leads us to cultivating a habit that fulfills the resolutions.
   (B) Because we are not discernable enough to tell the significance of a promise we make.
   (C) Because we not only benefit by the resolutions we make, but they also keep us from forming a bad habit.
   (D) Because it could lead to the formation of a new personality.

02 Which one is closest in meaning to the underlined sentence?
   (A) Losing chances are more foolish than lacking the willpower to keep resolutions.
   (B) Only when a resolve is accompanied by self-discipline to keep it, a chance is not lost.
   (C) Resolutions that are not fulfilled are nothing more than chances lost.
   (D) You'd better lose a chance than make an empty resolution.

03 What is the tone of the passage?
   (A) emphatic   (B) disparaging
   (C) reproachful   (D) conciliatory

Hollywood turns to Botox to smooth foreheads and other wrinkle zones, but as usual, beauty comes at a price. The cosmetic procedure can render you less able to read other people's emotions, says David Neal, a psychology professor at the University of Southern California and lead author of the research, according to USA Today. People read emotions partly by mimicking facial expressions, Neal says, so "if muscular signals from the face to the brain are <u>dampened</u>, you're less able to read emotions." Botox, a purified form of a nerve poison, paralyzes muscles, hindering certain facial movements that can cause wrinkles. Personally, we'd rather be clued into what other people are thinking and feeling than have a plastic-looking face.

01 Choose the one closest in meaning to the underlined "dampened."
   (A) disturbed   (B) weakened
   (C) stupefied   (D) disabled

02 What is the main idea of the passage?
   (A) The benefit of botox treatment is worth the potential side effects.
   (B) Social relationships may improve due to younger looking face.
   (C) Facial expressions are an effective form of nonverbal communication.
   (D) Botox may deaden your important ability to read the minds of people.

"Good" and "bad", "better" and "worse", are terms which may not have a verbal definition, but in any case first come to be understood ostensively. Let us then begin with an attempt to indicate their meaning, leaving the question of verbal definition to a later stage. A thing is "good" if it is valued for its own sake, and not only for its effects. We take nasty medicines because we hope they will have desirable effects, but a gouty connoisseur drinks old wine for its own sake, in spite of possible disagreeable effects. _____ When we have to choose whether a certain state of affairs is to exist or not, we have of course to take account of its effects. But the state of affairs, as well as each of its effects, has an intrinsic quality which inclines us to choose it or not to choose it, as the case may be. It is this intrinsic quality that we call "good" when we incline to choose it and "bad" when we incline to reject it.

01 Choose the one that best fills in the blank.
(A) The medicine is good but not useful, and the wine is useful but not good.
(B) The medicine is useful but not good, and the wine is good but not useful.
(C) The medicine is both good and useful, and the wine is neither useful nor good.
(D) The medicine is both useful and good, and the wine is good but not useful.

02 Which of the following cannot be inferred about "good" and "bad"?
(A) We can use "bad" means to accomplish "good" purposes.
(B) They are easier to understand in specific situations than to define by words.
(C) Something that has a "good" intrinsic quality can result in "bad" effects.
(D) They are absolutely objective, irrespective of our penchant for things or affairs.

What do you believe about copyright? [I] Is it an inherent right in which creators can legally protect their hard-earned and often underpaid efforts? [II] Or is it an erosion of democracy and a drain on culture where every time you want to use something created, you must first ask permission and then pay for it? [III] Creators like myself feel discouraged when we see our work copied illegally, mis-used out of context, or even plagiarized. We don't like it and we seek retribution. [IV] But educators and many business people have quite a different world view. The so-called Copy Left movement thinks that the public domain where works are freely available is an important part of cultural activity. Many educators believe that works should be available to all students to use as they wish. Some even argue that all creations are just recycled ideas, since there is really nothing new under the sun.

01 According to the passage, the attitude of educators toward copyright is _____.
(A) supportive
(B) critical
(C) neutral
(D) indecisive

02 Which of the following CANNOT be inferred from the passage?
(A) Copyright is a right that an author has over his creation.
(B) Copyleft is opposed to the proprietary nature of copyright.
(C) Copyright ensures that a work will be always available.
(D) Copyleft guarantees a work is free to copy and distribute.

03 Where would the following sentence best fit into?
These are not simple questions.
(A) [I]
(B) [II]
(C) [III]
(D) [IV]

The American Bondholder Foundation is demanding that China pay back more than 15,000 government bonds — dating back more than 90 years — that they say are worth $89 billion. The Foundation's claim tests the degree to which China will honor its obligations to foreign investors as the country benefits from trade and global capital markets. But the turmoil of China's 20th-century history has blurred official responsibility for the bonds. China's first modern republic issued the bonds in 1913, _____ 26 years later amid civil war and the Japanese invasion. Later, the government fled from a communist offensive to Taiwan in 1949. The Chinese government in Beijing has never accepted responsibility.

01 The best main idea of the passage is that _____.

(A) The American Bondholder Foundation's demand for the payback of the previous Chinese government bonds is absurd
(B) The Chinese government in Beijing ought to repay its previous bonds
(C) The American Bondholder Foundation's demand for the payback of the government bonds issued in 1913 has been refused by Beijing
(D) China entered into rivalry with the U.S. in the international financial market
(E) The international community needs to mediate the recent conflict between China and the U.S.

02 Which of the following is the best for the blank?

(A) compensating   (B) defaulting
(C) contracting   (D) merging
(E) refinancing

Britain's House of Lords voted against a bid to stop sales of the "morning after" contraceptive pill in support for a government strategy to cut Europe's highest teen-age pregnancy rate. Votes were 177 to 95 against a motion to bar over-the-counter sales of the pill. Proponents of the ban fear that sales of the pregnancy-preventing drug grant youngsters a license to do as they please. But lawmakers who argued against the proposed ban said it would _____.

01 The best main theme of the passage is _____.
(A) pros and cons regarding a proposal to ban sales of a particular anticonceptive pill
(B) increasing skepticism concerning effects of contraceptive pills
(C) how to prevent dissipated life of the teenagers in England
(D) controversies around effects of a particular anticonceptive pill on the lower birth rate in England
(E) unethical tricks used by pharmaceutical industry to boost sales of contraceptive pills

02 Which of the following is the best for the blank?
(A) please abortion-rights advocates
(B) help minors terminate pregnancies
(C) mean more unwanted pregnancies
(D) reduce the country's high abortion rate
(E) jeopardize pharmaceutical industry

For the first time that night, I was silent. 'How could I convince this woman to push, just so that she could deliver her dead child into the world?' After an hour, the resident returned and asked me why it was taking so long. I whispered that I could feel the infant's head, but the mother just wasn't pushing enough. I asked if I could speed up the delivery by doing an episiotomy, a small incision to enlarge the birth canal. She nodded her approval. I quickly made the incision and felt the baby pop into my hands. It was a lovely little girl, weighing about three kilos. As was normal practice, I placed the infant on a sterile sheet I had draped over the mother's abdomen. ①She looked at her dead daughter, then turned ②her head away. I was quiet the whole time.

As I started to suture the incision I had made, I heard a small cough. I looked up at the baby, who was still on the mother's belly. Then I heard the loveliest and loudest sound in my life. ③She was screaming her lungs out! All I could say was, "Mummy, your baby is alive!" over and over again. ④Her soft cries turned into convulsive happy tears. "Doctor, thank you for bringing ⑤my child to life," she said repeatedly. Nothing compares to that magical moment when I experienced the wonderful miracle of birth.

01 Which of the following would be the best title of this passage?
(A) An Episode on My First Night in the Hospital
(B) Delivery: The Biggest Challenge of Doctors
(C) Delivery: Sign of Motherhood
(D) A Wonderful Miracle of Birth
(E) The Necessity of Episiotomy for Safe Delivery

02 According to the passage, which of the following is true?
(A) The author was silent because she was afraid of unsuccessful delivery.
(B) In general, it takes a doctor less than an hour to deliver a dead baby.
(C) The author must have been a specialist in pediatrics.
(D) Doctors usually put a newborn baby beside its mother right after delivery.
(E) The baby cried with pain of lung disease.

03 Among ①, ②, ③, ④, and ⑤, which one differs from the others in what they refer to?
(A) ①
(B) ②
(C) ③
(D) ④
(E) ⑤

We've been under the impression that we would have robot maids, live on the moon, and zip around in flying cars before we hit the year 2000. We may have been _____, but at least the "flying car" fantasy is making some progress. Futuristic car-maker Moller International has invented a "flying saucer" car that it hopes will change the way we commute. If the Californian company gets its way, we'll be zipping about like the Jetsons sooner than we think. According to Moller spokes-people, this eight-engine craft is spacious, easy to operate, can run on petrol, diesel or even ethanol. It takes off and lands vertically like a helicopter and can hover up to three meters off the ground. Any higher and the driver would need a pilot's licence. A piece of the future can be yours from just $90,000. Moller hopes to begin selling this invention by next year and expand production to 250 annually.

01 Which of the following cannot be inferred about "a flying car" from the passage?
(A) The Jetsons are not real persons who have ridden a flying car.
(B) A flying car will be labeled a car, not an airplane.
(C) A flying car can not yet be mass-produced as other types of cars are.
(D) A car flying higher than three meters off the ground is technically unattainable.

02 Choose the one that best fills in the blank.
(A) presumptuous
(B) scrupulous
(C) chicken-hearted
(D) reserved

As conservative cultural critic Stanley Crouch astutely observed, when a black person commits a crime, it's a comment on race. When a white person commits a crime it's a comment on society or that one individual alone.

No matter how many times a disturbed white male shoots up a school, church or workplace, bombs an abortion clinic or is arrested for being a serial killer, nobody raises questions like: is something wrong with white suburban culture? The response is either: that's one sick individual, or it just goes to show you how bad society is getting.

If America is ever going to have a meaningful inter-racial conversation about the legacy of white supremacy and its impact on present day political and economic conditions, then we've got to have mental dexterity to keep track of some important distinctions. That's a tall order in these times when you can be accused of being a "black racist bigot" for simply daring to question the new PC — "color blindness."

01 What is the purpose of the passage?
(A) to describe some cases of racism
(B) to narrate a new black power movement
(C) to explicate a peculiar tendency regarding eye
(D) to argue against a new kind of color blindness

As our theories about the world around us have evolved and have become more useful, they have become, almost without exception, less teleological and more mechanistic. A teleological explanation of a phenomenon describes causes and effects in terms of desires or purposes: something happens simply because it serves a certain purpose, because it is "supposed" to happen, or because someone or something "wants" it to happen. A ball falls to earth because, as it is in the air, it perceives that its more proper place is on the ground, and not because anything pushes it. [I] Teleological explanations never survive as useful theories because they are backward: they place the cause after the effect. [II] A mechanistic explanation, on the other hand, requires that any discussion of causes and effects be restricted by the known laws of how physical objects and substances interact as time moves forward. [III] No right-minded chemist would say that trinitrotoluene explodes because it "wants to." [IV] It does so because the presence of heat and oxygen releases the potential energy stored in its bonds.

01 Which of the following can be an appropriate example of the underlined "they place the cause after the effect"?

(A) Water evaporates because it absorbs heat.
(B) An engine works because it burns fuel.
(C) A dog yelps because it perceives pain.
(D) A bird sings because it likes the sound.

02 Where could the following sentence go to be added to the passage?

"This is the language of the scientist."

(A) [I] (B) [II]
(C) [III] (D) [IV]

Scholars distinguish between manifest power and implicit power. Manifest power is based on an observable action by A that leads B to do what A wants. A police officer's signal that causes a driver to stop and wait is an example of manifest power. In the case of implicit power, B does what A desires not because of anything A says or does but because (1) B senses that A wants something done and (2) for any of a variety of reasons B wishes to do what A wants done. Many examples of implicit power are found in families, whose members are so attuned to one another that there is often no observable communication between members of the family who yet manage to read and comply with one another's wishes. A father may toss the car key to his daughter on Saturday morning completely unprompted except by his knowledge of her habits and his desire to comply with her wishes. As she drives, the daughter may obey the 55-mile-per-hour speed limit because she knows that her parents feel strongly about it. In neither case is there any overt signal from one family member to the other.

01 Which of the following is not associated with "implicit power"?
    (A) definiteness
    (B) sensibility
    (C) voluntariness
    (D) invisibility

02 Which of the following cannot be inferred about "manifest power" and "implicit power"?
    (A) If a country threatened another with military invasion, it would be an example of manifest power.
    (B) If gangsters who overheard their boss killed his foe, it would be an example of implicit power.
    (C) Implicit power is more likely to bring about misunderstanding and undesired results than manifest power.
    (D) The exercise of manifest power is more difficult to determine than that of implicit power.

Millennia ago, humans were doing pretty well for themselves, but it's when they settled around the basins of large rivers that civilizations really started to flourish. [I] Think of ancient Egypt, Mesopotamia, the Indus Valley: Humans got much smarter and more sophisticated when they lived closer to rivers. [II] Examining 260 subjects in their late 70s with no cognitive defects, a study found that the hippocampus — the learning center of the brain — was 14% larger in those who ate baked or grilled fish (not fried) on a weekly basis than in those who did not. [III] The omega-3 fatty acids contained in fish also improved the performance of neurons in the brain's frontal lobe, an area that is crucial for executive functions like short-term memory and task planning. [IV] If you have neurons that are bigger, stronger and can make better connections to other neurons, they're going to be able to do their job more effectively. Plenty of seafood is rich in omega-3s — you can complement your salmon with oysters, trout and even sardines. Fish may be the secret to heftier brains, but variety remains the spice of life.

01 밑줄 친 "variety remains the spice of life"가 암시하는 것으로 적절한 것은?

(A) It is better to eat various seafoods including fish.
(B) It matters what kind of fish we eat regularly.
(C) The taste for fish tends to change over time.
(D) Fish is just one of the various marine life forms.

02 아래의 문장이 들어갈 곳으로 가장 알맞은 곳은?

So it's not entirely surprising that consuming fish can actually enhance the physical size of the brain.

(A) [I]   (B) [II]
(C) [III]   (D) [IV]

In recent times, it has been increasingly the custom for advertisers to borrow the prestige of science and medicine to enhance the reputation of their products. The American people have come to feel for the laboratory scientist and the physician an awe once reserved for bishops and statesmen. The alleged approval of such men thus carries great weight when it is a question of selling something, or (which is the same thing) inducing someone to believe something. Phrases such as "leading medical authorities say..." or "independent laboratory tests show..." are designed simply to transfer the prestige of science, which presumably is incapable of either error or corruption, to a toothpaste or a cereal. Seldom if ever are the precise "medical authorities" or "independent laboratories" named. But the mere phrases have vast weight with the uncritical.

01 Why is the tactic of using alleged approval of scientist successful?
(A) Because the public is uncritical and credulous.
(B) Because products allegedly endorsed by scientists are better than products that are not.
(C) Because scientists make more attractive models than politicians.
(D) Because scientists are more trustworthy than priests.

02 Which of the following is part of the author's contention?
(A) Today bishops and statesmen are held in contempt by the public.
(B) We cannot always be sure whether the doctors and scientists have really testified to the efficiency of the advertised products.
(C) Scientists are easily bribed to endorse products of inferior quality.
(D) Scientists gain more prestige by remaining invisible.

It's human nature to believe that successful people have never made mistakes. But it's not so. Someone facing difficulty needs to be reminded of the challenges and failures that haunt us all. I decided to go to a certain seminary because of a teacher there named Howard Hendricks. His personality, candor, wit and confidence shone through in everything he said. He proved to be the greatest teacher I'd ever had. After a while, though, I grew discouraged, thinking that I could never live up to what he had accomplished. One day, Hendricks seemed to spot my mood and perhaps the whole class's mood. He stopped everything in the middle of a lecture and began to talk heart to heart. He quietly spoke of his failures and how he was tempted several times to give up teaching. He had us laughing one moment and feeling sad and sympathetic the next. I realized he was a man of clay. "Life isn't a hundred-yard dash," he said to us. "It's a marathon and those who win are often just plodders like you and me."

01 Which of the following is the main idea of this passage?

(A) Success depends upon a man's personality and flawlessness.
(B) The road to success is open to only a few privileged people.
(C) A successful man has been struggling in a slow and steady manner.
(D) A Jack-of-all-trades is less likely to succeed than a common man.

02 Which of the following is closest in meaning to the underlined part?

(A) a man in the street
(B) a man with many faults
(C) a man susceptible to temptation
(D) a man of weak character

The Western mind is bent on the notion that we must do something all the time. However, when we remember that consciousness precedes matter, we recognize that serenity is more than a beautiful feeling. It's an essential strength. An agitated mind creates an agitated world, which then creates more agitated minds, which then create a more agitated world. But moments of sacred silence break the vicious cycle. And that is why the cultivation of such moments is one of our wands. It harmonizes everything.

Advertisements constantly hawk the latest pharmaceutical answers to our lack of inner peace. Yet all of us know, deep within, that psychic pain, like physical pain, is there for a reason. We don't heal a broken leg by numbing it, and we don't heal a broken heart that way, either. Ultimately, only the alchemical processes of spirit can actually disentangle the thought forms that cause our distress, guiding us to forgive one another.

01 Which of the following is LEAST consistent with the passage?
(A) Western people cherish serenity despite their busy daily life.
(B) Serenity prevents our mind from being disturbed by the world.
(C) An emotional pain needs serenity as a broken leg needs treating.
(D) Serenity can drive the thoughts of revenge out of our mind.

Franklin: Despite rising costs in construction and a long-lasting recession, a record number of first-time area home buyers (33%) had their houses built rather than buying existing houses. This compares to 21% in the previous 6 years. This is surprising considering the numerous factors that can drive up the overall cost of building a new home. Included in new construction costs are the *impact fees*, which the community often charges to help pay for development costs (such as sewer and road developments.) These can add up to 5% to overall costs, which buyers may not be aware of until after the purchase is made because they are not included in the mortgage.

In addition to these high costs, there are additional, physical and financial deterrents that might normally keep new home buyers from building. Some of these include lack of land or space to build, difficulty finding reputable developers, and the high costs involved in continuing to pay one mortgage or rent while paying for a new house to be built.

One would expect these challenges to lead home buyers to decide to purchase existing housing. In spite of everything, however, more and more home buyers are opting to build.

01 Why is it surprising that so many people are having new homes built?
(A) Developers have increased their fees as the cost of materials has risen.
(B) Less land is available in the downtown area now than six years ago.
(C) Forecasters predicted that fewer people would have houses built this year.
(D) It is more expensive to have a house built than to buy an existing one.

02 What is mentioned as a common challenge of having a house built?
(A) Locating good neighborhoods and roads
(B) Finding workers who have time to build
(C) Paying for rent and a mortgage at the same time
(D) Having a high tax rate

Charles Darwin was both a naturalist and a scientist. Darwin's *Origin of Species* (1859) was based on twenty-five years of research in testing and checking his theory of evolution. "Darwinism" had a profound effect on the natural sciences, the social sciences, and the humanities. Churchmen who feared for the survival of religious institutions rushed to attack him. However Darwin never attempted to apply his laws of evolution to human society. It was the social Darwinist who expanded the theory of evolution to include society as a whole. The social Darwinist viewed society as a "struggle for existence" with only the "fittest" members of society able to survive. They espoused basically a racist and elitist doctrine. Some people were naturally superior to others; it was in the "nature of things" for big business to take over "less fit," smaller concerns.

01 The final sentence of the passage beginning "Some people …" is the author's attempt to _____.

(A) summarize one point of view
(B) discredit Charles Darwin's theory
(C) voice his or her own point of doctrine
(D) explain the modern prominence of big business

02 The underlined word espoused is closest in meaning to _____.
(A) disregarded   (B) emphasized
(C) alleviated   (D) adopted

03 The author's primary purpose in this passage is to _____.
(A) give an example of Darwinian evolution
(B) warn of the dangers of having one's ideas abused
(C) explain how Darwin's theory was applied to society
(D) defend Darwin against modern charges of racism and elitism

Comparative psychology has identified a number of symptoms that may help to distinguish intelligent, conscious imitation from automatic copying. In the first case, the solution comes instantly in the form of insight not requiring repetition. Such a solution pertains to all characteristics of intellectual action. It involves understanding the field structure and relations between objects. On the contrary, automatic drill imitation is carried out through repeating trial-and-error series, which show no sign of conscious comprehension and do not include understanding the field structure. In this sense, it can be said that animals are unteachable.

In the child's development, on the contrary, imitation and instruction play a major role. They bring out the human qualities of the mind and lead the child to new developmental levels. In learning to speak, as in learning school subjects, imitation is indispensable. What the child can do in cooperation today he can do alone tomorrow. Therefore the only good kind of instruction is that which marches ahead of development and leads it.

01 밑줄 친 indispensable과 의미상 가장 가까운 것은?
 (A) useless
 (B) impossible
 (C) essential
 (D) feeble

02 본문에서 제시되고 있는 모방의 역할을 가장 잘 설명한 것은?
 (A) 모방이 인성 교육과 학습에 중요한 이유는 아이들이 어른들의 행위를 따라함으로써 협동정신을 기를 수 있기 때문이다.
 (B) 모방은 아이들의 학습 과정에서 개별적으로 배운 내용을 차후에 보다 강화해 주는 중요한 보조역할을 한다.
 (C) 근본적으로 모방은 효율적인 학습에 방해가 되기 때문에 학습과정에서 배제되어야 하지만 때로는 효과적인 문제해결 방법을 제시해 준다.
 (D) 모방의 중요한 학습 기능은 아이들이 먼저 어른들이 하는 것을 따라한 후에 혼자 그 일을 독자적으로 할 수 있다는 데에 있다.

Pure science may seem useless in the usual sense, but over a long period of time it surely leads to economic and technological benefits. If we stop paying for pure science today, there will be no applied science tomorrow. Charles Darwin's work on evolution and Gregor Mendel's on the heredity of plants laid the foundations for the science of genetics, which eventually led to the discovery of DNA, which led to genetic engineering, which is now exploding with unimaginable applications. Michael Faraday's discovery of how a magnet can produce electricity made possible the first hydroelectric power plant fifty years later. Yet Darwin and Mendel and Faraday were not supported with any such profit in mind, nor could they have been. A nation cannot bet on pure scientists like betting on horses. It can, however, build stables.

01 According to the passage, which of the following does not belong to pure science?
    (A) science of genetics
    (B) discovery of DNA
    (C) genetic engineering
    (D) electromagnetism

02 According to the passage, a nation can support pure science by _____.
    (A) focusing grants on the most productive pure scientists
    (B) leading applied scientists to patronize pure scientists
    (C) awarding pure scientists for applications created by them
    (D) providing pure scientists with good research conditions

03 What is the main idea of the passage?
    (A) Pure science is developed by curiosity-driven research, regardless of benefits.
    (B) Pure science has produced as many eminent scientists as applied science.
    (C) Pure science provides the soil from which applied science and technology grow.
    (D) Pure science cannot develop until a nation's economy is sufficiently developed.

In 1961, President Kennedy brought in the "brilliant" young head of Ford Motor Co., Robert McNamara, as secretary of defense. Faced with the problem of a growing communist influence in Vietnam, McNamara went right to work, confident in the powerful analytic tools that had been successful at Ford. In short order he silenced his critics, increased U.S. involvement and predicted confidently that we had the situation well in hand.

All this was done with little thought to the history of the region, the culture(s) of its people or the true motivations of our opponents. Now, of course, McNamara's name is a symbol for this prideful swagger.

Sound familiar? Only 40 years later a new crop of intelligent, forceful and supremely self-confident leaders has decided to do the same kind of thing in a different part of the world. And, in an eerily parallel way, they predict victory while the true situation goes south.

01 What is the main idea of the passage?
(A) New McNamaras bring us new hubris
(B) New foreign policy is brought home
(C) American foreign policies since 1960s
(D) Nothing changes in the America's world management

02 Which of the following best replaces the underlined "goes south?"
(A) improves
(B) deteriorates
(C) ameliorates
(D) travels toward the south

Without contact with temptation, virtue is worthless, and even a meaningless term. Temptation is an essential form of that conflict which is the essence of life. Without the fire of perpetual temptation no human spirit can ever be tempered and fortified. The zeal of the Moral Reformers who would sweep away all temptation and place every young creature from the outset in a temptation-free vacuum, even if it could be achieved (and the achievement would not only annihilate the whole environment but eviscerate the human heart of its vital passions), would merely result in the creation of a race of useless weaklings. Temptation is even more than a stimulus to conflict. It is itself, in so far as it is related to passion, the ferment of Life. To face and reject temptation may be to fortify life. To face and accept temptation may be to enrich Life. He who can do neither is not fit to live.

01 Choose the main idea of the passage.
    (A) Why should we build Temptation-free society?
    (B) Why is both Temptation and Virtue necessary?
    (C) Why is Virtue necessary?
    (D) Why is Temptation necessary?

02 According to the writer's point of view, which of the following is true?
    (A) Virtues only are absolutely right.
    (B) There is no Temptation-free society that we have made.
    (C) Challenge and overcome Temptation.
    (D) Deny the existence of Temptation.

Niuafo'o, which has been nicknamed "Tin Can Island," lies about 190 miles northeast of Suva, Fiji. It is five miles in diameter. The odd part of it is that, though Niuafo'o is purely volcano and has no reef, it is an almost perfect circle of land surrounding an almost equally circular lake in its center. The land rises from the sea in cliffs 60 to 70 feet high. From this elevation the land slopes upward for three-fourths of a mile and then rises abruptly to a ridge of about 400-foot elevation. The waters of the lake are alkaline and are said to rise and fall with the tide. There is no pure water on the island and the rain water is insufficient for the needs of the 1229 people. They do not suffer, however, because they are able to obtain liquid from coconuts. Landing on Niuafo'o is difficult. The island got its nickname because the natives swim or canoe out to passing mail ships and carry the mail from and to the island in a tin can lashed to pole.

01 Choose the best of the following titles for this selection.
(A) The Volcanic Islands
(B) The Geography of Niuafo'o
(C) Life in the Pacific Islands
(D) How Tin Can Island Got Its Name

02 Niuafo'o received its nickname of "Tin Can Island" because _____.
(A) water is stored in tin cans
(B) one of its volcanoes looks like a tin can
(C) its postal system is concerned with a tin can
(D) it is circular in shape similar to a tin can

They call it the Valley of Death. A sulfurous pall often hangs in the air, hiding a toxic inferno below. When the sun sets behind the nearby mountains, it is barely visible through a dense veil of pollution. Dead scrub blankets the once verdant hillsides. Fish pulled from the city's fetid rivers are blind and mutant. In Vila Parisi, a favela(shantytown) at the city's edge, open sewers foaming with hot industrial wastes flood regularly. The city's this transformation began when industries started moving in nearly 30 years ago. Petrobrás, the government-owned petroleum monopoly, came first, building an oil refinery in 1954. Others followed, including four U.S.-owned firms. French and Italian multinationals have also moved into the area and set up shop. Paulo Figueiredo, president of Union Carbide, explains: "Companies were attracted because of the availability of raw materials, the proximity of Santos harbor, and the largest market in Brazil, São Paulo. It is only natural that when you have this confluence of industry you will have pollution, and so the problem was born."

01 What is this passage mainly about?

(A) The Valley of Death
(B) Industrialization and Environmental disruption
(C) The advantage of Industrialization
(D) The damage of the sulfurous gas

02 What does the word "the Valley of Death" not refer to in this passage?

(A) a sulfurous pall hung in the air
(B) the radioactive wastes
(C) a dense veil of pollution
(D) the city's fetid rivers

The Bali road map contains no specific commitments or figures on the emissions reductions that developed countries will need to take, beyond language that "deep cuts" will be needed. Earlier in the week the EU fought hard to include a specific target of 25 to 40% cuts for developed nations by 2040, and a need to halve global emissions — two figures cited by the UN's Intergovernmental Panel on Climate Change's (IPCC) latest assessment of global warming science. Neither made it into the final text, thanks largely to determined opposition from the U.S., although a footnote points to the IPCC report. For environmentalists who had hoped that the recent avalanche of data underscoring the rising crisis of climate change might prompt tougher action, Bali was a disappointment. "It was a rather weak deal," said Meena Rahman, chair of Friends of the Earth International. "It's compromised."

01   What is the main topic of the passage?
(A) different responses to the Bali road map
(B) seriousness of global warming
(C) what wasn't achieved at Bali
(D) landmark achievements at Bali
(E) the conflict between environmentalists and the U.S.

02   According to the passage, which of the following is CANNOT be inferred?
(A) The Bali road map includes no statement about reduction in emissions.
(B) EU failed to set the specific target into the Bali road map.
(C) UN's Intergovernmental Panel on Climate Change recently presented the target for reduction in emissions.
(D) The U.S. didn't support adopting the specific target for developed countries.
(E) A huge number of data recently accentuated the mounting crisis of climate change.

If a man harms his family in a civilized country, the police are called in to stop him. If a gang of thugs terrorizes a neighborhood, the police mount an operation to shut them down. ①_____, if you are audacious enough to organize an even bigger gang of thugs, you can take over a whole country. Call yourself some sort of political party, and the world's media will obligingly use this title, thus helping legitimize your crimes, as most notoriously happened in Germany in the early 1930s. The governments and diplomats of the world will talk to you in the vain belief that because you claim to be a political organization, this somehow means you are reasonable people. ②_____, you will be able to abuse, torture, murder and rob the nation's people at will, as has happened on so many occasions in the past century.

01 빈칸 ①과 ②에 들어갈 말을 순서대로 바르게 짝지은 것은?
(A) However — Meanwhile
(B) Furthermore — Contrarily
(C) Nevertheless — Instead
(D) Similarly — Otherwise

02 이 글의 주제와 관련하여 이 글 뒤에 이어질 문장으로 가장 알맞은 것은?
(A) Is it necessary to forgive immoral or criminal politicians?
(B) Is human nature unalterable despite the advance of civilization?
(C) Is it impossible to clear despotic rulers of their hypocrisy?
(D) Is morality or criminality applicable only on a small scale?

Drinking more than three cups of coffee a day helps protect older women against some age-related memory decline, French researchers say, giving women more reason to love the world's most popular stimulant. Men did not enjoy the same benefit, they said. "The more coffee one drank, the better the effects seemed to be on (women's) memory functioning in particular," said Karen Ritchie at the French National Institute of Medical Research, whose work appears in the journal, *Neurology*.

The study found women who drank more than three cups of coffee per day, or its caffeine equivalent in tea, retained more of their verbal and — to a lesser extent — visual memories over four years. Women over 80 reaping more benefits from these beverages than those who were 10 to 15 years younger. Some studies in mice have suggested that caffeine might block the buildup of proteins that lead to mental decline. Ritchie is not sure why only women benefited in her study.

01 Which of the following would contiguously follow the passage?

(A) An effect of caffeine on the cognitive decline in women
(B) A reasoned guess about the reason that coffee offers no such benefits for men
(C) An average worldwide daily coffee consumption
(D) Some women's idiosyncratic metabolism

02 Which of the following can be inferred from the passage?

(A) The benefits of coffee for women increased with age.
(B) Caffeine prevents dementia.
(C) Coffee has been linked to reduced risks of the liver and diabetes.
(D) Coffee has side effects like other treatments for cognitive decline.

Psychology recognizes two types of research, experimental and differential. The former is concerned mainly with the overall processes governing human activities, and the latter sets out to establish individual differences in performance. More recent studies have demonstrated the need for a third type of psychological study, namely, that which has to do with human development. Rather than considering this aspect of human performance as a part of the first two types, scientists have noted that developmental research indeed belongs in a separate category in and of itself. Piaget's work would indisputably fall in the area of developmental theories that have had great impact on both experimental and differential research. When examining Piaget's studies, it is necessary to keep in mind that, while his theories have been highly influential, his methodology has been strongly criticized. The primary shortfall of his work had to do with a lack of definition and standardization in his data and experiment design.

01   According to the passage, what is the central goal of experimental research?

(A) To arrive at a general classification of individuals
(B) To analyze individual differences in human activity
(C) To establish the psychological processes governing humans
(D) To administer experiments on humans and processes

02   It can be inferred from the passage that the author is a proponent of _____.

(A) reversing current trends in research
(B) furthering a third branch of investigation
(C) abolishing experimental and differential studies
(D) assessing a need for human development

At 7:35 a.m. on November 13, 1872, in the port city of Le Havre, France, the art world changed forever. Claude Monet gazed out his hotel window and began to paint what he saw. The result was "Impression, Soleil Levant"("Impression, Sunrise") — and the birth of a movement.

How do we know exactly when Impressionism began? Because of Donald Olson, a Texas State University astrophysicist who uses astronomy to solve art and literary mysteries. When art historian Geraldine Lefebvre and Marmottan Monet Museum deputy director Marianne Mathieu asked Olson to help determine the painting's provenance, the self-styled "_____" began by poring over maps and photos to identify Monet's hotel and room. Then he turned to astronomy — using the rising sun and the moon to determine the tide, season, and time of day — and consulted digitized 19th-century weather observations. The final clues were the smoke plumes in the painting, showing the wind blowing east to west.

Those findings — plus the "72" by Monet's signature — closed the case and put a precise time stamp on a timeless work of art.

01 Choose the best phrase for the blank.
(A) terrain surveyor
(B) mystic hermit
(C) celestial sleuth
(D) divine messenger

02 Which of the following was NOT used to determine when "Impression, Soleil Levant" was created?
(A) astronomy
(B) cartography
(C) meteorology
(D) geography

White noise and other soothing sounds, once mainly played on machines to aid nighttime sleep, are increasingly helping make daytime hours more serene. Daytime white-noise listeners say the sounds serve two main purposes: to block out distractions and lessen sounds that cause anxiety, such as sirens. When played through headphones, the sounds help people tune out chatty co-workers, pounding jackhammers and the dentist's drill. White noise can be used to create a more relaxing environment, masking sounds and promoting a sense of privacy. To make the soothing sounds, developers take computer-generated sounds or sounds recorded in nature and make an audio file that usually is repeated. These digital files are then available at the iTunes store and on other websites. Most popular are sounds from nature: rain, wind, waves crashing on the beach and crickets.

01 The best title of the passage would be _____.
(A) White Noise to Tune Out Distractions
(B) Some Advantages from Nature Sounds
(C) The Various Aids for Improving Daytime Concentration
(D) An Unexpected Pleasure of Mixed Sounds
(E) Popular Uses for White Noise Generators

02 According to the passage, which of the following is true?
(A) Many people can feel the nature in the raw with relaxing sounds.
(B) Actively listening to white noise is one of the best ways to reform a criminal.
(C) Developers of soothing sounds go trekking in search of unique sounds.
(D) Natural ambient sounds to be used for relaxing can be downloaded from websites.
(E) Many prefer listening to computer-generated sounds to sounds from nature.

When my family and friends heard that I forgave the driver of the truck that hit me, they all said I was a very good person. Actually, I'm just like you. I figured I'd be really angry. But when you are so dramatically confronted with your own mortality, your perspective changes. I don't have time for bitterness. Life is too short to spend a second of it cultivating enemies. Annie Dillard wrote that how we spend our lives is how we spend our days. I choose to spend mine on the sunny side, not in a dark cave. And you know what? Forgiving the driver who struck me was as much of <u>a weight off my shoulders</u> as it was his. Maybe more. It was a cosmic win-win. I could have spent the rest of my life being bitter, sad and sorry. I could have.

01 Choose the one that CANNOT replace the underlined part.
    (A) taking a load off my mind
    (B) giving me the cold shoulder
    (C) alleviating my suffering
    (D) lifting a burden from my shoulders

02 Why does the author share the car accident story?
    (A) to explain retributive justice in the real world
    (B) to call for precautions against traffic casualties
    (C) to denounce the human obsession with the past
    (D) to give the lesson that forgiveness is freedom

03 Which explanation is most likely to be true of the author?
    (A) The author was distinguished from other people for his or her extraordinary neutrality.
    (B) The author turned the driver into an object of resentment and contempt.
    (C) The author learned to embrace optimism and turn away from pessimism.
    (D) The author complained about the occurrence of such a fatal accident.

PASSAGE

051—100

Late in the 19th century, and very briefly, there was an anti-realistic literary movement called "symbolism," also known as "neo-Romanticism," "idealism," or "impressionism." Symbolism was briefly popular in France, and it recurred occasionally in the 20th century. The idea behind symbolism is that truth can be grasped only by intuition, not through the senses or rational thought. Thus, ultimate truths can be suggested only through symbols, which evoke in the audience various states of mind that correspond vaguely with the playwright's feelings.

One of the principal dramatic symbolists, Maurice Maeterlinck, believed that every play contains a "second level" of dialogue which speaks to the soul. Through verbal beauty, contemplation, and a passionate portrayal of nature, great drama conveys the poet's idea of the unknown. Therefore, plays which present human actions can only, through symbols, suggest higher truths gained through intuition. The symbolists did not deal at all with social problems. Rather, they turned to the past and tried to suggest universal truths independent of time and space, as Maeterlinck did, for example, in *Pelleas and Melisande*.

01 위 글에서 Maurice Maeterlinck의 견해라고 유추할 수 없는 것은?

(A) Plays represent the immaterial realities of thought and feeling by using symbolic dialogues.
(B) Truth in literary works can be figured out by intuition and implicitly presented through symbols.
(C) Dramatists should reject imaginative idealization in favor of detailed descriptions of the society.
(D) Plays have a poetic fancy and deep inspiration which appeal to the audience's own feelings.

02 밑줄 친 "evoke"와 의미상 가장 가까운 것은?

(A) generate (B) involve
(C) reveal   (D) explain

A serious critic has to comprehend the particular content, unique structure, and special meaning of a work of art. And here she faces a dilemma. The critic must recognize the artistic element of uniqueness that requires subjective reaction; yet she must not be unduly prejudiced by such reactions. Her likes and dislikes are less important than what the work itself communicates, and her preferences may blind her to certain qualities of the work and thereby prevent an adequate understanding of it. Hence, it is necessary that a critic develop a sensibility informed by familiarity with the history of art and aesthetic theory. On the other hand, it is insufficient to treat the artwork solely historically, in relation to a fixed set of ideas or values. The critic's knowledge and training are, rather, a preparation of the cognitive and emotional abilities needed for and adequate personal response to an artwork's own particular qualities.

01 According to the author, a serious art critic may avoid being prejudiced by her subjective relations if she _____.

(A) treats an artwork in relation to a fixed set of ideas and values
(B) brings to her observation a knowledge of art history and aesthetic theory
(C) allows more time for the observation of each artwork
(D) takes into account the preferences of other art critics

02 The author implies that it is insufficient to treat a work of art solely historically because _____.

(A) doing so would lead the critic into a dilemma
(B) doing so can blind the critic to some of the artwork's unique qualities
(C) doing so can insulate the critic from personally held beliefs
(D) subjective reactions can produce a biased response

03 The passage suggests that the author would be most likely to agree with of the following statement?

(A) Art speaks to the passion as well as to the intellect.
(B) Most works of art express unconscious wishes or desires.
(C) The best art is accessible to the greatest number of people.
(D) The art produced in the last few decades is of inferior quality.

I find it takes the young writer a long time to become aware of what language really is as a medium of communication. He thinks he should be able to put down his meaning at once and be done with it, and he puts it down and release his feeling for it in language that is meaningless to anyone else. He has to learn that he can load almost any form of words with his meaning and be expressing himself but communicating nothing. He has to learn that language has grown naturally out of the human need to communicate, that it belongs to all those who use it and its communicative capacities have developed to meet the general need, that it is most alive when it comes off the tongue supported as it always is by the look and action of the speaker, that the tongue use of it is universal but the written use of it is relatively rare. He must come to see that tongue use is filled with cliches which are the common counters best serving the general need. Words and phrases that come off his tongue made alive by the living presence of himself become on paper dead transcriptions. Somehow he must overcome the capacity of words to remain dead symbols of meaning as they are in the dictionary. He must breathe life into them as he sets them on paper.

01 The title below that best expressed the ideas of this passage is _____.

(A) Why Cliches Are Valueless
(B) The Young Writer Speaks
(C) How Speech Aids the Writer
(D) Why Writing Is Difficult

02 The passage indicates that when words are spoken and then written _____.

(A) they become more powerful
(B) they become more understandable
(C) their effect is different
(D) their dictionary definitions have no value

03 The author implies that young writers are _____.

(A) in too much of a hurry to have their say
(B) lacking in confidence
(C) too critical in analyzing their own work
(D) too emotional in their approach to writing

[I] The causes of schizophrenia are not clear, but schizophrenia has long been attributed to faulty parenting. [II] In cases where schizophrenia developed, the parents were often considered responsible. [III] However, recent studies are now pointing to heredity and prenatal environmental factors as the chief culprits in this disease. [IV]

Recent studies of identical twins have been used to demonstrate that heredity plays a role in the development of schizophrenia. These studies have shown that in cases where one identical twin is afflicted with schizophrenia, the other twin has a 50 percent probability of also suffering from it.

However, heredity is not believed to be the only culprit. Studies of the fingerprints of identical twins have lent credence to the theory that prenatal environmental factors are likely contributors to the development of schizophrenia. In studies of pairs of identical twins in which one is afflicted with schizophrenia and one is not, abnormalities were found in the fingerprints of one-third of the twins. Since fingers develop in the second trimester of pregnancy, the hypothesis has been proposed that the abnormalities in the fingerprints were due to a second-trimester trauma.

01 The author's purpose in this passage is to _____.
    (A) enumerate examples
    (B) cause the development of schizophrenia
    (C) prove that faulty parenting is the main cause of schizophrenia
    (D) refute a common misconception

02 The following sentence can be added to paragraph 1. Choose the most appropriate place for the following sentence.
    They were faulted for having been uncaring, or manipulative, or emotionally abusive.
    (A) [I]   (B) [II]
    (C) [III]   (D) [IV]

03 This passage would probably be assigned reading in which of the following courses?
    (A) Criminology   (B) Psychology
    (C) Statistics   (D) Public Administration

One of the major changes in psychoanalysis since Freud's death has been the growing emphasis by a number of analysts on autonomous ego functions. This emphasis is reflected in the phrase "ego psychology." A prime mover in this development has been Heinz Hartmann. Whereas Freud saw the ego as essentially subservient to the demands of the id though the ego could gain some amount of control, Hartmann and his colleagues give greater autonomy to the ego. In fact, they consider the ego, as well as the id, as having origins in basic human inheritance. In their view, the ego has its own developmental course and operates on neutralized energy, which makes possible an interest in objects and activities that are not necessarily related to underlying sexual or aggressive drives. Though Freud at times also seemed to be suggesting that such interests are possible, his dominant theme is different: objects and activities are "interesting" to the person primarily because they are related, directly or indirectly, to the basic personality components of sex and aggression.

01 Which of the following statements about the new development on psychoanalysis after Freud's death is best supported by the passage?
(A) A strong social flavor to the theory is brought about.
(B) Psychoanalysis is dead and waiting for burial.
(C) The ego's development may be set prior to its existence.
(D) The patient is likely to be plagued by unconscious guilt.

02 The underlined word 'autonomous' is closest in meaning to which of the following?
(A) interrelated   (B) restricted
(C) elaborate   (D) free

We animals don't give plants nearly enough credit. When we want to dismiss a fellow human as ineffectual or superfluous, we call him a "potted plant." A "vegetable" is how we refer to a person reduced to utter helplessness, having lost most of the essential tools for getting along in life. Yet plants get along in life just fine, thank you, and did so for millions of years before we came along. True, they lack such abilities as locomotion, the command of tools and fire, the miracles of consciousness and language. To animals like ourselves, these are the tools for living we deem the most "advanced," which is not at all surprising, since they have been the shining destinations of our evolutionary journey thus far. But the next time you're tempted to celebrate human consciousness as the pinnacle of evolution, stop to consider where you got that idea. Human consciousness. Not exactly _____. In fact, there are some other pinnacles of evolution, the kind that would get a lot more press if natural history were written by plants rather than animals. For while we were nailing down locomotion, consciousness, and language, the plants were hard at work developing a whole other bag of tricks, taking account of the key existential fact of plant life: rootedness.

01 Choose the one that best fills in the blank.
   (A) a definite asset
   (B) a universal truth
   (C) an objective source
   (D) an ultimate goal

02 What is the main idea of the passage?
   (A) We are prejudiced against plants, but they deserve more research on their evolution.
   (B) As animals have achieved feats in their evolutionary course, so will plants in the future.
   (C) Though they have many differences, plants and animals diverged from a common ancestor.
   (D) Plants also have developed their own strategies for surviving and flourishing on the earth.

03 Which of the following is an animal's most salient difference from a plant according to the passage?
   (A) locomotion   (B) use of tools and fire
   (C) consciousness   (D) language

If we were perpetually conscious of the insecurity of life and happiness we might easily become morbid, and lose our ardour alike in work and in pleasure. If we are never conscious of it, however, we are likely to set a false value on what is really valueless, and to waste our years in pursuit of things that are not worth pursuing. Hence, it is an excellent medicine for the mind that we should occasionally realize that we are travelling through space on a fragile crust of earth that may one day subside, bringing a sudden end to ourselves, our possessions and our ambitions. Many of the philosophers, at least, have thought so, and have made it their business to remind us that we build up our business and pursue our dreams under the shadow of death. We are all condemned to die, it has been said, but under an indefinite reprieve, and we cannot measure the worth of anything in life by a standard which takes no account of this.

01 Choose the closest meaning to the underlined part of the passage.
   (A) Human cloning will be eventually made a futile achievement.
   (B) We have the only rule of philosophy to measure the depth of life.
   (C) Economic value cannot be a standard for your life.
   (D) We are the unhappiest but philosophical creature in the universe.

02 Choose the main idea of the above passage.
   (A) We sometimes need to be pessimists.
   (B) We have no standard to judge by for our life.
   (C) We are all fellow travellers on a journey to perpetuality.
   (D) We have no stake in the gaiety of life.

The visual system in the brain is too slow to process information if the images are slipping across the retina at more than a few degrees per second. Thus, for humans to be able to see while moving, the brain must compensate for the motion of the head by turning the eyes. Another complication for vision in frontal-eyed animals is the development of a small area of the retina with a very high visual acuity. This area is called the fovea, and covers about 2 degrees of visual angle in people. To get a clear view of the world, the brain must turn the eyes so that the image of the object of regard falls on the fovea. Eye movements are thus very important for visual perception, and any failure to make them correctly can lead to serious visual disabilities.

Having two eyes is an added ①_____, because the brain must point both of them accurately enough that the object of regard falls on corresponding points of the two retinas; otherwise, double vision would occur. The movements of different body parts are controlled by striated muscles acting around joints. The movements of the eye are no exception, but they have special advantages not shared by skeletal muscles and joints, and so are considerably different.

---

01 다음 중 첫 번째 문단의 주제로 적절한 것을 고르시오.

(A) visual system
(B) frontal-eyed animals
(C) retina
(D) importance of eye movements

02 빈칸 ①에 알맞은 것은?

(A) relaxation
(B) approximation
(C) precision
(D) tension

03 다음 빈칸에 가장 알맞은 것은?

To get the best view, the image of the object should fall on _____.

(A) retina
(B) fovea
(C) cornea
(D) iris

The latest scam in business is to make the customer do all the work. Of course, the customer-as-worker is an old lurk. Service stations were first in, when they removed the attendants and decided people could pump their own fuel. Next came the fast food restaurants, who decided the customers should clear their own tables and leave the trays neatly stacked. Business says, "We're trying to reduce costs, which we then pass on as savings to our customers."

Everywhere companies are in love with the idea of the customer as unpaid staffer. At Qantas, frequent flyer members are now asked to print out their own boarding pass, using their home computer. According to the airline, it's all for the convenience of the customer: no way is it just to save Qantas from using its own paper, ink and staff time. You now turn up at the airport, gripping your self-printed boarding pass, half-expecting them to throw you the keys and pilot's uniform. Where, exactly, does this stuff stop? The self-serve customer is like the self-milking cow: a great convenience for business but you do have to wonder what's in it for the cow.

01 The underlined sentence "you do have to wonder what's in it for the cow" implies that _____.

(A) customers have to require companies to reduce personnel expenditure
(B) companies have to take advantage of self-service because they can reduce their own cost
(C) it is necessary to think how business improves convenience of self-serving customers
(D) customers should consider what is advantageous for them rather than for business

02 Which of the following is true according to the passage?

(A) The idea considering the customer as the worker appears strange to old people.
(B) Both service stations and fast food restaurants are reluctant to use the self-service system.
(C) Qantas believes that self-printed tickets eventually bring benefit to their passengers.
(D) When you bring your boarding pass, Qantas will provide you with the keys.

03 Which of the following best describes the attitude of the author toward self-service?

(A) humorous
(B) evenhanded
(C) censorious
(D) sanguine

Writing for a broad audience is a constant struggle. Journalists today are well educated and have broad interests, and their natural inclination, if not checked by self-monitoring and good editing, is to _____. The marketplace does not discourage this elitist tendency as efficiently as it used to. That is because journalism is in slow transformation from appealing to a mass audience to tailoring its appeal to many different classes of audiences. As Alvin Toffler has said, we are moving from 'a few messages sent to many people' to 'many messages sent to a few people.'

Newspapers, and the advertisers who support them, still count for the most part on maximizing their reach, so clear writing is still important. The message was carried most forcefully to the media by a 1938 immigrant from Austria named Rudolf Flesch. His dissertation at Columbia University included a mathematical definition of readability based on sentence and word length, and it was published as *Marks of Readable Style*. But, being a dissertation, it was not itself a very good example of readability. When he realized this, Flesch rewrote it as *The Art of Plain Talk*, published by Harper and Brothers in 1946.

01 Choose the one that best fills in the blank.
(A) cover feature stories
(B) write for each other
(C) go beyond their newsbeat
(D) change their writing style

02 Which of the following can be inferred from the passage?
(A) We have more kinds of newspapers and magazines today than in the past.
(B) Alvin Toffler means that information is increasing but subscribers decreasing.
(C) Elitist writing serves to spread the influence of newspapers and advertisers.
(D) *Marks of Readable Style* is probably more readable than *The Art of Plain Talk*.

03 Which of the following is not associated with the readability in journalism?
(A) At United Press in the mid twentieth century, the maxim was "Write for the Omaha milkman."
(B) When Blanche Perkins taught journalism in the 1940s, she told her students to write for a 12-year-old child.
(C) The admonition "Seek truth and write it" is found in the 1996 revision of the code of ethics of the Society of Professional Journalists.
(D) Edwin A. Lahey, as the Washington bureau chief for Knight Newspapers in the 1960s, advised his reporters to write for people who move their lips when they read.

Being an unhappy person doesn't mean you must be sad or dark. You can be interested instead of happy. You can be fascinated instead of happy. The barrier to this, of course, is that in our super-positive society, we have an unspoken zero-tolerance policy for negativity. Beneath the catch-all umbrella of negativity is basically everything that isn't super-positive. Seriously, who among us is having a "great!" day every day? Who feels "terrific!" all the time? _____.

Instead of trying to alleviate some of the uncomfortable and unpleasant emotions you feel by "trying to be positive", try being negative. This will help you get in touch with how you actually feel: "I feel hopeless and fat and stupid. And like a failure for feeling this way. And trying to be positive and upbeat makes me feel angry, and feeling angry makes me feel like I am broken."

If that's how you feel — however you feel — then you have a baseline, you have established a solid floor of reference. Sometimes just giving yourself permission to feel any emotion without judgment or censorship can lessen the intensity of those negative emotions.

01 Choose the one that best fills in the blank.
    (A) It is these super-positive people that we need
    (B) We cannot feel happy at all on rainy days
    (C) Anger and negativity have their uses too
    (D) Happiness and success are nowhere to be seen

02 Which of the following is associated with "our super-positive society"?
    (A) an espousal of pluralism
    (B) a holistic world view
    (C) an acceptance of paradox
    (D) a unilateral mindset

03 Which of the following cannot be inferred about happiness and unhappiness?
    (A) We can enjoy some positive things even when we are unhappy.
    (B) Happiness has nothing to do with what kind of society we live in.
    (C) It can be a road to happiness to give up trying to be happy.
    (D) If we embrace unhappiness as it is, happiness comes closer to us.

It is as though each of us investigated and made his own only a tiny circle of facts. Knowledge outside the day's work is regarded by most men as a gewgaw. Still we are constantly in reaction against our ignorance. We rouse ourselves at intervals and speculate. We revel in speculations about anything at all — about life after death or about such questions as that which is said to have puzzled Aristotle, 'why sneezing from noon to midnight was good, but from night to noon unlucky.' One of the greatest joys known to man is to take such a flight into ignorance in search of knowledge. The greatest pleasure of ignorance is, after all, the pleasure of asking questions. The man who has lost this pleasure or exchanged it for the pleasure of dogma, which is the pleasure of answering, is already beginning to stiffen. One envies so inquisitive a man as Jowett, who sat down to the study of physiology in his sixties. Most of us have lost the sense of our ignorance long before that age. We even become vain of our squirrel's hoard of knowledge and regard increasing age itself as a school of omniscience. We forget that Socrates was famed for wisdom not because he was omniscient but because he realized at the age of seventy that he still knew nothing.

01 Choose the one closest in meaning to the underlined "a gewgaw."
   (A) something valueless
   (B) something wonderful
   (C) something practical
   (D) something obtainable

02 Which of the following is not true about "most of us"?
   (A) We endeavor to know more in our daily life, but are reluctant to admit that we are ignorant.
   (B) We respect those who try hard to learn something new at an old age, but forget our ignorance.
   (C) We boast of all our little knowledge, which we think will increase as we get older.
   (D) We think Socrates was a wise man who knew everything, but he knew nothing in reality.

03 What is the main idea of the passage?
   (A) We cannot distinguish what we should know from what we need not know.
   (B) We should be aware of our ignorance and never cease asking questions.
   (C) We cannot have the pleasure of ignorance without the pleasure of dogma.
   (D) We should acknowledge that we know nothing and that we can do nothing.

It probably comes as no surprise that Stephen Hawking, an <u>outspoken</u> atheist, remains unconvinced about life after death, but the 69-year-old physicist made his position on the subject explicit in an interview with *The Guardian*.

I have lived with the prospect of an early death for the last 49 years. I'm not afraid of death, but I'm in no hurry to die. I have so much I want to do first. I regard the brain as a computer which will stop working when its components fail. There is no heaven of afterlife for broken down computers; that is a fairy story for people who are afraid of the dark.

MSNBC notes that Hawking's "*The Grand Design*" claimed that the origin of the universe could be explained without God, but he didn't take a stance as aggressive as the one taken in *the Guardian* interview.

01 Choose the one closest in meaning to the underlined "outspoken."
 (A) straightforward
 (B) adamant
 (C) presumptuous
 (D) well-rounded

02 Stephen Hawking compares human brains to computers most probably in order to _____.
 (A) blur the boundary between humans and computers
 (B) dismiss the immortal life as a mere delusion
 (C) illustrate his theoretical arguments more scientifically
 (D) soothe the humans' abnormal fear of death

03 Which of the following CANNOT be inferred about "Stephen Hawking"?
 (A) He has been afflicted with some serious chronic disease.
 (B) He might have encountered considerable resistance from religious groups.
 (C) He explained the birth of the universe denying the existence of a creator.
 (D) He is becoming more and more hostile to his opponents in his contention.

Ernest Rutherford beamed charged particles at gold foil. He observed that while most particles went through foil, some bounced back. In 1911 he theorized that atoms must be mainly empty space with a small nucleus in the center. That being so, electrons must orbit the nucleus; yet wouldn't charged electrons lose all their energy and fall into the nucleus? In 1913 Niels Bohr proposed that electrons behaved in quantum fashion. They remained in fixed orbits and moved from one orbit to another — in quantum leaps — when they emitted or absorbed energy. The neutron, the atom's last part until accelerators revealed more, was found in 1932 by James Chadwick. Theorist and experimenter were united in the person of Enrico Fermi, who studied electrons and gases before building the first fission reactor that led to the atomic bomb and nuclear power.

01 Rutherford theorized that atoms must be mainly empty space because _____.

(A) electrons lose all their energy
(B) most electrons went through the foil
(C) the small nucleus occupies the center
(D) charged particles gathered at the gold foil

02 According to Bohr, charged electrons losing their energy _____.

(A) shifted orbits
(B) fell into the nucleus
(C) still remained in the same orbits
(D) either emitted or absorbed energy

03 The above passage is mainly about _____.

(A) the investigation of the structure of the atom
(B) the theorists who were concerned with nuclear power
(C) the relative merits among contending theories
(D) the complex orbit of the electron moving around the nucleus

I guess it is true that big and strong things are much less dangerous than small soft weak things. Nature (whatever that is) makes the small and weak reproduce faster. And that is not true of course. The ones that did not reproduce faster than they died, disappeared. But how about little fault, little pains, little worries. The cosmic ulcer comes not from great concerns, but from little irritations. And great things can kill a man but if they do not he is stronger and better for them. A man is destroyed by the duck nibblings of nagging, small bills, telephones (wrong number), athlete's foot, ragweed, the common cold, boredom. All of these are the negatives, the tiny frustrations and no one is stronger for them.

01 The best title for this passage is _____.
   (A) Negative Things
   (B) The Cause of Cosmic Ulcer
   (C) The Danger of Small Things
   (D) The Strength of Small Things

02 Which is NOT true of the passage?
   (A) Small things take less time to reproduce.
   (B) Things which died before reproducing eventually vanished.
   (C) Small things are dangerous because they reproduce at a great rate.
   (D) Men are more affected by small annoyances than by big disasters.

03 The underlined part, "no one is stronger for them" means here _____.
   (A) no one gains anything from them
   (B) no one can resist them
   (C) everyone is destroyed by them
   (D) no one rises above them

It seems to be characteristic of our period that norms and truths which were once believed to be absolute, universal, and eternal, or which were accepted with blissful unawareness of their implications, are being questioned. In the light of modern thought and investigation, much of what was once taken for granted is declared to be in need of demonstration and proof. The criteria of proof themselves have become subjects of dispute. We are witnessing not only a general distrust of the validity of ideas but of the motives of those who assert them. This situation is aggravated by a war of each against all in the intellectual "<u>arena</u>" where personal self-aggrandizement rather than truth has come to be the coveted prize.

01 Our period can be defined by _____.
   (A) the relative impregnability of norms and truths
   (B) the uncertainty of norms and truths
   (C) the unchangeableness of norms and truths
   (D) the dubious battle between norms and truths

02 According to the passage, men _____.
   (A) try to demonstrate and prove the rightness of old truths and norms
   (B) want to evolve a new way to prove the impeccability of truths and norms
   (C) cannot live without the proof to believe truths and norms
   (D) doubt both the established truth and norms and their premises

03 The underlined word "<u>arena</u>" is _____.
   (A) a premise
   (B) the general state of competition
   (C) a scene or place of competition or fighting
   (D) the general chaos resulting from competition

04 The author implies that modern thinkers doubt _____.
   (A) the validity of ideas and the motives of their proponents
   (B) the validity of ideas and the premises of their opponents
   (C) the validity of ideas and their premises
   (D) the validity of ideas only

Art, like words, is a form of communication. Words, spoken and written, render accessible to humans of the latest generations all the knowledge discovered by the experience and reflection, both of preceding generations and of the best and foremost minds of their own times. Art renders accessible to people of the latest generations all the feelings experienced by their predecessors and those already felt by their best and foremost contemporaries. Just as the evolution of knowledge proceeds by dislodging and replacing that which is mistaken, so the evolution of feeling proceeds through art. Feelings less kind and less necessary for the well-being of humankind are replaced by others kinder and more essential to that end. This is the purpose of art, and the more art fulfills that purpose, the better the art; the less it fulfills it, the worse the art.

01 The author develops the passage primarily by _____.
(A) theory and refutation
(B) example and generation
(C) comparison and contrast
(D) question and answer

02 According to the passage, knowledge is _____.
(A) evolutionary and emotional
(B) cumulative and progressive
(C) static and unmoving
(D) dynamic and cyclical

03 The style of the passage can be best described as _____.
(A) poetic
(B) speculative
(C) sarcastic
(D) explanatory

There is no law that states that the President of the United States must have a cabinet. The Constitution states only that the President "may require the opinion, in writing, of the principal officer in each of the executive departments, upon any subject relating to the duties of their respective offices." The President does not have to ask for this advice, and, when it is given, does not have to take it. Nevertheless, Presidents have often looked to this group of official councillors for information and advice, because no one person can know about everything that is going on in the nation.

Each President chooses the members of the cabinet with the "advice and consent" of the Senate, but these advisers serve at the President's pleasure and can be fired at any time. They are chosen for their knowledge, their experience, their special talents, or their general wisdom. They may be old and trusted friends, sometimes even relatives. They can be farmers, diplomats, scientists, or politicians. They meet weekly in the cabinet room next to the President's Oval Office in the West Wing of the White House.

01 According to the passage, why does the President have a cabinet?
   (A) It is useful for maintaining contact with the voters.
   (B) It is a valuable source of information.
   (C) It is required by the Constitution.
   (D) It was legislated by Congress.

02 The author suggests that the President chooses cabinet members based on _____.
   (A) voter support
   (B) his predecessor's recommendations
   (C) personal preference
   (D) political pressure

03 It can be inferred from the passage that each member of a President's cabinet is _____.
   (A) a past President
   (B) a scientist
   (C) a military officer
   (D) the head of an executive department

The rate at which the deforestation of the world is proceeding is alarming. In 1950 approximately 25 percent of the Earth's land surface had been covered with forests, and less than twenty-five years later the amount of forest land was reduced to 20 percent. This decrease from 25 percent to 20 percent from 1950 to 1973 represents an astounding 30 million square kilometers of forest land will be lost by 2040. The majority of deforestation is occurring in tropical forests in developing countries, fueled by the developing countries' need for increased agricultural land and the desire on the part of developed countries to import wood and wood products. More than 90 percent of the plywood used in the United States, for example, is imported from developing countries with tropical rain forests. By the mid-1980's, solutions to this expanding problem were being sought, in the form of attempts to establish an international regulatory organization to oversee the use of tropical forests.

01 The author's main purpose in this passage is to _____.
(A) cite statistics about an improvement on the Earth's land surface
(B) explain where deforestation is occurring
(C) make the reader aware of a worsening world problem
(D) blame developing countries for deforestation

02 Which of the following best describes the tone of the passage?
(A) Concerned
(B) Disinteresting
(C) Placid
(D) Exaggerated

03 This passage would probably be assigned reading in which of the following courses?
(A) Geology
(B) Geography
(C) Geometry
(D) Marine Biology

Some researchers think that one of the causes of alcoholism is a poor diet. They found that mice craved alcohol when they were given foods low in vitamin B.

At first, all of the mice in the experiment were put on the same diet. This diet was neither high nor low in vitamin B. The mice were given a choice of four liquids to drink. One was water and the other three were alcohol solutions. The alcohol concentration in the liquids ranged from the level found in beer to the level found in whiskey. Despite the fact that all of the mice ate the same food, they chose different liquids to drink. Some of them became alcoholics and some did not.

The researchers then gave the alcoholic mice a diet high in vitamin B. The mice that chose water were given food that was lower in vitamins and minerals than their original diet. The first group of mice stopped drinking whiskey and began to drink water. The second group stopped drinking water and began to drink whiskey. When vitamin B was added to the second group's diet, they again chose water and seemed to have no need for alcohol.

01 The researchers conducted this experiment to show that _____.
   (A) mice can become alcoholics
   (B) drunken mice are easier to catch
   (C) mice have the same diets as human beings
   (D) a lack of vitamin B might be one of the factors causing alcoholism in human beings

02 Which of these is NOT an example of what happened to the mice in this experiment?
   (A) They were given a choice of liquids to drink.
   (B) The alcoholic mice were given diets high in vitamin B.
   (C) Some of the alcoholic mice later chose water without having vitamin B added to their diet.
   (D) The mice which at first chose water chose alcohol to drink later in the experiment process.

03 What is the purpose of this passage?
   (A) To explain one of the possible causes of alcoholism.
   (B) To persuade people not to take vitamin B.
   (C) To describe what the hazard of alcoholism is.
   (D) To tell what the writer thinks causes alcoholism to the researchers through the experiment of mice.

04 How did the researchers find out that some mice would become alcoholics and some would not?
   (A) The mice chose different liquids to drink.
   (B) Some of the mice stuck to vitamins and minerals from the beginning.
   (C) Some of the mice were sorted to drink the alcohol concentrated liquids as an experiment.
   (D) The mice all ate the same food and drank the alcohol ranged from beer to whiskey by turns.

The great intellectual leaders in the past took the whole range of human experience as their domain. Aristotle, Aquinas, Erasmus, and Voltaire did not limit themselves to narrow fields of competency. They explored as experts the total of man's scientific, philosophical, and political knowledge.

The leaders of today seem to lack the ability to achieve equal excellence in more than one portion of today's areas of investigation. Einstein in physics achieved a different level from the one that Einstein achieved on the issues of the day. Bertrand Russell was an authority when writing his *Principia Mathematica*; Bertrand Russell was just another intellectual when writing on popular causes.

Could it be that today the amount of time required to master the accumulated data in one specialized field does not leave enough time, even for the genius, to think through the facts in more than one area? Possibly, when the computer becomes a matured tool of research, the process of assimilation of knowledge can be so speeded up that humanity will once again be able to profit from the encyclopedic minds that accept a total challenge from the universe around them.

01 The outlook expressed by the author is one of _____.
(A) joy
(B) confidence
(C) hopefulness
(D) disappointment

02 According to the author, it is desirable to _____.
(A) live a modest life
(B) specialize in one filed
(C) acquire practical knowledge
(D) be proficient in various areas of knowledge

03 Computers are superior to human beings in their ability to _____.
(A) handle many facts
(B) ask right questions
(C) come to conclusions
(D) reject erroneous data

Exposure to bright light may hold the key to helping people who suffer from jet lag and other sleep disorders. In a study of 14 men exposed to fluorescent lighting at various times during a 24-hour stretch, research scientists have determined that the body's natural alarm clock can be reset over a period of two to three days. This cuts a third of the time required for adjustments in the body after long international flights.

Dr. Charles Czeisler, director of the research team, concludes that light has a direct biological effect on the sleep-wake cycle of the body. The hypothalamus, the brain's sleep regulator, is connected straight to nerves in the eye's retina. Dr. Czeisler's theory is that light impulses are the primary factor in resetting the sleep-wake cycle. This stands in contrast to accepted belief that light only indirectly affects the cycle by making it more difficult to sleep.

01 What is the main subject of this passage?
(A) Various ways to avoid jet lag and sleep disorders
(B) Benefits of fluorescent lighting
(C) The nature of the sleep-wake cycle
(D) The effect of light on the internal clocks of humans

02 It can be inferred that resetting the body clock after long flights normally takes _____.
(A) between six and nine days
(B) almost exactly 24 hours
(C) around two to three days
(D) about four to five days

03 It can be inferred from the passage that Dr. Czeisler's theory _____.
(A) will completely eliminate all sleep disorders
(B) is not yet accepted principle
(C) has little practical application
(D) is based primarily on guesswork

Until recently, owning a fur coat, usually a mink, was an unquestioned emblem of luxury and social status. But lately a growing group of animal-rights protectionists has been aggressively denouncing such garments as "sadist symbols" that, they say, require the deaths of some 70 million helpless creatures each year — about 50 minks for each coat. That emotional claim has started a bitter battle that set the animal lobby against fur owners and the increasingly embattled fur industry. So nasty have the hostilities become that in some cities of the United States women wearing the fur coats are being publicly <u>jeered</u> or otherwise harassed.

The fur industry maintains that mink, which account for seventy five percent of the United States fur coats, are treated humanely and killed painlessly. Fur, the industry points out, is a natural fabric whose production does not pollute the environment or use fossil fuels, as does the creation of acrylic fibers. Nonetheless, the United States fur sales have remained stagnant — at an annual level of about $1.8 billion — over the past three years; during the Christmas season, many department stores slashing prices to move their furs.

01. What is the main topic of the passage?
    (A) Growing anti-fur movement
    (B) Lobbying for environmental protection
    (C) Endangered species of animal
    (D) New trends in fashion

02. What is the major problem faced by the fur industry?
    (A) The increasing difficulty to acquire minks
    (B) The fierce competition with textile industry
    (C) The government regulations against killing endangered species
    (D) The stagnant fur sales that seem to continue or worsen

03. Which of the following is NOT mentioned by the fur industry in their attempt to protect their business?
    (A) Fossil fuel is not used in the production of furs.
    (B) Minks are treated humanely and killed painlessly.
    (C) Minks are growing in number and are no longer endangered.
    (D) The production of furs does not pollute the environment.

04. Which of the following is closest in meaning to the underlined word "<u>jeered</u>"?
    (A) envied   (B) derided
    (C) esteemed   (D) disregarded

Few buildings in Tokyo are as easy to identify as the head office of staffing company Pasona in Tokyo's Marunouchi district. Plants burst from each of the building's balconies, enveloping it in greenery. The offices inside are equally _____, with pots hanging from ceilings and the staff cafeteria more like a greenhouse than an eatery. Then there's Pasona's staff-tended indoor farm. Covering about 1.5 hectares, this urban greensward grows an array of vegetables and even has rice paddies that, with the aid of indoor lighting, can be harvested three times a year.

As skeptics will rightly point out, it takes a lot of energy to power an indoor farm, but Pasona doesn't bill the project as a ready-made ecological solution. In part, it's a team-building exercise for the company's staff. It's also an attempt at promoting a greater understanding of environmental and food-supply concerns. More important, it's a pioneering experiment: How are we going to develop truly efficient urban farms if we don't start urban farming in the first place? Visits are free but need to be booked in advance; accessed via Otemachi or Nihonbashi stations.

01 Choose the one that best fills in the blank.
(A) messy
(B) verdant
(C) chimerical
(D) azure

02 According to the passage, what is true about "Pasona's indoor farm"?
(A) It almost entirely depends upon the sunlight from outside.
(B) It does not consume much energy thanks to eco-innovations.
(C) It is intended for both managerial and environmental purposes.
(D) It is a risky project undertaken by a budding venture company.

03 What is the purpose of the passage?
(A) to publicize an eco-conscious company and its indoor farming project
(B) to assess the Tokyo government's efforts to disseminate green workplaces
(C) to explain how an urban company can make a profit from its urban farm
(D) to show that there are more and more greenhouse-like buildings in Tokyo

The main streets of central Seoul were paralyzed last Sunday, hit by mass rallies organized by the Korean Confederation of Trade Unions, though the police had previously banned them. The demonstrators wielded wooden clubs and hurled stones at policemen in attempts to barge through the riot police. The Institute of International Management Development (IMD) based in Switzerland recently noted that the radical labor movement has been weakening the national competitiveness of Korea. Trade unions have been coming with excessive demands while the management has failed to gain their trust due to a lack of managerial transparency. The government has also failed to cope with labor issues with no concrete principles or policies.

Unionists have been claiming the right for assembly and demonstration to be guaranteed by the Constitution, _____ no one has the right to enjoy his or her freedom at the sacrifice of another person's freedom. The demonstrators who took to the streets on Sunday inflicted huge inconvenience to the general public and losses to proprietors of small shops and street vendors, in particular. The current government is responsible for the brewing dispute and confusion, as it has been adopting lenient policies toward unions. Now it needs to strictly crack down on unlawful collective activities to ensure social justice and the rule of law and principle instead of seeking populist policies.

01 What is the author's attitude toward "collective activities" in the passage?
    (A) grievous   (B) blameful
    (C) applausive   (D) revengeful

02 Choose the one that best fills in the blank.
    (A) otherwise   (B) as soon as
    (C) because   (D) even though

03 Choose the one that can best replace the underlined brewing.
    (A) lawless   (B) predictive
    (C) overcast   (D) impending

Legend has it Icarus fell from the sky because <u>hubris</u> led him too close to the sun, melting the wax that held the feathers on his wings. More likely, his arms just gave out. Uncounted numbers of "bird-men" have died over the centuries after leaping from tower or cliff, not realizing they could never flap homemade wings hard or fast enough to stay aloft. Their modern heirs, BASE jumpers, leap from buildings, cliffs, and bridges, plunge for a few exhilarating moments, and then throw out a parachute to slow their fall. Some don wing suits, with baffled fabric wings that generate enough lift to propel the wearer forward at up to 160 miles an hour while falling. J. T. Holmes of Squaw Valley, California, who has made about a thousand wing-suit jumps, says, "It's as close as human beings can get to flying like a bird." It's also extraordinarily dangerous: about 12 BASE jumpers die each year. Hitting the mountain while free-falling or after the parachute deploys is a common cause. The best success in purely human-powered flight came in 1988, when the Daedalus, a light-weight aircraft built by a team at the Massachusetts Institute of Technology, flew 71.5 miles from the Greek island of Crete to Santorini. The 69-pound craft, pedaled by a Greek Olympic cyclist, got caught in turbulence as it approached the beach at Santorini. It crashed in the sea, a few yards from the shore.

01 Choose the one closest in meaning to the underlined "<u>hubris</u>".
(A) carelessness (B) conceitedness
(C) dauntlessness (D) distractedness

02 According to the passage, what is true about "BASE jumpers"?
(A) Their predecessors jumped from heights with no means of flight.
(B) They enjoy free-falling for a while before throwing out the parachutes.
(C) They are safer when they use wing-suits than when they use parachutes.
(D) They often feel so excited that they forget to deploy parachutes in time.

03 What is the best title for the passage?
(A) The Wish to Fly Claiming A Cyclist
(B) The BASE Jumpers in Great Danger
(C) The Tragic Fall of Legendary Icarus
(D) The Daring Personal Flight Experiments

The body's internal clock, which controls when a person starts to feel tired, shifts after puberty, making it hard for most teens to fall asleep before 11 p.m. Class usually begins before 8:15 a.m., with many high schools starting as early as 7:15 a.m. To get to school on time, most teens have to get up by 6:30 a.m., guaranteeing they'll _____. Teens often sleep much later on weekends to catch up, making it even harder to fall asleep on Sunday night and wake up Monday morning. Playing catch-up on weekends also doesn't help teens stay alert when they need it most: during the week at school.

Since the 1990s, middle and high schools in more than two dozen states have experimented with later school start times. The results have been encouraging: more sleep, increased attendance, better grades and fewer driving accidents. For example, ninth graders' daily attendance rose from 83 percent to 87 percent and overall grades went up slightly when Minneapolis high schools moved the start time from 7:15 to 8:40 a.m. And car crashes involving teen drivers fell 15 percent when high schools in Fayette County, Ky., switched the high-school start time from 7:30 to 8:30 a.m. But most schools still start early, meaning teens have their work cut out for them if they want to get enough sleep.

01 Choose the one that best fills in the blank.
(A) be free of insomnia every night
(B) soon get accustomed to rising early
(C) be sleep-deprived during the week
(D) be much bothered by the punctuality

02 What does this passage mainly discuss?
(A) changes in adolescents' bio-rhythm
(B) importance of sleep habits during adolescence
(C) relations between sleep time and school life
(D) necessities for delaying the school start time

03 Which of the following cannot be inferred from the passage?
(A) Most of the teens have to reduce their school work to get enough sleep.
(B) It is not recommendable that teens make up for lack of sleep on weekends.
(C) Teenagers are allowed to drive a car in some parts of the United States.
(D) Babies and children go to bed earlier than adults owing to biological clocks.

Even when we try to be smart about fires, we often just make things worse. For more than a century, the U.S. Forest Service — the federal agency responsible for combatting wildfires — has pursued a policy of stamping out blazes wherever they occur and doing so all the more aggressively as population grows in the endangered regions. For those accustomed to living in urban areas, that makes sense — the job of a city fire department is to stop blazes before they damage property. But that's not how things work in the great Western forests. Paradoxically, trying to put out every minor blaze may raise the risk for the occasional megafire since the forests are not permitted to do their important work of occasionally clearing out accumulated vegetation. This is a little like letting newspapers pile up in your kitchen: if a fire occurs, the place is primed to blow. "These larger and more severe wildfires are an unintended consequence of a suppression policy that doesn't work," says Richard Minnich, a wildfire ecologist at the University of California at Riverside. "If anything, suppression actually endangers society."

01 What is the author's purpose in the passage?

(A) to point out that a wrong policy can lead to a conflagration in the great forests
(B) to urge that the government spend more money fighting wildfires in cities
(C) to argue that the urban society is more vulnerable to the unexpected wildfires
(D) to inform city dwellers of how huge and severe wildfires can be prevented

02 Which of the following cannot be inferred from the passage?

(A) Those in charge of fighting wildfires so far have tried just to put out all sizes of fires.
(B) The mere endeavor to extinguish fires does not always ensure better state of affairs.
(C) Fires, small and big, must be put out as soon as possible anywhere, especially in great forests.
(D) Accumulated vegetation in the forest is like something inflammable piled up in the kitchen.

03 What is the author's attitude toward "the suppression policy" in the passage?

(A) admiring   (B) deploring
(C) contemplating   (D) inquiring

Virginia, England's first colony in North America, was founded in 1607 at Jamestown. The ocean voyage from England to North America was long and dangerous, so the leaders of the colony lured Englishmen to Virginia with ①_____ promises of wealth.

Many of the first settlers were disappointed when they arrived. They did not become wealthy and they faced many hardships. The land was swampy and home to mosquitoes. The colonists led a very ②_____ existence; harsh weather and food shortages put the colony's future in doubt. Many suffered from disease, hunger, and cold. During the first year, half of the original settlers died.

In order to attract new settlers, the leaders of Virginia promised to ③_____ fifty acres of land to anyone who would come to the colony to live. Hoping to get land, thousands of the English sailed to Virginia between 1618 and 1622. By 1619, Virginia had its own assembly. Tobacco became an important industry. As the colony grew, the settlers and Native Americans got into ④_____ over land. In 1622, war broke out between the Native Americans and settlers. By 1625, the fighting was over. The settlers had won, and the Virginia colony had survived.

01 Which of the following is most suitable for the blank ①?
(A) temporary   (B) misleading
(C) shabby   (D) flexible

02 Which of the following is most suitable for the blank ②?
(A) fragile   (B) spacious
(C) impressive   (D) assiduous

03 Which of the following is most suitable for the blank ③?
(A) confiscate   (B) pine for
(C) dispose of   (D) distribute

04 Which of the following is most suitable for the blank ④?
(A) dealings   (B) pacts
(C) conflicts   (D) concession

Taking people for granted makes them very angry. Did you ever knock yourself out for someone, work hard to help, spend time and money — and get no appreciation? Instead, your extra effort is treated as if it was only what you were supposed to do.

Another turnoff is negative criticism. Negative criticism is when you are told a real, hard truth about yourself or something you've done but you are not told anything to make you want to improve or to do better. When someone tells you "I really liked your hair a lot better the other way," that's negative criticism. If a friend of yours has written a story and you tell him only what you didn't like and nothing of what you liked about it, that is also negative criticism.

Being taken for granted, or negatively criticized makes you want to take revenge. But you can turn it around, instead. Try to be the kind of person who is interested in everybody and shows it. Never ignore people who go out of their way to communicate or interact with you. Listen to them when they talk to you, make them feel that what they say matters, that they matter.

01 According to the passage negative criticism is _____.

(A) getting an answer back in a threatening way
(B) telling a lie to a person who is credulous
(C) criticism of disagreement at all points
(D) telling a person something true but destructive

02 The best thing to do after being taken for granted is to _____.

(A) take revenge
(B) go out of your way to open yourself to others
(C) ignore those who ignore you
(D) do something spectacular

03 Which of the following is the meaning of the "turnoff"?

(A) something which misleads
(B) a trick to escape something
(C) the condition of being relieved
(D) something that causes dislike

Everyone has a habit that once served them well but is now dragging them down. It might not be drink or drugs but it's an addiction nonetheless. Procrastination is an addiction. So is being defensive. Or refusing to accept responsibility for your mistakes.

My addiction was conflict avoidance. When I was growing up, I learned to give people what they wanted, and I was rewarded — pats on the back, good marks, team captain. But the flip side was that I didn't learn to ask what I wanted for myself. I was unable to say to a friend, "I'd rather not." Or to an employee, "John, your performance is not acceptable."

It was only after I diagnosed this behavior that I could enlist friends and supporters to help me change it. They practised with me on what to say to John and how to say it, paving the way for a productive, and easier, conversation. As a result, John altered his behavior and became a more effective member of the team.

01 Which of the following best expresses the main idea of the passage?
(A) Everything in life has both its bright side and dark side.
(B) Everyone does an addictive behavior in a period of life.
(C) You cannot change others until you come to change yourself.
(D) You must identify your addiction before you can get out of it.

02 Which of the following CANNOT be inferred from the passage?
(A) Some have a habit of protecting their own position in a conversation.
(B) If people pat a boy on the back, it shows that he has done as they want.
(C) Neither drinks nor drugs can be considered to be an addiction.
(D) The author perhaps was John's superordinate in the same company.

03 Which of the following best describes the author's attitude toward "conflict avoidance"?
(A) regretful
(B) doubtful
(C) advocating
(D) hesitating

Today, my children's best friends sometimes are not around because they're in Europe or skiing in Vail. My own children have been to Paris twice in the last three years. Everyone's cars are new and nobody does without. In a nation where many people are enjoying increasing affluence, there is some concern that our children are growing up with a ①twisted sense of the world. In this surreal economic expansion, how do we show our children that life won't always be easy? With children who are surrounded by a lot of wealth, they get stuck in a psychological prison, and they do not get anything that is valuable. Affluence is a problem that we all should have, but this may be a case of ② _____. It is great that we can provide for our families and that money has given us more freedom to fully enjoy our lives, but are our lifestyles giving our children a goal or an excuse? Children were just reacting rationally to our wealth. The more you get paid, the more you want to work to grab that income. But as income gets so high, you want to enjoy it. In terms of children with more affluence, there is less of a need to work and make money.

01   What is similar in meaning to the underlined ①twisted?
(A) devastating
(B) controlled
(C) renewed
(D) distorted

02   Which of the following is most suitable for the blank ②?
(A) penny wise and pound foolish
(B) too much of a good thing
(C) a stitch in time saves nine
(D) locking the stable door after the horse is stolen

03   Which of the following does the author most agree with?
(A) Reasoning power is accompanied by sense of the value of money.
(B) The value of things changes in proportion of the number of the things.
(C) The children with wealth are likely to lose their sense of value.
(D) Some social problems on poverty are hidden by the general affluence in the society.

Since trash can be dangerous to dolphins if ingested, some of the animals at Marine World Africa USA were trained to retrieve the trash and return it to the trainer for a reinforcement reward. One day the lead trainer went through the routine only to notice that the dolphin kept coming back with a piece of trash even though the tank appeared clean. The trainer asked a colleague to go below to the engineer's port to observe what the dolphin was doing when a trainer came out on the float. The trainer came out on the float and sure enough, the dolphin quickly showed up with a piece of trash and got his reward. The scam was revealed! This dolphin had established a savings account of sorts. He collected all the trash and stuffed it in a bag wedged in a corner of the tank near the intake of the filtering system. The amazing thing is that when he went to the *bank* he did not simply take a piece, rather he would tear a bit off to ①_____ the return. This behavior is particularly interesting because it shows that the dolphin had a sense of the future and delayed gratification. He had enough presence to realize that a big piece of trash got the same reward as a small piece, so why not deliver only small pieces to keep the extra food coming? ②He in effect had trained the humans.

01 Which of the following is best title of the passage?

(A) The Dolphin's Intelligence
(B) The Dolphin's Ability to Survive
(C) The Dolphin as a Friend to Humans
(D) The Dolphin's Habit of Cleaning

02 Which of the following is most suitable for the blank ①?

(A) correct   (B) praise
(C) maximize   (D) allocate

03 Which of the following CANNOT be inferred from the passage?

(A) The training was initiated to keep dolphins from swallowing trash.
(B) The dolphins with more experience of training learn more easily.
(C) The place the dolphin accumulated trash was not easily noticeable.
(D) The training brought an unexpected discovery to the trainers.

04 What does the underlined ②He in effect had trained the humans imply?

(A) The dolphin's talent was over the top.
(B) The dolphin was a cut above his trainers.
(C) The dolphin's trick wore his trainers out.
(D) The dolphin called for higher level of discipline.

The "soccer vs. football" argument is a century-long gripe. "Soccer" originated in England as Oxbridge slang, a contraction of the formal term "association football." In 1905, an indignant New York Times reader complained when the paper used the "undignified" term soccer when ①reporting a game. "It is ②to be hoped that this heresy will not spread," he wrote. But the word soccer was necessary to distinguish this foreign import from the already ③established American game of football. Arguing that we should stop saying soccer is like saying Americans should stop saying gasoline instead of petrol, or have a parliament, or ④adopting the metric system — changes that would be pointless, burdensome and culturally coward. America's lack of enthusiasm for soccer Ⓐis chalked up to racism, according to some U.S. bashers. But contrary to hooligan sniping, there is more of an ethnic mix on the average U.S. football team than almost any comparable soccer team.

01 Which of the following CANNOT replace the underlined part Ⓐ?
(A) is blamed for   (B) is attributed to
(C) is consigned to   (D) is ascribed to

02 Which of the following is NOT grammatically correct?
(A) ① reporting   (B) ② to be hoped
(C) ③ established   (D) ④ adopting

03 According to the passage, which of the following is true?
(A) U.S. football team shows moderately low levels of racial diversity.
(B) Most Americans disparage the term "soccer" as it is an abbreviation.
(C) The adoption of the word "soccer" was inevitable.
(D) "Soccer vs. Football" is the latest cultural conflict.

Today, Western civilization is almost never mentioned, _____ promoted, in political and intellectual discourse, either in America or in Europe. When it is mentioned amongst Western elites, the traditions of the West are almost always an object of criticism or contempt. Instead, real discussion of Western civilization is usually undertaken by the political, intellectual, and religious leaders of non-Western societies — most obviously, Muslim societies. Indeed, the idea of the West seems to be most charged with vital energy in the excited mind of our civilization's principal contemporary enemy, radical Islam. The most lively consciousness of the West actually seems to be found within the East. But within the West itself (i.e. the United States, Europe, and also Canada, Australia, and New Zealand) it sometimes seems that the Western civilization of fifty years ago has become a lost civilization today. What explains this great transformation in a great civilization? Which of the West's traditions remains a living reality today? And what might be the fate of these traditions in the future?

01 Which of the following is best for the blank?
(A) much less
(B) none the less
(C) all the more
(D) still more

02 Which of the following can be inferred from the passage?
(A) Courses on Western civilization are important in American universities.
(B) The leaders of radical Islam laud the idea of the West.
(C) Non-Western societies think of the West civilization's dominance as the inevitable consequences of globalization.
(D) It seems that the discourse on the Western civilization in the West has been a languid one.

03 What would be the most appropriate content for the paragraph following this passage?
(A) The point of the discussion made within the radical Islam.
(B) Some principles underlying the West civilization which exist as a living reality.
(C) An egalitarianism that can be used in reconciliation between the West and the East.
(D) The contribution of the West civilization especially in the East.

Political and economic _____ in the Arab world have sent gas prices skyrocketing in the United States in recent weeks, and some lawmakers are ready to tap into the country's Strategic Petroleum Reserve.

The reserve was formed after an energy crisis of a different era. In October 1973, the Organization of Arab and Petroleum Exporting Countries(OAPEC) shut off oil supplies in response to United States support of the Israeli military during the Yom Kippur War. The oil embargo, which lasted until the following March, caused a global energy and economic crisis. To prevent such a situation from arising again, the U.S. government created the Strategic Petroleum Reserve(SPR) in 1975. Several other countries also created oil reserves, but the American stockpile was and remains the biggest.

As of March 7, the SPR consists of 726.5 million barrels of crude oil stored in underground caverns at four secure locations along the Gulf Coasts. The biggest reserve site is Bryan Mound, near Freeport, Texas. There, 254 million barrels fill 20 manmade caverns that have been hollowed out beneath salt domes a few thousand feet underground. The other three reserve sites are Big Hill, Texas, West Hackberry, LA, and Bayou Chocktaw, LA.

01 Which of the following best fits in the blank?
(A) stability
(B) prosperity
(C) alliance
(D) unrest

02 What is the purpose of this passage?
(A) To explain what SPR is and the history of its foundation
(B) To criticize America's extravagant consumption of oil
(C) To warn us of global depletion of energy resources
(D) To show off the largest reserve the U.S. has in the world

03 Which of the following cannot be inferred from the passage?
(A) The global economy turned out to be interdependent during the oil crisis in 1973.
(B) Only a few people may have exclusive access to the storage sites of crude oil.
(C) Global efforts will be made to resolve the long-lasting Arab-Israeli conflict.
(D) OAPEC perceived oil as an effective weapon for the struggle against Israel during the War.

Sometimes, by way of birth, marriage or for another reason, a person may wish to be a citizen of both the United States, and ①another country. Whether or not the U.S. allows this depends on how the person intends to become a citizen of both countries.

If a U.S. citizen acquires nationality in ②another country because of marriage or birth, the United States allows citizenship in both countries. If a child of a citizen of another country is born in the U.S., the 14th Amendment of the U.S. Constitution grants them automatic citizenship, without giving up ③another.

The United States government will revoke American citizenship to any person who purposely pledges allegiance to ④another country. A person may do this through words, i.e. taking an oath of citizenship, or actions. Joining a foreign country's military service which is fighting against the U.S. can result in losing your U.S. citizenship.

Being a dual citizen or dual national is accepted by the U.S. government, but is not encouraged, because of problems it may cause. Dual citizens are expected to obey the laws of both countries they are citizens of and these laws may conflict with each other.

01 Which of the following is the main idea of the passage?
   (A) Can the dual citizen contribute to the America?
   (B) The dual national can do harm to both countries.
   (C) Does the United States allow the dual citizenship?
   (D) There are loopholes to become an American citizen.

02 The U.S. administration doesn't grant the dual citizenship when _____.
   (A) an infant whose parents have sojourned in the U.S. is born in the U.S.
   (B) dual nationals accept the laws of both countries and conform to them
   (C) an American tries to procure another citizenship after marrying a foreigner
   (D) dual nationals are deeply involved in espionage in the U.S. territory

03 Which of the following is grammatically incorrect?
   (A) ① another   (B) ② another
   (C) ③ another   (D) ④ another

Employees are rapidly demoralized after a company warns about layoffs — even if the job cuts won't happen for a while.

Just announcing the intent to "reduce head count" — as Bank of America Corp. and some other financial firms have done recently — can distract workers, hurt recruiting efforts and prompt top performers to head for the exit.

Bank of America Chief Executive Brian Moynihan told employees in an internal email last week that "overall employment levels" at the bank would come down by 30,000 over the next few years.

Rumors of massive layoffs had been rippling through the ranks for months, according to one senior analyst at Bank of America. "A lot of people are really scared about what's going to happen," he said. "①I don't know anybody who's not looking for another job."

He said managers have tried to send short notes to reassure employees but it seems they are nervous about their own positions. "They say it's going to be 30,000 over the next couple years. Does that mean that for the next several years we're supposed to wait for our number to be called?" A Bank of America spokesman declined to comment about this.

---

01 Which of the following can be inferred from the passage?

(A) Latest layoffs by Bank of America have affected the industry.
(B) Massive layoffs can spook managers as well as employees.
(C) Some companies announce layoffs and never do them.
(D) Layoff hints alone cannot enervate employees.

02 Which of the following does the sentence ① imply?

(A) My understanding is that people want to maintain the status quo.
(B) I don't know any top performers who are not heading for the exit.
(C) To my knowledge, everybody is trying to take up another employment.
(D) As far as I know, nobody intends to seek for a new job.

03 The most plausible reason why the Bank of America spokesman declined to comment would be that _____.

(A) the company would reverse the existing corporate policy
(B) the company wanted to keep harmony with the employees
(C) the spokesman couldn't accept the analyst's critical opinion
(D) the spokesman's opinion could disadvantage the company

When was the last time you flashed a fake smile at the office? For some, it may be just another mundane aspect of work life — putting on a game face to hide your inner unhappiness. But new research suggests that it may have unexpected consequences: worsening your mood and causing you to withdraw from the tasks at hand. In a study published this month in the Academy of Management Journal, scientists tracked a group of bus drivers for two weeks, focusing on them because their jobs require frequent, and generally courteous, interactions with many people. The scientists examined what happened when the drivers engaged in fake smiling, known as "surface acting," and its opposite, "deep acting," where they generated _____ smiles through positive thoughts. After following the drivers closely, the researchers found that on days when the smiles were forced, the subjects' moods deteriorated and they tended to withdraw from work. Trying to suppress negative thoughts, it turns out, may have made those thoughts even more persistent. But on days when the subjects tried to display smiles through deeper efforts — by actually cultivating pleasant thoughts and memories — their overall moods improved and their productivity increased.

01 Choose the one that best fills in the blank.
 (A) wry
 (B) authentic
 (C) feigned
 (D) constrained

02 What is the main idea of the passage?
 (A) Even a fake smile can be good for your health.
 (B) Drivers are encouraged to have pleasant thoughts and memories.
 (C) A pretended smile to hide unhappiness can further worsen your mood.
 (D) The new research led to a major breakthrough in health research.

03 Which of the following cannot be inferred from the passage?
 (A) Hiding negative emotions may create more strain.
 (B) Women are more emotionally expressive than men.
 (C) Making a fake smile may have aggravated the subjects' moods.
 (D) A genuine smile through positive thoughts may help you work agreeably.

Until long habit has blunted the sensibility, there is something <u>disconcerting</u> to the writer in the instinct which causes him to take an interest in the singularities of human nature so absorbing that his moral sense is powerless against it. He recognizes in himself an artistic satisfaction in the contemplation of evil which a little startles him; but sincerity forces him to confess that the disapproval he feels for certain actions is not nearly so strong as his curiosity in their reasons. The character of a scoundrel, logical and complete, has a satisfaction for his creator which is an outrage to law and order. I expect that Shakespeare devised Iago with a gusto which he never knew when, weaving moonbeams with his fancy, he imagined Desdemona. It may be that in his rogues the writer gratifies instincts deep-rooted in him, which the manners and customs of a civilized world have forced back to the mysterious recesses of the subconscious.

01 What is the main idea of the passage?
(A) The villain in a literary work can be a source of satisfaction for its writer.
(B) The writer should keep sensibility to depict evildoers in his work as they are.
(C) Shakespeare devoted more vigor to creating Iago than Desdemona.
(D) The writer's instinct tends to retreat to the subconscious through civilization.

02 The underlined word "<u>disconcerting</u>" is closest in meaning to _____.
(A) embarrassing   (B) beneficial
(C) persuasive   (D) decent

One of the most important arguments for trade barriers centers on national defense. Protectionists argue that without trade barriers, a country could become too specialized and end up being too _____ other countries. As a result, a country might not be able to get such critical supplies as food, oil, and weapons during wartime. The governments of such countries as Israel and South Africa have developed large armament industries for such crises. They want to be sure they will have a domestic supply source if hostilities break out or other countries impose economic boycotts. Free traders admit that national security is a compelling argument for trade barriers. They believe, however, that having a reliable source of domestic supply must be weighed against the reality that the supply will be smaller and possibly less efficient than it would be with free trade.

01 Choose the one that best fills in the blank.
(A) superior to
(B) ignorant of
(C) dependent on
(D) competitive with

02 Which of the following can be inferred about "trade barriers" according to the passage?
(A) They tend to be supported by free traders.
(B) They may be needed to the country whose security is in danger.
(C) They would guarantee more sources of wartime supplies.
(D) They are not necessary for the permanent neutral countries.

It often strikes me how different reading is when one has garnered the greater part of life's experiences, from what it was when one was still at the seed-time of life. When one is very young, to read is, as it were, to pour a continuous stream of water on a parched and virginal plain. The soil seems to have an endless capacity to drink up the stream, sometimes with prolonged perpetual rapture, sometimes with impartial calm indifference, endlessly, unpausingly, with never a disturbing echo. But when one is no longer young, to read is a very different matter. The parched plain has become a luxuriant forest with lakes and streams in the midst of it. Every image which enters it evokes ancient visions from the depth of its waters, and every tone rustles among the trees with a music so rich in haunting memories that one grows faint beneath their burden. So now, when I open a book, it often enough happens that I lay it down, satisfied, on the page at which I opened.

01 Why does the author behave as described in the last sentence?
   (A) Because he doesn't look at the forest but only the individual trees in it.
   (B) Because his reading is being hampered by every visual and auditory nuisance.
   (C) Because old visions and memories make him too weary to read any more.
   (D) Because what he is reading reminds him of too many past experiences.

02 Which of the following is figuratively referred to by the underlined "a parched and virginal plain"?
   (A) a book never read by anybody and full of esoteric things
   (B) a world newly found and filled with every kind of novelties
   (C) a mind empty and ready to receive whatever one reads
   (D) an environment where one finds it most difficult to read

A set of agreed-upon symbols is only one feature of language; all languages must define the structural relationships between these symbols in a system of grammar. Rules of grammar are what distinguish language from other forms of communication. They allow a finite set of symbols to be manipulated to create a potentially infinite number of grammatical utterances.

Another property of language is that its symbols are _____. Any concept or grammatical rule can be mapped onto a symbol. Most languages make use of sound, but the combinations of sounds used do not have any inherent meaning — they are merely an agreed-upon convention to represent a certain thing by users of that language. For instance, there is nothing about the Spanish word *nada* itself that forces Spanish speakers to convey the idea of "nothing". Another set of sounds (for example, the English word nothing) could equally be used to represent the same concept, but all Spanish speakers have acquired or learned to correlate this meaning for this particular sound pattern. For Slovenian, Croatian, Serbian/Kosovan or Bosnian speakers on the other hand, *nada* means something else; it means "hope".

01 다음 빈칸에 가장 알맞은 것은?

Languages can be distinguished from other forms of communication on the ground of _____.

(A) commonality (B) vocabulary
(C) grammar (D) symbols

02 위 글의 빈칸에 들어가기에 가장 알맞은 것은?

(A) fixed (B) mandatory
(C) widespread (D) arbitrary

In June 2020, I suffered an upper-respiratory infection. "It's no big deal." That's what I thought at first. But after the sniffles subsided, for almost a year ①_____. The effect was dramatic. One day, when I failed to turn off a burner on the stove properly, I couldn't smell the leaking gas. (Fortunately, my son, who dropped by four and a half hours later, noticed the fumes.) I stopped saving leftovers, as I no longer trusted my ability to detect rotten or rancid odors. Without aromas, food became a bland, tasteless mass, and life itself seemed equally monotonous. I was unable to enjoy the scent of coffee brewing, new-mown grass or the sweet smell of my baby grandson. Even my social life took ②_____. I stopped inviting friends to dinner, as I had no way of gauging whether my chili food was tasty or inedible. It was like cooking with plastic food because most of what we perceive as flavor in food does not come from the tongue, but the nose. It was apparent that something must be done to cure my sniffer.

01 Which is most appropriate for the blank ①?
(A) my family had to take care of me
(B) I had suffered from complications
(C) it was difficult to do any housework
(D) I had no olfactory sense
(E) something deprived me of the energy

02 Which is most appropriate for the blank ②?
(A) a fancy
(B) a hit
(C) pains
(D) responsibility
(E) prudence

03 What would the author do after this passage?
(A) hire a housemaid to help cook
(B) meet friends at an outside restaurant
(C) search a folk remedy to abate the sniffles
(D) see a doctor expert in orthopedic surgery
(E) find how to alleviate the symptoms

Over the past decade the media has been flooded with news about terrorist attacks, death and torture. It was before too, but now that American presence is so ㉮prominent abroad, more and more Americans read world news on a daily basis. For those people who follow international affairs, I'm sure death toll numbers aren't ㉯staggering until they reach near a hundred or more. The numbers do hurt, though, if the dead are Americans, or the tragedy happens in America. But if 21 are killed in a blast in Bangladesh, people tend to care more about who's responsible than about those now without family.

Now, as I read more and more world news, I find myself becoming ㉰susceptible to these death tolls. For example, when I read about the 52 Somalis who died in the recent smuggling attempt, I was more interested in the smuggling part than the dead 52. There is ㉱disconnection between the 52 and reality, and the number is just a number for me. People died, but I don't know their names, their faces, anything about them. Something that I couldn't control happened to 52 people.

01 What kind of news makes Americans feel grief according to the passage?
(A) terrorist attacks on embassies and diplomats
(B) the triumph of American military presence abroad
(C) the accident of hundreds of their fellow countrymen
(D) the death of a number of people due to the natural disaster

02 Among ㉮, ㉯, ㉰ and ㉱, choose the word that is NOT appropriate according to the context.
(A) ㉮ prominent   (B) ㉯ staggering
(C) ㉰ susceptible   (D) ㉱ disconnection

03 What is the author's attitude toward "the tragedy outside America"?
(A) compassionate   (B) apathetic
(C) critical   (D) ignominious

A small, unmanned vehicle makes its way down the road ahead of a military convoy. Suddenly it stops and relays a warning to the convoy commander. The presence of a deadly improvised explosive device, or IED, has been detected by ①sophisticated biochip technology incorporating living olfactory cells on microchips mounted on the unmanned vehicle. The IED is safely dismantled and lives are saved.

This scenario may become a reality, thanks to the work of three faculty researchers in the University of Maryland's James Clark School of Engineering who are collaborating across engineering disciplines to make advanced "②cell-based sensors-on-a-chip" technology possible. Pamela Abshire, electrical and computer engineering (ECE) and Institute for Systems Research (ISR); Benjamin Shapiro, aerospace engineering and ISR; and Elisabeth Smela, mechanical engineering and ECE; are working on ③new sensors that take advantage of the sensory capabilities of biological cells.

④These tiny devices, only a few millimeters in size, could speed up and improve the detection of everything from explosive materials to ⑤biological pathogens to spoiled food or impure water.

01 Which of the following is the best title of the passage?
(A) New Cell-based Sensors Sniff out Danger like Hunting Dogs
(B) A New Unmanned Vehicle Performing Transport Duty
(C) Technology-based Military Strategies
(D) A Newly Discovered Life Detecting Dangers
(E) New Findings about Human Olfactory Sense

02 Among ①, ②, ③, ④, and ⑤, which one differs from the others in what it refers to?
(A) ①
(B) ②
(C) ③
(D) ④
(E) ⑤

03 According to the passage, the new device is most distinctive because _____.
(A) it is shaped like living organism
(B) it adopts living cell functions
(C) it has a microchip embedded in it
(D) it is tiny and sophisticated
(E) it is a result of applied science

The difference between being and having is not essentially that between East and West. The difference is rather between a society centered around persons and one centered around things. The having orientation is characteristic of Western industrial society, in which greed for money, fame, and power has become the dominant theme of life. Less alienated societies — such as medieval society, the Zuni indians, the African tribal societies that were not affected by the ideas of modern "progress"— have their own Bashos. Perhaps after a few more generations of industrialization, the Japanese will have their Tennysons. It is not Western Man cannot fully understand Eastern systems, such as Zen Buddhism, but that modern Man cannot understand the spirit of a society that is not centered in property and greed. ①Indeed the writings of Master Eckhart and the Buddha's writings are only two dialects of the same language.

01 According to the passage, which of the following statements is NOT true?

(A) Western industrial society is after the life of the having orientation.
(B) Meeting with industrialization, even medieval society can be turned into the society centered around things.
(C) The difference between being and having is nothing but that between East and West.
(D) Modern Man cannot fully understand the spirit of the being-oriented society.

02 Which of the following is closest in meaning to ①?

(A) The spirits of Eckhart and Buddha pursue after the mode of being.
(B) Eckhart and Buddha use the same language even though they deal with different materials.
(C) The writings of Eckhart and Buddha which have different languages got to the point of master.
(D) Modern man can understand the true meaning of social value through Eckhart and Buddha's writings.

He did this better than anyone I'd ever known. Those who sat with him saw his eyes go moist when they spoke about something horrible, or crinkle in delight when they told him a really bad joke. He was always ready to openly display the emotion so often missing from my baby boomer generation. We are great at small talk: "What do you do?" "Where do you live?" ①_____ really listening to someone — without trying to sell them something, pick them up, recruit them, or get some kind of status in return — how often do we get this anymore? I believe many visitors in the last few months of Morrie's life were drawn not because of the attention they wanted to pay to him but because of the attention he paid to them. Despite his personal pain and decay, this little old man listened ②_____ they always wanted someone to listen.

01 The word this in the passage refers to _____.
(A) paying a visit to friends
(B) expressing his heart frankly
(C) listening to what people say as it is
(D) being patient with his suffering

02 Which of the following best fits into ① and ②?
(A) By the way — so
(B) But — the way
(C) Moreover — as
(D) In spite of — since

He sees. He walks. His heart pumps blood. But Rex, as he's called in the U.K., where he just debuted, is not human. In fact, he's not even alive. He is the world's most advanced bionic man, created as part of a three-month collaboration among scientists, researchers and a TV production company. Unlike the human-robot hybrids we're used to seeing on screen, this one is the real deal: his prostheses are already available; his organs are scientific prototypes; and his blood, made from plastic, is a harbinger of breakthroughs to come.

This is generally good news for patients. Kidney failure, for example, could be a nonissue if researchers create a working artificial replacement organ. Although prostheses are expensive (the U.K. bionic man cost roughly $1 million), prices should decrease with more evolved development. Still these advances raise all kinds of ethical questions. Like, What happens if a bionic limb surpasses the functionality of a human one? "Some may electively replace their healthy ones," says project leader Bertolt Meyer. That possibility is a long way off, but he wants to start that conversation before bionic tech goes mainstream. By then, of course, Rex might be able to participate.

01 What is the best title for the passage?

(A) The Rapid Progress of Biotechnology
(B) The Ergonomic Designs for Physical Health
(C) The High-Tech Future of the Human Body
(D) The Ethical Problems with Organ Transplant

02 Which of the following cannot be inferred from the passage?

(A) Rex is a humanoid robot made by state-of-the-art bionic, prosthetic technology.
(B) Rex's limbs are more advanced in popularization than his organs and blood.
(C) Ethical issues will arise when prostheses begin to outperform human body parts.
(D) Technological development limits the availability of prostheses to a selected few.

03 What is the author's attitude toward Rex?

(A) disparaging
(B) conservative
(C) admiring
(D) dissatisfied

In the past decade, baseball has experienced ①a data-driven information revolution. Numbers-crunchers now routinely use statistics to put better teams on the field for less money. Our overpriced, underperforming health care system needs a similar revolution.

Data-driven baseball has produced surprising results. Look at what's happened in baseball. For decades, executives, managers built their teams and managed games based on their personal experiences and a handful of dubious statistics. ②This romantic approach has been replaced with a statistics-based creed called ③sabermetrics. These are not the stats we studied as children on the backs of baseball cards. Franchises have used this data to answer some of the key questions in baseball.

Similarly, a health care system that is driven by robust comparative clinical evidence will save lives and money. America's health care system behaves like ㉑hidebound, tradition-based ball club that chases after aging sluggers and plays by the old rules: we pay too much and get too little in return. To deliver better health care, we should learn from the successful teams that have adopted baseball's ④new evidence-based methods. The best way to start improving quality and lowering costs is to study the stats.

01 Which of the underlined does NOT refer to the same thing?
(A) ① a data-driven information revolution
(B) ② This romantic approach
(C) ③ sabermetrics
(D) ④ new evidence-based methods

02 Which of the following CANNOT be inferred from the passage?
(A) Current health care is based on personal observation or tradition.
(B) Doctors can do better if they have evidence-based medical information.
(C) Data-driven health care can deliver the good quality care at the affordable cost.
(D) Evidence-based health care strips doctors of their decision-making authority.

03 Which of the following can be best replaced by the underlined word ㉑hidebound?
(A) lethargic   (B) dispassionate
(C) bigoted   (D) contentious

PASSAGE

**101
—
150**

James W. Pennebaker's interest in word counting began more than 30 years ago, when he did several studies suggesting that people who talked about traumatic experiences tended to be physically healthier than those who kept such experiences secret. He wondered how much could be learned by looking at every single word people used — even the tiny ones, the I's and you's, a's and the's. By counting the different kinds of words a person says, he is breaking new linguistic ground and leading a resurgent interest in text analysis.

[I] Take Dr. Pennebaker's recent study of Al Qaeda communications — videotapes, interviews, letters. [II] At the request of the F.B.I., he tallied the number of words in various categories — pronouns, articles and adjectives, among others. [III] He found, for example, that Osama bin Laden's use of first-person pronouns (I, me, my, mine) remained fairly constant over several years. [IV] "This dramatic increase suggests greater insecurity, feelings of threat, and perhaps a shift in his relationship with bin Laden," Dr. Pennebaker wrote in his report.

01 According to Dr. Pennebaker, a person's increased use of first-person pronouns can reflect his _____.

(A) personal preference (B) moral education
(C) mental state (D) brain injury

02 Where would the following sentences best fit into?

By contrast, his second-in-command, Ayman al-Zawahri, used such words more and more often.

(A) [I] (B) [II]
(C) [III] (D) [IV]

03 Which of the following is stated or implied in the passage?

(A) People who have shocking experiences may as well not keep silent about them.
(B) Dr. Pennebaker is interested in how sentences are put together to form a context.
(C) People show off their status as an important individual by using the first-person pronouns on purpose.
(D) Mr. al-Zawahri's more frequent use of first-person pronouns indicates his stubbornness.

Goethe, addressing the Society of German Sculptors in 1817, told them that "The topmost aim of all plastic art is to render the dignity of man within the compass of the human form. To this aim every nonhuman element, in so far as it lends itself to treatment in this medium, must subordinate itself. Such elements must first be assimilated to the dignity of man in order that they may set it off, instead of calling attention to themselves or even departing from it."

The intention was metaphysical — to render the dignity of man — and to this intention everything had to be sacrificed. Speaking at the beginning of a century in which virtually no sculpture of any permanent value was to be created anywhere in the civilized world, Goethe did not realize that he was demanding too much of the art of sculpture. It is true that there is nothing inherently incompatible between dignity and vitality, and conceivably the human figure can embody a human conception of the divine. A human figure carved by Michelangelo is both vital and dignified. We may say that it is a great work of art because it is dignified, but it exists as a work of art only because it is vital.

01 Choose the one closest in meaning to the underlined "metaphysical."
(A) abstract
(B) grandiose
(C) systematic
(D) essential

02 Which of the following cannot be inferred about "sculpture"?
(A) Goethe thought it must aim to represent the dignity of man in human form.
(B) It was not developed enough to meet Goethe's ideas of it in the 19th century.
(C) Animal figures, if full of vitality, can be works of sculpture, too.
(D) Dignity is a necessary condition for a subject to be a work of sculpture.

03 What is the tone of the passage?
(A) laudatory
(B) critical
(C) ambivalent
(D) satirical

However, quite often laughter shows negative intentions of a person. This issue is mostly analyzed by psychoanalysts. Sigmund Freud, for example, summarized it in his theory that laughter releases tension and "psychic energy" that had been wrongly mobilized by incorrect expectations. This theory is one of the justifications of the beliefs that laughter is beneficial for one's health, and explains why laughter can be a coping mechanism for when one is upset, angry or sad. Other psychologists like Karen Horney claim that it is a release of tension or even self-defense. For example, when someone is asked a difficult question and doesn't know how to answer it, he or she often may begin laughing and joking.

After discovering the facts related to laughter, research was conducted and some laughter therapies were invented. While it is normally only considered cliche that "laughter is the best medicine," specific medical theories attribute improved health, increased life expectancy, and overall improved well-being, to laughter. Perhaps we might know why it is man alone who laughs: He alone suffers so deeply that he had to invent laughter.

01 Which of the following would be the topic of the paragraph preceding this passage?
(A) the study of laughter as science
(B) laughter as a sign of enjoyment
(C) the growing popularity of laughter therapy
(D) laughter as an aspect of language activity

02 Which of the following can be inferred from the passage?
(A) The science of laughter is not well-known.
(B) Laughter is an acquired trait rather than innate one.
(C) Agony generates laughter, which helps lighten the burdens.
(D) The way a person laughs shows his or her personality.

03 Which of the following is similar in meaning to the underlined cliche?
(A) covert   (B) prodigy
(C) banality   (D) doctrine

Ancient athletes competed as individuals, not on national teams, as in the modern Games. The emphasis on individual athletic achievement through public competition was related to the Greek ideal of excellence, called "arete". Aristocratic men who attained this ideal, through their outstanding words or deeds, won permanent glory and fame. Those who failed to measure up to this code feared public shame and disgrace.

Not all athletes lived up to this code of excellence. Those who were discovered cheating were fined, and the money was used to make bronze statues of Zeus, which were erected on the road to the stadium. The statues were inscribed with messages describing the offenses, warning others not to cheat, reminding athletes that victory was won by skill and not by money, and emphasizing the Olympic spirit of piety toward the gods and fair competition.

01 According to the passage, why did ancient athletes compete individually?
(A) Because the Greek ideal of excellence emphasized on cooperative achievement.
(B) Because individual athletic achievement was the only way they could attain the ideal of excellence.
(C) Because they wanted to build everlasting reputation for the aristocratic value.
(D) Because they earned immortal honor if they reached their ideal through personal achievement.

02 Which of the following is LEAST likely to be carved in the statues of Zeus?
(A) Don't buy off your competitors before the competitions.
(B) The spirit of fair play is the true Olympic spirit.
(C) The game is not for money, but for glory of a nation.
(D) You can gain a victory if you enhance your athletic abilities.

Nearly 2,000 years after Mount Vesuvius buried Pompeii under pumice and steaming volcanic ash, some 2.6 million tourists tramp annually through this archaeological site, which is on Unesco's World Heritage list. Like many Italian excavations, Pompeii is accessible, allowing tourists to wander through the ruins unhindered — provided they can find elbow room. Frescoes in the ancient Roman city, one of Italy's most popular attractions, fade under the blistering sun or are chipped at by souvenir hunters. Mosaics endure the brunt of tens of thousands of shuffling thongs and sneakers. Teetering columns and walls are propped up by wooden and steel scaffolding. The padlocks deny access to recently restored houses, and custodians seem to be few and far between. On a recent April morning, a group of French tourists on the way out collided with some Germans trying to enter through the same narrow doorway. After much tussling, the umbrella-wielding tour guides broke the impasse. As you can see, the _____ also underscores one of Pompeii's most serious problems: overcrowding.

01 Which of the following is most suitable for the blank?
(A) destruction   (B) bottleneck
(C) gang fights   (D) racial conflicts

02 Which of the following is NOT the problem of Pompeii?
(A) too many tourists
(B) damages on paintings
(C) the lack of guardians
(D) no renovation and old facilities

03 What is the main topic of this passage?
(A) saving Pompeii from modern threats
(B) the tourists making troubles in Pompeii
(C) the problems of tourism in Pompeii
(D) Pompeii, the marvelous heritage

Some regions of the world have been marginalized by globalization. Economists once thought that, over time, inequalities between both regions and countries would naturally even out. Some believe that the global economy can be imagined to be a self-equilibrating mechanism of the textbook variety. Others believe that it can be recognized as subject to processes of cumulative causation whereby if one or more countries fall behind the pack, there may be dangers of them falling further behind, rather than enjoying an automatic ticket back to the equilibrium solution path. These two alternative, conflicting views of real-world economic processes have very different implications regarding institutional needs and arrangements. The same applies to regions. There is no reason in theory, nor evidence in practice, why they should enjoy virtuous circles of convergence rather than vicious cycles of divergence. Thus, at the time of the Brexit referendum it was said that income per head in Britain was back above pre-financial crisis levels. As Andy Haldane, the chief economist at the Bank of England, pointed out subsequently, this was true in aggregate, but at a disaggregated level it applied to only two of Britain's regions: London and the South-East.

01 According to the passage, which of the following is not true?

(A) All countries do not enjoy equal benefits from globalization.
(B) Different views of world economy result in different institutions.
(C) An economically unequal result can be a cause of greater inequality.
(D) Both regions and countries will be equally well off in the future.

02 The author cites the case of Britain to show that _____ is likely to occur.

(A) a vicious cycle of economic inequality between regions
(B) a vicious cycle of economic inequality between countries
(C) a virtuous circle of economic equality between regions
(D) a virtuous circle of economic equality between countries

In India, some marriages to non-resident Indians can be problematic. Brides going abroad can suffer from culture shock if they have had no prior exposure to the West. Their overseas-raised spouses, meanwhile, can find themselves pressured into a traditional marriage by émigré parents. The combination can result in loveless, incompatible relationships and eventually, divorce. The worst cases, however, are those where non-resident Indian men come to India seeking either huge doweries or 'holiday wives'. If they abandon their brides and return to their adoptive countries, the brides and their families, living in a culture of patriarchy and keen to preserve their honor, often do not approach the authorities. And even if they do, there are limited legal options before them.

Government agencies and NGOs are working to change that. The National Commission for Women has demanded that the government make it compulsory to register all marriages, which will provide women with a more solid legal standing. Meanwhile, activist groups are lobbying for changes in the law to criminalize the suppression of information about previous marriages, and urging the government to sign agreements with other countries to make marital fraud an _____ offense.

01 Which of the following can be inferred from the passage?

(A) In India, most young women want to marry men who reside in India.
(B) Bridegrooms returning to India suffer culture shock as much as their spouses.
(C) Indians think highly of the authority of fathers and the honor of families.
(D) Publicizing information about marriage will weaken women's legal standing.

02 Choose the one that best fills in the blank.

(A) impeachable   (B) ostracizable
(C) inexorable   (D) extraditable

The humble tomato may technically be a fruit, but lawmakers here consider it a vegetable. Members of the Assembly Agriculture and Natural Resources Committee on Monday approved a measure designating the Jersey tomato as the official state vegetable. A similar proposal is pending in a Senate committee.

Sponsors of the measure get around the fact that the tomato is considered a fruit by using a century-old U.S. Supreme Court ruling that slapped a vegetable tariff on tomatoes, similar to the tax placed on cucumbers, squashes and beans.

In squeezing tomatoes into the vegetable category, justices on the 1887 high court reasoned that if it's typically served with dinner, and not as a dessert, it must be a vegetable. "_____ it's a fruit, _____ it's a vegetable," said Sen. Ellen Karcher, who is co-sponsoring the Senate version of the bill. "Any of these bills that promote statewide pride is something we should embrace."

The Jersey tomato's ride through the Legislature began after a group of fourth-graders wrote letters urging lawmakers to adopt a state fruit. The beloved blueberry won out, and it — not the tomato — took its place last year as the official state fruit.

01 Which of the following pair best completes the sentence?
    (A) Technically — regrettably
    (B) Legally — actually
    (C) Regrettably — technically
    (D) Botanically — legally

02 Which of the following can be inferred from the passage?
    (A) Whether cucumbers are fruits is a matter of debate.
    (B) The tomato has been official state fruit.
    (C) Fruits are almost invariably served after dinner.
    (D) Tomatoes are juicy fruits most fourth-graders really enjoy.

Virtuosos are often praised with the statement that they make the music sound easy. The last 3 of Beethoven's 32 piano sonatas did not sound easy when Mitsuko Uchida played them on Sunday afternoon at the final concert of this year's Caramoor International Music Festival. The beginning of Sonata No. 30 sounded like a tangled wealth of notes that took all the work of 10 fingers to keep under control. This was, of course, an interpretive decision; if the music sounds difficult in the hands of Ms. Uchida, it is definitely because she wants it to.

Beethoven's music is commonly portrayed as a struggle. It was certainly a struggle to those confronting it for the first time. It can hardly be described as merely "pretty," and it still poses considerable challenges, both technical and dramaturgical, to players and listeners. Yet the struggle in many of the final works is precisely about the difficulty of achieving simplicity.

The intense emotion and complexity of these three sonatas blossom not in thorny counterpoint but, in the final movement of the final sonata, in a melting Arietta, opening like a flower, then gilded with the purity of the highest reaches of the keyboard. In all three pieces the simple line of a song is the ultimate musical value, but it is not something that is easily won. To present this kind of thinking too obviously would create not song but murkiness.

01 Which of the following is the writer's attitude toward Mitsuko Uchida's performance?
(A) disappointment
(B) admiration
(C) ambivalence
(D) condescension

02 Which of the following is the best title of the passage?
(A) Ms. Uchida's Most Fateful Performance
(B) Beethoven's Final Sonatas Blossom in Complex Simplicity
(C) Ponderous Proportions Swelled in Beethoven's Sonatas
(D) Beethoven's Sonatas Were Too Much for Ms. Uchida

I could introduce myself properly, but it's not really necessary. You will know me well enough and soon enough, depending on a diverse range of variables. It suffices to say that at some point in time, I will be standing over you, as genially as possible. Your soul will be in my arms. A color will be perched on my shoulder. I will carry you gently away.

At that moment, you will be lying there (I rarely find people standing up). You will be caked in your own body. There might be a discovery; a scream will dribble down the air. The only sound I'll hear after that will be my own breathing, and the sound of the smell, of my footsteps.

The question is, what color will everything be at that moment when I come for you? What will the sky be saying?

Personally, I like a chocolate-colored sky. Dark, dark chocolate. People say it suits me. I do, however, try to enjoy every color I see — the whole spectrum. A billion or so flavors, none of them quite the same, and a sky to slowly suck on. It takes the edge off the stress. It helps me relax.

01 Who is the narrator of the passage?
(A) chromatologist
(B) death
(C) candy maker
(D) climatologist

02 Which of the following does not characterize the narrator?
(A) He is too mean.
(B) He is supercilious.
(C) He enjoys doing his work.
(D) He loves chocolate.

If you assert that nature tends to take things from order to disorder and give an example or two, then you will get almost universal recognition and assent. It is a part of our common experience. Spend hours cleaning your desk, your basement, your attic, and it seems to spontaneously revert back to disorder and chaos before your eyes. So if you say that entropy is a measure of disorder, and that nature tends toward maximum entropy for any isolated system, then you do have some insight into the ideas of the second law of thermodynamics.

Some care must be taken about how you define ①_____ if you are going to use it to understand entropy. A more precise way to characterize entropy is to say that it is a measure of the ②_____ associated with the state of the objects. If a given state can be accomplished in many more ways, then it is more probable than one which can be accomplished in only a few ways. For a glass of water the number of molecules is astronomical. The jumble of ice chips may look more disordered in comparison to the glass of water which looks uniform and homogeneous. But the ice chips place limits on the number of ways the molecules can be arranged. The water molecules in the glass of water can be arranged in many more ways; they have greater multiplicity and therefore greater entropy.

01 Which of the following pairs fits best in the blanks ① and ②?

(A) order — probability
(B) disorder — uniformity
(C) order — homogeneity
(D) disorder — multiplicity

02 Which of the following CANNOT be inferred from the passage?

(A) The second law of thermodynamics is concerned with entropy.
(B) The entropy of an open system does not decrease.
(C) Things tend toward disorder if left to themselves.
(D) Water has a greater entropy than ice.

The Age of Categories is dead. Strangely, it never went by that name, or any name. Also curious is the fact that its boundaries are unclear: it overlapped the Age of Enlightenment, the Age of Reason and some others, but succumbed to the atomizing atmosphere of the Information Age. Knowledge, it held, went hand in hand with nomenclature and delineation. As science developed, branches formed. Elemental to the college and university were academic departments, each of which came surrounded by high walls. A datum was deemed to fit within the confines of chemistry or sociology or the history of spoons or whatever, and that was more or less that.

Now we perceive the _____ of those old categories and scoff; we value multidisciplinarianism and genre-bending. The life of the mind is more chaotic, but also more exhilarating. Often a new boundary-crossing perspective comes simply from going back to original sources — to the time before categories hardened. Study the famous late correspondence between Thomas Jefferson and John Adams, Steven Johnson notes, and you find only five references to Benjamin Franklin and three to George Washington, but 52 to Joseph Priestley, the scientist/theologian who is often credited with the discovery of oxygen.

01 Which of the following can be inferred from the passage?
(A) The boundaries of categories are still clear.
(B) The Age of Enlightenment and the Age of Reason existed in distinctly different time period.
(C) New boundary-crossing has a mixed blessing.
(D) Thomas Jefferson, John Adams, and Joseph Priestley all worked in the same field.
(E) Academic departments are incidental to colleges.

02 Which of the following best fits into the blank?
(A) corroboration   (B) development
(C) zenith   (D) limitation
(E) resurrection

New techniques for analyzing ancient DNA are helping scientists understand the evolution of the woolly mammoth and why these relatives of modern day elephants went extinct around 10,000 years ago. Paleolithic humans have often been blamed for hunting mammoths to extinction. The DNA studies, however, reveal that the cold-adapted elephants had very little genetic diversity, which may have made the species susceptible to being wiped out by disease. Stephan Schuster a genomicist at Pennsylvania State University says "The weather getting a little bit warmer can make a huge difference in humidity, and more humidity means more snow, then, animals can't find food anymore." He says, "A little bit warmer summer can also mean _____." Schuster doesn't let Paleolithic hunters off the hook entirely. He acknowledges that additional pressure from hunting could have been enough to finish off the last of the mammoths. The techniques that the research team to which Schuster belongs used may revolutionize the study of ancient DNA. Previous studies of genetic material from extinct species relied on samples taken from bone, which yielded samples that were heavily contaminated with DNA from fungus and microbes. The new study used a DNA sample taken from inside the shaft of a hair, which was 90 percent pure and much easier to analyze. The research team is still at work sequencing the last 30 percent of the mammoth genome, raising the possibility of cloning a mammoth from ancient DNA. "It is not what is really driving our science," says Schuster, "but everybody agrees that it is no longer impossible."

01 빈칸에 들어갈 가장 적합한 것을 고르시오.

(A) many more food for the mammoths
(B) a much higher pathogen load
(C) the mammoths got too thirsty
(D) they could give birth to more calves

02 위 글을 통해 추론할 수 없는 것으로 가장 적합한 것을 고르시오.

(A) The new study assembled 70 percent of the mammoth genome.
(B) Samples taken from bone are likely to have been contaminated with impurities.
(C) The mammoths lost their genetic diversity through the adaptation to cold.
(D) Humans might not have been the main culprit behind the extinction of mammoth, but they could have contributed to their demise.

In the decades before Europe went to war in 1914, the culture of the main powers was split in two. On the one hand, there was a body of thought — the one most often remembered now — that war had been effectively ended by progress, diplomacy, globalization, and economic and scientific development. They thought that no sane person would risk war and ruin the economic interdependence of the globalizing world. At the same time, each nation's culture was shot through with strong currents pushing for war: armaments races, belligerent rivalries and a struggle for resources. These arms races were massive and expensive affairs and were nowhere clearer than the naval struggle between Britain and Germany, where each tried to produce ever more and larger ships. Millions of men went through the military via conscription, producing a substantial portion of the population who had experienced military indoctrination. Nationalism, elitism, racism and other belligerent thoughts were widespread, thanks to greater access to education than before, but an education that was fiercely biased. Violence for political ends was common and had spread from Russian socialists to British women's rights campaigners. Violence for your country was increasingly _____, artists rebelled and sought new modes of expression, new urban cultures were challenging the existing social order. Europe was essentially primed for people in 1914 to welcome war as a way to recreate their world through _____.

01 Choose one that is most appropriate for the blanks.

(A) rejected — rationale
(B) transformed — configuration
(C) justified — destruction
(D) alleviated — division
(E) swayed — breach

02 According to the passage, which of the following is NOT the cause of the war in 1914?

(A) armament race between Britain and Germany
(B) competition for resources among the great powers
(C) prevalence of violence as a way to carry out political ends
(D) spread of aggressive nationalism
(E) economic interdependence of the main powers

Human hopes are always of two kinds. A human being ①has hopes for himself — hopes that are individual and personal. At the same time, he has suprapersonal hopes for the human race or for some fraction of it: his tribe, his family, perhaps, or his church.

These two kinds of human hopes are not always sharply distinguishable from each other. Self-centeredness, ②seems to be one of the characteristics of life, is ③so powerful a force that it invades even our suprapersonal hopes. In fact, "nosism" (or weism) as we may call this collective counterpart of "egotism," is the most _____ form of self-centeredness. Whether for good or for evil, man is far stronger when he is acting collectively than when he is playing a lone hand; and also, when he is acting collectively, he can behave selfishly without being pulled up short by his conscience, because he can delude ④himself into believing that he is subordinating his self-centeredness to the plural number from the singular. Thus self-centeredness may invade our suprapersonal hopes. On the other hand, our personal hopes may take the form of a moral reaction against self-centeredness and of an effort to transcend it.

01 Which of the following is most appropriate for the blank?
(A) general
(B) delusive
(C) formidable
(D) pleasurable

02 Which of the following is grammatically incorrect?
(A) ① has hopes for himself
(B) ② seems to be
(C) ③ so powerful a force
(D) ④ himself into believing

As Cardinal Joseph Ratzinger, before he became pope two years ago, Benedict had expressed concern that on several fronts, including evolution, science was overstepping its competence, denying the existence of God and becoming its own system of belief. Though he did not reject evolution, he noted in the remarks quoted from the book that science could not completely prove evolution because it could not be duplicated in the laboratory. But, Reuters reported, he also ①<u>defended</u> what is known as theistic evolution, the idea that God could use evolutionary processes to create life, if not through the direct engineering suggested by "intelligent design," which posits that life is so complex that it requires an active creator. Benedict XVI, in his first extended reflections on evolution published as Pope, says that Darwin's theory cannot be finally proven and that science has unnecessarily ②<u>narrowed</u> humanity's view of creation. In a new book, *Creation and Evolution*, published in German, the Pope praised progress gained by science, but cautioned that evolution raises philosophical questions ③<u>science alone can answer</u>. "The question is not to make a decision either for a creationism that fundamentally excludes science, or for an evolutionary theory that covers over its own gaps and does not want to see the questions that reach ④<u>beyond</u> the methodological possibilities of natural science," the Pope said.

01 위 글의 제목으로 가장 적합한 것을 고르시오.

(A) The Philosophical Questions of Evolutionary Theory

(B) Theistic Evolution vs. Intelligent Design

(C) Pope Melds Faith with Science

(D) Pope's Appraisal for Science

02 위 글에서 논지의 흐름상 가장 적합하지 않은 것을 고르시오.

(A) ①   (B) ②
(C) ③   (D) ④

Philosophers need to argue not only the necessity for dialogue but also explain its nature. Dialogue is not just the exchange of ideas. A quarrelling group may be actively exchanging ideas, but will be far from dialogue; ①_____. In both cases the discussions are not dedicated to acquiring knowledge about truth or goodness for the sake of desirable human relations. These, then, are necessary conditions of dialogue. But there are other necessary conditions. Dialogue must be based on rational discussion. Such a discussion is impossible unless the parties acknowledge the possibility that they might be wrong and the other right. We all know this attitude of mind does not come easily.

One of the severest impediments to dialogue is dogmatism, and it is, or ought to be, the role of philosophers to find an antidote to it. Dogmatism is not just holding a belief with a strong conviction; rather it is holding it with a conviction so strong that it rules out the possibility of error. It can be encountered in all spheres of human thinking, including philosophy (in the broad acceptation of this term). And ridding human thought of dogmatism is one of philosophy's objectives, in the strict conception of the discipline.

01 Choose the expression that would fit best in ①.

(A) neither would a group indulging in mutual admiration
(B) neither a group indulging in mutual admiration would be
(C) so would a group indulging in mutual admiration
(D) so a group indulging in mutual admiration would be

02 위 글에 비추어 빈칸에 들어갈 가장 알맞은 것은?

Philosophy has a duty and ability to _____ the pretensions to infallibility.

(A) promote   (B) confront
(C) condemn   (D) dismantle

It is remarkable, but after the devastating floods which covered huge areas of Mozambique, news reports were saying a lot about nature but nothing about human action. It is ironic that at least one major television news programme claimed that this "natural" catastrophe was unusual in Africa, since in that continent most human misery is the consequence of human acts such as civil war and genocide. What the programme neglected to mention is that the floods, like so many recent "natural" disasters, are the result of global warming. And what is the cause of global warming? Could it be humanity, not nature? For years now there have been warnings that the increasing temperature of the earth will lead to extreme weather and disasters which are the result in changes in rainfall and temperature. Most of us have not been frightened enough by this. We have thought of these consequences as lying somewhere in the distant future, not next year, next month or next week. So we have continued to pump chemicals into the atmosphere, slowly turning up the heat on the global pressure cooker. How long can this grand delusion continue, while around the globe, the evidence of our folly mounts at an ever accelerating rate?

01 이 글의 주장을 가장 잘 표현한 것을 고르시오.

(A) People underestimate the importance of human action in natural disasters.
(B) Most human misery in Africa is caused by human action.
(C) Humans are deliberately harming the earth.
(D) The weather is a serious problem around the world.

02 지구 온난화에 관한 사람들의 태도들 가운데 본문의 내용과 가장 일치하지 <u>않는</u> 것을 고르시오.

(A) People think the problems lie in the distant future.
(B) People do not make the connection between global warming and local disasters.
(C) People have not made the changes necessary to stop global warming.
(D) People are too afraid of global warming.

The United Nations ranked Norway as the best country to live in for a sixth consecutive year Thursday, prompting the country's Aid Minister to tell Norwegians to stop _____ about wanting more. Oil-rich Norway, with its generous welfare state, topped the U.N. Development Program's human development index, based on such criteria as life expectancy, education and income. Iceland was No. 2, followed by Australia, Ireland, Sweden, Canada, Japan and the United States.

Despite wealth, high levels of education, low unemployment, and an economic boom, Norwegians often complain of high taxes and of weaknesses in their cradle-to-grave welfare state, such as waiting lists at hospitals and a shortage of public care for both children and the elderly.

According to the study, Norwegians earn 40 times more than the study's lowest-ranked country, Niger, live almost twice as long, and have nearly five times the literacy rate. "The top place should make us show humility," said Aid Minister Erik Solheim in an interview. "Norway should be seen as a modern, rich and successful society, but should also be seen as a generous country. The world must see us as rich and generous, not rich and miserly."

01 Which of the following best completes the blank?
    (A) whining   (B) bragging
    (C) concerning   (D) compromising

02 Which of the following would be the gist of what Solheim said?
    (A) Instead of complaining, Norwegians should try to share their wealth with poorer countries.
    (B) Norway is the best country to live in.
    (C) There are unsolved problems in Norway, so it's quite natural that people look at the future with pessimism.
    (D) Norway is already the world's most generous foreign aid donors per capita.

Arid regions in the southwestern United States have become increasingly inviting playgrounds for the growing number of recreation seekers who own vehicles such as motorcycles or powered trail bikes and indulge in hill-climbing contests or in carving new trails in the desert. But recent scientific studies show that these off-road vehicles can cause damage to desert landscapes that has long-range effects on the area's water-conserving characteristics and on the entire ecology, both plant and animal. Research by scientists in the western Mojave Desert in California revealed that the compaction of the sandy arid soil resulting from the passage of just one motorcycle markedly reduced the infiltration ability of the soil and created a stream of rain water that eroded the hillside surface. In addition, the researchers discovered that the soil compaction caused by the off-road vehicles often killed native plant species and resulted in the invasion of different plant species within a few years. The native perennial species required many more years before they showed signs of returning, and the scientists calculated that roughly a century would be required for the infiltration capacity of the Mojave soil to be restored after compacted by vehicles.

01 What is main topic of the passage?

(A) Types of off-road vehicles
(B) Problems caused by recreational vehicles
(C) Plant of the southwestern desert
(D) The increasing number of recreation seekers

02 Which of the following is NOT true according to the passage?

(A) The damage to plants is irreparable.
(B) Native plants in these areas are dying.
(C) The desert landscape is being damaged.
(D) Little water seeps through when the soil is compacted.

Although the architects Samuel McIntire and Charles Bullfinch designed notable buildings in Salem and Boston, respectively, Asher Benjamin, a carpenter from Greenfield, Massachusetts, is credited with having exerted more direct influence than any other single person on architecture in New England. In 1797 he published a book called *The Country Builder's Assistant*. It was not the first book on architecture printed in the United States, but it was the first genuinely American treatment of the subject. It was very much a "how-to-do-it" book since it contained plans and detailed drawings for various private and public structures. Carpenters throughout the Northeast were a literate breed. They acquired Benjamin's book and began to pattern their construction work on his plans. The First Congregational Church in Bennington, Vermont, one of the most admired of all New England churches, was built by the carpenter Lavius Fillmore and closely resembles one of the designs found in Asher's book. Like Fillmore, most local carpenters had souls of their own and were not given to automated reproductions from the book. But the total result is a pervasive pattern that continues to give New England its distinctive flavor.

01 Benjamin's relation to the carpenters of his day could best be compared with that of _____.

(A) a teacher to students
(B) a commander to troops
(C) an enemy to adversaries
(D) an idol to worshipers

02 Which of the following would be the best title for this passage?

(A) Architects Versus Carpenters in New England
(B) How Bennington's Church was Built
(C) The Influence of Asher Benjamin on New England Architecture
(D) The Colonial Buildings of Salem and Boston

Art, all art, has this characteristic, that it unites people. Every art causes those to whom the artist's feeling is transmitted to unite in soul with the artist, and also with all who receive the same impression. But non-Christian art, ① _____ uniting some people together, ② _____ between these united people and others; so that union of this kind is often a source, not only of division, but even of enmity toward others. Such is all patriotic art, with its anthems, poems, and monuments; such is all Church art, *i. e.* The art of certain cults, with their images, statues, processions, and other local ceremonies. Such art is belated and non-Christian art, uniting the people of one cult only to separate them yet more sharply from the members of other cults, and even to place them in relations of hostility to each other. Christian art is only such as tends to unite all without exception, either by evoking in them the perception that each man and all men stand in like relation toward God and toward their neighbor, or by evoking in them identical feelings, ③ _____ may even be the very simplest, provided only that they are not repugnant to Christianity and are natural to everyone without exception.

01 What fits best in ① and ③, respectively?
   (A) while — which
   (B) even if — that
   (C) since — that
   (D) as if — which

02 Which of the following phrases fits best in the blank ②?
   (A) makes that very enmity a cause of unity
   (B) becomes increasingly commercialized the unity
   (C) makes a deep impression
   (D) makes that very union a cause of separation

One continuing problem in labor-management relations is the "us/them" mentality. In addition to fiscal constraints, continuing problems with the Fair Labor Standards Act, bad faith negotiations, bad management practices, poor union leadership, and a continued loss of management prerogatives will all combine to produce forces which will cause a significant increase in disruptive job actions in the near future. Neither side is blameless. The tragedy of the situation is that the impact of poor labor-management relations is relatively predictable and is thus avoidable.

Since the economic situation will not improve significantly in the next few years, the pressure on the part of union leaders to obtain more benefits for their members will be frustrated. As a result of the PATCO strike, management has learned that times are conducive to regaining prerogatives lost during the pervious decade. The stage for confrontation between labor and management in the public sector is set, and in many areas it only requires an incident to force disruptive job actions. The only solution to this seemingly intractable problem lies in the area of skilled negotiations and good faith bargaining. This requires commitment on the part of management and labor to live up to the terms of existing contracts.

01 The underlined word intractable could be best replaced by _____.
(A) obstinate
(B) equivocal
(C) abstruse
(D) arduous

02 Which of the following can be inferred from the passage?
(A) Fiscal constraints decrease disruptive job actions.
(B) The labor union regains its strength when the economy picks up.
(C) Existing contracts need to be revised in order to obtain more benefits.
(D) Skilled negotiations are the temporary remedy for poor labor-management relationship.

Ever since it was first spotted amid the factory smoke of western Europe's industrializing nations, the middle class has borne the hopes for progress of politicians, economists and shopkeepers alike. It remains hard to define, and attempts to do so often seem arbitrary. But in Brazil, the middle class describes those with a job in the formal economy, access to credit and ownership of a car or motorbike. This means households with a monthly income ranging from 1,064 reais($600) to 4,561 reais. Since 2002, the proportion of the population that fits this description has increased from 44% to 52%, which means that Brazil's ①_____ has now decreased. This social climbing is a feature mainly of the country's cities, reversing two decades of stagnation that began at the start of the 1980s. A sociologist suggests two factors behind the change. The first is education. The quality of teaching in Brazil's schools may still be poor, but those aged 15-21 now spend on average just over three more years studying than their counterparts did in the early 1990s. The second is a migration of jobs from the informal "black" economy to the formal economy. The rate of formal job creation is accelerating, with 40% more created in the year to this July than in the previous 12 months, which itself set a record. Together with cash transfers to poor families, this helps to explain why — in contrast with economic and social development in India or China — as Brazil's middle class has grown, so the country's ②_____ has lessened.

01 다음 중 위 글을 통해서 알 수 없는 것으로 가장 적절한 것을 고르시오.

(A) income range for the middle class in Brazil
(B) the exchange rate of real against dollar
(C) causes of the growth of Brazil's middle class
(D) the effects of migrant workers on Brazil's economy

02 빈칸 ①, ②에 공통으로 들어가기에 가장 적절한 것을 고르시오.

(A) income inequality
(B) racial discrimination
(C) social mobility
(D) job security

Are some people more helpful than others? When Daniel Santos's friends and co-workers learned of his heroics in jumping 150 feet off the Tappan Zee Bridge to save a stranger, they were not surprised. "That's just how he is," said one of his friends. "If he sees something, he is going to go and try to help out that person." A receptionist at the company where he worked as a mechanic added, "He will help anyone at any place and any time." His sister noted that he leaped into the water even though he is not a strong swimmer. "He has a good heart," she said.

Are there many people who are generally helpful across all situations? Are there others who are generally unhelpful? Although situational factors clearly can overwhelm individual differences in influencing helping behaviors, researchers have demonstrated some evidence of individual differences in helping tendencies. People who are more helpful than others in one situation are likely to be more helpful in other situations as well. In addition, a longitudinal study by Nancy Eisenberg and others suggests that this individual difference may be relatively _____ over time. Specifically, they found that the degree to which preschool children exhibited spontaneous helping behavior predicted how helpful they would be in later childhood and early adulthood.

01 What does the author imply with the description of Daniel Santos in the first paragraph?
   (A) People with altruistic personalities do not care about risking their own lives or the lives of others.
   (B) Altruistic people have certain personality traits in common.
   (C) People who have altruistic personalities are liked and admired by others.
   (D) People with altruistic personalities are just naturally willing to help others even in dangerous situations.

02 Which of the following is most suitable for the blank?
   (A) prompt   (B) stable
   (C) hidden   (D) meager

Einstein was more than a scientist. He was also a dedicated humanitarian, who wrote as much about ethical and social issues as about science. "Knowledge and skills alone cannot lead humanity to a happy and dignified life. Humanity has every reason to place the proclaimers of high moral standards and values above the discoverers of objective truth," he asserted. [I] Einstein was not only a great scientist, he was a great man. [II] The governments of the superpowers employ tens of thousands of people who know how to transform Einstein's equations into bombs, few who have studied his counsel on why the bombs should not be built. [III] To appreciate Einstein's qualities, we must peer behind the thunderheads of the myth. [IV] There stands an Einstein of Zen-like poise who was, first and last, pacific. Peace was the subject of hundreds of his essays, letters, and lectures. His last conversation with his old friend Otto Nathan, just a few hours before his death, concerned civil liberties. The last document he signed was a proclamation against the use of nuclear arms. He argued that the bomb had left the world with no choice but to renounce all-out war, which he called "the savage and inhuman relic of an age of barbarism."

01 Which of the following is the best title of the passage?
(A) The Great Philosophy of a Great Scientist
(B) Einstein Renowned for His Humanism
(C) The Disparity Between Science and Philosophy
(D) The Peace Threatened by Nuclear Arms

02 Which of the following would best fit into?

But the world has paid much closer attention to Einstein's science than to his humanitarianism.

(A) [I]   (B) [II]
(C) [III]   (D) [IV]

I am sorry you ascribe so much importance to the omission of your little paper on Dr. Reid's book. I did certainly intend to have inserted it, but the monstrous length of some other articles, and your unavoidable absence from home when the No. was finally filled up, prevented me. I think I shall give it a place in the next, though there is not much interest in the subject.

I feel that I am extremely to blame for not answering a former letter of yours on a subject more personal to yourself, and assuredly I do not feel it the less for your delicacy in saying nothing about it in your last; but I can safely say that it was not owing to indifference or unwillingness to give you all the information I had, but to a feeling of great uncertainty as to the justness of any information I had, and the hazard of the great error in any advice I might found on it. This made me hesitate, and resolve to reflect and inquire before I made any answer, and then came in the usual vice of procrastination and the usual excuse of other more urgent avocation, till at last it was half forgotten, and half driven willingly from my conscience when it recurred.

01 The writer is writing this letter _____.
(A) to express gratitude
(B) to prove he was not involved in the omission
(C) to explain why Dr. Reid's book no longer attracts the readers' attention
(D) to offer an apology and inform him that the paper will appear in the following issue
(E) to show that the paper was not of great significance

02 Which of the following is NOT suggested as reasons for not responding promptly?
(A) unwillingness to provide any information
(B) a feeling of great uncertainty on the justness of any information
(C) other more urgent things
(D) the possible error in any advice
(E) the writer's procrastination

Ambivalence, the alternation or simultaneous occurrence of positive and negative images, beliefs, feelings, and desires, is common — perhaps universal — in close relationships. The capacity to view the same person in opposite ways at different times is an expression of the dualistic organization of the primal information-processing systems. At the most obvious level, ambivalence becomes apparent when partners are loving one moment and in the next moment feel like tearing each other apart. It is often difficult to explain how or why people switch suddenly from affection to dislike, or why the previous warm feelings do not form a cushion against the experience of angry feelings. This kind of reversal of feelings in the relationship may not be apparent during the halcyon days of the romance, when all differences are submerged or sweetened by affection. [I] Potholes and rifts appear in the previously smooth landscape of their romance. [II] The balance between reciprocal interests and self-interest gradually shifts. [III] "What's best for you is best for me" becomes "What's best for me is best for you." [IV] Actually, both orientations may persist throughout a marriage, but the self-centered beliefs become more active than the altruistic beliefs in distressed relationships.

01 Choose the best location for the following statement.

"It becomes more obvious, however, as the partners become more involved in their own goals and desires."

(A) [I] (B) [II]
(C) [III] (D) [IV]

02 According to the passage, we are ambivalent when _____.

(A) we love someone at one time and someone else at another time
(B) we feel ourselves to be one person and to be another some time later
(C) we remain self-centered while saying we sacrifice ourselves for others
(D) we feel respect and disrespect about someone at the same time

Like other diseases that arouse feelings of shame, AIDS is often a secret, but not from the patient. A cancer diagnosis was frequently concealed from patients by their families; an AIDS diagnosis is at least as often concealed from their families by patients. And as with other grave illnesses regarded as more than just illness, many people with AIDS are drawn to whole-body rather than illness-specific treatments, which are thought to be either ineffectual or too dangerous. This disastrous choice is still being made by some people with cancer, an illness that surgery and drugs can often cure. A predictable mix of superstition and resignation is similarly leading some people with AIDS to refuse antiviral chemotherapy, which, even in the absence of a cure, has proved of some effectiveness (in slowing down the syndrome's progress and in starving off some common secondary illness), and instead to seek to heal themselves, often under the auspices of some "alternative medicine guru." But subjecting an emaciated body to the purification of a macrobiotic diet is about as helpful in treating AIDS as having oneself bled, the "holistic" medical treatment of choice in the Middle Ages.

01   The author's primary purpose is to _____.

(A) criticize the rise of "alternative medicine"
(B) contrast the medical treatment of AIDS with that of cancer
(C) discuss the effect that the attitudes of AIDS victims have on their choice of treatment
(D) analyze the responses of AIDS victims in the light of the reponses of victims of other diseases

02   The author uses the analogy between AIDS and cancer to _____.

(A) call for greater public and private acceptance of the diseases
(B) stress that AIDS symptoms differ markedly from those of cancer
(C) expose the superstitions many people have about these two diseases
(D) underscore the importance of illness-specific treatment for both AIDS and cancer

03   In presenting her argument, the author does all of the following EXCEPT:

(A) Refer to medical evidence supporting her contentions.
(B) Cite a treatment that is appropriate for AIDS victims.
(C) Sharply criticize whole-body and alternative medical treatments of AIDS.
(D) Note some common features that AIDS victims share with victims of other diseases.

The new school of political history that emerged in the 1960's and 1970's sought to go beyond the traditional focus of political historians on leaders and government institutions by examining directly the political practices of ordinary citizens. Like the old approach, however, this new approach excluded women. The very techniques these historians used to uncover mass political behavior in the nineteenth-century United States — quantitative analyses of election returns, for example — were useless in analyzing the political activities of women, who were denied the vote until 1920.

By redefining "political activity," historian Paula Baker has developed a political history that includes women. She concludes that among ordinary citizens, political activism by women in the nineteenth century prefigured trends in twentieth-century politics. Defining "politics" as "any action taken to affect the course of behavior of government or of the community," Baker concludes that, while voting and holding office were restricted to men, women in the nineteenth century organized themselves into societies committed to social issues such as temperance and poverty. In other words, Baker contends, women activists were early practitioners of nonpartisan, issue-oriented politics and thus were more interested in enlisting lawmakers, regardless of their party affiliation, on behalf of certain issues than in ensuring that one party or another won an election. In the twentieth century, more men drew closer to women's ideas about politics and took up modes of issue-oriented politics Baker sees women as having pioneered.

01   The primary purpose of the passage is to _____.

(A) identify a shortcoming in a scholarly approach and describe an alternative approach
(B) provide empirical data to support a long-held scholarly assumption
(C) compare two scholarly publications on the basis of their authors' backgrounds
(D) attempt to provide a partial answer to a long-standing scholarly dilemma

02   Which of the following best describes the structure of the first paragraph?

(A) A historical era is described in terms of its political trends.
(B) An argument is outlined, and counter-arguments are mentioned.
(C) An outmoded scholarly approach is described, and a corrective one is required.
(D) Two scholarly approaches are compared and a shortcoming common to both is identified.

03   Paula Baker and the 1960's and 1970's new political historians shared _____.

(A) a commitment to interest-group politics
(B) a disregard for political theory and ideology
(C) an emphasis on the political involvement of ordinary citizens
(D) a reliance on such quantitative techniques as the analysis of election returns

Another thing to remember in connection with concrete is that you are not allowed very much leeway for errors in either measurements or location. Once you have a solid mass of concrete set in place, it is going to stay there. You have a difficult job ahead of you if you try to remedy a mistake. Make very sure, before you fill the form, that everything is where and how you want it.

There are numerous rules regarding the proper mixing, handling, and finishing of concrete, but the essential one concerns the amount of water to use. The less water in the mix, the less the finished job will shrink. The less water used, the harder and more enduring the job after it has set.

The amateur concrete worker is plagued with two desires. One is to use enough water to have the concrete nice and soft and easy to push around. You have been warned against that. The second is to take off the wooden forms too early, to see what the job looks like. That is really fatal. If the forms are stripped off too soon, while the concrete is still "green," two things are likely to happen — you are almost sure to break off corners or edges, and you are likely to cause a major crack or defect in the body of the work. An excellent rule is to wait until you are sure the concrete is properly hardened, and then wait another day before removing the forms.

01 In mixing concrete, one of the desires the amateur must resist is to _____.
(A) break off a corner to see if the "green" has gone
(B) strip off the forms a day after the concrete has properly hardened
(C) use too much water
(D) use too little water

02 A human quality apparently *not* essential in someone who works with concrete is _____.

(A) sense of spatial relations   (B) patience
(C) inventiveness   (D) self-control

03 In instructing the reader in the intricacies of working with concrete, the author _____.
(A) understates the things that may go wrong
(B) allows the reader to find the solution to the problem from his own experience
(C) overstates the dire consequences of an error
(D) presents problem and gives solution

The deliberate violation of constituted law (civil disobedience) is never morally justified if the law being violated is not the prime target or focal point of protest. While our government maintains the principle of the Constitution by providing methods for and protection of those engaged in individual or group dissent, the violation of law simply as a technique of demonstration constitutes rebellion.

Civil disobedience is by definition a violation of the law. The theory of civil disobedience recognizes that its actions, regardless of their justification, must be punished. However, disobedience of laws not the subject of dissent, but merely used to dramatize dissent, is regarded as morally as well as legally unacceptable. It is only with respect to those laws which offend the fundamental values of human life that moral defense of civil disobedience can be rationally supported.

For a just society to exist, the principle of tolerance must be accepted, both by the government in regard to properly expressed individual dissent and by the individual toward legally established majority verdicts. No individual has a monopoly on freedom and all must tolerate opposition. Dissenters must accept dissent from their dissent, giving it all the respect they claim for themselves. To disregard this principle is to make civil disobedience not only legally wrong but morally unjustifiable.

01 The author's attitude toward civil disobedience is one of _____.
(A) indifference
(B) admiration
(C) hostility
(D) contempt

02 What would the author most likely feel about a demonstration against apartheid which resulted in the disruption of businesses not associated with the problem in any way?
(A) profound antipathy toward the goal of the demonstration
(B) severe condemnation of the location of the businesses
(C) tolerant acceptance of the demonstration's results
(D) regretful disapproval of the methods of protest

03 It can be inferred from the passage that _____.
(A) a just society cannot accept illegal civil disobedience
(B) a just society cannot accept immoral actions of any sort
(C) dissenters who use civil disobedience cannot use it merely to dramatize their cause
(D) civil disobedience is sometimes the right thing to do

Primitive mammals called monotremes are the only living representatives of the subclass *Prototheria*. This makes them the most likely living representatives of creatures that were part of the evolutionary transition from reptiles to mammals. They share some qualities with reptiles and birds, but are nevertheless true mammals. Like birds and reptiles, monotremes lay eggs rather than giving birth to live young. But, like other mammals, they have hair, large brains, and mammary glands that produce milk to nourish their offspring.

Their primitive organization and close relation to reptiles is manifested in their uncomplicated brian structure, egg-laying habits, and cloaca. (A cloaca is found in amphibians, reptiles, birds, certain fish, and monotremes, but not in placental mammals or most bony fishes. The animal's intestinal, urinary, and genital tracts open into this common cavity, which also functions as an outlet.)

Another feature that indicates they may be related to reptiles is their egg-laying behavior. Monotremes lay shelled eggs like those of reptiles and birds. The young are born in a relatively early stage of development and remain dependent upon the parent. The females have no teats; the milk that they secrete from their mammary glands passes directly through their skin.

There are only three types of monotremes in existence: the duck-billed platypus and two species of spiny echidna, or anteater.

01 The passage focuses on which of the following aspects of monotremes?
(A) the food they eat and their behavior in the wild
(B) the times of day when they are most active
(C) their relationship to both reptiles and mammals
(D) their mating behavior and reproductive organs

02 Which of the following is NOT mentioned as a quality that monotremes share with other mammals?
(A) hair on the body
(B) development of mammary glands
(C) a large brain
(D) egg-laying

03 The passage states that monotremes _____.
(A) are egg-laying mammals that are related to reptiles and birds
(B) are reptiles and birds
(C) have been exterminated
(D) are highly intelligent

People are going to be surprised at how different the Middle East is going to be in a few years. There's going to be more democratic development, undoubtedly turbulent, rocky, because that's how big changes are. When I look back on the fall of communism, I realize that we were just harvesting the decisions that had been made in 1946 and 1947. In 1946, the Italian Communists won 48% of the vote and the French Communists 46% of the vote. In 1948, Czechoslovakia fell to a Communist coup. In 1948, Berlin was permanently divided by the Berlin Crisis. In 1949, the Soviet Union set off a nuclear weapon five years ahead of schedule and the Chinese Communists won. If you had said to people at that time, "In 1989 and 1990, the Soviet Union is going to collapse, Eastern Europe is going to peacefully emerge as democratic, Germany will finally unify, Poland, Lithuania, Latvia, Romania are all going to be members of NATO," people would have said, "Are you out of your mind?" Now we're at the beginning of another great transformation. I don't know if it will be ten years or 20 or 30. But people will look back and say, "We're really glad that they didn't take the easy way, that they didn't decide stability was enough and insisted on democratic development."

01 Which of the following best expresses the main idea of the passage?

(A) It is right that we struggle to democratize the countries in the Middle East.
(B) We should ward off communism by spreading democracy in the Middle East.
(C) The decisions made in 1946 and 1947 will affect the future of the Middle East.
(D) The history of the Middle East has been a succession of great transformations.

02 Choose the one closest in meaning to the underlined "out of your mind."

(A) indifferent   (B) insane
(C) stupid   (D) oblivious

03 Which of the following CANNOT be inferred from the passage?

(A) There will be not a few troubles in the course of the democratization of the Middle East.
(B) In 1940s, most people did not expect Eastern Europe would be democratized about half a century later.
(C) The 1946 and 1947 decisions finally brought European communism to an end in the 1990s.
(D) People will someday feel regret for our current way of dealing with the Middle East problems.

As the work of Sigmund Freud became popular, artists became fascinated by the subconscious mind. By 1924, a surrealist manifesto stated some specific connections between the subconscious mind and painting. The metaphysical fantasies of Giorgio de Chirico have surrealist qualities. In works such as *The Nostalgia of the Infinite*, strange objects are irrationally juxtaposed: they come together as in a dream. These bizarre works reflect a world that human beings do not control.

Surrealism is probably more accurately represented by the paintings of Salvador Dali, however. Dali called his works, such as *The Persistence of Memory*, "hand-colored photographs of the subconscious," and the almost photographic detail of his work, coupled with the nightmarish relationships of the objects he pictures, has a forceful impact. The whole idea of time is destroyed in these "soft watches" (as they were called by those who first saw this work) hanging limply and crawling with ants. And yet the images are strangely fascinating, perhaps in the way we are fascinated by the world of our dreams. While the anti-art dadaism of Max Ernst may seem repulsive, the irrationality of de Chirico and Dali can be _____. The starkness and graphic clarity of their works speak of the unpolluted light of another planet, yet nonetheless it reveals a world we seem to know.

01 Choose the one that best fills in the blank.
   (A) aggressive   (B) entrancing
   (C) instrumental   (D) ostensible

02 Which of the following cannot be inferred about "surrealism"?
   (A) It reflects the subconscious mind or the world in a dream.
   (B) It tends to depict illogical scenes with photographic precision.
   (C) It deals with real objects in unexpected and strange ways.
   (D) It rejects all the traditional standards and definitions of art.

03 What is the best title for the passage?
   (A) Freud's Influence on Surrealism
   (B) Two Great Surrealist Artists
   (C) The Characteristics of Surrealism
   (D) The Relation of Surrealism to Dadaism

Once these preparations were completed, he was anxious to wait no longer before putting his ideas into effect, impelled to this by the thought of the loss the world suffered by his delay, seeing the grievances there were to redress, the wrongs to right, the injuries to amend, and the debts to discharge. So, telling nobody of his intentions, and quite unobserved, one morning before dawn — it was on one of those sweltering July days — he armed himself completely, mounted Rocinate, put on his badly-mended headpiece, slung on his shield, seized his lance and went out into the plain through the back gate on his yard, pleased and delighted to see with what ease he had started on his fair design. But scarcely was he in open country when he was assailed by a thought so terrible that it almost made him abandon the enterprise he had just begun.

For he suddenly remembered that he had never received the honor of knighthood, and so, according to the laws of chivalry, he neither could nor should take arms against any knight, and even if he had been knighted he was bound, as a novice, to wear plain armour without a device on his shield until he should gain one by his prowess. These reflections made him waver in his resolve, but as his madness outweighed any other argument, he made up his mind to have himself knighted by the first man he met, in imitation of many who had done the same, as he had read in the books which had so influenced him. As to plain armour, he decided to clean his own, when he had time, till it was whiter than ermine. With this he quieted his mind and went on his way, taking whatever road his horse chose, in the belief that in this lay the essence of adventure.

01   What is this passage mainly about?
   (A) The pleasure and delight of a man
   (B) The recklessness of a visionary man
   (C) The true courage of an adventurer
   (D) The greatness of a knight

02   Why did he come close to giving up what he had just planned?
   (A) Because he lacked courage.
   (B) Because he felt he was not ready to be engaged in a duel.
   (C) Because this was not what he had really been thinking of.
   (D) Because it came into his mind that he had not been knighted.

03   He decided to have himself knighted by the first man he met because _____.
   (A) he knew that he was a very reasonable man
   (B) his insanity was dominant over other factors
   (C) he was bound to be a knight after all
   (D) he firmly believed that he was a great adventurer

Astronomers have identified areas in space which they call black holes. They believe these black holes are super-dense stars from which nothing, not even light, can escape. Astronomers think black holes form when a very large star dies and begins to collapse inward upon itself. A star dies when it uses up its nuclear fuel and thus loses heat. As it cools, it begins to shrink. The collapsing star becomes more and more dense, and the pull of gravity becomes stronger. At the point when its density becomes a million billion times greater than that of water, the gravity becomes so strong that everything near the black hole, including light, planets or even other stars, is dragged into it. For our Sun, an ordinary-size star, to become a black hole, it would have to collapse to a point where its radius was a mere three kilometers. Surrounding any black hole is a spherical "horizon," a boundary through which light can enter but not escape. Because no light can leave the star, it appears to be totally black. Black stars can be detected only because, just before material enters the hole, it becomes hot and gives off X-rays, which can be detected from Earth. The only other way to detect these "invisible" black holes is by their influences on other stars. Black holes may be small, but they exert the same gravitation attraction as an ordinary, uncollapsed star of the size would, and so large black holes can be powerful enough that they can pull visible stars into orbit around them, and the movements of this second, visible star can be observed. Astronomers are now suggesting that all large galaxies may have gigantic black holes in their center.

---

01   According to astronomers, black holes are _____.
   (A) stars which are far darker than ordinary stars
   (B) stars of a very large size
   (C) areas in space which are as black as night
   (D) super-dense stars from which nothing can escape

02 The basic reason why a star begins to collapse and shrink is that _____.
 (A) light can enter but can not escape
 (B) a star runs out of fuel
 (C) the pull of gravity becomes stronger than that of water
 (D) the weight is added by planets and nearby stars

03 According to the passage, why can't light escape from a black hole?
 (A) The pull of gravity is so strong.
 (B) The sun has little nuclear fuel.
 (C) It is obstructed by the falling planets and stars.
 (D) Material blocks the hole.

If it's a question of someone's wanting the right to die, I say jump off a building. But as soon as you bring in somebody else to help you, it changes the equation. Just don't ask a doctor to help you do it. That would violate the traditions of medicine and raise doubts about the role of the physician.

One of my worries is that people will be manipulated by a doctor's suggesting suicide. A lot of seriously ill people already feel they're a burden because they're costing their families money. There is no coercion there, but you build on somebody's guilt. We'd have a whole new class of people considering suicide who hadn't thought about it before.

Then, too, I don't believe that you could successfully regulate this practice. The relationship between the doctor and the patient begins in confidentiality. If they decide together that they don't want anybody to know, there is no way the government can regulate it. The presumption is that physicians would only be helping people commit suicide after everything else had failed to end their suffering. But a lot of people won't want to be that far along. None of the proposed regulations takes into account a person who is not suffering now, but who says, "I don't want to suffer in the future. Let me commit suicide now." I can imagine a doctor who would say, "Yes, we're going to make sure that you don't have to suffer at all."

01 Which of the following questions does the passage answer to?
(A) How do doctors recognize their role as a physician?
(B) Should doctors be allowed to help terminally ill patients commit suicide?
(C) Should the government financially support severely ill patients?
(D) Why is it so controversial to disapprove assisted suicide?

02 According to the author of the passage, _____.
(A) many doctors have neglected their duty at the hospital
(B) committing suicide should be prohibited by the government
(C) serious patients might choose suicide in order to avoid financial burdens for their family
(D) the number of people committing suicide has increased

03 According to the author of the passage, this practice could be conducted by doctors and patients _____.
(A) openly
(B) effectively
(C) revengefully
(D) thoughtlessly

Another strategy is to ambush the bacteria with an unlikely ally: viruses. Vincent Fischetti at Rockefeller University, New York City, is enlisting the help of bacteriophages, viruses that infect only bacterial cells, leaving human ones alone. They hijack the bacterium's genetic machinery and within minutes start to pump out hundreds of copies of themselves. When enough _____ build up inside the cell, the phages produce an enzyme that chews through the cell wall, causing it to explode with the force of a popping champagne cork and spew out the viral intruders. Treating humans with live viruses — even ones that shouldn't harm us — is always risky, so Fischetti decided to isolate just the bacteria-puncturing enzyme and use it to kill bacteria from the outside. So far, he has developed compounds against pneumococcus, streptococcus and anthrax and hopes to eventually treat infected patients by squirting the enzymes in nasal-spray form weekly. None of these agents are quite ready for the pharmacy, and until they are, researchers are focusing on new ways to maximize the power of drugs we do have. By studying bacterial DNA, scientists at the U.S. Naval Research Laboratory are decoding the genetic battle plans that the bugs use to develop resistance. These secrets can help doctors prescribe antibiotics more effectively by knowing which strains are most susceptible to which drugs.

01 What is the best title for this passage?
(A) Battles Between Bacteria and Viruses
(B) A Great Achievement by A Bacteriologist
(C) Research for More Effective Antibiotics
(D) Strategies in the Battles Against Bacteria

02 Choose the one that best fills in the blank.
(A) progeny
(B) progenitors
(C) bacteria
(D) antibiotics

03 Which of the following cannot be inferred from the passage?
(A) Bacteriophages are very selective in attacking bacteria.
(B) Using enzymes is safer than using bacteriophages.
(C) The ultimate goal is to maximize the power of existing antibiotics.
(D) Different varieties of bacteria have different plans to develop resistance.

ID fraud — stealing someone's personal details to raid their bank or credit card accounts, or even to open new ones in their name — is increasing steadily throughout Asia, so the idea of insurance against it is appealing. AIG, for instance, offers ID Guard insurance that covers up to $3,500 per occurrence when any fraudulent purchases are made with your credit card numbers or ID card details and up to $7,000 for legal fees, loss of wages or other incidental costs. This costs a relatively low $35 a year.

However, many experts remain sceptical for the need for such insurance. MarketWatch.com's Chuck Jaffe points out that insurers make money off such policies because _____ remain small, particularly for someone who is concerned with the problem in the first place. A consumer who is concerned with identity theft would regularly check credit reports to look for unauthorized activity, would guard personal account information, shred documents with account numbers or any significant details, review bank statements and more. Those actions go much further towards protecting the consumer from identity fraud than insurance.

01 What is the best title for the passage?
   (A) The Severity of ID Fraud in Asia
   (B) The Precautions Against Insurance Fraud
   (C) The Dubious Necessity of ID Theft Insurance
   (D) The Insurance Policies in the Information Age

02 Which of the following cannot be inferred from the passage?
   (A) The increasing occurrence of ID theft in Asia is due to its economic downturns.
   (B) Frequent credit card users would probably be interested in ID Guard insurance.
   (C) It is more important to handle your personal information with care than to be insured.
   (D) Credit reports show you if someone else has bought things with your credit card.

03 Choose the one that best fills in the blank.
   (A) the coverages of identity theft insurances
   (B) the revenues from getting consumers insured
   (C) the odds of being an identity theft victim
   (D) the opportunities for new ones to enter the market

Aghast at the atrocities committed by US forces invading the Philippines, and the rhetorical flights about liberation and noble intent that routinely accompany crimes of state, Mark Twain threw up his hands at his inability to wield his formidable weapon of satire. The immediate object of his frustration was the renowned General Funston. "No satire of Funston could reach perfection," Twain lamented, "because Funston occupies that summit himself … [he is] satire incarnated."

It is a thought that often comes to mind, again in August 2008 during the Georgia-Ossetia-Russia war. George Bush, Condoleezza Rice and other dignitaries solemnly invoked the sanctity of the United Nations, warning that Russia could be excluded from international institutions "by taking actions in Georgia that are inconsistent with" their principles. The sovereignty and territorial integrity of all nations must be rigorously honored, they intoned — "all nations," that is, apart from those that the US chooses to attack: Iraq, Serbia, perhaps Iran, and a list of others too long and familiar to mention.

01 Which of the following cannot be inferred from the passage?

(A) The United Nations is actually under the control of the United States.
(B) The United States threatens to kick Russia out of the UN.
(C) The Georgia-Ossetia-Russia war may lead to another Cold War.
(D) The United States has honored the foreign sovereignty.

02 Which of the following characterizes Twain's attitude toward General Funston?

(A) awe
(B) trust
(C) admiration
(D) condescendence

03 According to the passage, which of the following does the US government's position on the Georgia war bring to mind?

(A) Actions speak louder than words.
(B) The pot calls the kettle black.
(C) A bad workman always blames his tools.
(D) Liars should have good memories.

Aaron Swartz made access to ideas a lifelong crusade. In adolescence, it drove him to become a top programmer. But as a young adult, it brought him face to face with a potential sentence of 35 years in prison on 13 counts of fraud, cybercrime and other charges after he allegedly stole a massive database of academic journals. On Jan. 11, as Swartz was months from trial and suffering from what friends say was a renewed bout of depression, his crusade came to an end when he took his life in his Brooklyn apartment. He was 26.

Despite his history of depression, friends say Swartz's death is the result of abuse by prosecutors seeking to make an example of him. They say the prosecution was overwhelming and too much for him to bear. The prosecutors and their supporters say they acted within their discretion and that the $58 billion in annual lost revenue from U.S. copyright violations _____ on computer-related intellectual-property crime. Idealistic loose cannon or Robin Hood of the open Internet, Swartz has come in death to personify the debate over how much information should be freely available and how aggressively the government should punish those who "liberate" it. Swartz's death dramatically illuminates his lifelong push to increase access to ideas and innovations that could better the world, but it is not clear whether it has advanced that cause.

---

01 Choose the one that best fills in the blank.

(A) forestalls a drastic crackdown
(B) necessitates a tough line
(C) nullifies vindicatory sanctions
(D) justifies lenient law enforcement

02 Choose the one closest in meaning to the underlined "loose cannon."

(A) a person who has much knowledge and gives advice to other people
(B) a person who pretends to be a professional so as to trick people
(C) a person who believes in helping the needy by giving money to them
(D) a person who tends to do unexpected things that can cause problems

03 Which of the following is true about Aaron Swartz?

(A) Not depression but prosecutorial overreach was a main cause of his death.
(B) He has struggled to shut down the websites accused of copyright violations.
(C) Before trial, he committed suicide, which fuels the online copyright fight.
(D) His death has made a breakthrough in ensuring free access to ideas.

J.R.R. Tolkien was a lifelong devout Catholic who poured his Catholic heart into the writing of the myth ①that is now captivated by a new generation half a century after its first publication. Tolkien insisted that the fact that he was a Christian and in fact a Roman Catholic was the most important and really significant element in his work.

If, however, *The Lord of the Rings* is fundamentally religious and Catholic, why is Christ never mentioned in its pages? To answer this question, Christ is never mentioned by name simply because ②Tolkien's myth takes place many thousands of years before the incarnation. He is not mentioned in *The Lord of the Rings* for the same reason that he is not mentioned in the Old Testament. He had not yet revealed himself in the flesh and, consequently, is present implicitly through grace, not explicitly in person. Christ is, however, king of Tolkien's myth. *The Lord of the Rings* is best understood if it is read through the prism of the Gospel, in much the same way that the Old Testament is best understood if it is read in the light of the Gospel. Certainly one can read it without such an insight ③but to do so is to miss the fundamental purpose. One can read *The Lord of the Rings* as an atheist or an agnostic, or indeed as a New Age neo-pagan, but one will not understand its fundamentally religious and Catholic significance. One will be paddling in the shallows of the shadows, ④instead of plunging headlong into the glorious depths of the light.

01 What does this passage mainly suggest?

(A) Tolkien was a lifelong devout Roman Catholic.
(B) *The Lord of the Rings* is an indisputable classic.
(C) Christ is never mentioned in *The Lord of the Rings*.
(D) *The Lord of the Rings* should be read in the light of the Gospel.

02 According to the passage, which of the following is NOT grammatically correct?

(A) ① (B) ②
(C) ③ (D) ④

03 According to the passage, which of the following is NOT true?

(A) *The Lord of the Rings* is an explicitly Christian work.
(B) *The Lord of the Rings* is set in a time long before Christ.
(C) *The Lord of the Rings* carries Christian overtones and themes.
(D) *The Lord of the Rings* was first published more than 50 years ago.

I was a mere child when the classic tear gusher *Love Story* hit theaters in 1970, but I wept along with the adult audience as the dying Ali MacGraw told the darling Ryan O'Neal, "Love means never having to say you're sorry."

Two years later, I saw another movie, *What's Up, Doc?*, in which Barbra Streisand's character repeated the very same line to the very same actor. This time, however, O'Neal had an answer. "That's the dumbest thing I ever heard," he said. For me, that was a lightbulb moment. Young as I was, something was telling me that real lovers say they're sorry quite often. Sincerely. Fervently, even.

This is not because dismal feelings like shame and regret are necessary components of a relationship, but because without apology no relationship would be free of them. Everyone does things that bother or hurt others; a bit of inconvenient procrastination, or a grumpy comment at a stressful moment. When we lack the ability to say we're sorry, minor offenses eventually accumulate enough weight to sink any relationship.

①_____ the simple act of apologizing can reestablish goodwill even when our sins are grave. Of course, it must be done right. A lame, badly constructed apology can do more damage than the original offense. ②_____, the art of effective apology is simple, and mastering it can mean a lifetime of solid, resilient relationships.

01 Which of the following is NOT answered by the author?

(A) What may happen when we lack the ability to apologize
(B) Why we should sincerely say we are sorry if needed
(C) How we can master the art of effective apology
(D) What we can secure by mastering the art of effective apology
(E) Why an apology must be done right

02 Which of the following is the best title of the passage?

(A) What is a Sincere Apology
(B) The Tips Not to Bother or Hurt Others
(C) How to Catch the Right Moment to Apology
(D) Two Movies Giving Insight into Touching Apology
(E) Why the Two Words, "I'm Sorry" Can Be Most Rewarding

03 Which of the following best fits into ① and ②?

(A) On the other hand — Accordingly   (B) Therefore — In fact
(C) But — Fortunately   (D) Similarly — In a word
(E) Moreover — In other words

Nicolas Baumard used a computer to check people's reactions to a modern morality tale. Dr Baumard's volunteers read about a beggar asking for alms, and a passer-by who did not give them. In some cases the pedestrian was not only stingy, but hurled abuse at the poor man. In others, he was skint and apologetic. Either way, he went on to experience some nasty event (anything from tripping over a shoelace, via being tripped up deliberately by the beggar, to being run over by a car).

The question asked of each volunteer was whether the second event was caused by the passer-by's behaviour towards the beggar. Most answered "no", the assumption being it was the shoelace, or the beggar's foot, or the car. But Dr Baumard also measured how long each volunteer thought about the answer — and he found that when the passer-by had behaved badly to the beggar and then suffered an unrelated bad incident, volunteers spent significantly longer thinking about their answers than when the passer-by had behaved well, or the beggar had tripped him up deliberately.

Dr Baumard's interpretation, though he cannot prove it, is that the volunteers were indeed making a mental connection, during this extra thinking time, between the passer-by's actions and his _____. In other words, they were considering the idea that he was getting his just deserts, dished out by some sort of universal fate.

01 What is the best title for the passage?
    (A) An Inconsistent Idea about Good Triumphing over the Evil
    (B) Sensational Scientific Research Concerning Religion
    (C) The Universal Lesson That Justice Will Prevail in the Long Run
    (D) Mental Relation between Behaviour and the Price of It

02 Choose the one that best fills in the blank.
    (A) mysterious ways
    (B) subsequent fate
    (C) religious orientation
    (D) racial prejudice

03 Which of the following cannot be inferred from the passage?
    (A) Dr Baumard's interpretation will require a lot of further testing.
    (B) The idea of universal just deserts is instinctive according to Dr Baumard.
    (C) Being observed had an effect on the pedestrians' behaviour.
    (D) People somewhat believe in the idea that evil is divinely punished according to Dr Baumard.

The dance of foraging honeybees — a zigzagging figure eight maneuver performed in the hive — provides cues as to the direction and distance of the trove of flowers so the other bees can locate it. There is only one problem: Many bees seem to ignore the information. Instead, researchers in Argentina have found, the bees rely on their own memories of where to find food. In addition to its waggle moves, which provide location information, a dancing bee carries the odor of the flowers it visited. And flower scents have a known effect on bees: if the insects haven't been foraging for a few days, the scent drives them to resume, often at a food source they have visited before. What happens when the dancer provides information about a new location, but the flower odor reminds the watching bees about food that they remember is at another location? In their experiments, the researchers found that in almost every case, the bees went to the familiar source. Even if the scent was unfamiliar — and thus the bee had no location memory for it — the dance only spurred the bees to return to a familiar source, not a new one. This showed that ①_____ the high degree of sociality in a hive, it was the ②_____ information in the bees' memories that was often most important.

01. Which of the following is most suitable for the blanks ① and ②?

(A) in spite of — accessible
(B) regardless of — personal
(C) prior to — exceptional
(D) contrary to — collective

02. Which of the following can be inferred from the passage?

(A) The information given by the dancing bees is often misguided.
(B) Bees never visit the food source that they visited once before.
(C) The dance of honeybees varies from one bee to another.
(D) Bees' dormant memory of a food source can be triggered.

03. Which of the following is the best title of the passage?

(A) Prize for the Work of Dancing Bees
(B) Efforts of Dancing Bees in Vain
(C) An Account of Senses of Honey Bees
(D) Dancing Bees: Marvels of the Animal Kingdom

147

Cheapness has many manifestations. A perfect example is the 1950s monster movie cheapness that Frank Zappa once sang about, with creatures that looked like giant poodles and visible nylon strings attached to the jaw of a giant spider. "I love that sort of cheepnis." as Zappa put it. Who doesn't? The cheapness was appealing precisely because it was an affront to pomposity and pretension.

I have a different theory of cheapness as it applies to wine: Often in New World regions and increasingly in the Old World, a producer's most expensive red wines are also the most done up — spiffed and polished and reeking of oaken vanilla and chocolate like too much makeup or hair pomade. _____, the wines are made from grapes so overripe that the prevailing flavors are of baked fruit and jam. Either way, creating a flavor profile to fit a preconceived notion of an expensive wine diminishes any sense of place and individuality.

That is why I'm often more interested in a producer's less expensive wines. If you can dodge the minefields of oak substitutes and other winemaking tricks that are intended to imitate expensive wines — "true cheepnis" in the monster movie sense — you just might find some wines in which you can taste simple essences. I love this kind of cheapness, too. It is sincerity rather than affectation, but it is likewise an affront to pretension because you are not playing the game. Let others spend the extra money; you get the more enjoyable wine.

01 Which of following is the intention of the writer mentioning the story of Frank Zappa?
(A) to show how crude the monster movie was at that time
(B) to reinforce his idea about the uselessness of cheapness
(C) to compare his idea of the cheapness of wine with that of the monster movie
(D) to describe the popularity of cheapness among the public

02 Which of the following is most suitable for the blank?
(A) Consequently   (B) Alternatively
(C) Allegedly   (D) Conversely

03 Which of the following is NOT true according to the passage?
(A) The cheapness is attractive to people because it insults pomposity.
(B) The high-priced red wine is elaborately made in the Old World.
(C) Some methods of making expensive wine derogate the quality of wine.
(D) There are some tricks for producing the taste of more expensive wine.

Several years ago, certain scientists developed a way of investigating the nature of the atmosphere of the past by studying air caught in the ice around the North or South Pole. According to their theory, when snow falls, air is trapped between the snowflakes. The snow turns to ice with the air still inside. Over the years more snow falls on top, making new layers of ice. But the trapped air, these scientists believed, remains exactly as it was when the snow originally fell.

To find what air was like three hundred years ago, you use a drill in the shape of a hollow tube to cut deep into the layers of ice. When you pull up the drill, an ice core made of many layers comes up inside it. Then, back at the laboratory, you count the layers in the core—each layer represents one year—to find ice formed from the snow that fell during the year to be studied. Using this method, these scientists suggested that the amount of carbon dioxide (CO_2), one of the gases which may cause global warming, had increased greatly over the last two hundred years.

A Norwegian scientist, however, pointed out that there might be a problem with this method. He claimed that air caught in ice does not stay the same. In particular, he said, the quantity of CO_2 does not remain stable, since some of it is absorbed by ice crystals, some enters water, and some locks itself up in other chemicals. If this were true, then there could have been more CO_2 in the past than we thought. Even so, measurements taken over the past thirty years show that CO_2 has increased by over ten percent during this short period.

01 Certain scientists claimed that _____.

   (A) atmospheric gases increase the yearly amount of snow
   (B) the air held between snowflakes keeps its original nature
   (C) falling snowflakes change the chemical balance of the air
   (D) the action of atmospheric gases causes snow to turn into ice

02 In order to study atmospheric gases for a particular year, these scientists had to _____.

   (A) identify a particular layer in the ice core
   (B) examine the different kinds of snowflakes
   (C) measure how hollow each layer was within the core
   (D) count how many cores were necessary for measuring trapped air

03 A Norwegian scientist questioned the usefulness of ice-core analysis, claiming that _____.

(A) ice absorbs more CO_2 when the core is pulled out
(B) ice has effects on global warming by reducing CO_2
(C) the amount of CO_2 within the ice changes in several ways
(D) the quality of the ice might be affected during the drilling

There are so many healthy reasons to eat vegetables that it feels redundant to keep enumerating them. But if a stronger immune system, cancer-fighting antioxidants and heart-healthy fiber aren't reason enough for some, perhaps we can appeal to their vanity: a study published in the journal *Evolution and Human Behaviour* found that eating foods high in carotenoids — a nutrient found in some fruits, leafy greens and root vegetables — gave them a healthy glow that rivaled a sun tan and made them more attractive in tests.

"We found that, given the choice between skin color caused by suntan and skin color caused by carotenoids, people preferred the carotenoid skin color," Dr. Ian Stephen, the study's lead researcher, said in a statement. "So if you want a healthier and more attractive skin color, you are better off eating a healthy diet with plenty of fruit and vegetables than lying in the sun."

People with diets high in fruits and vegetables had demonstrably yellower skin, the researchers found. But the scientists weren't sure if the veggie glow would be perceived differently than one achieved by sitting in the sun. So they asked study participants to look at 51 different Caucasian faces and adjust the skin tones to the hues, ranging from those typical of a day in the sun to the glow from a carotenoid-rich diet, that they thought looked healthiest. Reported California Watch: The students could adjust the skin tone of the photographed faces, making them more yellow, more suntanned or more pale. According to the new study, the students found yellower faces more attractive and healthy looking. Want the glow? Try upping your intake of carrots, tomatoes, sweet potatoes, bell peppers, cantaloupe, spinach and kale.

01 Which of the following is not mentioned as a reason of eating vegetables?

  (A) helping prevent heart disease
  (B) giving a glowing complexion
  (C) boosting the immune system
  (D) extending the life span

02 Which of the following can be inferred from the passage?

  (A) Carotenoids have no significant effect on a healthy glow.
  (B) People getting a tan outnumber people with diets high in fruits and vegetables.
  (C) There is a considerable link between veggie-rich diet and beauty.
  (D) Skin color caused by carotenoids is virtually identical to skin color caused by suntan.

03 What is the purpose of the passage?

(A) to challenge conventional views on eating vegetables
(B) to inform people about the new benefits of eating vegetables
(C) to persuade vegetarians to eat less vegetable
(D) to identify the reasons why eating vegetables is beneficial to health

The sleeping must be important because all animals do it. There is no clear evidence of an animal species that does not sleep. Even the dolphin — which is sometimes held up as an animal that doesn't sleep because it moves continuously — will show "unihemispheric sleep" with one eye closed and one half its brain showing the slow ㉮waves characteristic of deep sleep. The very fact that dolphins have developed the remarkable specialization, rather than merely getting rid of sleep altogether, should count as evidence that sleep must serve some essential function and cannot be eliminated.

Sleep is strictly regulated by the brain, because sleep deprivation is followed by a rebound, in which the sleep-deprived animal either sleeps longer, or spends more time in the deeper sleep characterized by large slow brain waves. Prolonged sleep deprivation has been shown to kill rats, flies and cockroaches. Humans who have a genetic insomnia can also die. In less extreme cases, sleep deprivation affects cognitive function in animals ranging from flies to rodents. Rats ㉯kept waking will engage in "micro-sleep" episodes, and sleep-deprived humans tend to fall asleep even in the most dangerous circumstances.

The sleep may be the price you pay so ①your brain can be plastic the next day. This hypothesis is that sleep allows the brain to regroup after a hard day of learning ㉰by giving the synapses, which increase in strength during the day, a chance to damp down to baseline levels. Sleep may be important for consolidating new memories, and to allow the brain to forget the random, unimportant impressions of the day, ㉱so there is room for more learning the next day.

01 Which of the following is true according to the passage?

(A) The sleep is a way to impose an immobile state and is important by itself to animals.
(B) The sleep has some essential function including rearranging synapses and relieving stress.
(C) Dolphins actually sleep although it seems that they do not sleep because of their intermittent movement.
(D) Some kinds of sleep-deprived animals can either sleep longer and deeper or doze off.

02 Which of the following does underlined ①"your brain can be plastic the next day" mean?

(A) You can forget consequential things which happened and were experienced during the day.
(B) The sleep can cause the brain to create synapses and enhance memories.
(C) Your brain can have enough room for new memories for the next day.
(D) The synapses can give strength to the brain which has complex memories.

03 Which of the underlined ㉮, ㉯, ㉰ and ㉱ is grammatically incorrect?

(A) ㉮ waves characteristic
(B) ㉯ kept waking
(C) ㉰ by giving
(D) ㉱ so there is room

PASSAGE

151—200

The revelation more than 60 years ago that most of the world's bats can "see with sound" made clear that echolocation contributed significantly to the great evolutionary success and diversity of bats. But which of the two key bat adaptations — flight and echolocation — came first? By the 1990s three competing theories had emerged. The flight-first hypothesis holds that bat ancestors evolved powered flight as a way of improving mobility and reducing the amount of time and energy required for foraging. Under this scenario, echolocation evolved subsequently to make it easier for early bats to detect and track prey that they were already chasing in flight.

In contrast, the echolocation-first model proposes that gliding protobats hunted aerial prey from their perches in the trees using echolocation, which evolved to help them track their quarry at greater distances. Powered flight evolved later, to increase maneuverability and to simplify returning to the hunting perch.

The tandem-development hypothesis, for its part, suggests that flight and echolocation evolved ①_____. This idea is based on experimental evidence showing that it is energetically very costly for bats to produce echolocation calls when they are stationary. During flight, however, the cost becomes nearly ②_____, because contraction of the flight muscles helps to pump the lungs, producing the airflow that is required for intense, high-frequency vocalizations.

01 What does the passage mainly discuss?

(A) theories about natural selection of bats
(B) the evolutionary origins of bat adaptations
(C) eyesight and auditory capacity of bats
(D) hypotheses on ecology of bat ancestors

02 Which of the following is most suitable for the blanks ① and ②?

(A) concurrently — invincible
(B) intrinsically — piddling
(C) spontaneously — infinitesimal
(D) simultaneously — negligible

03 Which of the following is NOT the cause of bat adaptations suggested by the theories?

(A) to improve hunting efficiency through boosting mobility and maneuverability
(B) to use geographical features that enable the bats to hunt in the air
(C) to save the amount of time and energy when the bats search for food.
(D) to make powerful vocalizations more easily

But let us turn to the different, but equally grave, plight of the modern historian. The ancient or mediaeval historian may be grateful for the vast winnowing process which, over the years, has put at his disposal a manageable corpus of historical facts. As Lytton Strachey said in his mischievous way, "ignorance is the first requisite of the historian, ignorance which simplifies and clarifies, which selects and omits." When I am tempted, as I sometimes am, to envy the extreme competence of colleagues engaged in writing ancient or mediaeval history, I find consolation in the reflection that they are so competent mainly because they are so ignorant of their subject. The modern historian enjoys none of the advantages of this built-in ignorance. He must cultivate this necessary ignorance for himself — the more so the nearer he comes to his own times. He has the _____ task of discovering the few significant facts and turning them into facts of history, and of discarding the many insignificant facts as unhistorical. But this is the very converse of the nineteenth-century heresy that history consists of the compilation of a maximum number of irrefutable and objective facts. Anyone who succumbs to this heresy will either have to give up history as a bad job, and take to stamp-collecting or some other form of antiquarianism, or end in a madhouse.

01   Which of the following is most appropriate for the blank?
(A) boring
(B) dual
(C) insurmountable
(D) omniscient

02   Which of the following is not stated or implied according to the passage?
(A) The modern historian doesn't enjoy what Lytton Strachey called the advantages of ignorance.
(B) When it comes to working with facts, some modern historians have to be able to do a task of giving up some facts as unhistorical.
(C) The task of modern historians is in direct opposition to the nineteenth-century heresy.
(D) Anyone, who will faithfully follow the nineteenth-century heresy, may think of history as of great significance.

A severely ill toddler at the center of a legal battle between his parents has died days after his father agreed to switch off his ventilator. The 13-month-old boy, known as Baby RB, suffered from congenital myasthenic syndrome, a rare genetic condition that means he cannot breathe on his own. Cristopher Cuddihee, a solicitor who represents the father, confirmed the baby's death early Sunday but did not provide any more details. The baby's father had been battling his mother and the hospital in London's High Court because they wanted the child's life support switched off "in his best interests." He disagreed, saying the baby could play and recognize his parents. The father withdrew his objection Tuesday and allowed the ventilator to be switched off. The hospital defended its stance in a statement last week, saying the baby's birth defect "causes severe muscle weakness, feeding and respiratory problems, and the disease is progressive." Baby RB's lungs filled with fluid every few hours, giving him the sensation he is choking and causing the child to suffer, lawyers representing the hospital said in court November 2. _____, the father agreed with the mother and the hospital that the best thing was for the baby to die "in a planned way, with the _____ of a large dose of sedative, the removal of the ventilation tube and his consequent death," Judge Andrew McFarlane said Tuesday. The baby's parents, who are separated, cannot be named because of a court order protecting their privacy.

01 Which of the following is <u>not</u> stated or implied according to the passage?

(A) The severely ill toddler has died days after his father agreed to turn off his ventilator.
(B) The 13-month-old boy suffered from the disease that didn't allow him to breathe on his own.
(C) The baby's mother and the hospital said that they wanted the child's respirator to be switched off for the baby's father.
(D) Eventually, the father agreed that the best thing was for the baby to die in a planned way.

02 Which of the following is most appropriate for the blanks?

(A) Therefore — intake
(B) By contrast — prescription
(C) Ultimately — administration
(D) Moreover — assignment

Severe storms and rising sea levels forced the Inupiat of Point Hope, Alaska, to relocate from Old Town to New Town several kilometers away in the 1970s. That relocation left a lasting cultural trauma, as the townspeople watched their traditional homes slowly vanish beneath the waves. Environmental transformations caused by climate change now _____.

The Inupiat have their stories about small human-like beings known as the Little People, who have long been known among the Alaska Natives as tricksters and miracle-makers. The abandonment of Old Town was followed by increasing reports of the Little People appearing in and around the ruins of Old Town. Unlike the urban views of the environment, the Inupiat still see the natural world as filled with animal spirits, trolls, shape-shifters and the Little People. They tell stories explaining their coexistence with all the forces within the natural environment, which help people anchor their emotions to their eroding homeland and changing natural landscape. According to one of their stories, dragons that had once lived in a nearby lake became homeless and either died or moved off after the lake drained of water. The story reflects how Arctic lakes drain or emerge in response to climate change. Now the storytelling has become one of the Inupiaq people's best strategies for adapting to the harsh reality of climate change, not to mention dealing with the trauma of losing their ancestral home. The stories have allowed the Inupiaq people to make sense of their changing world as they continue to fortify their eroding homeland against the rising seas as the Netherlands and other countries have done.

01 What is the best title for the passage?
   (A) Tragedies Caused by Climate Change
   (B) Climate Change and Cultural Trauma
   (C) Storytelling As an Adaptive Strategy
   (D) A Tribe's Stories about Environments

02 Choose the one that best fills in the blank.
   (A) drive them to find food somewhere else
   (B) make them hold on to religious rituals
   (C) reinforce their ties with neighboring tribes
   (D) threaten the core of their cultural identity

03　Which of the following cannot be inferred about "the Inupiat"?
　　(A) Climate change led them to move near the seashore.
　　(B) They think of themselves as part of their environment.
　　(C) Their cultural heritage helps them cope with new challenges.
　　(D) They are faced with the same fate as the Dutch have been.

　　　It's hard to stir up controversy when you've been dead for tens of thousands of years, but 15 protohumans did just that in 2015, after their fossils were found in Johannesburg. They were hard to place on the human evolutionary ladder, with a jumble of relatively modern skeletal features but a brain as small as a gorilla's. Many questions arose over their estimated age, a matter that was at last resolved on May 9, when it was revealed that they are roughly 236,000 years old.

　　　That matters a lot, because it means that the prehumans might have been living right alongside early modern humans, or *Homo sapiens*. Taken together with what we already know about Neanderthals and *Homo sapiens'* coexisting, it essentially debunks the old idea that modern humans evolved from a single line of prehumans. Instead, there were competing human models on the road together, with only one equipped to win.

　　　The fossils that made the latest news belong to a protohuman species called *Homo naledi* and were uncovered in a cave by paleoanthropologist Lee Berger. He initially pegged their age at approximately 2 million years, but that was just an educated guess; Berger's latest research used isotopic dating — a far more accurate tool — to place his finds at the less-than-a-quarter-million-year mark.

　　　Nevertheless, Berger believes *Homo naledi* may be part of a more ancient line, one that could have emerged 2 million years ago but winked out — or was wiped out — when modern humans arose. We are a competitive, resource-gobbling species today, and the new research helps confirm that, for better or for worse, we always have been.

01 Which of the following is NOT true about protohumans?
   (A) Their bones sometimes give rise to controversies after being dug out.
   (B) They were composed of a single strain destined to be our ancestors.
   (C) They would often be extinguished when more evolved species appeared.
   (D) They fiercely competed for survival, depleting resources on the earth.

02 Which of the following is true about *Homo naledi*?
   (A) It must be excluded from the human evolutionary ladder.
   (B) It appeared on the earth as the first human model millions of years ago.
   (C) It had been immune to the principle of survival of the fittest.
   (D) It would probably have coexisted with other protohuman species.

03 Which of the following is Lee Berger trying to find in the passage?
   (A) fossils believed to bridge the evolutionary split between primates and humans
   (B) a common origin of all the species that have lived and are living on the earth
   (C) evidence showing that original forms of life came from the outer space
   (D) a more precise tool for dating the fossils of protohumans recently discovered

As the author Anthony Powell said, "Growing old is like being increasingly penalized for a crime you haven't committed." After decades of hard labor and long service to the government in the form of taxes, you finally start to get ready for a deserved rest — and what happens? Your body starts to play up and your senses start to weaken — and you can only sleep properly in the middle of a conversation. To add insult to injury, some people start to say that you are placing a burden on the health service. No wonder you might begin to mutter bitterly every now and then! [A] Of course, there is a serious point here. Old people are as deserving of health resources as anyone, if not more so, because they have paid their tax contributions all their lives. The ethos of the National Health Service (NHS) is that it provides free health care for all, and old people should not be exceptions to this policy. It's quite simple: if they are ill, they should be treated. [B] Unfortunately, the NHS does not always live up to this ideal. A recent survey by the British Geriatric Society of British doctors suggested that more than half would be worried about how they might be treated when they were older — because of the way they see old people being treated now. [C] Most doctors surveyed believe that older people are much less likely to have symptoms properly investigated. When old people feel ill, there is a tendency to assume that the problem is 'just old age' rather than examining them properly for signs of a treatable illness. Three-quarters of the doctors asserted that older people are less likely to be properly treated and referred to the right specialists. [D] Of course, many of the health problems faced by older people are an inevitable part of growing old. But this does not mean they cannot be treated in any way. Old people may also respond less well to treatment for some ailments than younger people do. [E] It is therefore sometimes suggested that limited NHS resources should be steered towards younger people where they can give more obvious improvements to quality of life. Indeed, there is some evidence that this is how the NHS does indeed respond, often treating old people as second-class patients.

Where would the best points be to divide this essay into paragraphs?

(A) at points [A], [B], and [D]
(B) at points [A], [C], and [D]
(C) at points [B], [C], and [D]
(D) at points [A], [C], and [E]
(E) at points [B], [D], and [E]

02 Which of the following sentences incorrectly paraphrases an idea from the passage?

(A) Ageing is an increasingly painful physical phenomenon which can not be blamed on those who experience it.

(B) Given their lifelong fulfillment of obligations as taxpayers, older people deserve more than apathy and undertreatment.

(C) The NHS has to offer free health care to all residents in the country, regardless of their sex, class, job, or age.

(D) Older people tend to look upon symptoms of illness as the result of their own old age and avoid visiting a doctor.

(E) Older women with breast cancer are less likely to receive the full range of cancer therapy than younger women.

The world has warmed more than one degree Celsius since the Industrial Revolution. The Paris climate agreement — the nonbinding, unenforceable and already unheeded treaty signed on Earth Day in 2016 — hoped to restrict warming to two degrees. The odds of succeeding, according to a recent study based on current emissions trends, are one in 20. If _____ we are able to limit warming to two degrees, we will only have to negotiate the extinction of the world's tropical reefs, sea-level rise of several meters and the abandonment of the Persian Gulf. The climate scientist James Hansen has called two-degree warming "a prescription for long-term disaster." Long-term disaster is now the best-case scenario. Three-degree warming is a prescription for short-term disaster: forests in the Arctic and the loss of most coastal cities.

Robert Watson, a former director of the United Nations Intergovernmental Panel on Climate Change, has argued that three-degree warming is the realistic minimum. Four degrees: Europe in permanent drought; vast areas of China, India and Bangladesh claimed by desert; Polynesia swallowed by the sea; the Colorado River thinned to a trickle; the American Southwest largely uninhabitable. The prospect of a five-degree warming has prompted some of the world's leading climate scientists to warn of the end of human civilization.

01 Which of the following is most appropriate for the blank?
(A) through the united efforts of mankind
(B) using science and technology
(C) by some miracle
(D) by scientists' efforts
(E) by international convention

02 The underlined "three-degree warming is the realistic minimum" means _____.
(A) keeping the temperature rise below 3 degrees minimizes global warming
(B) 3-degree warming must be accepted as a de facto reality and we should be prepared for the possibility of higher temperatures
(C) it is a pessimist's view of the future that temperatures will rise above 4 degrees
(D) it is an idealistic view to see a rise in temperature below 2 degrees
(E) the temperature rise will stop at 3 degrees and we should be prepared for that

03 The main theme of the passage would be _____.

(A) failure of the Paris climate agreement
(B) fragmentation of scientists' views on rising temperatures
(C) responsibility of the government to keep up with rising temperatures
(D) scientists' doomsday scenario
(E) global warming and the harsh future

Witches, as they are most commonly portrayed, are evil, ugly, unmarried, and old. They are the manifestation of every misogynistic conceptualization of woman. They are unworthy of male desire and demonstrate what happens when a woman dares to have power or assert her authority. The dangerous bitch and the hideous old witch are complementary representations, intended to show up women's iniquities and punish them, but also to warn and frighten men. The male counterpart to a witch is often considered to be a wizard or a warlock. While they can be evil, they aren't often depicted as such, instead they are pictured as necromancers or alchemists, serious seekers after the truth; they age with dignity and grow beards. Old crones [or witches] sometimes have beards, too, but grow snakes instead of hair on their heads, wreaking destruction on kings and commoners alike. Similar to the idea of a femme fatale, if a woman has power (as do witches in the form of magic) it is more often than not used for evil purposes. The messages behind conceptualizations of witches are "Ladies, if you don't want to be labeled a witch, then follow feminine gender roles like a good little girl." Depictions of witches are thus intimately connected to misogynistic ideals of what constitutes perfect womanhood: submitting to male authority, marrying and bearing children, remaining attractive to men, etc.

01 Which of the following is the purpose of the passage?

(A) To reveal the cruelty of witch hunts
(B) To criticize the misogynistic conceptualizations of witches
(C) To commemorate the victims of witch hunts
(D) To explain the origin of misogynistic attitudes by analyzing witchcrafts

02 According to the passage, which of the following is true?

(A) People depict witches as unattractive married women.
(B) Most witches are feeble old women who don't have any power.
(C) A wizard is considered as a good being whose mission is eliminating evil.
(D) A misogynist wants to disclose women's iniquities using the notion of witches.

03 Which of the following can be inferred from the passage?

(A) The idea of witches reflects the fear of a male toward female dominance.
(B) A femme fatale is likely to take a submissive attitude to her male counterpart.
(C) Without the help of alchemists, most wizards cannot use evil magic powers.
(D) The intention of conceptualizations of witches is to spread feminism.

I felt a challenge to plan, and build, an organization that could help to cure the black man in North America of the sickness which has kept him under the white man's heel.

The black man in North America was mentally sick in his cooperative, sheeplike acceptance of the white man's culture.

The black man in North America was spiritually sick because for centuries he had accepted the white man's Christianity, which asked the black so-called Christian to expect no true Brotherhood of Man, but to endure the cruelties of the white so-called Christians. Christianity had made black men fuzzy, nebulous, confused in their thinking. It had taught the black man to think, if he had no shoes and was hungry, "we gonna get shoes, milk, honey and fish fries in Heaven."

The black man in North America was economically sick and that was evident in one simple fact: as a consumer, he got less than his share, and as a producer, gave least. The black American today shows us the perfect _____ image — the black tick under the delusion that he is progressing because he rides on the udder of the fat, three-stomached cow that is white America.

The black man in North America was sickest of all politically. He let the white man divide him into such foolishness as considering himself a black "Democrat," a black "Republican," a black "Conservative," or a black "Liberal" when a ten-million black vote bloc could be the deciding balance of power in American politics, because the white man's vote is almost always evenly divided. Listen, let me tell you something! If a black bloc committee told Washington's worst "nigger-hater," "We represent ten million votes," why, that "nigger-hater" would leap up: "Well, how are you? Come on in here!"

---

01   Which of the following best fits in the blank?

(A) savior   (B) parasite
(C) scapegoat   (D) host

02   Which of the following is NOT true about the black man in North America?

(A) He is acquiescing in the white man's dominance.
(B) He has been sacrificed by the white man's Christianity.
(C) His role in America's economy is insignificant.
(D) He is as politically conscious as the white man.

03   What is the author's attitude toward the black man in North America?

(A) laudatory   (B) sympathetic
(C) contemptuous   (D) denunciatory

"The walkways are like waves, curving up and down, people can trip and fall," says Ridwan, a Muara Baru resident who often visits the fish market. As the water levels underground are being depleted, the very ground market-goers walk on is sinking and shifting, creating an uneven and unstable surface. "Year after year, the ground has just kept sinking," he said, just one of many inhabitants of this quarter alarmed at what is happening to the neighbourhood. Fortuna Sophia lives in a luxurious villa with a sea view. The sinking of her home is not immediately visible but she says cracks appear in the walls and pillars every six months. "We just have to keep fixing it," she says, standing beside her swimming pool with her private dock just a few metres away. "The maintenance men say the cracks are caused by the shifting of the ground." She's lived here for four years but it has already flooded several times: "The seawater flows in and covers the swimming pool entirely. We have to move all our furniture up to the first floor."

But the impact on the small homes right by the sea is magnified. Residents who once had a sea view now see only a dull grey dyke, built and rebuilt in a valiant attempt to keep seawater out. "Every year the tide gets about 5cm higher," Mahardi, a fisherman, said. None of this has deterred the property developers. More and more luxury apartments dot the North Jakarta skyline regardless of the risks. The head of the advisory council for Indonesia's Association of Housing Development, Eddy Ganefo, says he has urged the government to halt further development here. But, he says, "so long as we can sell apartments, development will continue". The rest of Jakarta is also sinking, albeit at a slower rate. In West Jakarta, the ground is sinking by as much as 15cm annually, by 10cm annually in the east, 2cm in Central Jakarta and just 1cm in South Jakarta.

01 According to the passage, which of the following is NOT correct?
(A) As the ground subsides, cracks and changes are appearing on roads and buildings.
(B) There is no warning about ground subsidence and its risk.
(C) Construction on dyke to protect the villages adjacent to the beach is under way.
(D) Real estate developers are ignoring the risk of land subsidence as they pursue profit through development.
(E) The subsidence rate in the northern part of Jakarta is the fastest.

02 The best topic of the passage would be _____.

(A) a marvelous effort by humans to fight ground subsidence
(B) Jakarta's gap between rich and poor revealed by the subsidence problem
(C) a warning against Jakarta's ground subsidence
(D) Indonesian government's response to the risk of subsidence
(E) the conflict between developers and residents over the causes of subsidence

The French economist J. B. Say was a highly regarded member of the Classical School. To this day, he is best known for Say's Law of Markets. Thanks to John Maynard Keynes, in the popular lexicon, this law simply states that "supply creates its own demand." But Keynes' rendition of Say's Law distorts its true meaning and leaves its main message on the cutting room floor.

Say's message was clear: a demand failure could not cause an economic slump. This message was accepted by virtually every major economist, prior to the publication of Keynes' *The General Theory of Employment, Interest and Money* in 1936. So, before *The General Theory*, even though most economists thought business cycles were in the cards, demand failure was not listed as one of the causes of an economic downturn.

All this was _____ by Keynes. Keynes set J. B. Say up as a straw man so that he could remove Say's ideas from economic discourse and the public's thinking. Keynes had to do this because his entire theory was based on the analysis of demand failure, and his prescription for putting life back into aggregate demand — namely, a fiscal stimulus.

Keynes was widely successful. With the publication of *The General Theory*, the supply side of the economy almost entirely vanished. It was replaced by aggregate demand, which was faithfully reported in the national income accounts. In consequence, aggregate demand has dominated economic discourse and policy ever since. The structure of the economy — the supply side — is nowhere to be found.

01 Which of the following is true about J. B. Say?

(A) He was thrown out by Keynes from the mainstream of the Classical School.
(B) He owed the completion of his Law of Markets to Keynes' interpretation of it.
(C) His Law of Markets was rooted in the supply-oriented classical economics.
(D) He failed to predict that an economy would experience business fluctuations.

02 Which of the following is NOT true about J. M. Keynes?

(A) He believed that demand failure was one of the causes of economic slump.
(B) He defined Say's Law as "supply creates its own demand" in Say's favor.
(C) His *General Theory* drastically altered the way economists view recession.
(D) His economics was policy-oriented and interested in aggregate demand.

03 Which of the following best fits in the blank?

(A) manifested (B) bolstered
(C) underlined (D) overturned

Ignorant and inexperienced, it is not strange that in the first years of our new life we began at the ①_____ instead of at the ②_____; that a seat in Congress or the state legislature was more sought than real estate or industrial skill; that the political convention or stump speaking had more attractions than starting a dairy farm or truck garden. A ship lost at sea for many days suddenly sighted a friendly vessel. From the mast of the unfortunate vessel was seen a signal, "Water, water; we die of thirst!" The answer from the friendly vessel at once came back, "Cast down your bucket where you are." A second time the signal, "Water, water; send us water!" ran up from the distressed vessel, and was answered, "Cast down your bucket where you are." And a third and fourth signal for water was answered, "Cast down your bucket where you are." The captain of the distressed vessel, at last heeding the injunction, cast down his bucket, and it came up full of fresh, sparkling water from the mouth of the Amazon River. To those of my race who depend on bettering their condition in a foreign land or who underestimate the importance of cultivating friendly relations with the Southern white man, who is their next-door neighbor, I would say: "Cast down your bucket where you are" — cast it down in making friends in every manly way of the people of all races by whom we are surrounded.

01 What is the main idea of the passage above?
(A) In order to enhance our racial status, we black Americans should widen our perspectives.
(B) In order to resolve the racial conflict, we should try to give any help to other races.
(C) In order to gain a functioning independent nation, we need an educated elite society.
(D) More than anything else, we should secure what we need most: elementary necessities.
(E) Since we have attained some rights as a race, now it's a time to get along with other races.

02 Which pair best fits ① and ②?
(A) bottom — top   (B) top — bottom
(C) front — back   (D) back — front
(E) politics — economies

03 Which of the following CANNOT be inferred from the passage?
(A) The black race has been interested only in its own problems.
(B) Black Americans have tried to produce politicians who can represent their interests.
(C) It would be possible to find a sense of fulfillment in a variety of jobs.
(D) To make money through real estate development has been held in high esteem.
(E) The writer argues that the racial movement should begin at the bottom of life.

Although I've discussed this issue a number of times over the years, every now and then a new study comes out that provides further evidence of the limitations of body mass index(BMI) as a measure of health, or even adiposity (level of fat in the body). While it is great when used in epidemiological studies across thousands of people, it's a pretty _____ measure on an individual basis. In this cross-sectional study the authors assessed the BMI, body fat percentage, and cardiometabolic risk factors of 6,123 (924 lean, 1,637 overweight and 3,562 obese, classified according to BMI) Caucasian subjects (69% females) between the ages of 18 and 80 years.

What did they find? First, 29% of subjects classified as normal weight and 80% of individuals classified as overweight according to BMI had a body fat percentage within the obese range. Thus, on an individual basis BMI tends to consistently underestimate a person's adiposity. This data implies that there are many individuals who don't weigh that much on an absolute scale, but a large proportion of their weight is composed of fat tissue. These are people who may look thin, but tend to be soft, with little muscle tone. Secondly, when compared to individuals who were actually lean (both on BMI and body fat), those with a high levels of adiposity, regardless of their BMI (normal weight, overweight or obese BMI) had poorer cardiometabolic profiles, including elevated blood pressure, blood glucose and lipid levels, as well as markers of systemic inflammation.

01 Which of the following is the main idea of the passage?
(A) BMI is an unreliable standard for an individual's health.
(B) New studies use body fat percentage and cardiometabolic risk factors.
(C) It is necessary to replace old health standards.
(D) Some BMI normal weight and most overweight have body fat percentage in the obese range.
(E) BMI is not a good measure to judge muscle mass.

02 Find expression that best fits in the blank.
(A) alternative
(B) lousy
(C) authentic
(D) conscientious
(E) pectoral

03 Which of the following can be inferred from the passage?

(A) Doctors may miss signs of poor health if they rely too much on BMI.
(B) Since weight and body fat are meaningful, doctors should focus on BMI as a relevant marker of health.
(C) In order to maintain health, you should watch your weight and height.
(D) Muscle mass has nothing to do with health, so it should not be regarded as an index of health.
(E) BMI knows better than to mistake muscle mass for obesity.

Older generations often sign up for internet access to stay in touch with children, nieces, nephews and grandchildren. We talk about this kind of contact like it's some old-fogey activity, but it is exactly why younger people use social media. The truth is most people use social media to gently keep tabs on one another, to see how those they care about are doing without needing to ring them up on the phone every night. It's true that the communications of 15-year-olds often end up being more dramatic than those of 30-year-olds, 50 year-olds or 75-year-olds. The more seniors that join, the more relevant the conversations taking place on these sites will become for their contemporaries. And this is another secret of social media: everyone gets to use it their own way. Newcomers, younger and older, who worry about getting it right are assuming there's a right way to get it. Turns out, there isn't. Even inveterate users take to some online activities over others. Some people talk a lot on Twitter and others on Facebook. Plenty of people use both. Many younger users are moving to Instagram. And some people post nothing but are avid consumers of social media as readers. Social media companies seldom promote the idea of mere readership, since they'd rather see people pumping their networks full of pictures and posts, but there's no rule against being ①a fly on the wall. It's a fine way to engage. We're quick to forget that the web wasn't invented by 13-year-olds; it was created by today's seniors. I'd never try foisting social networks on those with no interest or with an inherent aversion to frivolous twittering. But don't let the talk of age divides put you off. There's nothing to stop boomers from reclaiming the network their own generation created.

01 Which of the following would be best for the title?

(A) Social Media Has No Age Limit
(B) The Young Do Not Reclaim the Internet
(C) There Are Two Types of Internet Users
(D) The Elderly Hate Frivolous Twittering

02 Which of the following best describes ①?

(A) a user who censors another's internet contents
(B) a user who only posts his own internet contents
(C) a user who both reads and posts internet contents
(D) a user who just reads or sees internet contents

03 Which of the following is NOT true?

(A) The young and the old are using social media for the same reasons.

(B) Newcomers to social media should learn the right ways to use it.

(C) Merely reading what is posted is undesirable, but not impermissible.

(D) The internet was invented by today's senior citizens, or baby boomers.

The traditional explanation of intelligence is that human flesh is suffused with a non-material entity, the soul, usually envisioned as some kind of ghost or spirit. But the theory faces an insurmountable problem: How does the spook interact with _____? How does an ethereal nothing respond to flashes, pokes, and beeps and get arms and legs to move? Another problem is the overwhelming evidence that the mind is the activity of the brain. The supposedly immaterial soul, we now know, can be bisected with a knife, altered by chemicals, started or stopped by electricity, and extinguished by a sharp blow or by insufficient oxygen. Under a microscope, the brain has a breathtaking complexity of physical structure fully commensurate with the richness of the mind.

Another explanation is that mind comes from some extraordinary form of matter. Pinocchio was animated by a magical kind of wood found by Geppetto that talked, laughed, and moved on its own. Alas, no one has ever discovered such a wonder substance. At first one might think that the wonder substance is brain tissue. Darwin wrote that the brain "secretes" the mind, and recently the philosopher John Searle has argued that the physico-chemical properties of brain tissue somehow produce the mind just as breast tissue produces milk and plant tissue produces sugar. But recall that the same kinds of membranes, pores, and chemicals are found in brain tissue throughout the animal kingdom, not to mention in brain tumors and cultures in dishes. All of these globs of neural tissue have the same physico-chemical properties, but not all of them accomplish humanlike intelligence. Of course, something about the tissue in the human brain is necessary for our intelligence, but the physical properties are not sufficient, just as the physical properties of bricks are not sufficient to explain architecture and the physical properties of oxide particles are not sufficient to explain music. Something in the patterning of neural tissue is crucial.

According to the passage, which of the following is correct?

(A) Despite overwhelming evidence that the mind is the result of brain activity, the writer believes that there is a soul in man.
(B) The writer agrees with Darwin's explanation of the relationship between brain and mind.
(C) The claim that the soul is the source of human intellect adequately explains the interaction of soul and matter.
(D) The writer is looking for such an extraordinary substance to prove that the mind is derived from extraordinary substances.
(E) There is something that makes the human brain special, although it has the similar tissue to that of other animals.

02 The best expression for the blank would be _____.

(A) solid matter
(B) divine intervention
(C) immaterial consciousness
(D) incorporeal object
(E) spiral evolution

The crowd was like a turbulent water forcing itself through one tiny outlet. The men in the rear, excited by the success of the others, made frantic exertions, for it seemed that this large band would more than fill the quarters and that many would be left upon the pavements. It would be disastrous to be of the last, and accordingly men with the snow biting their faces, writhed and twisted with their might. One expected that from the tremendous pressure, the narrow passage to the basement door would be so choked and clogged with human limbs and bodies that movement would be impossible. Once indeed the crowd was forced to stop, and a cry went along that a man had been injured at the foot of the stairs. But presently the slow movement began again, and the policeman fought at the top of the flight to ease the pressure on those who were going down.

A reddish light from a window fell upon the faces of the men when they, in turn, arrived at the last three steps and were about to enter. One could then note a change of expression that had come over their features. As they thus stood upon the threshold of their hopes, they looked suddenly content and complacent. The fire had passed from their eyes and the snarl had vanished from their lips. The very force of the crowd in the rear, which had previously vexed them, was regarded from another point of view, for it now made it inevitable that they should go through the little doors into the place that was cheery and warm with light.

01 According to the passage, all of the following are true EXCEPT that _____.
(A) the change of expression over the faces of the men was caused because they knew that they would make it into the shelter
(B) the passage refers to the crowd as "a large band" which has nothing to do with a real marching band
(C) it is reasonable to assume that the men waiting to get in out of the cold are hostile or snarling with anger
(D) the men were going down the stairs because they wanted to escape from the police

02 The general tone of the second passage can be best described as _____.
(A) fathomless   (B) frantic
(C) relieved   (D) vexed

When we talk about having a "dark side," we're generally calling attention to our most aggressive, or lustful, anti-social instincts. Or the mean-spirited, bloodthirsty belligerence presumably lurking deep within us. Or our acting out impulses that would disrupt others' lives — if not outright decimate them. Rape; mutilation; murder; unconscionable acts of thievery, betrayal, treachery, sadism, masochism; unbounded greed; incest; and so on. But what I'd like to suggest here is that perhaps your darkest fantasies shouldn't be understood as all that demonic. Or at least that they can be much more compassionately appreciated as audacious, disinhibited, primitive, grandiose, or hedonistic — as opposed to, say, degrading, disgraceful, or nefarious. To live harmoniously with others, we must subdue our impetuous desires. Given that our dark side embodies our more primitive, pleasure- or power-seeking instincts, must we zealously avoid disclosing it, or reject it as despicable and therefore to be shunned and repudiated?

In the end, such "dark" predilections really can't be seen as intrinsically _____, in that most of them merely represent "appetites" or "urges" innate in all of us. Many psychology researchers have written about the practical utility of daydreams. For, as already suggested, they can function positively as a much needed outlet for our frustrations. And so our simply "entertaining" such fantasies doesn't really reflect any disastrous potential that must be viewed as dark or depraved. The reason that horror movies are perennially popular (especially among the young) is that they, too, enable us to experience a safe release from our more primitive, anti-social instincts.

01 Which expression best fits the blank?
(A) conspicuous
(B) credulous
(C) obscure
(D) culpable
(E) prominent

02 Why did the author argue that "perhaps your darkest fantasies shouldn't be understood as all that demonic" in paragraph one?
(A) Because they are our most aggressive anti-social instincts.
(B) Because they are urges innate in all of us.
(C) Because they can be easily shunned by power-seeking instincts.
(D) Because they do not reflect our disastrous potential.
(E) Because they can distort our more primitive instincts.

03 Which of the following performs the same role as horror movies?
(A) bloodthirsty belligerence
(B) betrayal and treachery
(C) sadism and masochism
(D) daydream
(E) appetite

In his heart Philip hoped that Foinet would look at his picture, and that rare smile would come into his face, and he would shake Philip's hand and say: "You have talent, real talent." Philip's heart swelled at the thought. Foinet sat down; and Philip without a word placed before him the picture which the Salon had rejected; Foinet nodded but did not speak; then Philip showed him the two portraits he had made of Ruth Chalice, two or three landscapes which he had painted at Moret, and a number of sketches. "That's all," he said presently, with a nervous laugh. Monsieur Foinet rolled himself a cigarette and lit it. "You have very little private means?" he asked at last. "Very little," answered Philip, with a sudden feeling of cold at his heart. "Not enough to live on." "There is nothing so degrading as the constant anxiety about one's means of livelihood. I have nothing but contempt for the people who despise money. They are hypocrites or fools. Money is like a sixth sense without which you cannot make a complete use of the other five. Without an adequate income half the possibilities of life are shut off. The only thing to be careful about is that you do not pay more than a shilling for the shilling you earn. You will hear people say that poverty is the best spur to the artist. They have never felt the iron of it in their flesh. They do not know how mean it makes you. It exposes you to endless humiliation, it cuts your wings, it eats into your soul like a cancer. It is not wealth one asks for, but just enough to preserve one's dignity, to work unhampered, to be generous, frank, and independent. I pity with all my heart the artist, whether he writes or paints, who is entirely dependent for subsistence upon his art."

01 According to the passage, which of the following is true?
   (A) Foinet would help Philip for he recognized his picture and liked him.
   (B) Philip had wanted to hear he had real talent with which Foinet was very satisfied.
   (C) Foinet thought that Philip had to despise creating work of art for money.
   (D) Foinet would like those artists who are entirely dependent for subsistence upon his art, whether he writes or paints.

02 Which of the following best describes Foinet's opinion on money?
   (A) It seems that poverty stimulates the sensitivities of artists most effectively.
   (B) Those who love money excessively are hypocrites.
   (C) Money is important for a decent life.
   (D) Most people may overestimate the power of money in the modern world.

03 According to the passage, what is the meaning of "the iron"?
   (A) the freedom
   (B) the happiness
   (C) the pain
   (D) the money

The build-up of energy and heat in Earth's system is important to track because of its bearing on current weather and future climate. Greenhouse gas emissions were rising during the decade and satellites showed there was a growing gap between how much sunlight was coming in and how much radiation was going out. Some heat was coming to Earth but not leaving, and yet temperatures were not going up as much as projected.

So where did the missing heat go? To figure out where the heat was going, scientists ran five simulations on a computer model that portrays complex interactions between the atmosphere, land, oceans and sea ice.

Computer simulations suggest most of it was trapped in layers of oceans deeper than 1,000 feet during periods like the last decade when air temperatures failed to warm as much as they might have. The heat has not disappeared and so it cannot be ignored. It must have consequences.

These simulations all indicated global temperature would rise several degrees this century. But all of them also showed periods when temperatures would stabilize before rising. During these periods, the extra heat moved into deep ocean water due to changes in ocean circulation.

---

01 Choose the one closest in meaning to the underlined "bearing".
   (A) hazard   (B) derision
   (C) tolerance   (D) impact

02 What is the purpose of the passage?
   (A) to explain the complicated system of the Earth
   (B) to allay the growing fear of global warming
   (C) to clear up the mystery of missing heat
   (D) to stress the importance of the deep ocean

03 Which of the following is NOT true according to the passage?
   (A) The long-term trend of global warming will eventually come to an end within the next decade or so.
   (B) When greenhouse emissions kept increasing, global temperatures did not rise correspondingly.
   (C) Global warming is temporarily on hold as the deep oceans capture the sun's extra heat before releasing it finally.
   (D) Earth's missing heat can conceal the effects of global warming for the time being and haunt us later.

It's known as the French ①_____: people who live in France eat lots of saturated fat (in the form of butter, cheese and other milk products), yet they have one of the lowest rates of cardiovascular disease. One explanation is that the French also drink wine, usually in moderation.

Too much alcohol can destroy just about every organ in the body, the heart included. But investigators have discovered through clinical trials that people who have taken an occasional nip have about a 20% lower risk of heart disease than do teetotallers.

The mechanism isn't entirely clear, but alcohol may boost blood levels of HDL, the good cholesterol that cleans plaque off arterial walls. Two of four drinks a week seem optimal for men, one to three for women. Since excess alcohol consumption is the second leading cause of preventable death in the US, says Dr. Charles Henekens of Harvard Medical School, "I'm opposed to a wide public health recommendation to drink alcohol. But I'm ready to consider it for a particular patient after going over his or her risks and benefits."

01 With what topic is the passage mainly concerned?
(A) The effects of alcohol on reducing the risk of heart disease
(B) The power of alcohol to destroy every body organ including the heart
(C) Preventing immoderate alcohol consumption in the United States
(D) Opinion on the wide public health recommendation to drink alcohol

02 Which of the following statements is NOT true according to the passage?
(A) Drinking too much alcohol can seriously damage body organs.
(B) The reason why the French have extremely low rates of heart-related disease is that they usually drink a lot of wine.
(C) The appropriate frequency of drinking is, on an average, three times a week for men, and twice a week for women.
(D) People who sometimes drink just a moderate amount of alcohol have been found to have about a one-fifth lower risk of heart disease than do nondrinkers.

03 Which of the following is most appropriate for the blank ①?
(A) paroxysm   (B) revolution
(C) orthodox   (D) paradox

Hostility to Gypsies has existed almost from the time they first appeared in Europe in the fourteenth century. They had come from northern India to the Middle East some 200 years previously, working as minstrels and mercenaries, metalsmiths and servants. But because their real origins were shrouded in mystery, Europeans misnamed them Egyptians, soon shortened to Gypsies. While Gypsy activists prefer to be called Roma, from the Romany word for "man," others still refer to themselves as Gypsies.

Their _____ began quickly, the church seeing heresy in their fortunetelling, the state seeing anti-social behavior in their nomadism. In some countries they were reduced to slavery — it wasn't until the mid-1800s that Gypsy slaves were freed in Romania. Perhaps half a million perished in the Holocaust. Their women have been sterilized, their children forcibly given for adoption to non-Gypsy families (a practice in Switzerland until 1973).

With very few exceptions Gypsies have expressed no great desire for a country to call their own. "Romanestan," said Ronald Lee, the Canadian Gypsy writer, "is where my two feet stand." A clan system, based mostly on their traditional crafts and geography, has made them a deeply fragmented and fractious people, only really unifying in the face of enmity from non-Gypsies, whom they call *gadje*.

01 Which of the following is the best title for the passage?
(A) The Rise and Fall of Gypsies
(B) The History and Traits of Gypsies
(C) The Artistic Talents of Gypsies
(D) The Long-awaited Wish of Gypsies: Independence

02 Which of the following is most appropriate for the blank?
(A) persecution   (B) suspicion
(C) struggle   (D) prosperity

03 According to the passage, which of the following is true about Gypsies?
(A) They first appeared in the Middle East about two centuries ago.
(B) Because of their wandering lifestyle, they were ill-treated by the church in Europe.
(C) Until 1973, it was not unusual for Swiss families to adopt Gypsy children.
(D) They kept their society integrated, especially when confronted with the outsiders' hostility.

[Ⅰ] And then, luckily, my fingers, still wandering in the corners of my pockets, lighted on a shilling, and the account was squared. But the fact did not lessen the glow of pleasure which ㉮so good-natured an action had given me.

[Ⅱ] Having searched my pockets in vain for stray coppers, and having found I was utterly penniless, I told the conductor with ㉯as an honest face as I could assume that I couldn't pay the fare, and must go back for money. But "Oh, you needn't get off; that's all right." said he. "All right," said I, "but I don't have any copper on me." "Oh, I'll book you through," he replied. "Where do you want to go?" he said and handled his bundle of tickets with the air of a man who was prepared to give me a ticket for anywhere from the Bank of England to Hong Kong.

[Ⅲ] One day when I jumped onto a bus, I found that I had left home without any money in my pocket. Everyone has had the experience and knows the feeling which the discovery arouses. You are annoyed because you look like a fool at best, and like a knave at worst. You would not be surprised at all if the conductor eyed you coldly ㉰as if to say, "Yes, I know that stale old trick. Now then, off you get."

[Ⅳ] I said ㉱it was very kind of him, and told him where I wanted to go, and as he gave me the ticket, I said, "But where shall I send the fare?" "Oh, you'll see me some day all right," he said cheerfully, as he turned to go.

01 Which of the following is the correct order of the four paragraphs above?
(A) [Ⅱ] — [Ⅳ] — [Ⅲ] — [Ⅰ]
(B) [Ⅲ] — [Ⅰ] — [Ⅱ] — [Ⅳ]
(C) [Ⅲ] — [Ⅱ] — [Ⅳ] — [Ⅰ]
(D) [Ⅳ] — [Ⅰ] — [Ⅲ] — [Ⅱ]

02 Which of the following is grammatically incorrect?
(A) ㉮   (B) ㉯
(C) ㉰   (D) ㉱

03 Which of the following is true about the author of the passage?
(A) He expected the conductor would stare at him, making cynical remarks.
(B) He was asked by the conductor where he had had his purse stolen.
(C) He found a shilling in a corner of a pocket, but it was too late to pay the fare.
(D) In revenge for the conductor's rudeness, he decided not to pay the fare even after he found a shilling.

The ailanthus is sometimes called the "tree of heaven," but O. Henry, who was not known for his nature writing, referred to it merely as the "backyard" tree. The bark is gray, and the coarse, rather crooked branches carry exotic looking leaves. These, late to come and late to go, have a tropical appearance, especially when dancing in a breeze. Thick leafstalks measure up to a yard long, and carry many leaflets, which are of a brilliant green no matter what the weather. In June the trees produce pale yellowish green flowers that are all but invisible. By late summer large clusters of fruit hang heavy on the trees. The seed, so light that seventeen thousand of them are needed to make a pound, is a small black dot at the center of a pair of twisted wings a much more efficient flying machine than, for example, the single bladed maple seed. Winds take it surprisingly high. The tree's characteristic branches can occasionally be spotted hanging over the masonry of rooftops a hundred feet up. The tree may be found not only in back yards, but in waste places where other trees would fail. It thrives in cracks between bricks.

A poet once suggested that two dead vine leaves, a cigarette butt, and a paper clip provide ideal growing conditions for an ailanthus. Several years ago a fifteen foot specimen was found flourishing on a corner of a garage roof, sustaining itself on dust and roofing cinders.

01 What does the author of the passage imply about O. Henry?
(A) He was responsible for giving the name "tree of heaven" to the ailanthus.
(B) He thought of the ailanthus as quite an ordinary tree.
(C) He included a description of the ailanthus in his nature writing.
(D) He believed that the ailanthus was a tropical tree.

02 It is clear from the passage, compared with the ailanthus, most other trees have leaves that _____.
(A) sprout later in the spring
(B) are more abundant
(C) fall earlier in the year
(D) grow nearer the stalk

03 We may conclude from the passage that, in contrast to the seed of the ailanthus, the seed of the maple tree _____.

(A) is more viable
(B) is less buoyant
(C) needs more water in order to take root
(D) needs less wind to carry it one hundred feet high

Goods are becoming transformed into pure services, the end of property as a defining concept of social life. As goods become more information-intensive and interactive, and are continually upgraded, they change character. They lose their status as products and metamorphose into evolving services. The nature of services is also changing. Now, with the advent of electronic commerce, services are being reinvented as long-term multifaceted relationships between servers and clients. The changes taking place in the structuring of economic relationships, according to Jeremy Rifkin, are part of an even larger transformation occurring in the nature of the capitalism system. We are making a long-term shift from industrial production to cultural production and a transition into what economists call an experience economy — a world in which each person's own life becomes, in effect, a commercial market. If, for example, one contracts for an air-conditioning service rather than buying the air conditioner itself, one pays for the experience of having air-conditioning. The new capitalism, then, is more temporal than material. Instead of commodifying places and things and exchanging them in the market, we now secure access to one another's time and expertise and borrow what we need, treating each thing as an activity or event that we purchase for a limited period of time. Capitalism is shedding its material origins and increasingly becoming a temporal affair.

01 위 글의 내용과 가장 일치하는 것을 고르시오.
(A) As the nature of capitalism changes, the nature of goods is also being transformed in a way that strengthens the concept of property.
(B) As the service industry expands, one-time and unilateral services are becoming mainstream in the service market.
(C) As the experiences and expertise of people are mainly traded, the essence of capitalism is changing from material commodity trading to temporal information trading.
(D) The market for directly purchasing goods is gradually increasing, while the market for renting goods is shrinking.

02 The underlined word "temporal" is closest in meaning to _____.
(A) time-related   (B) temporary
(C) spatial   (D) permanent

The Middle East lives among vanished glories, present prejudices and future fears. Scrabble in its soil with a hoe and you will find relics of empires long, long gone birthplaces of civilization that have waxed and waned and monuments to religions almost as old as recorded history.

From the Nile to the Euphrates, where trans-world air routes now cover much the same trails as the plodding camel caravans of the past, Man — persistent, passionate, prejudiced — carries on the age-old plot of the human drama. Almost all has altered, yet nothing has changed in the Middle East since centuries before Christ.

Palmyra, the caravan city of Queen Zenobia, is now a magnificent but melancholy reminder of the dreams of men long dead. Baalbek, where even the gods of yesterday have died, is but a tourist attraction, though today no tourists come. The Pyramids themselves, grandiose monuments to man's eternal hope of immortality, are scuffed and wrinkled now — cosmetically patched against the cruelty of the centuries.

Yet, essentially nothing has changed. Man and his emotions, Man and his ignorance and knowledge, Man in his pride, Man at war with other men, set the scene and dominate the stage of the turbulent Middle East.

---

01 According to this passage, problems in the Middle East have been due to the _____.
(A) disappearance of belief in immortality
(B) collapse of former civilization
(C) waning of civilization
(D) weakness of man

02 According to this passage, the men of the ancient Middle East were _____.
(A) vain
(B) irreligious
(C) melancholy
(D) unimaginative

03 We can conclude from this passage that ancient civilizations _____.
(A) embraced one God
(B) existed before Christianity
(C) were democratic in nature
(D) relied on agriculture as their industry

Most animals prey on more than one species as food. Therefore, the term "food web" is a better description of food relationships than "food chain." A food web is a complex feeding system that contains a number of food chains. For instance, hares and deer eat plants. Owls eat hares. Mountain lions eat hares and deer. These four species are parts of food chains that together form a food web.

The first link in a food chain is always a green plant. Only organisms with chlorophyll, such as green plants, can make food. For example, the first link in aquatic food chains is algae. Most algae are microscopic green plants that produce food by photosynthesis. In photosynthesis, energy from sunlight converts carbon dioxide and water to sugar. Tiny fish in lakes or oceans eat algae. In turn, these tiny fish are eaten by larger fish. The larger fish are eaten by still larger fish. The food supply for fish is made by algae. This food is then passed through the food chains as one animal eats another.

Organisms may be divided into three groups based on how they obtain food. These groups are producers, decomposers, and consumers. Organisms containing chlorophyll are producers. Thus, green plants are producers. Animals that eat other animals and plants are consumers. Microbes, one-celled organisms that cause the decay of dead plants and animals, are decomposers. Since decomposers can not make their own food, they are also consumers.

01 What is the main purpose of this passage?

(A) To describe the interconnected food relationships among organisms
(B) To explain how organisms are categorized into different groups
(C) To illustrate the process of photosynthesis in green plants and organisms
(D) To support the position of conservationists in maintaining the bio-diversity
(E) To argue for the superiority of food web as a term for food relationships

02 Which of the following does the underlined expression This food refer to?

(A) energy from sunlight
(B) sunlight
(C) algae
(D) tiny fish eating algae
(E) larger fish eating tiny fish

03 According to the passage, a decomposer would also be a consumer because _____.

(A) it can terminate other animals
(B) it needs to feed on other organisms
(C) it cannot catch other animals
(D) it can covert sunlight into food
(E) it need not depend on other organisms for food

In 1912 Frederick G. Hopkins and Casimir Funk suggested that specific human diseases, such as beriberi, rickets, and scurvy, were caused by the absence of certain nutritional substances in the diet. These were termed vitamines("vital amines"), because the first such substance isolated, thiamin(vitamin B1), was an amine(a compound containing an amino group). When other such essential substances were isolated and analyzed, they proved not to be amines, but the term vitamin was retained to refer to any essential growth factor required in very small amounts. Many vitamins have been discovered since that time. Although the functions of some vitamins are unknown, many have been shown to be coenzymes. Although the functions of some vitamins are unknown, many have been shown to be coenzymes.

Letters of the alphabet were first used to describe the mysterious nutritional factors. These letters (A, B, C, D, E, K, and others) have persisted. It was found, however, that some factors actually consisted of more than one substance. The original B factor has been shown to consist of more than a dozen entities. These factors are now designated as specific substances, for example, thiamin (B1), riboflavin (B2), pantothenic acid (B3), and three related substances, and niacin. Because these commonly occur together, they are referred to as the B-complex vitamins.

01 The author's main purpose in this passage is to _____.
(A) compare and contrast nutritional substances
(B) define vitamins and relate their history
(C) identify the vitamins humans need
(D) argue in favor of taking vitamins

02 It can be concluded from this passage that _____.
(A) vitamins cannot be used to treat disease
(B) vitamins work separately in the body
(C) most vitamins are not essential to good health
(D) scientists still don't know everything about vitamins

03 Which of the following statements best describes the organization of the passage?
(A) A general concept is defined, and examples are given.
(B) Persuasive language is used to argue against a popular idea.
(C) Suggestions for the use of vitamins are given.
(D) Several generalizations are made from which several conclusions are drawn.

Most women need to work for financial reasons. And today they have more career options than ever. They are well educated, confident and technologically savvy, and they are entering a labor market that still desperately wants them. According to the Census Bureau, in 1998 nearly 60 percent of all women over 16 worked, compared to 43 percent in 1970. New mothers are, on average, returning to work more quickly: in 1998 nearly 62 percent of mothers with children under the age of 1 were working, up from 31 percent in 1975. And they are having children — or at least planning for them — at an earlier age: Andrea Truncali, 27, says she began thinking about having kids during her first year of medical school, when she learned about the risks of advanced maternal age. Indeed, the new generation places great importance on establishing their families. "These young people on the whole have grown up as children of divorce," says Sheila Washington. "They may tend to value family more."

01 Which of the following can best replace savvy?
   (A) salient
   (B) saline
   (C) converse
   (D) imbecile
   (E) versed

02 Based on the above passage, which of the following best describes women today?
   (A) Most women sacrifice marriage and children to career.
   (B) Most women want to work for pleasure.
   (C) Most women are attracted to the idea of not working.
   (D) Most women try to keep balance between family and work.
   (E) Most women undergo painful marriage crisis.

03 Comparing with the year 1970 or 1975, which of the following is NOT true of the characteristic of the women in 1998?
   (A) The number of working mothers with babies has doubled.
   (B) More than half of women over 16 years have jobs.
   (C) More women want to have children after they succeed in their job.
   (D) More women are ready to recognize the importance of family.
   (E) Women are more qualified in education, thus more confident.

Introducing oneself as a psychologist often invites questions such as "What is psychology?" or "What do you do?" Psychology seems to belong to a group of terms that sound familiar to many but are understood by far less.

A standard psychology textbook would tell you that psychology is the scientific study of the human mind and human behavior. More questions, though, may be raised by such a definition. First of all, you would notice the abundant psychological resources listed under the title "Animal Psychology." Studying animal behavior and animal mental states, and comparing them with human's can shed light on our understanding of the human psyche. Studying the relationship between humans and their companion animals can help us find more ways to enhance the ethological well-being of humans. Psychology has a way of outgrowing its formal definitions. It has been and will continue to be working its way into many cross-fields in the scientific frontier.

It sounds right to say that psychology is the scientific study of behavior and mental processes of — but not limited to — human beings. Under this umbrella are numerous psychology sub-fields. Clinical psychology, developmental psychology, cognitive psychology and social psychology are just several well-known examples. There are many more. In fact, the American Psychological Association has 53 divisions at present time. Psychology has many relatives, too. They include sociology, anthropology, biology and psychiatry. This last one, psychiatry, is another source of confusion in understanding the role and identity of a psychologist.

01 What is the passage mainly about?

(A) what psychology is
(B) the goal of psychology
(C) the broader range of psychology
(D) the problems psychologists are faced with
(E) how to study psychology efficiently

02 Which of the following is NOT mentioned as a sub-field of psychology?

(A) clinical psychology
(B) developmental psychology
(C) social psychology
(D) cognitive psychology
(E) psychiatry

03 What is the opinion of the author about psychology?
   (A) It is impossible to define psychology in mundane terms.
   (B) More confusion will occur whenever we try to define psychology.
   (C) Psychology will be combined into more and more fields in science.
   (D) The formal definition of psychology will remain in the future.
   (E) Psychiatry has nothing to do with psychology.

Robots have been a part of the manufacturing work force for decades. One in ten auto-workers, for instance, is now made of metal and electronics. Robots for the home have been slower to come. Household chores are less predictable and repetitive than those of the assembly line, making ①them difficult to explain in the simple language of a machine. One answer is to design robots that are flexible for specific tasks, such as vacuuming. Another is to figure out a way to make robots simple and cheap for ordinary people to build ②their own from parts and program them to do whatever ③they please. That's the tack scientists at Carnegie Mellon University in Pittsburgh are taking, through an educational development project they call TeRK (Tele-presence Robot Kit). With funding from Google, Intel and Microsoft, ④they have created a series of building-it-yourself robots which they say are simple and cheap enough for almost anyone to create. It starts with a black box called Qwerk — the robot "brain" that CMU built and sells for $349 on its Web site. Using off-the-shelf parts and some simple instructions, anybody can build a 10-centimeter-high robot and program the Qwerk brain. You might make a wheeled robot with a video camera that can keep an eye on your house and sound the alarm in case an intruder enters, or make sure ⑤Fido doesn't steal food from the kitchen counter. A stationary robot might sniff the air for pollutants.

01 What is the passage mainly about?

(A) Robots
(B) Industrial robots
(C) Robot engineers
(D) Robots for the home
(E) Homemade robots

02 Which of the following is NOT correct?

(A) Them in ① refers to "household chores."
(B) Their own in ② means "their own robots."
(C) They in ③ refers to the same thing as "them" in "program them."
(D) They in ④ refers to "scientists at CMU."
(E) Fido in ⑤ means "a pet dog."

03 Which of the following questions is NOT answered by the author?

(A) What percentage do robots account for of the automobile industry workers?
(B) How can we design robots that are adaptable for specific tasks?
(C) What policy are scientists at CMU taking through their project called TeRK?
(D) What is Qwerk?
(E) What are the examples of building-it-yourself robots we can make easily?

You might think that emotions are the enemy of decision making, but in fact they're integral to it. Whenever you make up your mind, your limbic system — the brain's emotional center — is active. A neurologist has studied people with damage to only the emotional parts of their brains, and found that they were unable to make basic choices about what to wear or eat. He speculates this may be because our brains store emotional memories of past choices, which we use to inform present decisions. However, making choices under the influence of an emotion can seriously affect the outcome. Take anger for example. Angry consumers are more likely to opt for the first thing they are offered rather than considering other alternatives. It seems that anger can make us impetuous, selfish and risk-prone. All emotions affect our thinking and motivation, so it may be best to avoid making important decisions under their influence. Yet strangely there's one emotion that seems to help us make good choices. The American researchers found that sad people took time to consider the various alternatives on offer, and ended up making the best choices. In fact, many studies show that depressed people have the most realistic take on the world. Psychologists have even coined a name for it: depressive realism.

01 밑줄 친 "impetuous"와 뜻이 가장 가까운 것은?
    (A) rash   (B) bold
    (C) dull   (D) fussy

02 이 글의 요지를 가장 잘 나타낸 것은?
    (A) 화가 날 때는 의사 결정을 미루어야 한다.
    (B) 슬플 때는 의사 결정을 잘 할 수 있다.
    (C) 의사 결정을 할 때는 감정을 고려해야 한다.
    (D) 의사 결정의 종류에 따라 감정의 영향이 다르다.

03 이 글 마지막에 제시된 depressive realism에 가장 잘 부합하는 설명은?
    (A) 슬픈 현실을 직시해서 의사 결정을 해야 한다.
    (B) 슬픈 감정은 현실적인 의사 결정을 방해한다.
    (C) 슬픈 사람이 현실에 대한 대안을 잘 제시한다.
    (D) 슬픈 사람이 세상을 가장 현실적으로 본다.

Business is changing. The long-held notion that companies should focus solely on the bottom line is being challenged by a new generation of corporate-dwelling social entrepreneurs who believe that ①doing well and doing good are inextricably linked. Worldwide problems as diverse as poverty, disease, lack of education and pollution, which were historically addressed by political and social activists, are now being tackled by businesses as well.

②The call for involvement is coming from within corporate walls, led by CEOs and employees. They believe ③social responsibility should be an integral part of every organization's mission. Many companies report that new hires are asking not just about salaries and benefits, but about the opportunities they'll have to make social contributions through their jobs. Facing projected shortages of key workers in years ahead, companies may find that ④caring corporate cultures attract the brightest and most committed employees.

Technology will play a key role in change, such as battling the lack of education that consigns many children in developing countries to poverty. A number of technology firms have contributed $2 million apiece to the nonprofit "One Laptop per Child" effort, which plans to manufacture $100 laptop computers that will be sold to governments and given to children in poor countries. Because a half-billion children have no access to electricity, the laptop's battery can be recharged with a crank, a pedal or a pull-cord.

01   Which of the following does the passage mainly discuss?
(A) a change in the way companies hire new employees
(B) effective ways to eliminate worldwide problems
(C) the importance of technological breakthroughs
(D) a new trend where businesses feel a sense of obligation to society

02   Choose the one which refers to different meaning from the others.
(A) ①   (B) ②
(C) ③   (D) ④

03   How can technology contribute to the change according to the passage?
(A) by establishing a charity for permanent aid
(B) by hiring new employees interested in social contributions
(C) by having employees volunteer in the developing countries
(D) by inventing products that bring education to those without money or resources

Since the turn of the century, digital technology has conquered the world. Sales of DVDs far outstrip those of videotapes, and digital cameras are favored by consumers and professionals alike. But digital still has its enemies, and the biggest one may be the film industry. The majority of films made for cinematic release are still shot using traditional 16mm or 35mm film cameras, with prominent directors like Martin Scorsese and Steven Spielberg refusing to cross over to the new format.

Why is Hollywood resisting? By now, most people agree that digital technology is cheaper; for the struggling film-maker, using a low-scale digital-camera model can mean a difference of thousands. But some still think the technology falls short esthetically, while others dispute its perceived flexibility: unlike compact digital photo cameras, digital film equipment can be bulky. And if a director's not familiar with its workings, it can be hard to calculate the outcome of a shot. "You have to be confident you know what you're doing," says Nic Morris, a British cinematographer. "And many of us are still trying to find our way around." Still, the most likely reason for the hesitance is that the Scorseses and Spielbergs just don't care; the general perception is that film still offers a richer image than digital, which more than makes up for its higher cost. The savings may matter to young, struggling film-makers, but not to Hollywood's elite.

01 Choose the one closest in meaning to the underlined 'cross over to the new format'
(A) newly use digital cameras to shoot films
(B) turn over a new leaf of the film industry
(C) break with their predecessors in film making
(D) make their way toward new media other than films

02 What is the point Nic Morris makes in the second paragraph?
(A) Everything requires foresight, which many modern directors lack.
(B) Directors must know the significance of making a film, but they actually don't.
(C) Directors are not so good at handling digital film equipment as they should be.
(D) The recession of film industry has a way out, which many directors are trying to find.

03 Which of the following can be inferred from the passage?
(A) Digital technology has a long history of more than one century.
(B) Steven Spielberg doesn't pursue a low-cost strategy for his film-making.
(C) More beautiful and richer images can be obtained through digital technology.
(D) Nowadays, most movies are made by young directors with digital cameras.

In the wake of the Romantic revolution in literature came a similar revolution in music. About 1820, Beethoven began to write passionate compositions which often threatened to burst asunder the classical forms in which he worked. His 1824 Symphony No. 9 is notable not only for its length and complexity, but for the fact that he experimentally introduced vocal soloists and a chorus into the final movement, as if the purely instrumental form of the classical symphony could not express all that he felt. [I]

Beethoven is also significant in the history of music for being the first composer to earn his living directly from his own work without being subsidized by a church or aristocrat. He benefited from the emergence of the new bourgeois audience which could not afford to retain a composer on salary as Haydn was retained by Prince Esterhazy, but who eagerly bought tickets for Beethoven's concerts. [II] With the money he received from lessons, from the sale of his compositions, and from his public performances, Beethoven was able to survive if not to prosper. This was a crucial factor in allowing him to express his extreme individualism, rejecting the role of artistic servant within which even giants like Haydn and Mozart had been confined. He could write as he pleased and challenge the public to follow him. [III]

The rise of the new middle classes created a new audience seeking fresh sensations. It was also an audience, which was powerfully drawn to emotion in the arts, and music more than any of the other arts has the capacity to elicit powerful emotions. Although forms like the sonata continued to be used by Romantic composers, the new audiences were less to appreciate the details of the development of themes than to be swept along on waves of melody, harmony, and rhythm. [IV]

01 Which of the following is the most appropriate title for the passage?

(A) Beethoven's Personality and Music
(B) Beethoven: Classical or Romantic
(C) Beethoven: The Magnificent Master
(D) Beethoven: The First Romantic Composer

02 Which is the most appropriate place for the sentence below?

After this radical departure from classical tradition, many composers felt free to experiment.

(A) [I]   (B) [II]
(C) [III]   (D) [IV]

03 What does the underlined This refer to?

(A) to express his extreme individualism
(B) to be subsidized by a church or aristocrat
(C) to earn his living directly from his own work
(D) to write as he pleased and challenge the public to follow him

There is little in life that the human psyche either welcomes with more enthusiasm than, or dreads so profoundly as change. People past the age of thirty have long been accepted to be less adaptable, less open to changes great or small. That perception does not reflect the current generation; how do we go about updating the notion that older adults are stagnant and notoriously conservative? Mohandas Gandhi said, "You must be the change you want to see in the world." It is clear that Gandhi said we have to walk the walk, not just talk the talk.

For the most part, I believe that people in all age groups are open to reasonable change. I think the difference in the generations may be how each age group defines "reasonable." What change are you seeking? Or, what change would you find acceptable? What are you willing to do, or not do, for the changes you seek? Have you ever said to yourself that you are too old, tired, poor, or insignificant, to affect a change? Would you accept any of those excuses from a friend, a mate, a government leader?

Change is not merely necessary to life; it is life. And it doesn't have to be large scale to affect us; a simple thing such as a change to one's daily routine can put a person out of sorts — and perhaps more so than a change of global proportions. Again, though, it is a person's attitude about change itself that influences the reactions to changes in daily life. It is necessary to understand that change does happen and will continue to do so.

01 Which of the following is the purpose of the passage?

(A) to advise how to adapt to unexpected changes
(B) to persuade people to take advantage of changes
(C) to argue that changes bring some hardship
(D) to urge people to take active stance toward changes

02 Which of the following does the underlined sentence mean?

(A) we should keep trying to renew old concepts
(B) we should show our belief through our actions
(C) we should articulate specific plans to enact change
(D) we should be aware of circumstances and be prepared

03 Which of the following would the author most agree with?

(A) Modern society has faced more changes than before.
(B) Change occurs more often to those who are more willing to change.
(C) Each generation has its own standards for what to change.
(D) The bigger the scale of change is, the more influenced we are.

There are in work all grades, from mere relief of tedium up to the profoundest delights, according to the nature of the work and the abilities of the worker. Most of the work that most people have to do is not in itself interesting, but even such work has certain great advantages.

Most people, when they are left free to fill their own time according to their own choice, are at a loss to think of anything sufficiently pleasant to be worth doing. And whatever they decide on, they are troubled by the feeling that something else would have been more pleasant.

To be able to fill leisure intelligently is the last product of civilization, and at present very few people have reached this level. Moreover, the exercise of choice is in itself tiresome. Except to people with unusual ①initiative it is positively agreeable to be told what to do at each hour of the day, provided the orders are not too unpleasant. Most of the idle rich suffer unspeakable boredom as the ②_____ of their freedom from drudgery. At times, they may find relief by hunting big game in Africa, or by flying round the world, but the number of such sensations is limited.

01 What is similar in meaning to the underlined ①initiative?
(A) feature
(B) reputation
(C) plan
(D) drive

02 Which of the following is most suitable for the blank ②?
(A) meaning
(B) delight
(C) price
(D) purpose

03 Which of the following would the author most agree with?
(A) Poor people are offended by rich people with a lot of free time.
(B) Work is mostly aimed at recovering stolen property.
(C) Most people are not aware of the value of their free time.
(D) Work filling many hours of the day saves the trouble of deciding what one shall do.

Synthetic Genomics, a company aimed at creating modified microbes, was founded by Craig Venter. Venter and his colleagues want to synthesize the entire DNA sequence of an individual bacterium, with crucial modifications to make the organism do new and interesting things and try to implant artificial chromosomes into empty bacterial cells, in the hope that they will come alive. Venter talks in computer jargon about this project. "It is installing the software — basically we have to boot up the genome, get it operating"

The idea that life is just genetic information is sobering. What we need to reflect on is the balance between potential benefit and possible risk in work on artificial organisms. The aims of Synthetic Genomics are honorable. It wants to modify bacteria so that they can capture carbon dioxide from the atmosphere or produce new, clean fuels. But there are reasons for concern. The technology to synthesize DNA from publicly available sequences is getting cheaper and simpler. Genetic information — the sequence of the bird flu virus, for instance — is available on the internet. That's good for science, but it means that anyone with the capacity to synthesize DNA and with less ①_____ motives than Venter and his colleagues could ②_____ use this information to make new and deadly infectious organisms.

01 Which of the following is NOT discussed in the passage?
(A) the intent of Synthetic Genomics
(B) the example of the genetic information on view
(C) the potential gains offered by Synthetic Genomics
(D) the criterion for choosing a bacteria to be modified

02 What is the rhetorical device used in the underlined sentence?
(A) simile   (B) paradox
(C) metaphor   (D) oxymoron

03 Which of the following is most suitable for the blanks ① and ②?
(A) imprudent — tactfully
(B) benevolent — maliciously
(C) lucrative — spontaneously
(D) altruistic — lawfully

Think of life as one long afternoon at the mall, shopping. We all spend a good amount of time contemplating value. Is that mocha latte really worth four bucks? Will you finally write a $200 check to your chosen candidate? Not a day goes by that we don't ask ourselves the question "So, what is it worth?" Such questions have no absolute and universal answers, of course. Judgments of worth and value are a complex meld of attitudes and feelings about both money and thousands of commodities that defy comparison.

A lot of people are very interested in ①_____, including psychologists. How does the brain sort through the impossible confusion of life's marketplace and arrive at a choice? Two Princeton University scientists have been exploring this problem and may have some clues to the subtle and surprising nature of these everyday decisions. They believe that many of the economic decisions we make have little to do with objective value. Market choices have much more to do with the brain's basic, internal perceptions of the world and the way those perceptions shape our feelings of comfort and ease. In this view, even currency has no clear and absolute value; regardless of those numbers on bills and coins, they ②_____.

01 Which of the following is most suitable for the blank ①?

(A) what we set much value on
(B) which is worth the trouble
(C) how we value stuff
(D) why we classify the value

02 Which of the following is true according to this passage?

(A) The money has clear and absolute value.
(B) We always question ourselves about the worth of something.
(C) The universal value comes from everyday decisions.
(D) There is no relationship between objective value and market choices.

03 Which of the following is most suitable for the blank ②?

(A) derive their true value from the individual mind
(B) have only mundane value
(C) don't need any perception of value in mind
(D) bring some value from other stuff

_____ has brought seismologists one step closer to being able to predict earthquakes. As part of an unrelated effort to measure underground changes caused by shifts in barometric pressure, a team of researchers found that increases in subterranean pressure preceded earthquakes along San Andreas Fault by as much as 10 hours. If follow-up tests advance the findings, seismologists may eventually be able to provide a few hours' notice for people to find safe haven prior to quakes.

Researchers used a high-tech equivalent of a stereo speaker lowered into a bore hole near Parkfield, California, a half-mile deep and five yards from a measuring device. For two months, researchers transmitted pulse signals three times per second, from the speaker to the measuring device, calculating travel time between the two stations. Scientists learned the seismic waves slowed dramatically on only two occasions: two hours prior to a magnitude-1 temblor, and a startling 10 hours before a magnitude-3 quake.

The research team theorizes that the immense amount of pressure building along the fault causes small cracks within the rock during the final hours before an earthquake, increasing rock density and slowing the transmission signals. "The more cracks you have, the slower the seismic velocity," says study co-author Paul Silver. Still unknown is whether there is any significance to the fact that the magnitude-3 quake had a much longer pre-seismic signal than the lower-magnitude quake, or whether it was simply because its magnitude was larger and its epicenter closer to the sensors.

01 What is the best title for this passage?

(A) An Experiment Finding the Causes of Earthquakes
(B) A New Clue in Predicting Earthquakes
(C) Various Technology Predicting Earthquakes
(D) The Relationship between Magnitude and Barometric Pressure

02 Which of the following is most suitable for the blank?

(A) Endeavor of researchers
(B) An accidental discovery
(C) The constant research of earthquakes
(D) The new finding in epicenter

03 What is NOT true according to the passage?

(A) If scientists can flesh out the new findings, it could make an early-warning system for quakes.
(B) The seismic waves slowed dramatically prior to magnitude-1 and magnitude-3 earthquakes.
(C) The researchers believe that cracks within the rock slow down the transmission signals.
(D) A magnitude-3 quake had a longer pre-seismic signal because of its larger magnitude.

In contemporary times, information technology and its associated systems have flooded the world with data. Information/knowledge components of organizations determine the success of military forces, businesses, states, and individuals. In fact, it is the speed of obtaining, processing, and use of information that has become more important than just having information. It has become one of the fundamental critical success factors for organizational survival. Because of this, it has also grown to be the prime target for combatants in any competitive or antagonistic situation. Information is now not only power but a weapon at all levels: strategic, tactical, and operational. In fact, the Information Age has made these terms become blurred as the speed of data production and the emphasis on the information component of organizations make strategy and operations become the same. Like all major weapons, information needs to be defended. Therefore, information should be protected as much as physical assets. In fact, it could be argued that it is more important to maintain the integrity and relevance of information and associated systems than it is to maintain physical assets. This book will discuss the concepts associated with the world of information warfare. It is about a world where organizations use information to build beneficial images of themselves and negative images of competitors or enemies. An environment where hackers attempt to break systems is the order of the day. It is a world that managers ignore at their peril.

01 According to the passage, which of the following needs to be protected the most?
(A) The origin of information
(B) The quantity of information
(C) The components of information
(D) The integrity of information

02 According to the passage, which of the following statements is CORRECT?
(A) Merely having information is more important now than using it.
(B) An organization can survive only if it multiplies its physical assets.
(C) This book is devoted to helping hackers break systems of information.
(D) The information war can be exploited to plant negative images of one's competitors.

03 In which part of a book would this passage most likely appear?
(A) epilogue   (B) preface
(C) acknowledgements (D) bibliography

[1] The president of a large company told me about an otherwise qualified job candidate he turned down because the candidate was groomed too meticulously. "I think good grooming is important," the executive explained. "But this guy was so perfect, he was scary. His clothes were perfect. His hair was perfect. His fingernails were perfect. Even his teeth were perfect. He was ①plastic, and I don't trust that. Nobody is perfect." Too many people think that if the boss sees a few imperfections their chances evaporate. They guard their speech, sit in the back row at meetings and stay as inconspicuous as possible for fear they will slip and reveal the horrible truth — that they are not perfect.

The only way to avoid making mistakes is never to do anything new. From my point of view, an employee who never makes mistakes suggests that his creativity is at a standstill, that he is immersed in the day-to-day details of the job and not thinking of the future. Employees who play it safe ②go nowhere.

[2] We often think that we need to be perfect for a job interview. Striving for perfection, however, is not only a misguided effort, but it is also an incorrect strategy. A job interview is not about perfect attire, skills or resume tricks. It is rather about personal relationships, about learning an applicant's personality and answering the question, "Do I want to work with this person?" And across most offices there is one constant: people hire applicants that will become productive and fun co-workers. Remember that in some strange sense we are more whole when we are missing something. And because of the limitations we have, we yearn, try, hope, and nourish our souls with the dream of something better. So, don't try to be too perfect. Admit a flaw and that makes you more human and genuine.

01 지문 [1]에서 각각의 밑줄 친 부분을 대신할 수 있는 표현으로 적절하게 짝지어진 것은?

　　　　　　①　　—　　②
(A) impressionable　—　are almost dead
(B) artificial　　　—　are coward
(C) fake　　　　　—　achieve nothing
(D) superficial　　—　will be dismissed

02 두 개의 지문에서 다음 중 신입사원 면접 시 중요하게 고려하는 점으로 옳게 짝지어진 것은?

(A) perfectionism　—　creativity
(B) creativity　　　—　personality
(C) meticulousness　—　loyalty
(D) simplicity　　　—　adroitness

When Irene Mendevil, a high school English teacher, shouts at her students, she said, ①she gets a sore throat. So she has begun to use an amplifier. "I had the experience of losing my voice completely," she said of her constant shouting. "No sounds came out of my mouth. I had to write on paper to tell my students what to do." Ms. Mendevil, 33, shouts because her class is so big that just getting the students to listen is a challenge. And the school itself is not unusual in a country whose population of 92 million is exploding so fast, and whose education budget is so small, that it cannot find space to teach its children. More children are also coming into the public schools as the economy tightens and families cannot afford the haven of private schools, with their smaller classes. This school year opened with a nationwide enrollment of 21 million students from elementary through high school, almost exactly a million more than in the previous year. Although the government began a classroom-building program three years ago, the schools are still 27,124 classrooms short, according to Juan Miguel Luz, a former under secretary of education who works with the National Institute of Policy Study, which advocates better education policies. To _____ all the students, many classrooms have been divided into two by partitions. Stairwells and corridors have been converted into miniature classrooms. In 2016, double sessions were introduced to take off some of the pressure.

01 Which of the following is closest in meaning to the underlined ①"she gets a sore throat"?
(A) She clears her throat.
(B) She gets a frog in the throat.
(C) She sticks in her throat.
(D) She gets a lump in her throat.

02 Choose the one that best fills in the blank.
(A) take after
(B) squeeze in
(C) hold off
(D) scavenge for

03 According to the passage, which of the following is NOT true?

(A) Irene had to write on paper to tell her students what to do because she had the experience of injuring her voice.

(B) More children are coming into the public school because of the country's poor economic conditions.

(C) The country's classroom building program pays off because its economy tightens.

(D) Juan Miguel Luz, who used to be a senior government official, works with the National Institute of Policy Study.

For the weary traveller, the Art Deco arches at the entrance to the Lincoln tunnel in New Jersey signal that the joys of midtown Manhattan are just an $8 toll away. Before October 1997 getting through those arches took a lot longer than it does now. But then E-ZPass, an automatic toll-payment system used across America's north-east, was installed at some of the tunnel's toll lanes.

The adoption of E-ZPass is reckoned to have reduced delays at the tunnel and other toll booths by around 85%. This meant less time and fuel wasted while drivers waited, engines idling, to pay their tolls. But speedier passage through toll booths has also meant less local pollution. A study by Janet Currie and Reed Walker of Columbia University finds this has had unexpected effects.

A lot of Americans live close to busy main roads. The researchers looked at medical data on all children born to women in New Jersey and Pennsylvania who lived within 2km of a highway during periods when most toll booths acquired E-ZPass. They found that almost 12% fewer babies with abnormally low birth-weights were born to women who lived within 2km of a toll booth after E-ZPass was introduced. There was no change for children born to mothers who lived further away from a toll booth. There was a similar effect on premature births. Reduced congestion, it seems, does a lot more than soothe ratty drivers. Those who signed up for E-ZPass _____.

01 Which of the following is the best title of the passage?

(A) Perceptions of Traffic Risk
(B) Struggle for Traffic Accident Reduction
(C) Effects of Traffic Congestion on Health
(D) Correlations between Driving and Aggression

02 Which of the following would best fill in the blank?

(A) were forced to observe the traffic regulations
(B) polluted our environment cleverly, if not deliberately
(C) were only concerned about their safety and convenience
(D) inadvertently did a large number of children a favour

03 According to the passage, it can be inferred that _____.

(A) new safety measures unexpectedly fail to work
(B) E-ZPass is effective for the prevention of traffic accidents
(C) unintended consequences caused by the automatic toll-payment system are not bad
(D) countries with a large number of vehicles are less polluted than expected

The Arctic tundra is one of the world's most extensive ecosystems, and the frozen soil known as permafrost, which underlies ⓐit, can be hundreds of meters deep. But as the world warms up in response to the millions of tonnes of carbon dioxide and other greenhouse gases being poured into the atmosphere each year, so does the permafrost. As the permafrost thaws, bacteria start chewing up the organic matter it contains. This releases yet more carbon dioxide, as well as methane, another greenhouse gas, which has 25 times the warming potential of CO_2. It is estimated that the world's permafrost contains twice as much carbon as ⓑits atmosphere. Nor is that all. Thawing permafrost also leaks nitrates and phosphates into the tundra, allowing novel plant species to get a foothold in what was, to start with, a fairly spartan habitat. It distorts the Earth's surface, too, creating a landscape of domes and pits known as thermokarst because of ⓒits resemblance to the karstic terrain of limestone-rich parts of the world. It also plays havoc with human structures, such as buildings, roads and pipelines, that sit on top of ⓓit. For all of these reasons, then, more research is needed into this icy realm. And that is the object of the project, which is led by Breck Bowden of the University of Vermont in Burlington, involves 17 research groups from America and Canada. The project will try to work out how thawing permafrost will affect the numerous streams, rivers and lakes of the Arctic. As water moves through affected areas, it picks up both nutrients and sediment that would otherwise be held in the permafrost's icy grasp. These, _____, have opposite effects on the growth of algae. The phosphates and nitrates stimulate it whereas the extra sediment suppresses it by trapping nutrients in the beds of such bodies of water.

01 다음 중 대명사 ⓐ ~ ⓓ가 지칭하는 것이 잘못 짝지어진 것을 고르시오.
(A) ⓐ it → the Arctic tundra
(B) ⓑ its → the world's
(C) ⓒ its → the Earth's surface's
(D) ⓓ it → permafrost

02 다음 중 윗글의 내용과 일치하는 것을 고르시오.
(A) 영구 동토층은 영양분이 거의 없는 척박한 토지이다.
(B) 영양분과 침전물은 조류의 성장을 억제하는 역할을 한다.
(C) 메탄은 이산화탄소보다 지구온난화에 훨씬 더 많은 영향을 미친다.
(D) 석회암이 풍부한 열크라스트의 생성으로 툰드라 지역이 위험해지고 있다.

03 빈칸에 들어갈 가장 적절한 단어를 고르시오.
(A) apparently
(B) proportionally
(C) consequently
(D) paradoxically

It is true that global warming demands an answer. We need to move away from fossil fuels and toward green energy. But we are wrong to believe that the current approach is achieving anything in that regard.

The European Union is applauded by many for implementing stringent targets that will reduce its emissions 25 percent by 2040 and will increase its green energy by equal measure. But the policy will reduce temperatures by just one tenth of one degree Fahrenheit in 2100, at a cost of about $380 billion a year for the rest of the century. The massive price tag exists because there is no affordable alternative to fossil fuel. Current green technology is so inefficient that — to take just one example — if we were serious about wind power, we would have to blanket most countries with wind turbines to generate enough energy. We would still have the massive _____: there would be no power when the wind doesn't blow.

A sensible energy policy should focus first on unleashing human ingenuity to solve the massive technological challenge before us. Both public and private investment is needed, including significant government spending on research and development aimed at developing new and cheaper low-carbon technologies.

It is extremely foolish to try to make fossil fuels so expensive that nobody wants to use them. Instead, we need to promote innovation so the price of green energy comes down and alternatives rapidly become cheap enough that everyone will buy them, including developing nations. Such a policy would be smarter than our current approach, and actually bring about green energy everywhere in the future.

01. Choose the one that best fills in the blank.
    (A) problem of storage
    (B) chances of windfall
    (C) need for weathercast
    (D) perils of pollution

02. What is the main idea of the passage?
    (A) We should replace fossil fuels with eco-friendly energy sources.
    (B) Green technology, in its infant stage of development, is ineffective.
    (C) Our energy policy should zero in on innovating current technology.
    (D) Price is a crucial factor in the worldwide spread of green energy.

03. The underlined word "ingenuity" is closest in meaning to _____.
    (A) happiness
    (B) inventiveness
    (C) calmness
    (D) kindness

It might sound like a joke, but Jimmy Kimmel might be on to something when he suggests National Unfriend Day. Thanks to Facebook, many of us have way too many friends. Well, actually, in most cases, they aren't even real ①friends at all.

[I] The average Facebooker has about 120 friends. Anthropologist Robin Dunbar, says that humans have an average of about 150 ②friends, and that the human brain can't really accept more than that. Dunbar says you have a core of about five, then another ten close ones beyond that, and then the outer circle is 35, complemented by about another 100 who have some sort of "obligation of friendship." [II] So what about all these Facebook people with thousands of "friends?" Well, in their defense, it is Facebook that refers to them as ③friends, not you. [III] In many cases, people are friended in order to network either socially or professionally, although there are many who only want the big headcount. [IV]

So on Wednesday, Nov 17, National Unfriend Day, you might want to think twice before you get rid of those annoying Facebook friends who you just accepted only to be nice, because not only might they be interesting enough to get to know better, but there is another study that reports that the more ④friends you have, the wealthier you will be.

01 Which of the following can be inferred from the passage?
(A) Many friends guarantee us that we will be more wealthier.
(B) We regard all friends as equal to us and treat them equally.
(C) It is difficult to unfriend many friends in Facebook.
(D) Some users only want the popularity of their Facebooks.

02 Which is the best place in the passage for the following sentence?

Many people I didn't initially know, but who friended me for some reason have become friends — people I now care about and with whom I am interested in pursuing an ongoing social obligation.

(A) [I]   (B) [II]
(C) [III]   (D) [IV]

03 Among ①, ②, ③, and ④, which one differs from the others in what they refer to?
(A) ① friends   (B) ② friends
(C) ③ friends   (D) ④ friends

Cancer is the common lay term to name the most aggressive, and usually fatal, forms of a larger class of diseases known as neoplasm. A neoplasm is described as being relatively ①_____ because it does not fully obey the biological mechanisms that govern the growth and metabolism of individual cells and the overall cell interactions of the living organism. Some neoplasms grow more rapidly than the tissues from which they arise; others grow at a normal pace but, because of other factors, eventually become recognizable as an abnormal growth and not normal tissue. The changes seen in a neoplasm are heritable ⓐ_____ these characteristics are passed on from each cell to its ②_____. The principal classification of neoplasms as either benign or malignant relates to their behavior. Several relative differences distinguish these two classes. A benign neoplasm, for instance, is encapsulated but malignant neoplasms are not. Malignancies grow more rapidly than benign forms and invade adjacent, normal tissue. Tissue of a benign tumor is structured in a manner similar to that of the tissue from which it is derived; malignant tissue, however, has an abnormal and unstructed appearance. Most malignant tumors, in fact, exhibit abnormalities in chromosome structure — that is, the structure of the DNA molecules that constitute the genetic materials duplicated and passed on to later generations of cells. Most importantly, however, benign neoplasms do not metastasize — ⓑ_____, begin to grow at sites other than the point of origin — whereas malignant tumors do.

01 What is the prime difference between malignant and benign neoplasms?

(A) All malignant tumors have abnormal chromosome structures.
(B) Benign neoplasms only grow where they first appear.
(C) Malignant neoplasms are composed of abnormal tissue.
(D) Benign neoplasms grow more rapidly.

02 How can neoplasms be visually identified?

(A) They grow more rapidly in tissues.
(B) Their growth rate or forms are unusual.
(C) They don't fully obey biological mechanisms.
(D) They grow at a normal rate.

03 Which of the following best fits in ① and ②?
   (A) autonomous — progeny
   (B) ancillary — offspring
   (C) viscous — ascendant
   (D) disobedient — ancestor

04 Which of the following best fits in ⓐ and ⓑ?
   (A) because — for example
   (B) in that — that is
   (C) when it comes to — on the contrary
   (D) unless — that is to say

Natural selection describes the biological process in which the differences of individuals within a population influence their abilities to survive and reproduce in an environment. The difference in individuals is a result of their genetic inheritance from their parents. In a population, any characteristic which blocks reproduction success tends to decrease generation by generation. In time, the ill-adapted die out. On the other hand, the individuals who do survive and reproduce will tend to produce offspring which are better adapted to the environment. Natural selection tends to promote adaptations that will increase the organism's ability to survive in an environment.

Natural selection can serve to stabilize a population if the new traits, called mutations, are eliminated when they appear because they are not as well-adapted to the environment. The opposite effect is obtained when a new trait is introduced which allows individuals to adapt better. Over time, the species will change as this mutation becomes more widespread in the population. In human beings, increased brain size helped individuals to adapt better, and so brain size increased gradually in the species. Changes in the overall genetic makeup of a population are normal when there are environmental changes, especially severe environmental disruptions. Specialized adaptations to specific environments can lead, over time, to the development of subpopulations of individuals, ones who are better adapted to particular soil conditions, food sources and so on. Given enough time, these subpopulations may develop into separate species, such as zebras and horse, living in distinct environments and not interbreeding.

01 Individuals in a population differ from one another because _____.
(A) they have different success generation by generation
(B) they are ill-adapted and eventually die out
(C) they have different genetic inheritance
(D) they want to survive and reproduce successfully

02 Which of the following is NOT true about natural selection?
(A) Natural selection favors adaptions that help a species to survive.
(B) Natural selection works against extreme changes in a species.
(C) Natural selection allows helpful new traits to spread through a population.
(D) Natural selection occurs in periods of severe environmental disturbances.

03 On the basis of the passage, it would be most reasonable to infer that _____.

(A) the ancestors of horses and zebras were once members of the same species
(B) the greatest biological change occurs in stable environments
(C) individuals mutate when they need to adapt to a new environment
(D) we can control population size by adapting new traits

04 The topic of this passage would be _____.

(A) why natural selection leads to population increase over generations
(B) how natural selection maintains and changes the makeup of a population
(C) why natural selection created the large brain size in human beings
(D) how natural selection promotes individuals who care for their offspring

Parents try it often: more pocket money for good behavior, less for bad. Now the British government wants to introduce a similar scheme for the nation's teenagers. From 2008, it proposes that everyone aged between 13 and 19 should have an Opportunity Card, loaded with £12 ($21) worth of credits. Those from poor backgrounds and engaged in useful activity (such as voluntary work, or attending school regularly) will get more credits, perhaps another £12 per month. Those who misbehave (through truancy, vandalism and the like) will get fewer, or none. The credits will be ① _____ for sessions at sports centers, dancing lessons and other worthy pastimes.

This is a prime example of the government's favorite approach to public policy: interventionist, but delivered through a market mechanism. It sounds tempting, benefiting both the participants and, by keeping them out of trouble, everyone else too. The government cites academic research that shows a correlation between inactivity and misbehavior. Healthy hobbies such as sport, art and music, by contrast, give young people a sense of purpose.

But there are flaws. If the incentive for good deeds mutates into a mere "payment," it risks blunting goodwill. To link so tightly doing good to immediate material reward can end up ② _____ community spirit. As many parents find out, a child paid for being tidy soon learns to expect to be paid for other things, too. And bribing young people into education seems odd. Attending classes should be desirable for its own sake (and millions of young people in poorer countries than Britain make big sacrifices in order to do so). If British education is so unattractive then perhaps the supply side, rather than the demand, needs attention.

01 Which of the following set of words best fits both blanks ① and ②?
(A) converted — boosting
(B) redeemable — corroding
(C) cashed in — penalizing
(D) retrieved — eroding

02 Which of the following best describes the author's attitude toward the British government's scheme?
(A) neutral
(B) subjective
(C) critical
(D) approved

03 What does this passage mainly discuss?

(A) A new plan for the British teenagers
(B) How to save credits in an Opportunity Card
(C) The incentive for good deeds
(D) A matter of education in England

04 Which of the following CANNOT be inferred from the passage?

(A) Students can use credits for enjoying their healthy hobbies.
(B) The credits will be exchanged for a particular sum of money for sessions at gym.
(C) Teenagers can get their credits in accordance with their behavior.
(D) Backward country students will depend on their Opportunity Card issued by their government.

Abd Allah bin Hamad al-Attiyah, Qatari energy minister, voiced support for OPEC kingpin Saudi Arabia's call for an increase of 1.5 million barrels per day of the production ceiling of the organization. "I think this is a good indication that OPEC is doing its best to check the rise in oil prices," the minister said. Oil prices have risen sharply recently and on Friday, a barrel was selling at an all-time high of $41.56 in New York.

Attiyah, however, said the high prices were caused by political fears and not a shortage on the market. "The fear factor is adding $8 to prices," he said. "I checked with all our end users and asked one question: do you feel there is a shortage of oil? Their answer is no." Analysts have listed security fears over terrorist attacks in Iraq and Saudi Arabia as the main reasons for the price hike.

Attiyah said the Organisation for Petroleum Exporting Countries was already producing more than 1.5 million barrels per day above its official ceiling of 23.5 million barrels per day. But he refused to put a figure on OPEC's likely increase in production if the organization agrees on it at its meeting in Amsterdam or in Beirut.

01 What does the passage primarily discuss?
(A) the cause of recent price hike and OPEC's response
(B) the fear factors concerning oil price
(C) the roles of OPEC in affecting oil price
(D) OPEC's next meeting place

02 The underlined word "kingpin" is closest in meaning to _____.
(A) leader
(B) regime
(C) monarchy
(D) subordinate

03 To check the rise in oil prices, how much oil increase is needed?
(A) 1.5 million barrels per day
(B) 23.5 million barrels per day
(C) 25 million barrels per day
(D) Heaven knows

04 The underlined word "ceiling" is closest in meaning to _____.
(A) cover
(B) altitude
(C) top limit
(D) canopy

PASSAGE

201 — 250

There is a limit to how small an animal's body can be. Many of the constraints derive from the fact that for any given shape, the ratio of surface area to volume increases with decreasing size. This is a major issue for warm-blooded birds and mammals; the smaller they get, the faster they lose heat, so they have to generate heat faster to compensate. Minute birds and mammals push their metabolism to the absolute limits. The classic evidence of this size limitation is in the smallest shrews, where they are constantly eating to renew the energy that is being rapidly lost through their skin. This is why the smallest recorded bird, the 30mm-long bee hummingbird of Cuba and the smallest known mammal, the 40mm Etruscan pygmy shrew found across Europe, north Africa and Southeast Asia are much larger than the smallest known reptile, a dwarf gecko from the Caribbean that measures just 14mm from snout to anus. But while heat loss isn't an issue for cold-blooded creatures, water loss is. This is a special problem for amphibians. If a tiny frog gets out into dry air it could dry out in a matter of minutes. Fish would appear to have things easier. Being cold-blooded and aquatic, heat loss and desiccation are not a problem. There are other constraints that kick in at such sizes, though. Losing a few bones here or there might not make much difference to a very small animal, but all its parts still have to work. And there are fundamental limits on how far organs can be scaled down. One is that organs are made of cells, a certain number of which are needed to make complex organs like brains and eyes. The upshot is that an organ in a small animal is usually _____ its size than in a big animal.

01 Choose the one that best fills in the blank.
(A) smaller relative to
(B) larger relative to
(C) smaller regardless of
(D) larger regardless of

02 According to the passage, what does not influence an animal's body size?
(A) the time of the day the animal is active
(B) the ability to regulate body temperature
(C) the class which the animal belongs to
(D) the number of cells needed for organs

03 Which of the following can be inferred from the passage?

(A) Their volume being equal, a short animal loses heat faster than a long one.
(B) The smaller an animal's size is, the slower metabolism it should have.
(C) The frog is a cold-blooded animal which belongs to the amphibian class.
(D) The brains and the eyes of animals are made of the same number of cells.

04 What is the tone of the passage?

(A) admonitory   (B) introspective
(C) exclamatory   (D) descriptive

Muzafer Sharif performed some very interesting experiments with a group of 11-year-old boys to demonstrate group loyalty. The boys were fairly homogeneous in background and were total strangers to each other at the beginning of the experiment. The boys went to a summer camp under Sharif's supervision to take part in the project.

As is the norm, the boys quickly formed friendship groups spontaneously. Sharif then randomly divided the boys into large two groups and had them live relatively far from each other. The objective was to break the bonds the boys had established. The boys soon established new ties within the new groups. Sharif then had the groups compete against each other in sports and games. The boys were cooperative within their groups and hostile to the other group, which included, of course, some of their former friends. To culminate the experiment, Sharif created an emergency situation: the cutting ①_____ of the water supply. The groups were obliged to work together, and the situation was particularly successful in making the boys forget their recently acquired hatred for each other. Boys who were banished ②_____ a group were suddenly welcomed by it. Sharif's experiment gave him the opportunity to assess the dominion of situation over other elements which may also contribute to the formation of group boundaries. While it is impossible to quantify its influence, it would be utter stupidity to state that ③_____.

01 The best title of the above passage is _____.
(A) Situational Ethics
(B) Types of Behavioristic Experiments
(C) Effects of Situation on Group Dynamics
(D) Growing Peer Pressure among Boy Groups

02 Which would be most appropriate for the blanks ① and ②?
(A) in — toward
(B) by — with
(C) on — as
(D) off — from

03 Which would be most appropriate for the blank ③?
(A) all work and no play makes Jack a dull boy
(B) boys are apt to break the bonds they establish among themselves
(C) spontaneous friendship depends on individual differences in personality
(D) situation has little to do with group dynamics

04 Which of the following statements corresponds to the above passage?

(A) Mr. Sharif used to be a boy scout advisor.
(B) The boys did not cooperate with Mr. Sharif.
(C) The boys seem to adjust well to varying circumstances.
(D) Mr. Sharif had the boys enjoy playing some weird psychological games.

The recently identified planet, Gliese 581c, is the right distance from its sun to be capable of harboring liquid water, and may be the best hope yet for alien hunters. The Swiss team from the Geneva Observatory has concluded that small Earth-like planets are probably common. So is life also common among the stars? And should it matter to us?

Since the dawn of civilization, the status of the heavens has been central to man's concept of his place in the universe. The medieval "world" or cosmos consisted of a spherical Earth cocooned within a series of concentric spheres carrying the moon, the planets, the sun and, furthest away, the stars pinned on to the outermost firmament. Beyond that was God. The starry spheres had been invented to account for the nocturnal revolutions of the night sky. This was a cosy walled-in world with mankind occupying the centre. But then _____ when his solar system with the Sun at its centre allowed the Earth to spin and orbit the sun. If, as Copernicus argued, the Earth rotated rather than the stars, there was no need for all those spheres. Few would now defend an Earth-centered universe but, to many, mankind remains the central concern of the God. This would be harder to maintain if Gliese 581c and other worlds are teeming with life. But it would make the universe a more exciting place to live in.

01   Which is closest in meaning to the underlined word "cocooned"?
(A) damaged   (B) protected
(C) separated   (D) followed

02   Which of the following is NOT true according to the passage?
(A) The medieval Earth was believed to be surrounded by spheres.
(B) God was believed to exist beyond the starry spheres in the medieval universe.
(C) The Earth, within its spheres, circles the Sun according to Copernican theory.
(D) The Sun stays in the centre according to Copernican theory.

03   Which of the following is most suitable for the blank?
(A) Copernicus turned the medieval universe upside down
(B) Copernicus scientifically proved the medieval belief
(C) the existence of God was questioned among scientists
(D) Copernicus's theory strengthened the medieval belief

04 Which of the following best describes the author's attitude toward extraterrestrial life?
(A) doubtful
(B) assured
(C) hopeful
(D) reserved

204

As consumers hunker down to cope with hard economic times, an environmental group has offered a suggestion: ①_____. The Environmental Working Group released a report that charged that some bottled waters were "no different than tap water." And it found fertilizer residue, pain medication and other chemicals in some major brands.

While a lot of bottled water may be as pure as promised in those alluring commercials, the real problem is telling which is which. Public water supplies are regulated by the federal government. Not so for bottled water. The International Bottled Water Association, which represents most of the industry, has voluntary standards to make sure there are no contaminants. The association encourages (but does not require) bottlers to release pertinent information about what's in their water when consumers call and ask.

The federal government requires all public water works to tell consumers once a year what is in their water and whether it meets federal standards. Those public reports are not always as helpful as they should be. ②Some are printed in ant-size type and best understood by chemists. But at least they are readily available, and the same detail should be publicly available for bottled water. For the extra cost and the promise of added purity, that bottled water should be as good or even better than the less-expensive stuff that comes out of a tap. And consumers should be able to see certified data that prove it.

---

01 Which of the following is the purpose of the passage?
(A) to inform customers what kinds of contaminants are in the bottled water
(B) to criticize the International Bottled Water Association for releasing confidential information
(C) to recommend the best way to choose the bottled water which is pure
(D) to argue that information about the purity of bottled water should be provided

02 Which of the following is CANNOT be inferred from the passage?
   (A) Some famous bottled waters include material unsuitable for drinking.
   (B) The advertisements promise that the bottled water is clean.
   (C) Every water service must be monopolized by the federal government.
   (D) Giving information to customers is not compulsory for bottlers.

03 Which of the following is most suitable for the blank ①?
   (A) Stop using tap water provided by public water services
   (B) Buy cheaper bottled water instead of major brands
   (C) Get your water from the faucet not a bottle
   (D) Be careful when you choose the bottled water

04 Underlined expression ②"Some are printed in ant-size type and best understood by chemists" implies that some public reports on water are _____.
   (A) not abstruse for ordinary people
   (B) too difficult for mediocrities to comprehend
   (C) written by chemists for academic purpose
   (D) not accessible for people who are not chemists

205

I was playing in a company softball game in New York's Central Park, on one of those few brilliant blue evenings that make the city temporarily seem like a livable place in the summer. I had been stationed deep in right field, so naturally my thoughts began to migrate to subjects other than the game before me. I watched the tall trees sway in the breeze, and was instantly gripped by dread. The disaster is coming and it is all the fault of the trees, which kill everything in sight. For this, like much else, I blame M. Night Shyamalan. Those who have seen his most recent film, *The Happening*, know why — it is a paranoid thriller about a family on the run from a natural crisis that presents a large-scale threat to humanity.

It's not just my cinematic diet that tends to turn my thoughts dark. Environmental reporting will give you ①_____. There are the melting Arctic ice and rising sea levels, torched rainforests, polluted Chinese megalopolises, and animals going extinct up to 10,000 times faster than the rate believed over the past 60 million years. When we talk about climate change, we are not just talking about rising temperatures or altered landscapes. [Ⅰ] We are talking about the end of human civilization as we know it: we fear that we may be creating the conditions for our own end through day-to-day consumerist lives. [Ⅱ] Global warming is very scary because once it truly gets started, we may in the end be helpless to stop it. [Ⅲ] However, fear has never been a very good motivator, especially not for the decades-long societal changes we will need to make to slow climate change. [Ⅳ] What we need is positivity: a low-carbon world will bring benefits that go well beyond simple survival, and that is a message that needs to be heard.

01 The first paragraph is introduced as the example of _____.
(A) personal fear of the possible end of the world
(B) criticism of the urgent environmental situation
(C) an analysis of an immediate environmental risk
(D) an unquestioning acceptance of the story in a movie

02 Which of the following is most suitable for the blank ①?
(A) acute judgements
(B) an emotional inertia
(C) all-or-nothing mentality
(D) an apocalyptic mind-set

03 Where would the following sentence best fit into?

Put it simply, we are all digging our own graves, with every mile driven and every last bit of air conditioning.

(A) [I]   (B) [II]
(C) [III]   (D) [IV]

04 Which of the following best describes the opinion of the author?

(A) Everyone believes easily whatever they fear.
(B) Fears are based on illusion and future thinking.
(C) We should not let fears stand in the way of hope.
(D) We should realize that most of the world crises presented are exaggerated.

It is widely regarded as one of the wonders of the world, attracting millions of tourists a year, but the city of Venice faces ongoing problems that threaten its ability to stay above water. The city's flooding issues are well known: Each year water surges through its famous streets ①wreaking havoc on historic buildings, often damaging priceless art. But Venice also faces the problem of a dwindling population and an increasing influx of tourists that locals claim it is incapable of keeping up with. [I] Venice in Peril says that up to 60,000 tourists can enter into the city in any given day — doubling the population. [II] "There are no more people, there is no more culture, there is no Venetian way of life, and the city is every day more like a museum." said Matteo Secchi, spokesman for local protest group. Secchi and his followers are fighting to maintain Venice's population, which has dropped dramatically since 1951 when it was just under 175,000. [III] In 2009, when the population was estimated to have fallen below 60,000, Secchi and other locals staged a symbolic funeral procession for the city they felt had died. [IV] But Secchi doesn't blame the tourists; he is aware that the city needs them in order to survive. He and his supporters are lobbying Venice's Mayor, Giorgio Orsoni, to diversify the city's industry away from tourism so fewer residents will leave to take jobs on the mainland.

01 The following sentence could be added to the passage. Find the most appropriate place.

Those numbers can swell further during big cultural events like the biennale and city's famous film festival.

(A) [I] (B) [II]
(C) [III] (D) [IV]

02 Which of the following is NOT true according to the passage?

(A) Some Venetians have held a mock funeral for the slow death of Venice.
(B) The growing number of visitors has outnumbered the declining resident population.
(C) Venice's heavy reliance on tourism has made job-seekers head for the mainland.
(D) The finger of blame should be pointed at travelers for Venice in jeopardy.

03 Which of the following is the best title for the passage?

(A) The World's Best Veniceland Theme Park
(B) Campaign for Preserving Venice's Cultural Heritage
(C) Battling to Keep the Real Venice Afloat
(D) Sinking Venice with Rising Water Levels

04 Which of the following is closest in meaning to ①?

(A) ravaging (B) fortifying
(C) restoring (D) preserving

Once upon a time, we lived in a broadcast society, one in which the few transmitted information to the many. That information was controlled by gatekeepers — radio stations, newspapers, TV networks — that decided what we did and what we did not see, read or hear. There was the mainstream and there was no stream. ㉮ But then the World Wide Web came along and blew the gatekeepers away. Suddenly anyone with a computer and an Internet connection could take part in the conversation. Countless viewpoints ①_____. There was no longer a mainstream; instead, there was an ocean of information, one in which Web users were free to swim. ㉯ It's a wonderful idea. Except, as Eli Pariser argues in his new book *The Filter Bubble*(Penguin), it's no longer true. ㉰ Invisibly over the past few years, the major social networks and search engines, led by the behemoths Facebook and Google, have begun ②_____ their results to the individual Web user. ㉱ It's called personalization, and on the surface, it sounds like a good thing. Where once Google delivered search results based on an algorithm that was identical for everyone, now what we see when we enter a term in the big box depends on who we are, where we are and what we are. Facebook has long since done the same thing for its all-important News Feed: you'll see different status updates and stories float to the top based on the data Mark Zuckerberg and company have on you.

01 When the above passage can be divided into two paragraphs, which would be the best boundary?

(A) ㉮
(B) ㉯
(C) ㉰
(D) ㉱

02 According to the passage, which aspect is associated with customized search?

(A) It limits result diversity and possibly narrows users' perspective.
(B) It enables Web users to resist an advanced new form of gatekeepers.
(C) It makes other conventional broadcast media less competitive.
(D) It provides free and full access to all available information.

03 Which one is most appropriate for the blanks ① and ②?
(A) flourished — releasing
(B) dwindled — manipulating
(C) shriveled — concealing
(D) bloomed — tailoring

04 The paragraph following the passage would most likely deal with _____.
(A) some benefits of user profiling for target marketing
(B) structural problems of giant social networking sites
(C) negative consequences of an information filtering system
(D) the necessity to enforce privacy and data protection laws

Romantic art in England reached its greatest achievement in landscape painting. John Crome set the stage for the English style with his emphasis on light and air. The two most famous English landscape painters of this period, however, were John Constable and J. M. Turner. They were masters in portraying the "vaporous" English atmosphere. Constable's colors are rich and deep. He was the first to paint with daubs of broken color. This technique gave his paintings a unique brilliance. Delacroix greatly admired this technique, and it was later used by the French Impressionist painters to create similar effects. Although he is best known for his use of color, Constable is also highly regarded for his knowledge of form and structure. Turner studied many old masters of landscape painting. Perhaps his greatest influence came from the 17th century French landscape painter, Claude Lorrain. He often painted cool, luminous skies, which impressed Turner. Turner intensified the skies into a dramatic fever of light and color which spread throughout the entire painting. In Turner's paintings, "vaporous" clouds, water and colored light in swirling movement became symbols of the great forces of nature.

01 Which painter was the founder of the English style of Romantic landscape painting?
(A) Turner
(B) Crome
(C) Delacroix
(D) Constable

02 What characteristic of Constable's work had the greatest influence on later painters?
(A) his rich, deep colors
(B) his cool, luminous skies
(C) his daubs of broken color
(D) his knowledge of form and structure

03 The best meaning for the underlined word "vaporous" is _____.
(A) shiny
(B) misty
(C) decent
(D) depressing

04 Which of the following descriptions about J. M. Turner's paintings is appropriate?
(A) They are cool and luminous.
(B) The colors are rich and deep.
(C) They are similar to older styles of painting.
(D) They suggest motion and power.

The ①deadly tornadoes and rainstorms that tore across the Midwest last month combined with melting snow have left the Mississippi River ②bursting at the seams. Amidst the evacuations and extensive flooding along the river, experts know records are being broken, but they say they won't know the full extent of the flood — such as how much water has actually _____ the riverbanks — until things quiet down.

"We get rain across the Mississippi River basin all the time, and if it is spread out in time it will not cause a problem," said Tom Salem, science and operations officer at the National Weather Service in Memphis, Tenn. "It is when it comes at the same time and multiple rivers add to the total of the entire system ③that we have problems."

Some areas along the Mississippi River have seen 10 to 20 inches (25.4 to 50.8 centimeters) of rain during April, said Royce Fontenot, a hydrologist at the National Weather Service. While the river levels are currently reaching record levels, the extent of the damage won't be known until after the flooding stops, ④where could be well into June, Fontenot said. We don't know how much water has been overflowed onto land from the Mississippi River. This is not something we can get in real time; we'll need to survey the area after the fact.

01 Which statement can be inferred from the passage?
    (A) The Mississippi River has been constantly causing trouble to river towns.
    (B) Low-lying residents are charged premiums to construct a recovery system.
    (C) People in the potential flood zone are likely to make evacuation plans.
    (D) Inundation of the Mississippi River will rank as world's costliest disaster.

02 Which of the following is grammatically incorrect.
    (A) ① deadly   (B) ② bursting
    (C) ③ that   (D) ④ where

03 Flood in the Mississippi River is caused by _____ of rainfall.
    (A) unpredictability   (B) concentration
    (C) components   (D) abundance

04 Choose the one that best fills in the blank.
    (A) breached   (B) reinforced
    (C) transformed   (D) contaminated

The message began as ①_____ as thousands of other singles ads that are routinely posted on the Internet in Japan. "Seeking companion," wrote the lonely male undergrad student from Tokyo. He wasn't looking for his dream date. "I have everything prepared except sleeping pills," the posting concluded. Two weeks later, on May 21, the college student was found dead in a car on a road running through a Gunma Prefecture forest. With him were the bodies of two other young men who, after evidently answering his online invitation, committed ㉮collective suicide by carbon monoxide poisoning.

Many of the 30,000 Japanese who kill themselves every year no longer fit the stereotype of the jobless, middle-aged salaryman. Suicides are on the rise among young men and women and with the shift in demographics comes ㉯a new style of self destruction. Youth are using a bizarre Internet aberration — the suicide site — to hook up with desperate soulmates willing ㉰to share their bleak journey. In February, two women and a man, all in their 20s, met on a suicide site and killed themselves in a Saitama apartment. Since then there have been seven similar incidents and 14 deaths.

The website where the Saitama victims met — Shinju Keijiban (Suicide Pact bulletin board service) — has closed, but many other remain. "The method used by youths to construct human relationships has changed," says Takehiko Kikkawa, a psychiatry professor at Chubu Gakuin University — even in cases where the relationship is necessarily short-lived. Some victims never even meet face to face until the fateful day. Nevertheless, they all share ㉱a powerful bond: the fear of dying alone.

01 위 글의 제목으로 가장 적절한 것을 고르시오.
(A) The Influence of Internet on Youth
(B) The Internet Way of Death
(C) The Ways of Handling Fear of Death
(D) The Love Affairs Leading to Suicide

02 다음 중 빈칸 ①에 들어가기에 가장 적절한 것을 고르시오.
(A) indifferently   (B) inquisitively
(C) innocently   (D) incredulously

03 밑줄 친 ㉮, ㉯, ㉰, ㉱ 중 가리키는 내용이 나머지 셋과 다른 것을 고르시오.
(A) ㉮   (B) ㉯
(C) ㉰   (D) ㉱

04 다음 중 위 글에서 추론할 수 있는 내용이 <u>아닌</u> 것을 고르시오.

(A) Many singles are using the Internet to find their fit mates.
(B) Collective suicides are usually committed by those who know each other.
(C) Sleeping pills can be used as a means of suicide.
(D) Even though there are many illegal, harmful websites, it is not easy to eliminate them all.

211

The whole process of being exposed to society — and of absorbing that experience — is called "acculturation." Of course, the acculturation of any particular person is profoundly affected by their family's socioeconomic class, religious beliefs, political views, and other factors, but probably the greatest shaper of beliefs in modern times — and hardly a positive one at that — is television. By the time the average American graduates from high school, he or she will have spent 11,000 hours in school but more than 22,000 hours watching television. Television has a negative effect on viewers, especially young viewers, in a number of ways. First, by placing them in the role of spectators, TV encourages inactivity; it implies that satisfaction and amusement are to be had simply by passively receiving. Second, by bombarding young people with advertising — an estimated average of 750,000 ads by the age of eighteen — TV viewing tends to promote uncritical acceptance of consumer values: it promotes self-indulgence, impulsiveness, and the pursuit of instant gratification. Third, by building frequent scene shifts and advertisement breaks into programs, television prevents the development of young people's attention spans. Finally, by presenting talk show hosts and other figures of popular culture as authorities, television undermines the ability of people to distinguish between legitimate experts and mere media figures.

---

01 According to the passage, "acculturation" refers to _____.

(A) whether a person accepts culture
(B) how a person absorbs culture
(C) the ways in which a person views culture
(D) the manner in which a person approaches culture

02 Which of the following is NOT mentioned as a negative effect of television?
   (A) overexposure to advertising
   (B) underdeveloped attention span
   (C) rejection of moral authority
   (D) uncritical adoption of consumer values

03 Which of the following best describes the author's tone in this passage?
   (A) argumentative
   (B) complimentary
   (C) ironic
   (D) neutral

04 With which of the following statements would the author most likely agree?
   (A) American schools do a poor job of educating their students.
   (B) Television stations should not show advertisements.
   (C) American students should watch TV less and study more.
   (D) Family values are the most important influence on young people.

Although "lie detectors" are being used by governments, police departments, and businesses that all want guaranteed ways of detecting the truth, the results are not always accurate. Lie detectors are properly called emotion detectors, for their aim is to measure bodily changes that contradict what a person says. The polygraph machine records changes in heart rate, breathing, blood pressure, and the electrical activity of the skin(galvanic skin response, or GSR). In the first part of the polygraph test, you are electronically connected to the machine and asked a few neutral questions ("What is your name?" "Where do you live?"). Your physical reactions serve as the standard for evaluating what comes next. Then you are asked a few critical questions among the neutral ones ("When did you rob the bank?"). The assumption is that if you are guilty, your body will reveal the truth, even if you try to deny it. Your heart rate, respiration, and GSR will change abruptly as you respond to the incriminating questions.

That is the theory; but psychologists have found that lie detectors are simply not reliable. Since most physical changes are the same across the emotions, machines cannot tell whether you are feeling guilty, angry, nervous, thrilled, or activated from an exciting day. Innocent people may be tense and nervous about the whole procedure. They may react physiologically to a certain word("bank") not because they robbed it, but because they recently bounced a check. In either case, the machine will record a "lie." The reverse mistake is also common. Some practiced liars can lie without flinching, and others learn to beat the machine by tensing muscles or thinking about an exciting experience during neutral questions.

01 It can be concluded from the passage that a polygraph test _____.

(A) is the best way to determine a person's guilt
(B) can read a person's thoughts
(C) works in principle but not in practice
(D) is the only evidence needed in a court of law

02 Why did the author write the passage?

(A) To illustrate how a lie detector works
(B) To criticize the use of the lie detector
(C) To explain how innocent people are found guilty
(D) To propose ways of using a lie detector

03 The author would most probably agree with which of the following statements?

(A) Polygraphs have no place in our society.
(B) Physical reactions are not connected to thoughts.
(C) Machines are no match for psychologists.
(D) Polygraph tests should not be used as the sole evidence of guilt.

04 Which of the following statements best describes the organization of the last paragraph?

(A) Several generalizations are made from which several conclusions are drawn.
(B) A general concept is defined and examples are given.
(C) Suggestions for the use of lie detectors are given.
(D) Persuasive language is used to argue against a popular idea.

David Vanegas gravitated to large lecture classes where he wouldn't stand out. At mealtimes, he never seemed to have his ID card handy and relied on friends to let him into the dining hall. In the evenings, he persuaded students to let him stay overnight in their dorm rooms. But his schoolmates began to notice odd things about him, like he never seemed to have any homework. Then in September of his second year at Rice University, one friend discovered that Vanegas had used someone else's e-mail address to create his student Facebook page and challenged Vanegas to prove he was a student. He couldn't.

Student impostors are rare, but they have popped up in recent years at universities across the United States, including Princeton, Yale and USC. Whatever their motives, impostors like Vanegas exploit the open atmosphere of college, where young students, living on their own for the first time, are surrounded by new faces. In the dorms, overnight guests are common. On occasion, students who flunk out remain on campus for fear of returning home. But to pose as a student for months or years requires a special talent for deceit — and good fortune.

"Vanegas, who comes from a poor family, meant no harm." Enrique Gomez, Vanegas's lawyer said. "He just wanted his mother to be proud, and he socialized with the people at Rice," Gomez said. "Maybe he used poor judgment, but there was no _____."

01 Which of the following is the purpose of this passage?
    (A) to defend the right of people to learn
    (B) to warn against people pretending to be students
    (C) to report a man had turned out to be a fake student
    (D) to explain reasons a man had to deceive others

02 Which of the following cannot be inferred from the passage?
    (A) Vanegas tried to attend big classes not to be recognized.
    (B) Vanegas's friends had helped him out when he asked for help.
    (C) The friend of Vanegas who accused of him had been having a bad relationship with Vanegas.
    (D) The students living in the dorms have considerable freedom.

03 The underlined "popped up" could be best replaced by _____.
    (A) decreased unexpectedly
    (B) threatened seriously
    (C) escaped hastily
    (D) appeared suddenly

04 Which of the following is best suitable for the blank?
    (A) ill intent
    (B) alleged fraud
    (C) poor background
    (D) conclusive evidence

The new research by the University of East Anglia will challenge existing views of how and why civilization arose. Civilization was in large part an accidental by-product of unplanned adaptation to catastrophic climate change. ①Civilization was a last resort — a means of organizing society and food production and distribution, in the face of deteriorating environmental conditions. For many, if not most people, the development of civilization meant a harder life, less freedom, and more inequality. The transition to urban living meant that most people had to work harder in order to survive, and suffered increased exposure to communicable diseases. Health and nutrition are likely to have deteriorated rather than improved for many. The research also has profound philosophical implications because it challenges deeply held beliefs about human progress, the nature of civilization and the origins of political and religious systems that have persisted to this day. It suggests that civilization is not our natural state, but the unintended consequence of adaptation to climatic deterioration — a condition of humanity "in extremis". People found themselves faced with increased social inequality, greater violence in the form of organized conflict, and at the mercy of self-appointed elites who used religious authority and political ideology to bolster their position. ②These models of government are still with us today, and we may understand them better by understanding how civilization arose by accident as a result of the last great global climatic upheaval.

01 Which of the following is the main idea of the passage?
(A) Human intelligence is the main factor for the development of civilization.
(B) Severe climate change was the primary influence in the development of civilization.
(C) New research should be conducted to offer evidence against the conventional theory.
(D) Civilization contributes positively to modern society.

02 Which of the following does "①Civilization was a last resort" imply?
(A) Human beings had no choice but to develop civilization in the end.
(B) It took a long time for people to develop civilization.
(C) Otherwise civilization would have been easily developed.
(D) Civilization is one of the greatest achievements that humans have attained.

03 Which of the following is most likely to belong to "②These models of government"?
(A) revolution
(B) enthusiasm
(C) injustice
(D) superstition

04   Which of the following is NOT true according to the passage?

(A) Human beings did not plan to develop civilization.
(B) The change in lifestyle due to civilization led to a better quality of life.
(C) The new research influences philosophical ideas too.
(D) Insights into the origin of civilization can help us comprehend modern systems of government.

When the Amazon was aflame and the forests of Southeast Asia were being systematically clear-cut, biologists were clear about what posed the greatest threat to the world's wildlife, and it wasn't men with guns. For decades, the chief threat was ①_____. Whether it was from destitute locals burning a forest to raise cattle or a multinational destroying a tree-covered Malaysian hillside, wildlife was dying because species were being driven from their homes. However, that has changed. The problem now is that hunting. That threat has been escalating over the past decade largely because the opening of forests to logging and mining means that roads connect once impenetrable places to towns. It's easier to get to where the wildlife is and then to have access to markets. Economic forces are also at play. Thanks to globalization, meat, fur, skins and other animal parts are sold on an increasingly massive scale across the world. ②Smoked monkey carcasses travel from Ghana to New York and London, while gourmets in Hanoi and Guangzhou feast on turtles and pangolins (scaly anteaters) from Indonesia. Eating bushmeat is now a status symbol. Half of the major protected areas in Southeast Asia have lost at least one species of large mammal due to hunting, and most have lost many more. At the end of the week, UNESCO announced that it was sending a team to investigate the slaughter.

01 Which of the following does the passage mainly discuss?
(A) why bushmeat is popular
(B) ways to protect wildlife in danger
(C) what endangers wildlife
(D) how to search for rare animals

02 Which of the following is most suitable for the blank ①?
(A) a forest fire
(B) tourist industry
(C) habitat destruction
(D) environmental pollution

03 Which of the following can be inferred from the passage?
(A) Hunting animals in Southeast Asia is legal.
(B) Logging and mining in the forest have helped people gain access to wildlife.
(C) Bushmeat turned out to be a healthy food.
(D) UNESCO was sending a team to find out who eats bushmeat.

04 The fact that ②Smoked monkey carcasses travel from Ghana to New York and London, while gourmets in Hanoi and Guangzhou feast on turtles and pangolins (scaly anteaters) from Indonesia is quoted as a proof that _____.

(A) the number of wildlife has increased slowly
(B) the distribution of bushmeat is widespread
(C) hunting techniques have improved greatly
(D) eating bushmeat is limited to local people in Southeast Asia

Remember Thomas Friedman's McDonald's theory of international relations? The thinking was that if two countries had evolved into prosperous, mass-consumer societies, with middle classes able to afford Big Macs, they would generally find peaceful means of adjudicating disputes. ①They'd sit down over a Happy Meal to resolve issues rather than use mortars. The recent unpleasantries between Israel and Lebanon, which both have McDonald's operations, put an end to that reasoning. But the Golden Arches theory of realpolitick was good while it lasted.

②_____, I propose the Starbucks Theory of International Economics. The higher the concentration of expensive, nautical-themed faux-Italian branded frappuccino joints in a country's financial capital, the more likely the country is to have suffered catastrophic financial losses.

It may sound doppio, but work with me. This recent crisis has its roots in the unhappy coupling of a frenzied nationwide real-estate market, centered in California, Las Vegas and Florida, and a nationwide credit mania, centered in New York. If you could pick one brand name that personified these twin bubbles, it was Starbucks. The Seattle-based coffee chain followed new housing developments into the suburbs and exurbs, where its outlets became pitstops for real-estate brokers and their clients. It also carpet-bombed the business districts of large cities, especially the financial centers, with nearly 200 in Manhattan alone. Starbucks's frothy treats provided the fuel for the boom, the caffeine that enabled deal jockeys to stay up all hours putting together offering papers for Collateralized Debt Obligations, and helped mortgage brokers work overtime processing dubious loan documents.

01 Which of the following does the underlined sentence ① imply?
(A) The countries which have McDonald's stores are less likely to war with each other.
(B) Israel attacking Lebanon can be explained by the Golden Arches theory.
(C) McDonald's integrates into the world economy going to war with each other.
(D) People in countries with McDonald's franchises like to wait in line for burgers.

02 Which is most suitable for the blank ②?
(A) Consequently
(B) Randomly
(C) Similarly
(D) Presumably

03 According to the passage, it can be inferred that _____.
(A) McDonald's theory is profoundly linked to Starbucks theory
(B) countries without Starbucks are less likely to suffer from global economic downturn
(C) it is tough to find Starbucks in the disputed areas on the globe
(D) the economically mediocre countries have tons of Starbucks.

04 What is the main point of the passage?
(A) The more Starbucks a country has, the bigger its financial problems.
(B) Starbucks's frappuccino has an effect on mortgage brokers processing loan documents.
(C) Like the housing market, Starbucks has fallen gradually.
(D) The number of Starbucks doesn't have much to do with economic situation.

Being a leader is a good way to discover the validity of Murphy's law: "If anything can go wrong, it will." A leader is constantly required to solve numerous problems involving both people and things. Because of those problems and the difficulties attendant on solving them, many people find leadership positions enormously stressful. People in managerial positions also complain repeatedly that they are in charge of things over which they have little control. As a leader, for example, you might be expected to work with an ill-performing team member, yet you might not have the power to fire him or her. You might also be called on to produce a high-quality service or product but not be given the staff or the funds to get the job done effectively.

In addition, leadership limits the number of people in whom you can confide. It is awkward, not to mention unprofessional, to complain about one of your employees to another employee. Then, too, you need to be wary about voicing complaints against your superiors to the people who work for you. Such complaints are bad for morale. Even worse, they can threaten your job security. Not surprisingly, people in leadership positions complain that they miss being "one of the gang."

People at all levels of an organization, from the office assistant to the chairperson of the board, must be aware of political factors. Yet you can avoid politics more easily as an individual contributor than you can as a leader. As a leader you have to engage in political byplay from three directions: below, sideways, and upward. Political tactics such as forming alliances and coalitions are a necessary part of a leader's role.

---

01 What is similar in meaning to the underlined attendant on?

(A) stopping   (B) accompanying
(C) suggesting   (D) keeping

02 Which of the following is the purpose of the passage?

(A) to explain difficulties suffered by leaders
(B) to inform why leaders abandon their positions
(C) to argue that a leader should be respected
(D) to advise how to be recognized as a leader

03 Which of the following is NOT required to be a leader according to the passage?
(A) patience
(B) prudence
(C) indecision
(D) statesmanship

04 It can be inferred from the second paragraph that the higher you rise as a leader, the more _____ you are likely to be.
(A) biased
(B) solitary
(C) cowardly
(D) suspected

Historians often assume that they need pay no attention to human evolution because ①the process ground to a halt in the distant past. That assumption is looking less and less secure in light of new findings based on decoding human DNA. People have continued to evolve since leaving the ancestral homeland in northeastern Africa some 50,000 years ago, both through the random process known as genetic drift and through natural selection.

[I] In most cases, the source of selective pressure — forces acting on populations that determine that some individuals are more reproductively successful and contribute more genes to subsequent generations — is unknown. [II] However, researchers have found that people in the various continents adapted to pressures, such as new disease, changing climates, and altered diets. [III] Likewise, the genes under selective pressure found in one continent-based population or race are mostly different from those that occur in the others. [IV]

The emerging lists of the genetic changes may open new insights into the interactions between history and genetics. If we ask what are the most important evolutionary events of the last 5,000 years, they are cultural, like the spread of agriculture, which caused the changes in diets, or extinctions of populations through war or disease. These cultural events are likely to have left ②deep marks in the human genome.

01 Which of the following is the main idea of the passage?

(A) Human evolution influenced by cultural as well as environmental factors has continued.
(B) The major selective force on human evolution is the resistance to diseases.
(C) Human evolution will continue as long as there is a selective force.
(D) The evidence of human evolution has implications for how mankind survives.

02 What does the underlined sentence ① mean?

(A) The process has been in pause over the past few years.
(B) The process gradually came to a stop a long time ago.
(C) The process has not been fully studied since it started.
(D) The process suddenly accelerated with stunning speed at some point.

03 Where would the following sentence best fit into?

A striking feature of many of these changes is that they vary from place to place.

(A) [I] (B) [II]
(C) [III] (D) [IV]

04 What does the underlined ②deep marks refer to?

(A) genetic changes
(B) interactions
(C) new insights
(D) war or disease

The psychopath is one of the most fascinating and distressing problems of human experience. For the most part, psychopaths never remain attached to anyone or anything. They live a "predatory" lifestyle. They feel little or no regret, and little or no remorse — except when they are caught. They need relationships, but see people as obstacles to overcome and be eliminated. ①_____, they see people in terms of how they can be used. They use people for stimulation, to build their self-esteem and they invariably value people in terms of their material value (money, property, etc.).

A psychopath can have high verbal intelligence, but they typically lack "emotional intelligence". They can be expert in manipulating others by playing to their emotions. ②There is a shallow quality to the emotional aspect of their stories (i.e., how they felt or why they felt that way). The lack of emotional intelligence is the first good sign you may be dealing with a psychopath. A history of criminal behavior in which they do not seem to learn from their experience, but merely think about ways to not get caught is the second best sign.

01 Which of the following is true according to the passage?
(A) A psychopath feels attached to predators.
(B) A psychopath feels some regret when they are caught.
(C) A psychopath lacks verbal intelligence.
(D) A psychopath does not need any kind of relationship.

02 Which of the following is most suitable for the blank ①?
(A) Therefore
(B) Nevertheless
(C) Or
(D) For instance

03 Which of the following can be a sign of a psychopath according to the passage?
(A) A person has low verbal intelligence.
(B) A person is an incarnation of charity.
(C) A person has a sense of guilt.
(D) A person has low emotional intelligence.

04 Which of the following is the meaning of the underlined ②?

(A) A psychopath tells emotionally abundant stories.
(B) A psychopath's stories reflect their emotional vulgarity.
(C) A psychopath has a narrow range of emotions.
(D) A psychopath has difficulty controlling their emotions.

Prejudice may be defined as making negative prejudgments about other people or other groups. While in law a person is 'innocent until proven guilty', _____ as the individual who holds the prejudice believes them until they are proved false. Prejudice may be suppressed, but it may often come out in Ⓐunderlying attitudes, opinions and beliefs especially when under pressure. Our prejudices often stem from relying on our 'frame of reference' to fill in the gaps in our knowledge of other groups in society. This is called stereotyping and it can be about communities or individuals. Stereotyping is about making sweeping Ⓑgeneralizations about groups of people, where it is believed that just because people are members of a particular group or live in a particular community, they must, because of that fact, share particular traits which one thinks are characteristic of that group.

Gordon Allport identified five levels of prejudice. He related his scale particularly to the experience of the Jews in Nazi Germany. While this approach may be Ⓒresistant to criticism, it is still a useful tool to help understand the nature of prejudice against particular communities or individuals from within particular communities. The different scales of Allport's model are discussed below.

ⒹAnti-locution — Could be demonstrated by using phrases of color which equate whiteness with purity and blackness with bad or evil. Other examples include stereotypical language or ethnic jokes.

Avoidance — Quite simply this means to avoid another individual or group.

Discrimination — Means unequal treatment. This unequal treatment reinforces the power of the dominant group and disadvantages the minority group. Discrimination on the grounds of religion, gender, sexual orientation, disability and age is unlawful. The processes of discrimination can include denying employment or a less professional service delivered by a public body.

Physical attacks — These may range from attacks on the property of individuals to direct physical attacks.

ⒺExtermination — This is the ultimate violent expression of a prejudice. On an extreme level this could be demonstrated by the ethnic cleansing of a whole community.

01 밑줄 친 Ⓐ~Ⓔ 중 문맥상 낱말의 쓰임이 적절하지 않은 것은?
   (A) Ⓐ
   (B) Ⓑ
   (C) Ⓒ
   (D) Ⓓ
   (E) Ⓔ

02 빈칸에 들어갈 가장 적절한 것은?
   (A) people with guilt are less likely to commit crimes
   (B) prejudices tend to work in the opposite direction
   (C) the law of presumption of innocence has many legal problems
   (D) prejudice doesn't work for a prejudiced person
   (E) you should not have prejudice against crime

Since the dawn of time, a lot has been written about how our thoughts ultimately drive what we achieve. It is said that we need only believe without any doubt that our thoughts will come to fruition, and thus, they will. The difficult part is that we must believe without any doubt. Most times we will not know when nor how our thoughts will come to fruition. It requires a certain amount of faith that most of us just do not have.

It is the kind of faith held by the kid who uses a hairbrush as a mock microphone and pretends that she is a famous singer. She knows (not just believes) that she will surely become a famous singer. In fact, in her young mind, she is already a famous singer and it is only a matter of time before the rest of the world discovers her. It is the elementary school-aged boy who grew up to be an esteemed scientist because he knew that it was his ①_____. It is the golfer who focused on achieving and perhaps one day surpassing the accomplishments of his childhood golf idol to become one of the best golfers ever. It is the college-aged young woman who eventually led one of the world's largest, most successful publicly traded companies because she knew it was her ①_____.

What ②all of these individuals have in common is that they believed that it was only a matter of time before their dreams came true. In fact, they focused on a positive, immutable thought about their future self and this thought became an all-consuming part of what they thought about all day long.

01 Which of the following best fits in ①?
(A) specialty
(B) pipe dream
(C) destiny
(D) wishful thinking

02 Which of the following is NOT true about ②?
(A) They believed doubtlessly that their thoughts would become reality.
(B) They did not know whether they would succeed or fail in the future.
(C) They had a dream from an early age and focused on achieving that dream.
(D) They had a positive future self-image and continued thinking about it.

Kramer by no means invented the assumption that popular music is inherently lacking in long-range logical connection and is therefore lesser than classical music. Indeed, the assertion is an important one in a much earlier significant document arguing the assumed "high"/"low" split, Theodor W. Adorno's 1941 essay "On Popular Music." Adorno, like Kramer, is a master at constructing convincing arguments about musical phenomena. He is best understood as a social philosopher, but fully half of his writing are about music. For Adorno, music is tremendously fertile ground for thinking about and understanding society. In his view, the structure of a piece of music is inherently related to, and in a critical dialogue with the structure of the society in which the piece is created and functions. His perspective, which assumes that music is best understood not as art for art's sake but rather in a complex and potentially contradictory relationship with society, lies at the root of much study of popular music.

An infamous irony, though, is that Adorno's perspective on popular music is tremendously Ⓐ_____. Within the realm of classical music there is always much to criticize too, to be sure. Adorno's core belief is that society has become fundamentally broken and that from late Beethoven forward, good music would be music that, through its structure, would reflect this state of the world.

01 Which of the following CANNOT be inferred as Adorno's position?

(A) A symphony that exhibited coherence is an object for derision.
(B) The 20th century music should emphasize the primacy of rhythm of the mechanistic modern age.
(C) A music encompassing a sound true to contemporary society is a success.
(D) Standardized popular music which evokes old, familiar experience is to be disregarded.
(E) Music is an art; thus it should be rated as it is without any regard to society.

02 Which expression best fits Ⓐ?

(A) positivistic
(B) eclectic
(C) inhuman
(D) negative
(E) ahistorical

Symbiosis is the biological term used to describe two species which live together in a close, interdependent relationship. In a symbiotic relation, one member always benefits, but the second (called the host) may be harmed by, benefit from, or be unaffected by the association. The symbiotic relation is parasitic if one species injures the second. A parasite may destroy its host. An example is the hookworm which lives in the intestine of humans and other animals, stealing necessary food and nutrients from its host. The relationship is called commensalism if the host is not affected by the second species. An example is the tiny worm species that lives in the shell of the hermit crab with no ill-effects to its host. Many small plants and animals have a commensalistic relation with large-sized hosts, especially with trees, gaining protection and doing no damage. Mutualism is an interdependent relation that benefits both parties. For instance, all large ruminants (animals like cattle, goats, sheep, camels and such) have symbiotic bacteria in their intestines. These bacteria digest the plant matter ruminants eat and convert it into the vitamins and protein that the larger animals need to live. In mutualistic symbiosis, it is common for the host to be unable to digest certain materials without the help of the second species. Another kind of mutualistic relation is that of lichen. Lichen are actually partnerships. One partner is a fungus which provides water and the structure for the lichen. The other partner is algae, which uses the process of photosynthesis to make food that both organisms consume.

01 A symbiotic relation is commensalistic if _____.
(A) the second species doesn't destroy the host
(B) the second species gains protection from the host
(C) the host species does not benefit from the relation
(D) the host species is not changed by the relation

02 Which of the following is a characteristic of mutualism?
(A) The two species live independently of each other.
(B) One species helps the other to digest food.
(C) Each species provides something for the other's advantage.
(D) One species provides food, and the second gives protection.

03 Which of the following is the most reasonable statement?

(A) Cooperation is as common as competition between symbiotic species.

(B) Without bacteria, ruminants wouldn't have risen to their dominant position.

(C) The giant American forests couldn't live without small plants and animals.

(D) In symbiotic relations, it is always an advantage to be the smaller species.

04 Which of the following would make the best title for this passage?

(A) Types of Interdependent Species Relations

(B) How Species Provide Food for Other Species

(C) How the Small Defeat the Large

(D) The Need to Improve Relations between Species

Self-deception is the process of misleading ourselves to accept as true what is false. Self-deception, in short, is a way we justify false beliefs to ourselves. [I] To explain how self-deception works, philosophers and psychologists focus on self-interest, prejudice, desire, insecurity, and other psychological factors unconsciously affecting in a negative way the will to believe. [II] A common example would be that of parents who believe their child is telling the truth even though the objective evidence strongly supports the claim that the child is lying. [III] A belief so motivated is usually considered more flawed than one due to lack of ability to evaluate evidence properly. [IV] The former is considered to be a kind of moral flaw, a kind of dishonesty, and irrational. The latter is considered to be _____: some people are just not gifted enough to make proper inferences from the data of perception and experience.

However, it is possible that the parent in the above example believes the child because he or she has intimate and extensive experience with the child but not with the child's accusers. The parent may be unaffected by unconscious desires and be reasoning on the basis of what he or she knows about the child but does not know about the others involved. The parent may have very good reasons for trusting the child and not trusting the accusers. In short, an apparent act of self-deception may be explicable in purely cognitive terms without any reference to unconscious motivations or irrationality. The self-deception may be neither a moral nor an intellectual flaw. It may be the inevitable existential outcome of a basically honest and intelligent person who has extremely good knowledge of his or her child, knows that things are not always as they appear to be, has little or no knowledge of the child's accusers, and thus has not sufficient reason for doubting the child. It may be the case that an independent party could examine the situation and agree that the evidence is <u>overwhelming</u> that the child is lying, but if he or she were wrong we would say that he or she was mistaken, not self-deceived. We consider the parent to be self-deceived because we assume that he or she is not simply mistaken, but is being irrational. How can we be sure?

01 Where would the following sentence best fit into?

They, it is said, deceive themselves into believing the child because they desire that the child tell the truth.

(A) [I] (B) [II]
(C) [III] (D) [IV]

02 Which of the following is best suitable for the blank?

(A) free will (B) a matter of fate
(C) culture shock (D) moral hazard

03 Which of the following could best replace the underlined word "overwhelming"?

(A) detailed (B) inaccurate
(C) helpless (D) undeniable

04 Which of the following is most likely to follow the passage?

(A) the procedure of self-deception
(B) when children tell a lie to their parents
(C) how to develop skills in finding out if a child is lying
(D) the ways to see if parents are being illogical or not

Works of art are received and valued on different planes. Two polar types stand out; with one, the accent is on the cult value; with the other, on the exhibition value of the work. Artistic production begins with ceremonial objects destined to serve in a cult. One may assume that what mattered was their existence, not their being on view. The elk portrayed by the man of the Stone Age on the walls of his cave was an instrument of magic. He did expose it to his fellow men, but in the main it was meant for the spirits. Today the cult value would seem to demand that the work of art remain hidden. Certain statues of gods are accessible only to the priest in the cella; certain Madonnas remain covered nearly all year round; certain sculptures on medieval cathedrals are invisible to the spectator on ground level.

With the emancipation of the various art practices from ritual go increasing opportunities for the exhibition of their products. It is easier to exhibit a portrait bust that can be sent here and there than to exhibit the statue of a divinity that has its fixed place in the interior of a temple. The same holds for the painting as against the mosaic or fresco that preceded it. And even though the public ① _____ of a mass originally may have been just as great as that of a symphony, the latter originated at the moment when its public ② _____ promised to surpass that of the mass.

With the different methods of technical reproduction of a work of art, its fitness for exhibition increased to such an extent that the quantitative shift between its two poles turned into a qualitative transformation of its nature. This is comparable to the situation of the work of art in prehistoric times when, by the absolute emphasis on its cult value, it was, first and foremost, an instrument of magic. Only later did it come to be recognized as a work of art. In the same way today, by the absolute emphasis on its exhibition value the work of art becomes a creation with entirely new functions, among which the one we are conscious of, the artistic function, later may be recognized as incidental. This much is certain: today photography and the film are the most serviceable exemplifications of this new function.

01 빈칸 ①과 ②에 공통으로 들어가기에 가장 적합한 것을 고르시오.

(A) mimesis
(B) presentability
(C) mystery
(D) originality

02 위 글에서 저자가 주장하는 바와 가장 일치하는 것을 고르시오.

(A) The prehistoric men who painted the cave murals emphasized their cult value, so no other men than painters could see them.

(B) The essence of an artwork is absolute and cannot be changed.

(C) When the exhibition value of an artwork is dominant, it is very important where the artwork is displayed.

(D) As the exhibition value surpasses the cult value, people's perception of the nature or function of the artwork has also changed.

The coastlines on the two sides of the Atlantic Ocean present a notable parallelism: the easternmost region of Brazil, in Pernambuco, has a convexity that corresponds almost perfectly with the concavity of the African Gulf of Guinea, while the contours of the African coastline between Rio de Oro and Liberia would, by the same approximation, match those of the Caribbean Sea.

Similar correspondences are also observed in many other regions of the Earth. This observation began to awaken scientific interest about sixty years ago, when Alfred Wegener, a professor at the University of Hamburg, used it as a basis for formulating a revolutionary theory in geological science. According to Wegner, there was originally only one continent or land mass, which he called Pangea. Inasmuch as continental masses are lighter than the base on which they rest, he reasoned, they must float on the substratum of igneous rock, known as sima, as ice floes float on the sea. Then why, he asked, might continents not be subject to drifting? The rotation of the globe and other original forces, he thought, had caused the cracking and, finally, the breaking apart of the original Pangea, along an extensive line presented today by the longitudinal submerged mountain range in the center of the Atlantic. While Africa seems to have remained static, the Americas apparently drifted toward the west until they reached their present position after more than 100 million years. Although the phenomenon seems fantastic, accustomed as we are to the concept of the rigidity and immobility of the continents, on the basis of the distance that separates them it is possible to calculate that the continental drift would have been no greater than two inches per year.

01 The title that best expresses the ideas of the above passage is _____.

(A) A Novel Theory
(B) Two Inches per Year
(C) Static Africa
(D) A Notable Parallelism

02 Professor Wegener's theory is _____.

(A) an analysis of the lost continent
(B) based on a study of 100 years
(C) unsound
(D) revolutionary

03   Sima, as described in this passage, is _____.
    (A) the basic substance of Pangea
    (B) like an ice floe
    (C) the submerged mountain range
    (D) igneous rock

Every day in the media we see once-unthinkable science headlines. More than seven hundred cases of measles across 22 states in the U.S., largely due to vaccine deniers. Climate change legislation stalled in the U.S. Senate — due mainly to partisan politicians who routinely confuse climate and weather — even as scientists tell us that we have only until 2030 to cut worldwide carbon emissions by half, then drop them to zero by 2050. And, in one of the most incredible developments of my lifetime, the Flat Earth movement is on the rise. To make matters worse, scientists (and others who care about it) have not really found an effective way of fighting back against science denial. In this "post-truth" era — with headlines like "Why Facts Don't Change Our Minds" — it is an open question how to convince people who reject evidence, not just in science, but also on a host of other factual matters. In the empirical realm, scientists often choose to respond by presenting their evidence, then get upset and refuse to engage more when their data aren't accepted or their integrity is questioned. Perhaps this is understandable, but I also believe it is dangerous just to walk away and dismiss science deniers as irrational (even if they are.) Even worse is to react to their hectoring on the question of whether there is "100 percent consensus" on global warming, or whether we're "certain" that vaccines don't cause autism, by blustering about "proof," which only gives aid and comfort to one of the most damaging myths about science.

But we really can't afford to do this anymore, nor can we afford to defend science simply by talking about its successes. Climate change "skeptics" already know about the marvels of chemotherapy … but what does that have to do with the spike in global temperatures in 1998? And philosophers of science have spent the last hundred years looking in vain for some definitive logical "criterion of demarcation" between science and non-science. A better way to respond is to stop talking about proof, certainty, and logic, and start talking more about scientific "values." I defend the idea that what is most distinctive about science is not its method but its "attitude": the idea that scientists care about evidence and are willing to change their views based on new evidence. <u>This</u> is what truly separates scientists from their deniers and imitators.

01 Which is best title for the passage?
    (A) What to Trust in a "Post-truth" Era
    (B) How to Deal with the Rise of Science Deniers
    (C) Debunking Conspiracy Theories
    (D) How Media Make Us Believe in the Flat Earth
    (E) A Skeptical Response to Science Denial

02 What does the underlined This refer to?
    (A) holding on to your faith as factual evidence
    (B) convincing science deniers of countless scientific resources
    (C) establishing the standards of good empirical reasoning
    (D) defending science from pseudoscience
    (E) embracing possibilities of new ideas

The history of modern pollution problems shows that most have resulted from negligence and ignorance. We have an appalling tendency to interfere with nature before all of the possible consequences of our actions have been studied in-depth. We produce and distribute radioactive substances, "synthetic" chemicals, and many other potent compounds before fully comprehending their effects on living organisms. Our education is dangerously incomplete.

It is often argued that the purpose of science is to move into unknown territory, to explore, and to discover. It can be said that similar risks have been taken before, and that these risks are necessary to technological progress.

These arguments overlook an important element. In the past, risks taken in the name of scientific progress were restricted to a small place and a brief period of time. The effects of the progress we now strive to master are neither localized nor brief. Air pollution covers vast urban areas. Ocean pollutants have been discovered in nearly every part of the world. Synthetic chemicals spread over huge stretches of forest and farmland may remain in the soil for decades. Radioactive pollutants will be found in the biosphere for generations. The size and persistence of these problems have grown with the expanding power of modern science.

One might also argue that the hazards of modern pollutants are small compared to the dangers associated with other human activities. No estimate of the actual harm done by smog, fallout, or chemical residues can obscure the reality that the risks are being taken before being fully understood.

The importance of these issues lies in the failure of science to predict and control human intervention into natural processes. The true measure of the danger is represented by the hazards we will encounter if we enter the new age of technology without first evaluating our responsibility to the environment.

01 The author seems to feel that the attitude of scientists toward pollution has been _____.

(A) naive   (B) confused
(C) nonchalant   (D) concerned

02 The underlined word "synthetic" in means _____.

(A) new   (B) unsafe
(C) polluting   (D) man-made

03 The author believes that the risks taken by modern science are greater than those taken by earlier scientific efforts because _____.

(A) the effects may be felt by more people for a longer period of time
(B) science is progressing faster than ever before
(C) technology has produced more dangerous chemicals
(D) the materials used are more dangerous to scientists

In 1665, Robert Hooke, an English scientist, looked at thin slices of cork under a microscope. He saw a lot of empty spaces, which he called cells. During the 19th century, scientists with the improvement of the microscope began to see the cells more clearly. In 1831, Robert Brown, an English botanist, discovered the central part of the cell, the nucleus. A few years later, German biologists, Matthew Schleiden and Theodor Schwann, did experiments to see what kinds of living things had cells. Later biologists concluded that cells reproduced to form new cells. Their experiments and studies led to the cell theory acceptable today.

(1) All living things are made of one or more cells.
(2) Cells are the basic units of structure and function in living things.
(3) All cells come from the cells.

Cells have a variety of parts and functions. As major parts of animal cell, there are nucleus; endoplasmic reticulum; mitochondria; golgicomplex; microbodies; centrioles; and, ribosomes. The function of the nucleus is to control all the cell activities. Endoplasmic reticulum connects the nuclear membrane with the cell *membrane*, and its function is to move materials in the cell. Mitochondria as "powerhouses of the cell" produces energy when food is broken down. Golgi complex collects, packages, and distributes molecules that are synthesized at one location within the cell to another place. Microbodies carry enzymes. Centrioles help with cell reproduction. In cell reproduction, a single cell becomes two cells, and each cell must receive a set of chromosomes. Ribosomes are cell parts where proteins are made.

As major parts of plant cell, there are cell wall; vacuoles; chloroplasts; nucleus; mitochondria; golgi complex; and ribosomes. Cell wall gives a plant support while allowing oxygen, water, and minerals to enter the cell. Vacuoles store food, water, and minerals until the cell is ready to use them. Chloroplasts trap energy from the sun. The plant uses this energy to make food. The other cell parts, nucleus, mitochondria, golgi complex, and ribosomes have similar functions found in the animal cells.

01 A proper title of the passage is _____.
(A) Part of the cell
(B) Functions of cell
(C) Development of cell
(D) Facts about the cell

02 The cell parts that are not found in animal cells are _____.
(A) golgi complex
(B) cholroplasts
(C) mitochondria
(D) ribosomes

03 The cell parts that are involved with cell reproduction are _____.
(A) chloroplasts
(B) golgi complex
(C) mitochondria
(D) centrioles

04 The italicized word, *membrane* in the second paragraph refers to _____.
(A) thin piece of skin
(B) thick wall
(C) thick liquidity
(D) thick solidity

But one day he saw clearly for a little while. It was a day on which his two sons had come and after they had greeted him courteously. Now Wang Lung followed them silently, and they stood. Wang Lung heard his second son say in his mincing voice.

"This field we will sell and this one, and we will divide the money between us evenly. Your share I'll borrow at good interest, for now with the railroad straight through I can ship rice to the sea and I…" But the old man heard only these words, "sell the land," and he cried out and he could not keep his voice from breaking and trembling with his anger.

"Now, evil, idle sons! Sell the land?" He choked and would have fallen, and they caught him and held him up, and he began to weep. Then they *soothed* him and they said, soothing him, "No, no, we'll never sell the land." "It is the end of a family, when they begin to sell the land," he said brokenly. "out of land we came and into it we must go, and if you will hold your land you can live, no one can rob you of land." And the old man let his scanty tears dry upon his cheek and they made salty stains there. And he stooped and took up a handful of the soil and he held it and he muttered, "If you sell the land, it is the end." And his two sons held him, one on either side, each holding his arm, and he held tight in his hand the warm loose earth…. "Rest assured, our father, rest assured. The land is not to be sold." But over the old man's head they looked at each other and smiled.

01 The antonym of the italicized word, *soothed*, is _____.
(A) agitated
(B) alleviated
(C) appeased
(D) pacified

02 The underlined sentence, "Out of land we came and into it we must go" can be interpreted that the land is the basic source of _____.
(A) income
(B) life & death
(C) prosperity
(D) power

03 The underlined sentence, "But over the old man's head they looked at each other and smiled" can be inferred that Wang Lung's children _____.

(A) agreed with him
(B) respected his point
(C) despised his point
(D) had different ideas

04 One of the following statements that can serve as the best theme of this fiction is _____.

(A) Earth has no sorrow that Heaven cannot heal
(B) Those who really thirst for knowledge always get it
(C) The way of this world is to praise dead saints and persecute the living ones
(D) He who forgets his own roots wanders

When you go to the gym, do you wash your hands before and after using the equipment? Bring your own regularly cleaned mat for floor exercises? Shower with antibacterial soap and put on clean clothes immediately after your workout? Use only your own towels, razors, bar soap, water bottles?

If you answered "no" to any of the above, you could wind up with one of the many skin infections that can spread like wildfire in athletic settings. In June, the National Athletic Trainers' Association, known as N.A.T.A., issued a ①position paper on the causes, prevention and treatment of skin diseases in athletes that could just as well apply to anyone who works out in a communal setting, be it a school or commercial gym.

The authors pointed out that "skin infections in athletes are extremely common" and account for more than half the outbreaks of infectious diseases that occur among participants in competitive sports. And if you think skin problems are minor, consider what happened to Kyle Frey, a 21-year-old junior and competitive wrestler at Drexel University in Philadelphia.

Mr. Frey noticed a pimple on his arm last winter but thought little of it. He competed in a match on a Saturday, but by the next morning the pimple had grown to the size of his biceps and had become very painful.

His athletic trainer sent him straight to the emergency room, where the lesion was lanced. Two days later, he learned he had MRSA, the potentially deadly staphylococcus infection that is resistant to most antibiotics. Mr. Frey spent five days in the hospital, where the lesion was surgically cleaned and stitched and treated with antibiotics that cleared the infection. He said in an interview that he does not know how he acquired MRSA: "The wrestling mat might have been contaminated, or I wrestled with someone who had the infection."

If it could happen to Mr. Frey, who said he has always been health-conscious in the gym and careful about not sharing his belongings, it could happen to you.

01 What is the main idea of the passage?

(A) The hygiene in the gym can improve the efficiency of athletes.
(B) Skin diseases are more serious than what you think.
(C) Even when you exercise, make sanitation your priority.
(D) Exercise accompanied by bad habit can cause skin infections.

02 Which of the following CANNOT be inferred from the passage?

   (A) Participants in competitive sports are more likely to have infectious diseases than the other athletes.
   (B) What Mr. Frey got is not unique to Mr. Frey and can occur to anyone.
   (C) Because skin infections are contagious, one who got them should be isolated.
   (D) Small skin trouble can grow into the critical condition.

03 In which of the following would you most likely find this passage?

   (A) effective workout manual
   (B) televised campaign speech
   (C) regular checkup list
   (D) health feature in newspaper

04 Which of the following can replace ①"position paper"?

   (A) financial report
   (B) statement about skin diseases
   (C) cosmetic research paper
   (D) national address

Ever since the meteoric rise of social media, Brian Primack, director of the Center for Research on Media, Technology and Health at the University of Pittsburgh, has been interested in its impact on society. Along with Jessica Levenson, he examines the relationships between technology and mental health, looking at the good and the bad. When considering a link between social media and depression, they expected there to be a dual effect — that social media might sometimes alleviate depression, and sometimes exacerbate it, results which might plot out nicely in a "u-shaped" curve on a graph. However, a survey of almost 2,000 people revealed something much more surprising. There was no curve at all, the line was straight, and in an undesirable direction. Put another way, an increase in social media is associated with an increase in the likelihood of depression, anxiety, and a feeling of social isolation. "In an objective way, you might say: this person is interacting with friends, passing on smiles and emojis, you might say that person has a lot of social capital, that they are very engaged. But we found those people seem to have more feelings of perceived social isolation," says Primack.

What is unclear, however, is the exact causal direction: does depression increase social media use, or does social media use increase depression? Primack suggests it could be working both ways, making it even more problematic as "there's a potential for ①_____". The more depressed a person is the more social media they might then use, which worsens their mental health further. But there's another worrying impact. In a September 2017 study of over 1,700 young adults, Primack and colleagues found that when it comes to social media interaction, time of day plays a fundamental role. Engagement during the last 30 minutes before bed was found to be the strongest indicator of a poor night's sleep. "It was completely independent of the total amount of time of use in the day," says Primack. Something about keeping those last 30 minutes ②_____, it seems, is crucial to a restful slumber. There are several factors that could explain this. A now well-told caution is that the blue light emitted from our screens inhibits our melatonin levels — a chemical that effectively tells us that it's time to nod off. It could also be possible that social media use increases a person's anxiety as the day goes on, making it hard to switch off when we finally go to bed. "Then thoughts and feelings come back to haunt us as we try go to sleep," says Primack. Or a more obvious reason might be that social media is deeply alluring and simply reduces the time we have for sleep.

01 빈칸 ①과 ②에 들어가기에 가장 적합한 것을 고르시오.

(A) stress-related depression — taking an over-the-counter sleep aid
(B) mental derangement — having a daily spiritual practice
(C) diversionary tactics — saying goodbye to social media friends
(D) a vicious cycle — tech-free

02 위 글의 내용과 가장 일치하는 것을 고르시오.

(A) Social media can be said to have a dual effect because they sometimes alleviate depression and sometimes aggravate it.
(B) As the time spent on social media increases, so does the sense of social isolation.
(C) There is a clear causal relationship between increased depression and increased use of social media.
(D) People who spend more time in a day on social media are less likely to sleep well at night.

Until after the middle of the nineteenth century, cancer was thought to do its killing by stealth. Its lurking force lay under the cover of hushed darkness, and its first sting felt only when murderous infiltration had strangled too much normal tissue to restore the overwhelmed defenses of its host. The perpetrator regurgitated as malignant gangrene the life it had noiselessly chewed up.

We know better now, because we have come to recognize a different personality when our old enemy is seen through the microscope of contemporary science. Cancer, far from being a clandestine foe, is in fact berserk with the malicious exuberance of killing.

The disease pursues a continuous, uninhibited, circumferential, barn-burning expedition of destructiveness, in which it heeds no rules, follows no commands, and explodes all resistance in a homicidal riot of devastation. Its cells behave like the members of a barbarian horde run amok — leaderless and undirected but with a single-minded purpose: to plunder everything within reach.

This is what medical scientists mean when they use the word *autonomy*. The form and rate of multiplication of the murderous cells violate every rule of decorum within the living animal whose vital nutrients nourish it only to be destroyed by this enlarging atrocity that has sprung newborn from its own protoplasm.

In this sense, cancer is not a parasite. Galen was wrong to call it *praeter naturam*, "outside of nature." Its first cells are the bastard offspring of unsuspecting parents who ultimately reject them because they are ugly, deformed, and unruly. In the community of living tissues, the uncontrolled mob of misfits that is cancer behaves like a gang of perpetually wilding adolescents. They are the juvenile delinquents of cellular society.

01. According to the passage, what was cancer thought to be before the middle of the nineteenth century?

(A) a secret killer
(B) a normal tissue
(C) a noisy predator
(D) an overwhelmed host

02 According to the passage, how can we, modern people, know better about the characteristic of cancer?

(A) From the data of the earlier nineteenth century
(B) From the complaints of the patients with cancer
(C) With the help of high-tech scientific machines
(D) With the help of the government that has funded cancer research

03 According to the passage, which one is NOT proper to characterize cancer?

(A) a bastard
(B) a parasite
(C) a barbarian
(D) a juvenile delinquent

04 Choose the best title of the passage?

(A) The Malevolence of Cancer
(B) The Misunderstanding of Cancer
(C) How People Come to Recognize Cancer
(D) An Outsider of Nature

Keenly alive to this prejudice of hers, Mr. Keeble stopped after making his announcement, and had to rattle the keys in his pocket in order to acquire the necessary courage to continue. He was not looking at his wife, but he knew just how forbidding her expression must be. This task of his was no easy, congenial task for a pleasant summer morning.

"She says in her letter," proceeded Mr. Keeble, his eyes on the carpet and his cheeks a deeper pink, "that young Jackson has got the chance of buying a big farm... in Lincolnshire, I think she said... if he can raise three thousand pounds."

He paused, and stole a glance at his wife. It was as he had feared. She had congealed. Like some spell, the name had apparently turned her to marble. She was presumably breathing, but there was no sign of it.

"So I was just thinking," said Mr. Keeble, producing another *obbligato* on the keys, "it just crossed my mind... it isn't as if the thing were speculation... the place is apparently coining money... present owner only selling because he wants to go abroad... it occurred to me... and they would pay good interest on the loan..."

"What loan?" inquired the statue icily, coming to life.

01. Which of the following is the intended effect of the pauses, in Mr. Keeble's conversation?
(A) It demonstrates that he is a feeble man.
(B) It makes his speech disjointed.
(C) It shows his hesitancy in approaching his wife.
(D) It slows the rhythm of the conversation.

02. All of the following represent metaphors used by the author EXCEPT _____.
(A) "like some spell"
(B) "inquired the statue icily"
(C) "coming to life"
(D) "presumably breathing"

03. All of the following are physical manifestations of Mr. Keeble's anticipation of his wife's response EXCEPT _____.
(A) "had to rattle the keys"
(B) "was not looking at his wife"
(C) "keenly alive"
(D) "his eyes on the carpet"

04 The last sentence implies which of the following?
(A) Mr. Keeble's wife is not interested in lending money.
(B) Mr. Keeble's wife is interested in the proposition.
(C) Mr. Keeble's wife wants to hear more about the loan.
(D) Mr. Keeble's wife is keeping an open mind about the loan.

The growth of cities, the construction of hundreds of new factories, and the spread of railroads in the United States before 1850 had increased the need for better illumination. But the lighting in American homes had improved very little over that of ancient times. Through the colonial period, homes were lit with tallow candles or with a lamp of the kind used in ancient Rome — a dish of fish oil or other animal or vegetable oil in which a twisted rag served as a wick. Some people used lard, but they had to heat charcoal underneath to keep it soft and burnable. The sperm whale provided a superior burning oil, but this was expensive. In 1830 a new substance called "camphene" was patented, and it proved to be an excellent illuminant. But while camphene gave a bright light it too remained expensive, had an unpleasant odor, and also was dangerously explosive.

Between 1830 and 1850 it seemed that the only hope for cheaper illumination in the United States was in the wider use of gas. In the 1840's American gas manufacturers adopted improved British techniques for producing illuminating gas from coal. But the expense of piping gas to the consumer remained so high that until mid-century gaslighting was feasible only in urban areas, and only for public buildings or for the wealthy.

In 1854 a Canadian doctor, Abraham Gesner, patented a process for distilling a pitchlike mineral found in New Brunswick and Nova Scotia that produced illuminating gas and an oil that he called "kerosene." Kerosene, though cheaper than camphene, had an unpleasant odor, and Gesner never made his fortune from it. But Gesner had aroused a new hope for making an illuminating oil from a product coming out of North American mines.

01. Which of the following is NOT mentioned as a reason why better lighting had become necessary by the mid-nineteenth century?

(A) Development of railroads
(B) Demand for better medical facilities
(C) Increases in the number of new factories
(D) Growth of cities

02 What can be inferred about the illuminating gas described in the second paragraph?

(A) It was first developed in the United States.
(B) It was not allowed to be used in public buildings.
(C) It was not widely available until mid-century.
(D) It had an unpleasant smell.

03 According to the passage, what advantage did the kerosene patented by Gesner have over camphene?

(A) Kerosene had a more pleasant smell.
(B) Kerosene was less expensive.
(C) Kerosene burned more brightly.
(D) Kerosene was safer to use.

04 Which of the following best describes the organization of the passage?

(A) A description of events in chronological order
(B) A comparison of two events
(C) The statement of a theory and possible explanations
(D) An analysis of scientific findings

The United States Constitution makes no provision for the nomination of candidates for the presidency. As the framers of the Constitution set up the system, the electors would, out of their own knowledge, select the "wisest and best" as President. But the rise of political parties altered that system drastically — and with the change came the need for nominations.

The first method that the parties developed to nominate presidential candidates was the congressional caucus, a small group of members of Congress. That method was regularly used in the elections of 1800 to 1824. But its closed character led to its downfall in the mid-1820's. For the election of 1832, both major parties turned to the national convention as their nominating device. It has continued to serve them ever since.

With the convention process, the final selection of the President is, for all practical purposes, narrowed to one of two persons: the Republican or the Democratic party nominee. Yet there is almost no legal control of that vital process.

The Constitution is silent on the subject of presidential nominations. There is, as well, almost no statutory law on the matter. The only provisions in federal law have to do with the financing of conventions. And in each state there is only a small body of laws that deal with issues related to the convention, such as the choosing of delegates and the manner in which they may cast their votes. In short, the convention is very largely a creation and a responsibility of the political parties themselves.

In both the Republican and Democratic parties, the national committee is charged with making the plans and arrangements for the national convention. As much as a year before it is held, the committee meets (usually in Washington, D. C.) to set the time and place for the convention. July has been the favored month; but each party has met in convention as early as mid-June and also as late as the latter part of August.

Where the convention is held is matter of prime importance. There must be an adequate convention hall, sufficient hotel accommodations, plentiful entertainment outlets, and efficient transportation facilities.

01 Which of the following motivated a change in the original method of selecting a President of the United States?

(A) The framers of the Constitution
(B) The rise of the congressional caucus
(C) The emergence of the party system
(D) The establishment of national conventions

02 What can be inferred about why the congressional caucus system was terminated?

(A) It was not efficient to carry on.
(B) It took too much time.
(C) It did not conform to the Constitution.
(D) It did not include enough citizens.

03 According to the passage, the only aspect of political conventions addressed by federal law involves _____.

(A) organization
(B) choosing delegates
(C) voting procedures
(D) funding

04 In paragraph 4, the author compares _____.

(A) nominations and conventions
(B) finances and the Constitution
(C) delegates and candidates
(D) federal and state laws

05 The passage refers to all of the following as necessary in the city where the convention is held EXCEPT _____.

(A) an acceptable meeting place
(B) politically aware citizens
(C) an easy way of traveling around the city
(D) sufficient amusement opportunities

Ernest Hemingway and William Faulkner, contemporary to each other, were America's two greatest 20th-century novelists. Both writers are distinctly representative of the modern world and share some common concerns, yet each is different from the other in significant ways. Hemingway's stories are individualistic, portraying man as adrift and alone; in Hemingway's world the hero typically faces the Great Enemy — usually meaninglessness and modernity — as bravely as he can. Faulkner, on the other hand, sought to depict an entire society that embraced persons of differing colors and classes. Whereas Hemingway's work comprises novels that are largely independent of each other, Faulkner's work constitutes an integrated southern epic based on life in his native Mississippi. Many of Faulkner's same characters reappear in story after story.

Of course, both writers were concerned with moral values. For Hemingway personal courage and fortitude was the most important virtue. Most of the time a man cannot win the struggles which he must undergo such as when contending with nature or society. The paramount question, therefore, is how he strives. If he meets defeat without flinching, then he achieves "grace under pressure," which is a sort of triumph that gives meaning and dignity to his life.

By contrast, Faulkner's morality was more social than individualistic. Since Faulkner's South had inherited the curse of slavery, which gave rise to deep-rooted and far-reaching problems both before and after the Civil War, Faulkner had a much different view of human nature. He depicts "good people" — whites, blacks, and Native Americans — as striving against social force larger than themselves. Although women and men seek to do what is right, they are often helpless before the conniving, unscrupulous people who dominate their lives.

In terms of style Hemingway's sentences are short and exact, made mainly of nouns and verbs; adjectives and adverbs are avoided. As a result, the effect of the description is power and compression. Hemingway also believed that the strength of a story was in what lay beneath its surface — in what was unstated but implied. Faulkner's style was quite the opposite. His prose is colorful, convoluted, and complex. His sentences are extremely long — sometimes a single sentence may cover half a page — and he uses many adverbs and adjectives. He fully and explicitly develops his themes and narratives — indeed, his works could be said to offer an overabundance of thought and feeling.

01 What does this passage mainly discuss?

(A) The historical background to Hemingway's and Faulkner's works
(B) Why Hemingway and Faulkner are considered great writers
(C) Differences between Hemingway's and Faulkner's writings
(D) The influence Hemingway and Faulkner had on each other

02 According to the passage, which of the following traits did Hemingway most value?

(A) Audacity   (B) Self sacrifice
(C) Bravery   (D) Competence

03 The passage implies that compared with Hemingway Faulkner's portrayal of human characters had greater _____.

(A) accuracy   (B) scope
(C) feeling   (D) clarity

04 The passage refers to all of the following as differences between the writing styles of Hemingway and Faulkner EXCEPT _____.

(A) length of sentences
(B) use of adverbs and adjectives
(C) view of audience
(D) development of theme

05 Which of the following conclusions is best supported by the passage?

(A) Twentieth century America produced many great writers.
(B) Neither Faulkner nor Hemingway considered himself as essentially an "American" writers.
(C) Faulkner and Hemingway were equally skillful but Faulkner probably has a wider appeal.
(D) Hemingway and Faulkner differed but both were exceptional writers.

In medicine, the prevailing biological idea has been that the body seeks equilibrium, a steady state. When it is ill, say, with a fever, it tries to return to health by sweating and other means of cooling itself. This is the homeostatic view. It states that in each bodily function there is an ideal mean, and that a healthy person's functions will flutter randomly about that middle number.

According to the discipline of chronobiology, this approach is faulty, or at least incomplete. Bodily functions do fluctuate, but not randomly. They move up and down quite regularly. They keep in order among themselves, and the varying numbers they produce may result in all sorts of different interpretations by doctors who are unaware of this wide, normal variation.

Since so much of the chemistry and biology of the body changes each day, and changes by as much as tenfold, biologists have gradually come to realize that an animal — whether human or guinea pig — is virtually a different creature, physically and chemically, at different times of day.

Chronobiology has already begun to transform the way biological research is being conducted, and it is expected to have a major effect on all of medicine as well. It can alter results at every stage of practice, from preventing time-linked illnesses, to improving diagnoses, to improving treatment. Some conventional medical rules of thumb may have to be abandoned; for example, drugs are now given three times a day or four times a day, completely without regard for the differing effects they produce at different hours.

01 The main purpose of the passage is to _____.
(A) describe recent advances in the treatment of fevers
(B) compare the chemistry of different animals
(C) list common misconceptions about chronobiology
(D) indicate the significance of the body's natural rhythms

02 The passage states that the fluctuation of many bodily functions is _____.
(A) incomplete   (B) regular
(C) unnecessary   (D) faulty

03 The author most likely believes that many doctors are _____.

(A) relying too much on drug therapies
(B) not doing enough research on animals
(C) not knowledgeable about the body's rhythms
(D) arguing with one another too much

04 In determining the effectiveness of a drug, which of the following would most likely be considered more important by a chronobiologist than by a medical doctor?

(A) Who administers it
(B) When it is taken
(C) Whether the patient is sweating
(D) What the patient's diet is

05 Which of the following is closest in meaning to the phrase "rules of thumb" that appears in the last sentence of the passage?

(A) Authoritative regulations
(B) Customary practices
(C) Finger exercises
(D) Moral principles

Climatic conditions are delicately adjusted to the composition of the Earth's atmosphere. If there were a change in the atmosphere — for example, in the relative proportions of atmospheric gases — the climate would probably change also. A slight increase in water vapor, for instance, would increase the heat-retaining capacity of the atmosphere and would lead to a rise in global temperatures. In contrast, a large increase in water vapor would increase the thickness and extent of the cloud layer, reducing the amount of solar energy reaching the Earth's surface.

The level of carbon dioxide, CO_2, in the atmosphere has an important effect on climatic change. Most of the Earth's incoming energy is short-wavelength radiation, which tends to pass through atmospheric CO_2 easily. The earth, however, reradiates much of the received energy as long-wavelength radiation, which CO_2 absorbs and then remits toward the Earth. This phenomenon, known as the greenhouse effect, can result in an increase in the surface temperature of a planet. An extreme example of the effect is shown by Venus, a planet covered by heavy clouds composed mostly of CO_2, whose surface temperatures have been measured at 430℃. If the CO_2 content of the atmosphere is reduced, the temperature falls. According to one respectable theory, if the atmospheric CO_2 concentration were halved, the Earth would become completely covered with ice. Another equally respectable theory, however, states that a halving of the CO_2 concentration would lead only to a reduction in global temperatures of 3℃.

If, because of an increase in forest fires or volcanic activity, the CO_2 content of the atmosphere increased, a warmer climate would be produced. Plant growth, which relies on both the warmth and the availability of CO_2, would probably increase. As a consequence, plants would use more and more CO_2. Eventually CO_2 levels would diminish and the climate, in turn, would become cooler. With reduced temperatures many plants would die; CO_2 would thereby be returned to the atmosphere and gradually the temperature would rise again. Thus, if this process occurred, there might be a long-term oscillation in the amount of CO_2, present in the atmosphere, with regular temperature increases and decreases of a set magnitude.

Some climatologists argue that the burning of fossil fuels has raised the level of CO_2 in the atmosphere and has caused a global temperature increase of at least 1℃. But a supposed global temperature rise of 1℃ may in reality be only several regional temperature increases, restricted to areas where there are many meteorological stations and caused simply by shifts in the pattern of atmospheric circulation. Other areas, for example the Southern Hemisphere oceanic zone, may be experiencing an equivalent temperature decrease that is unrecognized because of the shortage of meteorological recording stations.

01 The passage supplies information for answering which of the following questions?

(A) Why are projections of the effects of changes in water vapor levels on the climate so inaccurate?
(B) What are the steps in the process that takes place as CO_2 absorbs long-wavelength radiation?
(C) How might our understanding of the greenhouse effect be improved if the burning of fossil fuels were decreased?
(D) What might cause a series of regular increases and decreases in the amount of CO_2 in the atmosphere?

02 The author refers to Venus primarily in order to _____.

(A) show that the greenhouse effect works on other planets but not on Earth
(B) show the extent to which Earth's atmosphere differs from that of Venus
(C) support the contention that as water vapor increases, the amount of CO_2 increases
(D) support the argument that the CO_2 level in the atmosphere has a significant effect on climate

03 The passage suggests that a large decrease in the amount of CO_2 in the atmosphere would result in _____.

(A) at least a slight decrease in global temperatures
(B) at the most a slight increase in short-wavelength radiation reaching the Earth
(C) a slight long-term increase in global temperatures
(D) a large long-term increase in the amount of volcanic activity

04 All of the following can be found in the author's discussion of climate EXCEPT _____.

(A) a statement about the effects of increased volcanic activity on the Earth's temperature
(B) a generalization about the efficiency of meteorological recording stations
(C) a contrast between two theories about the effects of a lowering of CO_2 levels in the atmosphere
(D) an indication of the effect of an increase in water vapor in the atmosphere

Those who criticize the United States government today for not providing health care to all citizens equate health-care provision with medical insurance coverage. By this standard, 17th and 18th century America lacked any significant conception of public health law. However, despite the general paucity of bureaucratic organization in preindustrial America, the vast extent of health regulation and provision stands out as remarkable.

Of course, the public role in the protection and regulation of 18th century health was carried out in ways quite different from those today. Organizations responsible for health regulation were less stable than modern bureaucracies, tending to appear in crises and ①_____ in periods of calm. The focus was on epidemics that were seen as unnatural and warranting a response, not on the many endemic and chronic conditions that were accepted as ②part and parcel of daily life. Additionally, religious influence was significant, especially in the 17th century. Finally, in an era that lacked sharp demarcations between private and governmental bodies, many public responsibilities were carried out by what we would now consider private associations. Nevertheless, the extent of public health regulation long before the dawn of the welfare state is remarkable and suggests that the founding generation's assumptions about the relationship between government and health were more complex than is commonly assumed.

Which of the following best expresses the author's point of contention with "those who criticize the United States government today for not providing health care to all citizens"?

(A) Their standard for measuring such provision is too narrow.
(B) They underestimate the role that insurance plays in the provision of health care today.
(C) They fail to recognize that government plays a more significant role today in health care than in previous eras.
(D) They lack any significant conception of public health law.

Which of the following would be most appropriate for the blank ①?

(A) withering away
(B) withered away
(C) wither away
(D) were withered away

03 What is the meaning of the underlined expression ②?

(A) a common and tedious part
(B) a rare and insoluble part
(C) a stressful and depressing part
(D) an essential and unavoidable part

04 What is the main point of the passage?

(A) The government's role in health care has not expanded over time to the extent that many critics have asserted.
(B) History suggests that the United States government has properly played a significant role in provision of health care.
(C) Health problems plaguing preindustrial America resulted largely from inadequate public health care.
(D) Private insurance is an inadequate solution to the problem of health care.

[I] One of the disturbing trends in the media and among public officials is the tendency to dispense depressing information that, although not untrue, is only partially accurate. They peddle incomplete or selective information that inspires misleading exaggerations or <u>unwarranted</u> inferences. People begin to feel that something is wrong, and this new sensation becomes an <u>irrefutable</u> fact, or worse, the basis for a misguided policy. [II] Crime is one area where such misinformation abounds. Most people would agree that there is too much crime, but the best surveys show that the crime rate has not worsened. In fact, some victimization rates have dropped. For example, the annual number of murders has not increased since 1980. Furthermore, 86 percent of the populace has not been victims of violent crime. Yet, we continue to purchase security systems for our homes and vehicles and to pass bond initiatives to build more prisons. Despite evidence to the contrary, we feel less safe. [III] Every danger or adverse social trend is not as ghastly as it seems. Consciousness-raising can be truth-lowering. We create synthetic truths from a blend of genuine evidence, popular prejudice and mass anxiety. If the media does not display data in an unbiased way, we will need to be discerning before we make judgments. [IV]

01 What is the main idea of the passage?

(A) Facts can be misused to form inaccurate impressions.
(B) The media misstates information.
(C) People need to make judgments with great caution.
(D) Facts are often stranger than fiction.

02 Which of the following is closest in meaning to the underlined words "<u>unwarranted</u>" and "<u>irrefutable</u>"?

(A) gratuitous — debatable
(B) pertinent — inarguable
(C) mistreated — unreliable
(D) groundless — unquestionable

03 Where would the following sentences best fit into?

We have been also told for years that the American standard of living is dropping. Yet over the past 25 years, the median family income has risen by 20 percent. But the increase is much slower than we expected, so slow that it is often imperceptible during any one year. Again, we feel decline instead of increase.

(A) [I] (B) [II]
(C) [III] (D) [IV]

04 What is the author's view toward disturbing news?

(A) It should be taken seriously.
(B) It may not be as bad as it is portrayed.
(C) It should cause deep reflection.
(D) It may be worse than it is being portrayed.

Audrey was out of town when Owen arrived in London, but she returned a week later. The sound of her voice through the telephone did much to cure the restlessness from which he had been suffering since the conclusion of his holiday. But the thought that she was so near yet so inaccessible produced in him ①_____ which enveloped him like a cloud that would not lift. His manner became distrait. He lost weight.

If customers were not vaguely pained by his sad, pale face, it was only because the fierce rush of modern commercial life leaves your business man little leisure for observing pallor in bank-clerks. What did pain them was the gentle dreaminess with which he performed his duties. He was in the Inward Bills Department, one of the features of which was the sudden inrush towards the end of the afternoon, of hatless, energetic young men with leather bags strapped to their left arms, clamouring for mysterious crackling documents, much fastened with pins. Owen had never quite understood what it was that these young men did want, and now his detached mind refused even more emphatically to grapple with the problem. He distributed the documents at random with the air of a preoccupied monarch scattering largess to the mob, and the <u>subsequent chaos</u> had to be handled by a wrathful head of the department in person.

Man's power of endurance is limited. At the end of the second week the overwrought head appealed passionately for relief, and Owen was removed to the Postage Department, where, when he had leisure from answering Audrey's telephone calls, he entered the addresses of letters in a large book and took them to the post. He was supposed also to stamp them, but a man in love cannot think of everything, and he was apt at times to overlook this formality.

01 Which would be most appropriate for blank ①?
   (A) a state of euphoria
   (B) a meditative melancholy
   (C) a helpless idleness
   (D) a ceaseless strain

02 We can assume from the passage that Owen lost weight because _____.
   (A) Audrey refused to talk to him
   (B) he despised Audrey
   (C) Audrey was unreachable in person
   (D) he disliked his new job in the Postage Department

03 The underlined "<u>subsequent chaos</u>" was a result of _____.
   (A) Owen's romantic preoccupation
   (B) Owen's loss of weight
   (C) Owen's detachment and involvement
   (D) Owen's impending transfer to the Postage Department

04 The style of this passage can best be described as _____.
   (A) devilish invective
   (B) profound irony
   (C) light satire
   (D) reflective musing

In the early 1950s, Liu Binyan was a tall, eloquent young man deeply devoted to the ideals of socialism and set for a brilliant career in the People's Republic of China. When he was purged from the Communist Party in 1957 for writing about corruption and banished to a poor mountain village, he suddenly found that there were "two diametrically opposed kinds of truth" in China. The "longings of the peasants" formed one kind, the "policies of the higher-ups" the other. The rest of Liu's life — his sufferings as well as his remarkable achievements — followed from his choice to side with the first kind of truth. Many Chinese saw a widening gap between the language of socialism and the hard, sometimes disastrous, realities of daily life. While some chose to lie low and compromise, Liu insisted on writing about what he saw. If there is bullying, say so. If corruption exists, give the details. If newspapers carry falsity, don't pretend it's a different kind of truth.

The cathartic effect of Liu's writing brought him two huge waves of popularity, once in 1956 and again in the early 1980s. But his truth-telling cost him dearly. He lived 22 of his 80 years (1957-1979) in domestic exile, and another 17 years (1988-2005) in forced exile abroad. Chinese leaders ignored his requests to come home during his waning years. Why did he opt for such a life? In a 1979 speech, Liu said, "I have awoken to a hard fact: in today's China, if one speaks or writes and does not incur somebody's opposition, one might as well not have spoken or written at all. The only alternative is to cower in a corner and fall silent. But if we do that, why live?" _____ was not his only virtue. He wrote meticulously and had incisive analytic powers. Few could rival his grasp of Chinese society, or his abiding affection for China's common folk.

01 What's the best title for the passage?
(A) The Democratization of A Communist Country
(B) The Crisis of Freedom of Speech in China
(C) The Heroic Life of A Chinese Writer
(D) The Serious Corruption of Officials in China

02 Choose the one that best fills in the blank.
(A) Ideology
(B) Honesty
(C) Wisdom
(D) Learning

03 Which of the following describes Liu Binyan wrong?

(A) He was a zealous socialist.
(B) He suffered persecution due to his outspokenness.
(C) He was in exile for about half his life.
(D) He lacked affection for the lower class of China.

With 80 percent of women experiencing some form of impaired cognitive function during pregnancy, it's no surprise the idea of "pregnancy brain" has taken hold. But a recent paper suggests that the memory loss, stress, and general fuzzy-headedness of the prenatal period may actually have a crucial role in getting women ready to be mothers.

Since the 1940s, doctors have suspected that the hormonal bath of pregnancy helps prepare women for the demands of motherhood. But while there's plenty known about how hormones affect the teenage and the menopausal brains, the pregnant brain is poorly understood and little studied in humans. Recent research has mostly been done on pregnant rodents, with studies finding that the hormone rush of pregnancy improved spatial skills (leading to better and quicker foraging food) and multitasking, as well as increased boldness and decreased anxiety. These rats enjoyed the positive effects of having been pregnant throughout their lifetimes, long after their pups grew up.

Now scientists are attempting to apply the animal findings to people. In a new paper, Laura M. Glynn, a professor of psychology at Chapman University, argues for the existence of "maternal programming," a process by which the pregnant woman's hormone-soaked brain prepares for the challenges of parenthood. As it turns out, some of the worst parts about pregnancy — vague but nagging cognitive and memory lapses that are often dismissed as imaginary or just stress — may actually be side effects of the _____ that happen as a woman becomes a mother. In other words, you may be losing your memory at the same time you're gaining new capacities to bond with and care for an infant.

01 Choose the one that best fills in the blank.
    (A) mental disorders   (B) physical recoveries
    (C) mental shifts   (D) physical malfunctions

02 What is the best title for the passage?
    (A) What Should Be Prepared for Motherhood
    (B) How Pregnancy Transforms the Brain
    (C) What Roles Hormones Play in Pregnancy
    (D) How Pregnant Women Gain New Capacities

03 Which of the following is not characteristic of "pregnancy brain"?
    (A) abundant hormone secretion
    (B) impaired cognitive function
    (C) baby-rearing capacities
    (D) imaginary memory lapses

04 What is the author's attitude toward Laura M. Glynn's argument?
    (A) agreeing					(B) doubtful
    (C) criticizing					(D) conservative

The conservatism of the early English colonists in North America, their strong attachment to the English way of doing things, would play a major part in the furniture that was made in New England. The very tools that the first New England furniture makers used were, after all, not much different from those used for centuries — even millennia: basic hammers, saws, chisels, planes, augers, compasses, and measures. These were the tools used more or less by all people who worked with wood: carpenters, barrel makers, and shipwrights. At most the furniture makers might have had planes with special edges or more delicate chisels, but there could not have been much specialization in the early years of the colonies.

The furniture makers in those early decades of the 1600's were known as "joiners," for the primary method of constructing furniture, at least among the English of this time, was that of mortise-and-tenon joinery. The mortise is the hole chiseled and cut into one piece of wood, while the tenon is the protruding element shaped from another piece of wood so that it fits into the mortise; and another small hole is then drilled (with the auger) through the mortised end and the tenon so that a whittled peg can secure the joint — thus the term "joiner." Panels were fitted into slots on the basic frames. This kind of construction was used for making everything from houses to chests.

Relatively little hardware was used during this period. Some nails — forged by hand — were used, but no screws or glue. Hinges were often made of leather, but metal hinges were also used. The cruder varieties were made by blacksmiths in the colonies, but the finer metal elements were imported. Locks and escutcheon plates — the latter to shield the wood from the metal key — would often be imported.

Above all, what the early English colonists imported was their knowledge of, familiarity with, and dedication to the traditional types and designs of furniture they knew in England.

01 The relationship of a mortise and a tenon is most similar to that of _____.
(A) a lock and a key
(B) a book and its cover
(C) a cup and a saucer
(D) a hammer and a nail

02 For what purpose did woodworkers use an auger?
(A) To whittle a peg
(B) To make a tenon
(C) To drill a hole
(D) To measure a panel

03 The author implies that colonial metal workers were _____.

(A) unable to make elaborate parts
(B) more skilled than woodworkers
(C) more conservative than other colonists
(D) frequently employed by joiners

04 The author implies that the colonial joiners _____.

(A) were highly paid
(B) based their furniture on English models
(C) used many specialized tools
(D) had to adjust to using new kinds of wood in New England

ⓐA snowflake originates from countless water molecules that initially come together in small groups as a result of a weak attractive force between oxygen and hydrogen atoms. The same forces subsequently organize the groups into a frozen molecular crystal, a perfectly organized lattice of molecules. Finally, several molecular crystals join to form a snowflake. Scientists have realized for some time that the forces that assemble molecules into natural crystals can be utilized to produce a variety of important materials. ⓑThey have determined the structure of more than 90,000 different molecular crystals, the most common examples of them are aspirin and mothballs.

In recent years, researchers have studied how molecules organize themselves to form crystals in the hope of better understanding what types of molecules and what conditions will produce molecular crystals with unusual and useful properties. ⓒScientists are aware that the material properties of a crystal depend in large part on the organization of the molecules in the crystal, yet they know little about the factors controlling the assembly of such crystals.

Synthesizing a molecular crystal is similar to designing a building. Before construction can begin, the architect must specify the shapes and sizes of the girders and the number and placement of the rivets. Similarly, to produce new molecular crystals, chemists must choose molecules of the appropriate sizes and shapes and select the molecular forces that will hold the crystals together. ⓓA chemist can normally find many molecules of various shapes and sizes, but the challenge is to find ones that assemble in a predictable manner.

By making use of forces that assemble molecules into natural crystals, scientists can _____.

(A) find molecules of various shapes and sizes
(B) determine the structure of different molecular crystals
(C) organize molecules into a perfect lattice
(D) create new and useful materials

According to the passage, what reason do researchers have for studying how molecules organize themselves to form crystals?

(A) To assemble molecules into natural crystals
(B) To learn how to synthesize molecular crystals
(C) To make aspirin and mothballs
(D) To change the material properties of a crystal

03 To produce new molecular crystals, chemists must choose all of the following EXCEPT _____.

(A) molecules of the right size
(B) molecules of the appropriate shape
(C) the right molecular organization
(D) the proper molecular forces

04 According to the passage, which one is grammatically incorrect?

(A) ⓐ   (B) ⓑ
(C) ⓒ   (D) ⓓ

The Food and Drug Administration has recently proposed severe restrictions on the use of antibiotics to promote the health and growth of meat animals. Medications added to feeds kill many microorganisms but also encourage the appearance of bacterial strains that are resistant to anti-infective drugs. Already, for example, penicillin and the tetracyclines are not as effective therapeutically as they once were. The drug resistance is chiefly conferred by tiny circlets of genes, called plasmids, that can be exchanged between different strains and even different species of bacteria. Plasmids are also one of the two kids of vehicles (the other being viruses) that molecular biologists depend on when performing gene transplant experiments. Even present guidelines forbid the laboratory use of plasmids bearing genes for resistance to antibiotics. Yet, while congressional debate rages over whether or not to toughen these restrictions on scientists in their laboratories, little congressional attention has been focused on an ill-advised agricultural practice that produces known <u>deleterious</u> effects.

01 In the passage, the author is primarily concerned with _____.

(A) discovering methods of eliminating harmful microorganisms without subsequently generating drug-resistant bacteria
(B) explaining reasons for congressional inaction on the regulation of gene transplant experiments
(C) describing a problematic agricultural practice and its serious genetic consequences
(D) evaluating recently proposed restrictions intended to promote the growth of meat animals

02 According to the passage, the exchange of plasmids between different bacteria can result in which of the following?

(A) Microorganisms resistant to drugs
(B) Therapeutically useful circlets of genes
(C) Anti-infective drugs like penicillin
(D) Vehicles for performing gene transplant experiments

03 The author's attitude toward the development of bacterial strains that render antibiotic drugs ineffective can best be described as _____.

(A) indifferent   (B) perplexed
(C) pretentious   (D) apprehensive

04 In the last sentence of the paragraph, the word "deleterious" could best be replaced by which of the following?

(A) accurate
(B) indirect
(C) restricted
(D) harmful

During the nineteenth century, occupational information about women that was provided by the United States census — a population count conducted each decade — became more detailed and precise in response to social changes. Through 1840, simple enumeration by household mirrored a home-based agricultural economy and hierarchical social order: the head of the household (presumed male or absent) was specified by name, ①_____ other household members were only indicated by the total number of persons counted in various categories, including occupational categories. Like farms, most enterprises were family-run, so that the census measured economic activity as an attribute of the entire household, rather than of ②_____.

The 1850 census, partly responding to antislavery and women's rights movements, initiated the collection of specific information about each individual in a household. Not until 1870 was occupational information analyzed by gender: the census superintendent reported 1.8 million women were employed outside the home in "gainful and reputable occupations." In addition, he arbitrarily attributed to each family one woman "keeping house." Overlap between the two groups was not calculated until 1890, when the rapid entry of women into the paid labor force and social issues arising from industrialization were causing women's advocates and women statisticians to press for more thorough and accurate accounting of women's occupations and wages.

01   Which would be most appropriate for ①?
(A) so
(B) because
(C) whereas
(D) once

02   Which would be most appropriate for ②?
(A) age
(B) individuals
(C) gender
(D) social class

03   Each of the following aspects of nineteenth-century United States censuses is mentioned in the passage EXCEPT the _____.
(A) year in which data on occupations began to be analyzed by gender
(B) year in which specific information began to be collected on individuals in addition to the head of the household
(C) way in which the 1890 census measured women's income levels and educational backgrounds
(D) way in which household members were counted in the 1840 census

04 It can be inferred from the passage that the 1840 United States census provided a count of which of the following?

(A) Women who worked exclusively in the home
(B) People engaged in nonfarming occupations
(C) People engaged in social movements
(D) Women engaged in family-run enterprises

05 The passage suggests which of the following about the "women's advocates and women statisticians"?

(A) They wanted to call attention to the lack of pay for women who worked in the home.
(B) They believe that previous census information was inadequate and did not reflect certain economic changes in the United States.
(C) They had conducted independent studies that disputed the official statistics provided by previous United States censuses.
(D) They thought that census statistics about women would be more accurate if more women were employed as census officials.

Situated in the central mountains of Alaska, a peak named Denali rises 20,320 feet above sea level. It is the highest peak in North America and the center of Denali National Park. One of America's greatest wilderness areas, the park has had limited access to visitors, but in spite of this tourism rose from under 6,000 visitors in 1950 to over 546,000 visitors in 1990. The increasing popularity of this park is ①_____ serious discussions about the future use of Denali as well as how to preserve wilderness areas in general.

One important issue of land use ②_____ when parts of National Parts are owned by individuals. In Denali, though most of the land in this vast tract of more than a million acres is owned by the National Park Service, several thousand acres are still privately owned as mining tracts. These mining tracts in Denali were once abundant sources of gold, but they were sources of heavy metals such as arsenic and lead that polluted rivers and streams. Environmentalists were successful in getting the government to require mining companies to submit statements showing the potential impact of a mining project before they are allowed to begin mining. Because of this requirements, many individuals closed their mines and some sold their land to the National Park Service. Some land owners, however, are wondering if it is better to sell their land to the government or keep it for possible future use. Tourism in this previously remote area is bound to rise, as more roads are built to provide easier access to the park. This increase in the number of visitors creates a demand for hotels and other real estate development. The economic implications of this are of interest to the land owners, but are dismaying to those interested in preserving the wilderness.

01 Which of the following best fits into ① and ②?
(A) promising — surrenders
(B) sanctioning — volunteers
(C) prompting — arises
(D) trapping — prospers

02 What is the author's purpose in writing this passage?
(A) to demonstrate the changes in Denali National Park
(B) to use Denali as a example of common park issues
(C) to introduce the wonders of the wilderness area of Denali
(D) to explain the problems occurring in Denali Park

03 The author infers that some mine owners might hesitate to sell their land to the Park Service for which of the following reasons?

(A) There may be increasing demand for the ore in the mines.
(B) They might want to move to the towns.
(C) They might receive more money selling their land to developers.
(D) They might want to build a house on their property.

The ideal for humanity often has been characterized as a well-rounded individual with multiple interests and talents — the "Renaissance man." This flattering term has long been used to describe persons with rich and varied interests. The concept of the Renaissance man or woman may originate from Baldassare Castiglione's 1518 work, *The Book of the Courtier*. Courtiers were noblemen and noblewomen who had the means to pursue personal and cultural refinement. Castiglione felt that the ideal male courtier should be skilled not only in writing and oratory, but in the arts, sports, and use of weapons as well. In all things the courtier should be confident and suave, reflecting his command of any situation. The ideal court woman was to be familiar with literature and art, have the utmost moral character, and always act in a feminine manner.

If anyone embodied the Renaissance man, it was without a doubt Leonardo da Vinci. ①_____ his famous artistic skills that produced the Mona Lisa, da Vinci also studied anatomy, astronomy, botany, and geology, and drew up designs for hundreds of mechanical inventions. The American counterpart to da Vinci might be Benjamin Franklin, who was an accomplished writer, inventor, and statesman himself. ②_____ in modern times, few men or women can approximate the breadth of learning and achievement shown by da Vinci or Franklin. In a time of increasing technology and specialization, the Renaissance man or woman is unfortunately an endangered species.

01 The underlined word well-rounded means _____.
   (A) having desirably varied abilities
   (B) being disposed to diligent study
   (C) being excessively aware of being observed by others
   (D) being inclined to associate with the company of others

02 Which of the following would be most appropriate for ① and ②?
   (A) Despite — Therefore
   (B) Besides — Also
   (C) In addition to — Yet
   (D) As a result of — However

03 What is the author's attitude toward the ideal of the Renaissance man?

(A) strong admiration
(B) outright disdain
(C) sentimental nostalgia
(D) biased romanticism

04 According to the passage, why might Renaissance men or women be difficult to find today?

(A) People today simply do not value a balanced life.
(B) Our culture is no longer influenced by the Renaissance.
(C) They would tend to be modest people and thus difficult to identify.
(D) People's skills are so specialized today that they cannot be as versatile.

PASSAGE

251
—
300

The fact that superior service can generate a competitive advantage for a company does not mean that every attempt at improving service will create such an advantage. Investments in service, like those in production and distribution, must be balanced against other types of investments on the basis of direct, tangible benefits such as cost reduction and increased revenues. If a company is already effectively on a par with its competitors because it provides service that avoids a damaging reputation and keeps customers from leaving at an unacceptable rate, then investment in higher service levels may be wasted, since service is a deciding factor for customers only in extreme situations.

This truth was not apparent to managers of one regional bank, which failed to improve its competitive position despite its investment in reducing the time a customer had to wait for a teller. The bank managers did not recognize the level of customer inertia in the consumer banking industry that arises from the inconvenience of switching banks. Nor did they analyze their service improvement to determine whether it would attract new customers by producing a new standard of service that would excite customers or by proving it difficult for competitors to copy. The only merit of the improvement was that it could easily be described to customers.

01 The primary purpose of the passage is to _____.
(A) contrast possible outcomes of a type of business investment
(B) suggest more careful evaluation of a type of business investment
(C) illustrate various ways in which a type of business investment could fail to enhance revenues
(D) criticize the way in which managers tend to analyze the costs and benefits of business investments

02 The passage suggests that bank managers failed to consider whether or not the service improvement _____.
(A) was too complicated to be easily described to prospective customers
(B) could be sustained if the number of customers increased significantly
(C) was an innovation that competing banks could have imitated
(D) was adequate to bring the bank's general level of service to a level that was comparable with that of its competitors

03 Which of the following is closest in meaning to the underlined word "tangible"?
   (A) concrete
   (B) sustaining
   (C) exuberant
   (D) negligible

04 The author uses the underlined word "only" most likely in order to _____.
   (A) highlight the oddity of the service improvement
   (B) emphasize the relatively low value of the investment in service improvement
   (C) single out a certain merit of the service improvement from other merits
   (D) point out the limited duration of the actual service improvement

Whenever I succeeded in the American world, my brothers were supportive, whereas Papa would be disdainful, undermined by my obvious capitulation to the ways of the West. I wanted to be like my Caucasian friends. Not only did I want to look like them, I wanted to act like them. I tried hard to be outgoing and socially aggressive and act confidently, like my girlfriends. At home I was careful not to show these personality traits to my father. For him it was bad enough that I did not even look Japanese: I was too big, and I walked too assertively. My behavior at home was never calm and serene, but around my father I still tried to be as Japanese as I could.

As I passed puberty and grew more interested in boys, I soon became aware that an Oriental female evoked a certain kind of interest from males. I was still too young to understand how or why an Oriental female fascinated Caucasian men, and of course, far too young to see then that it was a form of "not seeing." My brothers would warn me, "Don't trust the Western boys. They only want one thing. They'll treat you like a servant and expect you to wait on them hand and foot. They don't even know how to be nice to you." My brothers never dated Caucasian girls. In fact, I never really dated Caucasian boys until I went to college. In high school, I used to sneak out to dances and parties where I would meet them. I wouldn't even dare to think what Papa would do if he knew.

What my brothers were saying was that I should not act toward Caucasian males as I did toward them. I must not "wait on them" or allow them to think I would, because they wouldn't understand. In other words, be a Japanese female around Japanese men and act as American around Caucasian men. The ①_____ within a "②_____" resulted not only in confusion for me of my role, or roles, as a female, but also in who or what I was racially. With the admonitions of my brothers lurking deep in my consciousness, I would try to be aggressive, assertive and "come on strong" toward Caucasian men. I mustn't let them think I was submissive, passive, and all-giving like Madame Butterfly. With Asian males I would tone down my natural enthusiasm and settle into patterns instilled in me through the models of my mother and sisters. I was not comfortable in either role.

01 The author's father reacted negatively to her successes in the Western world because _____.

(A) his expectations were that she could do even better than he had done
(B) he realized worldy success alone could not make her happy
(C) he envied her for having opportunities that he had never known
(D) he felt her Westernization was costing him his authority over her

02 By describing the white boy's fascination with Oriental women as "not seeing", the author primarily wishes to convey that _____.

(A) the white boys were reluctant to date their Oriental classmates or see them socially
(B) they had no idea what she was like as an individual human being
(C) the boys were too shy to look the girls in the eye
(D) the boys could not see her attractions because she was too large to meet Japanese standards of beauty

03 Which of the following would be most appropriate for ① and ②?

(A) double race — single expectation
(B) double identity — double standard
(C) single race — double expectation
(D) single nationality — single standard

04 The figure of Madame Butterfly can best be described as _____.

(A) a model the author sought to emulate
(B) the pattern the author's brothers wished her to follow
(C) a role the author eventually found comfortable
(D) an ethnic stereotype

Years ago, immigrants in the United States believed in the American Dream: the idea that through hard work, courage and determination anyone could achieve prosperity. [I] The American Dream did not immediately turn out for most immigrants, but their diligence and willingness to sacrifice for their families became an investment that yielded dividends in following generations. [II] Life became much easier for their sons and daughters, grandchildren and great-grandchildren, who (because of their parents) were able to earn college degrees and pursue successful professions. It was once common for every new generation to aspire to live better than its parents did. [III] Becoming an American meant learning another language; learning and obeying the laws and customs of the land; embracing the U.S. over native countries and siding with America in war. [IV] Today, the American Dream has radically changed — and some would argue shattered. Many immigrants come to the U.S. to find a better life, while others come strictly for employment, sending their wages back home to their families in the native lands. Foreigners once came to America to become Americans, to be "Americanized." They instilled this desire in their children as they became part of society. Their culture fused into the greater American culture, which became the Great Melting Pot. And that, many argue, is precisely why so many who come to the U.S. no longer desire to ①_____. They fear losing their national culture and traditions, their identity. And so they cling to their languages and customs, even to the point of insisting — that street signs and driver's tests and government forms be given in their native language. Speaking, reading and writing in English — once considered necessary to fulfilling the American Dream — is now viewed as obsolete, intrusive, even an infringement upon one's "right" to live however he or she may choose. A cultural war of opposing ideologies is being waged, polarizing government and dividing the nation.

01 If the above passage is divided into two, which would be the boundary?
(A) [I]   (B) [II]
(C) [III]   (D) [IV]

02 Which of the following is NOT mentioned in the passage?
(A) the definition of the American Dream
(B) the government's reaction to illegal immigrants
(C) the immigrants' attitude toward the American culture in the past
(D) the reason immigrants stick with their homeland culture

03 Which of the following is most appropriate for the blank ①?

(A) sacrifice
(B) volunteer
(C) segregate
(D) assimilate

04 Which of the following best exemplifies "the Great Melting Pot"?

(A) Texas in the U.S. where some of street signs are written in Spanish for the Hispanic immigrants
(B) Americans discriminating against immigrants who refuse to be "Americanized"
(C) Immigrants from different cultures identifying themselves as Americans and living in an American style
(D) The young generation in Korea enthusiastic about American culture such as songs, movies, and food, etc.

05 The author is most likely to agree with which of the following statements?

(A) It does not take long for immigrants to achieve the American Dream.
(B) Poverty among immigrants tends to be handed down to their children.
(C) Immigrants in the U.S. do not welcome the American Dream as they used to, which may destabilize the country.
(D) Recently, more and more immigrants in the U.S. think that their original culture is inferior to the American culture.

Morality may be a hard concept to grasp, but we acquire it fast. Marc Hauser, professor of psychology at Harvard University believes that all of us carry what he calls a sense of moral grammar — the ethical ①_____ of the basic grasp of speech that most linguists believe is with us from birth. However, merely being equipped with moral programming does not mean we ②_____ moral behavior. Something still has to boot up that software and configure it properly. ③Just as syntax is nothing until words are built upon it, so too is a sense of right and wrong useless until someone teaches you how to apply it. It's the people around us who do that teaching. Our species has a very conflicted sense of when we ought to help someone else and when we ought not, and the general rule is: "Help those close to home and ignore those far away." That's in part because the plight of a person you can see will always feel more real than the problems of someone whose suffering is merely described to you. But part of it is also rooted in you from a time when the welfare of your tribe was essential for your survival but the welfare of an opposing tribe was not. One of the most powerful tools for enforcing group morals is the practice of shunning. If membership in a tribe is the way you ensure yourself food, family and protection from predators, being ④blackballed can be a terrifying thing. Clubs, social groups and fraternities expel undesirable members, and the U.S. military retains the threat of discharge as a disciplinary tool, even grading the punishment as "dishonorable," darkening the mark a former service person must carry for life. Human beings were small, defenseless and vulnerable to predators. Avoiding banishment would be important to us.

01 Which of the following is best suitable for the blanks ① and ②?

(A) consistency — exercise
(B) equivalent — practice
(C) precedent — retain
(D) disposition — alter

02 Which of the following best describes the underlined sentence ③?

(A) Nothing is complete unless you put it in final shape.
(B) Many a little makes a mickle.
(C) A stitch in time saves nine.
(D) Actions should go hand in hand with words.

03 Which of the following best replaces the underlined word ④blackballed?

(A) harassed
(B) excluded
(C) threatened
(D) suspected

04 According to the passage, morality functions _____.

(A) as a symbol of humanity
(B) as a criterion of performance
(C) as a means of security
(D) as a way of obtaining success in life

Alchemy in general was forbidden in a bull issued by Pope John XXII in 1317, a prohibition which indicates that the practice of alchemy must have been fairly widespread. In the theories of the medieval alchemists there was not a great deal that was new. The metals, they believed, were generated by the union of the male principle of sulphur and the female principle of mercury, and the base metals could be ennobled by a process of death and resuscitation. Inorganic substances in general were living beings, made up of a body and a soul, or matter and spirit. The constituents of substances could be separated by heating, when the spirit came off as a vapour which could be condensed into a liquid in some cases. The characteristics and properties of a substance were determined by its spirit, and so a liquid obtained by distillation contained the concentrated essentials of the substance from which it came.

Such liquids were therefore highly active and potent agents, giving new life to old bodies, and conferring noble properties upon base matter. Thus, in theory, a transmutation could be effected by transferring the spirit of a noble metal to the matter of base metals. However, of the various metals only mercury would distil and give an isolatable 'spirit'. In accordance with the theory of the alchemists, mercury vapour silvered the surfaces of base metals, and so mercury was regarded as the spirit of silver, the progenitor of the metals, and indeed the origin of all things.

01 Which of the following is true according to the passage?
(A) Alchemy must have been widespread.
(B) The theories of the alchemists were progressive.
(C) The base metals were generated by the union of principle of sulphur and mercury
(D) A transmutation was effected by transferring the spirit of base metals to the matter of noble metals.

02 Which of the following is implied in the underlined word "essentials"?
(A) the constituents of substances
(B) the spirit of a noble metal
(C) the soul and spirit of inorganic substances
(D) the origin of all things

03   According to the passage, which about alchemy cannot be inferred?

(A) The medieval alchemists believed the base metals could be ennobled by a process.
(B) Roman Catholicism didn't acknowledge alchemy.
(C) Not only mercury but other metals could be separated into matter and spirit.
(D) The constituents of substances could be separated by heating.

The sociologist Melvin H. Kohn cites discipline as one of the most significant value differences between middle-class and working-class parents: "Working-class parents want the children to conform to externally imposed standards, while middle-class parents are more attentive to internal dynamics." Hence, working-class parents tend to emphasize the consequences of children's actions, whereas middle-class parents tend to emphasize intentions. Middle-class mothers, for instance, are much more likely to punish their youngsters when they "lose their temper" than when they engage in "wild play." They view "temper tantrums" but not wild play as a loss of self-control and inner restraint. Working-class mothers, in contrast, punish their children in both situations because they are concerned with the disruptive consequences of the behavior. Kohn suggests that these differences in values and child-rearing practices stem in large part from differences in occupational conditions. Working-class parents anticipate that as adults conformity and obedience will become highly valued traits. Middle-class parents tend to envision their children in professional careers, where initiative and self-discipline are thought to bring success. Recently, James D. and Sonia R. Wright carried out a partial replication of Kohn's study and confirmed the finding that the tendency to value self-direction increases with social rank. The Wrights argue, however, that Kohn exaggerates the importance of occupation, adducing instead level of education as the source of the link between social class and the values parents transmit to their children.

Social class differences show up not only in child-rearing practices but also in the relationships parents establish with their children. For instance, both middle-class parents are expected to be responsive to the psychological needs of their children. Consequently, the parenting roles of middle-class fathers and mothers are not vastly different: both concentrate their energies and efforts on the inner development of the child.

In working-class families, however, where socialization practices center on constraint and obedience, the mother is more likely to be supportive with the father the disciplinarian, though recent forces of social change, such as the women's movement, rising levels of education, and greater educational opportunities to women and ethnic minorities, have begun to influence young working-class people, blurring the traditional correlation between class and the division of labor in parenting.

01 The primary purpose of the passage is to _____.

(A) review the arguments in a recent sociological debate over whether economic class differences affect child-rearing
(B) outline some appropriate child-rearing methods for different economic classes
(C) present illustrations of recent ideas of the connection between class and parent-child relationships
(D) refute a prevalent theory about economic class as a source of differences in child-rearing

02 Which of the following best summarizes the differences between parents of the working class and those of the middle class?

(A) Working-class parents punish more severely.
(B) Middle-class parents place a greater emphasis on education.
(C) Middle-class parents establish closer relations with their children.
(D) Working-class parents place a greater emphasis on external features of children's behavior.

03 What attitude does the author of this passage assume toward the studies of Kohn and the Wrights?

(A) The author questions the accuracy of the terms "temper tantrum" and "wild play," but acknowledges the general validity of both studies' conclusions.
(B) While citing the specific examples as instructive, the author disagrees with the basic argument of both studies.
(C) The author presents the arguments of both studies without expressing a preference, while implying an acceptance of the fundamental idea.
(D) Both studies are presented as ideologically sound though questionable in terms of their methods.

In 1906, German neurologist Alois Alzheimer described what he had seen in a recently deceased female patient. At age 51, she could no longer write her name without prompting, was unable to run her household and had signs of increasing disorientation and progressive impairment of memory, judgment, decision making, language and physical skills.

[I] When he saw slices of the brain under the microscope, three features struck him. The brain itself was severely shrunken. Secondly, the brain tissue revealed a strange accumulation of a peculiar substance. Thirdly, inside the brain's neurons, or nerve-signal transmitters, were stringy tangles of another substance that looked like gnarled twine. These substances, which we refer to as plaques and tangles, are now considered the two essential features that distinguish Alzheimer's disease from other neurological disorders.

[II] By the 1960s, however, scientists began to realize that the plaques and tangles were not normal even in the elderly and that an insidious disease process was occurring.

[III] To Alzheimer, she seemed prematurely senile. She was too young to be showing symptoms of the dementia then thought to be a normal part of aging. He called it pre-senile dementia. Her symptoms got worse until she was comatose. When she died at 55, he examined her brain.

[IV] For over 50 years, however, the symptoms of Alzheimer's were thought to be a normal part of aging, and a true disease only in people who had it before age 65. Those sufferers represent five to seven per cent of cases. They have familial Alzheimer's, explains Dr Jack Diamond, a professor at McMaster University and scientific director for the Alzheimer Society of Canada.

01 이 글의 제목으로 가장 적절한 것은?

(A) Differences Between Dementia and Alzheimer's Disease
(B) Understanding of Alzheimer's As A Neurological Disease
(C) Achievements of Alzheimer and Other Medical Scientists
(D) The Two Substances in the Brain Contributing to Aging

02 이 글의 첫 단락에 이은 나머지 네 단락들의 적절한 순서는?

(A) [I] — [III] — [II] — [IV]
(B) [III] — [I] — [II] — [IV]
(C) [III] — [I] — [IV] — [II]
(D) [IV] — [II] — [III] — [I]

03 다음 중 이 글의 내용과 일치하지 않는 것은?

(A) Alzheimer's patient described above could not write her own name unless someone told it to her.
(B) Among the symptoms of dementia is that the patient does not know where he is or where he should go.
(C) Alzheimer's disease can be caused by hereditary factors and can progress without being noticed.
(D) Alzheimer's disease is not a true disease but just a result of aging if it occurs after the age of 65 years.

"Your eyes are getting heavy... you are becoming sleepy..."

Hypnotists use these or similar words to induce a trance called hypnosis. For a long time, hypnosis was considered a trick. A few enthusiasts believed it could be used to heal the sick, but most doctors scoffed at such notions. They had no faith in what they called "mind games." Now, however, times have changed. Doctors understand the importance of the mind-body connection and are willing to take a second look at hypnosis.

Just what is hypnosis? Most reference books define it as an altered state of consciousness. Some people believe that definition is accurate. Others say it is all wrong. Doctor Robert Baker has been practicing hypnosis for more than 20 years, but he doesn't believe it produces an altered state. "It's _____ to argue that hypnosis involves some sort of special state," Baker says, "when we can't find it no matter how long we look." Indeed, researchers have found no evidence that the brain changes during hypnosis. People like Baker think that the hypnotized mind plays a trick on itself. Hypnosis, they say, occurs when one part of the brain shuts down and another part remains highly focused.

Other people define hypnosis as a state of repose. The body relaxes, the mind is more open and attentive, and breathing becomes more regular. Doctor Robert Fisher, a psychiatrist, says hypnosis is like going to the movies. You are aware of everything when you enter the theater. You can hear the crackle of candy wrappers. You notice the head of the person in front of you. You feel the spilled popcorn under your feet. But, says Fisher, "Once the screen fills with images, you gradually become absorbed and you're in a state of focused concentration."

Most people don't care whether or not hypnosis is an altered state of consciousness. They are not looking for the perfect definition. They only ask: Will it work for me? Will hypnosis help me stop smoking or lose weight?

On this practical level, there is lots of evidence that hypnosis works. There is proof that it can change certain behaviors. Cigarette smoking is one example. Psychotherapist Laura Foster Collins uses hypnosis to help her clients kick the habit. Some of them gave up smoking completely and even lost the urge to smoke. Still, only about one smoker in five quits for good as a result of hypnosis. Anyone who has ever smoked knows how difficult it is to break the habit. Hypnosis can help, but it must be combined with a strong desire to quit.

01 Which of the following is best suitable for the blank?
(A) absurd
(B) reliable
(C) impartial
(D) interesting

02 Which is closest in meaning to the underlined expression "Hypnosis, they say, occurs when one part of the brain shuts down and another part remains highly focused"?
(A) Hypnosis occurs when the brain completely goes to sleep.
(B) Hypnosis occurs when a part of the brain sleeps while another concentrates intensely.
(C) Hypnosis occurs when the brain shuts down completely and is then able to become highly focused.
(D) Hypnosis occurs when the brain becomes highly focused on sleep.

03 People who want to use hypnosis to quit smoking must _____.
(A) be able to hypnotize themselves
(B) promise that they won't smoke after being hypnotized
(C) listen to music while under hypnosis
(D) be motivated to give up the habit

04 Which of the following best describes the author's attitude toward hypnosis?
(A) doubtful
(B) assured
(C) hopeful
(D) reserved

Studying Mahatma Gandhi's use of clothing as a metaphor for unity, empowerment and liberation from imperial subjugation, Salesian edu-communicator Peter Gonsalves' latest work *Khadi: Gandhi's Mega Symbol of Subversion* investigates the power of a symbol to qualitatively transform society.

Threading together historical evidence by discussing the complex challenges in Gandhi's highly polarized environment, Gonsalves examines the symbolic potential for change — through khadi — as a strategic ploy to achieve independence. The book is intimately connected to his previous work, *Clothing for Liberation*. The point of departure is the same: Gandhi's communication through clothing — a choice that Gonsalves claims was "an extremely courageous strategy intended to destabilize unjust authoritative systems in the pursuit of ①purna swaraj." However, the present work is noteworthy for the originality of its approach, the richness of the documentation it supplies, and the clarity with which the relevance and depth of Gandhi's thoughts and actions are demonstrated.

The author adopts a multi-disciplinary approach to bring together historical evidence of Gandhi's search for ②a semiotics of attire in his quest for personal integrity and socio-political change and closely examines the subversion underlying his ③_____ communication. He also discusses the complex challenges in Gandhi's highly polarized environment, such as the conflict between the British Empire and the Indian National Congress, the Hindu-Muslim tensions, the rural-urban divide and the role of the caste in fragmentation of the Hindu identity.

01 Which is true according to the passage?

(A) Peter Gonsalves recently wrote a book review titled "*Khadi: Gandhi's Mega Symbol of Subversion.*"
(B) Mahatma Gandhi liked to wear clothes of khadi, which made it an integral part of Indian textile industry.
(C) Gonsalves believes that Gandhi recognized khadi as a symbol of spiritual emancipation as well as bodily bondage.
(D) Gonsalves depicts colonial India as a mutually antagonistic society divided in terms of class, race, and religion.

02 Which phrase can best define ①purna swaraj, according to the passage?

(A) imperial subjugation
(B) total independence
(C) complete acquiescence
(D) indisputable authority

03 Which phrase is closest in meaning to ②a semiotics of attire in the passage?
    (A) the use of clothing as a metaphor
    (B) what it means to clothe people well
    (C) the meaning of a leader's frugal life
    (D) what attracts people to a common goal

04 Choose the best word for blank ③ above.
    (A) apocryphal   (B) florescent
    (C) sartorial   (D) resplendent

Most societies, especially nation states, seem to have some notion of social class. However, class is not a universal phenomenon. Many hunter-gatherer societies do not have social classes, often lack permanent leaders, and actively (가)avoid dividing their members into hierarchical power structures.

The factors that determine class vary widely from one society to another. Even within a society, different people or groups may have very different ideas about asked when trying to define class include 1) the most important criteria in distinguishing classes, 2) the number of class divisions that exist, 3) the extent to which individuals recognize these divisions if they are to be meaningful, and 4) whether or not class divisions even exist in the US and other industrial societies.

The theoretical debate over the definition of class remains an important one today. Sociologist Dennis Wrong defines class in two ways — realist and nominalist. The realist definition relies on clear class boundaries to which people adhere in order to create social groupings. They identify themselves with a particular class and interact mainly with people in this class. The nominalist definition of class focuses on the characteristics that people share in a given class — education, occupation, etc. Class is therefore determined not by the group in which you place yourself or the people you interact with, but rather by these common characteristics.

The most basic class distinction between the two groups is between the powerful and the powerless. People in social classes with greater power attempt to cement their own positions in society and maintain their ranking above the lower social classes in the social hierarchy. Social classes with a great deal of power are usually viewed as elites, at least within their own societies. In the less complex societies, power/class hierarchies may or may not exist.

01 밑줄 친 (가)avoid와 의미가 같지 않은 것을 고르시오.
(A) convert   (B) evade
(C) avert   (D) shun

02 다음 중 계급을 정의함에 있어 제기되는 의문들에 해당하지 않는 것을 고르시오.
(A) criteria in distinguishing classes
(B) number of class divisions
(C) the degree to which people recognize the divisions
(D) history of class divisions

03 위 글의 내용으로 보아 아래에 제시된 주장이 해당하는 것은?

I belong to the class A because I like the people here.

(A) realist definition
(B) nominalist definition
(C) all of the above
(D) none of the above

04 위 글의 내용과 일치하는 것은?

(A) Societies have social classes without an exception.
(B) Every society has the same class factors.
(C) Power serves as a criterion for the most fundamental class distinction.
(D) According to nominalist definition, class is determined by the group you interact with rather than common characteristics.

There's an animal apocalypse afoot in the northeastern U.S. Between 5.7 million and 6.7 million bats are estimated to have died since 2006 from white-nose fungus — an infection marked by the telltale white fuzz around their noses — in 16 U.S. states and Canada, according to officials at the U.S. Fish and Wildlife Service. The new estimate finds that the death toll is far worse than wildlife biologists believed, perhaps five to six times as high as previous count in 2009, and it could spell disaster — not just for the animals but for humans as well.

The deadly fungus has the potential to erase entire species of bats in the Northeast. Biologists who have painstakingly counted bat carcasses in mines and caves each winter since the infection was first detected more than five years ago in a cave near Albany, N.Y., found that in some affected caves, not a single night flyer remained. The most vulnerable species include the little brown bat, the tricolored bat and their northern long-eared cousins, all usually long-lived species, scientists say.

As alarming as the possible extinction of these bat species is, even more worrisome is the potential loss of a critical part of the ecosystem. A female bat of reproductive age can consume her weight in insects each year. If the bats are wiped out, insect populations could explode, including pests that can decimate food and agriculture yields and infest forests, not to mention the swarms that plague summer barbecues and spread disease to humans.

So far, bat populations in the Western U.S. seem to have been spared the fungus, but biologists are concerned that it is poised to spread. More than 140 partners from government and academic institutions met recently to devise a response to white-nose syndrome, but at the moment there is no treatment for it. Scientists are studying the bodies of afflicted bats to find a remedy, hopefully before it's too late.

01 Choose the one closest in meaning to the underlined "afoot."
(A) approaching
(B) finishing
(C) happening
(D) deepening

02 Which of the following is not a possible aftermath of the spread of the fungus?
(A) increasing sterility of female bats
(B) sharp decrease of food production
(C) forest damage caused by pests
(D) outbreaks of plagues among humans

03 Which of the following can be inferred about "white-nose fungus"?

(A) It has spread across the United States but is on the verge of decline.
(B) Many scientists have tried to come up with a cure for it but it's too late.
(C) It does an equal amount of damage to the entire bat species in the Northeast.
(D) Wildlife biologists didn't expect it would claim the lives of this many bats.

04 What is the main idea of the passage?

(A) A fungus that would devastate bat communities was found in a cave in the Northeastern U.S.
(B) Fungus-infected bats are dying in record numbers, heralding a real problem for human beings.
(C) We should worry more about the loss of the ecosystem than about the extinction of bat species.
(D) Scientists have planned a response to combat white-nose syndrome with the aid of government.

In the Apartheid era, political violence in South Africa was invariably seen in black and white. But in the wave of anti-immigrant carnage that swept the country in late May, all 62 of those killed were black. The hatred and violence that has shaken a country that optimistically proclaims itself the Rainbow Nation was not about racism — it was symptom of globalization. "Globalization might be creating rich countries with poor people," economist Joseph Stiglitz has noted. That is apparent in South Africa, whose postapartheid government adopted an open-market economy that drew cheers from Wall Street and the international banking community and helped achieve an impressive, steady annual economic growth rate of 4-5%. But that growth has done little to reverse inequality or dangerously high levels of unemployment. Globalization was supposed to be the tide to lift all boats, but (a)<u>the evidence in South Africa suggests that millions of boats are not merely missing the tide, they're in an entirely different ocean.</u> Your experience of globalization depends on what you have in the bank. In business class, the world is your village, and you're connected with your (b)<u>counterparts</u> from all corners. For those whose journey involves a long truck ride through a desert or a dangerous boat ride across open sea, globalization is often much less forgiving. Millions of people every year seek to migrate, legally and illegally, from poor countries, either to the industrialized world or to more prosperous developing countries such as South Africa. But the poor in the developing world are determined not to diminish the little they have by sharing it with foreign migrants and, like many in the rich world, are erecting _____ to outsiders settling in their midst.

01. Which of the following is <u>not</u> true about South Africa?

(A) The recent anti-immigration sentiments in South Africa reflect globalization's damaging side.
(B) "The Rainbow Nation" reflects the South Africans' rosy view of their future.
(C) Postapartheid policy of the South African government fueled open-market economy.
(D) Globalization in South Africa has had two-fold effects.

02 Find the sentence that best exemplifies the underlined sentence (a)"the evidence in South Africa suggests that millions of boats are not merely missing the tide, they're in an entirely different ocean."

(A) Tens of thousands lost their homes as a result of anti-immigrant violence.
(B) In November last year, the South African Institute of Race Relations estimated 4.2 million South Africans were living on $1 a day in 2005, up from 1.9 million in 1996.
(C) The proportion of people living on less than 2 dollars a day shrank from 67% in 1981 to 47% in 2004.
(D) Annual growth rate has risen steadily in South Africa with the result that the average persons are better off.

03 To which of the following does the word (b)counterparts refer?

(A) bank managers involved in a deal
(B) immigrant people around the globe
(C) business class people
(D) boat riders from poor countries

04 Which of the following would fit best in the blank?

(A) barriers
(B) circumspections
(C) vestiges
(D) commotions

05 Which of the following might be the best title of the passage?

(A) Symptoms and Effects of Globalization
(B) The Globalization Trap in South Africa
(C) Anti-Immigration Hostility in South Africa
(D) Past and Present of the Rainbow Nation

A recent, influential paper argued that the straightforward interpretation of money is that it works like a tool, in that it enables the owner to get what he wants. But that's not quite exactly correct. A genuine tool enables you to do things, directly. It doesn't matter what other people think about a tool. But money depends utterly on what other people think about it. Unless they agree to recognize it as having a particular kind of value, it is just useless paper and metal. Money, psychologically speaking, is our projection onto coins, bills, bank accounts and other financial instruments of our beliefs, hopes and fears about how those things will affect who we are, what will happen to us and how we will be treated by others or by ourselves. Money is control over the environment by means of the social system. You have control to make the system give you what you want.

What causes us to be so concerned about money is largely our beliefs about what will be the attitudes and behaviors of others toward us, as well as how we believe we will treat ourselves, depending upon whether or not we have enough of it. Clearly, thoughts about the _____ of money have important personal and interpersonal meanings. Otto Fenichel, a psychoanalyst, pointed out that depression is often associated with compulsion neurosis and that very often fear of _____ plays a role in the clinical picture of depression.

01 According to the passage, money psychologically would function as _____.
(A) a tool for self-sufficiency
(B) a mental ground for social interactions
(C) an indicator of financial success
(D) an expression of suppressed desires
(E) a springboard for cooperation among people

02 Which of the following CANNOT be inferred about money?
(A) Money indirectly enables us to do what we want to.
(B) Having much money can make us believe others will be kind to us.
(C) Having little money directly drives us into depression.
(D) Money can influence our future as well as our present.
(E) The value of money is not determined by its owner's thought.

03 Choose one which is most appropriate for the blanks.

(A) source — robbery
(B) sufficiency — poverty
(C) merit — penury
(D) waste — bankruptcy
(E) quantity — greed

04 According to the passage, the pragmatic value of money would depend on _____.

(A) the amount of money in circulation
(B) what the structure of an economy is like
(C) the absolute value established by authorities
(D) the value of materials that make up money
(E) the acceptance by people in a society

The big turning point was when I was thirteen, and Richard was in graduate school. He had been at home, and had left to go back to Princeton. There was a book lying on the table, and I said to my mother, "Richard's forgotten one of his books." I opened it, and inside was my name in Richard's handwriting, and a bookplate with my name on it. It was astronomy. A college textbook on astronomy. He had bought it secondhand in Princeton and left it for me, without saying anything.

Well, I asked him, "How can I read it? It's so hard." He said, "You start at the beginning and you read as far as you can get, until you are lost. Then you start at the beginning again, and you keep working through until you can understand the whole book."

My great ambition for years was to be an assistant to some man, just to be allowed to look at the stars. Not to do any science, but just to be his assistant — this was my child goal. I couldn't imagine anything further than that. My ambition was to be the person that fixed the telescopes so somebody else could look at the stars.

Richard always encouraged me. When I realized that what I really wanted was a telescope, I told Richard, and he said he would buy a piece of glass for me. I could grind the telescope lens at home, and then he would test it at Princeton on the machines there. I was all excited, but my mother and father decided that I couldn't grind it in my room. I don't remember why, but probably because glass dust gets all over everything. But we lived in an apartment block, and downstairs in the basement there were storage-bin rooms for furniture and so on, which were like little rooms. One of the boys who lived in the building had made a wonderful chemistry lab down there in one of these bins, and I used to go see it sometimes. So I figured I could go down there and grind my lens. Wonderful! I told my parents, and the answer was no. No, because they were afraid that I would be raped in the basement. Well, if I had been a boy they would have raised heaven and hell to get me to grind that lens. So I never had a telescope.

In the book there was mention of a woman called Celillia Payne-Gaposhkin. She was at Harvard, she was an astronomer, and she was good enough to be in this book. So ①<u>there was something wrong with this theory of my parents</u>. I figured, if somebody else could do it, I could do it too. And I did. So — just because things are impossible isn't any reason not to do them!

01 Who do you think Richard is in the passage?
   (A) a boyfriend   (B) a visitor
   (C) a brother   (D) a teacher

02 Which of the following is most likely to precede the passage?
   (A) In spite of my dream, my mother dissuaded me from being an astronomer.
   (B) My father thought science was such a wonderful thing.
   (C) I was always original like that — I did almost everything by myself, getting clues from books as to what was an interesting subject.
   (D) My father loved nature when I was a kid, although he was ill by then.

03 Which of the following is the best title for the passage?
   (A) Father's Great Influence on His Child
   (B) Overcoming Obstacles
   (C) Love of Nature and Astronomy
   (D) Environment As Well As Heredity Makes Genius

04 Which of the following best describes the underlined sentence ①?
   (A) My parents had impractical mind comparing with young generation.
   (B) My parents' knowledge was one thing and their deed was another.
   (C) My parents did not allow because of prejudice against women.
   (D) The wrong scientific theory caused my parents to make a false judgment.

It has long been said that if American economy sneezes, the rest of the world gets pneumonia. To escape from ①this syndrome, some foreign leaders have warned against becoming too intertwined with American financial vehicles and markets. But now that the credit contraction US financial firms have provoked is infecting economies around the world, even foreign leaders hostile to Washington have reason not to gloat over America's comeuppance.

In Europe, the credit squeeze brought to the fore latent quarrels between those who seek European Union-wide solutions to the crisis and countries that do not want their euros to be spent rescuing banks elsewhere on the continent. French President Nicolas Sarkozy, who currently occupies the six-month rotating presidency of the EU, recently proposed a common EU bailout fund for banks of all 27 members; Germany and Britain were ardently opposed.

Worse yet, once-proud German officials learned over the past few days that one of their biggest lending institutions, an outfit called Hypo Real Estate, needed a bailout that would take more than $70 billion. This unnerving revelation came barely two weeks after ②Germany's finance minister mistakenly assured his compatriots that the United States was "the source and the focus of the crisis."

Specific as it may be to the EU's internal debates about national sovereignty, the European reaction to the financial turmoil offers a crucial lesson for Americans. The next president will have to seek multilateral cooperation not only on terrorism and nuclear proliferation, but also on rules and regulations for an ever more globalized economy. If America is too big to fail, it is also too connected to the rest of the world to go it alone.

01 Which of the following would be the best title for the passage?

(A) The Worst Financial Crisis Since the Great Depression
(B) The Financial Conflicts Between the US and EU
(C) The US Financial Crisis and Its Impact on Europe
(D) The US Market Plunge Inducing Crisis Fears

02 Which of the following does ①this syndrome mean?

(A) A recessionary crisis in the US can bring worse problems to all countries.
(B) The made-in-USA financial crisis sweeps the US with the force of "one-hundred hurricanes."
(C) English or German investors do not shake in their shoes every time Wall Street sneezes.
(D) Americans are proud of themselves for infecting people from all over the world.

03 What lesson can we get from ②Germany's finance minister's behavior?

(A) Do to others as you would have them do to you.
(B) Don't count your chickens before they're hatched.
(C) One should examine oneself before condemning others.
(D) The manner of giving is worth more than the gift.

04 Which of the following is NOT stated or implied in the passage?

(A) America's financial turmoil and economic mess is now spreading wide across the Globe.
(B) America gets its comeuppance for economic over-dependence on the rest of the world.
(C) Germany was opposed to the proposal of a common EU bailout fund for banks in other countries.
(D) When the banks of one nation face financial risks, the businesses of the rest of the world can be threatened.

White holes are similar to black holes except that white holes are ejecting matter whereas black holes are _____ matter. The existence of white holes is implied by a negative square root solution to the Schwarzschild metric for space-time-matter continuum. It is important to remember that black and white holes can be composed from matter and antimatter. [I]

A worm hole, which joins white holes, is known as the Einstein-Rosen bridge and is one of the most fascinating concepts in theoretical physics. Theoretically, a worm hole could be stabilized to allow a safe equilibrium between matter and antimatter white holes. To stabilize the worm hole, the throat of the singularity contains matter and antimatter white holes, which are spherical in nature. The antimatter has a negative mass and exerts a positive surface pressure. [II]

The Einstein-Rosen bridge keeps the matter and antimatter black holes separated. The oscillations between the black holes at opposite ends of the worm hole force the black holes to become white holes that eject matter and antimatter in opposite directions forming the spiral arms of stars within the galactic disk. [III]

The antimatter negative mass ensures the throat of the worm hole lies outside the protected region and the positive surface pressure prevents the throat of the worm hole from completely collapsing. [IV] Einstein's equations specify what the energy-momentum content of matter must be in an area to produce the needed geometry. Matter and antimatter white holes can stabilize a worm hole.

01 What does the passage mainly discuss?

(A) the difference between white and black holes
(B) fascinating concepts in theoretical physics
(C) matter and antimatter white holes
(D) the origin and evolution of black holes

02 Which of the following is most suitable for the blank?

(A) evacuating   (B) offering
(C) releasing   (D) absorbing

03 Where would the following sentence best fit into?

The matter and antimatter properties are not arbitrary or purely theoretical for producing a stable worm hole.

(A) [I] (B) [II]
(C) [III] (D) [IV]

04 Which of the following is NOT true according to the passage?

(A) Matter and antimatter black holes are separated by a worm hole.
(B) The actual existence of white holes is confirmed.
(C) The properties of white holes help the stabilization of a worm hole.
(D) Black holes can be converted into white holes.

Censorship was hardly a concern of educators, although it was an obvious concern for librarians in the United States. Before World War II, censorship rarely surfaced in schools, although some works — such as John Steinbeck's *Of Mice and Men* and *The Grapes of Wrath* — did cause some discussion in the newspapers of the time. When students began to read the books, the furor spread into the schools. Norman Mailer published *The Naked and the Dead* in 1949, and J. D. Salinger wrote *Catcher in the Rye* in 1951, which described the society of that day as overly permissive, lax, and even immoral. Youth and young adults were caught up in that description. Most of the objections were aimed at the writers and publishers, and certainly some were aimed at the bookstores stocking the books. Few high school teachers taught the controversial books for many years; even fewer librarians would stock them.

Perhaps as important, until about 1967, young-adult books were generally safe, pure, and simplistic, devoid of the reality that young people faced daily violence, pregnancy, alcohol, and drugs, etc. Then, in 1967, Ann Head's *Mr. and Mrs. Bo Jo Jones* and S.E. Hinton's *The Outsiders* appeared and the face of young-adults literature changed. The books that followed were not always great or honest, but a surprising number were. Teachers and librarians, who had accepted the possibility of censorship with adult authors popular with their students, now learned that the once-safe young-adult novel was no longer "safe." Censorship attacks soon began. Many of the works were denounced.

01 Which of the following CANNOT be inferred from the passage?
   (A) Educators were seldom concerned with censorship until students started reading controversial books.
   (B) It was difficult to find controversial books in libraries and schools in the early 1950s.
   (C) Some of the books which were heavily censored have been acknowledged as masterpiece.
   (D) Young-adult books changed greatly after *Mr. and Mrs. Bo Jo Jones* and *The Outsiders* were published.

02 The author's mention of Steinbeck's works is intended to _____.
   (A) remind the reader to avoid his works as questionable
   (B) portray Steinbeck as an innovative writer whose works are generally appealing
   (C) illustrate what "bad" books really are and warn students to shun them
   (D) present works that are familiar as an example of what censorship really is

03 What does the underlined sentence Youth and young adults were caught up in that description mean?

(A) They were aware of the social changes of the times.
(B) They were enthralled by the outspoken portrait of the society.
(C) They were involved in writing against the society.
(D) They were intelligent enough to understand difficult books.

04 According to the passage, information contained in young-adult novels until 1967 can be considered _____.

(A) old-fashioned but vulgar
(B) forthright and inspiring
(C) surprisingly exaggerated
(D) more superficial than thorough

Philosophy, like all other studies, aims primarily at knowledge. The knowledge it aims at is the kind of knowledge which gives unity and system to the body of the sciences, and the kind of knowledge which results from a critical examination of the grounds of our convictions, prejudices, and beliefs. But it cannot be maintained that philosophy has had any very great measure of success in its attempts to provide definite answers to its questions. If you ask a mathematician, a mineralogist, a historian, or any other man of learning, what definite body of truths has been ascertained by his science, ①his answer will last as long as you are willing to listen. But if you put the same question to a philosopher, he will, if he is candid, have to confess that his study has not achieved positive results such as have been achieved by other sciences. It is true that this is partly accounted for by the fact that, as soon as definite knowledge concerning any subject becomes possible, this subject ceases to be called philosophy, and becomes a separate science. The whole study of the heavens, which now belongs to astronomy, was once included in philosophy. ②_____, the study of the human mind, which was, until very lately, a part of philosophy, has now been separated from philosophy and has become the science of psychology. Thus, to a great extent, the uncertainty of philosophy is more apparent than real: those questions which are already capable of definite answers are placed in the science, while those only to which, at present, no definite answer can be given, remain to form the residue which is called philosophy.

01 Based on the passage, which of the following is NOT true about philosophy?

(A) It is different from science in the kind of knowledge it aims at.
(B) It has not been so successful in finding definite answers to its questions.
(C) Some of the sciences were once included in the part of it.
(D) It is changed into a part of sciences when its answers become dubious.

02 Which of the following can be the best title for the passage?

(A) Uncertainty of Philosophy
(B) Need for Philosophical Knowledge
(C) The Comprehensibility of Philosophy
(D) Similarity between Philosophy and Science

03 Which of the following is implied by the underlined expression ①?

(A) Scientists tend to explain in a lengthy way.
(B) Answers by scientists are hard to understand.
(C) Patience is needed to listen to scientists.
(D) There are numerous definite truths ascertained by the sciences.

04 Which of the following is the most appropriate for the blank ②?

(A) For example
(B) However
(C) Similarly
(D) Therefore

Thomas Robert Malthus, the namesake of such terms as "Malthusian collapse" and "Malthusian curse," was a mild-mannered mathematician, a clergyman, and, his critics would say, the ultimate glass-half-empty kind of guy. When a few Enlightenment philosophers, giddy from the success of the French Revolution, began predicting the continued unfettered improvement of the human condition, Malthus ①cut them off at the knees. Human population, he observed, increases at a geometric rate, doubling about every 25 years if unchecked, while agricultural production increases arithmetically — much more slowly. Therein lay a biological trap that humanity could never escape.

"The power of population is indefinitely greater than the power in the earth to produce subsistence for man," he wrote in his *Essay on the Principle of Population* in 1798. "This implies a strong and constantly operating check on population from the difficulty of subsistence." Malthus thought such checks could be voluntary, such as birth control, abstinence, or delayed marriage — or involuntary, through the scourges of war, famine, and disease. He advocated against food relief for all but the poorest of people, since he felt such aid encouraged more children to be born into misery. That tough love earned him a nasty cameo in English literature from _____ Charles Dickens. When Ebenezer Scrooge is asked to give alms for the poor in *A Christmas Carol*, the heartless banker tells the do-gooders that the destitute should head for the workhouses or prisons. And if they'd rather die than go there, "they had better do it, and decrease the surplus population."

01 Which of the following might be the best title of the passage?
  (A) Thomas Robert Malthus and Ebenezer Scrooge
  (B) Malthusian Ideas Embodied in English Literature
  (C) Malthus' View of Food Supply and Population
  (D) The Effect of Malthus' Character on His Writing

02 Which of the following is not true to Malthus?
  (A) He coined "Malthusian collapse" in his writing.
  (B) He was gentle, theistic, and allegedly pessimistic.
  (C) He influenced one of Charles Dickens' works.
  (D) He gave the cold shoulder to the poor people.

03 Which is implied by Malthus' opinion shown in the second paragraph?

(A) noblesse oblige
(B) natural selection
(C) gravitational law
(D) butterfly effect

04 Which is the most suitable for the blank?

(A) anyone other than
(B) none other than
(C) anyone other else
(D) none other else

05 Which is the closest in meaning to ①cut them off at the knees?

(A) welcomed them
(B) supported them
(C) doubted them
(D) silenced them

The emphatic fertility drop is _____. Notwithstanding concerns over the planet's growing population, close to half the world's population lives in countries where the fertility rates have actually fallen to below replacement rate, the level at which a couple have only enough children to replace themselves — just over two children per family. They've dropped rapidly in most of the rest of the world as well, with the notable exception of sub-Saharan Africa. However, for demographers working to understand the causes and implications of this startling trend, what's happened in Brazil since the 1960s provides one of the most compelling case studies on the planet. Brazil spans a vast landmass, with enormous regional differences in geography, race, and culture, yet its population data are by tradition particularly thorough and reliable.

Although there are many reasons Brazil's fertility rate has dropped so far and so fast, central to them all are tough, resilient women who set out a few decades back, without encouragement from the government and over the pronouncements of their bishops, to start shutting down the factories any way they could. Encountering women under 35 who've already had sterilization surgery is an everyday occurrence in Brazil, and they seem to have no compunctions about discussing it. "I was 18 when the first baby was born — wanted to stop there, but the second came by accident, and I'm done," said a 28-year-old crafts shop worker. She had her tubal ligation, which is irreversible contraception, at a young age of 26. And it's not simply wealthy and professional women who have stopped bearing multiple children in Brazil. There's a common perception that the countryside and the urban slums are still crowded with women having one baby after another — but it isn't true.

01 Choose the one that best fills in the blank.

(A) not just a Brazilian phenomenon
(B) something peculiar to Brazil
(C) a drag on Brazil's economic growth
(D) not a recent development in Brazil

02 Choose the one closest in meaning to the underlined "shutting down the factories."

(A) going on a strike
(B) giving up their jobs
(C) fighting for maternity rights
(D) stopping their childbearing

03 Which of the following can be inferred from the passage?

(A) The fertility rates have dropped exceptionally sharply in sub-Saharan Africa.
(B) Despite its vast territory, Brazil has effectively taken censuses of its population.
(C) The Catholic authorities have supported the practices of birth control in Brazil.
(D) More country women do not want the second child than professional women.

04 What is the main idea of the passage?

(A) The fertility rates have greatly fallen in most parts of the world including Brazil.
(B) Demographers try to understand why and how Brazil's population has decreased.
(C) Brazil's fertility rate has dropped mainly due to women's efforts for birth control.
(D) There's a trend of Brazilian women having sterilization surgery at younger ages.

It is often said that the second half of the twentieth century was an era dominated by left-brain thinking. The skills to build bridges or design computers, to get to the moon or design new financial instruments, all make use of linear thinking and logic. Engineering, law, and finance all are "classic" left-brain activities, and while all of these fields remain important today, some feel that they will need to transform, especially as computers take over more and more of the analysis that has traditionally characterized left-brain thinking. In contrast, pundits argue that in the future right-brain thinking — nonlinear, intuitive, visual — will dominate. Daniel Pink argues convincingly that in an era when production becomes cheap, design dominates and helps to determine the winners. (a)Apple has surpassed Microsoft in market capitalization in part because design is at the heart of its work.

This left-brain/right-brain dichotomy has led to considerable discussion about gender roles in the work force. The engineering and finance professions, dependent on analysis, have traditionally been male dominated, while those professions stereotypically right-brain in character — the arts, writing, design — have been (b)more open to women. In the past, the latter professions and, we might add, academic departments, carried lower status. Now, however, many would argue that they represent the best chance of competing in the future, when analysis can be programmed or outsourced. This has in turn led some to predict a reversal of male and female social roles and even some handwringing about the future of the male sex. Hanna Rosin, in an *Atlantic* article (c)entitled "The End of Men," asks "What if the modern, postindustrial economy is simply more _____ to women than men?" She posits that "the attributes that are most favorable today — social intelligence, open communication, the ability to sit still and focus — are, at a minimum, not predominantly male."

While it is important to understand the distinct areas of the brain and the effect of right-brain and left-brain activities on education and society, ultimately the people who will be successful are those who can integrate both hemispheres, relying on creativity and intuition as well as discipline and focus. Consider the approach a pianist takes to learning a difficult piece; the inspirational insight into the music requires the synthetic activity of the right brain, but hard, disciplined work, (d)applied in a linear fashion to one section of music at a time, underlies the successful performance. While some would assign "creativity" to the right brain, I would argue that successful creative people integrate both hemispheres of their brains effectively; intuition works together with logical methods to achieve significant results. Unlike Daniel Pink, I do not think that right-brainers will rule the future; rather, individuals with fully integrated brains, or teams of individuals with different strengths (e)which can, together, blend analysis and synthesis, will be the best positioned to succeed.

01 Which of the following would be the best title for the above passage?

(A) Lateralization of Brain Function
(B) The Age of Creativity via Integrated Brains
(C) Sex Differences and Activity of the Left and Right Brain
(D) The Left-Brain/Right-Brain Dichotomy
(E) Left Brain vs. Right Brain Dominance

02 Which of the following can be inserted into the blank?

(A) parsimonious   (B) aloof
(C) fawning   (D) congenial
(E) detached

03 Choose the underlined phrase that must be changed for the sentence to be correct.

(A) (a) Apple has surpassed Microsoft
(B) (b) more open to women
(C) (c) entitled "The End of Men,"
(D) (d) applied in a linear fashion
(E) (e) which can, together, blend

04 According to the above passage, which of the following is NOT true?

(A) The financial sector, which utilizes linear thinking and logic, is suitable for left-brained humans.
(B) In the future, computers will do more analytical work on behalf of humans.
(C) Creativity is based entirely on intuition as a characteristic of the right brain.
(D) For the pianist's practice, collaboration between the left and right brain is necessary.
(E) According to Hanna Rosin, the attributes favorable to the economy of the postindustrial society are mainly feminine ones.

To get a better understanding of why women are so poorly represented in tech and other high-growth businesses, I asked National Center for Women & Information Technology (NCWIT) to help me analyze data on the background and motivations of 549 successful entrepreneurs.

Female and male entrepreneurs differ in some subtle ways. Women were more motivated by a business partner who encouraged them. Women put a higher value on their professional/business networks. Finally, women were more cautious and expressed more concern about protecting their company's intellectual capital. On the other hand, financial pressure to keep a steady job was more acutely felt by men than women.

ⓐ_____, men and women entrepreneurs are similar in many respects, the results show. They had equivalent levels of education, the same early interest in starting their own business, and similar other advantages. Men and women also had similar motivations to launch a business.

ⓑ_____ all the similarities in background and motivation for men and women entrepreneurs — and the fact that women now outnumber men in universities — we remain perplexed by the lack of female startup executives. Evidence suggests that this does not reflect a failure on the part of women but rather a societal failure. Consider the contrast with India, a country that is in many respects more conservative than the U.S. Yet there, women are rapidly rising through the top ranks of the business community. India's finance industry is newer, and women there may contend with fewer ⓒentrenched players, says Cindy Padnos who has been researching the role of women in high tech.

Padnos is optimistic that the tide will turn in the U.S. as more people recognize that having women at the helm makes good business sense. Women-led high-tech startups generate higher revenues per dollar of invested capital and have lower failure rates than those led by men, her research shows.

01 What would be the most appropriate word pair to fill in ⓐ and ⓑ?

(A) Yet — Given
(B) Despite — Nevertheless
(C) However — As to
(D) Moreover — Under

02 Which of the following is the best title for the passage?
   (A) The Comparison of Male and Female Entrepreneurs
   (B) Under-representation of Male Executives in IT
   (C) The Dearth of Female High-tech Entrepreneurs
   (D) Female-dominated High-tech Industry

03 Which of the following CANNOT be inferred from the passage?
   (A) There will be no significant turnaround in female participation in IT.
   (B) Female-led businesses outperform those run by men in high-tech startups.
   (C) Much more should be done to encourage talented women to pursue IT entrepreneurship.
   (D) Both men and women seem to launch their enterprises under many of the similar conditions.

04 Choose the word closest in meaning to ⓒentrenched.
   (A) exclusive   (B) competent
   (C) naive   (D) well-established

Solar mystery is the curious nature of solar flares. Equivalent to millions of 100-megaton hydrogen bombs detonated simultaneously, solar flares are the most intense and energetic explosions that occur in our solar system. [Ⅰ] These explosions occur on the sun's photosphere and are difficult to view through layer's bright emissions, even with specialized equipment. Solar flares are directly linked to another more easily observable solar phenomenon — sunspots. With the invention of the telescope in 1608, astronomers were finally able to look into the face of the sun and see that it is not a perfect and unchanging yellow disc as they had expected, but that it is often marred by discernable ①blemishes or dark spots. [Ⅱ] These dark areas are the coolest regions on the sun's photosphere and are characterized by intense magnetic activity. The frequency of sunspot occurrences follows an eleven-year solar or sunspot cycle. [Ⅲ] At the minimum end of the cycle, there is very little sunspot activity and at the maximum end, there might be hundreds of visible sunspots. An increased number of sunspots indicate a correlated increase in solar flare activity. [Ⅳ] This period of activity can pose a serious danger to satellites and astronauts. One solar flare can emit enough magnetic energy to cause serious damage to a satellite, or change the satellite's orbit. ②It can also shake to the Earth's magnetic field and cause dangerous surges in power lines, resulting in blackouts over large areas. Because of these dangers and our increasing reliance on satellites, it has become even more important for scientists to understand the nature of solar weather and to determine more accurate methods of predicting solar activity.

01 Why does the author mention ①blemishes in the passage?

(A) To suggest that sunspots are flaws on the surface of the sun
(B) To illustrate that the sun is thought to have a face
(C) To emphasize that sunspots are indicative of illness
(D) To explain that microscopes are strong enough to see sunspots

02 According to the passage, what is the relationship between solar flares and the eleven-year sunspot cycle?

(A) Solar flares are not related to the sunspot cycle.
(B) There is more solar flare activity at the maximum end of the cycle.
(C) The sunspot cycle fluctuates with sporadic solar events like solar flares.
(D) The sunspot cycle indicates where on the sun the solar flares will occur.

03 Where does the following sentence fit best in the passage?

We were recently in the 23rd solar cycle, which was predicted to end in the first few months of 2007.

(A) [I] (B) [II]
(C) [III] (D) [IV]

04 The word ②It in the passage refers to _____.

(A) satellite (B) solar cycle
(C) sunspot (D) solar flare

Cognitive approaches to creativity focus on the mental processes by which creative works are generated. These processes include concept combination, expansion of concepts, imagery, and metaphor. While most psychologists believe that creativity involves a combination of expertise, chance, and intuition, they differ in the degree to which they emphasize these factors. Expertise theorists point to evidence that creativity is often achieved only through ①an extensive practice and learning. This is commonly referred to as the *10-year rule* on the basis of evidence that 10 years' experience in a domain is necessary for creative success. Experts are more able than beginners to detect and remember domain relevant patterns, and generate effective problem representations. Expertise theorists believe that creativity involves everyday thought processes such as remembering, planning, reasoning, and restructuring; they claim that no special or unconscious thought processes are required for creativity ②beyond familiarity with and skill in a given domain.

Others note that entrenchment in established perspectives and approaches may make experts more prone than beginners to phenomena such as functional fixedness, set, and confirmation bias. Some emphasize the role of chance meetings, opportunities or situations that invite creative ideation. Still others view creativity as not so much a matter of expertise or chance but of listening to intuitions and following them through from an ill-defined state of potentiality to a well-defined state of actualization. This view emphasizes how the association-based structure of memory provides a scientific basis for the phenomenon of intuition, and for findings that creative individuals tend to have flat associative hierarchies, meaning they have better access to ③close associates: items that are related to the subject of interest in indirect or unusual ways.

Some of the earliest efforts to think systematically about creativity came from computer scientists, who viewed creativity as a process of heuristic search in which ④rules of thumb guide the inspection of different states within a state space (a set of possible solutions) until a satisfactory solution is found. In heuristic search, the relevant variables of the problem or task are defined up front; thus, the state space is generally fixed. Examples of heuristics include breaking the problem into sub-problems, and working backward from the goal state to the initial state. It has since been proposed that creativity involves heuristics that guide the search for, not just a new possibility in a predefined state space, but a new state space itself.

01 위 글의 내용과 일치하는 것을 고르시오.

(A) Expertise theorists argue that no inspiration, intuition or chance is required for creativity.
(B) Those who emphasize the role of chance in creativity advise developing potential while listening to intuition.
(C) People with flat associative hierarchies excel in everyday thinking processes such as remembering, planning and reasoning.
(D) Most computer scientists today believe that creativity follows heuristics.

02 글의 흐름상 가장 적합하지 않는 것을 고르시오.

(A) ①
(B) ②
(C) ③
(D) ④

In the film *Proof*, the central character — Martin, who is blind — takes photographs of things in order to test their existence. The film centers on the relationship between Martin and his housekeeper, Celia: he withholds the love and affection she craves; Celia responds with small acts of sadism — positioning objects so he will stumble over them, enticing away his guide-dog, continually watching him, and, eventually, seducing his one friend. The malice and humor evident in *Proof* revolve around Martin's rejection of Celia and her minor cruelties, but underpinning all this is the theme of trust, and ⓐphotography is central to this issue. Martin does not trust the sighted, because he is unable to verify their descriptions. As far as he is concerned, sighted people are able to deceive him with false, or inaccurate, accounts of appearances. He believes his mother was embarrassed by him and suspects that she took her revenge by describing things that were not there (he even claims that she faked her own death to escape from him). Martin photographs things and events, subsequently he has an independent witness describe the images — firstly Celia, and then his friend Andy. In so far as these people did not witness the things represented, but corroborate what he knows of events and what people have said to him, he is able to verify the situations he experienced. He is, of course, also testing the describers of the pictures. (As the plot unfolds, this becomes complicated, because Andy and Celia increasingly wish to keep secrets from Martin). Photography performs this role in *Proof* because it is assumed to be an automatic and mechanical recording technology, which accurately reproduces the appearance of things. In this film, the camera is presented as an objective and independent witness, operating independently of the photographer and his desires (he can't even see what it sees). Eventually, through the medium of an old black-and-white image, Martin discovers what he took to be a key example of his mother's descriptive deceit was, in fact, an accurate account.

01. According to the passage, which is true?
    (A) Martin's mother died trying to avoid him.
    (B) Celia distorts Martin's perception of the situation.
    (C) Martin trusts the words of his loved ones more than what the pictures tell him.
    (D) Celia's sadistic behavior is getting worse and worse.

02 According to the passage, which is NOT true about the underlined ⓐphotography?

(A) It's a technology that the main character even trusts more than his family.
(B) It's an automatic and mechanical technique that accurately penetrates a person's psychology.
(C) The main character took the pictures himself, but he needed someone to testify about them.
(D) The main character found his mother's deception to be true through a black-and-white photo.

03 What CANNOT be inferred about the film *Proof*?

(A) The film deals with the theme of how we can gain trust in a situation of distrust.
(B) The main character symbolizes the existence of human beings who have no choice but to rely only on other people's interpretations.
(C) Celia and Andy indicate that the interests of those who participate in the interpretation inevitably affect the interpretation.
(D) In the movie, photography shows that depending on the photographer's interests, it can distort the truth.

Nearly everything we understand about global warming was understood in 1979. By that year, data collected since 1957 confirmed what had been known since before the turn of the 20th century: Human beings have altered Earth's atmosphere through the indiscriminate burning of fossil fuels. The main scientific questions were settled beyond debate, and as the 1980s began, attention turned from diagnosis of the problem to refinement of the predicted consequences. Compared with string theory and genetic engineering, the "greenhouse effect" — a metaphor dating to the early 1900s — was ancient history, described in any Introduction to Biology textbook. Nor was the basic science especially complicated. It could be reduced to a simple axiom: The more carbon dioxide in the atmosphere, the warmer the planet. And every year, by burning coal, oil and gas, humankind belched increasingly obscene quantities of carbon dioxide into the atmosphere.

Why didn't we act? A common boogeyman today is the fossil-fuel industry, which in recent decades has committed to playing the role of villain with comic-book bravado. An entire subfield of climate literature has chronicled the machinations of industry lobbyists, the corruption of scientists and the propaganda campaigns that even now continue to debase the political debate, long after the largest oil-and-gas companies have abandoned the dumb show of denialism. But the coordinated efforts to bewilder the public did not begin in earnest until the end of 1989. During the preceding decade, some of the largest oil companies, including Exxon and Shell, made good-faith efforts to understand the scope of the crisis and grapple with possible solutions.

Nor can the Republican Party be blamed. Today, only 42 percent of Republicans know that "most scientists believe global warming is occurring," and that percentage is falling. But during the 1980s, many prominent Republicans joined Democrats in judging the climate problem to be a rare political winner: nonpartisan and of the highest possible stakes. The issue was unimpeachable, like support for veterans or small business. Except the climate had an even broader constituency, composed of every human being on Earth.

01 According to the passage, _____ claim or claimed "global warming is occurring."
 (A) Exxon and Shell in 1980s
 (B) the fossil-fuel industry lobbyists
 (C) most of veterans
 (D) most Republicans today
 (E) the corrupted scientists

02 What does the underlined An entire subfield of climate literature mean?
(A) articles on global warming since 1989
(B) writing that ignores the seriousness of global warming
(C) novels about climate change
(D) political debates over global warming
(E) articles scientifically predicting the consequences of climate change

03 According to the passage, global warming _____.
(A) was unknown until the end of 1989
(B) is true for most Republicans
(C) has been nonpartisan and of the highest possible stakes
(D) was more a matter of diagnosis than a matter of prediction in 1980s
(E) is not much different from what we knew almost 40 years ago

The world's most abundant creatures are the insects, and the known species of insects outnumber all the other animals and the plants combined. Insects have been so successful in their fight for life that they are sometimes described as the human race's closest rivals for domination of the earth. Small size, relatively minimal food requirements, and rapid reproduction have all helped to perpetuate the many species of insects. Entomologists have named almost 1,000,000 species — perhaps less than one-third of the total number.

Insects thrive in almost any habitat where life is possible. Some are found only in the Arctic regions, and some live only in deserts. Others thrive only in fresh water or only in brackish water. Many species of insects are able to tolerate both freezing and tropical temperatures. Such hardy species are often found to range widely over the earth. Few insects, however, inhabit marine environments.

Certain parasitic insects spend much of their lives on or within the body of an animal host where all the necessities of life, such as food, moisture, warmth, and protection from enemies, are optimal. Other kinds of insects spend all or some part of their lives securely enclosed in a food plant.

Some species have become remarkably versatile as they adapt in order to meet the changing demands of the environment. Various water bugs and water beetles, for example, are able to fly and swim as well as crawl. Many types of insects, such as the bees, ants, and wasps, depend upon a complex social structure and defensive behavior. Nonpredatory species frequently have defenses such as an unpleasant taste or odor, venomous spines, and camouflage that help protect them from enemies.

Although they are adaptable and versatile as a group, insects are often unable to adjust to weather extremes such as excessive rain, early frost, and extended drought that can quickly wipe out or drastically reduce insect populations in a region. Because insects are an important part of the diet of many animals — birds, reptiles, amphibians, and fish, as well as other insects — the number is constantly held in check.

The number of factors unfavorable to the survival of individual insects is overwhelming. As a result, in some species, only a few individuals out of hundreds of eggs laid by a single female reach adulthood. The survival of some species is enhanced by the large numbers of eggs laid.

01 _____ are scientists who study the insects.
   (A) Entomologists
   (B) Nutritionists
   (C) Archaeologists
   (D) Meteorologists

02 The insect's greatest advantage is probably _____.
   (A) size
   (B) habitats
   (C) adaptability
   (D) minor food requirements

03 According to the above article, to enhance survival, some insects _____.
   (A) migrate constantly
   (B) lay large number of eggs
   (C) fight against their enemies
   (D) avoid extreme environmental conditions

04 We can conclude from the article that insects outnumber other animals because _____.
   (A) they are smarter
   (B) man do not eat them as food
   (C) more species have been named
   (D) they have developed better survival skills

Energy alone is not enough to support life. Imagine, for example, that some plants such as algae were sealed into a sterilized jar full of pure water and exposed to plenty of sunlight. The plants would use carbon dioxide and release oxygen during photosynthesis. Soon the carbon dioxide would be used up and the plants would die. If the experimenter added carbon dioxide, the plants still would not survive. They would starve for lack of other chemicals necessary for life. The life in the jar might continue, however, if some plant consumer (a snail, for example) were introduced, and the pure water were replaced by pond water to supply nutrients and decay organisms. Assuming that the right number of snails were added, the jar might now perhaps become a balanced, stable ecosystem. Nutrients would be continuously recycled.

Algae use water, carbon dioxide, sunlight, and dissolved nutrients to support life and build tissue. Snails eat the plants. Oxygen is one major waste product of algae and at the same time is essential for snails. In turn, snails release carbon dioxide, which is needed by the algae. When plants and snails die, they are eaten by decay organisms and the nutrients are recycled. We see that the nutrients in the sealed jar cycle from plants to animals to decay organisms and back to plants to be reused again. Thus, the community can exist indefinitely. In fact, sealed aquariums, in which life has survived for a decade or more, can be seen in some biology laboratories.

01 What is the best title for the passage?
(A) Nutrient Cycles
(B) Nitrogen Cycle
(C) The Ecological Niche
(D) Carbon-Oxygen Cycle

02 In the passage, the author uses an example of plants in a sterilized jar and pure water to _____.
(A) simplify the natural ecosystem
(B) show the importance of food web
(C) show a common case in nature
(D) contrast with a well-designed experiment

03 The author suggests that pure water _____.
   (A) is best for plants living in it
   (B) prevents plants' photosynthesis
   (C) absorbs the necessary carbon dioxide for plants
   (D) is not nutritious enough for plants

04 What is the main topic of the passage?
   (A) Carbon and oxygen cycle in a natural system
   (B) A continuous energy recycle in a stable ecosystem
   (C) An organism's interaction with the physical environment
   (D) Social and environmental factors in establishing the niche

Seeing in the universe a wonderfully designed organism, in which each member held its proper place and fulfilled its God-given function by virtue of a "pre-established harmony," Leibniz has designated the world we know as "the best of all possible worlds." Schopenhauer, on the other hand, weighing the actual amount of good and evil in the world against each other, arrived at the pessimistic conclusion that life was "a business whose profits do not nearly cover its expenses" and that therefore this world of ours was "the worst of all possible worlds." For him the prevalence of evil was the most obvious of facts and he considered the supposed rationality of the universe as an assumption and a product of wishful thinking of armchair philosophers.

Schopenhauer was a native of Danzig. He traveled in France, England, and Italy for some time to acquire cosmopolitan tastes and to perfect his natural ability in the command of foreign languages. He was a great admirer of Lord George Gordon Byron, but envied the English poet his luck with women and therefore refused to make his personal acquaintance. As a student of philosophy he attended Fichte's and Schleiermacher's lectures in Berlin and was so unfavorably impressed that he developed a lifelong antagonism against all the representatives of idealistic philosophy.

When he temporarily settled down in Berlin as *Privatdozent*, Hegel and Schleiermacher had become the favorites of the academic world, while Schopenhauer's lectures and writing found no response. He gave vent to his disappointment in bitter attacks against "the professional philosophy of the philosophy professors" in general and against Hegel in particular, who he dubbed a quack, a charlatan, and a servile creature of the Prussian government. The cholera epidemic of the year 1831, which claimed Hegel as one of its victims, caused Schopenhauer to move to Frankfurt, where he spent the rest of his "solitary" life, with his faithful black poodle as his only companion.

01 We can assume that the material directly preceding our sample was concerned with _____.

   (A) the philosopher Leibniz
   (B) Lord Byron and Schopenhauer
   (C) the universe as a well-designed organism
   (D) a pre-established harmony ordained by God

02 According to the passage, Schopenhauer experienced all of the following in his life EXCEPT _____.

(A) admiration of Lord Byron
(B) extensive travel and education
(C) rejection of Leibniz's philosophy
(D) academic acceptance and recognition

03 The passage states that Schopenhauer became a lifelong antagonist toward _____.

(A) solitude
(B) his fellow men
(C) idealistic philosophers
(D) only Hegel and Schleiermacher

04 It can be inferred from the passage that Arthur Schopenhauer's personality included which of the following.

[I] jealousy	[II] bitterness
[III] conviviality	[IV] great intelligence
[V] diffidence	

(A) [I], [III], and [V]
(B) [II], [III], and [IV]
(C) [I], [II], and [IV]
(D) [II], [IV], and [V]

A large part of our lives is spent in talk. From morning till night, or even in some cases through the night, the words pour out — in offices, classrooms, and homes, at meetings, parties and family meals. A certain amount of all this talk has a practical purpose — for giving information, instructions or explanations. Yet even when there is a definite purpose, a lot more talking usually goes on than is necessary to the subject. The truth is that an amazing amount of talk consists of speaking simply for the pleasure of speaking.

What do people most enjoy talking about? Above all else, themselves — their likes and dislikes, their opinions, their hopes. Whatever the topic — food, movies, cars, jobs, and anything under the sun, people want to talk about their own impressions and experiences. When a popular subject such as baseball is under discussion, it can sometimes seem as if everyone were talking and no one listening. The noise may get louder until one of the speakers cries out, "Wait a minute! Just let me finish."

From cases like this we might conclude that talking is more important to people than listening. On the whole, though, people follow the unwritten rule that if they want to speak, they must also listen. Most of us are good talkers from childhood. As we grow up, we learn to be good listeners. Conversation is a matter of both speaking and listening. It is a good way of examining our own impressions and thoughts by finding out how they look to others. Conversation is therefore a social activity, a basic human one. It is natural, then, that it fills so large a part of our lives.

01 The writer says that _____.

(A) if people were more serious and talked less, they could achieve much more
(B) when they are talking, people often waste time by going off the subject
(C) a great deal of the talking people do is not for a practical purpose
(D) the subjects that people talk about usually depend on the situation

02 The writer's view is that _____.

(A) people often talk about subjects they know nothing about
(B) people have a natural tendency to enjoy the attention of others
(C) people always discuss their favorite subjects in loud voices
(D) people often make the mistake of thinking that a loud voice will impress others

03 The writer's comments suggest that _____.
   (A) it is not from written words that we learn our skills in talking and listening
   (B) we never become as good at listening as we are talking
   (C) the older we grow, the less talking we wish to do
   (D) for most of us, talking comes more easily than listening to others

04 The writer concludes that _____.
   (A) we can understand ourselves better by exchanging views with other people
   (B) it is safer to find out other people's views before we tell them our own
   (C) asking other people questions is the most important part of conversation
   (D) human beings spend more time communicating with each other than other animals do

Sleep is a biological imperative, but do people consider it as vital as food or drink? Not in the rock-around-the-clock world of today's U.S. Not in a society in which stores don't close, assembly lines never stop, TV beckons all the time, and stock traders have to keep up with the trends in Tokyo. For too many Americans, sleep has become a luxury that can be sacrificed or a nuisance that must be endured.

Yet, scientists are increasingly making the case that forgoing rest is a foolish and often perilous bargain. In fact, evidence is mounting that sleep deprivation has become one of the most pervasive health hazards. The U.S. researchers have not yet proved conclusively that losing sleep night after night directly causes physical illness, but studies show that mental alertness and performance can suffer badly.

A typical adult needs about eight hours of shut-eye a night to function effectively. By that standard, millions of Americans are chronically sleep-deprived, trying to get by on six or seven hours or even less. In many households, cheating on sleep has become an unconscious and pernicious habit. In extreme cases, people stay up most of the night, seeing how little sleep will keep them going. They try to compensate by snoozing on weekends, but that makes up for only part of the shortfall.

Perhaps the most insidious consequence of skimping on sleep is the irritability that increasingly pervades U.S. society. But there are far grimmer effects. Harrowing tales are told by hospital interns and residents, many of whom routinely work 120-hour weeks, including 36 hours at a stretch. Some admit that mistakes are frighteningly common. A California resident fell asleep while sewing up a woman's uterus — and toppled onto the patient. In another California case, a sleepy resident forgot to order a diabetic patient's nightly insulin shot and instead prescribed another medication. The man went into a coma.

The U.S. Department of Transportation reports that up to 200,000 traffic accidents each year may be sleep-related and that 20% of all drivers have dozed off at least once while behind the wheel. Truckers are particularly vulnerable. A long-haul driver covering up to 6,500 km in seven to ten days often averages only two to four hours of sleep a night.

01 Which of the following is the best title for the passage?
(A) The Biological Nature of Sleep
(B) The Importance of Scientific Research on Sleep
(C) The Americans' Attitude Toward Sleep Deprivation
(D) Lack of Sleep and Its Problematic Consequences

02 According to the scientists, _____.
   (A) more Americans believe that adequate sleeping is indispensable for keeping good health
   (B) inadequate sleep causes not only physical but also mental problems
   (C) they scientifically proved that lack of sleep is the major cause of physical illness
   (D) around-the-clock business is the major reason why people have less sleep in the modern society

03 When people have extremely little sleep, they try to make up for the lack of sleep by _____.
   (A) doing some physical exercises
   (B) taking sleeping pills
   (C) taking naps on weekends
   (D) sleeping late on Saturdays and Sundays

04 Which of the following can be the best summary of this passage?
   (A) People in the modern society tend to have less sleep because business activities are now around the clock.
   (B) As long as people can have a snooze on weekends, they will have no health problems caused by inadequate sleep.
   (C) Medical doctors and truck drivers must be advised to have a good sleep every day so as not to have an accident.
   (D) Inadequate sleep causes both physical and mental illness, which sometimes results in medical mistreatment or traffic accidents.

Did the universe originate suddenly in an enormous primeval explosion thousands of millions of years ago? Or has the universe always been in the process of creation, without a definite beginning or end? Exponents of the first idea, called the "big bang theory," believed that all the matter in the cosmos once formed a compact mass, which some have likened to a huge "atom" of sorts. This mass then exploded, forming a vast fireball. In a few minutes, perhaps, matter was scattered across immense stretches of space. Today, the stars, galaxies, and planets that were formed from this material still have the motion that resulted from the explosion and are uniformly speeding away from each other at tremendous speeds. The different chemical elements developed from this primitive matter that exploded.

In this model of the universe, the expansion started at a unique moment in the past — the so-called big bang. On the other hand, followers of the continuous creation, or "steady state" theory, say that the universe has been much the same for ages and that matter, namely hydrogen, is constantly being created, apparently from nothing. This material forms the stars and galaxies and arises more or less uniformly throughout the cosmos. However, the amount of matter, according to this theory, is increasing very slowly — about one atom per thousands of millions of years in a volume of space equal to that of an average television set.

The steady state theory is in direct conflict with the big bang theory. In the latter theory, space becomes progressively emptier as the galaxies recede from one another. In the steady state theory, one must postulate that new matter is continuously created in the space between the galaxies, so that new galaxies may then form to take the place of those which have receded. The new material is believed to be hydrogen, which is the source from which stars and galaxies spring.

01   According to the passage, the steady state theory postulates that stars and galaxies are formed from which of the following?
(A) a compact mass
(B) immense stretches of space
(C) hydrogen
(D) a huge atom of space

02 All of the following beliefs are thought by supporters of the big bang theory EXCEPT that _____.

(A) the universe was suddenly created thousands of millions of years ago
(B) stars and galaxies move in space as a result of a violent explosion
(C) chemical elements in space were formed from exploding matter
(D) new galaxies are continually forming throughout space

03 It can be inferred from the passage that the steady state theory would probably be difficult to disprove directly because _____.

(A) the properties of hydrogen are not easily defined
(B) the exact number of galaxies is probably unknown
(C) many of the scientists that developed the theory have not lived
(D) matter is created too slowly to be measured

04 According to the big bang theory the expansion of the universe is most comparable to which of the following?

(A) When the driver of a car increases speed, the wheels of the car spin increasingly faster.
(B) When a balloon that is uniformly covered with specks of paint is blown up, all the specks move away from one another.
(C) When we drop balls from a tree, the smaller ball will continue to bounce longer.
(D) When a glass is smashed against a hard surface, the largest pieces of broken glass will fall nearest the point of impact.

In the early days of the United States, postal charges were paid by the recipient, and charges varied with the distance carried. In 1825, the United States Congress permitted local postmasters to give letters to mail carriers for home delivery, but these carriers received no government salary and their entire compensation depended on what they were paid by the recipients of individual letters.

In 1847 the United States Post Office Department adopted the idea of a postage stamp, which of course simplified the payment for postal service but caused grumbling by those who did not like to prepay. Besides, the stamp covered only delivery to the post office and did not include carrying it to a private address. In Philadelphia, for example, with a population of 150,000, people still had to go to the post office to get their mail. The confusion and congestion of individual citizens looking for their letters was itself enough to discourage use of the mail. It is no wonder that, during the years of these cumbersome arrangements, private letter-carrying and express businesses developed. Although their activities were only semilegal, they thrived, and actually advertised that between Boston and Philadelphia they were a half-day speedier than the government mail. The government postal service lost volume to private competition and was not able to handle efficiently even the business it had.

Finally, in 1863, Congress provided that the mail carriers who delivered the mail from the post offices to private addresses should receive a government salary, and that there should be no extra charge for that delivery. But this delivery service was at first confined to cities, and free home delivery became a mark of urbanism. As late as 1887, a town had to have 10,000 people to be eligible for free home delivery. In 1890, of the 75 million people in the United States, fewer than 20 million had mail delivered free to their doors. The rest, nearly three-quarters of the population, still received no mail unless they went to their post office.

01. Which of the following was seen as a disadvantage of the postage stamp?
(A) It had to be purchased by the sender in advance.
(B) It increased the cost of mail delivery.
(C) It was difficult to affix to letters.
(D) It was easy to counterfeit.

02 Why does the author mention the city of Philadelphia in line 10?

(A) It was the site of the first post office in the United States.
(B) Its postal service was inadequate for its population.
(C) It was the largest city in the United States in 1847.
(D) It was commemorated by the first United States postage stamp.

03 The private postal services of the nineteenth century claimed that they could do which of the following better than the government?

(A) Deliver a higher volume of mail
(B) Deliver mail more cheaply
(C) Deliver mail faster
(D) Deliver mail to rural areas

04 In 1863 the United States government began providing which of the following to mail carriers?

(A) A salary
(B) Housing
(C) Transportation
(D) Free postage stamps

Imagine a conservatory that offers unrivalled live performance opportunities, intensive training from leading musicians, and commitment to a full education — all for free. That's what Mary Louise Curtis Bok did when she first conceived Philadelphia's Curtis Institute of Music in 1924. Her goal, to which Curtis continues to aspire eight decades later, was "to train exceptionally gifted young musicians for careers as performing artists on the highest professional level".

Now a world-renowned center of excellence, Curtis holds firm on the belief that students "learn most by doing". This translates into over 100 concerts a year, including orchestral performances, operas, and solo and chamber music recitals — many of which are broadcast locally on television and radio.

The intake is based on the musicians needed for one symphony orchestra, a small opera department and select piano, organ, harpsichord, composition and conducting programs. Only five per cent of applicants meet the institute's strict criteria — reportedly the lowest acceptance rate of any college or university in the world. Annual enrollment is in the region of 165 to 170 students on average. "The numbers are not set in stone," says Curtis' current president Roberto Díaz. "We can take more if we want or if applicants are talented enough."

The institution's tough selection policy has proved its worth over the years: notable alumni include Leonard Bernstein, conductor Fritz Reiner and composers Gian Carlo Menotti and Samuel Barber. More recent graduates include Juan Diego Flórez, Lang Lang and Hilary Hahn, who joined Curtis in 1990 aged 10 and began working towards a Bachelor of Music degree at the age of 12. She stayed at Curtis for nine years, graduating in 1999.

Former Curtis president and director Gary Graffman entered the institute aged seven and stayed for 10 years. Entrants can join Curtis at any age, though the majority are between 17 and 22. Studies normally last between 3 and 10 years and end when a student's major teacher decides they are ready.

01 Which is NOT true of Curtis?

(A) It is one of the world's leading music schools.
(B) It offers full tuition scholarships to all students.
(C) It has produced many notable artists over the years.
(D) It sets a minimum age for the admission of students.
(E) It accepts about five per cent of applicants each year.

02 What does Curtis consider in selecting students for admission?
   (A) extracurricular activities
   (B) academic performance
   (C) SAT test score
   (D) financial ability
   (E) artistic promise

03 What makes Curtis a world-renowned center of excellence?
   (A) unrivalled live performance opportunities
   (B) intensive training from leading musicians
   (C) its tough selection policy
   (D) its notable alumni
   (E) all of the above

04 Which one would be the correct meaning of "The numbers are not set in stone"?
   (A) The numbers are too small.
   (B) The numbers can be altered.
   (C) The numbers are reasonable.
   (D) The numbers are carved in stone.
   (E) The numbers are not subject to change.

[Ⅰ] Augmented Reality does currently exist in rudimentary form. For instance, sports commentators can often use a light pen to "draw" on a football field and provide a visual aid to accompany their commentary. Another example is the first down line on football fields, drawn by computers in realtime and constantly updated. These aren't truly augmenting reality, however, because they only appear when you're staring at the TV screen. They do demonstrate proof of concept to some extent, however.

[Ⅱ] Augmented Reality refers to computer research that aims to produce information systems that merge real world information seamlessly with digital information. Augmented Reality is still in its ①_____, but many futurists and researchers expect it to experience a/an ②_____ sometime in the 2030s or 2040s.

[Ⅲ] Augmented Reality has the potential to eliminate the stationary computer as the primary means of accessing information systems. Just as desktops are being discarded in favor of laptops and mobile phone browsers, the next step could be to trade these in for an Augmented Reality system. In a sophisticated Augmented Reality scenario, you'd never need to leave the "real world" to access the Internet or do computer work — the two would be deeply intermixed. For now, though, computer users are mostly stuck staring at LED screens and sitting on our bums, not getting much exercise. An unfortunate state of affairs, really.

[Ⅳ] The central goal of an Augmented Reality system would be something like goggles or a retinal projector that provides the user with a heads-up display of relevant information, mapped onto the surrounding environment in realtime. For instance, when viewing a restaurant with Augmented Reality goggles on, one might immediately call up a list of reviews, or a menu from the restaurant's website.

01 위 글은 주로 무엇에 대한 내용인가?

(A) The present and future of Augmented Reality
(B) The technological defects of Augmented Reality
(C) Types of computers applied to Augmented Reality
(D) Differences between Augmented and Virtual Reality

02 다음 중 주어진 문단을 올바르게 배열한 것은?

(A) [Ⅰ] — [Ⅱ] — [Ⅳ] — [Ⅲ]
(B) [Ⅱ] — [Ⅳ] — [Ⅰ] — [Ⅲ]
(C) [Ⅲ] — [Ⅰ] — [Ⅱ] — [Ⅳ]
(D) [Ⅳ] — [Ⅲ] — [Ⅱ] — [Ⅰ]

03 빈칸 ①과 ②에 들어갈 단어를 짝지은 것으로 가장 적합한 것은?

(A) decline — increase
(B) disorder — regularity
(C) infancy — renaissance
(D) conflict — compromise

04 다음 중 위 글로부터 추론할 수 <u>없는</u> 것은?

(A) The future version of Augmented Reality will allow a user to move freely.
(B) Augmented reality enhances a user's perception of the real world.
(C) Augmented Reality is still in an early stage of research and development.
(D) Augmented Reality's most natural place is in the stationary computer world.

Barbie started as a toy, the kind of toy that got whisked off store shelves faster than Mattel, the doll's first maker and now, thanks to Barbie, the world's largest toy manufacturer, could restock those shelves. Barbie's star rose with post-war U.S. hegemony that made everyone in the world want fast-food, appliances, Coca-Cola, and, if you were a woman, blond hair, big breasts, impossibly long legs and the latest in sunglasses and sports cars. Barbie never got pregnant, fat, or old. She stood her own in stores as the mute brassy standard not just of beauty but of lifestyle.

Around the world, she became an icon aspired to by both mothers and their daughters; mothers and daughters who, no matter what size, shape, color, language or culture, identified desperately with the rich, blonde Barbie from that rich, blonde country. With their purchasing power they voted against their own perceived repulsive shapes, colors, and cultural identity. Barbie the bimbo, Barbie the liberated woman, it didn't matter. Barbie found herself in the bizarre position of defining culture.

While there have been significant and frequent Yankee Go Home uprisings, wars of liberation, and all sorts of anti-imperial hatred spewed and spat at the United States since it first asserted itself as a world power, there has been no corresponding popular movement against the Barbie culture. Book burnings, flag burnings, hostage taking, terrorist bombs and hijacking, all were aimed to force the Yankee home forever. Barbie, however, maintained her hegemony. Barbie has not only survived the flames; she has been rescued from them by women everywhere yearning to be free, beautiful, and cosmopolitan — just like Barbie.

01 Which of the following is NOT true according to the passage?

(A) Mattel became the world's largest toy manufacturer because of Barbie.
(B) Women around the world identified themselves with Barbie.
(C) There were no significant popular movements against the Barbie culture.
(D) Barbie was a symbol of the liberated woman.

02 Which of the following is NOT mentioned as one of the reasons of Barbie's popularity?

(A) Barbie has blond hair, big breasts and impossibly long legs.
(B) Barbie never gets pregnant, fat or old.
(C) Barbie is a bimbo.
(D) Barbie is rich.

03 The underlined bizarre could be best replaced by _____.
(A) peculiar   (B) enviable
(C) influential   (D) absurd

04 Which of the following can be inferred from the passage?
(A) Women around the world have supported U.S. hegemony.
(B) There is a possibility that Barbie will fuel racism.
(C) Barbie is a reflection of the ordinary woman.
(D) Barbie reflects the ideal beauty of each country.

Not long ago, I had a chance to watch a surgeon perform a delicate brain operation. [I] A slight slip of his hand would have meant paralysis or death for the patient. What impressed me about the doctor was not his skill but his amazing calmness. [II] I knew that only a few moments before the operation he had been nervous. [III] Such feats of concentration are, of course, routine with every outstanding person in every walk of life. [IV] At any given moment, the leader, the man of excellence, concentrates his whole being on the one job that he has to do. Most of the rest of us allow ourselves to be distracted by nervousness, preoccupations or conflicting interests. Not infrequently, we read of men who, successful in their own field, can also paint a little, write a bit of verse, play tennis or bridge well, make an impromptu after-dinner speech — who are, in a word, enviably versatile. We envy them that versatility because we think it a special aptitude. It may be so in part, but mainly these people have acquired facility in concentration. To each successive activity of the day they give not scattered attention but all their faculties, smoothly and intensely. Today, more than ever, concentration is essential not only to effective work but also to the full enjoyment of pleasures. This is an age of distraction, with interruptions by telephone, by friends, by noise, by scares and by our own flightiness. Increasingly, work must be done under conditions which are _____ concentration — yet on concentration depends, more and more, a man's success in our specialized world. It is vital not only in work but also in the enrichment of the inner life.

01 Which of the following is most appropriate for the blank?

(A) compatible with
(B) favorable to
(C) inhospitable to
(D) of great significance

02 Where does the following sentence fit best in the passage?

But once he stood at the operating table, he worked with a machinelike surety that dumbfounded me.

(A) [I] (B) [II]
(C) [III] (D) [IV]

03 What is the passage mainly about?

   (A) how to overcome distraction
   (B) importance of concentration
   (C) qualifications for becoming a successful man
   (D) results of concentration

①A shortened form of a word or group of words used in writing to save time and space is called an abbreviation. Some abbreviations are also used in speaking.

Abbreviations often consist of the first letter of a word, or of each important word in a group, written as a capital letter. Sometimes abbreviations are followed by a period. For example, *P.O.* stands for post office and *C.O.D.* for cash on delivery.

Sometimes an abbreviation is a small letter that may or may not be followed by a period. Examples include *b.* for born and *d.* for died. The same abbreviation may be used for different words. For example, *m.* may stand for married, masculine, and meter. When an abbreviation can be used for more than one word, the reader can use context to determine its meaning.

②Sometimes abbreviations are made up of more than one letter of a word. Examples include *ms.* for manuscript and *ft* for foot. Some abbreviations form a new word, as with *NATO* (North Atlantic Treaty Organization) and *OPEC* (Organization of Petroleum Exporting Countries). Such abbreviations are called ⓐ_____. Letters in abbreviations may be doubled for the plural form, as in *ll.* for lines and *pp.* for pages. For certain frequently used abbreviations, small capital letters are usually used, as in *A.D., B.C., A.M.,* and *P.M.*

Abbreviations are often used for common words such as the names of days, months, and states. Abbreviations may be used for long words and phrases, for example, *Lieut.* for Lieutenant and *R.F.D.* for Rural Free Delivery. ③Academic degrees and titles are usually abbreviated, as in *D.D.* for Doctor of Divinity and *Dr.* for doctor. Businesses use *Co.* for company, *Inc.* for Incorporated, and *Ltd.* for Limited.

Abbreviations for many Latin phrases in common use are made up of just the first letter of each word, as in *n.b.* for nota bene ("note well") and *i.e.* for id est ("that is"). An ⓑ_____ is *etc.* for *et cetera* ("and others").

Ancient monuments and manuscripts show that humans began to abbreviate words soon after alphabetic writing became general. In the United States, abbreviations have long been accepted. *OK* and *C.O.D.* date from the 19th century. ④Even agencies of the federal government are now commonly referred by their initials. For example, *FHA*, for Federal Housing Administration, and *NASA*, for National Aeronautics and Space Administration, have become household words.

01 When the same abbreviation is used for different words, the meaning can be determined from _____.
   (A) the dictionary   (B) the context
   (C) capitalization   (D) guesswork

02 The purpose of abbreviations is to _____.
   (A) make the writer look erudite
   (B) indicate when something was written
   (C) confuse the reader or listener
   (D) save time and space

03 Long official names are increasingly referred to by their initials, which suggests that _____.
   (A) people are getting lazier
   (B) it is easier and quicker to refer to initials
   (C) long names are becoming obsolete
   (D) people are getting smarter to make many abbreviations

04 The decision to change state abbreviations, such as *Mass.* to *MA*, was most likely due to a _____.
   (A) desire to simplify mailing addresses
   (B) decrease in the size of envelopes
   (C) post office error
   (D) mailing cost

05 According to the passage, which of the following is most appropriate for the blanks ⓐ and ⓑ?
   (A) pseudonyms — excerpt
   (B) cryptonyms — exception
   (C) homonyms — excerpt
   (D) acronyms — exception

06 According to the passage, which one is grammatically incorrect?
   (A) ①   (B) ②
   (C) ③   (D) ④

The making of classifications by literary historians can be a somewhat risky enterprise. When Black poets are discussed separately as a group, for instance, the extent to which their work reflects the development of poetry in general should not be forgotten, or a distortion of literary history may result. This caution is particularly relevant in an assessment of the differences between Black poets at the turn of the century(1900-1909) and those of the generation of the 1920's. These differences include the bolder and more forthright speech of the later generation and its technical inventiveness. It should be remembered, though, that comparable differences also existed for similar generations of White poets.

When poets of the 1910's and 1920's are considered together, however, the distinctions that literary historians might make between "conservative" and "experimental" would be of <u>little significance</u> in a discussion of Black poets, although these remain helpful classifications for White poets of these decades. Certainly differences can be noted between "conservative" Black poets such as Countee Cullen and Claude Mckay and "experimental" ones such as Jean Toomer and Langston Hughes. But Black poets were not battling over old or new styles; rather, one accomplished Black poet was ready to welcome another, whatever his or her style, for what mattered was racial pride.

However, in the 1920's Black poets did debate whether they should deal with specifically racial subjects. They asked whether they should only write about Black experience for a Black audience or whether such demands were restrictive. It may be said, though, that virtually all these poets wrote their best poems when they spoke out of racial feeling, race being, as James Weldon Johnson rightly put it, "perforce the thing the Negro poet knows best."

At the turn of the century, by contrast, most Black poets generally wrote in the conventional manner of the age and expressed noble, if vague, emotions in their poetry. These poets were not unusually gifted, though Roscoe Jamison and G. M. McClellen may be mentioned as exceptions. They chose not to write in dialect, which, as Sterling Brown has suggested, "meant a rejection of stereotypes of Negro life," and they refused to write only about racial subjects. This refusal had both a positive and a negative consequence. As Brown observes, "Valuably insisting that Negro poets should not be confined to issues of race, these poets committed (an) error...they refused to look into their hearts and write." These are important insights, but one must stress that this refusal to look within was also typical of most White poets of the Untied States at the time. They, too, often turned from their own experience and consequently produced not very memorable poems about vague topics, such as the peace of nature.

01 According to the passage, most turn-of-the-century Black poets generally did which of the following?

(A) Wrote in ways that did not challenge accepted literary practice.
(B) Aroused patriotic feelings by expressing devotion to the land.
(C) Expressed complex feelings in the words of ordinary people.
(D) Interpreted the frustrations of Blacks to an audience of Whites.

02 It can be inferred from the passage that classifying a poet as either conservative or experimental would be of little significance when discussing Black poets of the 1910's and the 1920's because _____.

(A) these poets all wrote about nature in the same way
(B) these poets were fundamentally united by a sense of racial achievement despite differences in poetic style
(C) such a method of classification would fail to take account of the influence of general poetic practice
(D) such a method of classification would be relevant only in a discussion of poets separated in time by more than three decades

03 According to the passage, an issue facing Black poets in the 1920's was whether they should _____.

(A) seek a consensus on new techniques of poetry
(B) write exclusively about and for Blacks
(C) withdraw their support from a repressive society
(D) turn away from social questions to recollect the tranquility of nature

04 The author quotes Sterling Brown in order to _____.

(A) present an interpretation of some Black poets that contradicts the author's own assertion about their acceptance of various poetic styles
(B) introduce a distinction between Black poets who used dialect and White poets who did not
(C) disprove James Weldon Johnson's claim that race is what "the Negro poet knows best"
(D) suggest what were the effects of some Black poets' decision not to write only about racial subjects

05 The author would be most likely to agree that poets tend to produce better poems when they _____.

(A) express a love of nature
(B) avoid technical questions about style
(C) emulate the best work of their predecessors
(D) write from personal experience

Not that fanaticism is a new development in American politics. If someone accused Bill Clinton of personally driving the bomb to Oklahoma, it wouldn't be much worse than what was said about Franklin Roosevelt, Harry Truman, Lyndon Johnson, Richard Nixon — or George Washington. Our standard for civic comity remains the placid 1950's, the decade most commonly cited by Americans, especially white Americans, as a time when "people in this country felt they had more in common... than Americans do today." But the three-and-a-half decades of chaos that followed should have given Americans the idea that upheaval and turmoil is in fact their country's normal condition. Nor was the 1950's as empty of conflict as we like to recall. This year's rebels — Western ranchers who aren't about to let government bureaucrats tell them where their cattle can step — had their counterparts 45 years ago in a Montana draft board that (가)took it upon itself to withhold inductions unless General Douglas MacArthur was given nuclear weapons to use against North Korea. Later in the decade, America didn't seem like an especially harmonious place to black children who needed federal troops to protect them on their way to elementary schools in the South. Perhaps unsurprisingly, a plurality of blacks in the Newsweek Poll chose the 1960s as the nation's halcyon era. But both groups — as well as Hispanics — agreed by wide margins that the American "national character" has gotten worse since 20 years ago.

Over the centuries, various institutions have held America together against the centrifugal tug of its sheer size and diversity. In successive generations these have been the Protestant religion, the English language, the Constitution, the shared experience of war, the three television networks and Disney World, of which only the last remains a universal, unchallenged touchstone of national identity. The Constitution is still in effect, naturally. But in the May decision striking down term limits a forceful minority of the Supreme Court seemed intent on radically reinterpreting it as a compact among sovereign states rather than the people — an inherently separatist view that has been out of favor at least since the Union won the Civil War.

01 The underlined part (가)"took it upon itself" means _____.
(A) asked another group for permission
(B) blamed itself
(C) made its own decision
(D) possessed itself
(E) passed the buck

02 Of the following things that held America together, which is still indisputably considered a touchstone of American identity?

(A) the Protestant religion
(B) the English language
(C) the Constitution
(D) television networks
(E) Disney World

03 Which of the following is NOT true according to the passage?

(A) Fanaticism has been in succession in American politics.
(B) There was no conspicuous conflict in the 1950's in America.
(C) The 1960's was considered a peaceful decade to a majority of blacks.
(D) All walks of life in America agree that in the past 20 years the American "national character" has grown worse.
(E) To substantiate his position the author takes examples of Western ranchers and a Montana draft board.

04 In the May decision, the minority opinion of the Supreme court was regarded as a separatist view because _____.

(A) the Constitution was reinterpreted as a compact among sovereign states rather than the people
(B) term limits were made possible
(C) it was accepted as a reflection of the original purpose of the Constitution
(D) it was a ruling for the weak
(E) None of the above

Everyday the mailboxes of America are filled with millions of solicitations provided by the direct marketing industry. Most often, they are straightforward advertisements for goods and services. America's response to this deluge has been strangely mixed. On the negative side, poorly executed direct marketing produces unwanted, annoying and wasteful solicitations, also known as "junk mail."

Even worse, aggressive direct marketing techniques represent a serious threat to informational privacy. Rapid increases in technology have allowed direct marketers to have access to the personal characteristics of virtually everyone. Further, sophisticated computer matching programs can produce intrusive personal profiles from information which, standing alone, does not threaten individual privacy. Direct mailers disseminate this personal information originally revealed with an expectation of privacy. This information is disclosed without the subject's consent, and the target is typically never notified of the transfer.

The 1991 Harris-Equifax Consumer Privacy Survey addressed popular attitudes toward direct mailing practices and their impact on informational privacy. When asked how they viewed direct mail offers in general, 46 percent said they were a "nuisance," 9 percent considered them to be "invasions of privacy," and only 6 percent said they were "useful." But if Americans have such a negative opinion of the direct marketing industry, they have a strange way of showing it.

Direct marketing is an effective technique that has grown in influence. Direct mail advertising expenditures rose from $7.6 billion in 1980 to $23.4 billion in 1990. The laws of market dictate that companies would not have made these efforts without prospects of success.

Moreover, in the Equifax survey mentioned above, almost half of the citizens who considered direct mail offers to be "invasions of privacy" had themselves bought something in response to a direct mail ad in the past year. Why, then, did not more of them express more positive opinions of direct marketing offers?

Still, direct marketing offers real advantages over other means of shopping. Even those who believe that the direct mailing industry has a generally negative societal impact probably would prefer to remain on the some mailing lists. _____.

01 Which of the following is the main idea of the passage?
(A) The mixed response stems from aggressive marketing techniques that threaten individual privacy.
(B) Despite its drawback, direct marketing has had an overall positive effect on American society.
(C) Concerns over privacy issue have influenced the way direct marketers have targeted their audience.
(D) The success of the direct marketing industry in the face of public opposition can be explained in the light of consumer tendencies.

02 Which of the following is NOT true according to the 1991 Harris-Equifax Consumer Privacy Survey?

(A) Nearly half of the public thought direct mail offers were vexing them.
(B) 6 percent embraced direct mail offers and actually purchased commodities.
(C) 9 percent thought direct mail offers encroached upon their rights of privacy.
(D) Those who thought direct mails useful were outnumbered by those who did not.

03 What can be inferred from direct mail advertising expenditures in the years between 1980 and 1990?

(A) The rise in expenditure during this time is suggestive of the expectations of direct marketing companies.
(B) The rise in expenditure during this period closely offends the laws of the market.
(C) Direct marketing companies expect this pattern to continue in the decades to come.
(D) The profit derived from sales in 1990 was more than double the profit derived from sales in 1980.

04 According to the passage, the public's stated views of a direct mail are _____ to individual's actual reaction to it.

(A) congruous
(B) compatible
(C) parallel
(D) contradictory

05 Which of the following best fits in the blank?

(A) We are really concerned about the problem caused by direct mailing industry.
(B) The negative side of direct marketing is so trivial that we should ignore it.
(C) Direct mailing companies should prepare ways to prevent "invasions of privacy".
(D) We like shopping by mail, and we don't want to throw out the good with the bad.

06 Which one of the following can be inferred from the passage?

(A) Direct marketing has had an overall positive effect on American society.
(B) Everyone who would prefer to remain on mailing lists thinks that direct marketing negatively affects society.
(C) There isn't a consistency between what people say about direct marketing and how they act in relation to it.
(D) The boom in direct marketing is not likely to be continued.

Efficiency means getting the most out of a given input. The inputs in productions are human effort, the services of physical capital such as machines and buildings, and the endowments of nature like land and mineral resources. The outputs are thousands of different types of goods and services. If society finds a way, with same inputs, to turn out more of some products, it has scored an increase in efficiency. The economic institutions relying on market-determined incomes have generated substantial Ⓐ_____ among citizens in living standards and material welfare. Meanwhile, the differentials in income are meant to serve as incentives — rewards and penalties — to promote efficiency in the use of resources and to generate a great, and growing, national output.

Equality implies smaller Ⓑ_____ among families in their maintainable standard of living, which in turn implies lesser Ⓒ_____ in the distribution of income and wealth, relative to the needs of families of different sizes. The equal standard of living, however, would not mean that people would choose to spend their income and allocate their wealth identically. It would secure the standard of living for all citizens. John Stuart Mill insisted that he would be communist if he believed that economic misery and deprivation were inherent in a capitalistic economy. One of main roles of any state is to provide universally distributed rights and privileges that proclaim the equality of all citizens. The political institutions relying on the domain of rights have secured the maintainable standard of living for all citizens to promote equality and to enhance human dignity.

At many points along the way, society confronts choices that offer somewhat more equality at the expense of efficiency or somewhat more efficiency at the expense of equality. In the idiom of the economist, a tradeoff emerges between equality and efficiency. The resulting mixture of equal rights and unequal incomes creates tensions between the political principles of democracy and the economic principles of capitalism. Money is used by some big winners of market rewards in an effort to acquire extra helping of those rights that are supposed to be equally distributed. For some of them, it obtains head starts that make opportunities unequally. For some who incur penalties in the marketplace, the result is a degree of deprivation that conflicts with the democratic values of human dignity and mutual respect. The society that stresses equality and mutual respect in the domain of rights must face up to the implications of these principles in the domain of dollars.

Yet some economic policies designed to reduce the scope and magnitude of inequality weaken incentives to produce and otherwise impair economic efficiency. The prizes in the marketplace provide the incentives for work effort and productive contribution. In their absence, society would thrash about for alternative incentives. Conceivably, the nation might instead stop caring about achievement itself and hence about incentives for effort. In that event, the living standard of the lowly would fall along with those of the mighty. A democratic capitalist society will keep searching for better ways of drawing the boundary lines between the domain of rights and the domain of dollars. And it can make progress. To be sure, it will never solve the problem, for the conflict between equality and economic efficiency is inescapable.

01 Which of the following is the best title of the above passage?
(A) The Future of Democratic Capitalism
(B) Equality and Efficiency: The Big Tradeoff
(C) Difficulty in Solving Inequality
(D) Confrontation between Communism and Capitalism
(E) The Balance between Duties and Rights

02 Which word best fits the blanks Ⓐ, Ⓑ and Ⓒ?
(A) freedom
(B) breach
(C) equality
(D) disparities
(E) equilibrium

03 According to the first paragraph, which of the following is NOT true?
(A) Reward and penalties damage economic motivation.
(B) Market efficiency is enhanced when the income gap in the market is allowed.
(C) Efficiency means that the maximum output is obtained from the same input.
(D) Under the market economy, the difference in income between individuals is almost inevitable.
(E) Human endeavor is one of the main factors of production.

04 Which of the following is TRUE about the above passage?
(A) Equality means that consumption patterns are the same in all classes.
(B) John Stuart Mill thought that economic misery and deprivation were inherent in the capitalism.
(C) The main goal of the state and political institution is to promote the equal life of the people.
(D) The principles of economic equality and human dignity have nothing to do with each other.
(E) By setting a boundary between efficiency and equality, conflicts between the two can be resolved.

A John Rawls reasons as follows: Suppose we gathered, just as we are, to choose the principles to govern our collective life — to write a social contract. What principles would we choose? We would probably find it difficult to agree. Different people would favor different principles, reflecting their various interests, moral and religious beliefs, and social positions. Some people are rich and some are poor; some are powerful and well connected; others, less so. Some are members of racial, ethnic, or religious minorities; others, not. We might settle on a compromise. But even the compromise would likely reflect the superior bargaining power of some over others. There is no reason to assume that a social contract arrived at in this way would be a just arrangement.

B Now consider a thought experiment: Suppose that when we gather to choose the principles, we don't know where we will wind up in society. Imagine that we choose behind a(n) "_____" that temporarily prevents us from knowing anything about who in particular we are. We don't know our class or gender, our race or ethnicity, our political opinions or religious convictions. Nor do we know our advantages and disadvantages — whether we are healthy or frail, highly educated or a high-school dropout, born to a supportive family or a broken one. If no one knew any of these things, we would choose, in effect, from an original position of equality. Since no one would have a superior bargaining position, the principles we would agree to would be just.

C This is Rawls's idea of the social contract — a hypothetical agreement in an original position of equality. Rawls invites us to ask what principles we — as rational, self-interested persons — would choose if we found ourselves in that position. He doesn't assume that we are all motivated by self interest in real life; only that we set aside our moral and religious convictions for purposes of the thought experiment. What principles would we choose?

D First of all, he reasons, we would not choose utilitarianism. Behind the _____, each of us would think, "For all I know, I might wind up being a member of an oppressed minority." And no one would want to risk being the Christian thrown to the lions for the pleasure of the crowd. Nor would we choose a purely laissez-faire, libertarian principle that would give people a right to keep all the money they made in a market economy. "I might wind up being Bill Gates," each person would reason, "but then again, I might turn out to be a homeless person. So I'd better avoid a system that could leave me destitute and without help."

E Rawls believes that two principles of justice would emerge from the hypothetical contract. The first provides equal basic liberties for all citizens, such as freedom of speech and religion. This principle takes priority over considerations of social utility and the general welfare. The second principle concerns social and economic equality. Although it does not require an equal distribution of income and wealth, it permits only those social and economic inequalities that work to the advantage of the least well off members of society.

---

01 Which of the following would be the best title for the above passage?

(A) Rawls' Thought Experiment
(B) How to Determine Principles for Social Contracts
(C) The Limits of Utilitarianism and Libertarianism
(D) From Primitive Equality to Social Inequality
(E) Strategies for Attaining Superior Bargaining Position

02 Which word best fits the blanks in paragraph B and D?

(A) well-established persona
(B) war of all against all
(C) anonymity control
(D) veil of ignorance
(E) process of mimesis

03 According to paragraph D, we would not choose utilitarianism and a purely laissez-faire, libertarian principle because these two principles _____.

(A) compel principle of majority rule and economic equality
(B) persecute other religious people and do not accept people living under other economic systems
(C) justify the dominance of the majority by the minority and do not correct the minority's occupying most of the wealth
(D) violate political suffrage and economic equality
(E) do not rule out the possibility that people's interests could be unequally undermined or economic inequalities might not be corrected

04 Which of the following best matches the Rawls' assertion in paragraph E?

(A) The most important principle of equality is to make the most needy people benefit most.
(B) Income and wealth should be distributed equally within the society.
(C) The greatest happiness of the greatest number is the most important social contract principle.
(D) Freedom of speech and religion must be provided equally to all citizens regardless of their social and economic status.
(E) No economic and social inequalities should be allowed at all.

A Smell is a sociocultural phenomenon, endowed with variegated meanings, symbolic associations and values by different cultures. Whether we like it or not, we remain as odoriferous beings despite all our cleaning regimes, and these odors play important roles in virtually every realm of our everyday life social experiences, running the gamut from gustatory consumption, personal hygiene, the home, the city, to class, gender and racial dimensions of social life. Perhaps smell is the only sense we cannot turn off. We can shut our eyes, cover our ears, or eschew touching or tasting. But we smell constantly and with every breath. Smell, however, is a highly elusive phenomenon, regarded as the mute sense, the one *sans* words. [I] Smells envelope us, enter our bodies, and emanate from us. Yet when we try to describe smells, olfactory epithets do not quite provide accurate descriptions. For instance, Miller points out: "The lexicon of smell is very limited and usually must work by making an adjective of the thing that smells. Excrement smells like excrement, roses like roses…What is missing is a specially dedicated qualitative diction of odor that matches the richness of distinctions we make with the tactile such as squishy, oozy, gooey … dank and damp". As Simmel opines similarly: "Smell does not form an object on its own, as do sight and hearing, but remains, as it were, captive in the human subject, which is symbolized in the fact that there exist no independent, objectively characterizing expressions for fine distinctions. If we say 'it smells sour', then this only means that it smells the way something smells which tastes sour". In other words, smells are more often than not described based on cause or effect, or flavors. [II]

B Furthermore, there is not even a scientific classification system for the sense of smell as there is for the other senses. Our sense of taste is governed by four paradigms of sweet, sour, salty and bitter. Light and wavelength variations ascertain sight. Sound is determined by assorted vibrations, and touch is determined by pressure, pain thresholds and other varying factors. There is, however, no agreement about olfaction. There is no consensus on the number of odor classes. [III] As Ackerman points out: "Those without hearing are labeled 'deaf', those without sight 'blind', those without speech 'mute', but what is the word for someone without smell?" She lets on that *anosmia* is what scientists label one without smell; a simple Latin/Greek combination comprising "without" and "smell". But how many of us are familiar with this term? [IV]

C Inasmuch as smell has been an elusive yet distinct component in our everyday life experiences, sociologists have seldom researched the senses or olfaction. Perhaps such negligence is due to the low status of smell in the sensory hierarchy, as

Synnott and Miller contend. Synnott, for example, argues that an indication of the low status of smell is the lack of a specialized vocabulary of olfaction. [V] As discussed previously, odors are often defined in terms of other senses through different sensorial gradations of sweet or sour (taste), or strong or weak (touch). Without an independent vocabulary, Synnott acknowledges, it is hard to broach the topic. A related point associated with producing an odor-inventory lies in the observation that instead of being independent entities, odors are "highly contextualized concepts" where their meanings are to be understood through a "culturally inscribed context".

01 The following sentence was removed from the passage. In which part may it be inserted to support the argument made by the author?

In terms of labeling an absence of the sense of smell, we also lack an equitable term for smell as compared to the other senses.

(A) [I]
(B) [II]
(C) [III]
(D) [IV]
(E) [V]

02 According to the passage, which of the following is NOT true?

(A) Smells are often described in connection with objects that give off the smell.
(B) A system that scientifically classifies the sense of smell or a vocabulary describing the difference in smell is absolutely lacking.
(C) The word *anosmia* used by scientists is rarely known among the public.
(D) Olfaction is considered relatively important in the hierarchy of importance compared to other senses such as sight, hearing and touch.
(E) In developing content related to odors, the fact that odors are understood in accordance with socio-cultural context should be taken into account.

03 Which of the following can the underlined word broach in paragraph C be best replaced with?

(A) perjure
(B) satiate
(C) occlude
(D) recant
(E) moot

One historically interesting case, which highlights the ethical issues faced when determining genetic facts about the dead, is that which centers on Abraham Lincoln. Medical geneticists and advocates for patients with Marfan syndrome have long wondered whether President Lincoln had this particular genetic disease. After all, Lincoln had the tall (a)gangly build often associated with Marfan's syndrome, which affects the connective tissues and cartilage of the body. Biographers and students of this man, whom many consider to be our greatest president, would like to know whether the depression that Lincoln suffered throughout his life ①_____ to the painful, arthritis-like symptoms of Marfan syndrome.

Lincoln was assassinated on April 14, 1865, and died early the next morning. An autopsy was performed, and samples of his hair, bone, and blood were preserved and stored at the National Museum of Health and Medicine; they are still there. The presence of a recently found genetic marker indicates whether someone has Marfan syndrome. With this advancement, it would be possible to use some of the stored remains of Abe Lincoln to see if he had this condition. However, would it be ethical to perform this test? And, if we should not test without permission, then how can we obtain permission in cases where the person in question is dead? In Honest Abe's case, the "patient" is deceased and has no immediate survivors; there is no one to consent. But allowing testing without consent sets a dangerous precedent.

It may seem a bit strange to apply the notions of privacy and consent to the deceased. But, considering that most people today agree that consent should be obtained before these tests are administered, do researchers have the right to (b)pry into Lincoln's DNA simply because neither he nor his descendants are around to say that they can't? Are we to say that anyone's body ②_____ whenever a genetic test becomes available that might tell us an interesting fact about that person's biological makeup? Many prominent people from the past ③_____; for instance, Sigmund Freud locked away his personal papers for 100 years. Will future Lincolns and Freuds need to (c)embargo their mortal remains for eternity to prevent unwanted genetic (d)snooping by subsequent generations?

And, when it comes right down to it, what is the point of establishing whether Lincoln had Marfan syndrome? After all, we don't need to inspect his genes to determine whether he was presidential timber — Marfan or no Marfan, he obviously was. The real questions to ask are, Do we adequately understand what he did as president and what he believed? How did his actions shape our country, and what can we learn from them that will benefit us today? In the end, the genetic basis for Lincoln's behavior and leadership might be seen as having no relevance. Some would say that genetic testing might divert our attention from Lincoln's work, writings, thoughts, and deeds and, instead, require that we see him as a (e)jumble of DNA output. Perhaps it makes more sense to encourage efforts to understand and appreciate Lincoln's legacy through his actions rather than through reconstituting and analyzing his DNA.

01 Which of the following would be the best title for the above passage?
(A) Why Was Abraham Lincoln So Tall?
(B) Predicting the Outcomes of Genetic Tests
(C) Should Genetics Researchers Probe Abraham Lincoln's Genes?
(D) The Genetic Secret behind Abraham Lincoln's Towering Success
(E) Did Abraham Lincoln Have a Genetic Mutation?

02 Which of the following pairs includes an expression that CANNOT replace the underlined expression in the passage?
(A) (a) gangly, lanky
(B) (b) pry into, inquire
(C) (c) embargo, ban
(D) (d) snooping, sneezing
(E) (e) jumble, assortment

03 Which of the following pairs would best fit in the blanks ① and ② to make the flow of the argument acceptable?
(A) might have linked — is opened to exam
(B) might have been linked — is open to examination
(C) should have linked — is open to exam
(D) could have been linked — is opened to examination
(E) could have linked — is open to be examined

04 Which of the following would best fit in the blank ③?
(A) opposed any tests or studies of human genes
(B) have applied for intellectual property rights in their research work
(C) welcomed their remains to be used freely for later research
(D) have taken special precautions to restrict access to their diaries, papers and letters
(E) realized the high value of genetic research on medicine

Philosophers have long noted the inconsistency in our regard for animals, but (a)it is only in recent decades that the systematic consideration of human-animal relations has really flourished and entered the public domain. Our relationships with animals have been called "speciesist" — a term introduced and popularized in the 1970s and specifically intended to draw a parallel with other forms of unjustified discrimination, such as racism and sexism. Speciesism, in the philosophical literature, refers to the assignment of different inherent moral status based solely on an individual's species membership.

As implicit in the definition of speciesism and its very name, speciesism can be understood in both a descriptive and a normative sense. Descriptively, speciesism is a concept that explains how people behave; namely that they do, as a matter of fact, assign moral worth to individuals on the basis of species membership, such that people can therefore be accurately described as having speciesist attitudes. Normatively, much work on speciesism is rooted (b)in the claim that people should not assign different moral values to individuals based solely on their species membership, with analogies made with treating people differently solely based upon their race (racism) or gender (sexism).

Speciesism manifests itself in the near universal belief that humans are intrinsically more valuable than individuals of other species. It also manifests itself in the belief that differential treatment of species that have comparable mental and emotional capabilities, such as pigs and dogs, is morally justifiable. These manifestations of speciesism are ubiquitous, (c)underpinning practices such as the mass factory farming of animals for food, the use of animals for human entertainment in circuses, and legal systems that view animals as property and deny them basic rights such as the right to bodily integrity. For example, we treat dogs with special moral status while simultaneously factory farming and eating pigs — despite the fact that dogs and pigs have similar mental and emotional capabilities. Such manifestations of speciesism are, descriptively, familiar to all, even if one might deny there is anything, normatively, wrong with this. Speciesism — like racism and sexism — is observed throughout history and across cultures.

Just like ethnic prejudice is observed in all societies but is directed against different groups based on local traditions and history, speciesism appears evident across cultures but is expressed differently across the world. Consider dogs and cats: in China (d)they are considered food and thus akin to other animals like pigs, but in Western societies they are seen as 'one of the family' and thus have a much higher status than pigs. Or consider cows: routine fare on the dinner plate in many Western countries, but (e)forbidden from eating and revered as sacred animals in Hindu societies. These culturally determined manifestations of speciesism occur not just across cultures but also across time. Horses were once routinely consumed in Western countries for centuries, but now horsemeat consumption has substantially declined and the perceived moral status of horses has increased.

01 Which of the following is the best title for the above passage?
(A) Declaration on the Elimination of Speciesism and Animal Rights
(B) The Domestication of Animals and Its Influence on Culture
(C) The Interaction Between Human and Nature through Speciesism
(D) Speciesism Rooted in Human History and Culture
(E) Normative Criticism of Speciesism

02 Choose the underlined phrase that must be changed for the sentence to be grammatically correct.
(A) (a) it is only in recent decades
(B) (b) in the claim that people should not assign
(C) (c) underpinning practices such as the mass factory farming of animals for food
(D) (d) they are considered food and thus akin to other animals
(E) (e) forbidden from eating and revered as sacred animals

03 According to the passage, which of the following is NOT true?
(A) In recent decades, systematic consideration of the relationship between humans and animals has begun.
(B) It is speciesism to assign moral status according to which species an individual belongs to.
(C) The descriptive understanding of speciesism is that individuals should not be discriminated against based solely on their species membership.
(D) The different human attitudes toward dogs and pigs are a kind of contradiction derived from speciesism.
(E) The difference in attitudes between Westerners and Hindus toward cattle is an example of how speciesism culturally determined.

After basic skills for many, and more advanced skills for some, education for economic growth needs a very rudimentary familiarity with history and with economic fact — on the part of the people who are going to get past elementary education in the first place, and who may turn out to be a relatively small elite. But care must be taken lest the historical and economic narrative lead to any serious critical thinking about class, about race and gender, about whether foreign investment is really good for the rural poor, about whether democracy can survive when huge inequalities in basic life-chances obtain. So critical thinking would not be a very important part of education for economic growth, and it has not been in states that have pursued this goal relentlessly, such as the Western Indian state of Gujarat, well known for its combination of technological sophistication with docility and group-think. The student's freedom of mind is dangerous if what is wanted is a group of technically trained obedient workers to carry out the plans of elites who are aiming at foreign investment and technological development. Critical thinking will, then, be discouraged — as it has so long been in the government schools of Gujarat.

History, I said, might be essential. But educators for economic growth will not want a study of history that focuses on injustices of class, caste, gender, and ethno-religious membership, because (a)<u>this will prompt critical thinking about the present</u>. Nor will such educators want any serious consideration of the rise of nationalism, of the damages done by nationalist ideals, and of the way in which the moral imagination too often becomes numbed under the sway of technical mastery — all themes developed with scathing pessimism by Rabindranath Tagore in Nationalism, lectures delivered during the First World War, which are ignored in today's India, despite the universal fame of Tagore as Nobel Prize-winning author. So the version of history that will be presented will present national ambition, especially ambition for wealth, as a great good, and will downplay issues of poverty and of global accountability. Once again, real-life examples of this sort of education are easy to find.

A salient example of this approach to history can be found in the textbooks created by the BJP, India's Hindu-nationalist political party, which also pursues aggressively an economic-growth- based development agenda. These books (now, fortunately, withdrawn, since the BJP lost power in 2004) utterly discouraged critical thinking and didn't even give it material to work with. They presented India's history as an uncritical story of material and cultural triumph in which all trouble was caused by outsiders and internal "foreign elements." Criticism of injustices in India's past was made virtually impossible by the content of the material and by its suggested pedagogy (for example, the questions at the end of each chapter), which discouraged thoughtful questioning and urged assimilation and regurgitation. Students were asked simply to absorb a story of unblemished goodness, bypassing all inequalities of caste, gender, and religion.

---

01 Which of the following is the best title for the above passage?
(A) The Unexpected Effects of History Education on the Public Goal
(B) Education: Driving India's Economic Growth
(C) The Need for Critical History Education for Democracy
(D) India's Education: Fiction and Reality behind Economic Growth
(E) The Liberal Education vs. Education for Economic Growth

02 According to the passage, which of the following is NOT true?
(A) In education for economic growth, basic history education for a small number of elites is needed.
(B) History education on past injustice will trigger critical thinking about the present.
(C) Early on, Tagore recognized the problems that Indian nationalism could cause.
(D) Textbooks compiled by the BJP attributed almost all of India's problems to the outside world.
(E) Tagore maintains his reputation as a Nobel laureate, and his comments are widely accepted in Indian society today.

03 Which of the following is the best example of *critical thinking* in (a)this will prompt critical thinking about the present?
(A) The statistical finding that women are less capable of accomplishing a certain task is used as a valid reason for treating them in a discriminatory way.
(B) Hindus and Muslims neither intermarry nor eat together, and indeed they belong to two different civilizations which are based mainly on conflicting ideas and conceptions.
(C) It is desirable that the caste system has spilled over into other religions in India, with Christians, Muslims, Sikhs and Jains all employing similar forms of social stratification.
(D) There should be a system of affirmative action that reserves a quota of higher education places, public sector jobs, and legislative seats for lower castes.
(E) It is not wrong to propagate a religion on the basis of statistical findings that people who believe in a particular religion have higher educational and living standards.

Excercise and physical fitness are obviously necessary for athletes, soldiers, firefighters, and all those whose jobs require hugh levels of physical performance. Then why should a sedentary person living in a comfortable, industrialized society exercise?

Medical and health professionals have determined that everyone, depending on the individual's metabolism, has minimum level of physical activity that must be maintained to prevent serious physical deterioration. The human body and all of its parts, like any living organism, must be used or they atrophy. The loss of structure and function that occurs when a broken arm is immobilized in a cast clearly demonstrates what happens when body parts are not exercised and used.

Basic survival once required the output of enormous physical energy by people on many levels of society. Modern technology has simplified life's physical demands in various ways. Machines from washing machines to automobiles and elaborate industrial equipment have reduced the amount of labor required of people. In more primitive times, most individuals burned up the calories gained from the food they consumed through the rigors of their daily activities. This is no longer true for most people, particularly those living in industrialized nations who do not do strenuous work.

Many people have retained their capacity for physical work. Even those who have been physically inactive for a long time can restore lost physical capability with just a month or two of daily physical training. People who exercise and reach their near-maximum physical capability can maintain it by exercising vigorously on alternate days.

Physical fitness and exercise are important for good physical and mental health, including weight control. Exercise helps the individuals develop and maintain a strong self-image and a sense of emotional balance. As a person gets older, exercise becomes more important because after 30 the heart's blood-pumping capacity declines at a rate of about eight percent every ten years or so.

Most common forms of exercise, such as bicycling and swimming, rarely cause serious injury. But contact sports, such as football and judo, can cause wear on the on the joint that can lead to articular disease, or joint problems. The problems for most beginners is overexercise. Many people experience stiffness after the first day of exercise, but this is harmless and does not last long. People who are overweight or past middle age or who suffer from heart disease should consult a physician before starting any exercise program.

01 Compared to people in the past, people today generally _____.
   (A) expend less physical energy on a daily basis
   (B) work more strenuously
   (C) burn calories faster
   (D) are medical and health professionals

02 Lost physical capability can be restored with _____.
   (A) two days of exercise
   (B) a week of daily physical training
   (C) a month or two of daily physical training
   (D) only bicycling

03 Modern technology has resulted in _____.
   (A) a more simple way of life for most people
   (B) less need for strenuous work
   (C) an increase in overweight people
   (D) stiffness after exercise

04 You can conclude from the article that the benefits of exercise are _____.
   (A) mostly physical
   (B) mental as well as physical
   (C) experienced mainly by professional athletes
   (D) none of the above

05 You can conclude from the article that the potential dangers of physical activity are _____.
   (A) outweighed by the advantages
   (B) not worth the risk
   (C) not worthy of consideration
   (D) non existent

Americans will not feel quite the same about the Orient, which for them is much more likely to be associated very differently with the Far East (China and Japan, mainly). Unlike the Americans, the French and British — less so the Germans, Russians, Spanish, Portuguese, Italians, and Swiss — have had a long tradition of (가)_____ I shall be calling Orientalism, a way of coming to terms with the Orient that is based on the Orient's special place in European Western experience. The Orient is not only adjacent to Europe; it is also the place of Europe's greatest and richest and oldest colonies, and one of its deepest and most recurring images of the Other.

In addition, the Orient has helped to define Europe (or the West) as its contrasting image, idea, personality, experience. Yet none of this Orient is merely imaginative. The Orient is an integral part of European material civilization and culture. Orientalism expresses and represents that part culturally and even ideologically as a mode of discourse with supporting institutions, vocabulary, scholarship, imagery, doctrines, even colonial bureaucracies and colonial styles. In contrast, the American understanding of the Orient will seem considerably less dense, although our recent Japanese, Korean, and Indochinese adventures ought now to be creating a more sober, more realistic "Oriental" awareness. Moreover, the vastly expanded American political and economic role in the Near East (the middle East) makes great claims on our understanding of that Orient.

It will be clear to the reader (and will become clearer still throughout the many pages that follow) that (나)_____ Orientalism I mean several things, all of them, in my opinion, interdependent. The most readily accepted designation for Orientalism is an academic one, and indeed the label still serves in a number of academic institutions. Anyone who teaches, writes about, or researches the Orient — and this applies whether the person is an anthropologist, sociologist, historian, or (다)philologist — either in its specific or its general aspects, is an Orientalist, and what he or she does is Orientalism. Compared with Oriental studies or Oriental area studies, it is true that the Orientalism is less preferred by specialists today, both because it is too vague and general and because it connotes the high-handed executive attitude of the nineteenth-century and early twentieth-century European colonialism. Nevertheless books are written and congresses held with "Orient" as their main focus, with the Orientalist in his new or old guise as their main authority. The point is that even if it does not survive as it once did, Orientalism lives on academically.

01 The author's chief purpose in writing this passage was _____.
   (A) to compare the West with the East
   (B) to criticize orientalism
   (C) to give information on Oriental studies in America
   (D) to justify the colonial rules by European countries
   (E) to support orientalism and show the need for it

02 According to the passage, which is NOT true?
   (A) Orientalism lives on academically.
   (B) The Spanish, Portuguese, and Italians have had a weaker tradition of Orientalism than the French and British.
   (C) The Orient remains as one of its deepest and most recurring images of the Other among Europeans.
   (D) In contrast to the Europeans, the Americans' understanding of the Orient will seem more deep-rooted.
   (E) None of the above

03 Which of the following pairs fits best in the blanks (가) and (나)?
   (A) what — by   (B) what — in
   (C) which — with   (D) which — to
   (E) which — in

04 Why are Oriental studies or Oriental area studies preferred to the Orientalism among specialists? The reason is that _____.
   (A) compared with Oriental studies or area studies, the Orientalism is more specific
   (B) the Orientalism implies the autocratic attitude of the previous European imperialists
   (C) Orientalism is a style of thought based upon an ontological and epistemological distinction
   (D) Orientalism symbolizes the integral part of European material civilization
   (E) None of the above

05 Choose the one closest in meaning to the underlined (다)philologist.
   (A) a person who specializes in the study of words, especially the history and development of the words
   (B) a person who collects and studies postage stamps of foreign countries
   (C) a person who studies how people vote in elections
   (D) a person who studies old maps
   (E) a person who researches money

The history of systematic human thought is largely a sustained effort to formulate all the questions that occur to mankind in such a way that they will fall into one or other of these two great baskets: the empirical, that is, questions whose answers depend, in the end, on the data of observation; and the formal, that is, questions whose answers depend on pure calculation, untrammeled by factual knowledge.

But there are certain questions that do not easily fit into this classification. "What is an okapi?" is answered easily enough by an act of empirical observation. Similarly, "What is the cube root of 729?" is settled by a piece of calculation in accordance with accepted rules. But if I ask "What is a number?", "What is the purpose of human life on earth?", "Are you sure that all men are brothers?" how do I set about looking for the answer?

There seems to be something queer about all these questions — as wide apart as those about number, or the brotherhood of man, or purpose of life; they differ from the questions in the other baskets in that the question itself does not seem to contain a pointer to the way in which the answer to it is to be found. The other, more ordinary, questions contain precisely such pointers — built-in techniques for finding the answers to them. The questions about number and so on (가)reduce the questioner to perplexity, and annoy practical people precisely because they do not seem to lead to clear answers or useful knowledge of any kind.

This shows that between the two original baskets, the empirical and the formal, there is an intermediate basket, in which all those questions live which cannot easily be fitted into the other two. These questions are of the most (나)_____ nature; some appear to be questions of fact, others of value; some are questions about words, others are about methods pursued by scientists, artists, critics, common men in the ordinary affairs of life; still others are about the relations between the various provinces of knowledge; some deal with the presuppositions of thinking, some with the correct ends of moral or social or political action.

The only common characteristic which all these questions appear to have is that they can not be answered either by observation or calculation, either by inductive methods or deductive; and as a crucial corollary of this, that those who ask them are faced with a perplexity from the very beginning — they do not know where to look for the answer; there are no dictionaries, encyclopedias, compendia of knowledge, no experts, no Orthodoxies, which can be referred to with confidence as possessing unquestionable authority or knowledge in these matters. Such questions tend to be called philosophical.

01 Which of the following is closest in meaning to (가)"reduce the questioner to perplexity"?

(A) make the questioner feel smaller
(B) make the questioner less puzzled
(C) make the questioner understandable
(D) make the questioner completely puzzled
(E) make the questioner unperturbed

02 Which of the following is NOT true according to the passage?

(A) Some questions which do not contain a pointer to the way in which the answer may be found are called philosophical.
(B) The answers to formal questions depend on pure calculation.
(C) "Where is my English dictionary?" is an example of ordinary questions.
(D) The philosophical questions can not be answered through empirical means.
(E) There is no philosophical question that experts can not solve.

03 What is the best title of the passage?

(A) The Subject Matter of Philosophy
(B) The Apology for Philosophy
(C) The Importance of Philosophy
(D) The History of Human Thought
(E) Goals of Philosophy

04 Which of the following is the best for the blank (나)?

(A) approving   (B) diverse
(C) similar   (D) typical
(E) limited

05 Which of the following is NOT stated or implied according to the passage?

(A) Some questions can annoy practical people.
(B) If you do not know where to look for an answer, the question can be philosophical.
(C) There is a class of questions to which we can find the answer by applying formal principles.
(D) The one belonging to the intermediate basket of questions can not be explained by the empirical and formal methods.
(E) Ordinary questions don't have any pointer in themselves.

www.kimyoung.co.kr

정가 30,000원

해독제 Vol.1 초·중급 난이도 300개 독해지문 수록
해독제 Vol.2 중·고급 난이도 300개 독해지문 수록

13740

ISBN 978-89-6512-153-4

THE MORE, THE BETTER!
독해 실력은 투자한 시간과 노력에 비례한다!

편입빈출유형 핵심지문 300

해독제
Vol.2

김영편입
컨텐츠평가연구소
편저

편입영어 기출문제 최신 출제 경향 완벽 반영
실전에 가장 가까운 예상문제들로 구성
단문부터 중·장문까지 다양한 독해지문 수록
수준에 맞는 단계별 독해 학습 가능

해설편

다양한 길이
난이도별
독해지문!

기출문제 토대
실전대비
예상문제!

다양한 배경지식
분야별
독해지문!

김영편입 컨텐츠평가연구소

김영편입 컨텐츠평가연구소는 편입 시험의 다양한 문제 유형과 난이도를 분석하여 수험생에게 올바른 학습 방향을 제시해 줄 목적으로 설립된 메가스터디의 부설 기관입니다. 수십 년간 시행되어 온 대학별 편입 시험을 심층 분석하여 실전에 가까운 컨텐츠를 개발하고 있으며, 김영편입의 우수한 교수진과 축적된 컨텐츠를 기반으로 다양한 교재를 출판하고 있습니다.

주요 집필 교재

『편머리 기본편 시리즈(문법, 어휘, 논리, 독해)』, 『편머리 심화편 시리즈(문법, 어휘, 논리, 독해)』, 『편머리 실전편 시리즈(문법, 논리, 독해)』, 『편머리 FINAL 실전모의고사』, 『편머리 편입영어 기출문제』, 『MVP STARTER』, 『MVP Vol 1, 2』 등

해독제 Vol.2

인쇄 2022년 4월 15일 **발행** 2022년 4월 29일

편저자 김영편입 컨텐츠평가연구소

제작총괄 안진영 **제작진행** 김형석 **연구개발** 안진영, 신종규, 김진희, 김형석
디자인 서제호, 서진희, 조아현 **판매영업** 조재훈, 김승규, 권기원

발행처 ㈜아이비김영 **등록번호** 제 22-3190호
주소 (06728) 서울시 서초구 서운로 32, 5층 (서초동, 우진빌딩)
전화 (대표전화)1661-7022 (컨텐츠평가연구소)02-3476-0331 **팩스** 02-3456-8073

ⓒ ㈜아이비김영

이 책은 저작권법에 따라 보호받는 저작물이므로 무단전재와 무단복재를 금지하며,
책 내용의 전부 또는 일부를 이용하려면 반드시 저작권자의 서면동의를 받아야 합니다.

ISBN 978-89-6512-153-4 (13740)

정가 30,000원

잘못된 책은 바꿔드립니다.

해설편

THE MORE, THE BETTER!
독해 실력은 투자한 시간과 노력에 비례한다!

편입빈출유형 핵심지문 300

해독제
Vol.2

김영편입
컨텐츠평가연구소
편저

김영편입

CONTENTS

PASSAGE 001~010 ……… 6
PASSAGE 011~020 ……… 11
PASSAGE 021~030 ……… 16
PASSAGE 031~040 ……… 22
PASSAGE 041~050 ……… 28

PASSAGE 051~060 ……… 34
PASSAGE 061~070 ……… 41
PASSAGE 071~080 ……… 47
PASSAGE 081~090 ……… 54
PASSAGE 091~100 ……… 61

PASSAGE 101~110 ……… 69
PASSAGE 111~120 ……… 78
PASSAGE 121~130 ……… 86
PASSAGE 131~140 ……… 95
PASSAGE 141~150 ……… 105

PASSAGE 151~160 ……… 115
PASSAGE 161~170 ……… 125
PASSAGE 171~180 ……… 135
PASSAGE 181~190 ……… 144
PASSAGE 191~200 ……… 154

PASSAGE 201~210 ……… 164
PASSAGE 211~220 ……… 174
PASSAGE 221~230 ……… 184
PASSAGE 231~240 ……… 194
PASSAGE 241~250 ……… 204

PASSAGE 251~260 ……… 214
PASSAGE 261~270 ……… 224
PASSAGE 271~280 ……… 234
PASSAGE 281~290 ……… 245
PASSAGE 291~300 ……… 257

PASSAGE

001
—
300

001

　　법률 서비스 광고에 대한 제한이 적을수록, 더 많은 변호사들이 그들의 법률 서비스를 광고하게 되며, 구체적인 서비스를 광고하는 변호사들은 광고를 하지 않는 변호사들보다 대체로 그 서비스에 대해 더 적은 비용을 요구한다. 그러므로 정부가 수수료 협정을 명시하지 않는 광고 제한과 같은 현재의 규정을 제거한다면, 전체적인 소비자 법률 서비스 이용비용은 정부가 현재의 규정을 보유할 때보다 낮아질 것이다.

restriction n. 제한, 한정
arrangement n. 배열; 조정, 협정

01 ▶ (C)는 수수료 협약을 명시하지 않는 광고 제한이 없어지면 더 많은 변호사들이 법률 서비스를 광고한다고 했다. 본문 처음에 나와 있듯이 제한이 적을수록 더 많은 변호사들이 광고를 한다고 했으므로 (C)가 정답이 된다

》 정답 (C)

002

　　혼자 있는 것은 당신의 일부였던 모든 종류의 특성을 조용히 없애준다. 그 특성이란 무엇보다 사람들 앞에서 포즈를 취하고 싶은 욕망, 사람들에게 사실은 당신이 그렇지 않은데도 그런 사람이라고 생각하게 만들고 싶은 그런 사람이라는 인상을 주고 싶은 욕망이다. 내가 아는 어떤 사람들은 혼자 있을 때도 포즈를 취할 수 있다. 그들에게 옷 입는 것을 도와주는 하인이 있다면 그들은 틀림없이 그 하인들에게는 영웅(최고로 잘난 사람)일 것이다. 그러나 나 자신은 그런 일이 가장 어려우며 나는 게을러서 그러기를 그만두어버렸다. 보는 사람이 없는 데서 가장된 행동을 하는 것은 너무 성가시고 무익한 일이어서 점차 그러기를 그만두어버리고 마침내는 가장된 행동을 할 줄을 아예 잊어버리는 것이다. 왜냐하면 실재 있는 그대로의 자신의 모습을 알아가는 데 더 많은 관심을 갖게 되니까. 예를 들어, 당신이 어느 쪽인지 상관할 사람이라곤 하나님 외에는 아무도 없을 때에도 당신은 지저분하기보다는 깨끗하기를 더 좋아한다는 것을 안다는 것은 만족스런 일이다. 당신이 다소 충격 속에서 알게 되는 바로서, 옷은 당신에게 전혀 관심거리가 되지 못한다. 당신은 옷을 단지 몸을 가리는 예방 장비에 불과한 것으로 여길 줄 알게 된다. 당신은 옷의 색깔과 마름질은 전혀 상관하지 않는다.

eliminate v. 제거하다, 배제하다
trait n. 특색, 특성
pose v. 자세를 잡다; 포즈를 취하다
impress v. 감명을 주다; 인상지우다
gradually ad. 차츰, 서서히
acquaintance n. 익히 앎; 면식
gratifying a. 만족스러운
precaution n. 조심, 경계

01 ▶ 두 문장 앞에서 언급한 '혼자 있을 때도 포즈를 취하는 것'과 호응하는 것을 선택한다.

02 ▶ '옷을 단지 몸을 가리는 예방 장비에 불과한 것으로 여길 줄 알게 된다.'는 것은 옷의 실용적인 면과 관련이 있다.

》 정답 01 (A) 02 (C)

003

　　불합리한 허구에 의존하지 않는 예술은 하나도 없지만 연극이야말로 모든 예술 가운데 가장 불합리한 것이다. 우리가 16세기의 베니스에 가 있고 빌링턴씨가 무어인이며 그러한 그가 자신이 그토록 존중해마지 않던 헉커비양을 베개로 교살하려 하고 있다는 사실을 우리보고 믿으라고 요구하고 있다는 것을 생각해보라. 뿐만 아니라, 사람들이 무운시(無韻詩)나 혹은 그보다 더 멋진 어투로 이야기했다는 사실을, 사람들이 놀라울 정도로 분명하고 조리 있게 이야기 했다는 사실을 우리가 믿도록 만들려고 하고 있다는 것을 생각해보라. 연극은 거짓의 잡초더미에서 불가사의하게 솟아나는 백합이다. 그럼에도 불구하고 바로 이러한 모든 불합리한 것들에서 비롯되는 긴장으로 인해 그와 같은 시와 힘과 매력과 진실이 연극을 통해서 탄생할 수 있는 것이다.

---

preposterous a. 불합리한
Moor n. 무어인(모로코의 회교인종)
stifle v. 교살하다
pillow n. 베개
falsity n. 허위; 잘못
blank verse 무운시
articulate a. 분명한, 명료한
inexplicably ad. 불가사의하게, 설명할 수 없이
weedy a. 잡초더미의
absurdity n. 불합리, 어리석음

01 ▶ 첫 문장과 마지막 문장을 통해 알 수 있듯이 이 글은 불합리한 허구 즉 상상력을 통해 예술과 연극의 힘과 매력과 진실을 표현한다는 글이다.

02 ▶ 마지막 문장에서 허구적인 극적 상황을 통해 성취할 수 있는 측면을 긍정적으로 적고 있다.

03 ▶ '거짓의 잡초더미'라는 말은 연극의 허구성을 비유한 표현이고 이와 대조되는 '백합'은 극적 사실성을 표현한 것이다. 따라서 문제의 표현은 극적 진실성이 극적 허구성에서 비롯됨을 뜻하는 표현이다.

》 정답   01 (B)   02 (A)   03 (C)

004

　　3일째 되는 날 나는 그 섬의 먼 쪽을 답사하고 있었다. 나는 자기 영역을 지키는 동물과도 같은 내 자신의 모습 또한 관찰하고 있었다. 당시 상황은 매우 고요했고 적막하기까지 했었다. 갑자기 나뭇잎 사이에서 천둥 같은 소리가 났고, 내 바로 3피트 앞에 겁에 질려 얼어붙은 뇌조(雷鳥)가 있었다. 나도 그만큼 겁먹은 듯이 보였는지는 모르겠으나, 난 정말 매우 놀랐었다. 적막감은 소음으로 변해버렸고, 그 섬에 혼자 있었기에 그 순간의 나의 상상은 복잡 미묘했다. 그러나 나는 긴장을 풀었고, 뇌조는 그러지 못했다. 내가 막대기를 집으려고 손을 뻗칠 때, 원시 사냥꾼으로서의 인간의 신화가 펼쳐지기 시작했다. 그러나 어떤 행동을 취하기 전에 또 다른 신화가 자리 잡았고 생명의 탈취는 없었다. 굶주림을 해소하고자 하는 원초적인 욕구와 원초적인 생명력. 나는 그 마주침을 잊을 수 없다.

---

observe v. 관찰하다, 관측하다; 지키다, 준수하다
territory n. 영토, 영지; 지방
grouse n. 뇌조(雷鳥)
elaborate a. 공들인, 정교한; 복잡한
unfold v. 열리다, 벌어지다, 전개되다
encounter n. (우연히) 만남, 조우(遭遇)

01 ▶ 당시 상황에서 잡고자 한다면 얼마든지 잡을 수 있었지만, 생명을 존중하여 그러지 않았다는 내용이 글 후반부에 있다. 이를 통해 (B)를 답으로 하는 것이 가장 적절하다. 나머지 보기들은 글의 내용만으로는 단언하기 힘들다.

02 ▶ 바로 뒤의 내용 곧, 생명을 빼앗지 않았다는 내용을 통해 알 수 있다.

03 ▶ 자신이 뇌조를 잡을 수 있었음에도 그러지 않았던 상황, 두려움에 미동도 하지 못하던 뇌조의 모습 등을 단순한 하나의 사건으로 보지 않고 '생존의 본능과 굶주림을 해소하려는 원초적인 두 욕구의 만남'으로 본 것은 또 다른 해석과 인식으로 볼 수 있다.

》 정답   01 (B)   02 (D)   03 (B)

005

　　복지국가는 우리가 하나하나 독립된 국민들의 국가가 아니라 납세자들의 돈을 기름 부음 받은 자들(특별히 선택된 소수 엘리트 층)의 비전에 따라 나누어주는 관료들에 의해 그 삶이 통제되는 복지사업 수혜자들의 국가여야 한다고 말한다. 복지국가 옹호자들이 아무리 이것을 "변화"라고 공포해도, 이것은 오늘날 새로 생겨난 사상은 아니다. 인류 역사의 대부분은 소수 엘리트에 의해 삶이 통제되고 운명이 결정되는 보통 사람들의 역사였다. "인류를 지배하도록 (신에게) 내몰리고 격려 받아" 태어난 것처럼 행동한 사람들의 압제 하에서 벗어나기 위해 인류는 수 세기 동안 투쟁하고 피 흘려야 했다. 지금 우리는 사람들의 운명이 자신의 손이 아니라 몇몇 부풀려진(과대 선전된) 정치 "지도자들"의 손에 달려있는 그런 세상을 향해 뒷걸음질치고 있다.

bureaucrat n. 관료, 관료주의자
dispense v. 분배하다, 나누어주다
advocate n. 옹호자; 주창자
proclaim v. 포고하다, 공포하다
bloodshed n. 유혈참사; 살해
boot v. 내쫓다
spur v. 몰아대다; 자극하다, 격려하다
puffed-up a. 부풀려진

01 ▶ (D)의 and 이하는 복지국가의 관점과 무관하다.

02 ▶ anoint는 '머리에 성유를 부어 거룩하게 하다'라는 의미이다. 과거에 성직자들이 사회 계층의 맨 위에 있었음을 고려하면, '기름부음 받은 자들'이 가리키는 대상은 '소수의 특권층'이라 할 수 있다.

》》 정답　01 (D)　02 (D)

006

　　자아가 분열된 사람은 자극과 오락을 찾는다. 그는 강렬한 열정을 사랑하지만 그것은 건전한 이유에서가 아니라 강렬한 열정이 당분간 그를 그 자신 밖으로 끌어내어 고통스럽게 생각해야 할 필요가 없게 만들어주기 때문이다. 모든 열정이 그에게는 일종의 도취이다. 그리고 그는 근본적인 행복을 생각할 수 없기 때문에 모든 고통으로부터의 구원이 그에게는 단지 도취의 형태로만 가능한 것처럼 여겨진다. 그러나 이것은 뿌리 깊은 병의 증세이다. 그러한 병이 없는 곳에서 가장 큰 행복은 자신의 능력을 가장 완전히 소유함과 더불어 찾아온다. 정신이 가장 활동적이고 가능한 한 많은 것을 기억하고 있는 바로 그 순간에 가장 강렬한 기쁨을 맛보게 되는 것이다.

excitement n. 자극; 흥분
distraction n. 기분전환, 오락
intoxication n. 도취; 중독
malady n. 질병, 병폐

01 ▶ 자아가 분열된 사람이 병적 도취에서 벗어나 현실을 망각하지 말고 자신의 모든 능력으로 활동할 때 가장 행복해진다는 취지의 글이다.

02 ▶ (A) 강력한 열정이 부정적인 결과를 낳는 것은 자아가 분열된 사람의 경우일 뿐이다. (B)와 (C)는 둘째, 셋째 문장에서 알 수 있고 (D)는 마지막 문장에서 알 수 있다.

》》 정답　01 (D)　02 (A)

007

　　세계에서 가장 많은 관광객들이 몰려드는 관광지 중 하나와 나와의 예상 밖으로 친밀한 만남은 그렇게 시작되었다. 육중한 대문이 철커덩하고 내 뒤에서 닫히는 소리를 들었을 때 마지막 일광의 흔적이 사라지고 있었다. 벌레와 새들이 요란스레 울어댔다. 잉카문명의 석벽이 수백 미터 아래 우루밤바(Urubamba) 강의 어지러울 정도로 깊은 골짜기를 향해 곤두박질치고 있었다. 온 사방에는 칼날같이 날카로운 푸른 산들이 솟아 있고, 산정은 사라져가는 태양에 청회색으로 변한 짙은 솜털구름층에 가려 보이지 않았다. 바로 눈앞에는 큰 돌계단들이 사다리꼴 문을 지나 잉카인들이 약 500년 전에 지은 사원과 집과 뜰과 샘이 모여 있는 곳으로 경사져 있었다. 달은 이제 거의 머리 바로 위에서 길을 걸어갈 수 있을 만큼 밝은 빛을 비추며 구름 사이를 들락날락거리고 있었다. 바로 그곳 마추픽추의 유적지에 나는 완전히 홀로 와있었다.

overrun a. 너무 많은 사람들이 몰려드는
clank v. 철커덩하고 울리다
chirp v. (새, 벌레가) 울다
plunge v. 뛰어들다, (산길이) 갑자기 내리막길이 되다
headlong ad. 거꾸로, 곤두박이로
dizzyingly ad. 현기증 날 정도로, 어지럽게
gorge n. 골짜기
cottony a. 솜털 같은
trapezoidal a. 사다리꼴의
terrace n. 계단모양의 뜰
millennium n. 1000년

01 ▶ 이 글은 유적지의 모습을 눈에 보이는 그대로 '기술'하고 있다. (A) 감상적인 (C) 과장된 (D) 명상적인

02 ▶ (A) 첫 문장에서 most overrun이라 했다. (B) "마지막 일광의 흔적이 사라지고 있었다."나 "사라져가는 태양"에서 황혼 무렵임을 알 수 있다. 끝에 '이 머리 위에서 밝게 비춘 것'은 '이제(now)'로 보아 유적지 안으로 들어가면서 시간이 경과되었음을 나타낸다. (C) 약 500년 전이라 했으므로 15세기 말이나 16세기 초로 짐작할 수 있다. (D) 아름답긴 하지만 사방이 날카로운 산으로 둘러싸여서 easily accessible(접근하기 쉬운)하지는 않다.

》 정답　01 (B)　02 (D)

008

　　실제 사실에 근거한 진정한 불만을 갖고 있지만 자신의 경험에 비추어 일반화해서 자신의 불행이 우주(세상 전체)를 아는 열쇠를 제공한다고 결론지어버리는 사람이 있다. 이를테면, 그가 국가정보기관의 어떤 비리사실을 발견하는데, 정부로서는 그것을 숨기는 것이 이롭다고 하자. 그럴 경우 그는 발견한 사실을 좀체 세상에 알릴 수 없고, 분명 고위층에 속한 인사들은 그를 분노케 하는 그 악을 시정하기 위해 손가락 하나 까딱하지 않으려 한다. 여기까지는 그가 말하는 그대로가 사실이다. 그러나 그는 자신의 좌절에 너무나 깊은 인상을 받은 나머지, 권력자는 모두 전적으로 그리고 오로지 권력의 원천인 범죄를 감추는 데에만 몰두해 있다고 믿어버린다.

grievance n. 불만, 불평
let us say 이를테면
scandal n. 추문, 독직사건, 부정행위
Secret Service 정보기관, 첩보기관
obtain publicity for ~을 세상에 알리다, 공표하다
high-minded a. 고상한, 고결한, 거만한
rebuff n. 거절, 저지; 좌절

01 ▶ 비리사실을 알리고 싶은데 알릴 길이 막혀있을 때 '좌절'을 경험할 것이다.

02 ▶ 처음부터 the universe까지가 주제문이고 그 이하는 예를 들고 있는데, 자신의 경험만으로 일반화하는 것은 잘못이라는 점을 지적하고자 쓴 글이다.

》 정답　01 (D)　02 (B)

009

　　내가 말하려는 차이점은 분명 일반적인 것이지만, 예외도 있다. 일반적으로 말하자면, 약 10퍼센트의 여성들은 금성보다 화성에서 온 것에 더 관련이 있다. 이러한 연유는 이들이 종종 대부분의 다른 여성들보다 더 높은 남성 호르몬을 타고났기 때문이다. 이러한 경우이더라도, 이러한 여성들은 여전히 임신과 출산을 위한 여성 호르몬을 지니고 있다. 이 여성들을 위해 이 책은 그들의 여성적인 필요를 확인시키는 것을 돕고 그들의 여성적인 측면을 뒷받침해주고 키워주는 계시의 역할을 한다. 우리가 이러한 차이점을 함께 탐구해 감에 따라 나는 여성과 남성이 어떻게 해야 한다고 기술하지 않는다는 점을 염두에 두라! 나는 단지 양성 간의 차이점이 드러날 때 남성과 여성이 대개 서로 어떻게 그리고 왜 오해하는지를 지적하고자 한다.

testosterone n. 테스토스테론(남성 호르몬의 일종)
revelation n. 폭로; 누설; 계시
nurture v. 양육하다, 키우다
rebut v. 반박하다, 반증을 들어 논박하다

01 ▶ (A), (B), (D) 모두 남녀 관계를 주제어로 갖고 있지만, 위 글의 요지는 남녀의 차이점을 인정하고 여기에서 생기는 오해를 이해하려는 것이므로 (C)가 가장 유력하다.

02 ▶ 이 책은 남녀 간의 고정관념에 대해 전쟁을 선포한 것이 아니라, 남성성과 여성성을 인정하고 그것을 존중하는 데 목적이 있다.

》 정답 01 (C) 02 (D)

010

　　젊은이들의 사회화가 미약하고, 사회적 결속이 약화되는 경우에 수치심도 흐려진다고 우리는 예상할 수 있다. 현재 이 나라에서는 젊은이들을 사회화시키지 못한 어른들의 무능함으로 인해 청소년들은 그들의 충동에 따라 행동하고 그들의 환상을 실현하려 하고 있다. 그 결과가 뻔뻔함을 과시하는 듯한 젊은이들의 문화가 된 것이다. 우리를 당황케 하는 것은 수치심의 상실이 청소년들에게만 한정된 것이 아니라는 점이다. 어른들 대다수도 자신들의 비겁함과 태만함에 대해 수치스러워하지 않는다. 우리는 수치심을 모르는 사회가 되어버렸다. 우리의 지적 스승들은 우리에게 죄책감 — 가난한 이들, 공해에 대한 — 을 갖게 하려하는 반면, 수치심은 반동적이고 억압적인 것이라며 눈살을 찌푸린다. 그러나 죄책감이 우리를 더 나은 사람으로 만들어줄 지는 몰라도, 수치심의 상실은 문명화된 사회로서의 우리의 생존을 위협한다. 이는 우리가 부끄러워하는 행동의 대부분은 법률로 처벌받지 않기 때문이며, 문명화된 삶은 형벌할 수 없는 규칙을 준수하는 데 달렸기 때문이다. 우리는 또한 수치심이야말로 죄책감보다 훨씬 더 인간 고유의 특성이라고 느낀다. 죄책감에는 수치심보다 더 많은 두려움이 들어 있는데, 동물들도 두려움은 알고 있다.

blur v. 흐려지다, 희미해지다
cohesion n. 결합; 단결, 유대; 응집력; 결속성
flauntingly ad. 과시하여
disconcerting a. 당황케 하는
frown on ~에 대해 눈살을 찌푸리다
reactionary a. 반동의
repressive a. 억압적인
observance n. 준수
unenforceable a. 형벌[처벌]할 수 없는
materialize v. 실현[구체화]하다
disembody v. (영혼 등을) 육체로부터 분리시키다

01 ▶ 환상은 사회화되지 못한 청소년들이 지닌, 사회적으로 실현 불가능하거나 현실적으로 수용될 수 없는 욕망을 말한다고 볼 수 있다. 그들은 수치심을 느끼지 못한 채 그런 욕망을 실현하려 할 것이다. 한편, 죄책감에는 많은 두려움이 포함되어 있는데, 두려움은 인간이 아닌 동물에게서도 발견되는 속성이라고 하였다. 반면, 수치심은 인간에게만 더욱 고유한 감정이다.

》 정답 (B)

011

　　항상 나쁜 조언을 따르는 사람이 있다는 것은 다 아는 이야기이다. 과학자들에 따르면 그들은 원래 그렇게 타고났을 가능성이 있다. 『신경과학 저널(The Journal of Neuroscience)』의 새 연구논문은 경험상으로는 해서는 안 되는 줄 알면서도 사람들이 다른 사람의 제안을 그대로 따라 행동할지를 유전적 차이로 어떻게 예측 가능한 지 상세히 서술하고 있다. 사람들은 이런 류(類)의 추론에 두뇌의 두 부분을 사용한다. 전(前) 전두엽 피질은 (남에게서) 받은 조언을 관리하는 반면, 두뇌의 더 깊숙한 곳에 자리 잡은 선조체는 경험을 처리한다. 유전자에 따라 선조체는 전전두엽 피질의 말에 더 쉽게 넘어가기도 한다. 이 연구는 습득한 신념이 새로운 정보를 거부하는 경향을 보이는 확증편향이라 불리는 어떤 것을 이해하는 실마리를 제공한다. 그리고 정치적 성향으로부터 점성술에 빠지는 이유에 이르기까지 모든 것을 설명할지도 모른다.

genetic variation 유전적 차이
prefrontal cortex 전(前) 전두엽 피질
striatum n. 선조체(線條體)
window n. 관찰할 기회, 아는 수단
confirmation bias 확증편향
acquired a. 획득한; 후천적인
resistant a. 저항하는, 반항하는
astrology n. 점성학[술]

01 ▶ 유전적 차이로 인해 타인의 조언에 따라 행동할지의 여부를 예측할 수 있다는 것이 연구 논문의 주제이므로 '사람의 행동에 중대한 역할을 하는 유전자'가 이 글의 제목으로 적절하다.

》 정답 (E)

012

　　인간 경험의 공유라는 보도의 근본적인 목적 전부가 신문을 많이 팔아서 수입을 올리고자 하는 욕망에 꾸준히 종속되어 가고 있다. 자신의 의견을 널리 보급하기 위하여 신문에 대한 통제를 원하던 과거의 신문사주는 이제 대체로 여론형성에는 관심이 없고 가급적 신문을 많이 파는 데만 관심이 있다고 공언하는 그런 신문사주로 대체되어 왔다. 한때는 보다 큰 정책에 대한 수단이었던 것이 대부분의 경우 정책 그 자체가 되어버린 것이다.[수단이 목적으로 변해 버린 것이다.] 그래서 이제는 보도 기구[신문]가 여론형성의 도구로 사용하기 위해 있는 것이 아니라 돈을 벌기 위해[이익을 위해] 있는 것이 되었으며, 우리가 상황이 그와 반대인 척 해야 할 단계는 이미 지나 버렸다.[이제는 신문사 같은 언론기관이 돈을 벌기 위한 것이 아니라 여론 형성의 도구로 사용되기 위한 것이라고 우길 수 없게 되었다.]

steadily ad. 착실하게; 꾸준히
subordinate v. 종속시키다
proprietor n. 소유주; 경영자
propagate v. 보급하다
replace v. ~에 대신하다, 대체하다
pretense n. ~인 체하기

01 ▶ otherwise는 'not for use, but for profit'의 반대를 가정한다.
02 ▶ '신문이 돈벌이의 수단으로 변질되었다'는 것이 본문의 주제이므로 '(여론형성에는 관심이 없고 단지 가급적 신문을 많이 파는데 만 관심이 있다고 공언하는) 새로운 신문사주들이 수단과 목적을 혼동하고 있다'고 한 (D)가 본문의 내용에 부합한다.

》 정답 01 (B) 02 (D)

013

　우리들 중의 많은 사람들이 유명하게 될 것 같지도 않고 기억에도 남을 것 같지 않다. 그러나 한 나라의 국민 또는 한 나라의 문학이 새로운 업적을 이룩하도록 인도하는 소수의 영광스러운 사람에 못지 않게 중요한 것은, 끈기 있는 노력으로 이 세상이 역행하는 것을 막아내는 다수의 무명(無名) 인사들인데, 그들은 설령 새로운 가치를 획득하지 못한다 하더라도 오래된 가치를 지키고 유지하며, 조상으로부터 물려받은 것을 손상시키지 않고 또한 감소시키지 않고 자손에게 전해 주는 것이 그들의 눈에 띄지 않는 승리이다. 우리들 거의 모든 사람들로서는, (생명의) 햇불을 떨어뜨리지 않고 다음 사람에게 넘겨줄 수 있다면 그것으로 충분하며, 만일 가능하다면, 우리들을 아는 몇몇 사람들로부터 사랑을 받고 그 사람들이 (이 세상을) 떠날 차례가 와서 사라지면 잊혀져 버리고 마는 것에 만족한다.

brilliant a. 찬란하게 빛나는; 훌륭한, 화려한
conquer v. 정복하다; (노력해서) 획득하다
inconspicuous a. 두드러지지 않은
hand on ~을 넘겨주다
torch n. 햇불
vanish v. 사라지다

01 ▶ 글의 요지는 '위인들 못지않게 무명의 사람들도 세상과 문명에서 중요한 역할을 하고 있다'는 것이다.

》 정답 (B)

014

　목성의 4대 갈릴레이 위성은 일찍이 강력한 충격을 받았을 것이다. 그래서 가장 오래된 칼리스토의 표면에는 충돌 크레이터(운석 구덩이)들의 흔적이 남아있다. 좀 더 젊고 다양한 표면의 가니메데는 밝고 어두운 지형이 뚜렷이 구별되는데, 홈과 능선이 교차하는 구조가 특징인 밝은 지형은 후에 일어난 얼음 표면의 대류에 의한 것일 것이다. 유로파의 충돌 부분은 거의 사라졌는데, 내부로부터 물이 유출되자마자 즉각적으로 광대한 얼음 바다를 형성했기 때문이다. 목성에 가장 가까운 이오의 위성 사진은 많은 것을 보여준다. 그 사진들은 매우 활발한 화산활동 결과로 태양계에서 지질구조상으로 가장 활발한 활동을 하고 있는 이오의 모습을 보여준다. 이오는 다른 3개의 갈릴레이 위성과 목성 사이에 존재하는 엄청난 인력에서 기인하는 조석력에 지배당하고 있다

bombardment n. 포격, 폭격; [물리] 충격
scar v. ~에 상처를 남기다
crater n. 분화구; (달 표면의) 크레이터
groove n. 홈; 도랑
ridge n. 능선; 융기
erase v. 지우다; 없애다
revelatory a. 계시의, 보여주는
tectonically ad. 지질구조상으로
solar system 태양계
engulf v. 삼켜 버리다

01 ▶ (A) 이오가 태양계에서 지질구조상 가장 활발한 위성이라고 했다. (B) 마지막 문장 Io is engulfed by tides 참고 (C) 두 번째 문장 the very ancient surface of Callisto ~ 참고. (D) 본문에 이오의 충돌 크레이터에 관한 내용은 없다.

02 ▶ 본문의 세 번째 문장 The younger, more … from later iceflows를 보면 가니메데의 밝은 지형은 어두운 지형이 형성되고 난 후 표면에 얼음 지대가 형성되면서 생겼다는 것을 알 수 있다.

》 정답 01 (D) 02 (A)

015

　　여성의 영혼에게 말을 걸고 그 영혼을 즐겁게 하는 특별한 문체가 있다. 이러한 책을 찾기는 어려울 수 있지만 발견된다면 그야말로 보물이다. 나는 작가 수 몽크 키드(Sue Monk Kidd)의 소설 『The Secret Life of Bees』의 등장인물들과 함께 웃고 울었다. 나는 소설 속 여성들과 깊게 연결되어 있다고 느꼈으며, 소설이 결말에 이를 때 나의 친구들이(등장인물) 떠나는 모습을 보기가 너무 슬펐다. 수 몽크 키드는 엄청난 재능을 살려 진정으로 이 책에 생명을 불어 넣었다. 나는 단지 나의 소중한 친구들이 현재 어떻게 지내는지 볼 수 있도록 속편을 간절히 바라고 있다. 당신이 여성이라면 이 책을 분명 좋아하게 될 것이라고 확신한다. 문체는 여성스럽고 아름답다. 나는 속으로 이제는 강력한 여성의 시각에서 쓴 글을 읽어야 할 때라는 생각이 들었다. 나에게 있어 이 책을 읽는 일은 호흡을 하듯 자연스러운 것이었다.

rejoice v. 기쁘게 하다, 즐겁게 하다
character n. 특성; 인격, 성격
come to an end 끝나다, 죽다
tremendous a. 무서운; 엄청난; 멋진
long v. 간절히 바라다; 열망하다
sequel n. (소설 등의) 속편; 결과
feminine a. 여자의, 여성의
perspective n. 전망; 시각

01 ▶ 책을 읽고 난 후 그 느낌을 1인칭 형식으로 서술하고 있으므로 정답은 (B) '잡지 속 서평 섹션'이 적절하다.

02 ▶ 책을 읽는 데 호흡하는 것처럼 자연스럽다는 언급은 그만큼 책 읽기가 '수월했다(effortless)'는 것을 의미한다.

　　　　　　　　　　　　　　　　　　　　　　　》 정답　01 (B)　02 (D)

016

　　빛이 색의 원천이라는 사실은 태양 광선을 유리 프리즘에 통과시켜 무지갯빛 가시(可視) 스펙트럼을 만들어낸 아이작 뉴턴에 의해 1666년에 처음으로 입증되었다. 이러한 현상은 뉴턴 이전에도 관찰되었지만, 그것은 항상 프리즘의 유리 속에 존재하는 것으로 믿어졌던 잠재적인 색채와 관련이 있었다. 그러나 뉴턴은 한 단계 나아가 간단한 실험을 했다. 그는 자신의 소형 무지개를 두 번째 프리즘에 통과시켰는데, 이 프리즘은 원래의 백색 광선을 복원시켰다. 색채는 빛 속에 있고 유리 속에 있지 않다는 그의 결론은 혁명적이었다.

demonstrate v. 증명하다
beam n. 광선
hue n. 색조
visible a. 눈으로 볼 수 있는
latent a. 잠재적인
miniature a. 축소된, 소형의
reconstitute v. 복원하다

01 ▶ 혁명적인 결론을 이끌어 낸 것은 '한 단계 나아간 간단한 실험'이다.

02 ▶ 첫 번째 문장에서 나타난 '빛이 색의 원천'이라는 증명이 뉴턴의 혁명적인 결론이다.

　　　　　　　　　　　　　　　　　　　　　　　》 정답　01 (E)　02 (B)

017

　　노예제도에 대한 해결책은 노예제도의 폐지가 아니다. 적어도 폐지가 완전한 해결책은 아니라는 것이다. 왜냐하면 새로운 형태의 노예제도가 또 다른 이름하에 만들어졌기 때문이다. 해가 뜰 때부터 질 때까지 유독한 환경 속에서 힘들게 일하고 침묵으로 순종하면서 일요일을 제외하고는 빛을 전혀 보지 못하는 공장의 노동자들은 아마도 많은 고대의 노예들보다 더 열악한 삶을 살았을 것이다. 그리고 오늘날 그들 스스로 생각해서 책임을 지기 보다는 오히려 지시받은 일을 하기를 더 좋아하는 모든 사람들은 ― 여론 조사에 의하면 영국인들 중 3분의 1이 자기들은 그런 일을 하기를 더 좋아한다고 말한다 ― 러시아의 자발적인 노예들의 정신적 후계자들이다. 자유롭다는 것은 사람을 지치게 만들고 괴로운 일이라는 것을 기억하는 것이 중요하다. 그리고 고갈의 시대에는, 자유에 대해 말뿐인 어떠한 호의를 보이더라도, 자유에 대한 애정은 항상 약해져왔다.

abolition n. 폐지
toil v. 힘써 일하다, 수고하다, 고생하다
poisonous a. 독성이 있는
heir n. 법정 상속인, 후계자
affection n. 애정, 호의; (pl.) 애착, 연모; 감정
wane v. (달이) 이지러지다, 작아지다; 약해지다
pay lip-service to ~에게 말뿐인 호의를 보이다

01 ▶ '책임을 지다[떠맡다]'라는 의미로 쓸 수 있는 동사는 take, assume, shoulder이다. put responsibility on somebody는 '책임을 누구누구에게 전가하다'의 의미이다.

02 ▶ (A)의 '자발적으로 노예가 된 사람들이 있었다'와 (B)의 '노예제도는 단지 신체적 여건의 문제는 아니다'와 (D)의 '어떤 현대인들은 고대 노예들보다 더 열악한 삶을 살고 있다'는 본문을 통해 추론할 수 있거나 언급되어 있다. (C)는 '자유에 대해 말뿐인 호의를 보이는 것은 우리들 중 어떤 사람도 그것을 원치 않는다'로 본문의 내용과 일치하지도 않고 추론할 수도 없다.

》 정답 01 (C) 02 (C)

018

　　교향악단은, 19세기 동안 음악 기술 발전으로 더욱 더 복잡한 악기가 더해지고 작곡가들이 그 새로운 소리를 가지고 열정적으로 실험하면서 크기와 규모가 커졌는데, 가장 이상적인 인간 사회의 모델이 되었다. 교향악단은 모든 음악가들이 하나의 공동 목적을 위해 함께 모일 것을 요구한다. 그 어떤 하나의 소리도 다른 한 소리보다 더 중요한 것은 아니다. 멜로디가 멜로디를 지탱하는 화음과 리듬보다 더 아름다운 것도 아니다. 만약 (교향악단이라는) 그 단일체가 청중들을 위해 강렬하고, 집중적이고, 열정으로 꽉 찬 하나의 체험을 만들어내지 못한다면, 각 연주자들의 평생의 업적은 없는 것이나 다름없다. 동시에, 그 최종 산물(연주)이 각 개인(개별 연주자)의 천재적 재능을 입증하는 증거다. 단 하나의 소리라도 시시하면 전체 사업(연주)이 망하게 된다.

dimension n. 크기, 규모
composer n. 작곡가
pull together 모으다, 모이다
entity n. 단일체
charged with ~로 꽉 찬
electricity n. 흥분, 열정
testimony n. 증언; 증거, 증명
genius n. 재능

01 ▶ 교향악단이 훌륭한 연주를 하기 위해서는 각각의 악기와 음악의 모든 요소들이 똑같이 중요한 역할을 하면서 일체성을 이루어 각자 최고의 연주를 할 때만 달성된다는 것을 강조하고 있다. 따라서 마지막 문장으로는 (B)가 들어가야 개별 연주자의 최고의 연주의 중요성을 강조한 앞 문장에도 자연스럽게 연결된다.

02 ▶ genius는 본문에서 '비범한 재능'이라는 뜻이므로, (A)의 talent(재능)가 정답이다.

》 정답 01 (B) 02 (A)

019

　　영국의 지방 교육 당국이 최근에 5~11세 아이들이 학교에서 읽도록 승인된 '규정된' 도서 목록을 발간했다. 많은 학부모들이 격분했는데, Sherry Blanchet이라는 아이들에게 매우 인기가 많은 작가가 그 목록에서 빠졌기 때문이다. 그 작가를 제외한 것에 대해 해명을 요구받자, 그 도서 목록의 준비를 책임졌던 위원장은 그 작가의 책은 "우리가 생각할 때 그 책들이 질이 떨어지고 아이들의 지적인 능력을 충분히 고취시키지 못한다고 생각해서 제외된 것이지, 정형화된 인물이 등장하거나 인종적 편견을 보여주어서가 아니다"고 말했다.

education authorities 교육 당국
issue v. 발간하다
prescribe v. 규정하다, 지시하다
approve v. 승인하다
furor n. 분노
inferior a. 열등한, 질 낮은
stimulate v. 도모하다, 자극하다
contain v. 포함하다
stereotype n. 정형, 판에 박힌 것
racial prejudice 인종적 편견

01 ▶ 위원장의 진술을 보면 Ms. Blanchet의 작품이 제외된 이유가 질적으로 떨어지고 어린이의 지적인 발달에 도움이 되지 않아서이지, 정형화되거나 인종차별적인 인물이 등장해서가 아니라고 하였다. 이것은 학부모들이 추측해서 제시한 이유가 아니라 다른 이유 때문이라고 위원장이 해명을 한다고 볼 수 있으므로, (B) "학부모들은 아마도 몇몇 등장인물들이 인종차별주의자여서 Blanchet의 작품이 제외되었을 것이라고 생각한다."가 옳다. 나머지는 본문을 통해서 알 수 없거나 잘못된 정보다.

≫ 정답 (B)

020

　　운동을 운동으로 생각하지 마라. 그렇게 생각하면 운동이 생활에서 멀어져 역효과를 낸다. 당신이 목표로 하는 강철 같은 복부를 아직 만들지 못한 것도 당연한 일이다. 활동량을 늘릴 생각을 하는 것이 더 좋다. 이 미묘한 생각의 변화가 장기적으로 건강해지고 체중을 줄이는데 더 도움이 되는 것 같다. 사우스캐롤라이나 대학 운동과학 교수인 러셀 페이트 박사는 두 사람을 비교했는데, 한 사람은 앉아서 일하는(그러나 하루 중 대부분 시간을 활동하는) 사람이었고 또 한 사람은 매일 60분씩 운동하는(그러나 그다지 활동적이지 않은) 사람이었다. 앉아서 일하는 사람이 운동을 하는 사람보다 에너지를 10퍼센트 더 많이 썼다. 그러니 만일 체육관에 가거나 운동을 할 시간이 없다는 생각이 계속 들면, 이 세상을 체육관으로 삼아라. 볼일을 걸어가서 보거나 리모컨 대신 손으로 차고의 문을 열어라. 활동이 새로운 운동기구인 셈이다.

counter-productive a. 비생산적인, 역효과의
abs of steel 강철 같은 복부(= abdomens of steel)
mind-set n. 심적 경향, 사고방식
conducive a. 도움이 되는
sedentary a. 앉아서 일하는
gym n. 체육관
work out 운동하다(= exercise)
errand n. 심부름, 볼일
remote ad. 멀리 떨어져서
fit n. (운동) 기구 한 벌

01 ▶ 활동이 새로운 운동기구인 셈이라는 말은 생활에서 분리된 운동이 아니라 생활 속의 활동이 좋은 운동효과를 낸다는 뜻인데, '이 세상을 체육관으로 삼아라'라는 말도 따로 운동을 하는 것이 아니라 생활 속의 활동을 운동하듯 활발히 하라는 것으로 같은 취지의 말이다.

02 ▶ 네 번째 문장 Better to think of being more active.가 이 글의 요지를 담은 주제문이다.

≫ 정답 01 (D) 02 (C)

021   당신이 세운 모든 결심을 실행에 옮길 수 있는 기회들 중 첫 번째를 잡아라. 그러면 당신은 매 감정적인 고무 단계마다 당신이 갖기를 열망했던 그 습관들의 방향으로 경험을 쌓게 될 것이다. 결심을 하고 그것을 지키지 않는 것은 아무 가치가 없다. 따라서 반드시 당신이 세운 모든 결심을 지켜야 하는데, 이는 당신이 그 결심으로 이익을 보기 때문만이 아니라 그렇게 함으로써 결심을 실행에 옮기는 데 필요한 습관을 형성시키는 두뇌 세포와 생리학적 상관물을 작동시키는 연습을 몸에 익힐 수 있기 때문이다. 행동에 옮기려는 경향은 행동이 실제로 발생하는 연속된 빈도에 비례해 효과적으로 우리 몸에 배고, 뇌는 그 사용에 맞춰 '성장'한다. 결심이나 타오르는 의지가 결실을 맺지 못하고 사라져 버리게 하는 것은 기회를 잃는 것보다 나쁘다.

resolution n. 결심, 결의
aspire v. 열망하다, 포부를 갖다
prompting n. 자극, 격려, 고무
resolve n. 결심, 결의
furnish v. 갖추다, 제공하다
physiological a. 생리학의
correlative n. 상관물
ingrained a. 깊이 베어든; 타고난
uninterrupted a. 연속된
discernible a. 인식[식별]할 수 있는
evaporate v. 증발하다, 소실하다; 자취를 감추다

01 ▶ 글쓴이는 우리가 결심을 실행할 수 있는 기회가 될 때마다 바로 실행에 옮기면 그것이 우리의 두뇌세포에 영향을 미쳐 습관을 형성할 수 있다고 말한다.

02 ▶ 결심을 하고 실행하지 않는 것은 기회를 잃어버리는 것보다 더 좋지 않다고 했다. 이는 '실행에 옮기지 못한 결심은 기회를 잃어버린 것에 불과하다.'와 다른 내용이며, '헛된 결심을 하느니 기회를 잃는 편이 낫다' 가 더 가까운 의미이다.

03 ▶ 한번 세운 계획을 왜 반드시 실천에 옮겨야 하는지에 대해 명확하고 단호하게 주장을 펼치는 글이다.

» 정답 01 (A) 02 (D) 03 (A)

022   할리우드는 이마와 다른 주름이 있는 부분들을 매끄럽게 하려고 보톡스에 의존하지만, 늘 그렇듯이 아름다움에는 대가가 따른다. 『USA Today』에 따르면, 보톡스 미용 시술은 다른 사람들의 감정을 읽을 수 있는 능력을 떨어뜨릴 수 있다고 서던캘리포니아 대학교의 심리학 교수이자 연구의 주 작성자인 데이비드 닐(David Neal)은 말한다. 사람들은 부분적으로 표정을 흉내내면서 감정을 읽기 때문에 "얼굴에서 뇌로 전해지는 근육의 신호가 약화되면, 감정을 읽기가 어려워진다"고 닐은 말한다. 신경독의 정화된 형태인 보톡스는 근육을 마비시켜서 주름을 야기할 수 있는 특정 얼굴 동작을 방해한다. 개인적으로는, 플라스틱처럼 보이는 얼굴을 하느니 다른 사람들이 무엇을 생각하고 느끼는지에 대한 실마리를 얻는 편이 낫다.

smooth v. 매끄럽게 하다; 주름을 펴다
render v. ~이 되게 하다(= make)
mimic v. 흉내 내다, 흉내 내어 조롱하다
paralyze v. 마비시키다
hinder v. 방해[저지]하다
clue v. 실마리를 주다

01 ▶ 밑줄 친 dampen은 '약화[둔화]시키다'는 뜻으로 마비시키거나 손상시키는 것은 아니므로 (B)가 정답으로 적절하다.

02 ▶ 본문은 보톡스의 이점보다는 그 단점에 대해 설명하고 있으므로 "보톡스가 사람의 마음을 읽는 중요한 능력을 둔하게 할지도 모른다"는 (D)가 주제로 적절하다. (C)는 본문을 통해 추론 가능한 내용이지만 주제로는 부적절하다.

» 정답 01 (B) 02 (D)

023

　　"좋은"과 "나쁜" "더 좋은"과 "더 나쁜"은 말로 정의내릴 수 없을지도 모르는 용어들이지만, 어쨌든 먼저 구체적으로는 이해되게 된다. 그렇다면, 말로 정의를 내리는 문제는 나중으로 남겨두고 우선 이 단어들의 의미를 나타내려고 해보자. 어떤 것이 그 결과 때문만이 아니라 그 자체 때문으로 귀중히 여겨지면 "좋은" 것이다. 우리는 바람직한 결과를 낳을 것으로 기대하기 때문에 쓴 약을 먹지만, 통풍에 걸린 감식가는 불쾌한 결과가 발생할 수 있는데도 불구하고 오래된 포도주 그 자체 때문에 오래된 포도주를 마신다. 약은 유용하지만 좋지 않고 포도주는 좋지만 유용하지 않다. 어떤 사태가 존재해야 하느냐 존재하지 말아야 하느냐를 선택해야 할 때 우리는 물론 그 결과를 고려해야 한다. 그러나 그 사태의 결과 하나하나 뿐 아니라 그 사태 자체도 우리로 하여금 경우에 따라 그 사태를 선택하고 싶도록 만들거나 선택하지 않고 싶도록 만드는 내재적인 특성을 갖고 있다. 우리는 그것을 선택하고 싶을 때 그 내재적 특성을 "좋다"고 여기고 그것을 거부하고 싶을 때 그 내재적 특성을 "나쁘다"고 여기는 것이다.

ostensively ad. 실물로, 구체적으로
sake n. 동기, 이유
nasty a. (약이) 먹기 힘든, 쓴
gouty a. 통풍(痛風)에 걸린
connoisseur n. 감식가, 전문가
disagreeable a. 불쾌한
take account of ~을 고려하다
as the case may be 경우에 따라

01 ▶ 앞의 진술에 의하면 그 자체로 귀중히 여겨지는 것이 좋은 것이고 그 결과가 바람직하면 유용한 것인데, 약은 그 자체는 모두 싫게 여기지만 약을 먹은 결과가 병이 낫는 바람직한 결과이고, 포도주는 결과는 불쾌할 수 있으나 그 자체는 좋아서 마시는 것이므로 (B)가 적절하다.

02 ▶ (A) 약의 경우이다. (B) 첫 문장에서 언급되었다. (C) 포도주의 경우이다. 마지막 부분에서 "좋다/나쁘다"는 판단에는 우리가 그것을 선택하고 싶다, 거부하고 싶다는 우리의 성향이 개입되어 있음을 알 수 있다. 따라서 "좋다"와 "나쁘다"는 사물이나 일에 대한 우리의 성향과 무관하게 절대적으로 객관적이라고 한 (D)는 추론할 수 없는 사항이다.

》 정답 01 (B) 02 (D)

024

　　여러분은 저작권이 무엇이라고 생각하는가? 저작권은 애써서 얻지만 종종 그에 합당한 보상을 받지 못하는 자신의 결과물을 창작자들이 법적으로 보호할 수 있는 고유의 권리인가? 아니면 저작권은 여러분이 어떤 창작물을 사용하고 싶을 때마다 먼저 허락을 받고 그 값을 지불해야 하는 것으로 민주주의를 침해하고 문화를 고갈시키는 것인가? <이러한 것들이 간단한 문제들은 아니다.> 나와 같은 창작자들은 우리의 작품이 불법 복제되거나 맥락을 벗어나 잘못 사용되거나 심지어 표절되는 것을 볼 때 좌절감을 느낀다. 우리는 이런 것을 좋아하지 않고 보복하려고 한다. 하지만 교육자들과 많은 사업가들은 완전히 다른 세계관을 가지고 있다. 이른 바 카피레프트(Copy Left) 운동에 의하면, 작품들을 자유롭게 이용할 수 있는 공공 영역은 문화 활동의 중요한 부분이다. 많은 교육자들은 모든 학생들이 원하는 대로 작품들을 이용할 수 있어야 한다고 생각한다. 심지어 일부 사람들은 하늘 아래 진정으로 새로운 것은 없기 때문에 모든 창작물들이 재생된 아이디어에 불과하다고 주장한다.

copyright n. 저작권, 판권
inherent a. 고유의; 선천적인
legally ad. 법적으로
erosion n. 침식, 부식
drain n. 고갈, 유출
plagiarize v. 도용하다, 표절하다
retribution n. 보복
domain n. 영역; 소유지; 분야
available a. 이용할 수 있는; 손에 넣을 수 있는

01 ▶ 교육자들과 많은 사업가들은 앞에서 언급한 창작자들과 다른 세계관을 지니고 있다고 언급하였으며, 모든 학생들이 자유롭게 작품을 이용할 수 있어야 한다고 하였다. 따라서 교육자들은 저작권에 대해 '비판적'인 태도를 나타내고 있다고 할 수 있다.

02 ▶ a work will be always available을 보장하려 하는 것은 '카피레프트 운동'이다.

03 ▶ These와 questions가 가리키는 것은 두 가지 측면에서 제시한 저작권에 대한 물음을 의미한다. 즉, 저작자 고유의 권한인가 아니면 자유를 침해하는 것인가를 묻는 것이다. 따라서 주어진 문장은 이러한 의문점이 모두 제시된 다음인 [Ⅲ]에 위치하는 것이 가장 적절하다. 뒤이어서 이 문제에 대해 서로 상응하는 creators와 Copy Left movement의 주장을 소개하는 흐름으로 이어진다.

》 정답 01 (B) 02 (C) 03 (C)

025

미국 채권자 재단은 중국이 90년 이상 전에 발행한 15,000여 개가 넘는 정부 채권들을 변제하라고 요구하고 있는데, 그들이 말하는 채권 총액은 890억 달러에 이른다. 그 재단의 요구는 중국이 무역과 국제 자본 시장에서 이익을 거둠에 따라 외국 투자자들에 대해 어느 정도까지 책임을 다할 것인가를 시험하고 있다. 하지만 중국의 20세기 역사의 혼란은 그 채권들에 대한 공식적인 책임 소재를 희미하게 했다. 중국의 첫 근대적 공화국은 1913년에 채권을 발행했으며 26년 후에 내전과 일본의 침략 와중에 변제를 이행하지 않았다. 훗날 그 정부는 공산주의자들의 공격으로 1949년 타이완으로 달아났다. 베이징에 있는 중국 정부는 책임을 인정한 적이 없다.

bondholder n. 채권 소지자
foundation n. 협회, 재단
turmoil n. 소란, 혼란
blur v. 흐려지게 하다, 희석시키다
issue v. 발행하다
default v. (약속, 채무 등을) 이행하지 않다
legitimacy n. 정통성
overdue a. 만기의, 지급 기한이 지난

01 ▶ 이 글의 전체적인 내용은 '중국이 역사적 혼란 때문에 1913년 발행한 채권에 대한 변제를 지금껏 이행하지 않았으며, 미국 채권자 재단이 이에 대한 변제를 요구하고 있다'는 것이다.

02 ▶ 다섯 번째 줄 마지막에서 '중국의 역사의 혼란은 그 채권들에 대한 공식적인 책임 소재를 희미하게 했다'고 언급하였으므로, 1913년에 발행된 채권은 내전과 일본 침략에 의해 '변제가 이행되지 못했음'을 짐작할 수 있다.

》 정답 01 (C) 02 (B)

026

영국 상원은 유럽에서 가장 높은 십대 임신율을 낮추려는 정부의 전략을 지지하여 사후 피임약의 판매를 금지하는 제안에 반대하는 표결을 했다. 표결 결과는 177대 95로 처방전 없이 피임약을 파는 것을 금지하는 제안에 대해 반대했다. 금지 조치를 옹호하는 사람들은 피임약의 판매가 젊은이들에게 그들이 원하는 대로 행동해도 된다는 허가증을 내주는 것이 될까 두려워한다. 하지만 발의된 금지 법안에 반대를 주장하는 의원들은 금지 법안이 원치 않는 임신을 낳을 수도 있다고 말했다.

House of Lords <영국> 상원
bid n. 입찰; 제안; 노력
contraceptive pill 피임약
motion n. 명령 신청; 동의; 제안
bar v. 금지하다
over-the-counter a. 처방전 없이 팔리는
proponent n. 제안자; 지지자, 옹호자
lawmaker n. 입법자, (국회) 의원

01 ▶ 표결에 부쳐진 사후 피임약 판매 금지 조치에 대해 찬성하는 사람들과 반대하는 사람들의 입장을 객관적으로 나열한 글이다.

02 ▶ '발의된 금지 법안(the proposed ban)'이란 '사후 피임약을 처방전 없이 판매하는 것을 금지하는 법안'이다. 이에 대해 '반대를 제기하는(argued against)'는 '의원(lawmakers)'들은 '표결에 참가하여 피임약 판매를 허용해야 한다는 입장을 취하는 177명의 사람들'이다. 여기서 '이것(it)'은 '발의된 금지 법안(the proposed ban)'으로, 이것이 미칠 파급 효과를 유추하면 된다. 즉 '피임약 판매 금지로, 약을 사지 못하게 되면, 원치 않은 임신이 늘어날 수도 있다'는 것이다.

》 정답 01 (A) 02 (C)

027

그날 밤 처음으로 나는 할 말을 잃었다. '어떻게 이 여인에게 그저 죽은 아이를 세상에 분만할 수 있도록 힘을 주라고 설득할 수 있단 말인가?' 한 시간이 지난 후 레지던트가 돌아와 왜 이렇게 시간이 오래 걸리느냐고 나에게 물었다. 나는 아기의 머리가 만져지지만 산모가 힘을 충분히 주지 않고 있다고 귓속말로 말해주었다. 나는 외음부절개술, 즉 약간 절개하여 아기가 나오는 길을 넓히는 수술을 해서 분만을 빨리 해도 좋을지 물어보았다. 레지던트는 고개를 끄덕여 동의해주었다. 나는 얼른 절개를 했고 아기가 불쑥 나와 내손에 들어오는 것이 느껴졌다. 체중 약 3킬로그램의 사랑스런 여자아이였다. 대개 그렇게 하듯이 나는 미리 산모의 배 위에 펴놓은 살균된 시트 위에 아기를 올려놓았다. 그녀는 자신의 죽은 딸을 보고는 고개를 돌려버렸다. 나는 내내 말이 없었다.

절개한 부위를 봉합하기 시작했을 때 나는 작은 기침 소리를 들었다. 아기를 올려다보니 아기는 여전히 엄마의 배 위에 있었다. 그런 다음 나는 내 생애 가장 아름답고 우렁찬 소리를 들었다. 아기가 자신의 폐활량대로 한껏 울어재끼고 있었다. 나는 "어머니, 아기가 살아 있어요."라는 말만 되풀이할 수 밖에 없었다. 그녀의 여린 울음이 행복에 찬 발작적인 울음으로 바뀌었다. 그녀는 "의사 선생님, 우리 아기를 살려주셔서 고마워요."라는 말을 되풀이 했다. 그 놀라운 분만의 기적을 경험한 그 마법 같은 순간에 비할 수 있는 것은 아무 것도 없다.

resident n. 레지던트, 전문의 수련자
episiotomy n. 외음부 절개술
sterile a. 메마른, 불모의; 살균한
drape v. (팔·다리 등을) 축 놓다[늘어뜨리다]
abdomen n. 배, 복부
suture v. 봉합하다
belly n. 배, 복부
convulsive a. 경련을 일으키는; 발작적인

01 ▶ 사산한 줄 알았는데 무사히 살아있는 아이를 분만하게 된 상황에 대한 글임을 감안하면, 제목으로는 (D)가 적절하다.

02 ▶ '한 시간이 지난 후 레지던트가 돌아와 왜 이렇게 시간이 오래 걸리느냐고 나에게 물었다'라는 말에는 대개는 한 시간보다 적은 시간이 걸린다는 의미가 내포돼 있다.

03 ▶ ③은 아기를 가리키고, 나머지는 산모를 가리킨다.

》 정답 01 (D) 02 (B) 03 (C)

우리는 서기 2000년이 되기 전에 로봇 가정부를 두고 달에서 살며 하늘을 나는 자동차를 타고 이리저리 날아다닐 것이라는 생각을 해왔다. 이런 생각은 주제넘은 생각이었을지도 모른다. 그러나 적어도 "하늘을 나는 자동차"에 대한 상상은 어느 정도 진척을 이루고 있다. 미래지향 자동차 제조업체인 몰러 인터내셔널(Moller International)사가 "비행접시" 자동차를 발명했는데, 이것이 사람들의 통근 방식을 바꾸어놓을 것으로 회사에서는 기대한다. 만일 캘리포니아에 있는 이 회사가 생각대로 잘 해나간다면 우리는 생각보다 더 빨리 젯슨 씨 가족처럼 이리저리 공중을 날아다니게 될 것이다. 몰러사 대변인들의 말에 의하면, 이 여덟 개의 엔진이 달린 이 자동차는 내부가 널찍하고 작동하기 쉬우며 가솔린이나 디젤, 심지어 에탄올로도 달릴 수 있다고 한다. 헬리콥터처럼 수직 이착륙을 하고 지상 3미터 높이에서 빙빙 돌 수 있다. 3미터 이상이면 운전자는 비행조종 면허증이 있어야 할 것이다. 이 미래 상품은 불과 9만 달러면 살 수 있다. 몰러사는 이 발명품을 늦어도 내년부터 시판하고 연간 생산량을 250대로 늘이기를 희망하고 있다.

under the impression that ~라고 생각하여
maid n. 하녀, 가정부
zip v. 소리를 내며 날다[달리다]
presumptuous a. 주제넘은, 뻔뻔스런
flying saucer n. 비행접시
commute v. 통근하다
get one's way 제멋대로 하다, 생각대로 하다
the Jetsons n. 우주 가족 젯슨(한나-바버라 프로덕션이 제작한 TV 애니메이션)
petrol n. 가솔린
vertically ad. 수직으로
hover v. 공중을 빙빙 돌다, 선회하다

01 ▶ (A) 이 글의 flying car가 이런 종류로는 최초의 것이며 아직 시판되지 않았으므로 젯슨씨 가족은 실제 인물들이 아닌 어떤 소설이나 만화영화의 등장인물들일 것으로 추론할 수 있다. (B) 3미터까지 올라갈 수 있고 그 이상이면 비행조종 면허증이 필요하다는 것은 이것이 비행기가 아닌 자동차로 분류될 것임을 의미하며, (C) 연간 생산량을 250대로 늘이기를 희망한다는 것은 대량생산되는 것이 아님을 말한다. (D) 지상 3미터가 자동차로 분류되는 한계이지 기술상의 한계는 아님을 의미한다.

02 ▶ 로봇 가정부, 달에서의 거주는 아직도 전혀 실현되지 않았고 비행자동차도 서기 2000년을 훨씬 넘긴 지금에야 실현되어가고 있으므로, 빈 칸 앞의 생각(impression)은 인간의 능력을 과대평가한 '주제넘은' 생각이었다고 할 수 있다.

» 정답 01 (D) 02 (A)

보수적 문화 평론가 스탠리 크라우치(Stanley Crouch)가 날카롭게 지적했던 것처럼, 흑인이 범죄를 저지르면 인종에 대한 논평이 이어진다. 백인이 범죄를 저지르면 사회에 대해, 아니면 그 개인에 대해서만 논평이 이어진다.

정신 장애를 겪는 백인이 학교, 교회, 직장에서 아무리 총을 난사하더라도, 낙태 전문 병원을 폭파시키더라도, 연쇄살인범으로 체포되더라도, 아무도 다음과 같은 질문을 던지지 않는다. 백인 교외 문화에 무슨 문제가 있는가? 반응은 저건 불량한 개인에 지나지 않아, 또는 얼마나 사회가 나빠지고 있는지 보여 주고 있는 거야 정도이다.

백인우월주의의 유산과 그것이 현재 정치, 경제적 상황에 미치는 영향에 대해 미국이 의미 있는 인종간의 대화를 갖기 위해서, 우리는 몇몇 중요한 차별에 대해 추적할 수 있는 정신적 기민함을 가져야만 한다. "색맹을 color blindness라고 부르지 말자, 그것이 인종 차별을 떠올리게 할 수도 있으니까"라고 문제를 제기하는 것만으로도 '고집불통 흑인 인종주의자'로 비난을 받게 되는 지금과 같은 때에 이는 가장 중요한 일이다.

astutely ad. 날카롭게
disturbed a. 정신 장애의
abortion n. 낙태
dexterity n. 기민함
tall order 무리한 요구
bigot n. 고집불통
PC(= Political Correctness) n. 정치적 공정성

01 ▶ 여전히 미국에 인종차별이 존재하고 있음을 이야기하면서 그러한 인종차별에 대해 반대하고 있는 글이다. 글의 성격상 자신의 주장을 펴고 있는 글이므로, argue하고 있는 글이다.

》 정답 (D)

---

030 주변 세계에 대한 우리의 이론이 진화하고 더 유용해지면서 그 이론들은 거의 예외 없이 목적론적인 성격을 덜 띠게 되고 더 기계론적이게 된다. 한 현상에 대한 목적론적인 설명은 원인과 결과를 욕망이나 목적의 관점에서 기술한다. 어떤 일이 일어나는 이유는 단지 그것이 어떤 목적에 부합하기 때문에, 즉 그것이 '일어나게 되어 있기' 때문이거나 누군가가 그 일이 일어나기를 '바라기' 때문이라는 것이다. 공이 땅에 떨어지는 이유는 공이 하늘에 있을 때 땅이 있기에 더 좋은 장소라고 생각하기 때문이지 뭔가가 그것을 땅으로 밀기 때문은 아니라는 식이다. 목적론적 설명은 유용한 이론으로 살아남을 수 없는데 그 이유는 이들이 역행하기 때문이다. 즉 목적론적 설명은 결과 뒤에 원인을 둔다. 반면에 기계론적 설명은 인과에 대한 논의가 시간이 앞으로 감에 따라 물리적 물체와 물질이 어떻게 상호 작용하는가에 관한 알려진 법칙에 국한될 것을 요구한다. <이것이 과학자의 언어인 것이다.> 정직한 과학자라면 누구도 트리니트로톨루엔이 폭발하는 이유가 그것이 '원해서'라고 말하지는 않을 것이다. 이것이 폭발하는 이유는 열과 산소의 존재가 그 화학물질 결합 속에 저장된 잠재 에너지를 방출시키기 때문이다.

theory n. 이론
evolve v. 진화하다
teleological a. 목적론의
mechanistic a. 기계론적인, 기계론의
phenomenon n. 현상
restrict v. 제한하다, 한정하다
release v. 방출하다
potential energy 잠재[위치] 에너지
bond n. (원소의) 결합

01 ▶ 밑줄 친 부분은 목적론적 설명의 예이므로 욕망이나 목적의 관점에서 쓰인 예문을 골라야 한다. 따라서 정답은 "새가 노래하는 것은 새가 노랫소리를 좋아하기 때문이다"가 된다.

02 ▶ "이것은 과학자의 언어이다"라고 했으므로 목적론 이후의 기계론적 설명 부분에 넣어야 하고 바로 뒤에 right-minded chemist라는 과학자의 이야기가 나오므로 [III]이 가장 적합한 자리이다.

》 정답 01 (D) 02 (C)

031

　　학자들은 명시적 권력과 암시적 권력을 구별한다. 명시적 권력은 A가 원하는 것을 B로 하여금 하게 만드는 A의 가시적인 행동에 기초해 있다. 운전자로 하여금 차를 멈추고 기다리게 만드는 경찰관의 신호가 명시적 권력의 한 예이다. 암시적 권력의 경우에도 B는 A가 바라는 것을 하지만 그것이 A가 하는 그 어떤 말이나 행동 때문이 아니라 (1) A가 어떤 일이 행해지기를 원한다는 것을 B가 감지하고 (2) 그 어떤 이유에서든 A가 행해지기를 원하는 것을 B가 하고 싶어 하기 때문이다. 암시적 권력의 많은 예는 가족에서 발견되는데, 가족 식구들은 서로에게 너무나 잘 맞추어져 있어서 종종 식구들 사이에 눈에 보이는 의사전달은 전혀 없어도 서로의 소원을 용케도 잘 읽고 응해 나간다. 토요일 오전에 아버지가 딸에게 자동차 키를 던져줄 수도 있는데, 이 경우 아버지는 완전히 자발적으로, 단지 딸의 습관을 알고 있어서 그리고 딸의 소원에 응하기를 바라서 그렇게 하는 것이다. 딸은 운전하면서 시속 55마일의 제한속도를 지킬 것인데, 이는 제한속도 준수에 대한 부모님의 생각이 확고하다는 것을 딸이 알고 있기 때문이다. 이 두 경우 모두, 한 식구에게서 다른 식구에게로 공공연하게 보내지는 신호는 전혀 없다.

manifest a. 명백한, 명시적인
implicit a. 은연중의, 암시적인, 내포된
observable a. 관찰할 수 있는, 가시적인
attune v. 맞추다, 조화[순응]시키다
comply with 응하다, 따르다
unprompted a. 지시받지 않고 하는, 자발적인
feel strongly about ~에 대해 확고한 생각을 갖고 있다
overt a. 공공연한, 겉으로 드러난

01 ▶ 암시적 권력에 대한 설명 중 (1)의 동사 senses에서 (B)의 sensibility (지각력, 감수성)를, 끝에서 세 번째 문장의 completely unprompted에서 (C)의 voluntariness(자발성)를, 그 앞 문장의 no observable communication에서 (D)의 invisibility(불가시성)를 각각 연관 지을 수 있다. (A)의 definiteness(확정성)는 명시적 권력과 관계있다.

02 ▶ 명시적 권력은 확연히 드러난 것이므로 무력침공으로 위협한 (A)가 좋은 예이고, 암시적 권력은 드러나지 않은 것이므로 두목의 말을 엿듣고 적을 살해한 (B)가 좋은 예이다. 암시적 권력은 드러나지 않은 것이므로 (C)처럼 오해와 원치 않은 결과의 가능성이 더 많고, 암시적 권력을 행사했는지 여부를 확정짓기가 더 어렵다.

》 정답 01 (A) 02 (D)

032

　　수천 년 전에도 사람들은 스스로의 힘으로 썩 잘 해가고 있었지만, 큰 강 유역을 중심으로 정착했을 때 문명이 사실상 번성하기 시작했다. 고대 이집트와 메소포타미아와 인더스 강 유역을 생각해보라. 인류는 강에 더 가까이 살게 되었을 때 더 똑똑해지고 더 정교해졌다. <그래서 물고기를 먹는 것이 뇌의 물리적 크기를 실제로 더 크게 해줄 수 있다는 것은 완전히 놀랄만한 일은 아니다.> 인지적 결함이 전혀 없는 70대 후반의 피실험자 260명을 조사한 한 연구는 팬에 굽거나 석쇠에 구운(튀기지 않은) 물고기를 매주 먹은 사람들의 뇌의 학습중추인 해마가 그렇게 하지 않은 사람들의 해마보다 14% 더 크다는 것을 밝혀냈다. 물고기에 함유된 오메가-3 지방산은 또한 단기기억과 업무기획과 같은 업무수행 기능에 중요한 부위인 뇌의 전두엽 안의 뉴런의 성능을 향상시켜주었다. 만일 당신의 뉴런이 더 크고 더 강하며 다른 뉴런과 더 잘 연결될 수 있으면, 그 뉴런은 제 기능을 더 효과적으로 수행할 수 있을 것이다. 해산물 중에는 오메가-3가 풍부한 것이 많이 있다. 당신은 연어를 먹으면서 굴과 송어와 심지어 정어리로 보충할 수 있다. 물고기가 더 큰 뇌의 비결일지 모르지만, 다양성은 여전히 인생의 묘미이다.

basin n. 분지, 유역
cognitive a. 인지적인
hippocampus n. 해마
grilled a. 석쇠[그릴]에 구워진
frontal lobe n. 전두엽
complement v. 보충[보완]하다
salmon n. 연어
oyster n. 굴
trout n. 송어
sardine n. 정어리
hefty a. 무거운, 큰
spice n. 양념, 묘미, 멋

01 ▶ 밑줄 친 부분은 '다양한 일을 하거나 일에 변화를 줄 때 인생은 재미있어진다(Doing many different things, or often changing what you do, makes life interesting.)'라는 의미인데, 문맥상 앞 문장과 관련하여 암시하는 것으로는 '생선을 포함한 여러 다양한 해산물을 먹는 것이 더 좋다'가 적절하다.

02 ▶ [Ⅰ] 앞뒤는 civilizations와 그 예들로 연결되어 있고, 인류가 강 가까이에서 살게 되었을 때 물고기를 먹어 두뇌력이 발달하여 문명이 발달하게 되었다는 의미이므로, 제시된 문장은 [Ⅱ]에 들어가는 것이 적절하다. 그리고 나서 이를 뒷받침하는 여러 실험의 과학적 사실들이 뒤이어지는 것이 자연스럽다.

≫ 정답 01 (A) 02 (B)

---

033 최근에 와서, 광고주들이 그들의 상품의 평판을 높이기 위해 과학이나 의학의 명성을 빌려와서 사용하는 일이 점차 관행처럼 되어 왔다. 미국인들은 한때는 주교나 정치가들에게서나 가졌던 경외감을 실험실의 과학자나 의사에 대해서도 느끼게 되었다. 이러한 사람들이 인정해 주었다고 하는 주장은 어떤 것을 판매하거나 (같은 이야기지만) 누군가로 하여금 어떤 것을 믿게 만드는 문제에 있어서는 엄청난 비중을 차지하게 된다. '일류 의학 권위자들에 따르면…'이나 '사설 연구소의 실험에 의하면…' 등과 같은 문구는 생각컨대 실수나 부패를 허용하지 않는 과학의 신망을 단지 치약이나 시리얼의 선전에 이용하기 위해 고안된 것이다. 아마도 정확한 '의학의 권위자'나 '사설 연구소'의 이름이 명기되는 경우는 거의 없을 것이다. 그러나 이러한 단순한 문구들은 무비판적인 사람들에게 대단한 비중을 가진다.

alleged a. (증거 없이) 주장된
induce v. 야기하다, 유발하다, 권유하다
presumably ad. 아마, 추측하건대
prestige n. 명성, 신망
reserve v. (어떤 목적을 위하여) 떼어두다
bishop n. (가톨릭의) 주교
statesman n. 정치가
transfer v. 옮기다; 변화시키다
corruption n. 부패; 타락

01 ▶ 과학자들이 인정해 주었다는 (증거 없는) 주장이 성공하고 있는 이유에 대해 마지막 문장에서 '무비판적인 사람들에게는 대단한 비중을 가진다'고 했다.

02 ▶ 본문 중간 부분의 Phrases such as …에서 '과학자들이 인정을 했다'는 문구는 선전을 위해 고안되었다고 했고, 밑에서 넷째 줄 Seldom if ever …에서 명확한 이름을 밝히지 않는다고 했다.

≫ 정답 01 (A) 02 (B)

034

　　성공하는 사람은 실수한 적이 없다고 믿는 것이 인지상정이다. 그러나 그렇지 않다. 어려움에 직면한 사람은 우리 모두를 항상 따라다니는 여러 도전과 실패를 상기할 필요가 있다. 나는 하워드 헨드릭스라는 성함의, 그곳에 계시는 한 선생님 때문에 어떤 세미나에 가기로 했다. 그가 하는 모든 말 속에 그의 인격과 솔직함과 기지와 자신감이 빛을 발했다. 그는 내가 그때까지 대해본 가장 훌륭한 선생님이셨다. 하지만 잠시 후, 나는 결코 그가 성취한 바에 맞게 살아갈 수 없다는 생각에, 나는 점점 기가 죽었다. 그러던 어느 날 헨드릭스는 내 기분과, 어쩌면 참석한 모든 사람의 기분을 알아차린 것 같았다. 그는 강연 도중에 모든 것을 멈추고 허심탄회한 이야기를 시작했다. 그는 조용히 자신의 실패담을 늘어놓았고 교직을 그만두고 싶은 마음도 여러 번 들었다고 했다. 그는 우리를 때로는 웃기기도 하고 때로는 슬퍼지고 연민의 정을 갖게도 했다. 나는 그가 보통 사람이라는 것을 알게 되었다. 그는 우리에게 이런 말을 했다. "인생은 단거리 경주가 아닙니다. 그것은 마라톤이어서 여러분과 나처럼 그저 꾸준히 일하는 자가 승리를 거둘 때가 많은 것입니다."

haunt v. ~에 늘 붙어 따라다니다
seminary n. 학교, 학원; 신학교; 세미나
candor n. 정직, 솔직
confidence n. 신용, 신뢰; 확신
discouraged a. 낙담한, 낙심한
spot v. 발견하다, 탐지해내다
tempt v. 마음을 끌다, 유혹하다
sympathetic a. 동정적인; 호의적인
clay n. 점토, 찰흙; 육체
plodder n. 터벅터벅 걷는 사람

01 ▶ 이 글의 요지는 마지막 인용문에 제시돼 있다.

02 ▶ clay가 육체라는 뜻으로 쓰였으며, 따라서 a man of clay는 '평범한 보통 사람'이라는 뜻이다. a man in the street도 '보통 사람'이라는 뜻이다.

》 정답 01 (C) 02 (A)

035

　　서구 정신은 우리가 언제나 무언가 일을 하고 있어야 한다는 생각에 열중하고 있다. 그러나 의식이 질료(質料)에 선행한다(정신적/영적 내면세계가 물질적/육체적 외부세계보다 먼저 존재하는 더 본질적인 것이라는 뜻)는 것을 기억할 때 우리는 평정심이 아름다운 감정 이상의 것임을 깨닫는다. 그것은 본질적인 힘이다. 동요된 내면의 마음이 동요된 외부세계를 만들고, 이 외부세계가 더욱 동요된 내면의 마음을 만들며 이것이 또 더욱 동요된 외부세계를 만든다. 그러나 성스런 침묵(평정심)의 순간이 그 악순환을 깨뜨린다. 그리고 바로 그런 이유 때문에 그런 (평정심의) 순간을 촉진하는 것이 우리가 가진 마법의 지팡이들 중 하나이다. 그것은 모든 것을 조화시킨다.

　　우리의 내면적 평화의 결여에 대한 해결책으로 최신 약품을 팔려는 광고가 끊임없이 나온다. 그러나 마음의 고통도 몸의 고통과 마찬가지로 이유가 있어서 있다는 것을 우리는 모두 마음 깊이 알고 있다. 우리는 부러진 다리를 마비시켜서 고치지는 않으며 상한 마음도 그런 식으로 고치지 않는다. 결국, 연금술적인(마법적인) 정신 (치료) 과정만이 마음의 고통을 야기하는 사고형태들을 실제로 해결해서 우리를 서로 용서하는 길로 이끌 수 있다.

be bent on ~에 열중하다
serenity n. 평온, 침착
agitated a. 동요된
vicious cycle 악순환
wand n. (마법의) 지팡이
hawk v. 외치고 다니며 팔다
psychic a. 마음의, 심적인
numb v. 마비시키다, 감각을 없애다
disentangle v. 풀어놓다, 해결하다
distress n. 마음의 고통, 고민

01 ▶ 이 글은 일에 몰두해 있는 서구인들의 정신적 문제(고통)에 대한 치유책으로 평정심을 갖기를 권하는 글이므로 (A)가 글의 내용과 일치하지 않는 진술이다. (B) 마음과 외부세계의 동요의 악순환을 평정심이 깨뜨려준다. (C) 부러진 다리를 고치는 것은 마취가 아니라 치료이듯이 상한 마음(마음의 고통)을 고치는 것이 평정심이다. (D) 마지막 문장의 '연금술적인 정신 과정'이 곧 평정심의 과정인데 이것이 서로를 용서하는 길로 이끌 수 있다고 했다.

≫ 정답 (A)

036

(프랭클린 기자) 건축비의 상승과 오랜 경기 침체에도 불구하고, 처음 단독주택을 장만하는 사람들 중 기존 주택을 구입하는 대신 자신들의 집을 신축하는 사람들이 기록적인 수치(33%)를 나타냈습니다. 이 비율은 지난 6년 동안의 21%와 비교되는 수치입니다. 신규 주택을 짓는 데 드는 총비용을 상승시키는 여러 요인들을 고려할 때, 이것은 놀라운 현상입니다. 신규 주택 건축비에는 "영향 평가금"이 포함되는데, 이것은 자치단체가 자체 개발비용을 충당하기 위해 종종 부과하는 돈(하수도, 도로 개발비 등)입니다. 이 요금으로 총 건축비가 5%까지 증가하지만, 주택융자금 안에는 이 요금이 포함돼 있지 않기 때문에 구입자들은 주택 구입이 완료된 후에야 비로소 이런 사실을 알 수 있습니다.

이런 큰 비용 이외에도, 일반적으로 신규 주택 구입자들로 하여금 직접 건축하는 것을 어렵게 만드는 물질적, 금전적 저해 요인이 더 있습니다. 이 요인들은 건축 부지의 부족, 믿을 만한 건축업자를 찾는 데 있어서의 어려움, 융자금이나 임대료를 계속 물면서 한편으로는 새 집을 짓는 비용을 따로 지불해야 하는 이중 부담 등입니다.

이런 난제들 때문에 주택 구입자들이 기존 주택을 구입할 것이라고 생각하는 사람들도 있습니다. 그러나 이런 모든 어려움에도 불구하고, 점점 더 많은 주택 구입자들이 자기 집을 새로 짓는 쪽을 선호하고 있습니다.

recession n. 경기 후퇴, 불경기
sewer n. 하수구, 하수도
mortgage n. 저당; 융자; 주택융자
deterrent n. 억제책; 방해물

01 ▶ 세 번째 문장, 'This is surprising ~ building a new home' 참조. 갖가지 비용 상승 요인이 많은데도 새로 집을 짓는 것이 놀랍다고 했다.

02 ▶ 두 번째 단락에 집을 짓는 데 있어서의 장애 요인이 언급돼 있다.

≫ 정답 01 (D) 02 (C)

037

　　찰스 다윈은 자연주의자이자 과학자였다. 다윈의 『종의 기원(1859)』은 자신의 진화론을 시험하고 확인하는 25년간의 연구에 기초를 둔 것이었다. "다윈설"은 자연과학, 사회과학, 인문과학에 심오한 영향을 끼쳤다. 종교제도의 존망을 염려한 성직자들은 다윈을 공격하려고 달려들었다. 그러나 다윈은 결코 자신의 진화론의 법칙을 인간사회에 적용시키려고 시도하지 않았다. 진화론을 확장시켜 사회를 전체로서 포괄하려던 이는 사회진화론자들이었다. 사회진화론자들은 사회를 가장 적합한 사회구성원들만이 살아남을 수 있는 "생존경쟁"으로 보았다. 그들은 근본적으로 인종차별주의와 엘리트주의의 노선을 취했다. 어떤 사람들은 선천적으로 다른 사람보다 우월했다. 대기업이 "덜 적합한" 소기업들을 합병하는 것은 "만물의 법칙"에 해당했다.

naturalist n. 자연주의자
profound a. 뜻깊은, 심원한
the humanities 고전문학, 인문학
institution n. 학회; 제도; 기관

01 ▶ 마지막 문장은 사회진화론자들의 입장을 설명하는 예에 해당된다.

02 ▶ espouse는 '신봉하다, 믿다; 받아들이다, 채택하다'의 의미이므로 (D) adopted가 정답이다.

03 ▶ 7째줄 이후 다윈의 이론을 사회에 적용시키는 사회진화론자들의 입장이 기술되어 있다.

》 정답　01 (A)　02 (D)　03 (C)

038

　　비교심리학에 따르면, 지적이고 의식적인 모방과 자동적인 모방을 구별해주는 여러 가지 증상들이 있다. 첫 번째 것의 경우, 반복을 요구하지 않는 통찰의 형태로 즉각적인 해결이 가능하다. 이러한 해결은 지적인 행동의 전형적인 특징에 속한다. 여기엔 장(場) 구조와 물체간의 관계에 대한 이해가 포함된다. 이와는 달리, 자동 연습 모방은 일련의 시행착오를 되풀이함으로써 이루어지며 여기서는 의식적인 이해의 조짐이나 장 구조에 대한 이해가 나타나지 않는다. 이런 의미에서 동물들은 교육이 불가능하다고 할 수 있다.

　　이와는 달리, 아동의 발달과정에서 모방과 교육은 주된 역할을 한다. 정신의 인간적 특질이 이를 통해 나오며 아동을 새로운 발달 단계로 나아가게 한다. 학교 과목을 배울 때처럼 말을 배울 때도 모방은 필수불가결하다. 지금은 함께 할 수 있는 일을 아동은 나중에는 혼자 할 수 있다. 그러므로 유일한 좋은 교육은 발달 단계보다 앞서 나아가 발달을 선도하는 것이다.

identify v. 확인하다; 인지[판정]하다
distinguish v. 구별하다, 분별하다
insight n. 통찰, 간파
pertain to 속하다; 어울리다
drill n. 훈련
imitation n. 모방, 모조; 모조품
comprehension n. 이해; 포함

01 ▶ indispensable은 '필수적인, 필수불가결한'이라는 뜻이므로, (C)의 essential이 정답이다.

02 ▶ 본문 두 번째 단락의 'What the child can do in cooperation … ahead of development and leads it' 참고

》 정답　01 (C)　02 (D)

039

　　순수과학은 보통의 의미로는 쓸모없게 여겨질지 모르지만 오랜 시간이 지나면 그것은 분명 경제적 기술적 이득을 가져다준다. 만일 오늘 순수과학에 대한 투자를 중단하면 내일 응용과학은 없을 것이다. 찰스 다윈의 진화 연구와 그레고어 멘델의 식물유전 연구가 유전학의 토대를 쌓아서, 결국 DNA의 발견을 초래했으며, 이것이 유전공학을 낳았는데, 유전공학은 지금 상상할 수 없을 정도로 많은 용도를 창출하며 폭발적으로 발전하고 있다. 마이클 페러데이가 자석이 어떻게 전기를 발생시킬 수 있는가를 발견한 것이 50년 후 최초의 수력발전소를 가능하게 했다. 그러나 다윈과 멘델과 페러데이는 그 어떤 그런 이득을 염두에 두고 지원을 받지는 않았고, 또 받을 수도 없었을 것이다. 국가는 경마에서 말에 돈을 걸듯이 순수과학자들에게 돈을 걸(지원을 할) 수는 없다. 그러나 마구간을 지을(연구 기반이나 여건을 지원할) 수는 있다.

pure science 순수과학
applied science 응용과학
heredity n. 유전, 형질유전
lay the foundation for ~을 위한 토대를 놓다
science of genetics 유전학
genetic engineering 유전공학
magnet n. 자석
hydroelectric power plant 수력발전소
stable n. 마구간
electromagnetism n. 전자기
eminent a. 저명한, 탁월한
regardless of ~에 관계없이

01 ▶ 다윈과 멘델의 연구로 세워진 (A)의 '유전학'은 순수과학이고 (B)의 'DNA의 발견'도 순수과학에서의 발견이지만 이로 인해 생겨난 (C)의 '유전공학'은 '상상할 수 없을 정도로 많은 용도를 창출하며 폭발적으로 발전하고 있다'는 말에서 알 수 있듯이 응용과학이다. 그리고 페러데이가 자석이 어떻게 전기를 발생시킬 수 있는가를 발견한 (D)의 '전자기학'은 순수과학이고, 이것의 기술적 응용이 수력발전소이다.

02 ▶ 마지막 문장에서 '국가는 경마에서 말에 돈을 걸듯이 순수과학자들에게 돈을 걸(지원을 할) 수는 없고, 마구간을 지을(연구 기반이나 여건을 지원할) 수는 있다'고 했으므로 (D)가 정답이다.

03 ▶ 이 글은 유전학과 전자기학을 예로 들어 순수과학은 응용과학과 기술의 발전을 가능하게 해주는 토양과 같은 역할을 한다고 설명하고 순수과학에 대한 투자를 강조한 글이다. 따라서 (C)가 이 글의 요지에 해당한다.

》 정답 01 (C)　02 (D)　03 (C)

040

　　1961년 케네디 대통령은 포드사의 '똑똑한' 젊은 두뇌 로버트 맥나마라를 국방장관으로 불러들였다. 베트남에서 점점 늘어나는 공산주의의 영향력 증대라는 문제에 직면하여 맥나마라는 포드사에서 성공적이었던 강력한 분석도구에 대한 확신을 가지고 바로 일에 착수했다. 얼마 안가서 그는 그의 비평가들을 잠잠하게 만들었고, 미국의 개입을 증대시켰으며 자신 있게 상황을 잘 통제하게 될 것이라고 예언했다.

　　이 모든 것은 그 지역의 역사, 그 나라 사람들의 문화, 우리의 반대자들의 진정한 동기에 대한 고려가 거의 없는 상태에서 행해졌다. 지금, 물론, 맥나마라의 이름은 이러한 자만에 넘치는 교만의 상징이다.

　　익숙한 소리로 들리는가? 40년도 지나지 않아, 지적이고, 강력하고 대단히 자신감 넘치는 새로운 지도자 무리들이 세계의 다른 곳에서 똑같은 일을 저질러 왔다. 그리고, 아주 섬뜩하게 유사한 방식으로, 그들은 진정한 상황은 악화되고 있는데도 승리를 예언하고 있다.

secretary of defense 국방장관
in short order 곧
have ~ in hand 통제하다
swagger n. 뽐냄, 교만
crop n. 무리
eerily ad. 섬뜩하게, 무시무시하게
parallel a. 같은, 유사한

01 ▶ 맥나마라와 같은 교만에 찬 지도자들이 오늘날 다시금 등장하고 있음을 이야기하고 있다.
02 ▶ go south 악화되다(= deteriorate)

》 정답   01 (A)   02 (B)

041

　유혹과의 접촉이 없다면 미덕도 가치 없는 것이고, 심지어는 의미 없는 것이기도 하다. 유혹은 인생에 있어 본질이라고 할 수 있는 대립의 필수적인 형태이다. 끊임없는 유혹의 불꽃이 없으면 인간의 정신은 단련되거나 강화될 수 없다. 모든 유혹을 없애버리고 우리의 젊은이들을 유혹으로부터 자유로운 지역의 출발점에 위치시키려는 도덕적 개혁주의자들의 열정은, 만일 그것이 달성된다고 하더라도 (그리고 그 결과는 환경을 전멸시킬 뿐 아니라, 인간의 심장에서 삶의 열정을 빼내는 일이 된다), 단지 쓸모없고 나약한 인류를 창조할 뿐이다. 유혹은 심지어는 앞서 말한 대립의 자극제 이상의 역할도 한다. 유혹은 열정에 관한 한, 그 자체로 삶의 촉진제가 될 수도 있다. 유혹에 마주쳤을 때, 그것을 거부하는 것이 자신의 삶을 강화하는 것이고, 그것을 받아들인다면 삶을 더욱 더 풍요롭게 하는 것이다. 이 두 가지 다 할 수 없는 사람은 살아가는 데 부적절한 것이다.

contact n. 접촉
temptation n. 유혹
perpetual a. 영속하는; 부단한
temper v. (사람을) 단련시키다
fortify v. 강하게 하다, 튼튼히 하다
zeal n. 열중, 열의
outset n. 착수; 시작
annihilate v. 절멸시키다, 전멸시키다
eviscerate v. 골자를[긴요한 부분을] 빼버리다
stimulus n. 자극; 격려
ferment n. 발효; 효소

01 ▶ 유혹의 가치와 역할에 대한 글이다.
02 ▶ 끝에서 세 번째 문장과 두 번째 문장의 내용과 호응하는 (C)가 정답으로 적절하다.

》 정답   01 (D)   02 (C)

042

　　　니우아포우는 '통조림 깡통 섬'이라는 별명을 갖고 있는데, 이 섬은 피지의 수바에서 북동쪽으로 190마일 떨어져 있다. 이 섬의 직경은 5마일이다. 이 섬이 이상한 것은 니우아포우가 순수한 화산이며 암초가 없는데도, 그 중심부의 거의 똑같은 원형 호수를 둘러싼 거의 완벽하게 원형을 이룬 섬이라는 점이다. 땅은 바다로부터 60에서 70피트 높이의 절벽으로 올라와 있다. 이 높이에서 땅은 3/4마일정도 위로 경사를 이루고 나서 불쑥 약 400피트 높이의 산마루로 상승한다. 호수물은 알칼리성이며 조수에 따라 오르내린다고 한다. 섬에는 맑은 물은 없고 빗물은 1229명의 사람들의 필요에는 불충분하다. 그러나 그들은 물을 코코넛에서 얻을 수 있으므로 고통을 겪지는 않는다. 니우아포우에 상륙하는 것은 어렵다. 니우아포우섬은 원주민이 수영을 하거나 카누를 타고 지나가는 우편선에 가서 우편물을 장대에 매단 통조림 깡통에 담아 나르기도 하고 섬으로 나르기도 한 데서 그 별명을 갖게 되었다.

diameter n. 직경, 지름
reef n. 암초; 광맥
tin n. 통조림
lash v. 묶다, 매다

01 ▶ 전체적으로는 니우아포우 섬의 지형적 특성을 자세히 기술하고 있으므로 (B)가 제목으로 가장 적절하다.
02 ▶ 수영을 하거나 카누를 타고 우편선에 가서 장대에 매단 통조림 깡통에 우편물을 담아온 데서 별명이 비롯되었다고 했다.

》 정답 01 (B) 02 (C)

043

　　　사람들은 그곳을 죽음의 계곡이라고 부른다. 유황의 장막은 아래에 있는 유해가스의 지옥을 가리우면서 종종 공중에 걸려 있다. 근처 산 너머로 해가 지면, 짙은 공해의 베일 때문에 거의 볼 수가 없다. 죽은 관목 숲은 한때 신록의 언덕 중턱이었던 곳을 온통 덮고 있으며, 그 도시의 악취 나는 강에서 잡아 올린 물고기들은 눈이 먼 돌연변이체다. 그 도시의 가장자리에 있는 빈민가(판자촌)인 빌라 파리시(Vila Parisi)에서는 뜨거운 산업폐기물로 거품이 이는 개방 하수로가 정기적으로 범람한다. 그 도시의 이러한 변화는 거의 30년 전 산업체들이 옮겨오면서부터 시작되었다. 정부 소유의 석유 독점기업인 페트로브라스사(Petrobrás)가 1954년 정유공장을 지으면서 제일 먼저 들어왔다. 4개의 미국 소유회사를 포함한 다른 회사들이 뒤따라 들어왔고 프랑스와 이탈리아의 다국적 기업들 또한 이 지역에 들어와 공장을 세웠다. 유니온 카바이드사(Union Carbide)의 사장인 파울로 피게이레두(Paulo Figueiredo)는 "원료를 쉽게 구할 수 있고 산토스 항구와 브라질 최대시장인 상 파울로가 가깝기 때문에 기업들이 유치되었다. 이렇게 산업이 집중되면 공해가 발생하고 문제가 저절로 생겨난다는 것은 당연한 일이다"라고 설명한다.

sulfurous a. 유황의, 유황을 함유한
pall n. 휘장, 장막
inferno n. 지옥, 지옥 같은 상태
verdant a. 푸릇푸릇한, 신록의
fetid a. 악취가 나는, 고약한 냄새가 나는
favela n. 빈민가
shantytown n. 판자촌, 판자집 지구

01 ▶ 본문은 산업화에 따른 환경오염과 관련된 글이다.
02 ▶ 방사능 폐기물은 언급하지 않았다.

》 정답 01 (B) 02 (B)

044

　　발리 로드맵(Bali road map)은 선진국이 맡아야할 배기가스 감축에 대해 '상당한 감축'이 필요할 것이라는 말 외에는 어떤 구체적인 책임이나 수치를 포함하지 않고 있다. 금주 초에 EU는 2040년까지 선진국들에 대한 25내지 40% 감축이라는 구체적인 목표와 전 세계적으로 배기가스를 절반으로 줄일 필요성을 포함시키려고 열심히 분투하였는데, 그 두 가지 수치는 유엔 정부 간 기후변화 위원회(IPCC)가 행한 지구 온난화 연구의 최근 평가에 의해 언급된 것이다. EU는 두 가지 수치를 최종 문서에 넣지 못하였는데, 그것은 주로 미국의 단호한 반대 때문이었다. 다만 하나의 각주가 IPCC 보고서에 언급되어 있다. 기후 변화에 관한 증대되는 위기를 강조하는 최근 자료의 쇄도가 더욱 강력한 조치를 촉발시키기를 희망했던 환경보호 운동가들에게, 발리 로드맵(Bali road map)은 실망스러운 것이었다. "불충분한 로드맵이었다. 그것은 원칙이 훼손된 것이다"라고 Friends of the Earth International의 의장인 Meena Rahman은 말했다.

cite v. 인용하다; 언급하다
footnote n. 각주
avalanche n. 눈사태; 쇄도
underscore v. 강조하다
compromise v. 손상시키다

01 ▶ 배기가스 감축에 관한 발리 로드맵의 한계에 대해 다루고 있는 글이다.
02 ▶ 첫 문장에서 배기가스의 상당한 감축이 필요하다고 언급했다.

▶ 정답　01 (C)　02 (A)

045

　　문명국가에서 어떤 사람이 자신의 가족에게 해를 입히면 경찰이 출동해 그를 저지한다. 한 무리의 악당들이 어느 동네를 공포에 떨게 하면 경찰이 작전을 개시해 그들을 진압한다. 그러나 만일 당신이 아주 뻔뻔스럽게도 이보다 훨씬 더 큰 악당들의 단체를 조직한다면 국가 전체를 손에 넣을 수 있다. 스스로를 무슨무슨 정당이라 불러보라, 그러면 1930년대 초 독일에서 가장 악명 높게 그랬던 것처럼, 세계 언론매체들이 이 명칭을 친절하게 사용해서 당신의 범죄행위들을 합법화하는 데 도움을 줄 것이다. 세계 각국의 정부와 외교관들은 당신이 스스로 정치 조직이라 주장하기 때문에 이것은 어쨌든 당신네가 합리적인 사람들이라는 것을 의미한다는 헛된 믿음 속에서 당신을 대화의 상대로 삼을 것이다. 그런 동시에 당신은, 지난 세기 때 너무나 많은 경우 그렇게 되었듯이, 국민들을 마음대로 학대하고 고문하고 죽이고 강탈할 수 있을 것이다.

gang n. 한 무리, 일당
thug n. 흉악범, 악당
terrorize v. 무서워하게 하다, 위협하다
mount v. (공격 따위를) 개시하다
audacious a. 대담한, 뻔뻔스런
take over 양도받다, 접수하다, 점거하다
obligingly ad. 친절하게, 자상하게
legitimize v. 합법화하다, 정당화하다
notoriously ad. 악명 높게

01 ▶ 빈칸 ①은 앞의 두 경우와 뒤의 경우가 상반되므로 However나 Nevertheless가 적절하고 빈칸 ②는 앞의 대외적 인정과 뒤의 내부적 범죄행위가 내용은 상반되어도 동시에 일어나는 것이므로 Meanwhile이 적절하다.
02 ▶ 이 글은 첫 세 문장에서 알 수 있듯이 범죄행위도 규모가 커지면 처벌할 수 없고 오히려 정당화되는 모순된 현실을 지적한 글이므로 (D)가 가장 적절하다.

▶ 정답　01 (A)　02 (D)

046

하루에 세 잔 이상의 커피를 마시면 나이든 여성들은 몇몇 나이와 관련된 기억력 감퇴로부터 보호받을 수 있다고 프랑스의 과학자들은 말한다. 여성들에게 세계에서 가장 인기 있는 자극제를 사랑할 이유를 또 하나 준 셈이다. 남성들은 같은 이익을 누리지 못한다고 이들은 말하고 있다. "커피를 많이 마실수록 특히 (여성의) 기억 기능에 미치는 효과는 증가하는 것 같다"라고 프랑스 국립 의학 연구소의 카렌 리치(Karen Ritchie)는 말했다. 그녀의 연구는 『Neurology』지에 실려 있다.

이 연구에 따르면 하루에 커피를 세 잔 이상, 혹은 그만큼에 상당하는 카페인을 차를 통해 섭취하는 여성들은 4년 정도 더 나은 언어 능력과, 그것보다는 조금 적은 정도의 시각적 기억력을 갖고 있다는 것이다. 80이 넘은 여성들은 그보다 10세 혹은 15세 더 젊은 여성들에 비해 이 음료에서 얻는 이익이 더 많았다. 몇몇 쥐에 대한 연구에 따르면 카페인이 정신적 쇠퇴를 낳는 단백질의 축적을 막을지도 모른다고 한다. 리치는 왜 여성들만이 이러한 이익을 얻을 수 있을까에 대해 확신하지 못하고 있다.

stimulant n. 흥분제, 자극물
equivalent n. 상당하는 것
retain v. 보유하다
reap v. 수확하다, 얻다
beverage n. 음료
buildup n. 축적

01 ▶ 마지막 문장에서 왜 여성들만이 이러한 이익을 얻는지 잘 모르겠다고 하였으므로, 그 다음에는 추측이나 설명이 나와야 한다. 이는 남성들이 이러한 이익을 얻지 못하는 것에 대한 추측이 될 수도 있다.

02 ▶ 80세 여성이 그보다 10세, 15세 어린 여성들보다 보다 많은 이익을 얻을 수 있다고 하였으므로 (A)가 정답이다. 다른 질병들에 대한 치료 또는 예방은 언급된 적이 없고, 부작용에 대해서도 나와 있지 않다.

》 정답 01 (B) 02 (A)

047

심리학은 두 가지 형식의 연구, 즉 실험적 연구와 차별적 연구를 인정한다. 전자(前者)는 주로 인간의 활동을 결정하는 전반적인 과정에 관여하고, 후자(後者)는 행동에 있어서 개개인의 차이를 확립하고자 한다. 더 최근의 연구에서는 심리학 연구의 제 3의 형식의 필요성을 드러냈는데, 즉 인간발달과 관련된 것이다. 과학자들은 인간 행동의 이러한 (발달적인) 측면을 처음 두 가지의 형식의 한 부분으로서 간주하기보다, 발달 연구는 그 자체로 확실히 독립적인 범주에 속한다고 언급해 왔다. 피아제(Piaget)의 연구는 실험적 그리고 차별적 연구 모두에 지대한 영향을 미치는 발달 이론의 분야에 분명히 해당된다. 피아제의 연구를 살펴볼 때, 비록 그의 이론은 매우 영향력이 있으면서도 그의 방법론은 강력히 비판받았다는 사실을 염두에 두어야 한다. 그의 연구의 근본적인 부족함은 자료 및 실험 계획에 있어서 정의와 표준화의 부족과 연관이 있었다.

have to do with ~와 관련이 있다
aspect n. 국면, 양상
indisputably ad. 명백하게
methodology n. 방법론
shortfall n. 부족, 부족액
definition n. 정의; 한정
standardization n. 표준화

01 ▶ 두 번째 문장을 참조한다. 실험적 연구(The former)는 "인간을 좌우하는 심리 과정을 확립하는 것"으로 요약할 수 있다.

02 ▶ 글쓴이는 기존의 두 가지 심리학적 연구에서 최근의 추세와 피아제에 대한 예를 들어가며 제3의 형식으로 인정될 수 있는 연구 방법을 제시하고 있다.

》 정답 01 (C) 02 (B)

048

　　프랑스 항구도시 르아브르에서 1872년 11월 13일 오전 7시 35분에 예술세계가 영원히 변했다. 클로드 모네는 호텔 창밖을 응시하다가 눈에 보이는 광경을 그리기 시작했다. 그 결과는 "인상, 해돋이"라는 작품이었고 하나의 운동(인상주의 운동)의 시작이었다.

　　인상주의가 정확하게 언제 시작되었는지 우리는 어떻게 아는가? 그것은 천문학을 이용하여 예술과 문학의 수수께끼들을 해결하는 텍사스 주립대학 천체물리학자 도널드 올슨 때문이다. 예술사가 제랄딘 레페브르와 마르모탕 모네 미술관 부관장 마리안 마티유가 올슨에게 그 그림의 기원을 확정짓는 데 도와달라고 부탁했을 때, 그 자칭 "하늘의 탐정"은 여러 지도와 사진을 꼼꼼히 살펴봄으로써 모네의 호텔과 방을 밝혀내는 일을 시작했다. 그런 다음 그는 천문학에 의지해, 떠오르는 태양과 달을 이용하여 간만의 조수와 계절과 하루 중의 시간을 판정했고, 지금은 디지털화되어 있는 19세기 때의 기상관측자료들을 찾아보았다. 마지막 단서는 그림 속의 굴뚝에서 나오는 연기기둥이었는데, 바람이 동에서 서로 불고 있음을 보여주고 있었다. 그 발견된 사실들과 모네의 서명 옆에 있는 '72'라는 숫자로 그 사건을 종결지었고 한 영원한 예술작품의 정확한 창작시점을 확정지었다.

gaze v. 응시하다
astrophysicist n. 천체물리학자
provenance n. 기원, 유래, 출처
self-styled a. 자칭(자임)하는
celestial a. 하늘의
sleuth n. 탐정
pore over 숙고하다, 열심히 연구하다
timeless a. 초시간적인, 영원한

01 ▶ 빈칸의 사람은 곧 도널드 올슨을 지칭하는데, 그는 천체물리학자여서 하늘과 관련되며 모네가 그림을 그린 호텔과 방을 탐정처럼 밝혀내는 일을 하게 된 것이므로 빈칸에는 (C) '하늘의 탐정'이 적절하다. (A) 토지 측량기사 (B) 신비한 은둔자 (D) 신의 전령사

02 ▶ 여러 지도를 꼼꼼히 살펴본다는 것은 지도를 제작하는 것과는 관계가 없으므로 (B) '지도제작법'이 이용하지 않은 것이다. 지도와 사진이 제공하는 그 지역의 여러 정보는 (D) '지리학과 관련이 있다. (A) 천문학 (C) 기상학

》 정답 01 (C) 02 (B)

049

　　한때 밤에 수면을 돕기 위해 기계에서 주로 울렸던 백색소음과 그 밖의 마음을 편안하게 해 주는 소리는 낮 시간을 보다 평온하게 만들어 주는 데 점점 도움이 되고 있다. 낮 시간에 백색소음을 듣는 사람들은 그 소리들이 두 가지에 도움이 된다고 말한다. 정신을 산만하게 하는 것을 차단해주고, 사이렌 소리 같이 불안감을 유발하는 소리를 줄여준다는 것이다. 헤드폰으로 이런 소리를 들으면 직장동료들이 떠드는 소리와 착암기를 두드리는 소리, 치과의사의 드릴소리 등을 차단해 줄 수도 있다. 백색소음은 보다 평온한 환경을 조성하고, 소음을 차단하고, 사생활을 보호할 수 있게끔 한다. 마음을 편안하게 해주는 소리를 만들기 위해서, 개발자들은 컴퓨터로 제작된 소리나 자연에서 녹음한 소리를 가지고 대개 반복되는 오디오 파일을 제작한다. 이러한 디지털 파일들은 아이튠즈 스토어나 다른 웹 사이트에서 이용 가능하다. 가장 인기 있는 소리는 비, 바람, 해안가에 부서지는 파도, 귀뚜라미 소리 등의 자연에서 나온 소리이다.

white noise 백색 소음
block out (빛·소리를) 가리다[차단하다]
tune out 안 들리게 하다; 잡음을 없애다
chatty a. 수다스러운, 이야기 좋아하는
pound v. 마구 치다[두드리다]; 두드려 부수다
mask v. 가리다, 감추다
soothing a. 달래는 듯한, 마음을 진정시키는 듯한

01 ▶ 수면을 돕기 위해서 사용되었던 백색 소음이 이제는 낮 시간을 보다 평온하게 만들어 주는 데 쓰이며 정신을 산만하게 해주는 것을 차단한다고 소개하고 있는 글이므로 (A)가 제목으로 적절하다.

02 ▶ natural ambient sounds는 white noise를 가리키며 개발자들이 만든 자연의 소리를 아이튠즈 스토어나 다른 웹사이트에서 이용가능하다고 하였으므로 (D)는 본문의 내용과 일치한다.

》 정답 01 (A) 02 (D)

---

050 나를 친 트럭 운전자를 내가 용서했다는 걸 내 가족과 친구들이 들었을 때, 그들 모두는 내가 굉장히 좋은 사람이라고 말했다. 실제로 나는 그저 당신과 같은 (평범한) 사람이다. 나는 내가 굉장히 화가 날 것이라고 생각했다. 그러나 당신이 바로 자신의 죽음에 너무나 극적으로 직면하게 되면, 당신의 사고방식은 변한다. 나는 비통해하는 데 쓸 시간이 없다. 삶은 적을 만드는 데 삶의 매 순간을 쓰기에는 너무나도 짧다. 애니 딜라드(Annie Dillard)는 하루하루를 어떻게 보내는가에 따라 우리의 인생이 결정된다는 명언을 남겼다. 나는 내 삶을 어두운 동굴에서가 아닌 좋은 면에다 쓰기로 결정한다. 그리고 당신은 나를 친 운전자를 용서하는 것이 그의 마음의 짐을 덜어주는 것만큼이나 나의 마음의 짐을 덜어주는 것이었다는 점을 아는가? 아마도 그보다 더 큰 내 마음의 짐을 덜어주었다. 그것은 포괄적 상생이었다. 나는 남은 일생을 원통해하고 슬프고 초라하게 보낼 수도 있었을 것이지만 그렇게 하지 않았다. 나는 정말 그렇게 보낼 수도 있었을 것이다.

be confronted with ~에 직면하다, ~와 마주하다
mortality n. 죽어야 할 운명; 사망자 수
perspective n. 전망, 시각; 견지
cultivate v. (재능 따위를) 신장하다, 계발하다; 수련하다
sunny side 바람직한 면; 좋은 면
cosmic a. 포괄적인, 보편적인
win-win a. 모두에게 유리한, 모두가 득을 보는
alleviate v. 경감시키다, 완화하다
lift a burden from ~에게서 짐을 덜어주다
retributive justice 인과응보
call for ~을 필요로 하다, 요구하다
casualties n. 사상자
denounce v. 비난하다
contempt n. 경멸, 멸시
turn away from ~을 외면하다

01 ▶ 나머지 보기들은 모두 '부담(심적 고통)을 덜어 준다'는 의미인 반면, (B)는 '쌀쌀한[냉담한] 태도를 보이다'는 뜻이므로 밑줄 친 부분을 대체할 수 없다.

02 ▶ 글쓴이가 자신의 교통사고 이야기를 공유한 이유는 And you know what? 이하에서 찾아볼 수 있는데, '자신을 다치게 한 운전자를 용서하는 것이 곧 자신의 마음의 짐을 덜어주는 것'이었다는 교훈을 주고 싶었기 때문이다.

03 ▶ 본문의 뒷부분에서 글쓴이는 자신의 삶을 좋은 면에 쓰기로 결정했다고 했으며 마지막 문장에서는 자신의 남은 일생을 원통해하고 슬프고 초라하게 보낼 수 있었지만 그렇게 하지 않았다고 했다. 따라서 (교통사고 후) 글쓴이가 비관적 태도로부터 멀어져 긍정적 태도를 수용하는 법을 배우게 됐다는 (C)가 올바른 사실이다.

》 정답 01 (B) 02 (D) 03 (C)

051

　19세기 후반, 아주 짧은 기간 동안, "상징주의"라고 불리는 반(反)사실주의 문학 운동이 있었는데, "신낭만주의", "관념주의", "인상주의" 등으로 알려져 있기도 하다. 상징주의는 프랑스에서 잠깐 인기를 얻었고, 20세기 때 가끔 다시 일어나기도 했다. 상징주의 이면의 사상은 진리는 감각이나 이성적 사고를 통해서가 아니라 직관에 의해서만 파악될 수 있다는 것이다. 그래서 궁극적 진리들은 상징들을 통해서만 암시될 수 있고, 상징들은 관객(독자)들에게 극작가의 감정과 어렴풋이 일치하는 다양한 마음의 상태들을 불러일으킨다.

　주요한 극적 상징주의자들 중 한 사람인 모리스 마테를링크(Maurice Maeterlinck)는 모든 희곡(연극)에는 영혼에게 말을 거는 "또 다른 차원"의 대화가 들어있다고 믿었다. 언어적 아름다움, 명상, 열정적 자연묘사 등을 통하여 위대한 희곡은 미지의 것에 대한 시인의 사상을 전한다. 따라서 인간의 행동을 보여주는 희곡들은 직관을 통해 얻은 더 높은 진리들을 상징을 통하여 암시할 수 있을 뿐이다. 상징주의자들은 사회 문제는 전혀 다루지 않았다. 대신, 그들은 과거에 의지했고, 예를 들어 마테를링크가 『펠레아스와 멜리장드』에서 그랬던 것처럼 시공간과 독립된 보편적 진리들을 암시하려고 했다.

recur v. 재발하다, 다시 일어나다
grasp v. 이해하다, 파악하다
intuition n. 직관
evoke v. 불러일으키다
vaguely ad. 희미하게, 어렴풋이
verbal a. 말의, 구두의
contemplation n. 명상
portrayal n. 묘사
convey v. 전달하다

01 ▶ 마테를링크는 상징주의 극작가인데 상징주의는 사실주의와 반대되는 문학 운동이라고 했으므로 사실주의의 특징인 '사회에 대한 상세한 기술을 지지해야 한다'고 한 (C)는 마테를링크의 견해라고 유추할 수 없다.

02 ▶ evoke는 '(영혼을) 불러내다, (감정을) 불러일으키다, 자아내다' 등의 '생겨나게 하다'는 뜻이므로 (A)가 가장 가까운 의미의 단어이다. (B) 관련시키다 (C) 드러내다 (D) 설명하다

》 정답 01 (C)　02 (A)

052

　진지한 비평가라면 예술작품의 특정한 내용과 독특한 구조, 그리고 특별한 의미를 파악해야 한다. 그런데 여기에서 비평가는 딜레마에 처하게 된다. 비평가는 주관적인 반응을 요하는 독특함의 요소들을 인식해야 하지만 그런 반응들로 인해 부당한 편견에 빠져서는 안 되기 때문이다. 비평가 자신의 호오(好惡)는 작품 자체가 전달하는 것보다는 덜 중요하다. 그리고 비평가는 자신의 편애로 인해 그 작품의 특정한 자질들을 못 보게 되고, 그로 인해 그 작품을 제대로 이해하지 못하게 될 수도 있다. 그러므로 비평가는 예술사와 미학이론에 정통하게 되어서야 얻어질 수 있는 감수성을 배양해야 할 필요가 있다. 다른 한편, 순전히 역사적인 견지에서, 즉 개념과 가치들의 고정된 집합과의 관계에서만 예술 작품을 다루는 것도 불충분하다. 비평가의 지식과 훈련은 오히려 예술작품의 고유한 자질들에 대해 적절한 반응을 보이는데 필요한 인식적, 정서적 능력을 준비하는 것이어야 한다.

critic n. 비평가
work of art 예술작품
dilemma n. 딜레마, 진퇴양난, 궁지
subjective a. 주관적인
unduly ad. 과도하게, 심하게; 부당하게
thereby ad. 그것에 의하여, 그것 때문에
sensibility n. 감성, 감수성
familiarity n. 잘 앎; 정통
aesthetic theory 미학이론
in relation to ~에 관하여
take into account ~을 고려하다

01 ▶ 주관적인 반응에 의해 편견을 갖게 되는 것은 객관성을 상실하는 것이다. 이 글에서 객관성을 보장해주는 요소로 거론되고 있는 것은 예술사와 미학이론의 도움을 받는 감수성이다. (D)의 경우도 객관성을 보장해주는 요소가 될 수 있지만 이 글에서는 전혀 언급돼 있지 않은 사실이므로 정답이 될 수 없다.

02 ▶ 역사적인 관점에서만 작품을 바라보면 그 작품의 개별적인 특수성을 간과하기 쉽다는 것이 필자의 생각이다.

03 ▶ 이 글은 근본적으로 주관성과 객관성 사이에서 균형을 취해야 하는 비평가의 딜레마를 다루고 있는 글이다.

≫ 정답 01 (B) 02 (B) 03 (A)

053

젊은 작가가 의사소통매체인 언어의 진정한 의미를 깨닫는 데는 많은 시간이 걸린다고 생각한다. 젊은 작가는 자신이 전하고자 하는 바의 의미를 즉각 적어버림으로써 그 일을 완료해 버릴 수 있어야 한다고 생각하고, 자신을 제외한 다른 모든 사람들에게는 무의미한 언어를 사용해서 자신이 전하려는 바의 의미를 적고 그에 대해 자신이 느끼는 바를 표출시킨다. 이러한 작가는 자신이 자신의 생각을 전달하기 위해 거의 아무렇게나 모든 말을 사용하고 있으며 자기 자신을 표현하고 있으나, 타인에게는 아무 것도 전달하지 못하고 있다는 사실을 알아야만 한다. 그는 언어가 의사를 전달하려는 인간의 필요에 의해서 자연스럽게 발전해 온 것이고 그러한 언어는 언어를 사용하는 모든 사람들의 것이라는 사실과 언어의 의사전달기능은 모든 사람들의 필요에 맞추어 발전해 온 것이라는 사실, 그리고 또한 언제나 그렇듯이 언어가 화자의 표정과 몸짓과 결합되어 입을 통해 나타날 때 그 언어는 가장 활기찬 것이 되며, 구어적 언어사용이 보편적인 데 반해서 문어적 언어사용은 상대적으로 드문 편이라는 사실을 알아야 한다. 그리고 구어적 언어 사용 시에는 모든 사람들의 필요를 충족시켜주는 공통적인 계기인 상투어들이 대단히 많이 사용된다는 사실도 알아야 한다. 작가가 구어로 사용하는 말과 어구들, 작가 자신의 살아있는 존재가 개입됨으로 인해 활력을 부여받은 말과 어구들은 지면 위로 옮겨지면서 죽은 글이 되어버린다. 따라서 작가는 어떻게 해서든 자신이 사용하는 말들이 사전속의 단어들처럼 각각의 의미를 지칭하는 죽은 기호가 되지 않도록 애써야만 한다. 작가는 지면 위로 말을 옮기면서 말속에 생명을 불어넣어야 한다.

put down 적어놓다; 제지하다
cliche n. 진부한 표현, 상투적인 문구
transcription n. 베낀 것, 복사
overcome v. 극복하다
breathe life into ~에 생명을 불어넣다

01 ▶ 이 글의 필자가 말하고자 하는 바는 마지막 두 문장에 압축되어있다. 진정한 글쓰기가 어떤 것이어야 하는가가 나타나 있는데, 이는 글쓰기란 것이 생각처럼 단순한 일이 결코 아님을 뜻하는 것이다.

02 ▶ 마지막에서 세 번째 문장을 통해 '입을 통해 말해진 뒤 글로 쓴 말은 색다른 영향을 미친다'는 것을 알 수 있다.

03 ▶ 둘째 문장에서 알 수 있듯이, 이 글의 필자에 의하면 젊은 필자들은 자기 목소리를 내려고 지나치게 서두른다.

≫ 정답 01 (D) 02 (C) 03 (A)

054   　　정신분열증의 원인은 명확하지 않지만, 정신분열증은 잘못된 양육 때문이라고 오랫동안 여겨져 왔다. 정신분열증이 발병하는 경우 부모들에게 책임이 있다고 종종 여겨졌다. 그러나 최근의 연구결과에 따르면, 유전과 태아기의 환경이 이 질병의 주요한 발병 원인이다.

　　일란성 쌍둥이들에 대한 최근의 연구들은 유전이 정신분열증 발병의 원인이라는 것을 증명하기 위해 행해졌다. 이러한 연구결과, 일란성 쌍둥이 가운데 한 명이 정신분열증을 앓고 있을 경우 나머지 한 명도 그 질병을 앓게 될 확률이 50%라는 것이 밝혀졌다.

　　그러나 유전만이 유일한 발병원인은 아닌 것으로 판단된다. 일란성 쌍둥이들의 지문에 대한 연구들은 태아기 때의 환경 요소들이 정신분열증의 발병 원인일 수 있다는 학설에 믿음을 가져다주었다. 일란성 쌍둥이 가운데 한 명은 정신분열증을 겪고 있고, 나머지 한 명은 그렇지 않은 쌍둥이들을 조사한 결과, 쌍둥이들의 3분의 1의 지문에서 변이가 발견되었다. 손가락은 임신기간 중 2기에 자라므로 지문의 변이는 임신기간 중 2기의 정신적 쇼크에 기인한다는 가설이 제기되었다.

---

schizophrenia n. 정신분열증
be attributed to ~에 기인하다
parenting n. 가정교육; 양육, 육아
heredity n. 유전
prenatal a. 태어나기 전의, 태아기의
culprit n. 죄인, 범죄자; 원인
afflict v. 괴롭히다
fingerprint n. 지문
credence n. 신용, 믿음, 신뢰
trimester n. 3개월, 3개월간
trauma n. 정신적 외상, 마음의 상처
enumerate v. 열거하다
refute v. 논박하다

01 ▶ 첫 번째 문단에 이 글의 요지가 드러나 있다. 정신분열증이 발병하는 경우 잘못된 양육을 한 부모에게 책임이 있다고 오랫동안 여겨져 왔으나, 최근의 연구결과에 따르면 유전과 태아기 때의 환경이 정신분열증을 일으킨다는 것이다. 따라서 (D) '흔히 있는 오해를 반박하기 위한 글'로 볼 수 있다.

02 ▶ However 이하는 잘못된 양육법이 아니라 유전적인 요소가 정신분열증을 일으킨다는 내용이므로 주어진 문장은 However 앞에 들어가야 한다. 주어진 문장의 They는 문맥상 parents를 가리키는데, 주어진 문장이 [I], [II]에 들어가게 되면 가리키는 대상이 없거나 부정확하므로 적절하지 않다.

03 ▶ 정신분열증은 심리학(Psychology)과 관련이 있다.

》 정답   01 (D)   02 (C)   03 (B)

055   　　프로이드가 사망한 이후 생겨났던 정신분석학의 주요한 변화들 중의 하나는 많은 정신분석학자들이 자율적인 자아의 기능을 점점 더 강조하게 되었다는 점이다. 이러한 점은 "자아 심리학"이라는 말에 그대로 반영돼 있다. 이러한 발전을 주도한 사람은 하인즈 하트만(Heinz Hartmann)이었다. 프로이드가 자아(ego, 에고)를 일정정도의 통제력을 가질 수 있긴 해도 본질적으로는 원초아(id, 이드)의 요구를 따르는 것으로 본 반면, 하트만과 그의 동료들은 자아에 더 큰 자율성을 부여했다. 사실, 그들은 자아도 원초아와 마찬가지로 기본적 인간의 유전적 속성에서 기원하는 것으로 간주하고 있다. 그들의 관점에서, 자아는 고유의 발전 과정을 가지고 있고, 중립적인 활력에 의거하여 움직여서, 기저의 성적(性的) 혹은 공격적 욕구와는 필연적 연관성이 없는 활동이나 대상에 대해 관심을 갖게 만든다. 때때로 프로이드 또한 그러한 흥미들이 가능하다고 하는 듯 했으나, 그의 주된 테마는 전혀 다른 것이다. 그는 대상과 활동이 그 사람에게 흥미로운 것은 그러한 것들이 본래부터 성(性)과 공격성이라는 기본적인 성격 구성 요소들에 직간접적으로 연관되어 있기 때문이라고 생각했던 것이다.

psychoanalysis n. 정신분석
emphasis n. 강조; 역설, 중요시
autonomous a. 자율의, 독립한, 자치의
subservient a. 도움이 되는; 비굴한
id n. 이드(개인의 본능적 충동의 원천), 원초아
inheritance n. 상속, 계승; 유전 형질
neutralize v. 중립화하다; 무효화하다

01 ▶ 프로이드 사후의 정신분석학자들은 '자아도 원초아와 마찬가지로 기본적 인간의 유전적 속성에서 기원하는 것으로 간주한다'고 했으므로, 이는 곧 자아가 유전적으로 결정된다는 의미이다. 이는 곧 존재하기 이전에 사전에 어느 정도 결정돼 있다는 것을 뜻하므로 (C)가 정답이다.

02 ▶ autonomous a. 자율적인(= free)

》 정답 01 (C) 02 (D)

056

우리 동물은 식물을 거의 충분히 신뢰하지 않는다. 동료 인간을 비능률적이거나 잉여적이라고 멀리하고 싶을 때 우리는 그를 "화분에 심은 식물"이라 부른다. "식물인간"은 생활을 해나가는 데 필수적인 수단을 대부분 잃어서 완전히 무력해져버린 사람을 가리키는 말이다. 그러나 걱정이야 고맙지만, 식물은 아주 멋지게 잘 살아가며 우리 인간보다 수백만 년 앞서 잘 살아갔다. 사실, 식물에게는 장소이동, 도구와 불의 사용, 의식과 언어의 기적 등과 같은 능력이 없다. 우리 같은 동물에게 이런 능력들은 우리가 가장 "발전된" 것이라 여기는 생활의 도구들이며, 이것들이 지금까지 우리의 진화 과정의 빛나는 도달점들이었기 때문에 그렇게 여기는 것도 전혀 놀라운 일이 아니다. 그러나 다음번에 인간의 의식을 진화의 정점으로 찬양하고 싶어지면, 어떤 근거에서 그런 생각을 하게 되었는지 잠시 생각해보라. 그것은 인간의 의식으로, 정확히 말해 객관적인 원천(근거)이 아니다. 사실, 진화의 또 다른 정점들이, 자연 역사가 동물이 아니라 식물에 의해 써진다면 훨씬 더 많이 대서특필될 그런 종류의 정점들이, 있다. 왜냐하면, 우리는 장소이동, 의식, 언어 등을 결정적인 것으로 하고 있었던 반면에 식물은 식물 생활의 핵심적인 실존적 사실인 착근(뿌리내림)을 고려하여 완전히 다른 부류의 책략들을 발달시키려고 노력하고 있었기 때문이다.

---

credit n. 신뢰, 신용
dismiss v. 일축하다, 멀리하다
superfluous a. 잉여인
potted plant 화분에 심은 식물
vegetable n. 채소, 식물, 식물인간
helplessness n. 무력함
locomotion n. 이동, 운동
pinnacle n. 정점, 절정
get press 언론에 보도되다
nail down 결정적인 것으로 하다

01 ▶ 빈칸 앞에서 인간의 의식을 진화의 정점으로 생각하게 된 근거가 인간의 의식이라고 했는데, 인간이 인간 자신의 의식(생각)으로 인간의 의식을 진화의 정점으로 생각한다는 것은 인간만의 주관적인 판단이라는 것이다. 즉 인간의 의식은 그런 생각의 객관적인 근거가 못 되므로 빈칸에는 (C)가 적절하다.

02 ▶ 이 글의 주제는 마지막 부분에 있다. 우리가 잘 몰라서 그렇지 사실, 식물도 식물 나름의 뛰어난 생존, 번성 책략을 발달시켜왔다는 것이다.

03 ▶ 네 보기 모두 식물과 다른 동물의 특징으로 언급되었지만 식물의 핵심적인 실존적 사실을 착근 즉 정지라 했으므로 동물의 가장 두드러진 특징은 '이동, 운동'이다. 사실 다른 특징은 인간이 아닌 동물에도 해당되는지 불확실한 면도 있다.

》 정답 01 (C) 02 (D) 03 (A)

057

　　우리가 항상 인생과 행복의 불확실성에 대해 의식하고 산다면, 우리는 쉽게 정신적으로 우울해질 것이며 일이나 기쁨에 대한 열정을 잃어버릴 것이다. 하지만 만일 이러한 것을 의식하지 않는다면 아무런 가치가 없는 것에 잘못된 가치를 부여하고 추구할 가치가 없는 것을 추구하며 세월을 낭비하기 쉽다. 그러므로 우리가 언젠가는 무너져서 우리 자신, 우리의 재산, 우리의 야망을 한순간에 앗아가 버릴지도 모르는 취약한 지구표면이라는 것을 타고 우주공간을 여행하고 있다고 생각하는 것은 우리의 마음에 아주 훌륭한 치료제이다. 많은 철학자들이 적어도 그렇게 생각해왔고, 우리가 죽음의 그늘 아래서 사업을 일으키고 꿈을 추구한다는 것을 우리에게 상기시켜주는 것을 자신들의 일로 삼았다. 우리는 모두 사형 선고를 받았지만, 무기한의 집행유예 하에 있다고 말한다. 그리고 이것을 고려하지 않은 기준으로는 인생의 어떤 것도 그 가치를 측정할 수 없다.

perpetually ad. 영구히; 끊임없이
insecurity n. 불안정성
morbid a. 병적인; 음침한, 우울한
ardour n. 열정
set a false value on ~에 그릇된 가치관을 두다
subside v. 가라앉다
bring a sudden end to ~을 갑자기 끝내다
possession n. 소유; 소유물
reprieve n. 형집행 정지

01 ▶ '우리 모두가 사형 선고를 받았지만, 무기한의 집행유예 하에 있다는 사실을 고려하지 않으면 인생의 어떤 것도 그 가치를 측정할 수 없다.'는 의미이므로, (B)가 가장 가까운 의미의 진술이다.

02 ▶ 글쓴이는 우리가 인생의 불확실성을 의식하고 살아야 한다는 입장인데, 이것은 어느 면에서는 비관론자의 생각과 유사하다.

》 정답 01 (B) 02 (A)

058

　　두뇌에 있는 시각체계는 이미지가 초당 몇 도 이상 망막을 가로질러 지나가 버리면 정보를 처리하기에 너무 늦다. 그래서 인간이 움직이면서 볼 수 있으려면 두뇌가 눈을 돌리는 것에 의해 머리의 움직임이 보상되어야 한다. 눈이 앞에 달린 동물에 있어서 또 다른 복잡한 문제는 높은 시력을 가진 작은 망막 영역의 발달이다. 이 영역은 중심와라고 불리며 사람들의 시각의 약 2도 정도를 담당한다. 세상을 더 분명히 보려면 두뇌는 물체의 이미지가 중심와에 일치하도록 눈을 돌려야 한다. 그래서 눈의 움직임은 시각적 인식에 매우 중요하며 눈의 움직임을 정확히 하지 못한다면 심각한 시각 장애를 야기할 수 있다.

　　두 눈을 갖는 것은 정밀성이 더해지는 것인데, 왜냐하면 두뇌는 양 눈을 정확히 향하게 해서, 주목하는 물체를 두 개의 상응하는 망막에 일치시켜야 하기 때문이다. 그렇지 않으면 복시현상이 생기게 될 것이다. 다른 신체 부위의 움직임은 관절 주위의 가로무늬근에 의해 통제된다. 눈의 움직임도 예외는 아니지만, 그들은 골격 근육과 관절이 갖지 않은 특별한 장점을 갖고 있고 그래서 상당히 다른 것이다.

visual a. 시각적인
slip v. 미끄러지다, 지나치다
retina n. 망막
compensate v. 보상하다
complication n. 복잡한 문제, 부작용
acuity n. 예민함, 예리함
fovea n. 중심와
corresponding a. 상응하는, 일치하는
otherwise ad. 그렇지 않으면
striated a. 평행으로 달리는 줄이 있는, 줄무늬의

01 ▶ 눈의 움직임의 중요성을 첫 문단에서 역설하고 있다.
02 ▶ 빈칸 뒤의 내용을 볼 때 정밀성이 더해져야 할 것이다.
03 ▶ 첫 문단의 후반부에서 중심와에 물체의 시야가 닿아야 한다.

》 정답 01 (D) 02 (C) 03 (B)

059

　기업에서 가장 최근에 일어나고 있는 사기는 고객이 모든 일을 하도록 시키는 것이다. 물론, 고객을 일꾼으로 쓰는 일은 오래된 사기였다. 주유소가 점원을 없애버리고 사람들이 스스로 연료를 주유해야 한다고 결정한 것이 최초였다. 다음으로 온 것은 고객이 자기가 쓴 테이블을 닦고 접시를 깨끗하게 쌓아 올린 후 떠나야 한다고 결정한 패스트푸드 음식점이었다. 기업들은 "우리는 비용을 줄이려고 노력하고 있으며 이것은 고객의 저축으로 환원될 것입니다"라고 말한다.

　어디에서나 기업은 고객을 무보수의 직원으로 여기는 생각에 푹 빠져 있다. 콴타스(Qantas) 항공사에서는 상용 고객 멤버들에게 이제 탑승권을 집 컴퓨터를 사용해서 스스로 인쇄할 것을 요구하고 있다. 그 항공사에 따르면 이는 모두 승객의 편의를 위한 것이지 단지 자신들의 종이, 잉크, 그리고 직원들의 시간을 아끼기 위한 것은 아니라고 한다. 이렇게 되면, 이제 당신은 자신이 인쇄한 탑승권을 들고 공항에 나타나서 그들이 열쇠와 조종사 유니폼을 던져주는 상황(비행기도 고객이 몰고 가는 상황)도 반쯤은 예상하게 된다. 이런 일이 대체 어디에서 멈출까? 셀프서비스 고객은 스스로 우유를 짜는 소나 다름없다. 그것은 사업의 편의를 위한 것이지만 당신은 거기에 과연 정말로 소를 위한 것이 있는지 생각해봐야 할 것이다.

---

scam n. 사기, 편취
lurk n. 잠복, 밀행; 편취, 사기
remove v. 제거하다; 치우다
tray n. 식판; 음식 접시
neatly ad. 깔끔하게, 말쑥하게
stack v. 쌓아 올리다
frequent flyer (비행기의) 단골 고객
boarding pass (여객기의) 탑승권
turn up 나타나다
grip v. 꽉 쥐다, 꼭 잡다

01 ▶ 이 문장은 사업적인 편리함을 위해 셀프서비스를 시행하는 회사들의 행태를 비유적 표현을 써서 우회적으로 비난한 말이다. 앞에서 self-serve customer와 self-milking cow를 같은 선상에 놓고 있으므로 여기서 말하는 cow는 customer이다. 따라서 소를 위한 게 있는지 생각해봐야 한다는 말은 정말로 고객을 위한 것이 무엇인지 생각해봐야 한다는 의미이다.

02 ▶ 두 번째 문단 셋째 문장의 According to the airline, it's all for the convenience of the customer를 통해 콴타스 항공사가 탑승권을 직접 인쇄해서 오는 것이 결국 승객들에게 이득이 된다고 생각한다는 사실을 알 수 있다.

03 ▶ 두 번째 문단에서 셀프서비스에 대한 필자의 생각이 잘 드러나 있다. 필자는 콴타스 항공사의 셀프서비스가 결국 고객에게 열쇠와 조종사 유니폼을 던져주는 상황까지 갈 것이라고 비꼬면서, 셀프서비스를 수행하는 고객은 self-milking cow와 마찬가지라고 셀프서비스에 대해 '비판적인' 태도를 보이고 있다. (A) 익살스러운 (B) 공정한 (D) 낙천적인

》 정답 01 (D) 02 (C) 03 (C)

폭넓은 독자를 위해 글을 쓰는 것은 끊임없이 노력하는 일이다. 오늘날 기자들은 교육수준이 높고 관심의 폭이 넓은데, 그들의 타고난 성향은, 자기감시와 훌륭한 편집으로 억제되지 않는다면, 기자들 서로를 위해 글을 쓰는 것이다. 시장은 이런 엘리트적 경향을 과거만큼 능률적으로 저지하지 못한다. 그 이유는 저널리즘이 다수 독자들의 마음을 사로잡는 것에서 서로 다른 많은 각 계층의 독자들의 마음을 사로잡는 것으로 서서히 옮겨가고 있기 때문이다. 앨빈 토플러가 말했듯이, 우리는 '소수의 메시지를 다수의 사람들에게 보내는 것'에서 '다수의 메시지를 소수의 사람들에게 보내는 것'으로 옮겨가고 있다.

신문들이, 그리고 신문들을 지지하는 광고주들이, 여전히 대체로 자신들의 영향력 범위를 극대화하기를 기대하다보니 명료한 글쓰기는 여전히 중요하다. 이런 뜻은 1938년 오스트리아에서 이민 온 루돌프 플레쉬라는 사람에 의해 언론 매체에 가장 강력하게 전달되었다. 그가 콜롬비아 대학에서 쓴 학위논문에는 문장과 단어 길이에 기초한 가독성에 대한 수학적 정의가 포함되어 있었으며 그것은 『가독문체의 특징들』이라는 제목으로 출판되었다. 그러나 그것은 학위논문이어서 그 자체가 가독성의 그다지 좋은 예가 아니었다. 플레쉬는 이것을 깨닫고 『알기 쉬운 말의 기술』이라는 제목으로 다시 썼으며 1946년에 하퍼 앤드 브라더스 사에 의해 출판되었다.

---

inclination n. 성향
self-monitoring n. 자기감시
appeal to (사람의) 마음에 호소하다, 마음에 들다
tailor v. ~에 맞추어 만들다, ~에 맞게 하다
count on 의지하다, 기대하다
maximize v. 극대화하다
reach n. (영향력 등의) 범위[권한]
dissertation n. 논문
readability n. 가독성, 읽기 쉬움
feature story 특집기사
newsbeat n. 취재담당구역
writing style 문체

01 ▶ 빈칸에 들어갈 말은 그 다음 문장의 this elitist tendency가 가리키는 것이다. 즉 교육수준이 높은 기자들이 서로에게 쓰는 글이 엘리트적인 글이 될 것이다. 따라서 (B)가 적절하다. 기자들은 스스로 감시, 점검하지 않으면 자꾸 독자의 수준은 생각지 않은 자기들끼리의 글이 될 것이다. (A) 특집기사를 취재보도하다 (C) 그들의 취재담당구역을 넘다 (D) 그들의 문체를 바꾸다

02 ▶ (A) 첫 단락에서 "저널리즘이 다수 독자들의 마음을 사로잡는 것에서 서로 다른 많은 각 계층의 독자들의 마음을 사로잡는 것으로 서서히 옮겨가고 있다"고 했으므로 지금은 다양한 독자들을 사로잡기 위해 신문과 잡지의 종류가 더 많아졌을 것이다. (B) 정기구독자 수의 증가감소 여부는 알 수 없다. (C) 엘리트인 글은 소수 식자층만 알 수 있으므로 신문잡지의 영향을 확산시키지 못할 것이다. (D) 전자의 가독성이 좋지 않아 후자로 다시 써진 것이므로 후자가 more readable하다.

03 ▶ (C)의 "진실을 찾아서 써라"는 것은 거짓기사를 쓰지 말라는 기사의 '정확성(accuracy)'과 연관된 것이고 다른 것은 모두 독자들이 읽어서 이해할 수 있는 기사의 '가독성(readability)'과 연관된 것이다. (A)의 '오마하지방의 우유배달부'나 (B)의 '12살짜리 아이'나 (D)의 '읽을 때 입술을 움직이는 사람들'은 모두 글을 읽는 능력이 낮은 사람들로 이들을 위해서는 쉽고 명료한 글을 써야 한다.

» **정답** 01 (B) 02 (A) 03 (C)

061

불행한 사람이라는 것이 반드시 슬프거나 어두운 사람이라는 말은 아니다. 행복하지 않으면서도 무언가에 흥미를 가질 수 있으며 행복하지 않으면서도 무언가에 매혹될 수 있다. 이렇게 되지 못하게 하는 장벽은 물론 초(超)긍정적인 우리 사회에서는 부정적인 것을 전혀 용납하지 않는 방침을 암암리에 갖고 있다는 것이다. 부정적인 것이라는 포괄적인 우산 아래에는 초긍정적이지 않은 모든 것이 기본적으로 들어간다. 진정으로 하는 말인데, 우리 가운데 날마다 "멋진" 날을 보내고 있는 사람이 누가 있는가? 항상 "너무 좋은" 기분인 사람이 누가 있는가? 분노와 부정적인 것도 쓸모가 있다.

당신이 느끼는 얼마간의 불편하고 불쾌한 감정을 "긍정적으로 되려고 애씀"으로써 완화하려 하지 말고 그냥 한번 부정적으로 되어 보라. 이것이 당신의 실제 감정을 접해보도록 도와줄 것이다. "나는 절망적이고 얼빠지고 어리석다는 느낌이 들어. 이런 느낌이 드니까 내가 낙오자 같아. 그리고 긍정적이고 명랑해지려고 애쓰니까 화가 나고, 화가 나니까 완전히 망가진 기분이네."

만일 어떤 감정이든 그것이 당신의 감정이라면, 그러면 당신은 하나의 기준선을 가진 셈이고, 참고할(기준으로 삼을) 견고한 밑바닥(근거)을 확립한 셈이다. 때로는 어떤 감정이든 판단하지 않고 검열하지 않고 그냥 스스로 느끼도록 놓아두는 것이 그 부정적인 감정들의 강도를 줄여줄 수 있다.

---

unspoken a. 암암리의, 말없는
zero-tolerance n. 무관용
catch-all a. 포괄적인
alleviate v. 완화하다
get in touch with ~와 접촉하다
fat a. 얼빠진, 우둔한
upbeat a. 낙관적인, 명랑한
baseline n. 기준선
floor n. 층, 바닥
reference n. 참고, 기준
censorship n. 검열

01 ▶ 빈칸 바로 앞의 두 의문문은 수사의문문으로 부정 평서문과 같은 의미이다. 그리고 빈칸 앞까지의 요지는 행복하지(긍정적이지) 않다고 모두 불행한(부정적인) 것은 아니라는 것이므로 빈칸에는 '행복하지(긍정적이지) 않음'을 긍정적으로 평가하는 말인 (C)가 적절하다.

02 ▶ 초(超)긍정적인 사회는 가장 긍정적인 것이 아닌 모든 것을 부정적인 것으로 보고 오로지 가장 긍정적인 것만을 인정하고 추구하는 사회이므로 '일면적 사고방식'이라는 (D)가 관련된 사항이다. bipolar mindset(양극적 사고방식)라 할 수도 있다.

03 ▶ 초긍정적인 사회에서는 가장 행복한 상태가 아니면 행복한 것이 아니게 되므로 행복해지기가 어려울 것이다. 따라서 (B)는 추론할 수 없는 진술이다. (A)는 첫 세 문장에서, (C)는 둘째 단락에서, (D)는 마지막 단락에서 각각 추론할 수 있다.

» 정답 01 (C) 02 (D) 03 (B)

062

우리들은 각자 작은 영역의 사실들만을 조사하여 자신의 것으로 만드는 것 같다. 일과(日課) 밖의 지식은 대부분의 사람들이 허울뿐인 지식으로 간주한다. 그래도 우리는 항상 우리의 무지에 반발한다. 우리는 때때로 분발하여 깊이 생각한다. 우리는 사후의 삶이나 아리스토텔레스를 당황케 했다고 하는 '왜 재채기는 정오부터 자정 사이에 하면 이롭고 밤부터 정오 사이에 하면 불길한가'와 같은 문제 등, 어떤 것에 대해서나 생각하기를 즐긴다. 인간이 알고 있는 가장 큰 기쁨 중 하나는 지식을 찾아 무지 속으로 뛰어드는 것이다. 무지의 가장 큰 즐거움은 결국 질문을 던지는 즐거움이다. 이 즐거움을 잃어버렸거나 답변을 하는 즐거움인 교의(도그마)의 즐거움과 바꾸어버린 사람은 이미 경직되어가고 있다. 우리는 조웨트만큼 탐구적인 사람을 부러워하는데, 그는 60대의 나이에 생리학 연구를 시작했다. 우리들 대부분은 그 나이가 되기 오래 전에 우리의 무지에 대한 의식을 잃어버렸다. 우리는 심지어 다람쥐가 물어다 놓는 도토리 같은 알량한 지식을 자랑하게 되며 늘어나는 나이 자체를 전지(全知)의 학교로 여긴다. 우리는 소크라테스가 지혜로 유명했던 이유가 그가 모든 것을 알고 있었기 때문이 아니라 70세의 나이에 여전히 아무 것도 모른다는 것을 깨달았기 때문이라는 것을 잊어버린다.

---

rouse oneself 분발하다
at intervals 때때로
speculate v. 숙고하다, 생각하다
revel in 기뻐하다, 즐기다
sneeze v. 재채기하다
inquisitive a. 호기심이 많은, 탐구적인
sit down to ~에 착수하다
physiology n. 생리학
be vain of ~를 자랑하다
omniscience n. 전지(全知), 박식

01 ▶ gewgaw는 '겉만 번지르르하고 실제로는 가치 없는 것'이라는 뜻이므로 (A)가 가장 가깝다. 단어의 뜻을 모르더라도 문맥상 부정적인 의미라는 것은 알 수 있다.

02 ▶ (A)는 첫 두 문장에서, (B)는 끝에서 넷째와 셋째 문장에서, (C)는 끝에서 둘째 문장에서, 각각 사실임을 알 수 있다. (D)는 everything으로 more than anyone else로, but 이하를 and he realized that he knew nothing로 고쳐야 할 것이다.

03 ▶ 우리는 우리의 무지를 알고 지식을 찾아 무지 속으로 뛰어들어 계속 질문을 던져야 한다고 한 (B)가 이 글의 요지이다.

» 정답   01 (A)   02 (D)   03 (B)

063

거침없이 의견을 말하는 무신론자인 스티븐 호킹 박사가 사후세계에 대해 여전히 확신하지 못하는 것은 아마도 놀라운 일로 다가오지 않을 것이다. 그러나 69세의 그 물리학자는 『가디언』과의 인터뷰에서 그 주제에 대한 자신의 입장을 뚜렷하게 밝혔다.

나는 지난 49년 동안 요절할 가능성을 가진 채 살아왔다. 나는 죽음이 두렵지 않지만 서둘러서 죽을 생각은 없다. 나는 우선 하고 싶은 일들이 너무 많다. 나는 인간의 뇌를 부품이 고장 나면 작동을 멈출 컴퓨터로 여긴다. 완전히 망가진 컴퓨터에게는 사후세계라는 천국은 존재하지 않는다. 그것은 암흑을 무서워하는 사람들을 위한 꾸며낸 이야기이다.

MSNBC는 호킹 박사의 『위대한 설계(Grand Design)』가 우주의 기원이 신(神)이 없어도 설명되어질 수 있다고 주장했으나 그가 『가디언』과의 인터뷰에서 취했던 것만큼 공격적인 태도를 취하지는 않았다고 말한다.

atheist n. 무신론자
unconvinced a. 확신하지 못하는
physicist n. 물리학자
explicit a. 명백한; (표현 등이) 솔직한
prospect n. 예상, 기대
component n. 성분; (기계 등의) 부품
origin n. 기원
stance n. (육체적, 정신적인) 자세
aggressive a. 공격적인; 적극적인
adamant a. 요지부동의, 단호한
presumptuous a. 주제넘은, 건방진
well-rounded a. 균형이 잡힌; 다재다능한

01 ▶ outspoken a. 거리낌 없이 말하는; 솔직한(= straightforward)

02 ▶ 인간의 뇌를 컴퓨터에 비유한 것은 작동을 멈춘 컴퓨터에게 사후세계가 존재하지 않듯, 죽음으로 인해 뇌의 기능이 정지한 인간에게도 천국과 같은 사후세계란 존재하지 않음을 말하기 위해서이다. 따라서 (B)의 '영생이란 한낱 망상이라고 일축하기 위해서'가 정답으로 적절하다.

03 ▶ 둘째 단락 첫 문장에서 요절의 가능성을 갖고 살아왔다고 했으므로 (A)를 추론할 수 있다. 호킹 박사는 『위대한 설계』에서 신이 없어도 우주의 기원을 설명할 수 있다고 주장했는데 이는 신(조물주, 창조자)의 존재를 부정하는 것이므로 (B)와 (C)를 유추할 수 있다. 반면, 마지막 문장을 통해 호킹 박사가 본인 주장의 정도나 수위를 조절할 수 있다는 점을 미루어, (D)는 추론할 수 없다.

》 정답 01 (A) 02 (B) 03 (D)

064

어니스트 러더퍼드는 전하를 띤 입자들을 금박지에 비췄다. 그는 대부분의 입자들이 금박지를 통과한 반면, 일부가 튀어나오는 것을 관찰했다. 1911년에 그는 원자는 중앙에 작은 핵이 있는 대체로 텅 빈 공간임이 분명하다는 내용의 이론을 내세웠다. 이것이 사실이라면, 전자들은 핵 주위를 궤도 비행할 것임에 틀림없는데, 그렇다면 전하를 띤 전자들이 그들의 모든 에너지를 잃고 핵 속으로 떨어지지 않을까? 1913년에 닐스 보어는 전자들이 양자의 방식으로 움직임을 나타낸다는 의견을 제시했다. 전자들은 고정된 궤도에 있다가 에너지를 방출하거나 흡수할 때에 한 궤도에서 다른 궤도로 — 양자 도약에서처럼 — 이동한다는 것이다. 가속장치로 인해 더 많은 것들이 밝혀질 때까지 원자의 마지막 부분으로 남아있었던 중성자는 1932년에 제임스 채드윅에 의해 발견되었다. 실험가 겸 이론가였던 엔리코 페르미는 전자와 가스를 연구하여 최초의 핵분열 원자로를 만들었는데, 이로 인해 원자탄과 핵발전소가 생겨나게 되었다.

charge v. 충전하다; 대전(帶電)시키다
observe v. 지키다, 준수하다; 보다; 말하다
nucleus n. 핵
quantum n. 양자(量子)
electron n. 전자
emit v. (빛, 열 등을) 발산하다, 방출하다
absorb v. 흡수하다, 빨아들이다
fission n. 분열; 핵분열

01 ▶ 바로 앞의 관찰내용에 해당하는 (B)가 정답이다.

02 ▶ 보어는 전자들이 고정된 궤도에 있다가 에너지를 방출하거나 흡수할 때에 한 궤도에서 다른 궤도로 이동한다는 의견을 제시했다.

03 ▶ 원자의 구조에 대한 여러 과학자들의 발견내용에 대한 글이다.

》 정답 01 (B) 02 (A) 03 (A)

065

크고 강한 것들이 작고 부드럽고 약한 것들보다 위험성이 훨씬 덜 하다는 것이 사실이라고 나는 생각한다. 자연은 (그게 무엇이든) 작고 약한 것들을 훨씬 더 빨리 번식시킨다. 물론 이것은 사실이 아니다. 죽는 것보다 번식속도가 빠르지 못했던 것들은 사라졌다. 그러나 (인간의) 사소한 잘못, 사소한 고통, 사소한 근심거리들은 어떠한가? 이 우주의 병폐는 심각한 우려에서 오는 것이 아니라 사소한 안달감에서 비롯된다. 그런데 큰 것들은 인간을 죽게 할 수는 있지만 그렇지 못한다면(인간을 죽이지 못한다면), 인간은 그것들에 비해 더 강하고 더 낫다는 것을 뜻한다. 인간은 잔소리, 소액 청구서, (잘못 걸려온) 전화, 무좀, 꽃가루 알레르기, 흔한 감기, 권태감 등에 의해 조금씩 갉아 먹힘으로써 파멸을 맞게 된다. 이 모든 것들은 부정적인 것들이며 사소한 좌절이지만 어느 누구도 이것들보다 더 강하지는 못하다.

- reproduce v. 번식하다
- athlete's foot 무좀
- ulcer n. 궤양; 병폐, 폐해
- ragweed n. 두드러기 쑥(꽃가루 알레르기 원인이 됨)
- irritation n. 짜증, 안달
- duck nibbling 오리처럼 조금씩 갉아먹기
- nag v. 잔소리하다
- frustration n. 좌절

01 ▶ 글의 요지는 '인간을 파괴시키는 병폐는 큰 것이 아닌 주변의 사소한 것들에서 비롯된다.'이므로, (C)가 제목으로 적절하다.

02 ▶ 번식속도가 빨라서가 아니라 인간을 조금씩 갉아먹음으로써 인간을 파멸시키기 때문에 위험하다.

03 ▶ "어느 누구도 이것들보다 더 강하지는 못하다"는 결국 '모든 사람이 그것들에 의해 파멸된다.'라는 의미이다.

≫ 정답 01 (C) 02 (C) 03 (C)

066

한때는 절대적이고 보편적이며 영원하리라고 여겨졌거나 혹은 다행스럽게도 의미도 모른 채 받아들여졌던 규범과 진리가 의심받고 있는 것이 우리 시대의 특징인 것 같다. 현대의 사상과 연구에 비추어 한때는 당연한 것으로 여겨졌던 것의 상당 부분이 입증과 증명을 필요한 것으로 선언되고 있다. 증명의 기준 자체도 논쟁의 대상이 되었다. 우리는 사상의 타당성에 대한 일반적인 불신뿐만 아니라 그것들을 주장한 사람들의 동기에 대한 불신도 목격하고 있다. 이런 상황은 자아확대가 진리보다 탐나는 상품이 되어버린 지적 무대에서 각자의 만인에 대한 투쟁으로 더욱 악화되었다.

- norm n. 기준; 규범
- blissful a. 더없이 행복한, 기쁨에 찬
- implication n. 내포, 함축, 암시
- in the light of ~의 관점에서
- take ~ for granted ~을 당연한 것으로 여기다
- demonstration n. 증명; 논증
- criterion n. (비판, 판단의) 기준, 표준
- validity n. 정당성, 타당성
- assert v. 단언하다, 역설하다
- self-aggrandizement n. 자기 확대, 자아 확대
- covet v. 몹시 탐내다, 바라다

01 ▶ '한때는 절대적이고 보편적이며 영원하리라고 여겨졌거나 혹은 다행스럽게도 의미도 모른 채 받아들여졌던 규범과 진리가 의심받고 있는 것이 우리 시대의 특징인 것 같다.'라고 했다.

02 ▶ 당연한 것으로 여겨 왔던 규범과 진리에 입증과 증명을 요구하고 있는 상황을 달리 표현할 수 있는 것을 선택한다.

03 ▶ arena n. 경기장, 투쟁이나 활동의 장소

04 ▶ '우리는 사상의 타당성에 대한 일반적인 불신뿐만 아니라 그것들을 주장한 사람들의 동기에 대한 불신도 목격하고 있다'고 돼 있다.

≫ 정답 01 (B) 02 (D) 03 (C) 04 (A)

067

　　말과 같이 예술도 의사 전달 형식이다. 말과 글은 앞선 여러 세대들과 당대 최고의 지성인들이 경험과 숙고를 통해 발견한 모든 지식을 가장 최근 세대의 사람들로 하여금 접해 볼 수 있게 해준다. 예술은 선조들이 경험한 모든 감정과 최고의 동시대인들이 느낀 감정을 최근 세대의 사람들로 하여금 접할 수 있게 해준다. 지식의 진보가 잘못된 것을 몰아내고 대체함으로써 이루어져 나가듯이, 감정의 진보도 예술을 통해 이루어져 나간다. 인류의 안녕에 덜 친절하고 덜 필요한 감정들은 그런 목적에 더 친절하고 더 필수적인 다른 감정들로 교체된다. 이것이 예술의 목적이며 예술이 그 목적을 더 많이 성취할수록 그만큼 더 나은 예술이 된다. 그리고 예술이 그 목적을 덜 완수할수록 그만큼 더 나쁜 예술이 된다.

render v. ~이 되게 하다
accessible a. 접근하기 쉬운; 입수하기 쉬운
reflection n. 반성, 숙고
preceding a. 이전의; 바로 전의
foremost a. 최초의; 일류의
predecessor n. 전임자, 선배
contemporary n. 동시대 사람
proceed v. 전진하다, 진행되다
dislodge v. 제거하다, 쫓아내다

01 ▶ 말과 예술을 비교하고 있으며, 마지막 문장에 대조의 기법이 사용되었다.
02 ▶ 잘못된 것을 몰아내고 대체함으로써 지식이 진보한다는 것은 지식의 '점증적, 발전적' 성격을 나타낸다.
03 ▶ 설명의 형식을 취하고 있다. (A) 시적인 (B) 사색적인 (C) 비꼬는

≫ 정답 01 (C) 02 (B) 03 (D)

068

　　미국 대통령이 내각을 두어야 한다고 명시하고 있는 법은 없다. 헌법에는 단지 대통령은 "각 부서의 직무와 관련된 문제에 관하여 각 행정부처 주무 관리의 의견을 서면으로 요구할 수 있다"라고 되어 있다. 대통령이 이러한 조언을 반드시 요구해야 하는 것은 아니며 조언을 들었을 때도 그것을 받아들일 필요는 없다. 그럼에도 불구하고 대통령들은 정보를 제공해주고 조언을 해줄 공식 자문 위원단을 자주 원한다. 왜냐하면 어느 누구도 국가에서 진행되고 있는 모든 일에 관해서 다 알 수는 없기 때문이다.

　　각각의 대통령은 상원의 '조언과 동의'를 통해 내각 구성원들을 선택한다. 그러나 이 자문 위원들은 대통령의 뜻에 따라 움직이며 언제라도 해고될 수 있다. 이들은 지식, 경험, 특별한 재능, 혹은 그들의 전반적인 지혜로 인해 선택된다. 이들은 오랫동안 신뢰하는 친구일 수 있고, 때때로 친척일 수도 있다. 이들은 농부, 외교관, 과학자, 정치가일 수 있다. 이들은 백악관 서쪽 건물에 있는 대통령 집무실 옆 내각 회의실에서 매주 회합한다.

cabinet n. 내각
constitution n. 헌법
respective a. 각각의, 각자의
look to 기대를 걸다
senate n. 상원
fire v. 내쫓다, 해고하다
relative n. 친척, 친지
diplomat n. 외교관
the Oval Office (백악관의) 대통령 집무실

01 ▶ 대통령들은 정보와 조언을 해줄 공식 자문 위원단(내각)을 자주 원한다고 했다.
02 ▶ 두 번째 단락을 통해 대통령은 내각 구성원을 마음대로 선택함을 알 수 있다. 조언과 동의는 부차적인 것이다.
03 ▶ 첫 번째 단락 두 번째 문장 중 the principal officer in each of the executive departments 참고.

≫ 정답 01 (B) 02 (C) 03 (D)

069

　　세계의 산림벌채가 진행되는 비율은 놀랍다. 1950년대에 지구의 육지표면 중 약 25%가 숲으로 덮여 있었는데, 25년도 채 못 되어서 산림지의 양이 20%로 감소되었다. 1950년에서 1973년까지 25%에서 20%이르는 이와 같은 감소는 2040년까지 놀랄만한 3천 평방킬로미터의 산림지가 사라지게 될 것을 나타낸다. 산림벌채의 대부분은 개발도상국가의 열대산림에서 발생하는데, 열대산림은 농경지의 증가에 대한 개발도상국들의 필요와 선진국의 입장에서는 목재와 목재생산품을 수입하려는 욕구에 의해 가속화되고 있다. 예를 들어서, 미국에서 사용하는 합판의 90%이상이 열대우림을 보유하고 있는 개발도상국으로부터 수입된다. 1980년 중반 무렵, 열대산림의 사용을 감독하는 국제적인 단속 기구를 설립하자는 시도로, 이렇게 확대일로에 있는 문제에 대한 해결책들이 모색되고 있었다.

deforestation n. 산림벌채, 산림개척
approximately ad. 약, 대략
astounding a. 깜짝 놀라게 할만한
plywood n. 합판, 베니어판
regulatory a. 규정하는
oversee v. 내려다 보다, 감독하다
placid a. 평온한, 침착한
exaggerated a. 과장된, 지나친

01 ▶ 점점 심해지는 산림벌채에 대한 우려를 독자에게 인식시키려 하고 있다.
02 ▶ 산림벌채에 대한 우려를 나타내고 있다.
03 ▶ 산림에 대한 내용을 다루는 학문은 지리학이다.

》 **정답** 01 (C)　02 (A)　03 (B)

070

　　어떤 연구원들은 알코올 중독의 여러 원인 중 하나가 좋지 않은 식습관이라고 생각한다. 그들은 쥐가 비타민 B가 부족한 음식을 먹었을 때 알코올을 원한다는 것을 알아냈다.

　　처음에는 이 실험에 쓰인 모든 쥐들에게 똑같은 음식물을 주었다. 이 음식물은 비타민 B가 높지도 낮지도 않았다. 이 쥐들에게 네 가지의 마실 것을 선택하게 했다. 하나는 물이고 나머지 세 개는 알코올 용액이었다. 그 액체 속의 알코올 농도는 맥주의 수준에서부터 위스키의 수준까지 다양했다. 모든 쥐들이 똑같은 음식을 먹었음에도 불구하고 그들은 서로 다른 마실 액체를 선택했다. 그 중 몇몇 쥐는 알코올 중독이 되었고, 어떤 쥐들은 그렇지 않았다.

　　그리고 나서 연구가들은 알코올 중독이 된 쥐들에게 비타민 B가 많이 들어 있는 음식을 주었다. 물을 선택한 쥐들에게는 원래 식단보다 비타민과 무기화합물이 더 낮은 음식을 주었다. 첫 번째 집단의 쥐들은 위스키 마시는 것을 멈추고 물을 마시기 시작했다. 두 번째 집단은 물을 마시는 것을 멈추고 위스키를 마시기 시작했다. 비타민 B가 두 번째 집단의 음식에 첨가되었을 때, 그 쥐들은 다시 물을 선택하였고 알코올에 대한 욕구는 없는 것처럼 보였다.

alcoholism n. 알코올 중독
diet n. 식사, 식습관
crave v. 열망하다, 갈망하다
solution n. 용액
concentration n. 집중; (액체의) 농도
alcoholic n. 알코올[술] 중독자
mineral n. 광물; 무기(화합)물
conduct v. (특정한 활동을) 하다
hazard n. 위험

01 ▶ 연구원들은 비타민 B가 결핍된 쥐가 알코올을 원한다는 것을 알아냈다. 첫 문장에서 알코올 중독의 한 가지 원인이 잘못된 식습관이라고 했으므로 보기 중에서 (D)가 정답이 될 수 있다.

02 ▶ 이 실험에서 쥐에게 일어난 사례가 아닌 것은 (C) "몇몇 알코올 중독에 걸린 쥐들은 비타민 B가 그들의 음식에 첨가되지 않았는데도 후에 물을 선택했다"라는 진술이다. without이 with로 바뀌어야 본문에 부합한다.

03 ▶ 이 글은 좋지 않은 식습관이 알코올 중독의 한 원인이라는 연구 결과를 설명하고 있다.

04 ▶ 연구원들은 쥐들에게 알코올 농도가 틀린 네 가지 마실 것을 주어 어떤 것을 선택하는지를 관찰하였다. 쥐가 알코올이 농축되어 있는 액체를 선택한다면 알코올 중독이라고 판정할 수 있을 것이다. (C)는 알코올이 농축되어 있는 액체를 마시도록 쥐를 강제로 분류한 것으로 본문의 실험 내용과 다르다.

» 정답 01 (D) 02 (C) 03 (A) 04 (A)

071

과거의 훌륭한 지적인 지도자들은 인간이 경험하는 전 영역을 자신들의 영역으로 설정했다. 아리스토텔레스, 아퀴나스, 에라스무스, 볼테르는 스스로의 능력 범위를 폭 좁게 국한시키지 않았다. 그들은 전문가로서 인간의 과학적, 철학적, 정치적 지식의 총체를 탐구했다.

오늘날의 지도자들은 오늘날의 연구 영역의 한 부분 이상에서 탁월한 능력을 발휘할 수 있는 능력이 부족한 듯 보인다. 아인슈타인은 그가 당대의 문제에 대해 성취했던 수준과는 다른 수준을 물리학 분야에서 성취했다. 버트란트 러셀은 『수학의 원리』를 쓸 때에는 권위자였으나, 대중적인 명분에 대해 쓸 때에는 단지 또 다른 한 명의 지성인에 불과했다.

오늘날에는 한 가지 전문분야에서 누적된 자료를 통달하는 데 소요되는 시간의 양 때문에 심지어 천재들에게도 한 분야 이상에서는 사실들을 숙고해 볼 충분한 시간이 없는 것일까? 어쩌면, 컴퓨터가 성숙한 연구수단이 될 때에는, 지식의 동화과정이 대단히 가속화되어, 그 결과 주변을 둘러싸고 있는 세계의 총체적 도전을 받아들일 백과사전적 지성으로부터 인류가 다시 한번 혜택을 얻게 될 지도 모른다.

intellectual a. 지적인, 총명한
domain n. 영토, 영역, 세력범위; (활동, 연구 등의) 분야
competency n. 적성, 자격, 능력; 권능
expert n. 전문가, 달인
portion n. 일부, 부분
investigate v. 조사하다, 연구하다
authority n. 권위, 권력; 권위자, 대가
accumulate v. (조금씩) 모으다, 축적하다
assimilation n. 동화, 흡수, 소화

01 ▶ 마지막 문단에 컴퓨터에 대한 기대감이 나타나 있다.

02 ▶ 글쓴이는 한 분야에 치우치지 않고, 많은 분야의 지식을 통달하는 것을 이상적으로 보고 있다.

03 ▶ 오늘날에는 오랜 시간에 걸쳐 지식이 누적돼 온 관계로 한 사람이 여러 분야의 지식을 마스터하는 것이 쉽지 않다. 그러하기에, 한꺼번에 많은 정보를 처리할 수 있는 컴퓨터에게 기대를 하고 있다는 내용이다. 따라서 컴퓨터가 인간보다 우월한 점은 여러 가지 것을 한꺼번에 다룰 수 있는 능력이다. 컴퓨터를 encyclopedic minds라고 칭한 데서도 짐작할 수 있다.

» 정답 01 (C) 02 (D) 03 (A)

072

　밝은 빛에 노출되는 것은 시차와 수면 장애로 고통 받는 사람들에게 도움을 줄 수 있는 실마리를 쥐고 있을지도 모른다. 24시간 동안 형광빛에 여러 번 노출시킨 14명의 사람들을 관찰한 연구에서 과학자들은 '신체알람시계'가 2~3일에 걸쳐 다시 정해진다고 결론지었다. 이 기간은 긴 시간 국제선을 탄 후 몸 상태를 조정하는 데 걸리는 시간의 3분의 1이다.

　이 연구팀의 책임자인 찰스 자이슬러(Charles Czeisler) 박사는 빛이 신체의 취침 및 기상 패턴에 직접적인 생물학적 영향을 끼친다고 결론 내린다. 뇌에서 수면을 조절하는 부위인 시상하부는 망막 신경과 바로 연결되어 있다. 자이슬러 박사의 이론은 빛의 자극이 수면 및 기상 패턴을 초기화하는 주요한 요인이라는 것이다. 이 이론은 빛은 잠자는 것을 어렵게 함으로써 오직 간접적으로만 취침 및 기상 패턴에 영향을 끼친다는 일반적으로 받아들여지는 생각과 대조를 이룬다.

exposure n. 노출; 폭로
jet lag 시차로 인한 피로
fluorescent a. 형광을 발하는; 빛나는
stretch n. 뻗기; 연속의 시간; 긴장
adjustment n. 조정, 정리; 조절
retina n. (눈의) 망막

01 ▶ 본문은 실험을 예로 들어가며 빛이 신체시계에 영향을 준다는 내용을 다루고 있다.

02 ▶ 실험에서 신체시계가 초기화되는 데 걸린 시간(2~3일)은 긴 비행시간 뒤에 몸 상태를 조정하는 데 걸리는 시간의 3분의 1이라고 하였으므로 정답은 (A)가 된다.

03 ▶ 마지막 문장에서 찰스 박사의 이론은 일반적으로 용인되고 있는 생각과 대조를 이루고 있다고 하였으므로 아직 그 이론이 받아들여지지 않았다는 것을 추론할 수 있다.

》 정답　01 (D)　02 (A)　03 (B)

073

　바로 얼마 전 까지 모피코트, 대개 밍크코트를 한 벌 갖고 있다는 것은 부유함과 사회적 지위에 대한 명백한 상징이었다. 그러나 최근 들어 증가하고 있는 동물권익 보호단체들은 그러한 옷을 "사디스트의 상징"이라고 공격적으로 비난하고 있는데, 그들의 주장에 따르면 옷을 만드는데 매년 약 7,000만 마리의 불쌍한 생명이 — 코트 한 벌에 약 50마리의 밍크가 소요됨 — 필요하다고 한다. 이러한 감정적인 주장은 동물보호단체와 모피 소유자 및 계속 싸울 태세를 강화하고 있는 모피 업계를 갈라놓는 격렬한 분쟁을 촉발시켰다. 그 적대감은 점점 거세져서 미국의 일부 도시에서는 모피코트를 입고 있는 여성들이 공공연히 조롱을 받거나 또는 암암리에 괴롭힘을 당하고 있다.

　모피 업계는 미국 모피코트의 75%를 차지하는 밍크가 인도적으로 다루어지고 있으며 고통 없이 도살되고 있다고 주장한다. 업계의 지적은 모피는 천연 직물이며, 그것의 생산은 아크릴 섬유의 생산이 그러한 것처럼 환경을 오염시키거나 화석 연료를 사용하지 않는다는 것이다. 그럼에도 불구하고, 지난 3년 간 미국의 모피 판매는 연간 약 18억 달러 수준에서 머물고 있다. 그래서 크리스마스 시즌에는 많은 백화점들이 모피 재고를 처분하기 위해 가격을 크게 인하하고 있다.

fur n. 모피
emblem n. 상징, 표상
denounce v. 비난하다, 매도하다
garment n. 의복
embattle v. 진을 치다, 방비하다
nasty a. 불쾌한, 싫은; (병 따위가) 심한, 중한; 위험한
hostility n. 적의, 적개심; (pl.) 적대 행위, 교전
harass v. 괴롭히다
account for (~의) 비율을 차지하다
stagnant a. 정체된
slash v. (예산·급료·쪽수 등을) (대폭) 삭감하다

01 ▶ 이 글은 '모피코트에 대한 동물보호단체의 냉소적 비난'을 중심적으로 다룬 글이다.
02 ▶ 둘째 문단에 언급되었듯이 모피 업계가 직면한 주요한 문제는 '모피 코트 판매가 계속 정체되고 떨어지고 있는 것'이다.
03 ▶ (C)는 모피 업계에 관한 내용이 아니며, 또 '밍크의 수가 늘어나고 있고 이제는 멸종 위기에서 벗어났다'는 언급은 없었다.
04 ▶ jeer v. 야유하다, 조롱하다(= deride)

▶ 정답 01 (A) 02 (D) 03 (C) 04 (B)

074

도쿄의 마루노우치 지역에 있는 파소나 인력용역전문회사의 본사 사옥만큼 알아보기 쉬운 건물은 거의 없다. 발코니마다 식물이 무성하게 자라 건물을 푸른 잎으로 가리고 있다. 건물 안의 사무실들도 마찬가지로 신록을 이루고 있는데, 천정에는 화분이 달려있고 직원식당은 식당이라기보다 온실에 더 가깝다. 그 다음에 파소나의 직원들이 돌보는 실내농장이 있다. 약 1.5 헥타르 면적의 이 도시 녹색들판에는 야채들이 줄지어 자라고 심지어 논도 있어서 실내조명의 도움으로 1년에 세 번 수확할 수 있다.

실내농장을 가동하는 데 에너지가 많이 든다고 회의론자들이 당연히 지적할 것이지만, 파소나는 이 사업을 준비된 환경문제 해결책으로 선전하지 않는다. 부분적으로 그것은 회사 직원들을 위한 팀워크 강화훈련이다. 그것은 또한 환경문제와 식량문제에 대한 더 큰 이해를 촉진하려는 시도이다. 더 중요하게도, 그것은 선구적인 실험이다. 우리가 제일 먼저 도시농업을 시작하지 않으면 어떻게 정말로 효율적인 도시농장을 발달시키겠는가? 방문은 무료이지만 미리 예약을 해야 하며, 오테마치 역이나 니혼바시 역을 경유해서 갈 수 있다.

identify v. 식별하다, 알아보다
staffing company 인력용역전문회사
greenery n. (집합적) 푸른 잎, 푸른 나무
eatery n. 간이식당
greensward n. 잔디
rice paddy 논
bill v. 광고(선전, 발표)하다

01 ▶ 앞 문장의 greenery(푸른 잎)와 문장 끝의 greenhouse(온실)가 단서이다. 빈칸에는 green과 동의어인 (B) '푸른 잎이 무성한, 신록의'가 적절하다. (A) 어질러진 (C) 공상의 (D) 하늘색의
02 ▶ 둘째 단락에서 팀워크 강화훈련은 이 사업의 경영상의 목적이고, 환경문제와 식량문제에 대한 더 큰 이해의 촉진은 환경보존의 목적이므로 (C)가 사실인 진술이다. (A) 첫 단락 끝에서 '실내조명의 도움으로'라 했다. (B) 둘째 단락 첫 문장에서 rightly라 했으므로 에너지 소비가 많다고 봐야 한다. eco-innovations는 '친환경적 기술혁신'의 뜻이다. (D) 선구적인 실험이라 했을 뿐 위험하다고는 하지 않았고, 이 회사는 용역회사이지 신진 벤처회사가 아니다.
03 ▶ 이 글은 파소나 회사와 그 실내농장을 소개하고 알리는 글이므로 (A)가 목적으로 적절하다. 마지막에 회사를 찾아가는 길을 안내한 것이 이를 뒷받침한다.

▶ 정답 01 (B) 02 (C) 03 (A)

075

경찰의 사전 저지에도 불구하고 지난 일요일 민주노총이 주관한 대규모 집회로 서울 중심가 일대가 마비되었다. 시위대는 경찰에 나무 방망이를 휘두르고 돌을 던지면서 시위 진압 기동대를 뚫으려고 했다. 스위스에 본부를 둔 국제경영개발연구원(IMD)은 최근 과격한 노조운동이 한국의 국가 경쟁력을 약화시키고 있다고 발표했다. 노조는 과도한 요구를 하고 있고 사측은 경영 투명성 부족으로 신뢰 획득에 실패했다. 정부 역시 구체적인 원칙이나 정책의 부재로 노동 문제 해결에 실패했다.

어느 누구도 타인의 자유를 희생시키면서 자신의 자유를 누릴 권리가 없음에도 불구하고, 노조원들은 헌법으로 보장된 집회 및 시위의 권리를 주장하고 있다. 지난 일요일 거리로 뛰쳐나온 시위대는 일반 시민들에게 커다란 불편을 야기했고 특히 작은 상점이나 가판대 소유주들에게 손실을 끼쳤다. 현 정부는 노조에 관대한 정책을 채택해서 일어나고 있는 분규와 혼란에 책임져야 한다. 이제는 대중에 영합하는 정책을 찾는 대신에 사회 정의, 법과 원칙의 지배를 확고히 하기 위해 불법 단체행동에 대해 엄격하게 단속을 할 필요가 있다.

paralyze v. 마비시키다
rally n. (정치적) 집회; 시위운동
hurl v. 세게 내던지다
inflict v. (상처 등을) 가하다, 입히다
proprietor n. (상점 등의) 소유자, 소유주
vendor n. 행상인
populist a. 대중에 영합하는 n. 대중 영합주의자

01 ▶ 글쓴이는 대규모 집회에 대한 '부정적인' 견해를 가지고 글을 서술하고 있다.
02 ▶ 문맥상 '~에도 불구하고'라는 의미의 접속사가 필요하다.
03 ▶ brewing a. 곧 일어날 것 같은(= impending)

≫ 정답   01 (B)   02 (D)   03 (D)

076

전설에 의하면 이카로스는 과도한 자만으로 태양에 너무 가까이 가서, 날개에 깃털이 붙도록 바른 밀랍이 녹아 하늘에서 떨어졌다고 한다. 아마 그의 두 팔은 힘이 다 빠졌을 것이다. 수세기 동안 수없이 많은 "인간 새들"이 손수 만든 날개를 아무리 열심히 빠르게 퍼덕거려도 높이 떠있을 수 없다는 것을 알지 못하고 탑이나 절벽에서 뛰어내리다가 목숨을 잃었다. 그들의 후계자들인 오늘날의 베이스점퍼들은 건물, 절벽, 교량에서 뛰어내려 잠시 동안 유쾌하게 곤두박질치다가 낙하산을 펼쳐 낙하 속도를 늦춘다. 더러는 윙수트를 입는데, 이 옷에는 기류를 조절하는 천으로 된 날개가 있어 낙하하는 동안 시속 160킬로미터나 되는 속도로 앞으로 나아가게 할 정도의 양력을 발생시킨다. 캘리포니아 주 스코밸리의 J. T. 홈즈는 윙수트 점프를 약 천 번 정도 한 사람인데, "윙수트 점프는 인간으로서 새와 가장 유사하게 나는 것입니다."라고 말한다. 그것은 또한 대단히 위험하다. 약 12명의 베이스점퍼가 매년 사망한다. 자유낙하 중이나 낙하산이 펼쳐진 후에 산에 부딪히는 것이 일반적인 사망원인이다. 순수하게 사람의 힘으로 난 가장 성공적인 비행은 1988년에 이루어졌는데, 당시 매사추세츠 공과대학 연구팀이 만든 경비행기인 데드러스 호는 그리스 크레타 섬에서 산토리니까지 71.5마일을 날았다. 그리스의 한 올림픽 사이클 선수가 페달을 밟은 69 파운드 무게의 그 비행기는 산토리니 해변에 접근하다가 난기류를 만나 해안에서 몇 야드 떨어진 바다에 불시착했다.

have it that절 ~라고 말하다, 주장하다
give out 기진맥진하다, 힘이 다 빠지다
bird-man n. 인간 새, 비행가
flap v. 퍼덕거리다
heir n. 상속인, 후계자
BASE jumper 베이스점퍼(고공 낙하자)
plunge v. 뛰어들다, 돌진하다, 곤두박질치다
exhilarating a. 유쾌하게 하는, 상쾌한
parachute n. 낙하산
don v. (옷을) 입다
wing suit 윙수트, 비행 옷
baffled a. 기류조절장치가 있는
lift n. 상승력, 양력
turbulence n. 난기류
crash v. (비행기가) 추락하다, 불시착하다

01 ▶ hubris n. 과도한 자신감, 자만(= conceitedness)
02 ▶ (A)는 셋째 문장에서 비행 수단으로 손수 만든 날개를 언급하므로, (C)는 윙수트와 낙하산의 안전도는 비교할 수 없으므로, (D)는 이 글의 내용만으로는 알 수 없으므로, 모두 사실이 아니다. (B)는 넷째 문장에서 plunge for a few exhilarating moments, and then throw out a parachute라고 언급하므로 사실이다.
03 ▶ 이 글은 옛날과 오늘날의 베이스점퍼들과 무동력 비행사들의 비행을 포함하여 인간의 오랜 꿈인 개인적으로 하늘을 나는 것을 시도한 모험에 대한 글이므로 (D)의 '용감한 개인 비행 실험'이 제목으로 가장 적절하다. (A)와 (C)는 너무 지엽적이고 (B)는 무동력 비행사가 제외되므로 부적절하다.

》 정답 01 (B) 02 (B) 03 (D)

077

몸의 생체 시계는 사람이 피곤을 느끼는 때를 지배하는 것으로서 사춘기 이후에 변하여, 대부분의 십대들은 밤 11시 전에 잠들기가 어려워진다. 수업은 대개 오전 8시 15분 이전에 시작되는데, 일찍이 7시 15분에 시작하는 고등학교도 많다. 정시에 학교에 당도하려면 대부분의 십대들은 늦어도 6시 30분에는 일어나야 하는데, 그러면 어김없이 주중에는 수면 부족이 될 것이다. 십대들은 종종 밀린 잠을 보충하려고 주말에는 훨씬 더 늦게까지 자게 되고, 그러면 일요일 밤에 잠들기와 월요일 아침에 일어나기가 훨씬 더 어려워진다. 주말에 밀린 잠을 보충하는 것은 또한 십대들이 가장 정신을 차리고 있어야 할 때인 주중의 수업 시간 중에 정신을 차리고 있는데 도움을 주지 못한다.

1990년대 이후 24개 이상의 주에서 중·고등학교의 수업 시작 시간을 늦추는 실험을 해보았다. 그 결과는 고무적이었는데, 학생들의 수면시간이 늘어났고 출석률도 높아졌으며 성적은 향상되고 운전 사고는 줄어들었다. 예를 들어, 미니애폴리스의 고등학교들이 수업 시작 시간을 오전 7시 15분에서 8시 40분으로 늦추자 9학년 학생들의 일일 출석률이 83퍼센트에서 87퍼센트로 늘어났으며 전반적인 성적도 조금 향상되었다. 켄터키 주 페이예트 카운티(Fayette County)의 고등학교들이 수업 시작 시간을 오전 7시 30분에서 8시 30분으로 바꾸자 십대 운전자가 연루된 자동차 사고가 15퍼센트 감소했다. 그러나 아직은 대부분의 학교가 수업을 일찍 시작하며, 이것은 십대들이 잠을 충분히 자기를 원해도 그렇게 하기가 힘들어진다는 것을 의미한다.

internal clock 생체 시계(= biological clock)
puberty n. 사춘기
sleep-deprived a. 수면부족의
insomnia n. 불면증
punctuality n. 시간엄수
catch up (밀린 일이나 잠을) 보충하다
attendance n. 출석(상황), 출석자수
have one's work cut out 벅찬 일이 맡겨지다

01 ▶ 생체 시계의 변화로 밤 11시 이후에야 잠이 들고 다음날 아침 일찍 일어나서 나타나는 결과는 주중의 수면부족이라 해야 그 다음에 이어진 주말의 수면 보충과 잘 연결된다.
02 ▶ 본문은 생체 시계의 변화로 중고등학생들이 밤에 일찍 잘 수 없다는 생물학적 요인과 수업 시작 시간을 늦추었을 때의 긍정적인 실험결과들을 들어 수업 시작 시간을 늦추어야 할 필요성을 설명한 글이다.
03 ▶ 마지막 문장은 잠을 충분히 자기 힘들어진다는 뜻이지 공부하는 양을 줄여야 한다는 뜻은 아니다.

》 정답 01 (C) 02 (D) 03 (A)

078

　　불에 대해 현명하려 애써도 사태를 악화시킬 때가 종종 있다. 산불 진화를 담당하고 있는 연방 정부 기관인 미국 산림청은 불이 나는 곳마다 불을 꺼버리는, 화재 위험 지역에 인구가 증가하면 더더욱 적극적으로 불을 꺼버리는 정책을 1세기 이상 동안 추구해왔다. 도시생활에 익숙해있는 사람들에게는 이것이 사리에 맞는 일이며, 도시의 소방서에서 하는 일은 불을 꺼서 재산상의 피해를 미연에 방지하는 것이다. 그러나 미국 서부 대(大) 산림지대에서는 일이 이렇게 되어가지 않는다. 역설적이게도, 작은 불을 일일이 다 끄려고 하다 보면 숲에 쌓인 식물을 가끔씩 제거하는 중요한 일을 숲이 하지 못하게 되므로 큰불이 이따금씩 일어날 위험이 높아지게 된다. 이는 부엌에 신문을 쌓아두는 것과 다소 유사하다. 불이 나면 부엌 전체가 순식간에 전소되어 버린다. "더 크고 더 심한 이런 산불은 실효성 없는 진압 정책의 본의 아닌 결과입니다. 진압은 사실 오히려 사회를 위험하게 만듭니다."라고 리버사이드 캘리포니아 대학(University of California at Riverside) 산불 생태학자인 리처드 민니치(Richard Minnich)는 말한다.

wildfire n. 산불
stamp out (불을) 밟아 끄다
blaze n. 불꽃, 불, 불길
property n. 재산
paradoxically ad. 역설적이게도
megafire n. 큰불
clear out 제거하다
prime v. 뇌관[도화선]을 달다
if anything 어느 편이냐 하면; 오히려, 아무튼

01 ▶ 본문은 지금까지 모든 불을 꺼버리려고만 한 진압 정책이 서부 산림지대의 대화재를 낳은 잘못된 정책임을 지적한 글이다.

02 ▶ (C)는 이 글의 취지와 반대되는 내용이다.

03 ▶ 필자는 진압 정책을 대화재를 낳을 수 있는 잘못된 정책으로 개탄스러워한다.

》 정답　01 (A)　02 (C)　03 (B)

079

　　북아메리카 최초의 영국 식민지였던 버지니아는 1607년 제임스타운에 건설되었다. 영국에서 북미까지 바다로의 항해는 길고도 위험해서 식민지 지도자들은 부(富)에 대한 그릇된 약속으로 영국인들을 버지니아로 유혹했다.

　　처음 이주한 많은 사람들은 그들이 도착했을 때 실망했다. 그들은 부유해지지 못했고 또 많은 어려움에 직면했다. 땅은 너무 습했고 집에는 모기가 들끓었다. 식민지에 이주한 사람들은 유약한[무너지기 쉬운] 생활을 영위했다. 거친 날씨와 식량 부족은 식민지의 미래를 의심하게 하였다. 많은 사람들이 병, 굶주림, 추위로 고생했다. 첫 해 동안 당초 이주자의 절반이 죽었다.

　　새로운 이주자를 끌어 모으기 위해 버지니아 지도자들은 식민지에 살기 위해 오는 사람이라면 누구에게나 50에이커의 땅을 나눠주겠다고 약속했다. (자기) 땅을 얻을 희망에 부푼 수천 명의 영국인들이 1618년과 1622년 사이에 버지니아로 항해했다. 1619년에 버지니아는 자체 의회를 가지고 있었다. 담배는 중요한 산업이 되었다. 식민지가 늘어나면서 이주자들과 아메리카 원주민들은 사이에는 땅을 놓고 충돌이 벌어졌다. 1622년 아메리카 원주민들과 이주자들 사이에 전쟁이 일어났다. 1625년에 전쟁이 끝났다. 이주민들이 이겼고 버지니아 식민지는 존속되었다.

lure v. 유혹하다
face v. 직면하다
hardship n. 고난, 고초, 곤란
swampy a. 늪[수렁]의; 늪이 많은; 습지의
harsh a. 호된, 모진. 가혹한
suffer from ~로 고생하다; (병 따위를) 앓다
attract v. ~의 마음을 끌다
assembly n. 집회; 의회
break out (전쟁 등이) 일어나다

01 ▶ '유혹했다(lured)'로 미루어 약속은 부정적인 내용이 되어야 한다. 다음 단락의 내용으로 미루어 '그릇된, 현혹시키는(misleading)'이 적절하다.

02 ▶ 앞의 '습지가 많고 모기가 들끓었다'와 뒤의 '거친 날씨와 식량부족'으로 미루어 '생활은 아주 힘들었거나 불안했다.'고 해야 한다. '유약한, 무너지기 쉬운'의 뜻인 fragile이 가장 적절하다.

03 ▶ '새로운 이주자를 끌어 모으기 위해'로 미루어 '50에이커의 땅을 무상으로 나누어 준다'고 했을 것이다.

04 ▶ 이어지는 단락의 '식민지 이주민들과 아메리카 원주민들과의 전쟁'으로 미루어 conflicts가 적절하다.

》 정답 01 (B) 02 (A) 03 (D) 04 (C)

080

사람들을 당연시 여기는 것은 그들을 매우 언짢게 만든다. 누군가 때문에 녹초가 되거나 도움을 주기위해 열심히 일하거나 시간과 돈을 들이고도 아무런 감사의 표시도 받지 못한 적이 있는가? 그 대신에 당신이 특별히 기울인 노력이 당신이 단지 해야 하는 것인 마냥 취급되어지면서 말이다.

또 한 가지 화나게 하는 것은 네거티브 비판이다. 네거티브 비판이란 당신 자신이나 당신이 한 일에 대해 사실적이고 혹독한 진실의 말을 듣지만 당신이 개선한다거나 더 잘하게끔 하는 말은 듣지 못할 때를 말한다. 어떤 이가 "그 반대로 했을 때의 머리가 정말 훨씬 나았던 거 같아"라고 말한다면 그것이 네거티브 비판인 것이다. 당신 친구가 어떤 이야기를 썼는데 당신이 그에게 당신이 좋아하지 않은 것만 말하고 그 이야기에 대해 좋았던 것은 말하지 않을 때, 이것 또한 네거티브 비판이다.

당연시 여겨진다거나 부정적으로 비판을 받는 것은 당신으로 하여금 복수를 하고 싶게 한다. 그러나 복수하는 대신 그러한 태도를 바꿀 수 있다. 모든 사람에게 관심을 갖고 또 그 관심을 보여주는 사람이 되도록 노력하라. 태도를 바꾸어 당신과 의사소통 또는 교류하려는 사람들을 절대로 무시하지 마라. 그들이 이야기할 때 들어주고 그들이 말하는 것과 그들이 중요하다고 느끼게끔 하라.

take ~ for granted ~을 당연하게 여기다
knock out 지치게 하다
appreciation n. 감사, 존중
negative a. 부정적인; 소극적인
criticism n. 비평, 비판
take revenge 복수하다, 보복하다
interact v. 상호작용하다

01 ▶ 두 번째 문단을 참고하면 네거티브 비판은 '사실이지만 상대방의 부정적인 측면을 드러낸다'는 것으로 종합할 수 있다.

02 ▶ 세 번째 문단에서 당연시 여겨지거나 비판을 받으면 복수하고 싶다는 느낌이 들지만 태도를 바꾸어 먼저 상대방의 의견을 잘 들어 주라고 언급하였다.

03 ▶ 첫 문단에서 사람을 언짢게 만드는 것 중의 하나로 당연시 여기는 것을 설명하였다. 두 번째 문단은 당연시 여기는 것 외에 네거티브 비판을 또 다른 예로 설명하고 있으므로 turnoff를 '언짢게 하다'와 문맥을 이루는 의미로 보아야 할 것이다. (D) '반감을 일으키는 것'이 가장 적절하다.

》 정답 01 (D) 02 (B) 03 (D)

081

　　과거에는 많은 도움을 주었지만 지금은 발전을 방해하는 그런 습관이 누구에게나 있다. 그 습관이 술이나 마약은 아니겠지만 그럼에도 그것은 마찬가지로 하나의 중독이다. 일을 미루는 습관은 중독이며, 방어적인 태도를 취하는 것이나 실수에 대한 책임을 인정하지 않으려 하는 습관도 또한 중독이다.

　　내가 가진 중독에 해당하는 습관은 충돌을 피하는 것이었다. 나는 자라면서 사람들에게 그들이 원하는 것을 줄 줄 알게 되었는데, 그러면 나는 등을 토닥인다거나 좋은 성적을 받는다거나 팀의 주장이 된다거나 하는 식으로 보상을 받았다. 그러나 그 이면에 나는 내가 나 자신을 위해 무엇을 원하는지 물어볼 줄 몰랐다. 나는 친구에게 "나는 그러지 않았으면 좋겠어."라든가 직원에게 "존, 자네의 업무 수행이 마음에 안 들어."라고 말할 수 없었다.

　　이런 행동에 대한 진단을 내리고 난 후에야 나는 이런 행동을 바꾸는 데 도움을 줄 친구들과 지지자들을 모을 수 있었다. 그들은 나와 함께 내가 존에게 무슨 말을 어떻게 해야 할지를 연습하여 생산적이며 더욱 손쉬운 대화를 나누는 길을 열어주었다. 그 결과 존은 자신의 행동을 바꾸었고 팀의 보다 더 능률적인 일원이 되었다.

drag down 끌어내리다
procrastination n. 지연, 지체
pat n. 쓰다듬기, 토닥거리기
flip side 뒷면, 반대의 면
acceptable a. 기준에 맞는, 마음에 드는

01 ▶ 첫 단락은 중독에 대한 일반적인 내용이고 둘째, 셋째 단락은 필자와 관련한 구체적인 내용이므로 요지는 둘째, 셋째 단락에서 찾아야 하는데, 셋째 단락 첫 문장이 요지를 담은 주제문이다. 이 글은 addiction에 대한 글이므로 addiction이 반드시 main idea에 들어있어야 한다.

02 ▶ (A) being defensive에 해당하며 (B) give people what they want에 대한 보상이다. (C) 너무나 큰 addiction이다. (D) 직원에게 그 직원의 업무수행에 대한 평가의 말을 한다는 것은 상위자임을 나타낸다.

03 ▶ 자신의 addiction으로 보상을 받았지만 부정적인 면을 알고 나중에 바꾸었다는 것은 '후회하는, 유감으로 생각하는' 태도에 해당한다.

》 정답　01 (D)　02 (C)　03 (A)

082

　　요즘, 우리 아이들의 가장 친한 친구들은 유럽에 있거나 베일(Vail) 스키장에서 스키를 타고 있기 때문에 가끔 주변에 없다. 나의 아이들은 지난 3년 동안 파리에 두 번 다녀왔다. 모든 사람들의 자동차는 최신형이고 아무도 차 없이는 지내지 못한다. 많은 사람들이 점점 더해가는 풍요로움을 즐기고 있는 나라에서, 우리의 아이들이 세상에 대해 왜곡된 시각을 가지고 자라나고 있다는 우려가 있다. 이러한 기상천외한 경제 성장 속에서 우리는 아이들에게 삶이 언제나 안락하지만은 않을 것이라고 어떻게 가르쳐 줄 수 있을까? 어린이들이 상당한 부(富)에 둘러싸여 있는 경우, 그들은 심리적 감옥에 갇히게 되며, 그 결과 가치 있는 그 무엇도 얻을 수 없다. 풍요로움은 우리 모두가 마땅히 가져야 할 문제이지만, 지금 이것은 과유불급일지도 모른다. 가족을 부양할 수 있고, 돈이 인생을 충분히 즐길 수 있도록 더 많은 자유를 제공한다는 점은 대단하지만, 우리의 삶의 방식이 자녀들에게 목표를 가져다주는가 아니면 핑계를 가져다주는가? 어린이들은 그저 우리의 풍요로움에 합리적으로 반응하고 있다. 당신이 더 많이 돈을 받을수록, 그 수입을 놓치지 않기 위해 더 많이 일을 한다. 그러나 수입이 너무 많아지면, 당신은 그 높은 수입을 누리려고 한다. 보다 풍요로운 어린이들의 견지에서는 일을 하거나 돈을 벌 필요성을 덜 느끼는 것이다.

do without ~없이 지내다
affluence n. 풍부함; 풍요
surreal a. 초현실적인; 기상천외한
get stuck 꼼짝 못하게 되다
provide for ~을 부양하다
excuse n. 핑계, 변명
rationally ad. 합리적으로, 이성적으로
grab v. 움켜잡다; 놓치지 않다
in terms of ~말로; ~의하여; ~의 견지에서
reasoning power 추리력

01 ▶ twist v. 왜곡하다(= distort)
02 ▶ 점점 더해가는 풍요로움이 자칫 아이들에게 가져올 문제를 우려하고 있다. 풍요로움은 좋은 것이지만 너무 풍요로워지면 곤혹스러운 일이 될지도 모른다는 것이다. penny wise and pound foolish 소탐대실 (小貪大失, 적은 금액을 절약하려다 큰돈을 잃는다는 뜻) too much of a good thing 과유불급(過猶不及, 도가 지나쳐서 넌더리나는 것) a stitch in time saves nine 호미로 막을 데 가래로 막기 locking the stable door after the horse is stolen 소 잃고 외양간 고치기
03 ▶ 상당한 부에 둘러싸인 어린이들은 심리적 감옥에서 갇혀 가치 있는 것을 얻을 수 없고, 일을 하거나 돈을 벌 필요성을 느끼지 못한다고 언급하였다. (C) "부유한 어린이들은 (돈의) 가치 판단 능력을 잃기 쉽다"는 생각과 일맥상통한다.

》 정답 01 (D) 02 (B) 03 (C)

083

돌고래들이 쓰레기를 먹게 될 경우 치명적일 수 있기 때문에 마린 월드 아프리카(Marine World Africa USA)에 있는 돌고래들은 쓰레기를 가지고 와서 조련사에게 주면 그것에 상응하는 상을 받는 훈련을 받았다. 어느 날 대표 조련사는 업무를 마치고 보니 수조가 깨끗해 보이는데도 불구하고 돌고래가 계속해서 쓰레기 조각을 가지고 오는 것을 알아차렸다. 그 조련사는 동료에게 기사실로 내려가 조련사가 물 밖으로 나왔을 때 돌고래들이 무엇을 하는지 관찰해 볼 것을 부탁했다. 조련사가 물 밖으로 나오자, 아니나 다를까 돌고래가 쓰레기 조각을 가지고 재빨리 나타나 그에 대한 상을 얻었다. 속임수가 밝혀졌다. 이 돌고래는 뭘까 '예금 계좌' 같은 것을 가지고 있었던 것이다. 그 돌고래는 쓰레기를 모두 모아서 여과 장치의 흡입구 부근의 탱크 모서리에 걸려 있던 가방에 쓰레기를 채워놨었다. 놀라운 것은 돌고래가 그 '은행'에 가서 단순히 쓰레기 조각을 가지고 온 것이 아니라 보상을 극대화하기 위해 쓰레기를 찢곤 했다는 것이다. 이러한 행동은 그 돌고래가 미래와 만족지연에 대해 이해를 했다는 것을 보여주기 때문에 특히 더 흥미롭다. 그 돌고래는 큰 쓰레기 조각이 작은 조각과 똑같은 보상을 얻는다는 것을 깨달았을 정도로 침착했으니 추가적으로 먹을 것이 계속 생기도록 작은 쓰레기 조각들만 나르면 되지 않겠는가? 그 돌고래는 사실상 인간들을 훈련시켰던 것이다.

ingest v. 섭취하다
retrieve v. 찾아 가지고 오다
reinforcement n. 보강, 강화; 상을 주는 학습
reward n. 보수, 포상; 보답
routine n. 판에 박힌 일, 일상의 과정
scam n. 사기
stuff v. 채우다
wedge vt. 끼어들게 하다; 밀어 넣다
intake n. (물·공기·연료 따위를) 받아들이는 입구[주둥이]
filter v. 거르다; 여과하다
delayed gratification 만족 지연
in effect 사실상
a cut above ~보다 한 수 위인

01 ▶ 본문은 보상의 극대화를 위해 쓰레기 조각을 모아두고 쓰레기 조각을 찢는 등의 행동을 한 돌고래의 지능에 관한 에피소드다.
02 ▶ 쓰레기 조각의 크기와 상관없이 똑같은 보상이 이루어지는 것을 알아내어 먹이가 계속 생길 수 있도록 하였다는 것이므로, 보상으로 제공되는 먹이를 '극대화'하고자 큰 조각을 작은 조각으로 찢는다는 것을 알 수 있다.
03 ▶ 훈련을 받은 경험에 따라 돌고래의 학습 능력이 어떻게 달라질 수 있는지는 전혀 다루어지지 않았다.
04 ▶ 인간이 미처 생각하지 못한 사이 돌고래는 훈련을 이용하고 있었다는 것을 의미한다. 즉, "돌고래가 조련사보다 한 수 위였다"와 일맥상통한다.

》 정답 01 (A) 02 (C) 03 (B) 04 (B)

084
　　'사커 대 풋볼' 논쟁은 한 세기에 걸친 불평의 표출이다. '사커'는 영국에서 유래한 영국 상류층에서 쓰는 속어이며 공식 용어인 'association football'의 줄임말이다. 1905년에 화가 난 한 독자는 뉴욕타임즈가 경기를 보도할 때 사커라는 '품위 없는' 용어를 사용했다고 항의했다. 그 독자는 "이런 이단이 확산되지 않기를 바란다."고 썼다. 그러나 미국에 수입된 외국 스포츠인 축구와 이미 자리를 잡고 있던 미국적인 미식축구 경기를 구분하기 위해 사커란 단어가 필요했다. 미국인들이 사커란 단어의 사용을 중단해야 한다고 주장하는 것은 (영국에서 휘발유를 의미하는) 페트롤이란 말 대신 미국에서 쓰는 개솔린이란 말의 사용을 중단해야 한다고 주장하는 것이나 마찬가지이거나 혹은 의회를 (영국처럼) 팔러먼트라고 부르고 미터법을 도입하라고 주장하는 것이나 같다. 이런 용어 변경은 무의미할 뿐만 아니라 부담스럽고 문화적으로 비겁한 짓이다. 미국을 맹렬히 비난하는 일부 사람들은, 미국인들의 축구에 대한 열성 부족을 인종주의 탓으로 돌린다. 그러나 축구장의 훌리건 방식의 비난과 반대로, 평균적인 미식 축구팀의 인종 구성은 거의 모든 비교 대상 축구팀보다 다양하다.

gripe n. 불만, 불평
contraction n. 수축, 수렴; 단축, 단축어
indignant a. 분개한, 성난
undignified a. 품위 없는
burdensome a. 무거운 짐이 되는, 번거로운
heresy n. 이교, 이단; 이설
basher n. 맹렬히 비난하는 사람
sniping n. (익명의) 비난, 공격

01 ▶ chalk A up to B는 'A를 B의 탓으로 하다'는 의미이다. consign A to B는 'A를 B에게 위탁하다'는 뜻이다.
02 ▶ ④의 adopting은 should stop~, or have~, or adopt~의 병렬구조에 맞게 동사원형으로 고쳐주어야 한다.
03 ▶ 기존 미식축구와의 구별을 위해 soccer라는 단어의 사용이 필요했다고 언급하고 있다.

》 정답 01 (C) 02 (D) 03 (C)

085
　　오늘날, 서구문명은 미국이나 유럽의 정치적·지적 담화에서 장려되기는커녕 거의 언급조차 되지 않는다. 서구 엘리트들이 서구문명에 관해 언급할 때, 언제나 서구 전통은 비판 혹은 경멸의 대상이 되고 있다. 오히려, 서구문명에 대한 실질적인 논의는 보통 비서구권의 — 특히 이슬람사회의 — 정치, 지식, 종교 지도자들이 떠맡는다. 사실상 서구라는 개념은 우리 문명의 현존하는 주요한 적대세력인 이슬람 근본주의자들의 과격한 정신 속에서 가장 커다란 비난을 받는 대상이 된 것 같다. 서구에 대한 가장 생생한 인식이 동방에서 발견되는 것처럼 보인다. 그러나 서구(다시 말해 미국, 유럽, 캐나다, 호주, 뉴질랜드 등)안에서는 50여 년 전의 서구문명은 이제 잃어버린 문명같이 비춰지고 있다. 한 거대한 문명 안에서 벌어지고 있는 이 거대한 변화는 무엇을 말하는가? 서구의 전통 가운데 아직도 살아있는 실체는 어떤 것이 있는가? 그리고 앞으로 이러한 서구전통의 운명은 어찌될 것인가?

discourse n. 담화, 토론; 강연
contempt n. 경멸
undertake v. (책임을) 떠맡다
be charged with ~라고 비난받다
all the more 그만큼 더
laud v. 칭송[찬미]하다
languid a. 흥미 없는, 활기 없는
egalitarianism n. 평등주의
reconciliation n. 화해

01 ▶ '~는 고사하고 ~조차 …않다'일 때, still less나 much less를 사용한다.
02 ▶ 서구 사회 내에서 서구문명에 대한 논의는 시들해지고 오히려 서구 사회를 적대적으로 보는 이슬람 근본주의자들의 서구사회에 대한 논의[비판]가 활발하다고 하였다.
03 ▶ 글 후반부에 "지금도 살아 있는 실체로서의 서구의 전통이 무엇인가?"라고 물었으므로 현대 문명의 근간이 되고 있는 주요 서구전통의 원리들이 제시될 것이라고 볼 수 있다.

》 정답 01 (A) 02 (D) 03 (B)

아랍 세계의 정치적, 경제적 불안은 최근 몇 주 동안 미국의 유가를 마구 치솟도록 했으며 몇몇 의원들은 (벌써) 미국의 전략 비축유를 활용할 준비가 되어있다.

전략비축유는 다른 시대의 에너지 위기 이후 형성되었다. 1973년 10월, 아랍 석유 수출국 기구(OAPEC)는 미국의 이스라엘군 지원에 대한 대응으로 욤 키푸르 전쟁(제4차 중동 전쟁) 동안 원유 공급을 중단했다. 다음해 3월까지 계속된 원유 금수조치는 세계적인 에너지 그리고 경제적 위기를 유발했다. 그러한 사태가 다시 일어나는 것을 예방하기 위해, 1975년 미국 정부는 전략비축유(SPR)를 만들었다. 여러 다른 국가들 또한 전략비축유를 만들었지만 미국의 비축량이 과거에도 그랬고 지금도 여전히 가장 크다.

3월 7일로 전략비축유는 미(美) 멕시코만 연안을 따라 4개의 안전한 장소의 지하 동굴에 저장된 7억 2650만 배럴의 원유를 보유하고 있다. 가장 큰 전략비축유 부지는 텍사스 주(州) 프리포트 근처의 브라이언 마운드이다. 그곳에는 2억 5400만 배럴이 수천 피트 지하의 암염(岩塩) 돔 아래 구멍이 뚫어진 20개의 인공 동굴을 가득 채우고 있다. 다른 3개의 비축유 부지는 텍사스의 빅힐(Big Hill), LA의 웨스트 핵베리(Hackberry), LA의 바이유 촉토(Bayou Chocktaw) 등이다.

skyrocketing a. 마구 치솟는
tap into ~에게 접근하다; ~을 이용하다
reserve n. 비축, 예비; 예비품
era n. 시대, 시기
shut off 끄다, 잠그다; 세우다
embargo n. 금수(禁輸) 조치, 통상 금지령
stockpile n. 비축량
secure a. 안전한, 보안이 철저한
cavern n. 동굴
hollow v. 후벼(파)내다, 도려내어 구멍을 뚫다(out)
alliance n. 동맹

01 ▶ 유가 상승의 원인으로 빈칸에는 부정적 의미의 단어가 필요하다. 따라서 (A)와 (B)는 정답이 될 수 없으며 포괄적 의미의 불안한 상태를 뜻하는 (D)의 unrest가 정답으로 적절하다.

02 ▶ SPR의 설립배경과 그것이 무엇인지에 대해 구체적으로 설명하고 있으므로 (A)가 정답이다. 미국의 원유 과소비나 에너지 고갈문제에 대한 언급은 없었다.

03 ▶ 두 번째 단락에서 원유공급의 중단으로 세계의 경제가 위기에 처했다고 했으므로 (A)의 1973년 석유위기로 세계경제가 상호의존적인 것으로 판명되었다고 유추할 수 있다. 마지막 단락의 비축유 부지에 대한 설명을 통해 (B) 역시 추론가능하다. 반면 미래의 잠재적 원유 공급 중단에 대비하기 위해 많은 다른 나라들도 비축유를 확보하고 있다 했을 뿐 (C) 아랍-이스라엘의 갈등 해결을 위한 세계적 노력이 이루어질 것이라고는 추측하기 어렵다.

》 정답 01 (D) 02 (A) 03 (C)

087

때때로 누군가가 출산, 결혼, 또는 다른 이유로 미국과 다른 나라의 국민 둘 다가 되기를 원할지도 모른다. 미국이 이것을 허락하는 지의 여부는 그 사람이 어떻게 양국의 국민이 되려고 하는가에 달려 있다.

만일, 미국 시민이 결혼이나 출산 때문에 다른 나라의 국적을 취득한다면, 미국은 양국의 국적을 허락해준다. 만일 다른 나라 시민의 아이가 미국에서 태어난다면, 미국 수정헌법 제14조에 따라 다른 나라의 국적을 포기하지 않고 자동으로 (미국의) 국적을 얻게 된다.

미국 정부는 고의로 다른 나라에 충성을 맹세할 경우 그 사람의 미국 국적을 취소할 것이다. 고의로 충성을 맹세하는 것에는 시민권 선서와 같은 말이나 행동이 해당된다. 미국과 싸우고 있는 외국의 군대에 입대할 경우 미국의 국적 상실로 이어질 수 있다.

이중국적자가 되는 것은 미국 정부에 의해 용인되긴 하나, 이중국적자가 일으키는 문제 때문에 장려되지는 않는다. 이중국적자들은 그들이 국민인 두 나라의 법을 준수하기로 되어 있어서 이들 양국의 법은 서로 충돌할 수도 있다.

by way of ~을 지나서, ~하기 위해
nationality n. 국적
the Amendment 미국 헌법 수정 조항
constitution n. 헌법
grant v. 허락하다, 인정하다
citizenship n. 국적, 시민권
revoke v. 취소하다
purposely ad. 고의로
pledge v. 서약하다
allegiance n. 충성
i.e. ad. 바꿔 말하면
take an oath 선서하다
dual citizen 이중국적자
espionage n. 스파이 활동
obey v. 복종하다, 따르다
conflict v. 충돌하다

01 ▶ 이 글은 어떤 경우에 미국이 이중국적을 허용하는지, 그리고 허용했던 이중국적을 어떤 경우에 박탈하는지에 관한 내용이다. 따라서 "미국은 이중국적을 허용하는가?"가 글의 주제로 적절하다.

02 ▶ (A) 미국 수정헌법에 따라 미국에서 태어나는 아기는 자동으로 미국국적을 가진다고 했다. (B) 이중국적이 양국 간의 마찰을 일으킬 수 있으므로 권장하지 않는다고 했을 뿐, 양국의 법을 준수할 경우 문제가 되지 않는다. (C) 미국 국민이 결혼 때문에 다른 나라의 국적을 취득할 경우 미국은 양국의 국적을 인정한다고 했다. (D) 이중 국적자가 고의로 다른 나라에 충성할 경우 미국 국적을 취소한다고 했으므로 (D)가 미국정부가 이중국적을 허락하지 않는 경우이다.

03 ▶ ①, ②, ④는 모두 미국과 비교되는 '막연한 다른 대상'을 가리키므로 옳게 쓰인 반면, ③은 본문에서 "다른 나라 국민의 아이가 미국에서 태어날 경우 그 나라의 국적을 포기하지 않고 미국 국적을 취득한다"고 했으므로 another는 '막연한' 대상이 아니라 '특정 국가'의 국민이 되므로 ③의 another를 두 국가 중 미국이 아닌 다른 국가를 지칭하는 the other로 고쳐야 한다.

» 정답 01 (C) 02 (D) 03 (C)

088

회사가 정리해고에 관해 예고한 이후 직원들의 사기는 급속히 저하된다. 비록 인력감축이 한동안은 일어나지 않을지라도 말이다.

뱅크오브아메리카나 다른 금융회사들이 최근에 실시한 것처럼, '인원수를 줄이겠다'는 계획을 발표하는 것만으로도 직원들의 마음을 혼란스럽게 할 수 있고, 직원들을 신규모집하려는 노력에 타격을 줄 수 있으며, 최고의 성과를 내고 있는 직원들이 회사를 떠나도록 부추길 수 있다.

뱅크오브아메리카 최고경영자인 브라이언 모이니헌(Brian Moynihan)은 지난주에 사내 메일로 직원들에게 전체 직원 수가 향후 수년 동안 3만 명 줄어들 것이라고 말했다.

뱅크오브아메리카의 한 선임 연구원에 따르면, 대량해고에 대한 소문이 수개월 동안 직원들 사이에 번져나갔다고 한다. "많은 사람들이 앞으로 무슨 일이 일어날지 정말로 두려워합니다. 제가 아는 사람 중에 다른 직장을 찾지 않는 사람들은 한명도 없습니다."라고 선임연구원이 말했다.

관리자들은 직원들을 안심시키려고 짧은 편지를 보내려고 애써왔으나, 관리자들은 자신의 일자리에 대해 안전부절 못하는 것처럼 보인다고 그 선임연구원은 말했다. "향후 수년 동안 3만 명이 될 것이라는 말이 있습니다. 이 말은 향후 수년 동안 우리의 번호표가 불리기를 기다려만 한다는 의미입니까?" 뱅크오브아메리카 대변인은 이에 대해 언급을 회피했다.

demoralize v. 사기를 저하시키다
layoff n. (일시적인) 해고
intent n. 의향, 목적, 의지
distract v. (마음·주의 등을) 산만하게 하다
prompt v. 자극하다, 격려하다, 고무하다
rip through 휩쓸고 지나가다
rank n. 사원
reassure v. 안심시키다
spokesman n. 대변인; 대표자

01 ▶ (A) 인원감축을 예고했을 뿐 아직 실시하지 않았으며, 금융업계에 영향을 주었다는 말은 본문에 언급되지 않았다. (C) 일부 회사들이 해고를 발표한 후 실행에 옮기지 않았다는 말은 본문에 언급되지 않았다. (D) 해고를 하겠다는 암시만으로 직원들의 사기가 급속히 저하된다고 했다. (B) 대규모로 인원감축을 하겠다는 발표 이후, 직원들을 안심시키려는 간부들조차 그들의 자리에 안절부절못한다고 했다. 따라서 대규모 해고는 일반 직원들뿐 아니라 관리자들까지 떨게 만들고 있다는 (B)가 정답이다.

02 ▶ 밑줄 친 문장은 "제가 아는 사람 중에 다른 직장을 찾지 않는 사람은 한명도 없습니다"는 의미이므로 "내가 알기로는, 모든 사람들이 다른 직장을 찾고 있다"라는 (C)가 정답이다.

03 ▶ 회사의 대변인이 언급을 회피한 이유는 해고에 관한 민감한 문제를 언급하면 자칫 회사에 불리하게 작용할 수 있기 때문이다.

》 정답 01 (B) 02 (C) 03 (D)

089

마지막으로 회사에서 가식적인 미소를 지은 적이 언제였는가? 몇몇 사람들에게는 내면의 불행을 감추기 위해 결의에 찬 표정을 짓는 것이 단지 직장생활의 또 다른 일상적인 양상일지도 모른다. 그러나 새로운 연구는 그것이 기분을 악화시키고 당장의 일에서 움츠러들게 하는 예상치 못한 결과를 가져올 수 있다고 제시한다. 경영학회저널에 이번 달에 발표한 연구에서, 과학자들은 한 무리의 버스 운전기사들을 2주 동안 따라다니며 그들에게 주의를 집중시켰다. 그들의 직업이 많은 사람들과 자주 일반적으로 공손한 상호관계를 필요로 하기 때문이다. 과학자들은 운전기사들이 '표면 연기'라고 알려진 가식적인 미소를 지을 때와 그것과 반대로 그들이 긍정적인 생각으로 진짜 미소를 만들어 내는 '깊은 연기'를 보일 때 어떤 일이 일어나는지 조사했다. 그 운전기사들을 가까이 따라다닌 후에 조사원들은 강제로 미소를 지은 날에는 피실험자들의 기분이 더 나빠지고 일에서 움츠러드는 경향이 있었다는 것을 알아냈다. 부정적인 생각들을 억누르려고 애쓰는 것이 그 생각들을 훨씬 더 지속되게 했을지도 모른다고 밝혀졌다. 그러나 피실험자들이 실제로 기쁜 생각과 기억을 함양하면서 깊숙한 내면의 노력에서 미소를 내보이려고 노력했던 날에는 그들의 전체적인 기분이 향상했고 생산성이 증가했다.

flash v. (시선·미소 등을) 흘낏 보내다
mundane a. 재미없는, 일상적인
game-face n. (운동선수의) 결의에 찬, 단호한 표정
subject n. 피실험자
deteriorate v. 악화되다, 더 나빠지다
persistent a. 끊임없이 지속[반복]되는
cultivate v. 양성[연마]하다; [품성]을 도야하다, 기르다
wry a. 얼굴을 찌푸린
feigned a. 거짓의; 꾸민
constrained a. 강제적인, 강요된

01 ▶ 운전기사들이 '표면 연기'라고 알려진 가식적인 미소를 지을 때와 반대라고 했으므로 그들이 긍정적인 생각으로 '깊은 연기'를 보일 때는 '진짜(authentic)' 미소를 만들어 낼 것이다.

02 ▶ 본문은 내면의 불행을 감추기 위해 가식적인 미소를 지으면 기분이 오히려 더 나빠지고 일에서 움츠러드는 경향이 나타난다는 사실을 주제로 다루고 있다.

03 ▶ 여성들이 남성들에 비해 더 감정적으로 표현이 풍부하다는 언급은 본문에 없다.

▶ 정답 01 (B) 02 (C) 03 (B)

090

오랜 습관에도 불구하고 작가의 지각력이 무뎌지지 않고 여전히 날카롭게 살아있는 한, 작가의 본능에는 작가를 당황케 하는 어떤 것이 있어서 이것이 작가로 하여금 인간 본성의 특이한 점들에 관심을 갖게 하는데 이 관심은 너무나 흡인력이 강해서 작가의 도덕의식을 무력케 한다. 작가는 악을 생각하는데서 예술적 만족을 진심으로 느끼고 약간 놀란다. 그러나 그는 정직하다보니 (작중인물의) 어떤 (악한) 행동에 대해 느끼는 반감보다는 그런 행동의 이유에 대한 호기심이 더 크다는 것을 솔직히 고백하지 않을 수 없다. 악한 인물의 성격, 즉 논리적이고 완벽하다는 것이 그 인물을 탄생시킨 작가를 만족시키는 점을 갖고 있다. 그러나 이 만족이 법과 질서에는 위배되는 것이다. 나는 셰익스피어가 자신의 공상으로 달빛을 짜며 데스데모나(선인)를 상상했을 때는 결코 알지 못했을 그런 기쁨으로 이아고(악인)를 만들었을 것이라고 생각한다. 작가는 작품 속의 악한 인물에서 자신 속에 뿌리 깊은 본능들을 만족시키는데 이 본능들이 문명 세계의 예절과 관습으로 인해 어쩔 수 없이 불가사이하게 잠재의식으로 물러나버린 것인지도 모른다.

singularity n. 기이한 점, 특이한 점
scoundrel n. 악당
outrage n. 침범, 위반, 폭행
gusto n. 기쁨, 활력
rogue n. 악당
gratify v. 만족시키다, 기쁘게 하다

01 ▶ 둘째 문장 전반부와 셋째 문장, 그리고 마지막 문장 전반부 등에 주제가 나타나있다.

02 ▶ disconcerting은 본문에서 '당황케 하는'이라는 뜻으로 쓰였으므로, (A)의 embarrassing이 정답이다.

》 정답 01 (A) 02 (A)

091

　　무역장벽을 지지하는 가장 중요한 주장들 중 하나는 주로 국방과 관련된 것이다. 보호무역주의자들은 무역장벽이 없으면 국가는 너무 전문화되어서 결국 다른 국가에 지나치게 의존하게 될 것이라고 주장한다. 그 결과, 국가는 전시에 식량, 석유, 무기와 같은 중대한 물자를 손에 넣을 수 없게 될지도 모른다. 이스라엘과 남아프리카 공화국과 같은 국가의 정부는 그러한 위기에 대비해 대규모 군수산업을 발달시켰다. 그들은 전쟁이 발발하거나 다른 국가가 경제봉쇄를 가해올 경우 확실히 자국 내에서 물자를 조달할 수 있게 되기를 원한다. 자유무역주의자들은 국가안보가 무역장벽을 지지해야 할 강력한 논거라는 점을 인정한다. 그러나 그들은 국내에 믿을만한 물자 공급원을 확보하는 것은 물자 공급이 자유무역의 경우보다 더 적어질 것이고 더 비능률적으로 될 수도 있다는 현실에 견주어 신중히 결정되어야 한다고 믿는다.

trade barrier 무역장벽
specialized a. 전문화된
armament industry 군수산업
hostilities n. (전쟁에서의) 전투, 교전
break out (전쟁 등이) 발발하다
boycott n. 보이콧, 불매운동, 배척, 봉쇄
national security 국가안보
compelling a. 강제적인; 강력한

01 ▶ 무역장벽이 없는 자유경쟁 세계시장에서는 한 국가가 비교우위에 있는 상품만을 생산하고 다른 상품은 수입하게 되는데, 이렇게 되면 그 수입하는 상품에 대해서는 다른 국가에 의존하게 된다. 의존성이 너무 크다고 해야 상대국이 수출금지 조치를 내릴 경우 일어나는 문제를 설명한 그 다음 문장과 잘 연결된다.

02 ▶ 보호무역주의자들은 국방과 관련하여 무역장벽을 지지하며, 국가안보가 위태로울 때 무역장벽이 필요할 수 있다는 것은 자유무역주의자들도 인정하고 있다.

》 정답 01 (C) 02 (B)

092

　　인생의 경험을 대부분 쌓았을 때의 독서는 아직 인생의 파종기에 있었을 때의 독서와 많이 다르다는 생각이 종종 든다. 아주 젊을 때의 독서는, 이를테면, 바싹 마른 처녀지에 물을 계속 붓는 것이다. 토양은 때로는 오래오래 영원한 기쁨에 젖어, 때로는 공정하고 고요한 무관심 속에서, 끝없이 쉬지 않고, 그러나 결코 불협화음을 내지 않고 그 물을 끝없이 마실 수 있는 것 같다. 그러나 나이가 들어버렸을 때 독서는 아주 다른 문제이다. 바싹 마른 평원은 울창한 숲이 되었고 그 안에는 호수와 개울이 있다. 숲으로 들어오는 모든 이미지는 호수와 개울 깊은 곳에 쌓여있는 과거의 광경들을 불러내고, 모든 음조들이 잊을 수 없는 너무나 많은 추억의 음악으로 나무들 사이에서 울려 퍼지면 그 추억의 무게로 정신을 잃을 지경이 된다. 그래서 이제 나는 책을 펼치면 (많은 페이지를 읽지 않고) 펼친 페이지 그대로인 채로도 만족스럽게 책을 내려놓는 일이 자주 있다.

garner v. 모으다, 축적하다
parched a. 바싹 마른
virginal a. 처녀의
rapture n. 기쁨, 환희
unpausingly ad. 중단 없이, 쉬지 않고
luxuriant a. 번성한, 울창한
evoke v. 불러일으키다, 불러내다
rustle v. 바스락거리다, 활발히 움직이다
haunting a. 자주 마음속에 떠오르는, 잊혀지지 않는

01 ▶ 바로 앞 문장의 every image which enters it과 every tone은 지금 책을 읽으면서 접하게 된 내용인데, 이것이 너무나 많은 과거의 경험들(ancient visions와 a music so rich in haunting memories)을 마음속에 불러일으키므로 한 페이지만 읽어도 감흥에 젖어 만족한다는 뜻이다.

02 ▶ 바싹 마른 처녀지는 쌓인 경험이 없어 비어있으며 읽는 모든 것을 받아들일 준비가 되어 있는 젊은이의 정신을 비유적으로 가리킨다.

》 정답 01 (D) 02 (C)

093

　　합의된 기호의 집합이라는 점은 언어의 한 가지 특징에 불과하다. 모든 언어는 문법 체계 속에서 이런 기호 사이의 구조적 관계를 정의해야 한다. 문법 규칙은 언어를 다른 형태의 의사소통과 구분하는 것이다. 문법 규칙은 유한한 일련의 기호들이 조작되어 잠재적으로 무한한 수의 문법에 맞는 발화들이 만들어질 수 있도록 해준다.

　　언어의 또 다른 속성은 그 기호가 임의적이라는 것이다. 어떠한 개념이나 문법 규칙도 기호에 일치시킬 수 있다. 대부분의 언어가 소리를 이용하지만 그 사용되는 소리의 조합은 내재적인 의미를 갖지 않고, 단지 언어의 사용자에 의해 뭔가를 나타내기로 합의된 관례일 뿐이다. 예를 들면, 스페인 단어 'nada' 그 자체에는 스페인어 사용자에게 '아무것도 아님'을 의미하도록 강요하는 것이 전혀 없다. 이와 다른 소리의 집합(예를 들면, 영어 단어인 nothing)도 같은 개념을 나타내기 위해 똑같이 사용될 수 있겠지만, 모든 스페인어 사용자들은 이 의미를 이 특별한 소리 형태와 관련짓는 것을 습득하고 배웠다. 다른 한편, 슬로베니아인, 크로아티아인, 세르비아/코소보인 혹은 보스니아인들에게는 'nada'가 '희망'을 의미한다.

finite a. 한정된
manipulate v. 조작하다, 조종하다
make use of 이용하다
combination n. 조합
convention n. 관례, 관습
convey v. (의미, 생각 등을) 전달하다

01 ▶ 두 번째 문장에서 언어가 다른 의사소통과 구분되는 것은 바로 '문법 규칙'이라고 했다.

02 ▶ 빈칸 뒤의 내용으로 볼 때 내재하는 것이 없고 단지 합의의 의미라고 했으므로 임의성을 뜻하는 (D)가 답이다.

》 정답 01 (C) 02 (D)

094

　　2020년 6월에 나는 상부 호흡기 감염증을 앓았다. 처음에 나는 "별일 아냐"라고 생각했다. 하지만 코 막힘이 가라앉은 뒤에도 거의 1년 동안이나 나는 후각을 잃었다. 그 영향은 막대했다. 하루는 난로 불을 제대로 끄지 못했는데, 나는 가스가 새는 냄새를 맡지 못했다.(다행히도 4시간 30분 후에 잠깐 들렀던 내 아들이 그 냄새를 눈치 챘다.) 나는 썩거나 고약한 냄새를 판별해내는 나의 능력을 더 이상 믿을 수 없었으므로 남은 밥을 보관하는 일을 그만두었다. 향이 없는 음식은 덤덤하고 맛없는 덩어리가 되었고 내 인생도 그것과 마찬가지로 단조롭게 느껴졌다. 나는 커피를 끓이는 향, 갓 베어낸 풀, 또는 갓난아기인 손자의 달콤한 향기도 누릴 수가 없었다. 나의 사교적인 생활조차 타격을 입었다. 나는 친구들을 저녁식사에 초대하는 일을 그만두었는데, 그 이유는 내 멕시코풍 요리가 맛있는지 아니면 먹을 수 없는 건지 판단할 방법이 없었기 때문이었다. 우리는 혀가 아닌 코로 대부분의 음식 맛을 지각(知覺)하므로 그건 플라스틱 음식을 가지고 요리를 하는 거나 다름없었다. 내 코를 치료하기 위해 무슨 수를 써야 한다는 것이 분명했다.

upper-respiratory infection 상부 호흡기 감염증
no big deal 별일 아니다
the sniffles 코 막힘, 코감기
subside v. 가라앉다, 잠잠해지다
fume n. 증기, 가스; 향기
leftover n. 나머지; 남은 밥
rancid a. 고약한 냄새가 나는
monotonous a. 단조로운
scent n. 냄새, 향기
brewing n. 양조(업), 양조량
new-mown a. (목초 따위를) 갓 벤
gauge v. 재다, 측정하다
inedible a. 식용에 적합지 않는, 못 먹는
sniffer n. 냄새 맡는 사람; 코

01 ▶ 호흡기 질환을 앓은 후에 1년 동안 냄새를 맡을 수 없어 고생했다고 말하면서 그 때문에 벌어진 몇 가지 해프닝을 제시하고 있다. 본문 여섯 번째 문장의 I couldn't smell을 참고하여 (D) "나는 후각을 잃었다"가 정답임을 알 수 있다.

02 ▶ 친구들을 더 이상 식사에 초대할 수 없었다고 했으므로, 사교적인 관계가 '타격을 입었음(took a hit)'을 알 수 있다.

03 ▶ 마지막 문장에서 something must be done to cure my sniffer라고 했으므로 증상을 완화하기 위한 방법을 찾는다는 (E)가 가장 적절하다. (C)의 경우, 코가 막히는 현상은 이미 가라앉았기 때문에 답이 될 수 없다. (D)는 정형외과 수술이므로 부적절하다.

≫ 정답 01 (D) 02 (B) 03 (E)

지난 10년 동안 미디어는 테러리스트의 공격, 죽음, 그리고 고문에 관한 뉴스로 넘쳐흘렀다. 전에도 그랬지만 지금은 미국의 해외 주둔이 매우 주목을 받고 있기 때문에 점점 더 많은 미국인들이 세계 뉴스를 매일 읽는다. 나는 확신하건대 국제적인 사건을 쫓는 이런 사람들에게 있어 사망자수는 100명 가까이 되거나 그 이상 되지 않는 한 놀라운 일이 아닐 것이다. 그러나 그 수들은 죽은 사람들이 미국인이거나 혹은 미국에서 일어난 비극적인 사건일 경우에는 가슴을 아프게 한다. 하지만 만약 방글라데시에서 21명이 폭발사고로 죽었다면 사람들은 이제 가족을 잃은 사람들보다는 누구에게 책임이 있는지에 대해 더 신경 쓰는 경향이 있다.

현재 나는 점점 더 많은 세계 뉴스를 읽을수록 이러한 사망자수에 대해 <영향 받기 쉬운> 나 자신을 발견한다. 예를 들어, 내가 52명의 소말리인이 최근에 밀입국을 시도하다 죽었다는 기사를 읽었을 때 나는 52명의 죽은 사람들보다는 밀입국 부분에 더 관심이 있었다. 52명과 현실성은 단절되어 있으며 내게 그 숫자는 단지 숫자일 뿐이다. 사람들이 죽었지만 나는 그들의 이름도, 얼굴도, 그들에 대해서는 아무것도 모른다. 내가 통제할 수 없는 무엇인가가 52명에게 일어난 것이다.

be flooded with ~로 넘쳐나다
torture n. 고문
presence n. 존재; (군대 등의) 주둔
prominent a. 눈에 잘 띄는, 두드러진
on a daily basis 매일
death toll 사망자수
staggering a. 어마어마한; 경이적인
blast n. 폭발
smuggle v. 밀수입[밀입국]하다
disconnection n. 단절
embassy n. 대사관
diplomat n. 외교관
ignominious a. 수치스러운, 창피한

01 ▶ 사망자수에 대한 사람들의 무감각을 언급한 뒤, 첫 문단 네 번째 문장에서 미국인들이 죽었을 경우나, 그 비극이 미국에서 발생한 경우에 한하여 사람들의 마음을 아프게 한다고(do hurt) 서술하였다. 따라서 '수백 명의 자국민의 사고'가 미국인들을 슬프게 만든다는 것을 알 수 있다.

02 ▶ ⓑ 뒤의 문장에서 예로 든 상황을 보면, 필자는 자신이 죽은 사람들에 대해 아는 것이 없으며 사망자수는 단지 숫자에 불과하다고 언급하고 있다. 따라서 사망자수에 대해 '정(情)에 무른', 혹은 '영향 받기 쉬운' 것이 아니라 '면역이 된' 상태라는 것을 알 수 있다. 따라서 ⓑ를 immune으로 고친다.

03 ▶ 첫 문단에서 미디어가 세계의 여러 끔찍한 상황을 보도하고 있지만 사람들은 별다른 감정을 느끼지 못한다는 점을 역설하고 있다. 이어서 미국인들이 죽었거나 미국에서 발생한 비극에 대해서는 마음 아파한다고 했는데, 필자도 일반적인 미국인들과 같은 태도이므로 미국 밖에서 일어난 비극에 대해서는 '냉담한, 무관심한' 태도가 정답이다.

》 정답   01 (C)   02 (C)   03 (B)

작은 무인 수송기구가 군대 수송대 앞에서 길을 인도한다. 갑자기 이 수송기구는 가던 길을 멈추고 수송대 지휘관에게 경고를 전달한다. 치명적인 사제폭발물, 즉 IED가 이 무인 기구에 탑재된 마이크로칩들에 살아있는 후각세포들을 심는 정교한 생물학적 칩 기술에 의해 탐지되었다. 그 사제폭발물은 안전하게 제거되고 생명을 구하게 된다.

공학의 여러 분야에 걸쳐서 협력하여 첨단의 '세포에 기초한 칩 센서' 기술을 가능하게 만들고 있는 메릴랜드(Maryland) 대학 제임스 클락(James Clark) 공대의 세 명의 교수 연구진의 업적에 힘입어, 이러한 시나리오가 현실이 될 것 같다. 전기 컴퓨터 공학부 교수인 동시에 시스템 리서치 연구소(ISR)에서 일하고 있는 파멜라 앱셔(Pamela Abshire), 우주공학부 교수이며 역시 ISR에서 연구하고 있는 벤자민 샤피로(Benjamin Shapiro), 그리고 기계공학부와 전기 컴퓨터 공학부의 엘리자베스 스멜라(Elisabeth Smela), 이 세 사람은 생물세포의 감각능력을 이용하는 새로운 센서들에 대해서 연구하고 있다.

몇 밀리미터의 크기에 불과한 이러한 작은 장치들은 폭발물에서 생물학적 병원체나 상한 식품 또는 깨끗하지 못한 물까지 모든 것에 대한 탐지력을 가속시키며 향상시킬 수 있을 것이다.

unmanned a. 무인의
convoy n. 수송대, 호위대
improvised explosive device(IED) 사제폭탄
incorporating a. 통합하는
olfactory a. 후각의
mounted a. 탑재된, 장착된
dismantle v. 제거하다, 분해하다
faculty n. 교수진
discipline n. 학문의 분야
pathogen n. 병원균, 병원체
spoiled a. 상한

01 ▶ "세포로 만들어진 새로운 센서가 사냥개처럼 위험을 냄새 맡다"라는 보기 (A)의 표현은 윗글의 핵심 주제를 드러내면서도 독자의 관심을 끌게 하는 좋은 제목이다. 제목이 짧을 수도 있지만 이렇게 문장으로 표현되는 경우도 빈번하다는 점에 유의한다.

02 ▶ ①~④는 모두 이 새로운 장치를 지칭하는 표현이지만, ⑤는 '생물학적 병원균'을 지칭한다.

03 ▶ 이 새로운 장치의 가장 큰 특징은 살아있는 세포를 이식한 칩 기술을 이용하여 생명체의 감각기관처럼 작동한다는 점이다.

》 정답 01 (A) 02 (E) 03 (B)

097

　존재와 소유의 다른 점이 반드시 동서양의 차이점에 있는 것은 아니다. 차이점은 오히려 인간 중심의 사회와 물질 위주의 사회에 있다. 소유의 지향은 서구 산업사회의 특징이다. 그 사회에서는 돈과 명예, 권력에 대한 탐욕이 삶의 지배적인 주제가 된다. 덜 소외된 사회, 예를 들어, 중세 사회, 주니(Zuni)족 인디언들 그리고 아프리카 부족 사회들처럼 현대의 '진보'라는 개념에 영향을 받지 않은 사회에는 그들만의 바쇼(Basho)와 같은 시인이 있다. 아마 산업화가 몇 세대 지난 후에, 일본에는 테니슨(Tennyson)과 같은 시인이 생길 것이다. 그 이유는 바로 서구인들이 선불교와 같은 동양적 체제를 전적으로 이해할 수 없는 것이 아니라, 현대인은 소유와 탐욕에 역점을 두지 않는 사회의 정신을 이해할 수 없기 때문이다. 실제로, 마이스터 에크하르트(Master Eckhart)의 글과 부처의 글은 단지 언어만 다를 뿐 똑같이 존재의 양식을 가리킨다.

property n. 재산, 소유물
Zen n. <불교> 선종, 선(禪)
alienate v. 멀리하다, 떼어놓다, 소외하다
medieval a. 중세의; 중세풍의

01 ▶ 소유와 존재 양식의 차이는 서두에 나와 있듯이, 반드시 동서양의 다른 점에 있지 않으므로 (C)가 본문의 내용과 다르다. (A)와 (B)는 산업사회와 더불어 소유와 물질 위주의 삶이 되어가고 있음을 밝히고 있다. (D)에서 현대인들은 에크하르트와 부처가 추구한 존재의 세계의 정신을 이해하지 못한다.

02 ▶ 이 글의 결론을 함축해 놓은 것으로 동서양을 불문하고 두 인물의 정신은 존재양식의 삶을 지향한다.

» 정답 01 (C) 02 (A)

098

　그는 내가 아는 어떤 사람보다 이것을 잘하였다. 그와 함께 앉은 사람들이 끔찍한 일에 대해 말할 때 그의 눈에 눈물이 고이고, 지독한 농담을 말할 때는 즐거워서 얼굴이 주름지는 것을 보았다. 그는 항상 우리 베이비 붐 세대들이 종종 간과하는 감정을 숨기지 않고 드러낼 준비가 되어 있었다. 우리는 예를 들면 "직업이 무엇입니까?" "어디에 사십니까?"처럼 잡담에 능숙하다. 그러나 사람들에게 물건을 팔려 하거나, 사람들을 선출하거나 충원하거나 어떤 지위를 대가로 얻으려 하지 않고 진실로 사람들의 말을 듣는 일을 우리는 얼마나 자주 하고 있는가? 모리(Morrie)의 생애 마지막 몇 달 동안에 방문객들은 그에게 관심이 있어서가 아니라, 그가 그들에게 기울인 관심에 이끌린 것이라고 나는 생각한다. 개인적으로 고통당하며 병마와 씨름을 한다 할지라도, 이 작은 체구의 노인은 사람들이 누군가가 들어주기를 바라는 방식대로 사람들의 말을 들었다.

moist a. 촉촉한
crinkle v. (종이 등이) 오그라들다, (얼굴이) 주름지다
display v. (감정 등을) 드러내다
small talk 잡담
status n. 신분, 지위; (사물의) 상태

01 ▶ 다음 문장에서 사례로 언급되었듯이 this는 '있는 그대로 사람들이 하는 말을 듣는 것'이다. 또한 this는 글의 전체적인 내용을 종합하는 문장으로, 본문에서 다른 사람들의 말을 경청하는 모리의 모습이 나타나 있으므로 (B)는 답이 될 수 없다.

02 ▶ ①의 경우, 우리는 잡담에 능숙하다고 긍정적인 측면을 이야기한 뒤에, 진실로 타인의 말을 듣는 일이 얼마나 있냐고 부정적인 어조로 반문하고 있다. 따라서 역접의 접속사(But)를 생각할 수 있다. ②에는 방식을 나타내는 관계부사(the way)가 타당하다.

» 정답 01 (C) 02 (B)

그는 보고 걸으며 심장이 피를 펌프질한다. 그러나 렉스 — 그가 막 첫 선을 보인 영국에서는 이렇게 불리는데 — 는 인간이 아니다. 사실 그는 살아있지도 않다. 그는 과학자, 연구원, TV 제작회사 사이의 3개월에 걸친 공동작업의 일환으로 만들어진 세계에서 가장 발전된 인조인간이다. 우리가 화면으로 보는 것에 익숙해져 있는 인간-로봇 혼성체와 달리 이것은 정말로 대단한 것이다. 그의 인공기관들은 이미 이용가능하며, 그의 장기는 과학적 표준이다. 그리고 그의 혈액은 플라스틱으로 만들어졌는데 앞으로의 획기적인 발전을 짐작케 하는 것이다.

이것은 환자들에게 일반적으로 희소식이다. 예를 들어 연구원들이 실용적인 인공 교체장기를 만들어내면 신장질환은 사소한 문제가 될 수 있을 것이다. 인공기관이 비싸긴 하지만(영국의 인조인간은 가격이 대략 100만 달러였다), 기술발전이 더 일어나면 가격이 낮아질 것이다. 그래도 이런 사태진전들은 온갖 윤리 문제를 제기한다. 인조 팔다리가 인간 팔다리의 기능을 능가하면 어떤 일이 일어나는가와 같은 문제이다. "일부 사람들은 그들의 건강한 장기들을 선택적으로 교체할지도 모릅니다."라고 프로젝트의 책임자인 버톨트 마이어는 말한다. 그럴 가능성은 먼 미래의 일이지만 그는 인공장기 기술이 주류가 되기 전에 그런 논의를 시작하기 원한다. 물론 늦어도 그때는 렉스도 그런 논의에 참여할 수 있을지 모른다.

debut v. (~로) 데뷔하다
bionic man 바이오닉 맨, 인조인간, 생체공학인간
hybrid n. 잡종; 혼성체
real deal 대단한 것
prosthesis n. (의족, 의치 같은) 보철, 인공기관
prototype n. 원형, 표준, 모범
harbinger n. 선구자, 전조
breakthrough n. 획기적인 진전, 돌파구
kidney failure 신장질환, 신부전
nonissue n. 사소한 문제
limb n. (하나의) 팔[다리]
surpass v. 능가하다, 뛰어넘다
functionality n. 기능성; 목적, 기능
electively ad. 선택적으로
go mainstream 주류가 되다
state-of-the-art a. 최첨단기술을 이용한, 최신식의
outperform v. ~을 능가하다
disparaging a. 얕보는; 헐뜯는, 비난하는

01 ▶ 최첨단 인조인간 렉스를 소개하면서 앞으로 신체장기를 대신할 인공장기의 기술이 더욱 첨단화하여 의학적으로 기여함과 동시에 윤리적 문제도 일으킬 것이라고 하므로 글의 제목으로는 (C)의 '인체의 최첨단 기술적 미래'가 적절하다. (A)는 Biotechnology가 너무 광범위하다. (B)는 사무용 가구 같은 것에 적용되는 인체공학적 디자인을 말한다. (D)는 '윤리문제'가 지엽적이고 '장기이식'이 아니라 인공장기로의 교체를 다룬 글이므로 부적절하다.

02 ▶ (A) bionic man은 곧 human-robot hybrid이고 또 humanoid robot이다. 모두 같은 말이다. state-of-the-art는 '최첨단'이라는 뜻이다. (B) 첫 단락 마지막 문장에서 prostheses(= limbs)는 이미 이용가능하다고 하고 organs는 과학적 원형(표준), blood는 앞으로의 획기적인 발전을 짐작케 하는 것이라고 한 것에서 prostheses(= limbs)가 다른 둘보다 대중화에 있어 앞서 있음을 알 수 있다. (C) 둘째 단락에서 윤리문제는 인조 팔다리가 인간 팔다리의 기능을 능가하면(outperform) 일어나게 될 문제라는 것을 알 수 있다. 인공기관이 비싸긴 하지만 기술발전이 더 일어나면 가격이 낮아질 것이라고 했으므로 (D)는 추론할 수 있는 것이 아니다.

03 ▶ 첫 단락에서 렉스는 지금까지 화면으로 보아온 것과는 비교가 되지 않을 정도로 정말 대단한 것이라 했으므로 (C)의 '찬미[감탄]하는'이 적절하다.

» **정답** 01 (C) 02 (D) 03 (C)

지난 10년 동안 야구는 데이터에 의한 정보 혁명을 경험했다. 현재 분석가들은 적은 돈으로 더 우수한 야구팀을 만들기 위해 관례처럼 통계학을 사용하고 있다. 너무 비싸고 제 역할을 하지 못하고 있는 우리의 의료 시스템도 이와 같은 개혁이 필요하다.

데이터에 의한 야구는 놀라운 결과를 가져왔다. 야구에서 무슨 일이 일어났는지 살펴보자. 수십 년 동안 구단주들과 감독들은 자신들의 개인적인 경험과 얼마 되지 않는 모호한 통계에 기초하여 시합을 관리하고 팀을 구성하였다. 이 비현실적인 접근은 컴퓨터를 이용한 야구 데이터 분석이라고 불리는 통계에 기초한 신조로 대체되었다. 이것들은 우리가 어렸을 때 조사했던 야구 카드 뒷면의 통계가 아니다. 프랜차이즈 야구팀들은 야구에서 중요한 몇 가지 주된 질문에 대한 답을 구하기 위해 이 데이터를 사용했다.

마찬가지로, 비교적 확고한 의료 증거들에 의한 의료 시스템은 생명을 구하고 돈을 절약해줄 것이다. 미국의 의료 시스템은 나이 든 강타자를 쫓고 오래된 규칙에 따라 시합을 하고 완고하고 전통적인 구단과 같다. 우리는 너무나도 많은 비용을 지불하는데, 그에 비해 돌아오는 성과는 너무나도 적다. 보다 나은 의료 혜택을 주기 위해, 우리는 야구의 새로운 증거에 입각한 방식을 채택해서 성공한 팀들로부터 배워야 한다. 질을 향상시키고 가격을 낮추는 가장 좋은 방법은 이런 통계를 연구하는 것이다.

---

data-driven a. (프로그램이) 데이터에 따라 처리를 하는
number cruncher n. 수치 계산하는 사람(분석가 등)
underperform v. 다른 것만큼 잘하지 못하다
statistics n. 통계; 통계학
sabermetrics n. 컴퓨터를 이용한 야구 데이터 분석(법)
lethargic a. 혼수상태의; 활발하지 못한
dispassionate a. 침착한, 냉정한
bigoted a. 편협한, 고집불통의
contentious a. 다투기 좋아하는, 토론하기 좋아하는

01 ▶ ①, ③, ④는 야구에서 적은 돈으로 우수한 팀을 관리하기 위해서 사용된 데이터 분석법을 가리킨다. ②는 개인적인 경험과 얼마 되지 않는 모호한 통계에 기초한 관리법을 의미한다.

02 ▶ 이 글에서는 부실한 의료 시스템에 야구에서처럼 데이터를 기초로 한 분석법을 도입해야 함을 주장하고 있다. 그러나 이 방법이 의사들의 의사결정의 권위를 빼앗을 것인지에 대해서는 추론할 수 없다.

03 ▶ hidebound a. 완고한, 편협한(= bigoted)

》 정답 01 (B) 02 (D) 03 (C)

101   단어의 수를 세는 것에 대한 제임스 펜베이커(James W. Pennebaker)의 관심은 30년도 전에 시작되었다. 그 때 그가 한 몇 번의 연구가 암시한 바는 잊을 수 없을 만큼 정신적 충격이 큰 경험에 대해서 말하는 사람들이 그런 경험을 비밀로 하는 사람보다 더 정신적으로 건강한 경향이 있다는 것이었다. 그는 사람들이 사용하는 모든 단어들, 심지어 대명사 I와 you, 관사 a와 the와 같은 사소한 단어들을 관찰함으로써 얼마나 많은 것을 알아낼 수 있을지 궁금히 여겼다. 사람들이 말하는 여러 종류의 단어를 세어봄으로써 그는 새로운 언어학 연구 분야를 개척하고 있고 텍스트 분석에 대한 관심을 부활시키고 있다.

알카에다 보도 내용이 있는 비디오테이프, 인터뷰, 서한들에 대한 펜베이커 박사의 최근 연구를 살펴보자. FBI의 요청으로 그는 다양한 범주, 그 가운데서도 특히 대명사, 관사, 형용사에 해당하는 단어의 수를 계산하였다. 예를 들어, 그는 오사마 빈 라덴(Osama bin Laden)의 1인칭 대명사(I, me, my, mine) 사용이 몇 년 동안 비교적 일정했음을 발견했다. <이와는 대조적으로 그의 부사령관인 아이만 알자와리(Ayman al-Zawahri)는 그런 대명사를 더욱 더 많이 사용했다.> 펜베이커 박사는 "이런 급격한 증가는 더 커진 불안감과, 위협감 그리고 아마도 빈 라덴과 그의 관계에 대한 변화를 암시한다."고 자신의 논문에 썼다.

traumatic a. 정신적 쇼크의; 상처 깊은
tally v. 계산하다
linguistic a. 언어의, 언어학의
resurgent a. 소생하는, 부활하는
analysis n. 분석
pronoun n. 대명사
article n. 관사
constant a. 변치 않는, 일정한
insecurity n. 불안전, 불안정

01 ▶ 펜베이커 박사는 1인칭 대명사 사용의 증가를 오사마 빈 라덴과 알자와리를 예를 들어 설명하였는데, 마지막 문장에서 이런 증가가 알자와리의 불안감, 위협감 등을 암시한다고 했으므로 '정신상태'를 반영한다고 하는 것이 적절하다.

02 ▶ by contrast는 앞 문장을 받아서 이와는 대조적이란 뜻으로 쓰이며 his는 오사마 빈 라덴을 지칭하고 있다. 따라서 제시된 문장은 [IV]에 들어가야 적절하다.

03 ▶ 정신적인 충격을 경험한 사람들이 그 경험에 대해서 이야기를 하면 정신적으로 건강한 경향이 있다고 했으므로, 그것에 대해 '침묵하지 않는 편이 좋음'을 알 수 있다.

》 정답 01 (C) 02 (D) 03 (A)

괴테는 1817년 독일 조각가 협회 연설에서 조각가들에게 이렇게 말했다. "모든 조형예술의 최고 목표는 인간의 위엄을 인간 형태의 범위 안에서 표현하는 것입니다. 모든 비인간적 요소는 이 매체(조각)로 다루어지기에 적합한 한, 이 목표에 종속되어야 합니다. 그런 요소들은 인간의 위엄을 드러내도록 우선 먼저 인간의 위엄에 동화되어야 하는 것이지, 그런 요소들 자체에로 주의가 쏠리게 한다거나 심지어 인간의 위엄에서 벗어나서는 안 되는 것입니다."

인간의 위엄을 표현한다는 의도는 형이상학적이었으며, 이 의도에 모든 것이 희생되어야 했다. 그 어떤 영원한 가치라도 있는 조각이 문명 세계 그 어디에서도 거의 창작될 수 없었던 세기(19세기) 초에 연설하면서 괴테는 자신이 조각이라는 예술에 너무 많은 것을 요구하고 있다는 것을 깨닫지 못했다. 사실, 위엄과 생명력 사이에 본래부터 양립할 수 없는 것은 아무 것도 없으며, 생각건대, 인간의 형상(인물상)은 신적인 것에 대한 인간의 생각을 구체적으로 표현할 수 있다. 미켈란젤로가 조각한 인물상은 생명력이 있으면서 위엄이 있다. 우리는 그 인물상이 위엄 있기 때문에 위대한 예술작품이라고 말할 수 있지만, 그것은 생명력 있다는 이유만으로도 예술작품으로 존재하는 것이다.

topmost a. 최고의, 최상의
plastic art 조형예술(조각, 도예 등)
render v. 표현하다
dignity n. 존엄, 위엄
compass n. 한계, 범위
lend oneself to ~에 적합하다
subordinate v. 종속(복종)시키다
set off 돋보이게 하다, 드러나게 하다
intention n. 의도, 목적
vitality n. 생명력
conceivably ad. 생각건대

01 ▶ metaphysical은 '형이상학적인, 극히 추상적인, 난해한'의 뜻이므로 (A)가 가장 가까운 의미이다.

02 ▶ (A) 첫 문장에 언급되었다. (B) 둘째 단락에서 19세기를 조각이 문명 세계 그 어디에서도 거의 창작될 수 없었던 세기라 하고 괴테는 자신이 조각에 너무 많은 것을 요구하고 있다는 것을 깨닫지 못했다고 했으므로, 당시 조각은 괴테가 생각한 조각의 개념에 부응할 정도로는 발달하지 못했음을 알 수 있다. (C) 마지막 문장에서 생명력만 있으면 예술작품이 될 수 있음을 알 수 있다. (D) 조각 작품이 될 필요조건은 vitality이고, dignity는 위대한 작품이 될 조건이다.

03 ▶ 이 글은 조각에 대한 괴테의 생각을 비판한 글이다. 둘째 단락에 비판의 논조가 잘 드러나 있다. (A) 찬미조의 (C) 양면가치적인 (D) 풍자적인

» 정답 01 (A) 02 (D) 03 (B)

그러나 웃음은 곧잘 사람의 부정적인 의도를 보여주기도 한다. 이러한 점은 대부분 정신분석학자들에 의해 분석되고 있다. 예를 들어, 지그문트 프로이드(Sigmund Freud)는 그의 이론에서 웃음은 어긋난 예상으로 인해 잘못 고조된 긴장과 '심적 에너지'를 해방시킨다고 요약했다. 이 이론은 웃음이 건강에 도움이 된다는 믿음을 정당화하는 이론 중 하나이며, 웃음이 어째서 우울하고 화나거나 슬플 때를 극복하는 장치가 될 수 있는지를 설명해준다. 카렌 호나이(Karen Horney)와 같은 심리학자들은 웃음이 긴장이나 심지어 자기 방어의 표출이라고 주장한다. 예를 들어, 어떤 사람이 어려운 질문을 받고 답변을 어떻게 할 지 모를 때 그는 종종 웃거나 농담을 하기 시작할 지도 모른다는 것이다.

웃음과 관련된 이러한 사실들을 발견한 후에 많은 연구가 이루어졌고 몇몇 웃음 치료가 개발되었다. "웃음은 만병통치약이다"라는 말은 대개 진부한 표현으로만 간주되지만, 어떤 의학 이론들은 건강 개선, 기대수명 연장, 그리고 전반적으로 건강해진 삶을 웃음 덕분으로 여긴다. 아마도 우리는 왜 사람만이 웃을 수 있는지 알 수 있을 것이다. 사람만이 너무나 괴로워서 웃음을 만들어내야 했을 것이다.

psychoanalyst n. 정신분석학자
psychic a. 마음의, 심적인
mobilize v. 동원하다; (기분 따위를) 고조시키다
justification n. 정당화; 변명; 변호
coping mechanism 대처기전
life expectancy 기대 수명

01 ▶ However로 시작하면서 웃음이 부정적인 상황을 나타낼 수 있다고 하였으므로, 앞에서는 이와 상반된 상황, 즉 '즐거움의 표시로서의 웃음'을 다루었음을 추론할 수 있다.

02 ▶ 본문은 웃음을 심적 고통을 표출하는 측면에서 설명하고 있다. 따라서 "고통은 우리의 짐을 덜어주게끔 하는 웃음을 발생시킨다"는 것을 추론할 수 있다.

03 ▶ cliche n. 상투적인 문구, 진부한 표현(= banality)

≫ 정답 01 (B) 02 (C) 03 (C)

고대의 운동선수들은 현대의 경기대회처럼 국가별 팀으로 겨루는 것이 아니라 개인별로 겨루었다. 공개적인 시합을 통한 개인 운동선수의 성취에 대한 강조는 '아레테(arete)'라고 불리는 탁월성에 대한 그리스적 이상(理想)과 관련이 있다. 뛰어난 언변과 행위를 통해 이러한 이상을 달성한 귀족 계급의 남자들은 영원한 영광과 명예를 얻었다. 이러한 규칙에 부응하지 못하는 자는 공개적인 수치와 불명예를 걱정해야만 했다.

모든 운동선수들이 이러한 탁월성의 규약에 따라 행동한 것은 아니었다. 속임수를 쓴 것으로 밝혀진 사람들은 벌금을 물어야 했고 그 돈은 경기장으로 가는 길에 세워진 제우스 청동상을 건립하는 데 쓰였다. 그 조각상에는 규칙위반에 대한 설명과 함께 부정을 저지르지 말 것에 대한 경고, 그리고 선수들에게 승리는 돈이 아니라 능력으로써 얻어진다는 것을 상기시키며 신에 대한 경건함과 공정한 경쟁이라는 올림픽 정신을 강조하는 문구가 새겨져 있었다.

emphasis n. 강조; 역설
attain v. 획득하다, 달성하다
outstanding a. 걸출한, 현저한
deed n. 행위, 행동
permanent a. 영구적인, 영속적인
disgrace n. 불명예, 치욕
statue n. 상(像), 조상
erect v. (몸·기둥 따위를) 똑바로 세우다, 직립시키다
inscribe v. (문자 따위를 비석 등에) 적다, 새기다
piety n. 경건, 신앙심

01 ▶ 첫 문단 두 번째 문장에서 개인의 성취에 대한 강조는 아레테라는 탁월성의 이상과 관련이 있다고 하였고 그다음 문장에서 그러한 탁월성의 이상을 달성하면 영원한 영광과 명예를 얻었다고 하였으므로, 그것이 개인적으로 경기에 임했던 이유가 되었음을 알 수 있다. 따라서 정답으로 가장 타당한 것은 (D)이다. (C)의 경우 arete가 귀족 계급만의 가치라고는 볼 수 없으므로 정답이 될 수 없다.

02 ▶ 둘째 문단 마지막 문장에서 제우스상에 새겨져 있었던 문구에 대해 설명하고 있다. (A)는 victory was won by skill and not by money에 해당하는 문구이고, (B)는 fair competition에 대한 설명이며 (D)는 reminding athletes that victory was won by skill에서 찾아볼 수 있다. (C)는 본문에 나오는 설명과는 부합하지 않는 내용이다.

≫ 정답 01 (D) 02 (C)

베수비우스(Vesuvius) 산이 폼페이(Pompeii)를 속돌과 김을 내뿜는 화산재 아래로 묻어버린 지 약 2천 년의 세월이 지난 후, 매년 약 260만 명의 관광객들이 유네스코의 세계유산 목록에 올라있는 이 고고학적인 장소를 답사한다. 이탈리아의 다른 많은 발굴유적지들과 마찬가지로 폼페이도 쉽게 찾아올 수 있는 곳으로 관광객들이 충분한 공간만 찾아낼 수 있다면 아무런 제약 없이 유적들 사이를 돌아다닐 수 있도록 허락하고 있다. 이탈리아에서 가장 인기 있는 관광지 중 하나인 고대 로마시대의 도시에 있는 프레스코 벽화는 타오르는 태양 아래 색이 바래거나 기념이 되는 물건을 노리는 사람들에 의해 뜯겨나갔다. 모자이크는 수많은 질질 끄는 고무 슬리퍼와 스니커즈의 공격을 견뎌내고 있다. 비틀거리는 기둥과 벽은 나무와 강철 뼈대에 의해 지탱되고 있다. 최근에 복구된 집으로 출입을 못하게 하는 것은 맹꽁이자물쇠이며, 관리인의 수는 극히 적어 보인다. 최근 4월의 어느 날 아침에 프랑스 관광객들이 밖으로 나가려다 같은 좁은 현관으로 들어오려는 독일인들 몇 명과 충돌했다. 옥신각신 끝에 관광 안내인이 우산을 휘둘러 곤경을 타파했다. 보다시피 병목현상 역시 폼페이가 가진 가장 심각한 문제 중 하나인 너무 많은 사람들로 붐비고 있다는 점을 부각시켜준다.

pumice n. 속돌, 부석(浮石)
tramp v. 도보여행하다
excavation n. 발굴; 구멍, 구덩이
unhindered a. 제약받지 않은
elbow room 몸을 편히 움직일 수 있는 공간
blistering a. 통렬한, 호된
brunt n. (공격의) 예봉; 날카로운 공격
shuffle v. 발을 질질 끌다
thong n. 가죽끈; 고무 슬리퍼
sneaker n. 고무바닥의 운동화
teeter v. 비틀비틀 서있다
prop v. 버티다, 버팀목을 대다
scaffolding n. 발판
padlock n. 맹꽁이자물쇠
tussle v. 격투하다, 싸우다
wield v. (칼 따위를) 휘두르다
impasse n. 막다른 골목, 곤경
underscore v. 강조하다

01 ▶ 빈칸 앞의 문장에서 관광객들이 서로 좁은 문으로 나가려다가 충돌하여 다투었다는 내용이 나와 있다. 이렇듯 폭이 좁아진 곳에서 나타나는 정체 현상을 교통체증에 비유하여 병목현상(bottleneck)이라고 부를 수 있다. 또한 overcrowding이라고 부연 설명을 해주고 있으므로 정답은 사람이 많이 붐빌 때 일어날 수 있는 현상인 (B)가 알맞다

02 ▶ recently restored houses라고 했으므로 전혀 수리공사가 이루어지지 않았다고는 볼 수 없으며, 시설이 낡았다는 이야기는 일절 꺼내지 않았으므로 (D)의 old facilities는 폼페이의 문제점으로 지적될 수 없다.

03 ▶ 앞에서 관광객들이 초래하고 있는 문제점들과 관리가 제대로 이루어지지 않고 있다는 문제점, 그리고 사람이 너무 붐벼 발생하는 문제점을 차례대로 지적하고 있다. (B) '폼페이에서 소란을 일으키는 사람들'의 경우는 문제점의 일부만 지적하고 있기 때문에 주제가 될 수 없으며, 전체를 아우를 수 있는 주제는 '폼페이의 관광 사업이 가진 문제점'이다.

» 정답 01 (B) 02 (D) 03 (C)

세계 일부 지역들은 세계화로 인해 뒤처지게 되었다. 경제학자들은 한때 지역과 지역 사이의 그리고 나라와 나라 사이의 불평등은 시간이 지나면 자연히 평등해질 것으로 생각했다. 일부 사람들은 세계경제가 교과서적인 자율균형 메커니즘인 것으로 생각할 수 있다고 믿는다. 그리고 또 다른 사람들은 세계경제가 누적적인 인과관계의 과정을 따르는 것으로 볼 수 있어서 만일 한두 나라가 다른 나라들보다 뒤처지면 균형을 찾는 해결의 길로 자동적으로 돌아가기보다 이 인과의 과정으로 인해 더욱 더 뒤처지게 될 위험이 있을지 모른다고 믿는다. 실제세계 경제 과정에 대한 이 두 가지 서로 대체적이고 상충하는 견해는 제도적 필요와 제도적 정비와 관련하여 매우 서로 다른 결과를 낳는다. 동일한 것이 지역에도 적용된다. 지역 간 격차가 벌어지는 악순환이 아니라 지역 간 격차가 좁혀지는 선순환이 있어야 할 이론상의 이유는 없으며 실제로 그렇다는 증거도 없다. 그래서 브랙시트 국민투표가 행해졌을 때 영국의 일인당 국민 소득이 금융위기 이전 수준으로 돌아갔다는 말이 있었다. 영국 은행 수석 경제 분석가 앤디 할데인이 뒤이어 지적했듯이, 이것은 전체 총계로서 맞는 말이었지만 지역별로 나누어 보면 영국의 두 지역, 즉 런던과 동남부 지역에만 맞는 말이었다.

---

marginalize v. 주변화하다; 뒤처지게 하다
even out 평평하게 고르다, 평등하게 하다
self-equilibrating a. 스스로 균형을 잡는
cumulative a. 점증적인, 누적적인
causation n. 원인, 인과관계
pack n. 한 무리, 일당
virtuous circle 선순환
vicious cycle 악순환
convergence n. (한 점으로의) 수렴, 집중
divergence n. 발산, 확산, 분기, 상이
Brexit n. 브렉시트 (영국의 EU 탈퇴)
referendum n. 국민투표
aggregate n. 총계
disaggregated a. 개별단위로 나눈

01 ▶ 지역 간과 나라 간의 경제 불평등이 시간이 지나면 자연히 사라질 것이라는 것은 일부 사람들의 믿음일 뿐 저자의 생각은 아니므로 (D)가 글의 내용과 일치하지 않는다.

02 ▶ 글의 마지막 부분에서 영국의 국민소득이 금융위기 이전 수준으로 낮아졌다고 해도 영국의 모든 지역이 똑같이 그렇게 된 것이 아니고 런던과 동남부 지역만 그렇게 되었다고 했으므로, 저자가 영국을 예로 든 것은 한 나라 안에서도 특정 지역이 다른 지역에 비해 점점 더 뒤처지는 경제적 불평등의 악순환이 일어날 가능성이 있음을 보여주기 위한 것이다.

» 정답 01 (D) 02 (A)

인도에서는 일부 국외 거주(국내에 거주하지 않는) 인도인들과의 결혼이 문제가 될 수 있다. 외국으로 시집가는 신부는 사전에 서방세계에 노출된 경험이 없으면 문화 충격의 고통을 겪을 수 있다. 한편, 해외에서 자란 배우자는 이민세대인 부모에게서 전통적인 결혼을 하라는 압력을 받을 수 있다. 그래서 이 결합은 사랑이 없고 양립할 수 없는 관계를 유지하다가 결국 이혼하게 되는 결과를 낳을 수 있다. 그러나 최악의 경우는 국외 거주 인도인 남성이 거액의 결혼 지참금이나 '휴가용 현지처'를 구하러 인도로 오는 경우이다. 이런 남성들이 신부를 버리고 자신이 귀화한 나라로 돌아가면, 신부와 그 가족은, 가부장제 문화 속에 살면서 명예를 지키는 데에 열성적이다 보니, 관계기관을 찾지 않는 일이 종종 있다. 그리고 찾아온다 해도 그들이 택할 수 있는 법적인 수단은 많지 않다.

정부기관과 비정부기구들은 이러한 사태를 바꾸려고 노력하고 있다. 국가여성위원회는 정부에게 모든 혼인 등록을 의무화하라고 요청했는데, 이렇게 하면 여성은 보다 견고한 법적 지위를 갖게 될 것이다. 한편, 여러 사회운동단체들은 법률 개정을 통해 과거 혼인경력에 대한 정보 공개를 막는 것을 범죄로 규정하도록 로비를 펼치고 있으며, 혼인사기를 본국으로의 인도가 가능한 범죄로 만들기 위한 조약을 다른 나라와 체결하라고 정부에 강력히 촉구하고 있다.

---

spouse n. 배우자
incompatible a. 양립 불가능한
dowery n. 신부 측의 결혼 지참금
holiday wife 휴가용 현지처
adoptive country 귀화국
patriarchy n. 가부장제
keen a. 예민한, 열심인
extradite v. 범인을 본국으로 인도하다
extraditable a. 본국으로의 인도가 가능한
offense n. 범죄

01 ▶ 첫 단락 마지막 부분의 living in a culture of patriarchy and keen to preserve their honor에서 (C)가 옳은 진술임을 알 수 있다.

02 ▶ 신부를 버리고 귀화한 나라로 가버린 남성을 인도로 붙잡아 와서 처벌할 수 있으려면 그 나라와 조약을 체결해 인도로 범죄인을 인도해올 수 있어야 한다.

≫ 정답 01 (C) 02 (D)

토마토는 기술적으로는 과일이겠지만, 이곳의 입법위원들은 토마토를 야채라고 생각한다. 미 하원 농업 및 천연자원 위원회 위원들은 월요일 저지(Jersy) 토마토를 주(州)의 공식 야채로 선정하는 조례를 승인했다. 이와 비슷한 조치가 상원 위원회에 계류 중이다.

이 조례의 발기인들은 토마토에 대해 오이나, 호박, 콩과 마찬가지로 야채 관세를 부과했던 100년은 더 된 미국 대법원의 판결을 이용하여 토마토가 과일로 간주된다는 사실을 피해나갔다.

토마토를 야채 범주에 밀어 넣으면서 1887년 고등 법원 판사들은 토마토는 디저트로 나오는 것이 아니라 대개 식사와 같이 제공되므로 야채임이 틀림없다고 말했다. "식물학적으로 토마토는 과일이죠, 하지만 법률적으로는 야채입니다"라고 상원에 제출한 법안의 공동 발기인인 엘렌 카쳐(Ellen Karcher) 상원의원은 말했다. "전국적인 긍지를 불러일으킬 수 있는 이러한 모든 법안을 우리는 채택해야 합니다."

저지 토마토가 입법부에 들어오게 된 것은 4학년 학생의 일단이 주를 대표하는 과일을 채택하자는 편지를 입법의원들에게 쓴 이후 시작되었다. 많은 사람들이 좋아하는 블루베리가 승리를 거두어서, 그것이 — 토마토가 아니라 — 작년에 공식 주 과일로 선정되었다.

designate v. 선정하다
pending a. 심의중의
sponsor n. 발기인
get around 빠져나가다
ruling n. 판결
slap v. 징수하다
tariff n. 관세
justice n. 재판관
reason v. 논하다
win out 성공하다

01 ▶ 토마토는 사실 과일인데, 법에 의해 야채가 되었다는 내용이므로, 뒤의 빈칸에는 법률적이라는 낱말이 필요하고, 앞의 빈칸에는 기술적, 생물학적, 식물학적, 과학적 등의 낱말이면 된다.

02 ▶ 과일과 야채를 구분하는 기준은 디저트 때 나오느냐, 식사를 하는 중에 먹을 수 있느냐는 것이라고 하였다. 과일은 디저트로 나오므로, 식사가 끝난 다음 나온다는 (C)가 옳다.

》 **정답** 01 (D) 02 (C)

거장들은 흔히 음악을 쉽게 들리도록 만드는 말을 해서 칭찬을 받는다. (하지만) 베토벤의 32개 피아노 소나타 중 마지막 세 곡을 미츠코 우치다가 연주했을 때 그것은 결코 쉽게 들리지 않았다. 이 연주는 토요일 저녁 Caramoor International Music Festival의 올해 마지막 콘서트였다. 소나타 30번의 시작 부분은 마치 지나치게 많은 음표들이 얽혀서 열 손가락 모두의 움직임을 완벽히 통제하는 능력을 요구하는 듯이 들렸다. 물론 이것은 해석상의 결정이다. 만일 우치다의 손에서 이 음악이 어렵게 들렸다면, 그녀가 그것을 분명 원했기 때문이다.

베토벤의 음악은 흔히 투쟁이라고들 말한다. 분명 처음으로 베토벤의 음악을 대하는 사람에게는 투쟁일 것이다. 그것은 그저 '예쁘다'라고 할 수만은 없는 구석을 갖고 있고, 연주자나 청취자 모두에게 기교적이고, 연출적인 상당한 도전을 여전히 제기하고 있다. 하지만 마지막 작품들에서의 투쟁은 바로 단순성을 성취한다는 것이 얼마나 어려운가와 관련된 것이다.

이 세 소나타들의 강력한 감정과 복잡성은 어려운 대위 선율에서 나타나는 것이 아니라, 마지막 소나타의 마지막 악장에서, 그 안의 애수를 불러일으키는 아리에타(Arieta)에서, 마치 꽃이 피어나듯 시작해서는 건반의 가장 높은 음의 순수한 소리로 빛나며 활짝 만개한다. 이 세 곡 모두에서 찾을 수 있는 단순한 멜로디야 말로 궁극적인 이 음악들의 가치이다. 하지만 이러한 단순한 멜로디는 쉽게 얻을 수 있는 것이 아니다. 이러한 생각을 지나치게 노골적으로 제시한다는 것은 듣기 좋은 음악을 만들어 내는 것이 아니라 오히려 뭔지 모를 모호한 음악만을 만들어 내게 될 것이다.

---

virtuoso n. 거장, 음악의 대가
tangled a. 엉킨, 꼬인
note n. 음표
confront v. 대면하다
dramaturgical a. 연출상의
thorny a. 고통스러운, 어려운
counterpoint n. 대위 선율
movement n. 악장
melting a. 애수를 자아내는
gild v. 치장하다, 빛나다
reach n. 미치는 범위
line n. 멜로디
murkiness n. 분명치 않음

01 ▶ 이 글은 미츠코 우치다의 베토벤 연주가 어렵게 들린 현상에 대해 설명하고 있는 평론인데, 이렇게 어렵게 들리도록 만든 것은 그녀의 기교 부족이 아니라 우치다가 원했던 바였다고 첫 번째 문단에서 말했고, 그 다음 문단에서 말하고 있는 것은 이 소나타들도 단순성을 성취한다는 것이 얼마나 어려운지를 보여주려는 것을 목적으로 하고 있다고 하였다. 따라서 우치다는 자신의 원했던 바와, 베토벤이 원했던 바를 완벽하게 보여 주고 있는 피아니스트이다.

02 ▶ 미츠코 우치다의 뛰어난 베토벤 해석과 연주에 대한 글이다. (B)는 그녀의 연주를 통해 베토벤의 complex simplicity에 대한 개념이 활짝 만개했다는 의미가 되므로 가장 알맞은 정답이다. (A)와 (D)는 형편없는 연주였다는 의미가 된다.

》 정답 01 (B) 02 (B)

나 자신을 제대로 소개할 수도 있지만, 별로 필요할 것 같지 않다. 여러 변수에 따라 다르긴 하겠지만, 당신은 금방, 나를 잘 알게 될 것이다, 그저 조만간이라고 말하는 것으로 충분한데, 어쨌든 나는 당신 위에 서 있게 될 것이다. 가능한 한 상냥하게 말이다. 당신의 영혼은 내 손 안에 있게 될 것이다. 하나의 색이 내 어깨에 걸쳐져 있게 될 것이고, 나는 당신을 부드럽게 들어 나를 것이다.

그 때가 되면, 당신은 누워 있게 될 것이다(서 있는 사람은 거의 보지 못했다). 당신은 육체 속에서 굳어가게 될 것이다. 그러면 어떤 발견이 있게 될 것이고, 절규가 하늘 아래로 뚝뚝 떨어질 것이다. 그 후 내가 듣게 될 유일한 소리는 나 자신의 호흡 소리, 냄새의 소리, 나의 발자국 소리가 될 것이다.

문제는, 당신에게 내가 다가갈 때 모든 것이 어떤 색이 될 것인가 하는 것이다. 하늘은 뭐라고 말할 것인가?

개인적으로는 나는 초콜릿 색 하늘이 좋다. 어두운, 어두운 초콜릿 말이다. 사람들은 그 색이 내게 잘 어울린다고 한다. 하지만 나는 내가 보는 모든 색, 모든 색 전체를 좋아해 보려고 노력하고 있다. 수십억 가지의 묘미, 그 중의 어떤 것도 같지 않고, 나는 그러한 하늘을 천천히 빨아 먹는다. 나의 스트레스는 좀 줄어든다. 하늘을 천천히 빨아 먹는 것은 나를 편하게 만들어 준다.

---

variable n. 변수
suffice v. 충분하다
genially ad. 상냥하게
perch v. 걸다
cake v. 굳히다
dribble v. 뚝뚝 떨어지다
suit v. 잘 어울리다
flavor n. 멋, 묘미
suck v. 빨다
take the edge off ~을 무디게 하다

01 ▶ 화자는 조만간 모두에게 찾아오는 존재라고 하고, 모든 사람의 영혼을 차지하며, 누워 있는 사람 위에 서는 존재이다.

02 ▶ 화자는 결국 모든 인간은 자신에게 굴복할 수밖에 없다는 생각을 갖고, 오로지 사람이 죽을 때, 자신이 먹게 될 하늘의 색에 관심을 갖는 오만하고, 심술궂은 존재이다. 형형색색의 하늘을 먹을 것을 기대하고 있으므로 사실은 그렇게 스트레스를 받는다고 할 수도 없다. 초콜릿을 즐기는 것이 아니라, 초콜릿 색 하늘이 좋다는 것이다.

》 정답 01 (B) 02 (D)

자연의 변화가 질서에서 무질서로 진행한다고 주장하면서 예를 한두 가지 든다면 여러분은 거의 전적인 인정과 동의를 얻을 것이다. 우리는 이를 일상에서 경험한다. 여러분이 책상, 지하실, 다락방을 몇 시간 동안 청소해놓으면 여러분의 눈앞에서 다시 무질서와 엉망진창인 상태로 저절로 돌아가는 것처럼 보일 것이다. 따라서 엔트로피가 무질서의 척도이고 고립계의 경우 자연이 최대 엔트로피 상태에 이르려 한다고 말한다면 여러분은 열역학 제2법칙의 이론을 간파하고 있는 것이다.

엔트로피의 이해를 위해 무질서라는 개념을 사용하려면 무질서에 대한 정의를 주의 깊게 내릴 필요가 있다. 엔트로피의 특성을 기술할 수 있는 더 정확한 방법은 엔트로피를 물질의 상태와 연관된 다양성의 척도로 보는 것이다. 다수의 방법으로 만들어질 수 있는 물질의 상태는 소수의 방법에 의해서만 만들어질 수 있는 물질의 상태보다 확률이 더 높다. 물 한 잔 속에 있는 분자의 수는 천문학적이다. 균일하고 고르게 보이는 물 한 잔과 비교했을 때 뒤섞여있는 얼음조각들이 훨씬 무질서해 보일 수도 있다. 하지만 얼음조각들은 분자들이 배열되는 방법의 가짓수를 제한한다. 물 한 잔 속에 있는 물 분자들은 훨씬 다양한 방식으로 배열될 수 있으므로 물 분자들의 다양성이 훨씬 크며 따라서 엔트로피도 더 크다.

---

assert v. 단언하다; 강력히 주장하다
assent n. 동의, 찬성
basement n. 지하실
attic n. 다락
spontaneously ad. 자연적으로, 무의식적으로
revert v. 본래 상태로 되돌아가다
insight n. 통찰력
thermodynamics n. 열역학
define v. 정의하다
associate v. 관련시키다
molecule n. 분자
astronomical a. (숫자가) 천문학적인, 엄청나게 큰
jumble n. 혼잡, 뒤범벅
uniform a. 균등한, 획일적인
homogeneous a. 동종의, 동질의
multiplicity n. 다수, 중복, 다양

01 ▶ 빈칸 ①의 경우, 본문 첫 번째 단락 마지막 문장에 entropy is a measure of disorder라고 기술되어 있다. 따라서 엔트로피를 이해하기 위해서는 disorder의 개념을 파악해야 한다. 빈칸 ②의 경우, 뒤에 얼음조각들과 물 한 잔의 예가 기술되어 있는데, 본문 두 번째 단락 마지막 문장의 they have greater multiplicity and therefore greater entropy를 통해 엔트로피가 multiplicity와 함수관계에 있음을 알 수 있다. 따라서 (D)가 정답이다.

02 ▶ 본문 첫 번째 단락 마지막 문장의 nature tends toward maximum entropy for any isolated system을 통해 자연이 isolated system의 경우 최대 엔트로피 상태에 도달하려고 한다는 것을 알 수 있다. 자연이 최대 엔트로피 상태를 지향한다는 말은 인위적인 개입 없이는 엔트로피가 감소하는 경우는 없다는 뜻이다. 하지만 open system의 경우 자연이 최대 엔트로피 상태에 도달하려고 하는지는 본문에 드러나 있지 않다. 따라서 (B)가 정답이다.

» 정답 01 (D) 02 (B)

범주의 시대는 끝났다. 이상하게도, 그것은 그 이름으로든 혹은 어떤 이름으로도 통용되지 않았다. 또한, 그 경계가 분명하지 않은 것도 흥미로운 사실이다. 그것은 계몽의 시대, 이성의 시대 등과 중첩되지만 정보화 시대의 세분화시키는 분위기에 굴복했다. 그것은 지식이 명명과 묘사와 조화한다고 생각했다. 과학이 발달하면서 여러 과학 분야들이 형성되었고 대학교에 필수적인 것은 각각이 높은 벽에 둘러싸인 학과들이었다. 하나의 데이터가 화학이나 사회학, 숟가락의 역사나 어떤 것의 범주 안에 들어맞는 것으로 보였고 어느 정도 그랬다.

이제는 우리가 그러한 낡은 범주의 한계를 인식하고 비웃는다. 우리는 다중 학문주의와 장르의 변화(파괴)를 소중히 여긴다. 지적 추구의 삶은 더 혼란스럽지만 더 흥미롭다. 자주 영역을 넘나드는 새로운 관점이 범주가 굳어지기 이전의 원래의 근원으로 돌아가는 것으로부터 나오게 된다. Steven Johnson이 지적하는 바로, Thomas Jefferson과 John Adams 사이의 서신을 보게 되면 Benjamin Franklin은 다섯 번, George Washington은 세 번 밖에 언급하지 않지만, 산소를 발견했다고 여겨지는 과학자이자 신학자인 Joseph Priestley에 대해서는 52번이나 언급된 것을 발견하게 될 것이다.

---

go by ~로 통용되다
overlap v. ~와 중첩되다
enlightenment n. 계몽
succumb to ~에 굴복하다
atomize v. 입자화하다, 세분화하다
nomenclature n. 명명
delineation n. 묘사
confine n. 제한, 한계, 영역
more or less 다소
scoff v. 비웃다, 조롱하다
exhilarating a. 흥미로운, 신나는
correspondence n. 서신(왕래)
theologian n. 신학자
be credited with ~의 공로, 업적 등이 인정되다

01 ▶ 범주의 영역이 불분명하다고 두 번째 문장에 있으므로 (A)는 곤란하고, 계몽의 시대와 이성의 시대가 중첩된다고 했으므로 (B)도 곤란하다. 또한 마지막 문장의 내용을 보면 Thomas Jefferson, John Adams 그리고 Joseph Priestley가 같은 분야에서 활동했다고 보기 어렵다. 둘째 단락 둘째 문장의 '지적 추구의 삶에서 지적 추구란 이 글에서는 영역의 경계를 넘는 것을 뜻한다. 그런데 이것이 혼란스럽긴 하지만 더 흥미롭다고 했으므로 장단점이 다 있다고 볼 수 있다.

02 ▶ 빈칸 뒤에 and가 있으므로 순접 관계로 연결되어 있고 비웃는다는 scoff가 제시되어 있으므로 범주에 대한 부정적인 서술이 되는 limitation이 적절하다.

》 정답 01 (C) 02 (D)

고대 DNA를 분석하는 새로운 기법의 도움을 받아 과학자들은 텁수룩한 매머드의 진화와 현대 코끼리의 친척인 이 매머드들이 왜 1만여년 전에 멸종했는지 이해하게 되었다. 구석기 시대 인간들은 그 동안 매머드들을 사냥하여 멸종에 이르게 했다고 종종 비난받아왔다. 그러나 DNA 연구 결과, 추위에 적응했던 이 코끼리들은 유전적 다양성이 매우 적었는데, 이로 인해 질병으로 절멸당하기 취약한 종이었다는 것이 드러났다. 펜실베이니아 주립대학의 게놈 연구학자 스테판 슈스터(Stephan Shuster)는 "날씨가 조금만 따뜻해져도 습도는 큰 차이가 나고, 습도가 높아진다는 얘기는 눈이 더 많이 내린다는 것이고, 그것은 곧 동물들이 먹이를 더 이상 찾지 못한다는 것이죠."라고 말한다. "여름에 약간만 기온이 상승하더라도 병원균의 양은 훨씬 더 커진다는 것을 의미하죠." 슈스터는 구석기 시대 사냥꾼들이 (매머드 멸종에 대한: 역주) 책임을 완전히 면하도록 하지는 않는다. 그는 사냥으로 인한 추가적 압박은 마지막 남은 매머드들을 완전히 절멸시키기에 충분했으리라는 점을 인정한다. 슈스터가 속한 연구팀이 사용했던 기법들은 고대 DNA 연구를 혁명적으로 바꿔놓게 될지도 모른다. 멸종된 종에서 나온 유전적 물질을 예전에 연구했을 때는 주로 뼈에서 채취한 샘플을 사용했는데, 이 샘플들은 진균류나 세균으로 심하게 오염된 DNA를 갖고 있었다. 새로운 연구는 털 자루에서 채취한 DNA 샘플을 사용했는데, 이 샘플은 90% 순수하고 훨씬 더 분석하기 쉽다. 연구팀은 지금 현재 매머드 게놈의 마지막 30%의 순서를 배열하는 작업을 진행 중으로, 고대 DNA로부터 매머드를 복제할 가능성을 점점 높여가고 있다. "우리의 과학을 몰고 가는 원동력이 매머드 복제는 아니지만, 그 일이 더 이상 불가능한 것은 아니라는 데 모든 사람들이 동의하고 있습니다"라고 슈스터는 말한다.

---

woolly a. 털이 많은
extinct a. 절멸한, 멸종된
paleolithic a. 구석기 시대의
genetic a. 유전적인
susceptible a. 취약한
wipe out 절멸시키다
organelle n. 세포 기관
humidity n. 습기; 습도
pathogen n. 병원균, 병원체
load n. 무거운 짐, 부담
off the hook 궁지(곤경)를 벗어나; 책임을 벗어나
fungus n. 진균류, 버섯
shaft n. 줄기; 깃촉; 자루, 손잡이
sequence v. 차례대로 나열하다
clone v. 무성 생식을 하다, 복제하다

01 ▶ 본문에서 매머드 멸종의 원인으로 크게 3가지가 지적되었다. 첫째, 질병 둘째, 적설량이 많아져 먹이 찾기가 어려워졌다는 점, 셋째, 인간의 사냥. 그런데 적설량과 매머드 멸종의 상관관계나 인간 사냥과의 상관관계는 언급되어 있지만 질병에 대한 언급은 본문 앞에 나온 뒤 서술은 뒤로 미루어졌다는 점에 주목해야 한다. 기후가 상승하면 병원균의 전파가 더 용이해졌으리라고 추측할 수 있다. (A), (D)는 매머드 생존이 더 용이해진다는 내용이므로 주제와 상반되고, (C)의 갈증을 많이 느낀다는 언급 역시 본문 속에서 상관관계를 찾기 어렵다.

02 ▶ (A) 매머드 게놈 연구의 마지막 30%가 남았다고 하였으므로, 이미 70%는 완성되었다고 추론할 수 있다. (B) 기존의 뼈 샘플은 진균류나 미생물에 심하게 오염된 DNA를 갖고 있다고 했다. (C) 본문에서 매머드를 '추위에 적응한 코끼리'라고 한 것은 그들의 서식처가 현대 코끼리에 비해 추운 곳이었다는 얘기일 뿐, 추위에 적응하면서 유전적 다양성을 상실했다고 보는 것은 근거를 찾기 어렵다. (D) 먹이를 찾기 어렵게 된 것, 질병에 취약해진 것 등이 주요 원인이겠지만 인간의 수렵이 매머드 멸종에 압박을 가했을 가능성은 충분히 있다고 지적하였다.

》 정답 01 (B) 02 (C)

1914년에 전쟁 속으로 빠져들기 전 10년 동안, 유럽 주요 강대국들의 문화는 두 갈래로 나누어졌다. 한편으로, 전쟁이 진보, 외교, 세계화, 그리고 경제적 및 과학적 발전에 의해서 사실상 끝이 났다고 생각하는 일련의 사조가 존재했는데, 현재 우리는 이들 사조를 가장 잘 기억하고 있다. 이 일련의 사조를 지지하는 사람들은 전쟁의 위험을 감수하고 세계화된 세계의 경제적 상호의존성을 파괴시킬 정도로 미친 사람이 유럽에 존재하지 않는다고 생각했다. 동시에 각 나라의 문화는 전쟁을 향해 가는 강력한 흐름으로 가득 차 있었다. 군비경쟁, 호전적인 경쟁관계, 그리고 자원을 확보하기 위한 투쟁 등이 있었다. 이 군비 경쟁은 규모도 크고 비용도 많이 드는 일이었다. 가장 대표적인 군비 경쟁은 더 크고 더 많은 배를 건조하고자 했던 영국과 독일 사이에 벌어진 해군 주도권 경쟁이었다. 수백만 명에 달하는 남자들이 징집을 통해 군대에 입대했는데, 이는 군대의 교화를 받은 경험이 있는 사람들이 인구의 상당 부분을 차지하게 만들었다. 민족주의, 엘리트주의, 인종주의, 그리고 그 외의 호전적인 사유들이 널리 퍼졌다. 이런 사유들이 널리 퍼지는 데 있어서 결정적인 역할을 한 것은 심한 편견으로 가득 차 있던 당대의 교육이었다. 정치적 목적을 위한 폭력은 흔했고 러시아의 사회주의자들에서부터 영국의 여성참정권주의자들에 이르기까지 폭넓게 퍼져 있었다. 조국을 위한 폭력은 점차 정당화되었고, 예술가들은 반항하면서 새로운 표현 방식을 찾았고, 새로운 도시문화는 기존의 사회질서에 도전했다. 본질적으로 1914년을 살았던 유럽인들은 파괴를 통해 세계를 재창조하는 하나의 문제 해결 방식으로 전쟁을 받아들일 준비가 되어 있었던 것이다.

shot through 가득 찬, 침투된
armament n. 무기; 군사력
indoctrination n. 주입, 가르침; 교화; 세뇌
prime v. 준비시키다, 대비시키다
rationale n. 논증, 추론
breach n. 위반; 갈라진 틈
configuration n. 구성, 배열, 배치
alleviate v. 완화시키다, 경감하다
division n. 분할, 분배; 나누기
sway v. 흔들다; 한쪽으로 기울다

01 ▶ 첫 번째 빈칸의 정답은 "정치적 목적을 위한 폭력은 흔했고 러시아의 사회주의자들에서부터 영국의 여성참정권주의자들에 이르기까지 폭넓게 퍼져 있었다."라는 단서로부터 추론할 수 있다. 두 번째 빈칸의 정답은 1914년의 유럽 사람들이 전쟁을 세계를 재창조하는 방식으로 받아들였다는 단서로부터 추론할 수 있다. 전쟁은 곧 파괴이다.

02 ▶ 열강들 간의 경제적 상호의존성은 전쟁의 위험을 감소시키는 역할을 한다.

》 정답 01 (C) 02 (E)

115

　　인간의 소망은 늘 두 가지 종류가 있다. 개인은 자신을 위한 소망을 가지고 있다. ― 개인적이며 사적인 소망을. 동시에 개인은 인류 혹은 인류의 일부인 종족, 가족, 교회 등을 위한 개인(자신)을 초월하는 소망도 지닌다.

　　이러한 두 종류의 인간의 소망은 늘 서로 엄격하게 구별되지는 않는다. 삶의 특징 중의 하나인 자기중심성이 매우 강력한 동력원이기 때문에 개인(자신)을 초월하는 소망으로 침투해 들어간다. 사실, 우리가 '이기주의'에 대한 집단적인 상대어로 사용하는 '우리주의'라는 말이 자기중심주의의 가장 강력한 형태다. 선을 위한 것이건, 악을 위한 것이건, 인간은 혼자 행동할 때보다 함께 행동할 때 훨씬 강하다. 그리고 또한 집단적으로 행동할 때 양심에 의해 갑자기 멈춰서는 일 없이 이기적으로 행동해갈 수 있다. 왜냐하면, 사람은 자신의 자기중심성을 개인으로부터 집단으로 종속시키고 있다고 스스로를 속일 수 있기 때문이다. 따라서, 자기중심주의가 개인을 초월하는 소망으로 침투해 들어갈 수 있는 것이다. 반면에 우리의 개인적 소망은 자기중심주의를 반대하고 넘어서려고 노력하는 도덕적 반응을 취한다.

suprapersonal a. 초개인적인
fraction n. 파편, 단편, 조각
distinguishable a. 구별되는
self-centeredness n. 자기중심성
nosism (or weism) n. 우리중심주의(we+ism)
egotism n. 자기중심주의
pull up short 갑자기 그만두다
delude v. 속이다, 미혹시키다
subordinate v. 복종시키다, 종속시키다
transcend v. 넘다, 초월하다

01 ▶ 빈칸 뒷 문장에서 '혼자 행동할 때보다 단체로 행동할 때 더욱 강력하고 더욱 이기적으로 행동할 수 있다'고 한 점에 착안하다.

02 ▶ ②가 들어있는 문장에는 주어인 Self-centeredness에 대한 동사로 seems와 is가 왔는데, 연결사 없이 한 문장 안에 두 개의 동사가 올 수 없다. 따라서 seems에 밑줄이 있으므로, ②를 which seems to be 로 고쳐서 주어를 수식해주는 형태로 고쳐야 한다.

》 정답　01 (C)　02 (B)

116

　　교황 베네딕토 16세는 그가 교황이 되기 2년 전, 조셉 라칭거(Joseph Ratzinger) 추기경으로서, 진화론을 포함한 몇몇 문제에 대해 우려를 표명하면서 과학은 자신의 능력의 한도를 지나쳐, 신(神)의 존재를 부정하고 스스로 독자적인 신앙 체계가 되어가고 있다고 하였다. 비록 그는 진화를 거부하지는 않았지만, 그 책에서 인용된 언급을 통해 과학은 진화를 실험실에서 재현해내지 못했기 때문에 진화를 완벽히 입증하지 못했다는 점을 지적하였다. 그러나 로이터 통신의 보도에 따르면, 그는 유신론적 진화론이라 알려진 것을 옹호했는데, 이것은 생명은 대단히 복잡해서 반드시 적극적인 창조자가 필요하다고 가정하는 '지적 설계론'이 주장하는 직접적 설계에 의한 것은 아니라고 할지라도, 신은 생명 창조를 위해 진화적 과정들을 이용했다는 사상이다. 베네딕토 16세는, 교황으로서 출간한 진화론에 대한 최초의 광범위한 저작에서, 다윈의 진화론은 결국 입증될 수 없으며 과학은 창조에 대한 인간의 견해를 불필요하게 제한시키고 있다고 말한다. 독일어로 출간된 신규 저서 『창조와 진화』를 통해 교황은 과학이 성취한 진보를 칭찬하면서도, 진화론은 과학만으로는 대답할 수 <있는> 철학적 질문들을 제기한다고 경고하였다. "문제는 과학을 근본적으로 배제시키는 창조론을 지지하는 결론도 내리지 않고, 진화론이 지닌 결함을 감추며 자연과학의 방법론적 가능성을 넘어서는 문제들을 외면하는 그런 진화론을 지지하는 결론도 내리지 않는다는 것이다"라고 교황은 말했다.

cardinal n. 추기경
overstep v. 지나가다; ~의 한도를 넘다
competence n. 적성, 자격, 능력
quote v. 인용하다
duplicate v. 복사하다; ~와 같은 것을 만들다
theistic a. 유신론의; 일신론의
posit v. 긍정적으로 가정하다, 단정하다
cover over (물건의 흠 등을) 가리다; (실책 등을) 감추다
methodological a. 방법론적인

01 ▶ 본문에서 교황은 진화론이 실험실에서 입증되지 않은 것이라고 하였으면서, 또 한편으로는 과학을 포용하는 창조론의 필요성 또는 유신론적 진화론 등을 수용하는 입장을 보여준다. 이는 창조론 혹은 신학의 틀 안으로 과학의 논리나 성과를 끌어들이겠다는 의도로 이해할 수 있다.

02 ▶ '과학만으로는 해결할 수 없는 문제들'을 신앙(또는 신학)적 틀 안에서 해결할 있을 것이라는 것이 교황의 입장이다. 따라서 ③에서 can을 cannot으로 바꾸는 것이 적절하다.

》 정답 01 (C) 02 (C)

---

117   철학자들은 대화의 필요성을 주장할 뿐만 아니라 대화의 본질을 설명할 필요가 있다. 대화는 단지 생각을 주고받는 것이 아니다. 말다툼하는 무리는 적극적으로 생각을 주고받을지 모르지만 대화와는 거리가 멀며 서로 칭찬하는 무리 또한 대화와 거리가 멀다. 두 가지 경우 모두에 있어서, 토론은 진리에 대한 지식 또는 바람직한 인간관계를 위한 덕을 습득하는 것에 전념하지 못하고 있다. 그런데 이것들은 대화의 필요조건이다. 하지만 다른 필요조건이 있다. 대화는 이성적인 토론에 기초해야 한다. 당사자들이 자신들이 틀릴 수도 있고 다른 쪽은 맞을 수도 있다는 가능성을 인정하지 않는다면 그런 (이성적인) 대화는 불가능하다. 우리 모두는 이런 마음가짐이 쉽게 생기지 않는다는 것을 알고 있다.

대화를 가로막는 가장 심각한 장애 중 하나는 독단론이며 독단론의 해결방법을 찾는 것이 철학자의 역할이며 또 역할이어야 하는 것이다. 독단론은 단지 강한 신념을 갖는 것이기보다는 잘못에 대한 가능성을 배제한 아주 강한 신념을 갖는 것이다. 그것은 넓은 의미에서의 철학을 포함한 인간사고의 모든 영역에서 마주칠 수 있는 것이다. 그리고 인간의 사고에서 독단론을 제거하는 것이 엄격한 학문적 개념에서의 철학의 목표 중 하나이다.

quarrel v. 싸우다, 다투다; 비난하다
for the sake of ~을 위해서
desirable a. 바람직한; 탐나는
necessary condition 필요조건
rational a. 이성적인, 합리적인
impediment n. 방해(물), 장애
dogmatism n. 독단(론); 독단주의
antidote n. 해독제; (해악 따위의) 교정[방어, 대항] 수단
hold a belief 신념을 갖다
conviction n. 신념, 확신
rule out 배제하다; 제거하다
sphere n. (활동) 영역, (세력) 범위

01 ▶ so/neither 구문은 'so/neither+동사+주어'의 형태로 '~도 또한 그렇다'의 의미를 갖는 도치된 생략형 문장이다. 이때 so는 앞문장이 긍정일 때, neither는 앞문장이 부정일 때 사용한다. 원래 문장은 a group indulging in mutual admiration would be far from dialogue, too 로 빈칸 앞의 will be far from dialogue를 will 대신에 would가 사용되었으며, so가 와서 주어와 동사가 도치된 (C)가 정답이다.

02 ▶ 첫 문장에서 "철학자는 대화의 필요성을 주장할 뿐만 아니라 대화의 본질을 설명할 필요가 있다"고 하며 철학이 대화에 있어서의 역할을 설명하고 있고, 본문의 마지막 문장에서 "인간 사고에서 독단론을 제거하는 것이 철학의 목표 중 하나이다"라고 했으므로 철학은 절대 확신하는 것을 '제거할 의무가 있다고 해야 옳다.

》 정답 01 (C) 02 (D)

모잠비크의 상당 지역을 뒤덮은 파괴적인 홍수를 겪은 후, 뉴스 보도에서 자연에 대해서는 많은 말을 하고 인간의 행위에 대해서는 별 말을 하지 않았다는 것은 놀라운 일이다. 어쨌든, 한 개의 주요 텔레비전 뉴스 프로그램에서 이 대륙에서 일어나는 대부분의 불행한 일들은 내전이나 대량 학살 등 인간 행위의 결과물이므로, 이 "자연" 재해가 아프리카에서는 드문 경우라고 주장한 것은 아이러니할 정도이다. 그 프로그램이 간과하여 언급하지 않은 점은 바로 그 홍수가 기타 최근의 많은 "자연" 재해들처럼 지구 온난화의 결과라는 것이다. 그렇다면 지구 온난화의 원인은 무엇인가? 자연이 아니라 혹시 인간일 수 있는가? 몇 해 째 지구 기온의 상승이 강우량이나 기온 변화의 결과로 나타나는 극단적인 날씨나 재난을 야기할 것이라는 경고가 있어왔다. 우리들 대부분은 이 경고에 그다지 두려움을 느끼지 않아 왔다. 우리는 이러한 결과적 현상들이 당장 내년이나 내달이나 내주가 아닌 먼 미래의 언젠가에 일어날 것으로 생각해 왔다. 그래서 화학물질을 공기에 방출시키면서 지구라는 압력솥을 서서히 가열해 온 것이다. 우리의 어리석음을 나타내주는 흔적이 지구상에 이렇게 엄청난 속도로 증가하고 있는데, 이 거대한 망상이 얼마나 오래도록 계속될 것인가?

remarkable a. 주목할 만한, 현저한, 남다른
devastating a. 파괴적인, 황폐시키는
catastrophe n. 파국; 대이변; 큰 재해
misery n. 불행, 고통; 빈곤, 비참함
genocide n. 대량학살
disaster n. 천재(天災), 재해
chemical n. 화학물질
delusion n. 망상, 착각
folly n. 어리석음, 우둔; 어리석은 행위

01 ▶ 사람들의 잘못으로 초래된 지구 온난화와 그에 따른 재난에도 불구하고 여전히 어떻게 하는 게 바른 것인지 사람들이 잘 모르고 있다는 내용이다.

02 ▶ 본문은 사람들이 지구온난화에 관심을 기울이지 않고 있음을 지적하는 내용이므로 (D)가 정답이 된다.

》 정답 01 (A) 02 (D)

UN은 목요일 6년 연속으로 노르웨이를 가장 살기 좋은 나라로 평가했다. 이에 자극받은 노르웨이의 원조 담당 장관은 노르웨이 사람들에게 더 많은 것을 원하는 푸념은 그만둬달라고 말했다. 관대한 복지국가이자, 기름이 풍부한 노르웨이는 UN 개발계획의 기대수명, 교육, 수입에 근거한 인간개발지수에서 맨 윗자리에 올랐다. 아이슬란드가 2위였고, 오스트레일리아, 아일랜드, 스웨덴, 캐나다, 일본, 미국이 그 뒤를 이었다.

부(富)와 높은 교육수준, 낮은 실업률, 경제호황에도 불구하고 노르웨이 사람들은 흔히 많은 세금과 요람에서 무덤까지 복지 국가의 취약함에 대해 불평을 한다. 예를 들어, 병원에서 줄지어 기다리는 것, 혹은 아이나 노인들을 위한 공공 치료시설의 부족에 대한 불평을 하고 있다.

이 연구에 따르면, 노르웨이 사람들은 이 연구에서 최저로 평가된 니제르에 비해 40배 더 많은 돈을 벌고, 두 배 더 오래 살며, 5배는 더 많은 비문맹률을 가지고 있다. 원조 담당 장관 에릭 솔하임은 한 인터뷰에서 "최고의 자리는 우리로 하여금 겸손을 보이게 한다."라고 말했다. "노르웨이는 근대적이고, 부유하며 성공적인 사회로 보여야 한다. 하지만 또한 너그러운 나라로도 보여야 한다. 세계는 우리를 부유하면서 인색한 나라가 아니라 부유하고 관대하게 보아야 한다."

rank v. 평가하다
consecutive a. 연속적인
prompt v. 자극하다; 격려하다, 고무하다
generous a. 관대한; 후한[너그러운]
top v. ~의 수석을 차지하다; ~의 선두에 서다
aid minister 원조 담당 장관
cradle-to-grave a. 요람에서 무덤까지의
humility n. 겸손, 겸양
miserly a. 인색한

01 ▶ '충분히 누릴 만큼 누리고 있는 상황에서 더 많은 것을 요구하고 있다'는 맥락이므로, '투덜대다'라는 의미의 whine이 적절하다.

02 ▶ 마지막 문단의 내용을 근거로 (A)를 정답으로 선택할 수 있다.

≫ 정답 01 (A) 02 (A)

120

미국 남서부의 건조한 지역들은 오토바이나 강력한 트레일 바이크와 같은 차량을 가지고 언덕 오르기 시합이나 사막에 새로운 길을 내는 데 열중하는 많은 오락 추구자들에게 점점 더 매력 있는 터전이 되어 왔다. 그러나 최근의 과학적 연구는 이런 오프로드 차량들이 사막지역의 물을 보존하는 특성과 동식물 모두의 생태 환경에 장기적인 영향을 미치는 사막 경관을 손상시킬 수 있다는 점을 보여준다. 캘리포니아의 서부 모하비 사막에서 행한 과학자들의 조사 결과, 단 한 대의 오토바이라도 지나가면 건조한 모래흙이 압축되어 토양의 물 흡수 능력을 현저하게 떨어뜨리고 언덕의 경사면을 침식시키는 빗물의 흐름을 만들어 내었다는 것을 밝혀냈다. 이외에도, 연구자들은 오프로드 차량들로 인해 토양이 압축되어 종종 토착 식물들을 죽여 몇 년 안 있어 다른 종의 식물이 침입한다는 사실을 알게 되었다. 다년생 토착 식물들이 되돌아올 조짐을 보이는 데는 이보다 더 많은 세월이 필요했는데, 과학자들은 차량들에 의해 압축된 후 모하비 사막의 토양이 다시 물을 흡수하는 능력을 회복하는 데는 대략 1백년이 걸릴 것이라고 추정하였다.

arid a. 건조한; 불모의
vehicle n. 수송수단, 탈 것
indulge in 즐기다, 탐닉하다
characteristic n. 특질, 특색
ecology n. 생태학
compaction n. 꽉 채움; 압축
markedly ad. 현저하게, 뚜렷하게
infiltration n. 침투
erode v. 좀먹다, 부식하다
species n. 종(種), 종류
perennial a. 연중 끊이지 않는
calculate v. 계산하다, 산정하다

01 ▶ 이 글은 과학자들의 연구결과를 바탕으로 사막에서 오토바이를 즐기는 사람들이 늘어남에 따라 초래된 동식물의 생태환경 파괴에 관하여 논하고 있다.

02 ▶ (B)는 문장 In addition, the researchers ~ killed native plant species에서, (C)는 두 번째 문장에서, (D)는 세 번째 문장 중 the compaction of the sandy soil ~ reduced the infiltration ability of the soil~에서와 같이 토양이 압축되면 물이 잘 스며들지 못한다는 사실을 알 수 있다. (A)는 이 글의 마지막 문장인 The native perennial ~에서 어떤 종류의 식물이 사라지면 그 자리에 그 식물이 다시 생겨나기까지는 오랜 시간이 소요된다고 하였으므로 '돌이킬 수 없다 (irreparable)'는 것은 아니다.

≫ 정답 01 (B) 02 (A)

121

건축가인 사무엘 매킨타이어와 찰스 불핀치는 각각 살렘과 보스턴의 유명한 건물들을 설계했지만, 메사추세츠 주의 그린필드 출신의 목수인 애셔 벤자민이 누구보다도 뉴잉글랜드의 건축에 더 큰 직접적인 영향을 끼친 것으로 평가되고 있다. 1797년에 그는 『국가건설의 보조원』이라는 책을 출간했다. 그 책은 미국에서 출간된 건축에 관한 최초의 문헌은 아니었지만, 그 분야를 진정으로 미국적인 입장에서 다룬 최초의 책이었다. 그 책은 다양한 개인 또는 공공 구조물에 관한 도면과 상세한 그림을 포함하고 있었기 때문에 다분히 "실용서적"이었다. 동북부 전역에 있는 목수들은 제법 학식이 있는 사람들이었다. 그들은 벤자민의 책을 구입하였고 벤자민의 설계를 모방하여 건설공사를 하게 되었다. 모든 뉴잉글랜드의 교회들 가운데서 가장 추앙받는 교회 중의 하나인 버몬트 주 베닝턴의 최초의 회중교회 건물은 목수인 래비우스 필모어에 의해 지어진 것이며, 그것은 애셔의 책에서 찾아볼 수 있는 디자인 중의 하나와 매우 유사하다. 필모어와 마찬가지로 대부분의 지방 목수들은 그들 나름의 열정을 가지고 있었으며, 애셔의 책을 통한 자동적 모방에만 몰두해 있지는 않았다. 그러나 전체적인 결과는 뉴잉글랜드 지방에 독특한 정취를 계속 부여해 주고 있는 하나의 건축 양식이 이 지역에 널리 파급됐다는 것이다.

architect n. 건축가
exert v. (힘 등을) 발휘하다, 쓰다; (영향력을) 행사하다
genuinely ad. 진짜로; 진심에서 우러나서
pervasive a. 퍼지는, 널리 미치는
distinctive a. 독특한, 특이한

01 ▶ 책에 있는 도면을 본따서 사용한 것이므로, 교사가 학생에게 미치는 것과 같은 역할이다.

02 ▶ 첫 문장을 통해 알 수 있다.

》 정답 01 (A) 02 (C)

122

예술, 즉 모든 예술은 사람들을 통합시킨다는 특성을 지니고 있다. 모든 예술은 예술가에 의해 전달된 감정을 받아들이는 사람들이 예술가나 혹은 같은 인상을 받은 사람들과 정신적인 유대를 지니게 하는 것이다. 그런데 비기독교 예술은 어떤 사람들을 함께 결속시키기는 하지만, 바로 그것이 결속된 이 사람들과 다른 사람들을 분리시키는 원인이 되고 있다. 따라서 이런 종류의 결속이란 사람들을 분열시키는 원천이 될 뿐 아니라, 다른 사람들에 대해 적의를 품게 하는 원인이 되고 있다. 그런 것은 모두 국수적 성격의 예술로서 그 나름의 축가, 축시, 기념물을 지니고 있다. 예를 들면, 모든 기독교 예술에서처럼, 우상이나 소유물 그리고 특유의 예식을 지니고서 일정한 제식을 행하는 예술을 일컬을 수 있다. 그러한 예술은 시대에 뒤지고 비기독교적 예술로서, 어느 한 종파의 사람들을 결속시키지만, 그들을 타 종파의 사람들과 더욱 철저히 분리시키고 있으며, 심지어 그들을 적대적인 관계에 놓기도 한다. 그러나 만인은 신과 그들 이웃에 대해 똑같은 관계에 서 있다는 인식을 불러일으킴으로써, 혹은 그들 사이에 일치단결된 감정 ― 기독교 정신에 어긋나지 않고 예외 없이 만인에게 합당한 것이라면 그 아무리 소박한 것일지라도 ― 을 불러일으킴으로써, 모든 사람들을 예외 없이 결속시키는 경향을 보이는 것, 그것이 바로 기독교 예술인 것이다.

transmit v. 내주다, 보내다, 전하다
enmity n. 증오, 적의
patriotic a. 애국의, 애국적인
anthem n. 국가, 찬송가
cult n. 제식, 숭배
statue n. 상(象)
procession n. 행렬, 행진, 진행
belated a. 시대에 뒤진
evoke v. 불러내다
repugnant a. 비위에 거슬리는; 모순된

01 ▶ 빈칸 ①의 경우, 빈칸이 포함된 문장이 앞 문장과 대조를 이루어야 하므로, 모든 사람에게 유대감을 갖게 하진 않는다는 의미가 되게 하는 while과 even if가 적절하다. 한편, 관계대명사 that은 계속적 용법으로 쓰이지 못하므로 빈칸 ③에는 which가 들어간다.

02 ▶ '사람들을 결속시킨다'와 상반되는 의미의 표현이 필요하다.

》 정답 01 (A) 02 (D)

노사관계의 한 가지 고질적인 문제는 '우리/그들'의 사고방식이다. 재정적 압박 이외에, 공정근로기준법(FLSA)과 관련해 지속적으로 발생하는 문제, 신의를 저버리는 협상, 부실 경영 관행, 무능한 노동조합 지도부, 경영진 특권의 지속적인 손실 등이 복합적으로 작용해, 노사관계를 악화시키는 태업이 머지않아 급증하게 된다. 이에 대해서는 노사 어느 쪽도 책임이 없다. 이러한 상황의 비극적인 측면은 분열된 노사관계가 이들 양측의 관계에 주는 영향이 상대적으로 예측 할 수 있고, 피할 수 있다는 것이다.

경제상황이 향후 몇 년 동안은 크게 나아지지 않을 것이기 때문에, 조합원들에게 더 많은 혜택이 돌아가게 하려고 하는 노조 지도부는 감당할 수 없을 정도로 많은 압박을 받게 될 것이다. 과거 전문항공관제사협회(PACTO)가 주도했던 파업을 경험한 회사의 경영진은, 지난 10년 동안 잃어버린 자신들의 특권을 되찾는 데 시간이 도움이 된다는 사실을 알게 됐다. 공공부문에서 노사 간 대립의 요건은 이미 갖추어졌다. 많은 지역의 경우, 노사 갈등을 악화시키는 태업의 강행에 불씨를 당길 수 있는 사건만 터지면 된다. 겉으로 보기에 손을 쓸 수 없어 보이는 이 문제를 해결할 수 있는 유일한 방법은 노련한 협상의 영역에 있다. 노련한 협상이 이루어지기 위해 요구되는 것은 기존 계약의 조항들을 지키겠다는 노사의 확고한 의지이다.

mentality n. 심리상태
fiscal a. 재정의
constraint n. 강제, 구속
prerogative n. 특권
disruptive a. 분열성의
job action 태업, 준법투쟁
conducive a. 이바지하는
commitment n. 관여, 참가, 실행
live up to 지키다, 실천하다

01 ▶ intractable a. 다루기 힘든, 고치기 힘든(= obstinate)

02 ▶ 본문에서 '향후 경제 사정이 크게 좋아지지 않을 것이기 때문에 노조 지도부는 감당하기 어려울 정도로 압박을 받게 될 것이다'라고 했기 때문에, 경제가 좋아지면 노조 지도부가 압박을 덜 받게 되고, 그만큼 더 힘을 쓸 수가 있어 노조의 힘이 더 강해진다는 것을 추론할 수 있다.

》 정답 01 (A) 02 (B)

중산층이 처음 서구 산업화 국가들의 공장 근로자들 가운데서 발견된 이래로 언제나 중산층은 정치인들, 경제학자들, 가게주인들에게 똑같이 발전의 희망을 갖게 하는 것이었다. 그것은 여전히 정의내리기 어려우며 정의 내리려는 시도들은 종종 자의적인 것 같다. 그러나 브라질에서는, 중산층이 공식 경제 안에서 일자리를 갖고 있고, 자유롭게 신용거래를 할 수 있고, 자동차나 오토바이를 소유한 사람들로 설명된다. 이것은 월 소득이 1,064레알(600달러)에서 4,561레알 사이인 가정을 의미한다. 전체 인구 중 이 설명에 부합하는 사람들의 비율이 2002년 이후 지금 44%에서 52%로 늘었는데, 이것은 브라질의 소득 불평등이 감소했음을 의미한다. 이런 사회적 지위 향상을 위한 노력은 브라질 도시들의 특징이며, 1980년대 초부터 20년간 계속된 경기침체를 역전시키고 있다. 한 사회학자는 이런 변화의 이면에는 두 가지 요인이 있다고 말한다. 첫째는 교육이다. 브라질 학교의 교육의 질은 아직도 열악할지 모르지만, 지금 15세에서 21세 사이의 사람들은 1990년대 초의 같은 연령대 사람들에 비해 평균 3년 이상 더 공부를 한다. 두 번째 요인은 비공식 '검은(지하)' 경제로부터 공식 경제로의 고용(일자리)의 이동이다. 공식 고용 창출이 가속적으로 늘고 있어, 올해 들어 7월 현재까지의 고용 창출이 지난해 12개월 동안의 고용 창출보다 40% 더 많은 수인데, 지난해도 늘어난 일자리는 기록적인 수였다. 가난한 가정으로 현금이 이전되는 것과 아울러 이렇게 일자리가 늘어나는 것은, 인도나 중국의 경제 사회 발전과는 대조적으로, 브라질의 중산층이 성장함에 따라 브라질의 소득 불평등도 마찬가지로 감소한 이유를 설명하는 데 도움을 준다.

spot v. 발견하다, 탐지해내다
bear v. 품다; 전하다, 제공하다
arbitrary a. 자의적인, 임의적인
access n. 접근, 접근하는 방법
reais n. real(브라질의 화폐단위)의 복수형
black economy 지하 경제

01 ▶ (A) 1,064레알에서 4,561레알 사이라 했다. (B) 1,064레알이 600달러이므로 1달러당 1.77레알의 환율이다. (C) 교육의 향상과 공식 경제로의 고용이동과 창출이 중산층 성장의 원인으로 언급되었다. (D) 이주노동자들이 브라질 경제에 미친 영향은 알 수 없다.

02 ▶ 중산층 비율이 증가한 결과로 감소되는 것은 소득 불평등이고, 빈곤층으로 현금이 이전되고 고용창출이 늘어난 결과로 감소되는 것도 소득 불평등이다.

▶ 정답 01 (D) 02 (A)

어떤 사람들은 다른 사람들보다 더 도움을 주는가? 다니엘 산토스(Daniel Santos)의 친구들과 동료들은 처음 보는 사람을 구하려고 타판교(Tappan Zee Bridge)에서 150피트를 뛰어내린 그의 영웅적인 면에 대해 알게 되었을 때 그다지 놀라지 않았다. "그는 원래 그래요. 그는 무언가를 보면 당장 가서 그 사람을 도우려고 합니다."라고 그의 친구 중 한명이 말했다. 다니엘이 정비사로 일하고 있던 회사의 접수원은 "그는 언제 어디서든 사람들을 도울 겁니다."라고 덧붙인다. 다니엘의 여동생은 "오빠는 용기가 대단하지요."라고 말하며 그가 수영을 잘 하지 못하면서도 물속에 뛰어 든 이야기를 했다.

어떤 경우에서라도 대체로 다른 사람들을 도와주는 사람들이 많이 있는가? 대개 다른 이들을 돕지 않는 사람들도 있는가? 도움의 행동에 영향을 미치는 데 상황적인 요소가 개인적 차이를 분명히 압도할 수 있음에도 불구하고, 연구원들은 도와주는 성향에 있어 개인적 차이에 대한 증거를 제시하였다. 어떤 상황에서 다른 사람들보다 도움을 많이 주는 사람들은 다른 상황에서도 그러할 가능성이 있다. 또한, 낸시 아이젠버그(Nancy Eisenberg) 및 여러 다른 연구원들에 의한 장기적인 연구에 따르면, 이러한 개인적 차이는 시간이 지나도 비교적 고정적일 수 있다. 보다 명확히 말하자면, 그들은 유치원 아이들이 자발적인 도움의 행동을 보여준 정도가 그 이후 어린 시절과 초기 성인기에 다른 이들을 얼마나 도와주는지를 예측케 한다는 것을 발견했다.

---

mechanic n. 기계공, 정비사
situational a. 상황의, 상황에 의한
factor n. 요인, 요소
overwhelm v. 압도하다, 제압하다
longitudinal a. 경도(經度)의; (변화 따위의) 장기적인
relatively ad. 상대적으로
specifically ad. 명확히; 특히
spontaneous a. 자발적인; 무의식적인

01 ▶ 위험한 상황에서 다른 이들을 도와주려는 다니엘 산토스를 설명하였다. 이어지는 문단에서, 도움의 행동에서 상황적 요소보다 개인적 차이를 발견한 연구 결과 및 유치원생 때의 성향이 성인이 되어서의 행동을 예측케 한다고 언급하며, 이러한 행동은 본래 타고난 특징이라는 것을 암시한다. 따라서 다니엘 산토스의 예는 상황에 따라 누구를 돕는 것이 아니라 "위험한 상황 속에서도 단지 자연스럽게 자발적으로 다른 사람들을 도와준다"것을 이야기해 준다.

02 ▶ 미래의 행동을 예측할 수 있는 조건은 그 행동이 '안정적(고정적)'이어야 가능할 것이다.

≫ 정답 01 (D) 02 (B)

아인슈타인(Einstein)은 단순한 과학자만은 아니었다. 그는 또한 헌신적인 인도주의자였으며 윤리나 사회문제에 관해서도 그가 과학에 관해서 쓴 것 못지않게 많은 글들을 썼다. "지식과 기술만으로는 인류가 행복하고 존엄한 삶을 누릴 수 없다. 인류가 높은 도덕 기준과 가치를 주장하는 사람들을 객관적 진리의 발견자들보다 높이 평가한다는 것은 지극히 당연하다"고 그는 언명했다. 아인슈타인은 위대한 과학자이었을 뿐만 아니라 위대한 인간이었다. <그러나 세계는 아인슈타인의 인도주의보다는 그의 과학에 훨씬 큰 관심을 기울였다.> 초강대국 정부들은 아인슈타인의 방정식을 핵폭탄으로 변형시키는 재주를 지닌 사람들을 수만 명씩이나 채용하고 있으나, 왜 핵폭탄을 만들지 말아야 하는가에 대한 아인슈타인의 조언을 곰곰이 생각해본 사람은 거의 아무도 채용하지 않고 있다. 아인슈타인의 진가를 제대로 알아보기 위해서는, 그를 구름같이 둘러싸고 있는 신화의 장막을 걷고, 그 속을 들여다보아야 한다. 그 안에는 철두철미 하게 평화를 사랑하는 선사(禪師)와 같은 모습의 아인슈타인이 있다. 평화야말로 수백을 헤아리는 그의 논설과 서신 및 강연들의 주제였다. 그가 별세하기 몇 시간 전 그의 오래된 친구 오토 나단(Otto Nathan)과 나누었던 대화의 내용도 시민의 자유에 관한 것이었다. 그가 서명한 마지막 문서는 핵무기 사용 반대를 천명하는 선언문이었다. 그는 핵폭탄이 이제 "미개했던 시대가 남겨 준 야만적이고 비인간적 유물"인 전면전쟁을 철폐하는 것 이외의 다른 아무런 선택의 여지도 이 세계에 남겨주지 않았다고 주장했다.

ethical a. 윤리적인
superpower n. 초강력; 초강대국
equation n. 방정식
peer v. 자세히 보다; 응시하다
thunderhead n. 적란운, 소나기구름
Zen n. 선(禪), 선종(禪宗)
first and last 전부 통틀어, 모두
proclamation n. 선언; 포고; 발포
renounce v. 포기하다; 부인하다; ~와 관계를 끊다
all-out a. 온 힘을 다한; 전면적인; 철저한
savage a. 야만의; 미개한; 잔혹한
relic n. 유적; 유물
barbarism n. 야만; 미개; 만행

01 ▶ 위대한 과학자이지만 인도주의자이기도 한 아인슈타인의 면모를 철학자로 비유하며 소개하고 있다. 따라서 (A)가 정답으로 적절하다. 본문은 아인슈타인의 인도주의가 그가 이룬 과학적 업적에 비해 잘 알려지지 않았다고 지적하고 있으므로 (B) '인도주의로 잘 알려진 아인슈타인'은 제목으로 적절하지 않다.

02 ▶ [ⅠⅠ] 뒤의 "강대국들은 인도주의자였던 아인슈타인의 사상을 거슬러 그의 방정식으로 핵폭탄을 개발한다"는 내용은 주어진 문장 "세계는 아인슈타인의 인도주의보다 그의 과학에 더욱 관심을 기울였다"의 하나의 예가 되므로 [ⅠⅠ]에 위치해야 한다.

» 정답 01 (A) 02 (B)

127

나는, 닥터 라이드의 책에 관한 당신의 소논문이 누락된 것을 당신이 그렇게 많이 중요시하는 것에 대해 유감스럽게 생각합니다. 나는 확실히 그것을 포함시키고자 했었지만, 다른 엄청난 양의 기사들과, 그리고 그 호(號)가 가득 찼을 때, 당신의 불가피한 출타로 인해 하지 못했습니다. 비록 그 주제에 많은 관심이 없을지라도, 저는 다음 호에 그것을 게재할 생각입니다.

나는 보다 더 사적인 주제에 대한 당신의 이전 편지에 답장을 드리지 않은 것에 매우 책임이 있음을 느낍니다. 당신의 마지막 편지에서 그것에 관해 언급하지 않은 당신의 배려로 인해 내가 그것을 덜 통감하는 것은 아닙니다. 내가 답장을 하지 않은 것은 내가 가지고 있는 정보를 모두 당신에게 제공하는 일에 무관심했다거나 또는 그것이 싫었기 때문이 아니라, 내가 가지고 있는 정보의 정당성 여부에 대해서 매우 불안한 감이 있었고 또 그 정보에 근거를 두고 내가 충고를 한다면 커다란 잘못을 저지를 위험이 있었기 때문입니다. 이것으로 인해 저는 주저하고, 그리고 제가 답변을 하기 전에 심사숙고와 상세한 조사를 하기로 결심하게 됐고, 그리고 나서 평소의 나쁜 버릇인 머뭇거림이 있었습니다. 그리고 보다 더 긴급한 다른 일이 있다는 흔한 변명이 있어, 결국에는 드디어 반쯤은 잊혀지고 그리고 그것이 다시 생각났을 때 그것은 내 양심에서 반쯤 사라졌습니다.

ascribe A to B A를 B의 탓으로 돌리다
omission n. 생략, 누락, 탈락
assuredly ad. 확실히, 의심 없이
delicacy n. 섬세함, 우아함, 고상함; 배려, 자상함
hesitate v. 주저하다, 망설이다
procrastination n. 지연, 지체; 미루는 버릇
avocation n. 부업; 직업
recur v. 마음에 다시 떠오르다; 재발하다

01 ▶ 첫 번째 단락의 첫 문장과 마지막 문장을 참고할 것.
02 ▶ 두 번째 단락의 "I can safely say that ~"의 문장을 참고할 것

》 정답 01 (D) 02 (A)

긍정적인 심상, 믿음, 감정, 욕망 등과 부정적인 이런 것들이 서로 번갈아 일어나거나 동시에 일어나는 현상인 반대 감정 병존은 친밀한 관계에서 보통 있는 것이고 어쩌면 보편적이기까지 하다. 동일 인물을 서로 다른 시점에 정반대로 볼 수 있다는 것은 주요한 정보처리(인지) 시스템이 이원적으로 조직되어 있다는 것을 나타내준다. 가장 명백한 차원에서 반대 감정 병존은 부부가 어느 순간에는 사랑하고 있다가 그 다음 순간에는 서로를 헐뜯고 싶어질 때 분명해진다. 사람들이 어떻게 혹은 왜 갑자기 애정에서 미움으로 바꾸는지, 아니면 왜 예전의 따뜻한 감정이 분노의 감정을 맛보지 않게 막아주는 완충물이 되지 않는지는 종종 설명하기 어렵다. 관계에 있어 이런 종류의 감정 반전은 애정에 의해 모든 차이가 수면 아래로 가라앉거나 달콤해지는 남녀 간 사랑의 황금기에는 분명하지 않을지 모른다. <그러나 그것은 부부가 각자의 목표와 욕망에 더욱 몰두할 때 더욱 명백해진다.> 예전에 평온했던 사랑의 풍경에 구멍과 균열이 나타난다. 상호이익과 자기이익 사이의 균형점이 점차적으로 옮겨간다. "너에게 가장 좋은 것이 나에게 가장 좋아"가 "나에게 가장 좋은 것이 너에게 가장 좋아"로 되는 것이다. 실제로, 두 가지 방향의 태도결정 모두가 결혼생활 내내 지속될 수도 있지만, 비참해진 관계에서는 자기중심적인 믿음이 이타적인 믿음보다 더 많이 작용하게 된다.

---

ambivalence n. 반대 감정 병존, (상반되는) 감정의 교차
dualistic a. 이원적인
primal a. 주요한, 근본의
tear apart 헐뜯다, 비난하다
switch v. 바꾸다
cushion n. 완충물
reversal n. 반전, 역전
halcyon days 평온하고 행복한 시대, 황금기
pothole n. 깊은 구멍, 웅덩이
rift n. 갈라진 틈
orientation n. 방위 결정, 태도의 결정
altruistic a. 이타적인
distressed a. 고뇌에 지친, 가난한, 비참해진

01 ▶ [I] 앞 문장이 감정 반전이 명백하지 않은 경우를 설명하고 제시된 문장은 however로 앞 문장과 연결되어 감정 반전이 더욱 명백해지는 경우를 설명하므로 제시된 문장은 [I]에 들어가는 것이 적절하다.

02 ▶ 첫 문장에서 Ambivalence와 is 사이에 삽입된 명사가 곧 ambivalence의 정의에 해당하는데 (D)가 'simultaneous occurrence of positive and negative feelings'의 경우라 할 수 있다.

》 정답　01 (A)　02 (D)

129　　창피하다는 감정을 불러일으키는 다른 질병들과 마찬가지로, 에이즈(AIDS)도 흔히 비밀로 다뤄지지만 환자에게는 아니다. 암 진단은 환자의 가족에 의해 환자에게 비밀로 하는 수가 많았다. 그러나 에이즈 진단은 환자들 쪽에서 가족들에게 비밀로 하는 수가 많다. 단순한 질병 이상으로 여겨지는 다른 중병을 앓고 있는 사람들처럼, 에이즈 환자의 대부분은 병 그 자체에 대한 치료보다는, 효과가 없다든가 너무 위험하다고 생각되는 전신 치료에 치닫게 된다. 암은 수술이나 약으로 치료 가능한 경우가 많긴 하지만, 일부 암 환자들 또한 이 비참한 선택을 하고 있다. 동일하게 에이즈 환자도 상상하기 어렵지 않은 미신과 체념에 뒤얽힌 감정에 사로잡혀, 치료제가 없는 경우에도 (증상의 진행을 늦추거나 발병하기 쉬운 2차 질환을 억제하는 데 있어) 일정한 효과가 있는 것으로 입증된 항바이러스 화학요법을 거절하고, 그 대신 "비정통 요법의 기도 선생"의 비호 아래 자신을 치료하려는 경우도 적지 않다. 그러나 쇠약한 육체로 자연식 요법을 행하는 것이 어느 정도 에이즈 치료에 도움이 되는가 하는 것은 기껏 중세의 "전체론적인" 치료 방법인 방혈 치료를 받는 것과 큰 차이가 없을 것이다.

conceal v. 숨기다, 비밀로 하다
illness-specific a. 질병 특유의
ineffectual a. 효과적이 아닌, 만족스런 효과가 없는
superstition n. 미신
resignation n. 단념, 체념
antiviral a. 항바이러스의
chemotherapy n. 화학요법
under the auspices of ~의 찬조로, 후원으로
alternative a. 양자택일의; 대신 택할
guru n. 지도자; (한정된 분야의) 권위자
emaciated a. 여윈, 쇠약해진
purification n. 깨끗이 하기, 세정, 정화
bleed v. 출혈하다, 출혈하게 하다
holistic a. 전체론적인

01 ▶ 본문에서는 여러 관찰 결과나 의견을 서술하고 있지만, 그것은 주로 에이즈 환자가 느끼는 독특한 치욕감이 치료 선택에 미치는 영향에 대해 이야기하고 있다.

02 ▶ 에이즈 환자와 암 환자 모두 병 그 자체에 대한 특수치료보다 전신 요법을 잘못 요구하기 쉽다는 점에서 에이즈와 암의 대비는 둘 중 어느 경우나 병에 대한 특수 치료의 중요성을 강조하는 것이 목적이므로 (D)가 답이다.

03 ▶ 항바이러스 화학요법을 에이즈 치료에 쓴다는 내용(B), 그리고 에이즈 치료를 위한 전신 요법과 비정통 요법에 대한 비판(C)과 에이즈 환자와 다른 병에 걸린 환자들은 수치심을 갖는다는 것과 걸핏하면 에이즈나 암의 전신 치료를 택한다는 점에서 공통적(D)이다. 그러나 저자의 논의를 입증하기 위한 의학적 근거(A)는 본문에 드러나 있지 않다.

》 정답　01 (C)　02 (D)　03 (A)

1960년대와 70년대에 등장한 새로운 정치역사 학파는 보통 시민들의 정치적인 실제 행동들을 조사함으로써 전통적으로 정치역사가들이 지도자들과 정부기관에 초점을 맞춰 온 것을 넘어서려 모색했다. 그러나 옛 접근법과 마찬가지로, 이 새로운 접근법에서도 여성은 제외되었다. 이런 역사가들이 19세기 미국의 대중 정치 행태를 밝히려 사용했던 바로 그 기법, 즉 예를 들면, 선거 개표 보고서에 대한 수량적 분석들이, 1920년이 되어서야 투표권을 갖게 된 여성들의 정치 활동을 분석하는 데는 소용이 없었다.

"정치 활동"을 다시 정의함으로써, 역사가 폴라 베이커는 여성을 포함하는 정치 역사학을 발전시켰다. 그녀는 보통의 시민들 가운데서, 19세기 여성들에 의한 정치 행동주의는 20세기의 정치 경향을 예표하는 것이었다고 결론짓는다. "정치"를 정부나 지역사회의 행동 과정에 영향을 미치기 위해 취해지는 모든 행동이라고 정의 내리면서, 베이커는 투표와 공직을 맡는 것이 남자들에게 국한되어 있던 동안, 19세기 여성들은 스스로 조직화하여 금주와 가난 같은 사회적 문제의 해결에 전념하는 단체를 만들었다고 결론 내린다. 다른 한편으로, 여성 활동가들은 비당파적 문제 지향 정치의 초기 개업의들(현장에서 뛰는 활동가)이었고 그래서 어느 정당이 선거에서 승리하도록 만드는 일에 관심을 두기보다는 어떤 문제를 위하여 의회 의원들의 정당 소속과는 관계없이 의원들을 동참하게 만드는 일에 더 관심이 많았다. 20세기에 와서는 더 많은 남성들이 여성들의 정치사상에 더욱 근접하여, 베이커가 여성들이 선구자 역할을 했다고 보고 있는 문제 지향 정치의 여러 방식들을 택했던 것이다.

school n. 학파, 유파
uncover v. 폭로하다, 밝히다
quantitative a. 양적인, 양에 관한
activism n. 행동주의, 실천주의
prefigure v. 예시하다, 예상하다
temperance n. 절제; 자제; 절주, 금주
practitioner n. 개업자
nonpartisan a. 당파에 속하지 않은
enlist v. 협력을 얻다, 도움을 얻다
affiliation n. 가입; 동맹
on behalf of ~을 대신하여, ~을 대표하여

01 ▶ (A) 어떤 학문상의 접근법의 단점은 첫 단락에 나온 여성을 제외한 정치학 접근법을 말하고 그 대안적 접근법은 둘째 단락에 나온 베이커의 접근법을 말한다.

02 ▶ (D) 두 접근법의 비교는 첫 문장에 나와 있고 모두에 공통된 단점은 둘째, 셋째 문장에 나와 있다.

03 ▶ '보통 시민의 정치 참여'라는 공통점이 있다. 다만, 전자는 여성을 배제한 반면 폴라는 여성을 포함시켜려 했다.

》 정답 01 (A) 02 (D) 03 (C)

콘크리트와 연관해서 기억해야 할 다른 하나는 측량이나 위치 선정에 있어서 실수를 만회할 여지가 썩 많지 않다는 점이다. 일단 굳은 콘크리트 덩어리를 제 위치에 놓고 나면, 그것은 계속해서 그 자리에 있을 것이다. 만약 실수한 것을 바로잡고자 한다면, 상당히 힘든 작업을 해야 한다. (그러므로,) 콘크리트를 거푸집에 붓기에 앞서서 모든 것들이 원하는 곳과 원하는 방식으로 돼 있는 지를 확인해야 한다.

콘크리트를 올바르게 혼합하고, 취급하고, 마무리하는 데 관해서는 여러 가지 규칙이 있지만, 가장 중요한 것은 사용할 물의 양에 관한 것이다. 혼합할 때 들어간 물의 양이 적을수록 완성품이 적게 수축하며, 물을 적게 쓸수록 굳어진 뒤 완성품이 보다 튼튼하고 견고해진다.

콘크리트로 작업하는 아마추어들은 두 가지 욕구에 사로잡혀 있다. 하나는 콘크리트를 멋있고 부드럽고 또한 다루기 쉽게 만들기 위해 물을 충분히 쓰려고 하는 것이다. 그렇게 하지 말라는 권고를 들은 적이 있을 것이다. 두 번째는 완성품의 모양이 어떤 지를 보려고 나무 거푸집을 너무 일찍 제거하는 것이다. 이것은 대단히 치명적이다. 콘크리트가 아직 완전히 굳어지지 않은 상태에서 거푸집을 너무 일찍 제거하면, 모서리나 가장자리를 부서뜨리거나 작품의 몸체에 큰 결함이나 흠을 남기는 두 가지 상황이 벌어질 가능성이 크다. 가장 좋은 규칙은 콘크리트가 완전히 굳었다고 확신할 때까지 기다린 다음, 하루를 더 기다린 후에 거푸집을 제거하는 것이다.

---

leeway n. (공간, 시간, 활동 등의) 여지, 여유
remedy v. 치료하다; 교정하다
shrink v. 오그라들다; 움츠리다
plague v. 애태우다, 괴롭히다
defect n. 결점, 결함
harden v. 굳다

01 ▶ '아마추어들은 물을 충분히 쓰려한다'고 했다.

02 ▶ 측량이나 위치 선정에 있어서 실수를 만회할 여지가 썩 많지 않으므로, 공간 감각이 필요하며, 진행상황을 확인하고자 하는 마음에 거푸집을 너무 일찍 제거하지 않으려면 자제력이나 인내심이 필요하다.

03 ▶ 콘크리트로 작업할 때 생길 수 있는 문제와 해법을 제시하고 있다.

》 정답 01 (C) 02 (C) 03 (D)

제정된 법률을 고의적으로 위반하는 것(시민 불복종)은 위반한 법률이 불복의 주목표나 초점이 아니라면 결코 도덕적으로 정당화되지 않는다. 정부가 개인이나 단체의 반대에 관련된 방법들을 보호하고 제공함으로써 헌법원칙을 지키는 한, 시위의 방법으로서 법률을 위반하는 것은 반란의 요소가 된다.

시민 불복종은 정의를 내리자면 법률위반이다. 시민 불복종 이론에서는 그 행동들이 정당성과는 관계없이 처벌되어야 한다고 인정하고 있다. 그러나 반대의 대상이 아니라 단지 반대를 극적으로 표현하기 위해서 이용된 법률위반은 법적으로 뿐만 아니라 도덕적으로도 용납할 수 없다고 간주되어진다. 시민 불복종에 대한 도덕적 옹호가 합리적으로 지지될 수 있는 것은 단지 인간의 근본적인 가치관을 훼손하는 법률에 관해서다.

공정한 사회가 존재하기 위해 관용의 원칙은 적절히 표현된 개인의 반대에 관련된 정부에 의해서, 그리고 법적으로 설정된 다수의 결정에 대해서는 개인에 의해서 받아들여져야만 한다. 어떠한 개인도 자유를 독점할 수 없으며 모두가 반대하는 측에 관용을 베풀어야만 한다. 반대자들은 자신들의 반대에 대한 반대를 인정해야만 하고 그 반대에 자신들을 위해서 주장한 모든 점을 제시해야 한다. 이런 원칙을 무시하는 것은 시민적 불복종을 법적으로 잘못되게 할 뿐 아니라, 도덕적으로도 정당화될 수 없게 만드는 것이다.

---

violation n. 위반
protest n. 항의
rebellion n. 반란, 폭동
disobedience n. 불복종
rationally ad. 이성적으로
tolerance n. 관용; 아량
monopoly n. 독점
dissenter n. 반대자
morally ad. 도덕적으로
apartheid n. 인종차별정책

01 ▶ 첫 문장에는 '위반한 법률이 불복종의 주된 대상이나 초점인 경우에는 불복종이 용인 가능하다'라는 의미가 내포돼 있다.

02 ▶ '반대의 대상이 아니라 단지 반대를 극적으로 표현하기 위해 이용된 법률위반은 법적으로 뿐만 아니라 도덕적으로도 용납할 수 없다고 간주되어진다'고 했다.

03 ▶ 사안에 따라서는 시민의 법률 위반을 긍정하고 있는 내용이다.

》 **정답** 01 (B) 02 (D) 03 (D)

단공류(單孔類)라 불리는 원시 포유류는 '원수류(原獸類)' 아강(亞綱)의 현생하는 유일한 구성원이다. 이는 원시 포유류를 파충류에서 포유류로 진화하는 과도기의 현생하는 가장 대표적인 생물로 만든다. 단공류는 파충류, 조류와 비슷한 점이 있지만 포유동물로 분류된다. 단공류는 새끼를 낳지 않고 알을 낳는다는 점에서 조류, 파충류와 비슷하다. 그러나 단공류는 다른 포유류처럼 털, 큰 뇌, 그리고 새끼를 키우는데 필요한 젖을 생산하는 젖샘을 가지고 있다.

그들의 원시 개체와 파충류와의 밀접한 관계는 복잡하지 않은 뇌 구조, 알을 낳는 습성, 그리고 배설강으로 증명된다. (배설강은 양서류, 파충류, 조류, 일부 어류, 그리고 단공류에서 볼 수 있지만, 태반 포유류와 대부분의 경골어류에는 없다. 그 동물의 장관, 요도관, 생식관이 항문관으로써의 기능도 하는 이 공통된 구멍으로 연결된다.)

단공류가 파충류와 밀접한 관련이 있다는 것을 증명하는 또 다른 특징은 알을 낳는다는 점이다. 단공류는 파충류, 조류와 같이 껍질이 두꺼운 알을 낳는다. 새끼의 부화기간은 상대적으로 짧으며 어미에 의존하게 된다. 암컷은 젖꼭지가 없다. 젖샘에서 분비되는 젖은 주위 피부에서 바로 흘러나온다.

현생하는 3종의 단공류는 오리너구리와 가시두더지 2종이다.

---

monotreme n. 단공류(單孔類) 동물(오리너구리 등)
Prototheria n. 원수류(原獸類)
mammary gland 젖샘
offspring n. 자식, 자손
cloaca n. (조류 등의) 총(總) 배설강(腔)
amphibian n. 양서류
placental mammals 태반 포유류
bony fishes 경골어류
urinary a. 비뇨기의; 오줌의
genital a. 생식(기)의
duck-billed platypus n. 오리너구리
spiny echidna n. 가시두더지

01 ▶ 이 글은 알을 낳는다는 점에서는 파충류와 비슷하지만 포유동물로 분류되는 단공류에 관한 내용이다. 특히 단공류가 가지는 파충류적 특성과 포유류적 특성에 포커스를 맞추어 자세히 설명하고 있다.

02 ▶ 첫 번째 문단 마지막 문장에 단공류는 다른 포유류처럼 털, 큰 뇌, 젖샘을 가지고 있다고 했다. 알을 낳는(egg-laying) 특성은 포유류가 아니라 파충류의 특성이다.

03 ▶ (C), (D)는 이 글에 전혀 언급되지 않은 내용이며, (B)는 이 글의 내용과 상반되는 주장이다. 단공류가 파충류와 조류처럼 알을 낳지만 포유류로 분류된다는 (A)가 정답이다.

» 정답 01 (C) 02 (D) 03 (A)

사람들은 몇 년 후 크게 달라질 중동의 모습에 놀랄 것이다. 민주주의가 더욱 발전할 것인데, 큰 변화는 의례 그런 법이니까 분명 그 발전 과정은 소란스럽고 많은 장애가 따를 것이다. 공산주의가 몰락하던 때를 되돌아보면 나는 당시 우리가 1946년과 1947년에 내린 결정들의 열매를 거두고 있었을 뿐이라는 것을 깨닫게 된다. 1946년에 이탈리아 공산당은 48%의 득표율을 기록했고 프랑스 공산당은 46%를 득표했다. 1948년에는 체코슬로바키아가 공산당 쿠데타에 쓰러졌고, 같은 해에 베를린은 베를린 위기로 영구 분단되었다. 1949년 소련은 예정보다 5년 앞서 핵무기 폭발을 단행했고 중국에서도 공산당이 승리를 거두었다. 그 당시 만일 당신이 사람들에게 "1989년과 1990년에는 소련이 붕괴될 것이고, 동유럽이 평화로이 민주국가로 등장할 것이며, 독일은 마침내 통일될 것이다. 그리고 폴란드, 리투아니아, 라트비아, 루마니아 등이 모두 나토 회원국이 될 것이다."라고 말했더라면 사람들은 "당신 미쳤소?"라고 말했을 것이다. 이제 우리는 또 하나의 변화의 시작점에 서있다. 10년이 걸릴지, 20년이 걸릴 지, 아니면 30년이 걸릴지 나는 모른다. 그러나 미래의 사람들은 (지금을) 뒤돌아보고 이렇게 말할 것이다. "과거 미국인들이 (중동문제에 대해) 쉬운 길을 택하지 않고, 그리고 (중동의) 안정으로 충분하다고 생각지 않고 (중동의) 민주 발전을 고집했던 것은 참으로 다행스런 일이다."

turbulent a. 몹시 거친, 사나운
rocky a. 장애가 많은
coup n. 쿠데타
set off 폭발시키다, 발사하다

01 ▶ 이 글은 1946년과 47년에 내린 결정이 40여년이 지난 후 공산주의의 몰락을 가져왔듯이 지금 미국이 중동에 대해 민주화의 길이라는 결정을 내리면 미래 언젠가 중동은 민주사회로 변해있을 것이라는 내용의 글이다.

02 ▶ out of one's mind 미친(= insane)

03 ▶ (D) regret이 아니라 happiness이다.

≫ 정답 01 (A) 02 (B) 03 (D)

지그문트 프로이드의 연구가 널리 알려지게 되자, 화가들은 잠재의식의 세계에 매료되었다. 1924년에는 이미 초현실주의 선언이 잠재의식과 회화 사이의 특수한 관련성을 언급했다. 조르지오 데 키리코의 형이상학적 환상들이 초현실주의의 특성을 갖고 있다. <무한한 공간의 향수> 같은 작품에서는 이상한 물체들이 비합리적으로 병렬되어 있는데, 그것들은 꿈에서처럼 함께 모여 있다. 이 별난 작품들은 인간이 통제하지 못하는 세계를 반영하고 있다.

그러나 초현실주의는 아마도 살바도르 달리의 그림이 더 정확히 표현하고 있을 것이다. 달리는 <기억의 지속> 같은 작품을 "손으로 물들인 잠재의식의 사진"이라 불렀으며, 그의 작품의 거의 사진에 가까운 상세함은 그가 그리는 사물들의 악몽 같은 관계들과 결부되어 강력한 충격을 던진다. 흐느적거리게 걸려있고 개미들과 함께 천천히 기어가고 있는 이 "흐믈흐믈한 시계들"(작품을 처음 본 사람들이 이렇게 불렀다) 속에서는 모든 시간 개념이 파괴된다. 그러나 이미지들은 어쩌면 우리가 꿈의 세계에 매력을 느끼는 것과 같이 이상하게 매력적이다. 맥스 에른스트의 반(反)예술적 다다이즘이 혐오스럽게 여겨질지도 모르는 반면에 데 키리코와 달리의 비합리성은 매혹적일 수 있다. 그들의 작품이 갖고 있는 경직성과 사실적 명료함은 다른 행성의 오염되지 않은 빛에 대해 얘기하지만, 그럼에도 그것은 우리가 아는 것 같은 세계를 보여준다.

manifesto n. 선언서
metaphysical a. 형이상학적인
surrealist a. 초현실주의의
juxtapose v. 나란히 놓다, 병렬하다
bizarre a. 기괴한, 별난
hand-colored a. 손으로 물들인
couple v. 연상하다, 결부시켜 생각하다
nightmarish a. 악몽 같은
limply ad. 흐느적거리게
repulsive a. 불쾌한, 혐오스러운
entrancing a. 황홀케 하는, 매혹적인
starkness n. 빳빳함, 경직성
graphic a. 사실적인, 생생한

01 ▶ 앞의 종속절 접속사가 상반관계의 while이므로 빈칸에는 repulsive(혐오스런)의 반대인 (B)의 '매혹적인'이 적절하다.

02 ▶ (A) 첫 단락 둘째 문장과 둘째 단락 끝에서 셋째 문장이 단서이다. (B) 첫 단락의 'strange objects are irrationally juxtaposed'와 둘째 단락의 'the almost photographic detail of his work'이 단서이다. (C) 달리의 작품에서 real object인 시계를 흐느적거리게 걸려있고 개미들과 함께 천천히 기어가게 그리고 있다. (D)는 오히려 다다이즘과 관련된 진술이다.

03 ▶ 이 글은 초현실주의가 프로이드의 영향으로 시작되었음을 언급하고 있고, 데 키리코와 달리라는 두 초현실주의 화가에 대해 논의하고 있지만, 결국 초현실주의가 어떤 특징의 사조인지를 설명한 글이므로 (C)가 제목으로 가장 적절하다.

» 정답 01 (B) 02 (D) 03 (C)

일단 준비가 끝나자 그는 자신의 생각을 실행에 옮기고 싶어 조바심이 났다. 그가 늦추면 세상이 크게 손해를 볼 것이라는 생각이 그를 밀어 붙였다. 시정되어야 하는 불만들, 바로 잡아야 할 옳지 못한 것들, 손 봐야 할 훼손된 사항들, 이행되어야 할 채무관계 등이 보이는 것 같았다. 그래서 그는 무더운 7월의 어느 날 아무에게도 자신의 의도를 말하지 않고 남의 눈에 띄지 않게 여명이 오기 전에 완전 무장을 하고, 로시난테(Rocinate)에 올라타고는 제대로 고치지도 못한 투구를 쓰고, 그의 방패를 걸치고, 창을 부여잡고서는 마당 뒷문을 통해서 들판으로 나갔다. 그는 자신의 철저한 계획이 쉽게 시작되는 것이 기쁘고 즐거웠다. 그러나 세상에 나오자마자 너무 끔찍한 생각이 엄습했기 때문에 그는 막 시작한 계획을 거의 포기할 정도였다.

그는 문득 자신이 기사 작위를 받은 적이 없음을 기억해냈다. 기사도법에 의하면 그는 어느 기사에게도 무기를 가지고 대항할 수 없었다. 그리고 기사 작위를 수여받는다 해도 초보자인 그는 자신의 용맹성에 의해 문장(紋章)을 얻기 전까지는 문장도 없는 방패와 복장을 해야만 했다. 이러한 생각으로 그의 결심이 흔들리긴 했지만 그의 광기가 그 무엇보다도 우세한 상황이었기 때문에, 그는 자신이 만나는 첫 번째 사람에게 기사 작위를 받기로 했다. 그에게 많은 영향을 끼친 책들에서 보았던 대로 그런 식으로 기사 작위를 받는 많은 사람을 모방하는 것이었다. 그리고 문장 없는 갑옷과 투구는 시간이 날 때 더욱더 깨끗하게 닦을 생각이었다. 이렇게 정리를 하고 나서 그는 마음을 가라앉히고 말이 가는 대로 길을 나아갔다. 모험의 요체가 이 안에 있으리라는 믿음을 갖고서.

---

grievance n. 불만
sweltering a. 찌는 듯이 더운
headpiece n. 투구
mount v. (말 따위에) 타다, 올라타다
lance n. 창
chivalry n. 기사도, 기사도적 정신
prowess n. 용감, 무용(武勇)
waver v. 망설이다, 주저하다
ermine a. 순백의

01 ▶ 엉뚱한 사람의 엉뚱한 행동들에 관한 내용이다. 내용을 통해 짐작하겠지만, 본문은 세르반테스 작(作) '돈키호테'의 일부이다.

02 ▶ 두 번째 문단 첫 줄부터 그 이유가 설명돼 있다.

03 ▶ 그의 광기가 그 무엇보다도 우세한 상황이었기 때문이다.

》 정답 01 (B) 02 (D) 03 (B)

137　　천문학자들은 자신들이 블랙홀이라고 부르는 지역을 우주공간에서 확인했다. 그들은 이 블랙홀이 안에서부터 그 어떤 것도, 심지어 빛조차도 빠져나올 수 없는 밀도가 큰 별이라고 믿고 있다. 천문학자들은 매우 큰 별이 소멸하고 안으로 수축할 때 블랙홀이 생성된다고 생각하고 있다. 별은 가지고 있는 핵연료를 다 쓰고 그로 인해 열을 잃게 되면 소멸하게 된다. 별은 식으면서 수축을 시작한다. 수축하는 별은 점점 더 밀도가 높아져서, 중력의 당기는 힘이 더 강해진다. 밀도가 물의 1,000조배에 이르면, 중력이 무척 강해져서 빛, 행성, 심지어 다른 별을 비롯하여, 블랙홀 주위의 모든 것들을 속으로 끌어당기게 된다. 보통 크기의 별인 태양이 블랙홀이 되려면, 반지름이 겨우 3킬로미터가 될 만큼 수축해야 할 것이다. 블랙홀은 모두 공 모양의 "층"이 둘러싸고 있는데, 빛이 이것을 통해 들어올 수는 있어도 빠져나가지는 못 하는 경계선이다. 블랙홀로부터는 빛이 전혀 나오지 못하기 때문에, 완전히 검게 보인다. 블랙홀을 발견할 수 있는 것은, 물질이 속으로 빨려들기 직전에 온도가 뜨거워지고 X선을 방출하는데, 그것을 지구에서 탐지할 수 있기 때문이다. 이 "보이지 않는" 블랙홀을 발견하는 유일한 다른 방법은 다른 별들에 미치는 영향을 통한 것뿐이다. 블랙홀은 크기가 작을 수도 있지만, 그렇더라도 중력은 같은 크기의 수축하지 않은 보통 별과 같으며, 그렇기 때문에, 큰 블랙홀은 매우 강력해서 눈에 보이는 별들을 자신 주위의 궤도로 끌어들일 수 있으며, 이러한 눈에 보이는 종속되는 별의 움직임을 관측할 수 있다. 오늘날 천문학자들은 규모가 큰 은하에는 모두 그 중심에 거대한 블랙홀이 있다는 가설을 내놓고 있다.

dense a. 밀집한, 조밀한
collapse v. 무너지다; 실패하다
gravity n. 진지함; 중력
drag v. 끌어당기다
radius n. 반지름; 행동반경; 범위
invisible a. 눈에 보이지 않는; 확실하지 않은
gravitation n. 인력(작용), 중력
galaxy n. 은하
gigantic a. 거인 같은, 거대한

01 ▶ 블랙홀이 무엇인지에 대해 설명하는 글이다. 두 번째 문장에서 과학자들은 어떠한 것도 빠져나올 수 없는 밀도가 큰 별이라고 했다. (A)에 관한 언급은 없었고, 블랙홀은 크기가 작을 수도 있다고 했다.

02 ▶ 별은 가지고 있는 핵연료를 다 쓰고 열을 잃게 되면 수축한다고 했다.

03 ▶ 블랙홀에서 빛이 빠져나올 수 없는 이유는 중력이 너무나도 강하기 때문이다.

》 정답　01 (D)　02 (B)　03 (A)

누군가가 죽을 수 있는 권리를 원하는 것에 대한 문제라면, 어떤 건물에서 뛰어내려버리라고 말할 것이다. 그러나 당신이 죽게끔 도와 줄 다른 누군가를 끌어들인다면 그 방정식은 달라지게 된다. 의사에게 당신이 죽는 것을 도와 달라고 요청하지 마라. 만약 그렇게 한다면, 그것은 의술의 전통을 해치고 의사의 역할에 대해 의문을 불러일으킬 것이다.

내가 우려하는 것 중의 하나는 사람들이 자살을 제안하는 의사들에게 조종당할 수 있다는 것이다. 중병에 걸린 많은 사람들은 그들로 인해 가족들이 돈을 너무 많이 쓰기 때문에 그들이 가족에게 부담이 된다고 이미 생각하고 있다. 강제적이지는 않지만, 한 사람의 죄책감을 가중시키는 것이다. 자살에 대해 전에는 한 번도 생각하지 않던 많은 사람들이 자살을 고려하게 될 지도 모른다.

또한 나는 이러한 절차를 성공적으로 통제할 수 있다고 생각하지 않는다. 의사와 환자의 관계는 비밀의 보장으로 시작된다. 만약 의사와 환자 모두가 다른 누군가는 모르게 하기로 결정한다면, 정부가 이것을 통제할 방법은 없다. 전제는 의사들이 환자들의 고통을 없애려고 시도한 모든 것이 실패한 후에야 환자의 자살을 도와준다는 것이다. 그러나 많은 사람들은 그렇게 너무 오래 걸리는 것을 원하지 않을 것이다. 제안된 규정 중 그 어느 것도 현재는 고통을 겪고 있지 않지만 "나는 미래에 고통 받기를 원하지 않으니까, 지금 자살하게 해주세요."라고 말하는 사람을 고려하고 있지 않다. 어떤 의사는 "그래요. 당신이 아무런 고통도 느끼지 않도록 우리가 만들어 드릴게요."라고 말할지도 모른다.

equation n. 방정식
manipulate v. 조종하다; 능숙하게 다루다
suicide n. 자살; 자살자
coercion n. 강제; 위압
guilt n. 죄책감; 유죄
confidentiality n. 기밀성, 비밀유지
presumption n. 추정, 가정; 추측
take into account ~을 고려하다
commit suicide 자살하다
revengefully ad. 복수심에 사무쳐

01 ▶ "But as soon as you bring in somebody else to help you", "Just don't ask a doctor to help you do it" 등에서 "의사가 중병의 환자들에게 안락사하는 것을 허용해야 하는가?"에 대한 대답임을 알 수 있다.

02 ▶ 두 번째 문단에서 중병에 걸리는 많은 사람들이 가족에게 경제적 부담이 되고 싶지 않아 전에는 생각하지 않던 자살을 고려할 것이라고 언급하였다.

03 ▶ 글쓴이는 의사들과 환자들이 모든 것을 시도해 보기도 전에 현재는 고통이 없지만 후일을 대비해 '무모하게(thoughtlessly)' 판단해 버리는 것에 대해 우려를 표하고 있다.

≫ 정답 01 (B) 02 (C) 03 (D)

또 하나의 전략은 영 아닐 것 같은 협력자로 박테리아를 습격하는 것인데, 그 협력자는 곧 바이러스이다. 뉴욕시 록펠러 대학의 빈센트 피셰티는 박테리아 세포만 감염시키고 인간 세포는 놔두는 바이러스인 박테리오파지의 도움을 구하고 있다. 박테리오파지는 박테리아의 유전자 작동부를 강점하여 몇 분 안에 수백 개의 자신의 복제물을 마구 만들어낸다. 세포 안에 복제한 자신의 새끼들이 충분한 수로 늘어나면 박테리오파지는 효소를 생산하는데, 이 효소가 세포벽을 물어뜯어 세포벽이 샴페인 병마개가 펑하고 터질 때처럼 힘차게 폭발하여 세포 안에 침입했던 바이러스들을 토해낸다. 우리 인간에게 해를 입히지 않는 바이러스라 하더라도 살아있는 바이러스로 사람을 치료하는 것은 항상 위험한 것이어서 피셰티는 박테리아를 파괴시키는 효소만을 추출하여 그것을 외부로부터 주입하여 박테리아를 죽이는 데 이용하기로 했다. 지금까지 그는 폐렴 쌍구균과 연쇄구균과 탄저균에 대한 효소화합물을 개발했고, 결국 효소제를 매주 코 안에 살포하는 형식으로 주입하여 감염된 환자들을 치료하게 되기를 바라고 있다. 이 약제들 중 바로 약국에서 시판되도록 나와 있는 것은 하나도 없으며, 그렇게 될 때까지는 지금 갖고 있는 약제들의 효력을 극대화하는 데 연구의 초점이 맞추어지고 있다. 미국 해군 연구소의 과학자들은 박테리아의 DNA를 연구하여 박테리아들이 약(항생제)에 대한 내성을 갖기 위해 사용하는 유전자 전투 계획 안의 암호를 해독하고 있다. 이 비밀들을 알면 의사들은 어느 종의 박테리아가 어느 항생제에 가장 취약한지를 알아서 항생제를 더욱 효과적으로 처방하는 데 도움을 받을 수 있다.

---

ambush v. 매복하여 습격하다
ally n. 동맹국, 협력자
enlist v. 병적에 편입하다, 도움을 얻다
bacteriophage n. 박테리오파지(세균 분해 바이러스)
hijack v. 공중납치하다, 강탈하다, 강제하다
chew v. 씹다, 깨물다
spew out 토해내다
puncture v. 구멍을 뚫다; 망쳐놓다
pneumococcus n. 폐렴 쌍구균
streptococcus n. 연쇄구균
anthrax n. 탄저균
squirt v. 분출하다, 주사하다, 퍼붓다
strain n. (박테리아나 바이러스의) 종

01 ▶ 이 글은 바이러스(박테리오파지)를 이용하는 등, 박테리아(세균)와의 전쟁에서 의학자들이 개발하거나 이용하는 여러 전략들을 설명한 글이다.

02 ▶ 앞 문장 끝의 copies of themselves를 달리 표현할 수 있는 것을 찾는다. progeny(자손)는 단수와 복수가 동형이며, 여기서는 복수형으로 쓰였다.

03 ▶ (A) 인간 세포는 놔두고 박테리아 세포만 공격하므로 선별적이다. (B) 박테리오파지는 살아있는 바이러스이므로 위험하다. (C) 기존 항생제의 효력 극대화는 효소화합물로 된 약제가 시판될 때까지만 시도될 뿐 궁극적 목표는 아니다. (D) 마지막 두 문장에서 알 수 있다.

» 정답   01 (D)   02 (A)   03 (C)

신용정보 사기 — 누군가의 상세한 개인 정보를 훔쳐서 그들의 은행계좌나 신용카드계좌를 침입하거나 심지어 자기 명의로 그런 계좌를 새로 개설하는 행위 — 가 아시아 전역에서 꾸준히 늘고 있다. 그래서 이에 대비해 보험에 가입한다는 생각이 설득력을 얻고 있다. 예를 들어 AIG 보험사는 ID Guard 보험을 내놓고 있는데, 이것은 당신의 신용카드 번호나 상세한 신분증 정보로 사기 구매가 행해질 때 건당 3,500 달러까지 보상해주고 법적(소송) 비용이나 임금손실이나 그 외 다른 부수적인 비용을 위해 7,000 달러까지 보상해준다. 이를 위한 보험료 비용은 1년에 35달러로 비교적 저렴하다.

그러나 많은 전문가들은 그런 보험의 필요성에 대해 여전히 회의적이다. 마켓워치닷컴(MarketWatch.com)의 처크 제이프(Chuck Jaffe)는 신용정보 절도(사기) 피해자가 될 가능성이 여전히 적기 때문에, 특히 신용정보 사기 문제에 대해 그 무엇보다 먼저 관심을 갖는 사람의 경우 피해자가 될 가능성은 적기 때문에, 보험회사들이 그런 보험에서 돈을 벌게 된다고 지적한다. 신용정보 절도에 대해 관심이 있는 소비자라면 정기적으로 자신의 신용보고서를 점검해서 자신의 신용정보가 무단으로 도용된 일은 없는지 살펴볼 것이고, 개인계좌 정보를 보호하고, 계좌번호나 상세한 중요 정보가 들어있는 서류는 파기하며, 은행 잔고 증명서를 자세히 살펴보고 그 이상의 조치도 취할 것이다. 보험에 드는 것보다도 그런 조치들이 소비자들을 신용정보 사기로부터 보호하는 데 더 많이 기여하는 것이다.

raid v. 침입[급습]하다
account n. 계좌
cover v. 망라하다; (손실을) 메우다; (경비를) 부담하다
fraudulent a. 사기의
incidental a. 부수적인
insurer n. 보험회사
insurance policy 보험증서
identity theft 신용정보 절도
credit report 신용보고서, 신용조회서
unauthorized activity 무단 사용 행위
shred v. 찢다
bank statement 은행잔고 증명서

01 ▶ 아시아에 신용정보 사기가 증가하여 관련 보험이 나왔는데 과연 그것이 필요한 것인가를 논한 글이다. 즉 두 번째 단락에 중점이 두어져 있다. (A) 심각성에 대한 이야기가 아니다. (B) 그냥 보험사기가 아니다. (D) '정보화 시대의 보험'은 너무 광범위한 제목이다.

02 ▶ 아시아 경제가 침체되어 신용정보 사기가 증가하고 있는 것은 아니다.

03 ▶ remain small이라 했으므로 (B)는 보험회사의 수익을 감소시키게 되고, 나머지는 보험회사의 수익을 증대시키는데, 그 중에 (C)만이 particularly for 이하와 잘 어울린다.

» 정답 01 (C) 02 (A) 03 (C)

141

필리핀을 침략하는 미군의 잔학 행위에 놀라고, 이러한 국가적 범죄에 일상적으로 동반되는 해방운동이나 고귀한 의도 등에 대한 수사학적 비약에 기가 막혀서 마크 트웨인(Mark Twain)은 그의 풍자라는 무기를 휘두를 수 없는 상황에 두 손을 다 들었다. 그의 좌절의 직접적인 대상은 유명한 펀스톤(Funston) 장군이었다. "펀스톤에 대한 어떠한 풍자도 완벽할 수 없다"라며 그는 애석해 했다. "왜냐하면 펀스톤이 바로 최고니까. 그는 정말이지 풍자의 화신이다."

2008년 9월 그루지야-오세티야-러시아 전쟁 동안 다시 한 번 이와 같은 생각이 떠올랐다. 조지 부시, 콘돌리자 라이스, 그 외 다른 고위 관료들은 진지하게 UN의 신성함에 호소하여, UN의 원칙에 '일치하지 않은 조치를 그루지야에서 행하고 있다는 이유 때문에' 러시아를 UN에서 축출할 수도 있다고 경고하였다. 모든 국가의 주권과 영토권은 엄격하게 존중되어야 한다. 이들은 '모든 국가'를 강조하여 말했다. 다시 말해, 이 모든 국가란 미국이 공격했던 이라크, 세르비아, 아마도 이란, 그 외의 너무나 많고, 너무나 잘 알고 있어서 언급하기도 뭐한 그런 나라들은 제외한 나라들을 가리킨다.

aghast a. 기가 막힌, 깜짝 놀란
atrocity n. 잔학 행위
wield v. 휘두르다
formidable a. 무서운, 가공할
incarnated a. 구현한, 육신을 갖춘
come to mind 떠오르다
dignitary n. 고위 관리
invoke v. 호소하다
sanctity n. 신성함
inconsistent a. 상반된
sovereignty n. 주권
territorial integrity 영토 보전
rigorously ad. 준엄하게, 엄격하게
intone v. 억양을 붙여 말하다

01 ▶ 이 글의 저자는 미국이 러시아를 비난할 만한 처지가 못된다고 지적하고 있다. 앞의 필리핀은 물론 뒤에 나온 이라크, 세르비아와 같은 나라들은 미국이 침공한 나라들의 예이다. 따라서 미국이 외국의 주권을 존중했다는 말은 거짓이다.

02 ▶ 마크 트웨인이 펀스톤에 대해 '풍자의 화신'이라고 부른 것은, 그의 말이 정말 얼토당토 않은 일방적인 미국의 입장을 옹호하는 수사학적 비약이라는 것, 그래서 그에게 두 손 두 발을 다 들었다는 의미이다. 마크 트웨인은 그를 칭찬하는 듯 하지만 사실은 그를 깎아 내리고 있는 것이다. 동사 condescend는 자신을 낮추는 듯 보이지만, 속으로는 다른 사람을 경멸하고, 비웃는다는 의미이다.

03 ▶ 이런 경우에 사용할 수 있는 속담은 '똥 묻은 개가 겨 묻은 개 나무란다'는 것이다.

≫ 정답 01 (D) 02 (D) 03 (B)

애론 스와르츠는 아이디어에의 접근을 필생의 운동으로 삼았다. 청소년기에 그것은 그로 하여금 최고의 프로그래머가 되게 했다. 그러나 청년이 되었을 때 그것으로 인해 그는 학술지의 방대한 데이터베이스를 훔친 것으로 전해진 후 사기, 사이버 범죄, 기타 혐의 등 13건의 기소 조항으로 징역 35년 형이 선고될 수도 있는 처지에 직면하게 되었다. 친구들의 말로는 우울증이 재발했다고 하는 스와르츠가 재판을 몇 달 앞둔 1월 11일에 브루클린에 있는 자신의 아파트에서 목숨을 끊었을 때 그의 운동도 끝나게 되었다. 그의 나이 26세였다.

그의 우울증 병력에도 불구하고 친구들은 스와르츠의 죽음이 그에게 본때를 보이려는 검찰관들이 저지른 학대의 결과라고 말한다. 그들은 그 기소가 기를 질리게 하는 것이었고 그가 감당하기에 너무 과한 것이었다고 말한다. 검찰관들과 그들의 지지자들은 자신들의 재량 범위 안에서 조치를 취했고 미국에서 저작권법 위반으로 잃게 되는 연간 세수입이 580억 달러에 달하다보니 컴퓨터 관련 지적재산권 범죄에 대해서는 강경 노선을 취하지 않을 수 없다고 말한다. 이상주의적인 위험인물이든 개방된 인터넷의 로빈훗(영웅)이든, 스와르츠는 얼마나 많은 정보가 자유롭게 이용될 수 있어야 하고 정부는 정보를 "자유화하는" 사람들을 얼마나 적극적으로 처벌해야 하는가 하는 문제들에 대한 논쟁을 죽음으로 구체화하게 되었다. 스와르츠의 죽음은 세상을 개선할 수 있는 아이디어와 혁신에의 접근을 증대하려는 그의 필생의 노력을 극적으로 조명해주지만, 그것이 그 운동을 진전시켰는지는 분명치 않다.

---

crusade n. 십자군; (개혁 등을 위한) 운동
adolescence n. 청소년기
sentence n. (형의) 선고
count n. 기소 조항
charge n. 고소, 혐의
allegedly ad. 전해진 바에 의하면
bout n. (병의) 발작
renewed bout 재발
prosecutor n. 기소자, 검찰관
make an example of ~에게 본때를 보이다
prosecution n. 기소
Robin Hood n. 의적, 영웅
personify v. 구체화하다
illuminate v. 조명하다
push n. 공격, 추진, 분발
better v. 개선하다
cause n. 대의, 운동

01 ▶ 검찰관들과 그 지지자들의 말을 나타내는 that절의 주어에서 '미국에서 저작권법 위반으로 잃게 되는 연간 세수입이 580억 달러에 달한다'고 했는데, 이것은 컴퓨터 관련 지적재산권 범죄에 대해 '강경 노선을 취하는 것을 필요하게 만들' 것이므로 빈칸에는 (B)가 적절하다.

02 ▶ 엉성하고 부정확한(loose) 대포(cannon)가 포탄이 언제 어디로 날아가 어떤 피해를 입힐지 모르듯이 loose cannon은 예상치 못한 말과 행동으로 문제를 일으키는 위험인물을 의미한다.

03 ▶ 첫 단락에서 '재판을 몇 달 앞둔 1월 11일에'라 했고 둘째 단락 끝에서 둘째 문장에서 '.... 논쟁을 죽음으로 구체화하게 되었다'라고 했으므로 (C)가 사실인 진술이다. (A) 우울증도 검찰의 무리한 수사도 자살 원인으로 추정되거나 주장될 뿐 정확한 자살 동기는 알려져 있지 않다. (B) 저작권침해 혐의를 받는 인터넷사이트를 폐쇄시키려 노력한 것이 아니라 인터넷상의 자유로운 정보이용을 위해 노력했다. (D) 마지막 문장 whether절의 it은 his death를, that cause는 his lifelong push to increase access to ideas and innovations를 가리키는데, 주절에서 it is not clear라 했다.

》 정답 01 (B) 02 (D) 03 (C)

143

J. R. R. 톨킨(Tolkien)은 신화 작품에 자신의 가톨릭 신앙을 쏟아 부은 한평생 독실했던 가톨릭교도로, 그 작품은 최초의 출판물이 발행된 지 반세기가 지난 후인 현재에도 새로운 세대를 사로잡고 있다. 톨킨은 자신이 기독교인이며 실제로는 로마 가톨릭교도라는 사실이 그의 작품에서 가장 중요하고 매우 의미 있는 요소라고 주장했다.

그러나 『반지의 제왕』이 본질적으로 종교적이고 가톨릭교적인 것이라면 왜 그리스도가 한 번도 책에서 언급되지 않은 것일까? 이 질문에 대답하자면 톨킨의 신화는 그리스도가 인간으로 나타나기 수천 년 전을 배경으로 하기 때문에 그리스도의 이름이 언급되지 않았다. 구약성서(그리스도의 탄생을 약속한, 그리스도 이전의 기록을 다룬 성서)에서 그리스도가 언급되지 않은 동일한 이유로 그리스도는 『반지의 제왕』에서 언급되지 않은 것이다. 그리스도는 아직 육신으로 자신을 드러내지 않았고 결과적으로 실물로 분명히 존재한 것이 아니라 은혜를 통해 은연 중에 존재한다. 하지만 그리스도는 톨킨 신화의 왕이다. 구약성서를 복음의 관점에서 읽으면 가장 잘 이해할 수 있는 것과 동일하게 복음의 프리즘을 통해 『반지의 제왕』을 읽으면 작품을 가장 잘 이해할 수 있다. 물론 그러한 식견 없이도 『반지의 제왕』을 읽을 수 있지만 그렇게 하면 근본적인 목적을 놓치게 된다. 무신론자, 불가지론자 혹은 뉴에이지 신이교도로서 『반지의 제왕』을 읽을 수 있겠지만 작품이 가지는 본질적으로 종교적이고 가톨릭교적인 의미를 이해하지는 못할 것이다. 그런 사람은 빛의 영광스러운 깊은 곳으로 곧장 뛰어드는 대신에 그림자의 얕은 곳에서 헤엄치게 될 것이다.

devout a. 독실한, 헌신적인
captivate v. ~의 마음을 사로잡다
incarnation n. 신이 인간의 모습으로 나타난 것; 구체화
the Old Testament 구약성서
implicitly ad. 은연중에, 암시적으로
explicitly ad. 명백하게, 분명하게
the Gospel 복음, 복음서
atheist n. 무신론자
agnostic n. 불가지론자
pagan n. 이교도
paddle v. 얕은 물속에서 뛰어다니다, 물장난을 치다
shallows n. 물이 얕은 곳, 여울
headlong ad. 곤두박이로, 신속하게

01 ▶ 본문의 주제는 두 번째 단락의 The Lord of the Rings is best understood if it is read through the prism of the Gospel에 단적으로 나타난다.

02 ▶ the myth가 a new generation을 사로잡는 것이므로 captivated by를 captivating으로 고쳐야 한다.

03 ▶ (A)의 경우, 반지의 제왕에서 그리스도의 이름이 언급되지 않았고 무신론자, 불가지론자 혹은 뉴에이지 신이교도로서 반지의 제왕을 읽는 것이 가능하기 때문에 반지의 제왕이 explicitly Christian work는 아니다. explicitly를 implicitly로 고쳐야 내용상 올바른 문장이 된다.

» 정답 01 (D) 02 (A) 03 (A)

1970년 모든 관객들을 눈물 젖게 했던 고전작품인 <러브스토리(Love Story)>가 극장을 강타했을 때, 나는 어린 아이였다. 그러나 여주인공 알리 맥그로(Ali MacGraw)가 죽어가면서 사랑하는 라이언 오닐(Ryan O'Neal)에게 "사랑은 결코 미안하다고 말할 필요가 없는 거예요"라고 말했을 때, 어른 관람객들과 함께 나도 눈물을 훔쳤다.

그로부터 2년 후, 나는 <왓츠업덕(What's Up Doc?)>이라는 또 다른 영화를 보았다. 그 영화에서는 바브라 스트라이샌드(Barbra Streisand)가 연기한 등장인물이 <러브스토리>에서 나온 바로 그 배우에게 똑같은 대사를 반복했다. 그러나 이번에는 오닐이 대답을 했다. 그는 "그 말은 내가 지금까지 들었던 말 중 제일 멍청한 말이야"라고 말했다. 나는 그 순간 깨달았다. 나는 비록 어렸지만, 진짜 연인들은 매우 자주 미안하다는 말을 한다는 것을, 그것도 진정으로, 심지어 열렬히 한다는 것을 무언가에서 깨닫고 있었다.

이것은 창피함이나 유감과 같은 우울한 감정이 인간관계에 필요하기 때문이 아니고, 사과 없이는 어떠한 관계도 그러한 우울한 감정들로부터 자유로울 수 없기 때문이다. 모든 사람들은 어떤 것들로 다른 사람들을 괴롭히거나 상처를 줄 수 있다. (약속시간에 늦는다든지 하는) 약간 불편하게 하는 지연이나 힘든 순간의 심술궂은 말 같은 것이 그것이다. 우리가 미안하다고 말하는 능력이 부족할 때, 작은 기분 상함이 결국에는 어떤 관계든지 침몰시킬 수 있는 무게를 축적하게 된다.

그러나 우리의 잘못이 중대할 때에도 간단한 사과의 행동을 통해서 좋은 관계를 회복할 수 있다. 물론, 사과는 올바른 방식으로 행해져야 한다. 불완전하고, 잘못 구성된 사과는 처음에 기분 상하게 했던 것보다 더 큰 상처를 줄 수 있다. 다행스럽게도 효과적인 사과의 기술은 간단하며, 이를 숙달하는 것은 평생 동안 견실하고, 탄력성 있는 관계를 유지할 수 있게 만들어준다.

---

gusher n. 분출
character n. 등장인물
lightbulb moment 무언가를 깨닫는 순간
fervently ad. 열렬하게
dismal a. 우울한
procrastination n. 지체
grumpy a. 심술궂은
accumulate v. 축적시키다
sink v. 침몰시키다
grave a. 중요한
resilient a. 탄력성 있는, 튀어 오르는

01 ▶ 위 글에서 효과적인 사과의 기술을 배우는 것은 간단하다고만 했지 그 기술을 숙달하는 법을 말하고 있지는 않다.

02 ▶ 위 글은 '인간관계에서 진심어린 사과의 중요성'을 말하고 있는 글이다.

03 ▶ 세 번째 문단에서 인간관계에서 작은 상처가 관계 자체를 침몰시킬 수 있다고 했고, 이어지는 네 번째 문단에서는 사과로 이를 회복할 수 있다고 했다. 따라서 반의 관계 접속사 But이 적절하다. 그리고 마지막 문장 앞에서 올바른 방식으로 사과하지 않으면 더 큰 문제를 초래한다고 했는데, 마지막 문장은 효과적 사과의 기술을 익히는 것이 쉽다고 말하는 것이므로 fortunately(다행스럽게도)가 적절한 표현이다.

» 정답 01 (C) 02 (E) 03 (C)

Nicolas Baumard는 현대 도덕 이야기에 대한 사람들의 반응을 확인하기 위해 컴퓨터를 이용했다. Baumard 박사의 실험의 지원자들은 동냥을 청하는 거지와 그들에게 동냥을 주지 않은 행인에 관하여 읽었다. 어떤 경우에 보행자는 인색했을 뿐만 아니라 그 가난한 사람에게 욕설을 퍼부었다. 다른 경우에 행인은 무일푼이라서 미안해했다. 어느 쪽이든 그 행인은 (신발 끈에 걸려 넘어지는 것부터 거지가 고의로 넘어뜨리는 것을 포함해 차에 치이는 것 까지) 어떤 불쾌한 일을 겪게 되었다.

각각의 지원자에게 물어본 질문은 두 번째로 일어난 (불쾌한) 일이 거지를 향한 행인의 행동이 원인이 된 것인지 아닌지 여부였다. 원인은 신발 끈이거나 거지의 발이거나 차라고 생각하며 대부분은 "아니오"라고 답했다. 그러나 Baumard 박사는 또한 각각의 지원자들이 답에 대해서 생각하는데 걸린 시간을 측정했고 그는 행인이 거지에게 나쁘게 행동하고 나서 관련이 없는 나쁜 사건을 겪었을 때가 행인들이 좋게 행동하거나 거지가 그를 고의로 넘어뜨렸을 때보다 지원자들이 답에 대해서 생각하는데 상당한 시간을 더 소비했다는 것을 알아냈다.

Baumard 박사의 설명은 증명할 수는 없지만 지원자들이 이 여분의 생각하는 시간에 행인의 행동과 그의 뒤따른 운명사이에 실제로 정신적인 연관을 지었다는 것이다. 다시 말해서 그들은 그 행인이 어떤 종류의 보편적인 운명에 의해 받는 응분의 벌을 받았다는 생각을 고려했었다는 것이다.

alm n. 자선품, 희사[구호]품
passer-by n. 행인
pedestrian n. 보행자
stingy a. 인색한[쩨쩨한]
hurl v. 욕, 비난, 모욕 등을 퍼붓다
skint a. 무일푼의
apologetic a. 미안해하는, 사과하는
trip v. ~를 넘어뜨리다
subsequent a. 차후의
get one's just deserts 응분의 대가를 받다
dish out 벌주다, 호통 치다, 꾸짖다

01 ▶ 이 글은 증명되지는 않았지만 Baumard 박사의 연구 결과, 지원자들은 거지에게 한 나쁜 행동과 그 후에 당한 불쾌한 사건 사이에 실제로 정신적인 연관을 지었다고 제시하고 있으므로, '행동과 그것의 대가 사이의 정신적인 연관성'이 제목으로 적절하다.

02 ▶ 지원자들은 나쁜 행동을 한 후 불쾌한 일을 겪은 행인이 어떤 종류의 보편적인 운명에 의해 받는 응분의 벌을 받았다는 생각을 고려했었다고 했으므로 지원자들이 여분의 생각하는 시간에 행인의 행동과 그의 뒤따른 운명사이에 실제로 정신적인 연관을 지었다고 해야 적절하다.

03 ▶ 실험 지원자들에게 제시된 사례에서 동냥을 청하는 거지에게 구호품을 주지 않은 행인이 누군가에게 목격되었는지 아닌지는 언급되지 않았으므로 목격되는 것이 행인들의 행동에 영향을 끼쳤는지는 알 수 없다.

» 정답 01 (D) 02 (B) 03 (C)

먹이를 찾는 꿀벌의 춤은 벌집 안에서 지그재그 형으로 추면서 8자를 그리도록 나아가는 춤인데, 꽃이 발견된 방향과 거리에 대한 단서를 제공하여, 다른 벌들이 꽃이 발견된 곳을 찾을 수 있다. 오직 한 가지 문제가 있는데, 상당수 벌들이 이 정보를 무시하는 것처럼 보인다는 것이다. 아르헨티나의 연구가들에 따르면, 이 벌들은 그 대신에 먹이를 어디서 찾을지에 대해 각자의 기억에 의존한다. 위치 정보를 제공하는 벌의 흔드는 동작 외에도 춤추는 벌은 그것이 다녀간 꽃의 향기를 지니고 있다. 그리고 꽃향기는 벌들에게 잘 알려진 한 가지 영향을 미치는데, 벌들이 며칠 동안 먹이를 찾아 나서지 않았다면 그 향기는 벌들이 그들이 전에 종종 다녀간 먹이 장소로 다시 먹이 찾기를 시작하게끔 한다. 그렇다면 춤추는 벌이 새로운 위치에 대한 정보를 제공하지만 그 꽃향기가 춤을 지켜보는 벌이 기억하기로는 다른 장소에 있는 먹이를 생각나게 하면 어떻게 될까? 실험에서 연구가들은 거의 모든 경우에 벌들은 익숙한 먹이 공급처로 간 것을 발견하였다. 그 향기가 익숙한 것이 아니어서 위치의 기억이 없더라도 벌의 춤은 다른 벌들에게 새로운 것이 아닌 전에 알던 먹이 공급처로 돌아가게 할 뿐이었다. 이 연구는 벌집 내 상당한 수준의 군거성(群居性)에도 불구하고, 가장 중요한 것은 벌들 기억에 있는 각자의 정보라는 것을 알려주었다.

forage v. 찾아다니다, 마구 뒤적여 찾다
maneuver n. 방향 조종, 곡예비행; 책략, 술책
hive n. 꿀벌통
trove n. 수집물, 발견물
waggle n. 흔들기
odor n. 냄새, 향기
scent n. 냄새, 향내
resume v. 다시 찾다, 다시 시작하다, 다시 계속하다
spur v. 박차를 가하다; 자극하다
sociality n. 사회성, 군거성(群居性)

01 ▶ 먹이 공급처를 찾는 데 동료의 정보보다 자신의(their own) 기억에 의존한다고 했다. 이러한 개인적인 성향은 'sociality(군거성)'와 상반되므로 ①에는 양보의 전치사 regardless of(~에도 불구하고)가 적절하다. ②에는 their own과 같은 personal이 적절하다.

02 ▶ 정보를 제공하는 벌이 풍기는 꽃의 냄새가 춤을 지켜보는 벌들로 하여금 전에 다녀간 먹이 공급처를 상기시킨다고 하였으므로 "벌의 먹이 공급처에 대한 잠재된 기억은 냄새로 환기될 수 있다"를 추론할 수 있다.

03 ▶ 정보를 제공하려는 벌의 춤은 종종 무시된다는 내용이므로 "춤추는 벌의 헛된 노력"이 제목으로 적절하다.

▶ 정답 01 (B) 02 (D) 03 (B)

싸구려인 것이 많이 있다. 한때 프랭크 자파(Frank Zappa)가 그 내용을 노래로 불렀던 1950년대 싸구려 괴물영화가 더 없이 좋은 예가 된다. 거기 나오는 동물들은 (괴물이 아니라) 큰 푸들처럼 생겼고 거대한 거미의 턱에 붙인 나일론 줄은 쉽게 눈에 띄었다. 자파는 "난 그런 싸구려가 좋아요"라고 노래로 말했다. 누가 좋아하지 않겠는가? 그런 싸구려는 대단한 척 우쭐대는 것을 욕보이는 싸구려였기 때문에 사람들의 마음을 사로잡았던 것이다.

포도주에 관해서라면 나는 이와는 조금 다른 싸구려론(論)을 가지고 있다. 미 대륙 지역에서는 종종 있는 일이고 유럽에도 갈수록 많아지고 있는 일인데, 포도주 생산자가 내놓는 가장 비싼 적포도주는 또한 가장 손질이 많이 간 것이기도 하며 멋진 모양에 윤이 나고, 화장이나 머릿기름을 너무 많이 바른 것 같은 오크바닐라와 초콜릿향이 나게 된다. 아니면 너무 익은 포도로 만들어서 포도주에서 주로 구운 과일과 잼 맛이 나게 된다. 어느 쪽이든, 비싼 포도주라는 선입관에 맞는 여러 맛을 만들어내면 생산지와 개성을 느끼는 감각이 약해진다.

바로 그런 이유로 나는 종종 생산자가 내놓는 덜 비싼 포도주에 관심이 더 많이 간다. 만일 오크 대용물을 피하고, 비싼 포도주의 모방(괴물영화 시각에서 보면 이것이 '진짜 싸구려'임)을 위한 또 다른 포도주 양조 기법들을 피할 수 있다면, 당신은 소박한 정수를 맛볼 수 있는 몇몇 포도주를 찾아낼 수도 있을 것이다. 나는 이런 종류의 싸구려도 좋아한다. 그것은 겉치레라기보다는 진실함이지만, 공명정대한 시합을 하고 있는 것은 아니기 때문에 이 경우도 마찬가지로 (승자의) 우쭐거림에 대한 모욕이다. 다른 사람들은 여분의 돈을 더 쓰게 하고 당신은 더욱 즐길만한 포도주를 구하도록 하라.

---

cheepnis n. 프랭크 자파가 부른 노래 제목
affront n. 무례, 모욕
pomposity n. 거만, 건방짐
pretension n. 가장, 허식
spiff v. 말쑥하게 하다, 멋 부리다
reek v. 연기를 내다; ~냄새가 나다
pomade n. 포마드, 머릿기름
prevailing a. 우세한
preconceived notion 선입관
dodge v. 피하다
minefield n. 지뢰밭
affectation n. ~인 체 함
conversely ad. 정반대로, 역으로
derogate v. 헐뜯다, 깔보다, 훼손하다

01 ▶ 필자는 프랭크 자파가 노래한 괴물 영화의 싸구려에 대해 언급한 뒤 자신이 포도주에 대해 갖는 생각은 이것과는 조금 다르다는 이야기를 하고 있다. 또한 마지막 문단에서 프랭크 자파가 노래한 true cheepnis를 비싼 포도주를 모방하는 것과 일맥상통한 단어로서 이야기하고 있다. 그러므로 필자가 프랭크 자파를 언급한 의도는 괴물영화와 포도주, 이 두 분야에서 그가 갖고 있는 싸구려에 대한 생각을 비교하기 위함이라고 할 수 있다.

02 ▶ 먼저 비싼 포도주의 특징을 언급한 뒤, 연이어 또 다른 특징을 이야기하고 있으므로 '대신으로', '아니면'이란 뜻의 alternatively가 가장 알맞은 연결어이다. 또한 either way라는 표현에도 나와 있듯이 두 문장은 모두 비싼 포도주에 대한 선입관을 맞추기 위한 방법이므로 순접의 열거 개념인 alternatively가 들어가야 한다.

03 ▶ 두 번째 문단 마지막 문장에서 비싼 포도주의 선입관에 맞추기 위한 맛을 만드는 것이 포도주 생산지와 개성을 느끼는 감각을 흐리게 한다는 말은 있지만 그것이 포도주의 질을 떨어뜨린다는 이야기는 본문에 나와 있지 않다.

》 정답 01 (C) 02 (B) 03 (C)

몇 년 전, 어떤 과학자들은 북극과 남극 주변에 있는 얼음 속에 갇힌 공기를 연구함으로써, 과거의 대기의 특성을 조사하는 방법을 발전시켰다. 그들의 이론에 의하면, 눈이 떨어질 때 공기는 눈송이 사이에 갇힌다. 그 눈은 여전히 속에 공기를 가진 채 얼음으로 변한다. 오랜 세월에 걸쳐 더 많은 눈이 그 위에 쌓여 새로운 얼음 층을 형성한다. 그러나 이들 과학자들은 갇힌 공기가 그 눈이 처음으로 떨어졌을 때와 똑같은 상태로 남아있게 된다고 믿었다.

300년 전의 공기가 어떠했었는지를 알아내기 위해, 얼음 층 깊숙이 절단할 수 있는 속이 빈 튜브 형태의 드릴을 사용한다. 드릴을 꺼내면, 많은 층으로 이루어진 얼음의 심(心)이 그 안에서 나온다. 그리고 나서 실험실로 돌아가 얼음심 안에 있는 층의 수를 세면 — 각각의 층은 1년을 나타낸다 — 연구하고자 하는 연도에 내린 눈으로부터 형성된 얼음을 알 수 있다. 이 방법을 사용하여, 이들 과학자들은 지구 온난화의 원인일 수도 있는 가스 중의 하나인 이산화탄소의 양이 지난 200년 동안 크게 증가했다고 주장했다.

그러나, 한 노르웨이 과학자는 이 방법에 문제가 있을 지도 모른다고 지적했다. 그는 얼음 속에 있는 공기가 그대로 있지 않는다고 주장했다. 특히, 이산화탄소의 경우 일부는 얼음 결정에 의해 흡수되고, 일부는 물에 녹고, 일부는 다른 화합물질과 결합하기 때문에 이산화탄소의 양은 일정하게 남아있지 않는다고 말했다. 만일 이것이 사실이라면, 우리가 생각했던 것보다 과거에 더 많은 이산화탄소가 있었을 수도 있다. 그렇다 할지라도 지난 30년 동안에 측정된 양은 이산화탄소가 이 짧은 기간 동안 10퍼센트 이상 증가했다는 것을 보여준다.

---

investigate v. 조사하다, 연구하다
atmosphere n. 대기; 공기; 분위기
hollow a. 속이 빈, 공동(空洞)의
carbon dioxide 이산화탄소
absorb v. 흡수하다
measurement n. 측량, 측정; 치수, 크기

01 ▶ 본문에 '눈 속에 갇힌 공기가 그 당시의 대기 특성을 나타낸다'라고 했다.

02 ▶ 각각의 얼음층은 1년을 나타내므로 특정 연도의 대기를 연구하기 위해서는 얼음심에서 그 연도에 해당하는 특정한 층을 확인해야 한다.

03 ▶ 여러 가지 이유로 얼음 속에 있는 이산화탄소의 양이 변할 수도 있다고 주장했다.

》 정답 01 (B) 02 (A) 03 (C)

149

채소를 먹어야 하는 건강상의 이유가 무수히 많이 있어서 그 이유를 계속해서 일일이 열거하는 것은 불필요하게 느껴진다. 그러나 만일 어떤 사람들에게는 더욱 강한 면역 체계, 암과 맞서 싸우는 산화방지제, 그리고 심장에 좋은 섬유질만으로는 채소를 먹어야 할 이유로 충분치 않다면, 아마도 그들의 허영심에 호소할 수 있다. 『진화와 인간행동』 저널에 게재된 연구결과에 의하면 카로티노이드 성분이 많이 함유된 음식을 섭취하는 것은 — 몇몇 과일, 잎이 많은 채소, 뿌리채소에서 발견되는 성분 — 선탠한 피부와 견주어도 손색이 없을 정도로 건강한 윤기를 띠게 하며 실험에서 더 매력적으로 보이게 하는 것으로 나타났다.

"선탠을 한 피부색과 카로티노이드에 의한 피부색 중 선택의 기회가 주어졌을 때 사람들은 카로티노이드에 의한 피부색을 선호한다는 것을 알게 되었습니다"라고 이 연구의 수석 연구원 이안 스티븐(Ian Stephen) 박사가 한 보고서에서 언급했다. "따라서 더 건강하고 더 매력적인 피부색을 원한다면 태양 아래 누워있는 것보다는 많은 과일과 야채를 곁들인 건강한 식사를 하는 것이 더 좋습니다."

과일과 채소를 많이 섭취하는 사람들의 피부색이 명백하게 더 노란빛을 띠는 것을 연구원들은 밝혀냈다. 그러나 과학자들은 채식에 의한 피부의 윤기가 태양 아래 앉아서 얻어지는 것과 다르게 인식되는지 확신하지 못했다. 그래서 과학자들은 실험 참가자들에게 51명의 백인 얼굴을 보고 그 얼굴 피부 색조를, 일반적으로 태양 아래서 하루를 보낸 색깔로부터 카로티노이드 함유량이 풍부한 식단을 통해 윤기 나는 색깔에 이르기까지 그들이 생각하기에 가장 건강해 보이는 색깔로 조절해 보라고 요청했다. California Watch의 보도에 따르면 학생들은 사진에 찍힌 얼굴의 피부색을 더 노란빛을 띠게 하거나, 더 선탠한 것처럼 보이게 하거나 더 창백하게 보이게 조절할 수 있었다. 새로운 연구에 따르면 그 학생들은 더 노란빛을 띠는 얼굴이 더 매력적이고 건강하게 보인다는 것을 알아내었다. 윤기 나는 피부를 원하는가? 당근, 토마토, 고구마, 피망, 멜론, 시금치, 케일의 섭취량을 늘려라.

---

redundant a. 불필요한
enumerate v. 열거하다
immune a. 면한, 면역성의
antioxidant n. 산화방지제, 노화방지제
vanity n. 허영심; 덧없음
greens n. 푸성귀, 야채
glow n. (피부의) 윤기, 건강한 혈색
veggie a. 채식주의(자)의
pale a. (얼굴이) 창백한
bell pepper 피망
cantaloupe n. 멜론의 일종

01 ▶ 첫 문단에서 채소를 먹는 이유로 강한 면역 체계, 암 투병에 좋은 산화방지제, 그리고 심장에 좋은 섬유질 때문이라고 하였으므로 (A), (C)는 적절하다. 또한 새로운 연구 결과에 따르면 채소를 먹으면 피부에 윤기가 난다고 하였으므로 (B)도 적절하다. 수명이 연장된다는 말은 본문에 언급되어 있지 않으므로 (D)가 정답이다.

02 ▶ 채소가 윤기 나는 피부에 도움이 된다고 하였으므로 채식 위주의 식단과 외모는 서로 관련성이 있다고 유추할 수 있다.

03 ▶ 채식 위주의 식단이 피부에 미치는 긍정적인 영향에 대한 새로운 연구 결과의 정보를 주기 위한 목적에서 쓴 글이다.

» 정답 01 (D) 02 (C) 03 (B)

모든 동물은 수면을 취하므로 잠이 중요한 것임은 틀림이 없다. 잠을 자지 않는 동물의 종(種)이 있다는 명확한 증거는 없다. 계속해서 움직이기 때문에 때때로 잠을 자지 않는 동물의 예로 언급되는 돌고래조차 한쪽 눈을 감고 뇌의 반쪽 부분이 깊은 잠의 특징인 느린 뇌파를 보여주는 '단일반구수면'을 취할 것이다. 돌고래가 단순히 잠을 완전히 없애버리지 않고 놀랄만한 특성화를 발달시켰다는 바로 그 사실은 잠이 필수적인 기능을 수행하는 것이 분명하며 없앨 수 없는 것이라는 증거로 채택될 수 있다.

잠은 뇌에 의해서 정밀하게 조정되는데, 이는 수면 부족 뒤에는 반동이 나타나서 수면이 부족한 동물들은 더 오래 자거나 굉장히 느린 뇌파를 나타내는 더 깊은 잠을 자는 시간이 더 길어지기 때문이다. 장시간 잠을 자지 못하면 쥐, 파리, 그리고 바퀴벌레들은 죽을 수 있다고 알려져 있다. 유전적인 불면증에 걸린 사람 역시 죽을 수 있다. 이것보다 덜 심한 경우이긴 하지만, 잠을 못자면 파리에서 설치류에 이르는 동물들의 인식 기능에 영향을 끼친다. 계속해서 깨어있는 쥐는 '깜박 조는' 증상을 보일 것이며, 수면이 부족한 사람은 가장 위험한 상황에서조차 잠이 드는 경향을 보인다.

잠은 뇌가 다음 날에 유연해지도록 하는 데 치르는 대가일 수도 있다. 이러한 이론은 열심히 학습하며 하루를 보낸 후, 잠은 낮 동안 강도가 상승한 시냅스가 기준선의 수준까지 내려갈 기회를 부여하여 뇌로 하여금 재조직화 되도록 한다는 것이다. 잠은 새로운 기억을 강화하고 뇌로 하여금 임의적이고 하찮은 하루에 대한 기억을 잊어버리게 하여 다음 날에 좀 더 학습할 기억 공간을 마련하기 위해서도 중요하다.

species n. 종(種), 종류
unihemispheric a. 단일반구의(單一半球)의
specialization n. 전문화
deprivation n. 박탈; 궁핍
prolonged a. 장기적인
cockroach n. 바퀴벌레
genetic a. 유전의, 유전학의
insomnia n. 불면증
rodent n. 설치류
hypothesis n. 가설, 가정
synapse n. 시냅스(신경 세포의 자극 전달부)
damp v. 축축해지다; 감쇠하다
baseline n. 기준선
consolidate v. 결합하다; 공고히 하다

01 ▶ micro-sleep은 '깜빡 졸다'라는 뜻으로 doze off와 같은 의미이다. 계속 깨어있어서 잠을 못 잔 쥐는 깜빡 조는 증상을 보일 거라고 했고 잠이 결핍된 동물들은 더 많이 깊은 잠을 잔다고 했으므로 (D)가 옳은 말이다.

02 ▶ plastic은 '유연한'의 뜻으로 쓰였다. 뒤의 부연설명처럼 이 문장의 의미는 잠을 자는 동안 뇌가 하루 동안 학습했던 것 중에서 중요하지 않은 부분을 없애고 뇌를 재조직해서 다음 날에 학습할 기억 공간을 만들어낸다는 것이다. 따라서 정답은 (C) "당신의 뇌는 다음날 새로운 기억을 저장하는 데 있어 충분한 공간을 가질 수 있다"가 정답이다.

03 ▶ ⓑ는 '계속 깨어있는'의 뜻으로 과거분사 kept와 보어의 결합인데 보어로 쓰이는 '깨어있는'은 서술적으로만 쓰는 awake여야 한다.

  ≫ 정답 01 (D) 02 (C) 03 (B)

전 세계에 있는 대부분의 박쥐가 '소리를 통해 볼 수 있다'는 사실이 60년 전에 밝혀지자, 반향정위(反響定位)가 박쥐의 진화적 성공과 다양성에 엄청나게 공헌했다는 것이 명확해졌다. 하지만 박쥐의 두 가지의 주요한 적응인 비행과 반향정위 중에 어떤 것이 먼저 왔을까? 1990년대까지 세 가지 경쟁 이론이 나타났다. 비행이 먼저라는 학설은 박쥐의 시조가 가동성을 향상시키고 먹이를 찾는 데 요구되는 시간과 에너지의 양을 줄이고자 동력 비행을 진화시켰다고 생각한다. 이 시나리오에서 반향정위는 초기 박쥐가 이미 비행을 하면서 쫓고 있었던 먹이를 더 쉽게 발견하고 탐지하기 위해 그 다음으로 진화했다.

반대로 반향정위가 먼저 왔다는 학설은 활주해 내려오는 원시 박쥐들이 반향정위를 이용하여 나무 위에 앉은 곳에서 공중에 있는 먹이를 사냥했으며, 반향정위는 멀리서도 사냥물을 추적하는 것을 돕기 위해 진화했다고 한다. 동력 비행은 기동성을 증가시키고 사냥을 하는 앉은 자리로 돌아오는 것을 간단하게 하고자 나중에 진화했다.

연계 발달 학설의 입장에서는 비행과 반향정위가 동시에 진화했다고 주장한다. 이 의견은 박쥐가 움직이지 않을 때 반향정위 소리를 만들어내는 일은 너무 힘이 많이 든다는 것을 보여주는 실험 증거에 기초를 둔다. 그러나 비행 동안에 그렇게 하는 데 드는 힘은 거의 없어지는데, 왜냐하면 비행 근육의 수축은 폐의 공기 주입을 도우며, 강렬하고 높은 주파수의 발성에 필요한 기류를 만들어내기 때문이다.

revelation n. 폭로; 누설
bat n. 박쥐
echolocation n. 반향정위, (박쥐의) 반향 위치 측정
adaptation n. 적응, 순응
hypothesis n. 가정, 가설
mobility n. 이동성, 가동성
forage v. 마초를 찾아다니다; 식량징발에 나서다
detect v. 발견하다, 간파하다
perch n. (새의) 횃대
quarry n. 채석장; 사냥감
maneuverability n. 기동성
tandem a. 직렬의; 연계한
stationary a. 움직이지 않는, 정지된
contraction n. 수축, 수렴
vocalization n. 발성, 발성법

01 ▶ 본문에서는 박쥐의 두 가지 주요 적응인 비행과 반향 정위 중 어떤 것이 먼저 진화했는지를 설명하는 세 가지 학설을 제시하면서, 어떻게 진화했으며 그 이유는 무엇인지를 설명하고 있다. 따라서 이 글에서 주로 이야기하고 있는 것은 '박쥐 적응의 진화적 기원'이다.

02 ▶ 움직이지 않는(stationary) 상태에 있을 때는 반향 정위가 힘들지만(costly) 비행 도중에는 비행 근육의 수축으로 강렬하고 높은 주파수의 목소리를 내는 일이 더 쉬어진다고 했으므로 이런 노력(cost)이 거의 '없어지게' 된다고 유추할 수 있다. 또한 이런 연계적인(tandem) 효과 덕분에 두 가지 능력이 '동시에' 발달했을 것이라고 알 수 있다.

03 ▶ '기동성과 가동성을 높여서 사냥의 효율성을 증가시키기 위해', '음식을 찾는 시간과 에너지를 아끼기 위해', '강력한 소리를 더 쉽게 만들어내기 위해'는 박쥐가 비행과 반향 정위라는 두 가지 적응을 한 이유로 제시되었지만 '지리적 특성을 이용하여 공중에서 사냥을 할 수 있도록'이라는 이유는 본문에 언급되지 않았다.

》 정답 01 (B) 02 (D) 03 (B)

그러나, 다르지만, 또한 중요하기도 한 현대 역사가의 고충을 살펴봅시다. 고대나 중세의 역사가는 여러 해에 걸쳐서 다루기 쉬운 역사적 사실의 자료를 자기 마음대로 할 수 있게 해준 그 엄청난 선별 과정에 대해 감사할지 모릅니다. Lytton Strachey가 짓궂게 말했듯이, "역사가의 첫 번째 필수 요건은 무지인데, 그 무지는 (역사적 사실의 자료를) 단순화하고 이해하기 쉽게 하고, 선택하고 생략하는 것입니다." 고대와 중세 역사를 쓰는 데 종사하는 동료들의 엄청난 능력에 대해, 내가 때때로 시샘을 하기도 하지만, 내가 시샘하고 싶은 유혹을 받을 때, 나는, 그들이 자신들의 주제에 대해 무지하기 때문에 그들이 매우 유능하다는 생각을 하며 위안을 찾습니다. 현대의 역사가는 이러한 고유한 무지의 장점을 누리지 못합니다. 현대의 역사가는 혼자 힘으로 이러한 필요한 무지를 배양해야만 합니다. ― 그렇게 더 많이 하면 할수록, 그는 자신의 시대에 더 가깝게 접근하게 됩니다. 역사가는 몇몇 중요한 사실들을 발견해서 그것들을 역사적 사실로 바꾸는 일과 그리고 많은 중요하지 않은 사실들을 비역사적 사실로 버리는 이중의 임무를 갖고 있습니다. 그러나 이것은 역사는 최대한의 반박할 수 없고 객관적인 사실들을 편집한 것으로 구성된다는 19세기의 이론(異論)과는 정반대입니다. 이러한 이론(異論)에 굴복하는 사람은 누구나 역사를 나쁜 일로서 포기하고, 우표수집, 혹은 다른 형태의 골동품 수집에 착수하거나, 정신병원에서 종말을 맞을 것입니다.

plight n. 고충; 어려운 입장[처지]
at one's disposal 마음대로
winnow v. 추려내다, 가려내다, 구별하다
corpus n. 자료, 전집
mischievous a. 유해한; 장난기 어린, 짓궂은
built-in a. 본래 갖추어진, 고유한, 뿌리 깊은
discard v. 버리다, 폐기하다
heresy n. 이론(異論), 이설
take to ~에 빠지다, 전념하다
antiquarianism n. 골동품 연구, 골동품 (수집) 취미
madhouse n. 정신병원

01 ▶ 역사가는 중요한 사실들을 발견해서 그것들을 역사적 사실로 바꾸는 일과 그리고 여러 가지 중요하지 않은 사실들을 비역사적 사실로 버리는 '이중의' 임무를 갖고 있으므로 빈칸에는 dual이 들어가야 한다.

02 ▶ 19세기의 이론(異論)을 따르는 사람들은 역사를 나쁜 일로 본다고 했으므로, 글의 내용과 일치하지 않는 것은 (D)이다.

≫ 정답 01 (B) 02 (D)

153

부모간의 법정싸움 와중에 중병에 걸린 아기가, 아버지가 인공호흡기의 전원을 끄기로 합의한 지 며칠 지나서 죽었다. Baby RB라고 알려진 그 13개월 된 남자아기는 선천성 근무력증, 즉 자기 스스로는 호흡을 할 수 없는 것을 의미하는 유전적으로 희귀한 증상을 앓고 있었다. 아버지를 대변한 변호사인 크리스토퍼 쿠디히는 일요일 일찍 그 아기의 사망을 확인했지만 더 상세한 사항을 제공하지 않았다. 그 아기의 아버지는, 어머니와 병원이 '그 아기를 위해' 인공호흡기의 전원을 끄고자 했기 때문에 런던의 고등법원에서 그들을 상대로 법정싸움을 해 왔었다. 그는 그 아기가 놀고 자신의 부모를 알아볼 수 있었다고 말하면서 동의를 하지 않았다. 그 아기의 아버지는 화요일에 자신의 반대를 철회하고 인공호흡기의 전원을 끄는 것을 인정했다. 그 병원은 아기의 선천적 신체결함이 "심한 근무력증, 음식섭취 문제 및 호흡기 질환을 야기하고 있고 그 병은 진행 중"이라고 말하면서, 지난주 한 성명에서 자신들의 입장을 옹호했다. 그 아기의 폐는 몇 시간마다 액체로 차서, 아기에게 숨이 막히고 있다는 느낌을 주어, 아기로 하여금 고통을 겪게 한다고, 병원을 대변하는 변호사들이 11월 2일 법정에서 말했다. 결국, 그 아기의 아버지는, "계획된 방법, 즉 다량의 진정제 투약과 호흡관의 제거, 그리고 그에 따른 사망"으로 아기가 죽는 것이 최선이라는 점에 아기의 어머니 그리고 병원과 합의를 했다고, 앤드류 맥팔레인 판사가 화요일에 말했다. 그 아기의 부모는 별거 중으로, 사생활을 보호하는 법원명령으로 인해 이름을 밝힐 수 없다.

toddler n. 유아, 아장아장 걷는 사람
congenital myasthenic syndrome 선천성 근무력증
life support 산소호흡기
ventilator n. 호흡장치
solicitor n. 법무관; 변호사
defect n. 결점, 결함
respiratory a. 호흡의, 호흡을 위한
sedative n. 진정제
consequent a. 결과로서 일어나는

01 ▶ 그 아기의 어머니와 병원은 아기 자신을 위해 죽는 것이 좋다고 했지 그 아기의 아버지를 위해, 인공호흡기를 떼서 아기가 죽는 것이 좋다고 말하고 있는 것은 아니다.

02 ▶ 첫 번째 빈칸 다음에서 그 아기의 아버지가 동의했다는 내용이 있으므로, '결국'의 의미를 갖는 Ultimately가 빈칸에 와야 한다. 그리고 두 번째 빈칸에 들어갈 '투약'을 의미하는 단어는 administration이다.

≫ 정답 01 (C) 02 (C)

1970년대에 심한 폭풍우와 해수면 상승으로 인해 알래스카 주 포인트 호프의 이누피아트 족은 구도시에서 수 킬로미터 떨어진 신도시로 옮기지 않을 수 없었다. 그 이주는 전통적인 가옥이 파도 아래로 서서히 사라지는 것을 지켜본 마을 사람들에게 지속적인 문화적 상처를 남겼다. 기후 변화로 인한 환경 변화들이 이제 그들의 문화적 정체성의 핵심을 위협한다.

이누피아트 족은 소인(小人)이라고 알려진 작은 체구의 인간 같은 동물에 대한 이야기들을 갖고 있는데, 그들은 오랫동안 알래스카 원주민들 사이에 사기꾼과 기적을 만드는 자들로 알려져 있었다. 구도시를 버린 후 소인들이 구도시의 폐허 주위에 출몰했다는 보도가 늘어났다. 도시인들의 환경에 대한 견해와 달리 이누피아트 족은 아직도 자연 세계를 동물의 정령과 난쟁이들과 자기모습을 바꾸는 것들과 소인들로 가득 차있는 것으로 여긴다. 그들은 자연 환경 안에서 모든 요소들과 공존하는 것을 설명하는 이야기를 들려주어 사람들이 그들의 침강하는 고향땅과 변화하는 자연 풍광에 그들의 감정을 정착시키도록 도와준다. 그들의 이야기 중 하나에 따르면, 한때 가까운 호수에 살았던 용들이 호수물이 고갈된 후에 집을 잃고 죽거나 딴 데로 옮겨갔다고 한다. 이 이야기는 어떻게 북극의 호수들이 기후 변화로 고갈되거나 출현하게 되었는지를 반영한다. 이제 스토리텔링(이야기하기)은 조상대대로 살아온 고향을 잃어버린 마음의 상처를 다루는 것은 말할 것도 없고 기후 변화의 거친 현실에 적응하는 것을 위해 이누피아트 족 사람들이 택한 가장 좋은 책략 중 하나가 되었다. 이야기는 이누피아트 사람들로 하여금 네덜란드와 다른 국가들이 그랬던 것처럼 상승하는 해수면에 맞서 그들의 침강하는 고향땅을 계속 튼튼하게 강화시키면서 그들의 변화하는 세계를 이해하도록 해주었다.

relocate v. 이동하다, 이전하다
trauma n. 정신적 외상, 마음의 상처
trickster n. 사기꾼, 트릭스터
troll n. 장난꾸러기 난쟁이
shape-shifter n. (늑대인간 같이) 자기 모습을 바꾸는 것
not to mention ~은 말할 것도 없고
make sense of ~을 이해하다
fortify v. 강화하다
erode v. 침식되다; 서서히 파괴되다

01 ▶ 이 글은 기후변화로 인해 이주가 일어났고 그 이주가 문화적 상처를 남겼으며 그 상처를 치유하고 새로운 환경에 적응하는 수단으로 스토리텔링을 이용하고 있다는 내용이므로 (C) '적응 전략으로서의 스토리텔링'이 제목으로 가장 적절하다.

02 ▶ 앞 문장에서 그 이주가 '지속적인 문화적 상처를 남겼다'고 했으므로 지금도 문화적 상처는 남아있을 것이다. 따라서 빈칸에는 문화적 상처와 관련된 (D)가 적절하다.

03 ▶ 기후변화로 인한 해수면 상승으로 살던 곳이 바다에 잠기게 되어 이주한 것이므로 해변에서 먼 곳으로 이주했을 것이다.

》 정답 01 (C) 02 (D) 03 (A)

죽은 지 수만 년이 지났으면 논쟁을 불러일으키기가 어렵지만, 15명의 원인(原人: 원형적 인간)은 2015년에 그들의 화석이 요하네스버그에서 발견된 이후 바로 그렇게 했다. 그들이 주워 모은 유골의 골격 특징들은 비교적 현대적이지만 뇌가 고릴라의 뇌만큼 작아서 인류의 진화 사다리에 자리를 정하기가 어려웠다. 그들의 추정 연대에 대해 많은 의문이 생겼는데 이 문제는 5월 9일에 그들이 대략 23만 6천년 된 것으로 밝혀졌을 때 마침내 해결되었다.

그것은 선행인류가 초기 현생인류, 즉 '호모 사피엔스'와 바로 나란히 함께 살고 있었을지도 모른다는 것을 의미하기 때문에 대단히 중요하다. 네안데르탈인과 '호모 사피엔스'의 공존에 대해 우리가 이미 알고 있는 것과 함께 생각해보면, 그것은 본질적으로, 현생인류가 단일 혈통의 선행인류에서 진화했다는 옛 생각이 잘못임을 보여준다. 사실은 그게 아니라 오히려, 진화의 도상에서 여러 인류 모형들이 함께 경쟁하고 있었으며 그 중 준비된 하나만이 승리를 거두었던 것이다.

가장 최근 뉴스가 된 화석들은 '호모 날레디'라 불리는 원인(原人) 종에 속하며 한 동굴에서 고인류학자 리 버거에 의해 발굴되었다. 그는 처음에는 그들의 연대를 대략 200만 년 전으로 어림잡았지만, 그것은 단지 경험에서 나온 추측이었다. 버거는 가장 최근의 연구에서 훨씬 더 정확한 도구인 동위원소 연대측정법을 이용하여 그의 발굴 화석의 나이를 25만 년이 채 안 되는 것으로 정했다.

그럼에도 불구하고 버거는 '호모 날레디'가 보다 더 오래된 혈통, 즉 200만 년 전에 출현했을 수도 있지만 현생인류가 발생하자 사라져버렸거나 멸종되어버린 혈통의 중요한 한 부분일지 모른다고 생각한다. 우리는 오늘날 심한 경쟁을 벌이고 자원을 닥치는 대로 고갈시키는 종인데, 이 새로운 연구는 우리가 좋든 나쁘든 언제나 그러해왔다는 것을 확증하는 데 도움을 준다.

---

protohuman n. 원인(原人)
jumble n. 뒤범벅, 주워 모은 것
skeletal feature 골격 특징
prehuman n. 선행인류(인류발생 이전의 동물(영장류))
debunk v. 정체를 폭로하다, 사실이 아님을 드러내다
line n. 혈통, 계열
paleoanthropologist n. 고인류학자
educated guess 경험에서 우러난 추측
isotopic a. 동위원소의
wink out 사라져버리다
wipe out 죽이다; 완전히 파괴하다
gobble v. 게걸스레 먹다

01 ▶ 둘째 단락에서 '그것은 본질적으로, 현생인류가 단일 혈통의 선행인류(원인)에서 진화했다는 옛 생각이 잘못임을 보여준다'고 했으므로 (B)가 사실이 아니다. (A) 첫 문장이 단서이다. (C) 호모 날레디도 원인(原人) 중 하나이므로 마지막 단락 첫 문장이 단서이다. (D) 마지막 문장이 단서이다.

02 ▶ 둘째 단락 마지막 문장에서 여러 인류 모형(원인, 선행인류)들이 함께 경쟁하고 있었다고 했고 호모 날레디도 그 중 하나이므로 (D)가 사실인 진술이다. (A) 자리를 정하기 어려울 뿐이다. (B) 첫 인류 모형이라는 언급은 없다. (C) 적자생존 원리는 모든 종들이 적용받았다.

03 ▶ 리 버거는 고인류학자로서 현생인류 이전에 존재한 선행인류 즉 원인들의 유골화석을 연구하여 완전히 동물인 영장류(고릴라, 침팬지, 원숭이, 오랑우탄)와 인간 사이를 연결지어주는 종의 화석, 즉 잃어버린 연결고리(missing link)를 찾고 있는 것이므로 (A)가 정답이다.

» 정답 01 (B) 02 (D) 03 (A)

작가 안소니 파웰(Anthony Powell)이 말했듯이, "점점 늙어가는 것은 저지르지 않은 범죄에 대해 점점 더 많은 처벌을 받는 것과 같다." 힘든 노동을 수십 년간 하고 세금의 형태로 정부에 오랫동안 봉사한 후, 이제 마침내 당연한 휴식을 취할 준비를 하기 시작하는데, 어떤 일이 벌어지는가? 몸은 나빠지기 시작하고 감각은 약해지기 시작하고 잠은 대화 도중에나 적당히 잘 수 있을 뿐이다. 엎친 데 덮친 격으로, 일부 사람들은 당신이 국가의 보건 서비스에 부담을 지우고 있다고 말하기 시작한다. 당신이 때때로 몹시 불평하기 시작하게 되는 것도 당연하다! [A] 물론, 여기서 진지하게 생각해봐야 할 점이 있다. 노인들은 평생토록 세금을 내었기 때문에 보건 자원을 누릴 자격이 그 누구보다 더 있지는 않다 하더라도 그 누구만큼은 있다. 국민 보건 서비스(NHS)의 윤리적 특성은 그것이 모두에게 의료혜택을 무료로 제공한다는 것이며, 노인들이 이 정책에 예외여서는 안 된다. 그것은 아주 간단하다. 노인들도 아프면 치료받아야 한다는 것이다. [B] 불행하게도, NHS는 이런 이상을 항상 실천하지는 못한다. 영국 노인병 협회가 영국 의사들을 대상으로 행한 최근의 한 조사는 반 이상의 사람들이 지금 그들이 보는 노인들의 치료 방식 때문에 그들이 늙으면 어떻게 치료받게 될까 걱정할 것이라는 것을 시사했다. [C] 조사에 응한 대부분의 의사들은 노인들이 증세를 적절히 조사받게 될 가능성은 훨씬 더 적다고 믿는다. 노인들이 아플 때에는 치료 가능한 질병의 징후를 찾으려고 적절히 진찰하기보다는 '그냥 노령' 때문이라고 생각해버리는 경향이 있다. 의사들 중 4분의 3은 노인들은 적절히 치료받고 옳은 전문의에게 보내질 가능성이 더 적다고 단언했다. [D] 물론, 노인들이 직면하는 건강문제들 중에는 노화의 불가피한 일부인 것이 많다. 그러나 이것은 그것들이 어떻게도 치료될 수 없다는 것을 의미하지는 않는다. 노인들은 또한 일부 질병의 경우 치료에 대한 반응이 젊은이들보다 더 더딜지도 모른다. [E] 따라서 제한된 NHS 자원을 젊은이들 쪽으로 돌려서 삶의 질 개선 효과를 더욱 분명히 낼 수 있게 하자는 제안이 때때로 제기된다. 사실, 이것이 NHS의 실제 대응 방식이어서 종종 노인들이 2류 환자 취급을 받는다는 증거가 어느 정도 있다.

deserved a. 당연한
play up (신체) 컨디션이 나빠지다
to add insult to injury 엎친 데 덮친 격으로
mutter v. 불평하다
ethos n. 윤리성, 기풍, 풍조
live up to ~를 실천하다
geriatric a. 노인병의
steer v. (~를 …쪽으로) 나아가게 하다

01 처음부터 [A]까지는 노화의 고통을 겪고 있는 노인들의 현 상태를 언급하고, [A]부터 [B]까지는 그들이 충분한 보건 서비스를 받아야 한다는 당위성을 말하며, [B]부터 [D]까지는 그들이 의료혜택을 제대로 받지 못하고 있는 현실을 설명하고, [D]부터 마지막까지는 이 현실을 개선시키기 어렵게 만드는 점으로 노인의 건강문제가 노화의 불가피한 결과라고 생각하는 인식과 의료의 효율성 문제를 언급하고 있다. 따라서 (A)가 정답이다.

02 셋째 단락은 의사들을 대상으로 실시한 조사에서 의사들이 응답한 내용이므로 넷째 문장에서 "노인들이 아플 때 '그냥 노령' 때문이라고 생각해버리는 경향이 있다."라고 한 것은 의사들이 그렇게 생각하는 경향이 있다는 말이다.

» 정답 01 (A) 02 (D)

세계는 산업혁명 이래 섭씨 1도 이상 상승하였다. 2016년 지구의 날에 서명된 강제력도 없고, 시행할 수도 없으며, 이미 무시되고 있는 파리 기후협약은 2도 상승으로 제한하기를 희망했다. 현재 (온실가스) 배출 추세에 입각한 최근의 연구에 따르면 그 목표가 성공할 가능성은 1/20이다. 만약 어떤 기적이 일어나 온난화를 2도로 제한할 수 있다면, 우리가 해야 할 일은 단지 세계 열대 산호초들의 멸종 문제와, 몇 미터에 이르는 해수면 상승, 페르시아만의 포기를 잘 처리하는 것이다. 기후 과학자 제임스 한센(James Hansen)은 2도 상승이 "장기적 재난에 대한 규정" 정도에 불과하다고 말한다. 장기적 재난이 지금으로서는 최선의 시나리오이다. 3도 상승은 단기적 재난에 대한 규정이다. 북극의 삼림지대에는 재앙이고, 대부분의 해안 도시들은 사라질 것이다.

국제연합 기후 변화에 관한 정부간 협의체(UN IPCC) 전직 임원이었던 로버트 왓슨(Robert Watson)은 3도 상승이 현실적인 최소한이라고 주장해왔다. 만약 4도가 상승한다면, 유럽은 영구적인 가뭄 상태가 될 것이고, 중국과 인도 및 방글라데시의 대부분 지역들이 사막화될 것이며, 폴리네시아는 바다에 잠길 것이고, 콜로라도 강은 실개울처럼 줄어들 것이며, 미국의 남서부는 대부분 거주가 불가능해질 것이다. 만약 5도가 상승한다면 일부 세계적인 기후학자들로 하여금 이는 곧 인류 문명의 종말이라고 경고하도록 자극할 것이다.

nonbinding a. 구속력이 없는
unenforceable a. 시행할 수 없는
unheeded a. 무시된
odds n. 가능성
negotiate v. (어려운 일을) 잘 처리하다
extinction n. 멸종
prescription n. 규정; 처방
drought n. 가뭄
claim v. 빼앗다
largely ad. 대부분, 주로
uninhabitable a. 거주가 불가능한

01 ▶ 빈칸 바로 앞 문장에서 '2도 상승으로 제한하려는 목표가 성공할 가능성이 1/20이다'고 하였으므로, 이는 사실상 현실적으로 거의 불가능하다는 것과 같다.

02 ▶ '현실적인 최소한'이라는 의미는 '보수적으로 판단하여 가장 낮게 잡은 것으로서 그것이 현실화될 가능성이 아주 높기에 사실상 현실로 받아들여야 하며, 그보다 더 높을 가능성도 염두에 두어야 한다'는 의미이다.

03 ▶ 글 전체에 걸쳐 객관적이면서 비관적인 분위기가 팽배해 있다. 어떤 기적이 일어나 기온 상승이 2도에 멈추면, 장기적 재난에만 대처하면 될 것이지만, 2도 상승은 거의 없고, 3도 상승이 '현실적인 최소한'인데 그럴 경우 대부분의 해안 도시들은 사라질 것이고, 4도 상승하게 되면 유럽, 아시아, 미 대륙 등이 황폐화되며, 5도 상승은 사실상 인류 문명의 종말을 뜻한다고 말하고 있다.

» 정답 01 (C) 02 (B) 03 (E)

마녀들은 일반적으로 흔히 사악하고 추하고 결혼도 못한 늙은 여자로 묘사된다. 그들은 여성에 대한 모든 여성혐오적인 개념화의 구현이다. 그들은 남성이 원할만한(남성욕망의 대상이 될 만한) 가치가 없는 존재이고 더 나가 여성이 감히 권력을 가지고자 하거나 자신의 권위를 주장할 때 무슨 일이 일어나는지를 보여주는 존재다. 위험한 계집과 끔찍한 늙은 마녀는 여성들의 사악함을 보여주고 그들을 처벌할 뿐만 아니라, 남성들에게 경고하고 남성들을 두렵게 만들고자 하는 의도를 가지고 있는 상호보완적인 재현(표상)이다. 마녀에 대해 상응하는 남자들은 종종 마법사나 요술쟁이로 여겨진다. 비록 그들도 사악할 수 있지만 그들은 사악하게 자주 묘사되지는 않는다. 대신에, 그들은 점쟁이, 연금술사, 진실을 추구하는 진지한 탐구자 등으로 그려진다. 그들은 위엄 있게 나이가 들어가고 수염을 기른다. 늙은 마녀도 때로 수염을 가지기도 한다. 그러나 그들은 머리에 머리카락을 기르는 대신 뱀을 기르고 왕과 평민 모두를 파멸에 이르게 한다. 팜므 파탈에 대한 생각과 유사하게, 여성이 힘을 가지는 경우(마녀들이 마법의 형태의 힘을 갖는 것처럼) 그 힘은 종종 사악한 목적으로 사용된다. 마녀라는 개념화 뒤에 있는 메시지는 "숙녀들이여 만일 그대들이 마녀라는 꼬리표를 달고 싶지 않다면, 착한 어린 소녀와 같은 여성적인 성 역할을 따르라."이다. 이처럼 마녀들에 대한 묘사는 완벽한 여성성을 구성하고 있는 여성혐오적인 생각들과 밀접하게 연계되어 있다. 이 경우 완벽한 여성성이란 남성의 권위에 복종하고 결혼해서 아이를 낳고 남성에게 매력적으로 남아있는 것 등을 의미한다.

manifestation n. 표명, 명시; 징후
misogynistic a. 여성 혐오증의
bitch n. 암캐, 계집
iniquity n. 부정, 불법; 사악함
counterpart n. 상대물, 상대방, 대응물[자]
warlock n. 요술쟁이, 마법사
necromancer n. (강령술에 의한) 점쟁이; 마술사
crone n. 쭈그렁 할멈, 늙은 암양
wreak v. (해·벌 등을) 가하다, 주다, (원수를) 갚다
femme fatale 팜므 파탈, 요부
commemorate v. 기념하다, 축하하다
submissive a. 순종하는, 유순한

01 ▶ 이 글은 여성주의적 관점에서 마녀에 대한 묘사(마녀의 개념화)가 여성혐오를 조장하고 있다는 요지의 주장을 펼치고 있다.

02 ▶ 여성 혐오주의자들이 마녀를 통해서 드러내고 싶어 하는 것은 여성의 '사악함'이다.

03 ▶ "위험한 계집과 끔찍한 늙은 마녀는 여성들의 사악함을 보여주고 그들을 처벌하고 더 나아가 남성들에게 경고하고 남성들을 두렵게 만들고자 하는 의도를 가지고 있는 상호보완적인 재현(표상)이다."라는 단서로부터 정답을 추론할 수 있다.

≫ 정답 01 (B) 02 (D) 03 (A)

나는 북미 흑인에게서 그를 백인한테 짓밟혀 있게 한 질병을 고쳐주는 데 도움을 줄 수 있는 기구를 계획하고 설립하라는 도전을 느꼈다.

북미 흑인은 그가 백인 문화를 협조적으로 양순하게 받아들임에 있어서 정신적으로 병들어 있었다.

북미 흑인은 그 어떤 형제애도 기대하지 말고 소위 백인 기독교인들의 가혹행위를 참으라고 소위 흑인 기독교인들에게 요구한 백인의 기독교를 그가 수세기 동안 인정해왔기 때문에 영적으로 병들어 있었다. 기독교는 흑인들을 흐릿하고 모호하고 생각이 혼란된 사람들로 만들었다. 그것은 흑인에게 만일 신발이 없고 배가 고프면 "우리는 천국에서 신발과 우유와 꿀과 생선튀김을 갖게 될 거야."라고 생각하라고 가르쳤다.

북미 흑인은 경제적으로 병들어 있었으며 그것은 소비자로서 그는 그의 몫보다 더 적게 획득했고 생산자로서 그는 가장 적게 주었다는 한 가지 단순한 사실에서 명백했다. 오늘날의 흑인은 우리에게 완벽한 기생충 이미지를 보여주는데, 백인 미국이라는 위가 셋인 살찐 소의 젖통에 올라타 있기 때문에 진보하고 있다는 망상에 빠진 검은 진드기의 이미지이다.

북미 흑인은 정치적으로 가장 크게 병들어 있었다. 그는 백인의 표는 거의 언제나 균등하게 나누어지기 때문에 천만 흑인 유권자 진영이 미국 정치에서 결정적인 힘의 균형이 될 수 있는데도 백인이 그를 분열시켜 그 자신을 한 사람의 흑인 "민주당원"이나 흑인 "공화당원"이나 흑인 "보수당원"이나 흑인 "진보당원"으로 생각하는 그런 어리석음에 빠지게 만들도록 허용했다. 좀 들어보시라, 분명히 말해두겠다! 만일 흑인 진영 위원회가 미국 정가에서 가장 심한 "흑인 혐오자"에게 "우리는 천만 표를 대표합니다."라고 말해주면, 그러면 그 "흑인 혐오자"는 뛰어 달려와 "아이고 이런, 안녕하세요? 이리 들어오세요!"라고 외칠 것이다.

---

cure A of B A에게서 B를 고치다
under ~'s heel ~에게 짓밟힌
sheeplike a. 양 같은
Christianity n. 기독교
brotherhood n. 형제애
fuzzy a. 흐트러진, 흐릿한
nebulous a. 불분명한, 모호한
parasite n. 기생충
tick n. 진드기
udder n. 젖통
why ad. (if ~, why) 그러면
leap up 약동하다, 날듯이 행동하다

01 ▶ 빈칸 뒤에서 소의 젖통에 올라타고 영양분을 섭취하는 검은 진드기가 예로 나오므로 '기생충'이란 의미의 (B)가 적절하다.

02 ▶ 마지막 단락에서 북미 흑인이 정치적으로 가장 크게 병들어 있다고 하고 정치적 의식이나 단결심이 없음을 설명하므로 (D)가 사실이 아니다.

03 ▶ 이 글의 저자는 북미 흑인이 백인의 억압을 받으면서도 저항하거나 개선하려는 의지가 없는 어리석음을 지적하면서도 그 병적 상태를 고쳐주고 싶은 마음이 있음을 첫 문장에서 말하므로 북미 흑인에 대한 태도로는 (B)의 '동정적인'이 적절하다.

» 정답 01 (B) 02 (D) 03 (B)

"인도가 물결처럼 울퉁불퉁해서 사람들이 걷다가 넘어질 수 있어요."라고 무아라 바루(Muara Baru)에 살면서 자주 어시장을 찾는 주민인 리드완(Ridwan)은 말한다. 지하의 수위가 고갈됨에 따라, 시장을 오가는 사람들이 걷는 지반이 침하되고 변화하면서 울퉁불퉁하고 불안정한 표면이 형성되고 있다. "매년 지반이 계속 가라앉고 있어요."라고 말하는데, 그는 지금 벌어지고 있는 일들에 관해 경고를 받은 이 지역 주민들 중의 한 사람이다. 포르투나 소피아(Fortuna Sophia)는 바다가 보이는 호화 빌라에서 살고 있다. 그녀의 저택이 침하되는 것이 바로 목격된 것은 아니지만 6개월마다 벽과 기둥에서 균열이 나타나고 있다고 그녀는 말한다. "계속 수리하고 있습니다."라고 개인용 도크에서 몇 미터 떨어져 있는 그녀의 풀장 옆에 서서 그녀는 말한다. "유지보수하는 사람들 얘기에 따르면 균열이 생긴 건 지반이 움직여서라는군요." 그녀는 이 집에서 산 지 4년이 되었지만 이미 여러 차례 침수되었었다. "바닷물이 흘러들어와 풀장을 완전히 뒤덮어요. 우리는 모든 가구를 2층까지 옮겨야 합니다."

그러나 바닷가에 바로 인접한 소형 주택들에 대한 영향은 커진다. 한때 바다를 보고 살았던 주민들은 이제 바닷물을 막기 위한 용감한 시도로 쌓고, 또 쌓은 밋밋한 회색 제방만 볼 수 있을 뿐이다. "매년 조수의 높이가 5센티미터 가량 높아지고 있어요."라고 어부인 마하르디(Mahardi)는 말했다. 상황이 이런데도 부동산 개발업자들은 단념하지 않고 있다. 위험에도 불구하고 점점 더 많은 호화 아파트들이 점점이 흩어져 세워져서 북부 자카르타의 스카이라인을 형성하고 있다. 인도네시아 주택개발 협회 자문위원회 위원장인 에디 가네포(Eddy Ganefo)는 이 지역의 추가적인 개발을 중단해야 한다고 정부에 촉구해 왔다. 그러나 그는 "아파트 매매가 계속되는 한, 개발은 계속될 겁니다."라고 말한다. 비록 그 속도는 더 느리지만, 자카르타 다른 지역들도 역시 침하 중이다. 서부 자카르타의 지반은 매년 15센티미터, 동부 지역은 10센티미터, 중부 지역은 2센티미터, 그리고 남부 자카르타는 1센티미터씩 침하하고 있다.

---

walkway n. 보도, 인도
deplete v. 고갈시키다
maintenance n. 유지, 보수
first floor 2층
dyke n. (바닷가) 제방
valiant a. 용감한, 씩씩한
deter v. 단념시키다
skyline n. 윤곽

01 첫째 단락에 '지금 벌어지고 있는 일들에 관해 경고를 받은 이 지역 주민들'이라는 표현이 나오고, 둘째 단락에 '이 지역의 추가적인 개발을 중단해야 한다고 정부에 촉구한' 조직이 있음을 알 수 있기에 (B)는 본문의 내용과 일치하지 않는다. 한편, 글의 마지막 부분에서 '비록 그 속도는 더 느리지만, 자카르타 다른 지역들도 역시 침하 중이다.'고 하면서 서부, 동부, 중부, 남부 자카르타 지역의 침하 속도를 소개한 것으로 보아 이 글에서 주로 다룬 지역은 북부 자카르타임을 알 수 있고, 북부 지역의 침하 속도가 가장 빠른 것으로 볼 수 있으므로 (E)의 진술은 본문의 내용에 부합한다.

02 이 글은 빠른 속도로 침하되고 있는 자카르타의 현재를 취재한 기사문이다.

» 정답 01 (B) 02 (C)

프랑스 경제학자 J. B. 세이(J. B. Say)는 대단히 존경받는 고전학파 학자였다. 지금까지 그는 세이의 시장 법칙으로 가장 잘 알려져 있다. 존 메이너드 케인즈(John Maynard Keynes) 덕분에 대중적인 말로 하면 이 법칙은 단지 "공급은 그 자체의 수요를 창출한다."는 말이 된다. 그러나 세이의 법칙에 대한 케인즈의 해석은 그 법칙의 진정한 의미를 왜곡하고 그 법칙이 지닌 주된 메시지를 함부로 편집하여 잘라내 버린다.

세이의 메시지는 분명했는데, 그것은 수요 부족이 경기 불황의 원인일 수 없다는 것이었다. 이 메시지는 케인즈가 1936년에 『고용, 이자 및 화폐의 일반이론』을 발표하기 전에는, 거의 모든 주요 경제학자들에 의해 인정되었다. 그래서 『일반이론』 전에는, 비록 대부분의 경제학자들이 경기순환이 예상된다고 생각했지만, 경기 후퇴의 원인 목록에 수요 부족은 들어있지 않았다.

이 모든 것이 케인즈에 의해 뒤집어졌다. 케인즈는 J. B. 세이를 거짓을 말하는 사람으로 몰아세웠고 그래서 세이의 사상을 경제 담론과 대중들의 생각에서 제거할 수 있었다. 케인즈는 그의 전체 이론이 수요 부족에 대한 분석에 기초해 있었기 때문에 이렇게 해야만 했고, 그래서 총수요에 다시 활기를 불어넣기 위한 그의 처방이 나오게 되었는데, 그것이 곧 재정지출을 통한 경기부양이었다.

케인즈는 널리 성공을 거두었다. 『일반이론』의 발표와 더불어, 경제의 공급 측면은 거의 완전히 사라졌다. 공급 측면은 총수요로 대체되었고 총수요가 국민소득계정에서 성실히 보고되었다. 그 결과, 지금까지 줄곧 총수요가 경제 담론과 경제 정책을 지배해왔다. 경제의 구조인 공급 측면은 어디에도 찾아볼 수 없다.

---

regarded a. 존경받는
lexicon n. 어휘
rendition n. 해석
distort v. 왜곡하다
cutting room 편집실
slump n. 불황, 불경기
business cycle 경기순환
in the cards 예상되는
downturn n. 하락, 후퇴, 침체
overturn v. 뒤집어엎다
set someone up 위험한 상황[유죄]으로 몰아세우다
straw man 짚 인형; 위증하는 증인; 보잘 것 없는 사람
aggregate demand 총수요
fiscal stimulus 재정지출 통한 경기부양

01 ▶ 케인즈의 경제학은 총수요를 중시하는 수요지향의 경제학인 반면에 세이의 시장법칙은 공급지향적인 것이라는 것을 마지막 두 단락에서 알 수 있다. 따라서 (C)가 정답이다. (A) 세이는 고전경제학의 주류였다. (B) 케인즈의 해석이 세이의 법칙의 완성을 도운 것이 아니고 오히려 그 의미를 왜곡시켰다. (D) 세이를 포함한 고전경제학자들도 경기순환을 예측하기는 했다.

02 ▶ 세이의 시장법칙을 "공급은 그 자체의 수요를 창출한다."라고 대중적으로 정의한 것은 케인즈가 맞지만 세이에게 유리하게 정의한 것은 아니다.

03 ▶ 세이의 메시지(사상)가 둘째 단락에서는 인정되었는데 셋째 단락에서는 경제 담론과 대중들의 생각에서 제거되었으므로 빈칸에는 반전의 의미인 (D) '뒤집어진'이 적절하다.

》 정답 01 (C) 02 (B) 03 (D)

무지하고 경험 없었던 우리가 아래에서부터가 아니라 위에서부터 새로운 삶을 시작하려고 했던 것은 놀라운 일이 아니다. 우리는 부동산이나 어떤 일을 위한 기술을 추구하기보다는 연방 의회의 한 자리, 그게 아니라면 주 의회의 한 자리라도 얻으려 노력해왔다. 목장이나 시장에 팔 채소밭을 가꾸는 것보다 전당대회의 한 자리, 가두연설의 한 자리가 더 매력이 있었다. 바다에서 며칠이고 길을 잃은 배가 갑자기 우호적으로 보이는 배를 보았다. 불운한 배의 마스트에는 "물, 물이 필요해요. 갈증으로 죽어가요!"라는 신호가 쓰여 있었다. 우호적인 배에서 당장 대답이 왔다. "지금 거기서 두레박을 내리세요." 조난 위기에 처한 배는 다시 한 번 "물, 물을 보내 줘요!"라는 신호를 보냈다. 대답은 "지금 거기서 두레박을 내리세요."였다. 세 번째, 네 번째 신호에도 마찬가지로, "거기에서 두레박을 내리세요."가 대답으로 돌아왔다. 위기에 처한 배의 선장은 마침내 그 권고에 주의를 기울였고, 두레박을 내렸다. 그랬더니 아마존 강어귀의 거품이 이는 강물로 가득 찬 두레박이 올라왔다. 외국 땅에서 자신의 처지를 개선하길 원하는, 혹은 남부에서 자신들의 이웃 백인들과 우호적인 관계를 설정하는 중요성을 과소평가하고 있는 나의 인종들에게 나는 말하고 싶다. "네가 있는 그곳에서 양동이를 내려라."라고. 우리를 둘러싸고 있는 모든 인종의 사람들과 친교를 맺는 모든 인간적인 방법으로 양동이를 내리라고.

---

state legislature 주 의회
real estate 부동산
convention n. 전당대회
stump speaking 가두연설
truck garden 시장판매용 채소밭
bucket n. 두레박, 양동이
distressed a. 어려운 상태에 처한
heed v. 주의를 기울이다
injunction n. 명령, 권고
fresh water 민물
sparkling a. 거품이 이는
better v. 개선하다
underestimate v. 과소평가하다
next-door a. 옆집의
hold ~ in high esteem 존중하다

01 ▶ 이 글의 중심사상(요지)은 To those of my race 이하에 나와 있다. 흑인이 미국 사회에서 자신들의 지위를 개선시키려면 자신의 생각에 갇혀있지 않고 주변의 이웃들에게 열린 자세로 나아가야 한다는 것이다.

02 ▶ 빈칸 ② 다음의 두 개의 that절에서 밑바닥의 생업에 필요한 기술과 능력보다 높은 정치적 지위를 더 많이 추구했음을 알 수 있으므로 ①에는 top이, ②에는 bottom이 적절하다.

03 ▶ 부동산을 통해 돈을 버는 것은 이제까지 무시되어 왔던, 아래로부터의 운동이다.

》 정답　01 (A)　02 (B)　03 (D)

나도 몇 년에 걸쳐 이 문제에 대해 여러 번 거론해 왔지만, 이따금씩 새로운 연구들이 등장하여 체질량지수(BMI)가 건강의 척도로서, 심지어 지방과다의 척도로서도 한계가 있음을 입증하는 근거를 제시하고 있다. 이 지수는 수천 명을 상대로 한 역학 연구에 사용될 때는 의미가 있지만, 개인들에 대해서는 정말 형편없는 기준이다. 이 단면 조사 연구에서 저자들은 18세에서 80세에 이르는 백인 실험 대상(그 중 여성은 69%였다)들의 BMI, 체지방 비율, 심혈관대사 위험요인을 살펴보았다. (BMI에 따르면 이들 중 924명은 여위고, 1,637명은 과체중, 3,562명은 비만으로 분류되었다.)

그들은 무엇을 발견했는가? 우선 BMI에 따르면 정상체중으로 분류된 피실험자의 29%와 과체중으로 분류된 사람들 중 80%가 비만 범위 내에 있는 체지방률을 가지고 있었다. 따라서 개인적인 측면에서 보자면 BMI는 체지방률을 일관성 있게 과소평가하고 있다. 이 자료는 절대적인 기준으로 보면 별로 무게가 나가지 않지만, 몸무게의 많은 부분이 지방 조직으로 이루어진 사람들이 많다는 것을 암시하고 있다. 이 사람들은 겉으로 보기엔 야위어 보이지만, 근육의 상태가 보잘것없어, 말랑말랑한 몸을 가지고 있는 사람들이다. 두 번째, (BMI나 체지방 둘 다에서) 실제로 마른 사람들과 비교해 볼 때, BMI와는 상관없이(BMI에 따라 정상이건, 과체중이건, 비만이건 간에) 지방과다인 사람들은 심혈관대사 상태가 좋지 않다. 혈압은 높고, 혈당과 혈중 지질, 전신염증의 표시도 있을 수 있다.

---

every now and then 때때로
adiposity n. 체지방률, 지방과다
epidemiological a. 역학의, 전염병의
cross-sectional study 단면 조사 연구
cardiometabolic a. 심혈관대사의
obese a. 비만의
caucasian a. 백인의
tone n. 근육의 긴장 상태
profile n. 농도, 수준, 상태
blood glucose 혈당
blood lipid 혈중 지질
systemic inflammation 전신염증

01 ▶ 이 글의 주제는 "BMI는 신뢰 가능한 건강 척도가 아니다"이다. (C)의 경우는 '낡은 건강 기준'이 무엇을 가리키는지 막연하다.

02 ▶ 내용상 '형편없다'는 의미의 낱말이 필요하다.

03 ▶ 마지막 문장에서 지방과다인 사람들은 건강에 대한 여러 위험 요소를 가지고 있는데, BMI는 이를 밝혀낼 수 없다고 하였다. 따라서 정답은 (A)이다. (E)는 BMI는 근육 양을 비만으로 착각할 정도로 어리석지 않다는 내용이다. 사실은 구별 못한다고 내용에 있다.

》 정답 01 (A) 02 (B) 03 (A)

노인 세대들은 종종 인터넷에 가입해 들어가 자녀들, 조카들, 손자손녀들과 계속 연락을 취한다. 우리는 이런 종류의 접촉에 대해 그것이 어떤 구식 사람의 활동인 것처럼 이야기하지만, 그것은 정확하게 젊은이들이 소셜미디어를 사용하는 이유이다. 사실은 대부분의 사람들이 소셜미디어를 사용하여 부드럽게 서로를 확인하고, 그들이 걱정하는 사람들이 어떻게 지내고 있는지를 매일 밤 전화를 걸어 일어나게 할 필요 없이 알아본다. 사실, 15세 사람들이 나누는 교신이 30세, 50세, 75세 사람들의 교신보다 종종 더 극적인 교신으로 끝나기도 한다. 대화에 동참하는 노인들이 많을수록 이들 사이트에서 일어나는 대화는 그들의 동시대인들에게 더욱 적합하게 될 것이다. 그리고 이것은 소셜미디어의 또 다른 비밀인데 모든 사람이 그것을 나름대로의 방식으로 사용하게 된다는 것이다. 나이가 많든 적든, 소셜미디어를 옳게 사용하는 것에 대해 걱정하는 소셜미디어 신참자는 소셜미디어를 사용하는 올바른 방법이 있다고 생각하지만 알고 보면 그런 것은 없다. 상습적인 사용자들조차도 어떤 인터넷 활동들을 다른 것들보다 더 좋아한다. 어떤 사람들은 트위터로 많은 이야기를 하고 또 다른 사람들은 페이스북으로 그렇게 한다. 많은 사람들은 이 두 가지를 모두 사용한다. 많은 젊은이들은 인스타그램으로 옮겨가고 있다. 그리고 일부 사람들은 인터넷에 아무 것도 올리지 않고 독자로서 소셜미디어의 열렬한 소비자이다. 소셜미디어 회사들은 사람들이 그들의(회사의) 네트워크를 퍼 날라 온 사진과 글로 가득 채우는 것을 보고 싶어 하기 때문에 단지 남의 글을 읽기만 한다는 생각은 좀체 장려하지 않지만, 벽에 앉은 파리(읽고 보고 듣기만 하는 사람)가 되지 못하게 막는 규정은 없다. 그것도 좋은 참여 방법이다. 우리는 인터넷망이 13세 사람들이 만든 것이 아니었다는 것을 재빨리 잊어버린다. 그것은 오늘날의 노인들이 만든 것이었다. 나는 전혀 관심이 없거나 경박한 트위터링에 본래부터 반감을 갖고 있는 사람들에게 소셜네트워크를 억지로 사용하게 하지는 않을 것이다. 그러나 (소셜미디어 사용과 관련하여) 나이 구분에 대한 이야기에 넘어가지는 마시라. 베이비부머 세대 사람들로 하여금 그들 자신의 세대가 만든 네트워크를 이용하지 못하게 막을 것은 아무 것도 없다.

---

sign up 가입하다
old-fogey n. 구식 사람
keep tabs on 확인하다; 감시하다
ring up 전화를 걸어 일어나게 하다
inveterate a. 상습적인
post v. 게시하다
avid a. 열렬한
foist v. 억지로 떠맡기다
boomer n. 베이비붐 세대 사람
reclaim v. 이용하다

01 ▶ 소셜미디어는 젊은이들의 전유물이 아니고 노인들도 사용해야 하는 것이라는 것이 특히 글의 첫머리와 끝부분에 잘 나타나 있으므로 '소셜미디어에는 연령제한이 없다'가 제목으로 적절하다.

02 ▶ ①은 벽에 앉은 파리가 방안을 구경하듯이 보고 듣기만 하는 수동적인 사람을 의미하므로 (D)가 가장 잘 설명한 것이다.

03 ▶ 소셜미디어 신참자는 소셜미디어를 사용하는 올바른 방법이 있다고 생각하지만 알고 보면 그런 것은 없다고 했으므로 (B)가 사실이 아니다.

》 정답 01 (A)　02 (D)　03 (B)

지성에 대한 전통적인 설명은 인간의 육체에는 일종의 유령 같은 존재로 상상되곤 하였던 비물질적 존재, 즉 영혼이 가득 차 있다는 것이다. 그러나 그 이론은 극복할 수 없는 한 가지 문제에 직면하게 된다. 유령이 어떻게 딱딱한 물질과 상호작용하는가? 아무런 형태가 없는 것이 어떻게 빛에, 찌름에, 경적에 반응하며 팔과 다리를 움직이게 하는가? 또 다른 문제는 정신이 뇌의 활동이라는 압도적인 증거이다. 우리가 비물질적이라고 여기고 있는 그 영혼(인간의 뇌)이 칼로 이등분할 수 있고, 화학물질로 변화시킬 수 있으며, 전기에 의해 시동이 걸리고 꺼질 수도 있고, 바람이 세게 불거나 산소가 부족하면 꺼져버릴 수도 있다는 것을 이제 우리는 알고 있다. 현미경으로 본 뇌는 정신의 풍요로움에 맞먹는 놀라우리만치 복잡한 물리적 구조를 지니고 있다.

또 다른 설명은 정신이 특별한 형태의 어떤 물질에서 유래한다는 것이다. 피노키오는 제페토가 발견한 일종의 마술적인 나무에 의해 생명이 불어 넣어지는데, 그 나무는 스스로 말하기도 하고 웃기도 하며 움직일 수 있는 나무였다. 슬프게도, 그런 기적의 물질을 발견한 사람은 없다. 우선 먼저 그 기적의 물질이 뇌 조직이 아닐까 생각해볼 수 있다. 다윈(Darwin)은 뇌가 정신을 "분비한다"고 썼고 최근에 철학자 존 썰(John Searle)은 마치 젖가슴 조직에서 젖을 만들고 식물 조직이 당분을 만들듯이 뇌 조직의 물리 화학적 특성에 의해 정신이 만들어진다고 주장하고 있다. 그러나 배양 접시에 담긴 뇌종양과 배양 조직은 말할 것도 없고, 똑같은 종류의 세포막과 기공, 화학물질들이 동물계 전반에 걸쳐 발견된다는 사실을 상기하자. 이 작은 신경 조직들은 동일한 물리 화학적 특성들을 가지고 있지만, 그 어느 것도 인간과 같은 지성을 성취하지는 못한다. 물론, 인간 뇌 조직의 어떤 것이 인간의 지성을 위해 반드시 필요하지만, 그 물리적 특성만으로는 충분하지 않다. 마치 벽돌의 물리적 특성만으로는 건축을 설명하기에 모자라고, 산화물 입자의 물리적 특성으로 음악을 설명하기에 충분치 못한 것과 같다. 신경 조직이 정형화됨에 있어서의 그 뭔가가 결정적으로 중요하다.

---

entity n. 실재, 존재
insurmountable a. 극복할 수 없는
spook n. 유령
ethereal a. 무형의
bisect v. 이등분하다
commensurate a. 상응하는
secrete v. 분비하다
membrane n. 세포막
pore n. 기공
tumor n. 종양

01 ▶ 필자는 인간의 뇌에서 정신 작용이 비롯되기 위해서는 '인간 뇌의 물리적 특성만으로는 충분하지 않다'고 했고, 마지막 문장에서 '어떤 것(something)이 결정적으로 중요하다'고 덧붙였다.

02 ▶ 빈칸 다음에 an ethereal nothing은 the spook을 받으며, 빛, 찌름, 경적에 반응하여 팔과 다리를 움직이게 한다고 했으므로 정신이 '물체의 형태'를 지닌 인간의 몸을 움직이게 한다고 볼 수 있다.

» 정답 01 (E) 02 (A)

군중은 조그만 배출구를 통해 빠져나오는 거친 물과 같았다. 다른 사람들의 성공에 흥분한 뒤쪽에 있던 사람들은 필사적인 노력을 했다. 왜냐하면 이 많은 무리의 사람들은 숙소를 가득 채우고도 남아서 사람들이 도로에 남겨질 것으로 보였기 때문이다. 마지막이 되는 것은 비참한 것일 것이다. 따라서 눈이 얼굴의 살을 에는 듯해서 사람들은 전력을 다해 몸부림치며 뚫고 지나갔다. 누구라도 그 엄청난 압력으로 인해, 지하실 문으로 통하는 좁은 통로는 사람들의 팔다리와 몸으로 너무나 가득 차서 그 결과 움직임이 불가능할 것이라고 예상을 했다. 한때, 정말로 사람들은 멈추어야 했다. 그리고 층계 밑바닥에서 한 사람이 부상을 당했다는 외침이 나왔다. 그러나 곧, 느린 움직임이 다시 시작되었고 경찰이 내려가는 사람들에게 가해지는 압력을 덜어주기 위해서 계단 맨 위에서 애를 썼다.

사람들이 순서대로, 마지막 세 개의 계단에 도달해서 막 들어가려고 했을 때, 창문에서 나오는 붉은색 빛이 사람들의 얼굴을 비추었다. 그때 어느 누구라도 그들의 얼굴에 나타난 표정의 변화를 알아차릴 수 있었다. 따라서 그들이 희망의 문턱에 섰을 때, 그들은 갑자기 만족하고 기뻐하는 듯 보였다. 불빛이 그들의 눈에서 스쳐갔고 욕설이 그들의 입술에서 사라졌다. 이전에는 자신들을 성나게 했던 뒤에 있던 사람들의 힘이 다른 관점에서 보였다. 왜냐하면 그것은 이제 자신들이 조그만 문들을 통과해 유쾌하고 빛으로 따뜻한 곳에 들어가는 것을 불가피하게 만들었기 때문이었다.

---

frantic a. 미친 듯이 날뛰는, 광란의
quarters n. 숙소
pavement n. 포장도로
writhe v. 몸부림치다, 몸부림치며 괴로워하다
at the foot of the stairs 층계 밑바닥에서
complacent a. 기뻐하고 있는
threshold n. 문지방, 입구; 발단, 시초
snarl n. 으르렁거리는 소리, 욕설

01 ▶ (C)는 'the snarl had vanished from their lips'로 미루어 알 수 있다. (D)는 "the policeman fought at the top of the flight to ease the pressure on those who were going down."의 문장을 참고한다.

02 ▶ 그들 얼굴의 표정이 갑자기 'content and complacent'했다고 했음에 유의하면 (C)가 답이 된다.

≫ 정답 01 (D) 02 (C)

167

우리가 가지고 있는 '어두운 면'에 관해서 대화를 나눌 때 우리는 일반적으로 우리의 가장 공격적이고 호색적이고 반사회적인 본능에 대해서 관심을 기울인다. 혹은 우리 안 깊은 곳에 숨어있다고 여겨지는 야비하고 피에 굶주린 공격성에 관심을 기울인다. 혹은 타인들의 삶을 완전히 절멸시키는 것까지는 아니지만 어찌되었든 타인들의 삶을 망치게 하는 공격적인 충동에 관심을 기울인다. 강간, 사지절단, 살인, 도둑질과 배신과 모반과 사디즘과 마조히즘 등의 비양심적인 행위들, 끝없는 탐욕, 근친상간 등등. 그러나 내가 여기서 말하고자 하는 것은 당신의 어두운 백일몽이 전적으로 악마적인 것으로 이해돼서는 안 된다는 것이다. 혹은 최소한 그것들은 예를 들어서 품위를 떨어뜨리고, 수치스럽고 사악한 것과는 반대되는 대담하고, 소심하지 않고, 원초적이고, 거창하고, 쾌락적이라고 훨씬 더 동정적으로 평가될 수도 있는 것이다. 타인들과 조화롭게 살기 위해서 우리는 우리의 충동적인 욕망을 억눌러야 한다. 우리의 어두운 면이 우리의 원초적이고 즐거움과 권력을 추구하는 본능을 구현하고 있는 것이라는 점을 고려한다면, 진정 우리는 광적으로 그 어두운 면이 드러나는 것을 피하고, 그 어두운 면을 비열하며 피하고 부인해야 할 것이라고 거부해야만 하는 것일까?

궁극적으로 그와 같은 '어두운' 본능에 대한 선호는 그 어두운 본능들 대부분이 단지 우리 모두가 타고난 '욕구'와 '충동'을 표상하는 것이라는 점에서 본질적인 정말로 비난받을 만한 것은 아니다. 많은 심리학 연구자들은 몽상들이 가지고 있는 실질적인 유용성에 대해서 언급해 왔다. 왜냐하면, 이미 앞에서 제시했듯이, 몽상들은 우리의 좌절을 위한 꼭 필요한 배출구로서 긍정적으로 기능할 수 있기 때문이다. 그리고 우리가 그와 같은 몽상들을 단순히 '즐긴다는 것'은 반드시 어둡고 타락한 것으로 여겨져야만 하는 파괴적인 잠재성을 정말로 반영하는 것은 아니다. (특히 젊은이들 사이에서) 공포영화가 지속적으로 인기를 누리는 이유는 우리로 하여금 우리의 보다 본능적이고 반사회적인 본능들을 안전하게 배출할 수 있는 경험을 할 수 있게 해 주기 때문이다.

---

lustful a. 호색적인
decimate v. 많은 사람을 죽이다
mutilation n. 손발 따위 절단
treachery n. 배반, 배신
incest n. 근친상간
hedonistic a. 쾌락주의의
nefarious a. 사악한
impetuous a. 충동적인
culpable a. 비난받을 만한
depraved a. 타락한

01 ▶ 어두운 면이 우리 내부에 존재하는 자연스러운 충동이란 단서로부터 정답을 추론할 수 있다.
02 ▶ 어두운 본능들은 우리 모두가 타고난 욕구를 표상하고 있기 때문이다.
03 ▶ 욕구를 분출시킨다는 점에서 공포영화와 몽상은 유사한 역할을 한다.

» 정답 01 (D) 02 (B) 03 (D)

Foinet이 그의 그림을 보고, 보기 드문 미소를 지으며 악수를 청하고 "당신은 진정한 재능이 있군요."라고 말해주길 Philip은 마음속에서 희망했다. Philip은 그 생각에 마음이 부풀어 올랐다. Foinet이 자리에 앉고, Philip은 말없이 전람회에서 거부했던 그림을 그 앞에 놓았다. Foinet은 고개를 끄덕였으나 아무 말도 하지 않았다. 그래서 Philip은 Ruth Chalice를 그린 두 개의 초상화와 Moret에서 그린 두서너 개의 풍경화, 그리고 여러 스케치를 보여주었다. "이게 다입니다." 긴장 섞인 웃음을 지으며 말했다. Foinet은 담배를 말아 불을 붙였다. 그리고 마침내 물었다. "거의 생계 수단이 없지요?" "아주 조금요."라고 갑작스러운 한기를 느끼며 Philip이 말했다. "먹고 살기 충분치 않습니다." "사람이 생계에 대해 늘 불안해하는 것보다 품위를 저하시키는 일은 없습니다. 저는 단지 돈을 하찮게 여기는 사람들을 경멸할 뿐입니다. 그들은 위선자이거나 혹은 바보들입니다. 돈이란 이것 없이는 나머지 다른 오감을 완전하게 사용할 수 없는 일종의 육감과 같습니다. 충분한 수입이 없다면 삶의 발전 가능성의 절반이 차단되고 만다는 것입니다. 유념해야 할 유일한 것은 당신이 벌어들이는 돈 이상은 쓰지 않는다는 것입니다. 당신은 흔히 사람들이 예술가들에게 있어 가난은 가장 좋은 자극이라고 말하는 것을 곧잘 듣습니다. 그런 사람들은 결코 가난의 고통을 몸으로 직접 느껴 본 적이 없는 사람들입니다. 그들은 가난이 얼마나 당신을 비참하게 만드는지를 모릅니다. 가난은 당신을 끝없는 굴욕으로 내몹니다. 가난은 당신의 날개를 잘라버리고 암처럼 영혼을 좀먹는 것입니다. 사람들이 바라는 것은 부(富)가 아니라 단지 어느 정도 자신의 품위를 유지하고, 구속받지 않은 채 일하고, 아량 있고, 솔직하며, 남에게 의지하지 않을 만큼의 돈입니다. 나는 글을 쓰건 그림을 그리건, 자신의 예술에 생계를 전적으로 의지하고 있는 예술가는 참으로 딱해 보입니다."

---

portrait n. 초상화
landscape n. 풍경화
private means 부수입, 과외 수입
have a contempt for ~을 경멸하다
hypocrite n. 위선자
shilling n. 실링(영국의 은화)
spur n. 자극, 고무; 동기
humiliation n. 굴욕; 창피
unhampered a. 방해[구속]받지 않은
subsistence n. 생존; 생계
obstacle n. 장애(물)
overestimate v. (능력을) 과대평가하다

01 ▶ 'had wanted to+동사원형'은 과거의 이루지 못한 소망을 나타내며 본문에서 Philip은 Foinet에게서 좋은 평을 원했지만 듣지 못했으므로 (B)가 옳다.

02 ▶ '사람이 살아가는데 어느 정도 자신의 품위를 유지하고, 구속받지 않은 채 일하고, 아량 있고, 솔직하며, 남에게 의지하지 않을 만큼 돈이 필요하다'는 것이 돈에 대한 Foinet의 입장이다.

03 ▶ '박차'란 말을 타는 기수의 장화 밑에 달려 있는 '쇠붙이'로 이것을 말에게 찍으면 말은 아파서 열심히 달리게 된다. 따라서 the iron은 '고통'을 의미한다.

》 정답 01 (B) 02 (C) 03 (C)

지구 생태계내의 에너지와 열의 축적 과정을 추적하여 파악하는 것은 중요한데, 이는 그것이 현재 날씨와 미래의 기후에 미치는 영향 때문이다. 온실가스 방출은 지난 10년간 증가했으며 인공위성들은 태양광선이 흡수된 양과 복사 에너지가 방출된 양 사이의 차이가 점차 증가하고 있음을 보여주었다. 일부 열은 지구에 흡수되어 방출되지 않았음에도 불구하고 기온은 예상만큼 증가하지 않았다.

그렇다면 사라진 열은 어디로 간 것인가? 그러한 열이 어디로 간 것인지를 파악하기 위해 과학자들은 대기, 대지, 해양 그리고 해빙 사이의 복잡한 상호작용을 나타내주는 컴퓨터 모델상의 다섯 가지 모의실험을 가동시켰다.

컴퓨터 모의실험 결과들은 사라진 열의 대부분이 대기의 온도가 예상됐던(가능했던) 것만큼 높아지지 않았던 지난 10년과 같은 기간 동안 1,000피트 이상 깊이의 해양층에 갇혀 있었음을 보여주었다. 그 열은 사라진 것이 아니므로 간과될 수 없다. 그 열은 반드시 영향을 끼칠 것이다.

이러한 모의실험의 결과들은 모두 지구 기온이 금세기 내로 몇 도간 올라갈 것임을 보여주었다. 그러나 그 결과들 모두 또한 기온이 상승하기 전 안정되는 기간을 보여주었다. 이렇게 기온이 안정되는 기간 동안, (사라졌다고 생각한) 여분의 열은 해양순환의 변화로 인해 해양심층수로 이동했다.

---

current a. 현행의; 널리 유행하고 있는
emission n. 방사, 발산, 방출
radiation n. (빛, 열 등의) 방사, 복사; 복사에너지
portray v. 그리다, 묘사하다
interaction n. 상호작용
consequence n. 결과, 결말; 중요성
indicate v. 가리키다, 지적하다, 보이다
stabilize v. 안정시키다, 견고하게 하다
circulation n. 순환; 유통

01 ▶ bearing n. 영향(= impact)

02 ▶ 둘째 단락의 문두에서 사라진 열의 행방에 대해 의문을 제기한 뒤 이를 파악하기 위해 활용한 컴퓨터 시뮬레이션의 결과들을 설명해 주었다. 따라서 사라진 열과 관련된 의아한 점을 설명하기 위함이 이 글의 목적으로 적절하다.

03 ▶ 온실가스 방출량이 증가한 만큼 지구 온난화가 진행되지 않은 것은 증가한 여분의 열이 심해로 이동해 일시적으로 기온이 안정화됐기 때문이라 했다. 그러나 그 열은 없어진 것이 아님으로 안정기가 지난 후 반드시 영향을 끼쳐 금세기에 기온이 몇 도간 올라갈 것이라고 했다. 따라서 지구 온난화의 장기적 현상이 향후 10년 정도 내로 멈출 것이라고는 말할 수 없으므로 (A)가 잘못된 진술이다.

》 정답 01 (D) 02 (C) 03 (A)

프랑스인들이 (버터, 치즈, 기타 유제품의 형태로) 포화지방산을 많이 섭취하지만 심혈관계 질환의 발병률이 매우 낮다는 것은 프랑스인의 역설로 알려져 있다. 이것을 프랑스인들이 적당히 와인을 마시기 때문이라고 설명하기도 한다.

과다한 음주는 심장을 비롯한 체내 각 장기를 손상시킬 수 있다. 그러나 연구원들은 임상실험을 통해 일상적으로 술을 조금씩 마시는 사람이 술을 전혀 마시지 않는 사람들보다 심장질환이 발병할 위험이 20%정도 낮다는 것을 발견했다.

이 메커니즘이 전적으로 명확한 것은 아니지만, 아마도 술이 동맥의 혈관벽에서 플라그를 없애는 좋은 콜레스테롤인 HDL(High density lipoprotein) 농도를 높이는 것 같다. 남자는 1주일에 2~4회의 음주가 최적이고, 여자는 1주일에 1~3회가 좋다. 과음이 미국에서 예방할 수 있는 사망원인 중 2번째에 해당하기 때문에, 하버드 의대의 찰스 헤네킨스(Charles Henekens) 박사는 "나는 공중보건을 위해 널리 음주를 권하는 데는 반대하지만, 특별한 환자에 대해서는 각각의 위험성과 이점을 감안한 후에 음주에 대한 추천을 고려하기도 한다."고 말하고 있다.

saturated fat 포화지방
cardiovascular a. 심장 혈관의
nip n. 술 따위의 한 모금, 소량
teetotaller n. 술을 전혀 못 마시는 사람
arterial a. 동맥의
go over 조사하다, 검토하다

01 ▶ 심장병의 발병 확률을 줄이는 데 적절한 음주가 도움이 된다는 내용이다.
02 ▶ 와인을 '적당히' 마신다고 했다.
03 ▶ '심장병을 일으키는 포화지방산을 많이 섭취함에도 불구하고 그 질환의 발병률이 낮은 것'은 역설(paradox)에 해당한다.

》 정답 01 (A) 02 (B) 03 (D)

집시들에 대한 적대감은 14세기 들어 그들이 유럽에 처음 등장한 거의 그때부터 존재해 왔다. 그들은 그로부터 약 200년 전에 북부 인도에서 중동으로 들어와서 음유시인, 용병, 금속세공인, 하인 등의 일을 했다. 그러나 그들의 진짜 기원은 신비에 가려져 있었기 때문에, 유럽인들은 그들을 이집트인이라고 잘못된 이름으로 불렀고, 곧 집시로 줄어들었다. 집시 활동가들이 집시말로 "인간"에 해당하는 단어에서 나온 로마(Roma)라고 불리기를 더 좋아하는 반면, 다른 사람들은 여전히 그들 스스로를 집시라고 부른다.

곧 그들에 대한 박해가 시작되었다. 교회는 그들의 점치는 행동에서 이단의 요소를 보았고, 국가는 그들의 방랑생활에서 반사회적 행동을 보았다. 일부 국가에서 그들은 노예가 되고 말았는데, 1800년대 중반에 와서야 집시 노예들이 루마니아에서 해방되었다. 나치의 유태인 대학살에서는 집시들이 50만 명 정도 목숨을 잃었을 것이다. 집시 여성은 강제불임시술을 받았고 자녀들은 집시가 아닌 가정에 강제 입양되었다.(스위스에서는 1973년까지 행해졌다.)

거의 예외 없이, 집시들은 자신들만의 나라에 대한 갈망을 전혀 나타내지 않았다. "집시의 나라는 나의 두 발이 딛고 서 있는 곳입니다."라고 캐나다의 집시 작가 로널드 리는 말했다. 대개, 그들의 전통적인 직업과 지리적 위치에 기초한 씨족 제도로 인해, 집시들은 대단히 분열되고 까다로운 민족이 되었으며, 단지 그들이 "gadje"라고 부르는 비집시인들로부터의 적개심에 직면해서만 정말로 단합할 뿐이었다.

---

minstrel n. (중세의) 음유시인
mercenary n. 용병
metalsmith n. 금속세공사
Romany n. 집시, 집시 말
shroud v. 수의를 입히다; 가리다, 감추다
heresy n. 이단, 이교(異敎)
fractious a. 성마른, 까다로운
enmity n. 증오, 적의

01 ▶ 집시들이 겪은 고난의 역사와 그들의 특성을 기술한 글이다.
02 ▶ 집시가 겪은 고초에 관한 배경과 내용이 이어지므로 '박해'라는 의미의 (A)가 빈칸에 적절하다.
03 ▶ 집시의 자녀들을 집시가 아닌 가정에 입양시키는 것이 스위스에서는 1973년까지 관행으로 행해졌다고 했다.

》 정답 01 (B) 02 (A) 03 (C)

[Ⅲ] 어느 날 나는 버스에 올라타서, 주머니에 돈 한 푼 없이 집을 나섰다는 것을 알게 되었다. 그런 경험은 누구나 한 적이 있으며, 그런 사실을 뒤늦게 알고서 마음속에 일어나는 감정도 누구나 알고 있다. 잘 해야 바보 같아 보이고 최악의 경우는 악당처럼 보이니까 기분이 불쾌해지는 것이다. 만일 차장이 마치 "그래, 그런 케케묵은 수법을 난 잘 알지. 그러니 이제 그만 내려주시지."라고 말하려는 듯이 냉담하게 노려본다고 해도 전혀 놀라지 않을 것이다. [Ⅱ] 굴러다니는 동전이라도 있나 해서 주머니들을 뒤져도 허탕, 그래서 완전 빈털터리라는 걸 알고서, 나는 최대한 정직한 얼굴로 차장에게 요금을 낼 수 없고 돈을 가지러 집으로 돌아가야 한다는 말을 했다. 그러나 그는 "아, 괜찮아요, 내리실 필요 없어요."라고 말했다. "좋습니다, 하지만 나한테 동전이 하나도 없거든요."라는 나의 말에 그는 "아, 표를 끊어드리지요."라고 대답했다. "어디 가시려는 겁니까?"라고 말하며 그는 차표 뭉치를 만졌다. 영국 은행에서 홍콩까지 어디라도 곧 표를 끊어줄 것 같은 태도였다. [Ⅳ] 나는 대단히 고맙다는 말과 함께 행선지를 말해주었다. 그리고 그가 나에게 차표를 주었을 때 나는 "하지만 요금은 어디로 보내드릴까요?" 하고 물어보았다. "아, 괜찮습니다, 언젠가 또 만나게 되겠지요 뭐." 그는 유쾌하게 말하고 몸을 돌려서 가려고 했다. [Ⅰ] 그때 다행히, 아직도 여러 주머니 구석구석을 헤매고 있던 내 손가락에 1실링짜리 동전 하나가 발견되었고, 그래서 계산을 치르게 되었다. 그러나 그렇게도 마음씨 착한 행동이 나에게 주었던 희열감은 (계산을 치렀다는) 그 사실에도 불구하고 줄어들지 않았다.

wander v. 헤매다, 방랑하다
account n. 계산, 계산서
square v. 청산하다, 결제하다
stray a. 길을 잃은; 뿔뿔이 흩어진
copper n. 구리; 동전; 잔돈
penniless a. 무일푼의, 몹시 가난한
conductor n. (버스, 열차의) 차장
assume v. (태도를) 취하다
knave n. 악한, 악당
stale a. 케케묵은, 흔해빠진

01 ▶ 버스에 타서 돈이 없다는 것을 알게 됨 → 차장에게 사정을 이야기하고 양해를 구함, 차장이 배려해 줌 → 차표의 값을 나중에라도 치르겠다고 하나 차장은 여전히 받지 않으려 함 → 주머니에서 동전을 발견하여 값을 치름. 차장의 마음씀씀이에 여전히 감동함.

02 ▶ ㉯는 as honest a face as로 고쳐야 한다.

03 ▶ 돈이 없다는 것을 케케묵은 속임수로 여기고 차에서 내리게 할 거라 예상했었다.

» 정답 01 (C) 02 (B) 03 (A)

173

　　가죽나무는 가끔 '천국의 나무'로 불리지만 자연 문학작품으로는 명성을 날리지 못했던 O. Henry는 그 나무를 단지 '뒤뜰' 나무라고 불렀다. 가죽나무의 나무껍질은 회색이고, 거칠고 약간 비뚤어진 가지에는 이국적 모습의 잎이 달려있다. 늦게 나고 늦게 떨어지는 이 잎들이 특히 미풍에 흔들릴 때는 열대 잎의 모습을 띤다. 두꺼운 잎 꼭지는 길이가 1야드까지 되며, 날씨가 어떠하든 간에 밝은 녹색을 띠는 많은 작은 잎들을 갖고 있다. 6월에 이 나무는 엷은 황록색 꽃을 피우는데, 눈에는 거의 띄지 않는다. 늦여름에는 커다란 열매 송이들이 이 나무에 주렁주렁 맺는다. 1만 7천개가 되어야 1파운드가 될 정도로 아주 가벼운 이 나무의 씨앗은 조그만 검은 점 같은 것의 양편으로 비틀어진 날개 한 쌍이 있는 형태인데, 이 날개는 예를 들어 날개가 하나인 단풍나무 씨앗보다 훨씬 더 효율적인 비행장치인 것이다. 바람을 타고 이 씨앗은 엄청나게 높은 곳까지 올라간다. 이 나무의 특징은 가지로 때때로 100피트의 석조건물 지붕 위까지 뻗쳐있는 것이 눈에 띈다. 이 나무는 뒤뜰에서 뿐만 아니라, 다른 나무들은 살지 못할 불모지에서도 발견될 수 있다. 이 나무는 벽돌 틈새기에서도 잘 자란다.

　　어떤 시인은 한 때, 완곡하게 두 개의 죽은 덩굴 잎과 담배꽁초, 그리고 서류 클립이 가죽나무에 이상적인 생장조건을 제공한다고 말했다. 몇 년 전 그 표본이 되는 15피트의 높이의 가죽나무가 차고(車庫) 지붕의 한쪽 구석에서 먼지에도 끄떡없이, 그리고 재를 지붕처럼 덮고 있으면서도 잘 자라고 있는 것이 발견되었다.

---

ailanthus n. 가죽나무속(屬)의 식물
bark n. 나무껍질
coarse a. (표면 등이) 거친
crooked a. 비틀어진, 뒤틀린
leafstalk n. 잎 꼭지
measure up to 길이[폭·높이]가 ~에 달하다
pale a. (색이) 엷은
hang heavy on ~에게 성가실 정도로 많다
maple n. 단풍나무
masonry n. 석조건물
cigarette butt 담배꽁초
cinder n. (나무나 석탄이 타고 남은) 재

01 ▶ O. Henry가 ailanthus를 뒤뜰의 나무라고 한 것은 평범한 나무로 간주했다는 뜻이다.

02 ▶ 세 번째 문장(These, late to come and late to go …)에서 다른 나무의 잎들이 더 일찍 진다는 내용을 유추할 수 있다.

03 ▶ Ailanthus의 씨가 단풍나무의 씨보다도 훨씬 더 효율적인 비행장치라고 했으므로 단풍나무의 부력(buoyant)이 적다.

》 정답 01 (B)　02 (C)　03 (B)

상품들은 순수 서비스로 변화해 가면서, 사회생활의 본질적인 의미를 규정하는 개념으로서의 소유 개념이 종식되어 가고 있다. 상품은 점점 더 정보 집약적이고 상호작용적으로 변해가고 있고, 지속적으로 업그레이드되면서 그 특성도 변하고 있다. 상품은 어떤 물건으로서의 지위를 상실하고 서비스 형태로 변형되고 있다. 서비스의 본성 역시 변화하고 있다. 이제, 전자 상거래가 출현하면서 서비스는 서버와 클라이언트 간의 장기적이고 다면적인 관계로서 재창조되어 가고 있다. 제레미 리프킨(Jeremy Rifkin)에 따르면 경제적 관계들의 구조화에서 일어나는 변화들은 자본주의 체제의 본성 안에서 일어나는 훨씬 더 큰 변화의 한 부분이라고 한다. 우리는 산업생산에서 문화생산으로 넘어가는 장기적 변화를 만들어가고 있으며, 각자의 삶이 사실상 상업적 시장이 되는 세상, 경제학자들이 경험 경제라고 부르는 시대로 이행하고 있다. 예를 들어, 어떤 사람이 에어컨을 구입하는 대신 에어컨 서비스를 받기 위한 계약을 맺는다면, 그 사람은 에어컨 서비스를 받는 경험에 대해 대가를 지불하는 것이다. 그렇다면 새로운 자본주의는 물질적이라기보다는 좀 더 시간적인 것이다. 장소와 물건을 상품화하고 그것들을 시장에서 교환하는 대신, 이제 우리는 타인의 시간과 전문 기술에 접근해 우리가 필요한 것을 빌리는데, 그 모든 것들을 우리가 제한된 시간만큼 구매하는 어떤 활동 혹은 행사로 다루게 되는 것이다. 자본주의는 자신의 물질적 기원들을 버리고 점점 더 시간적인 것으로 변해가고 있다.

defining a. 본질적인 의미를 규정하는
property n. 소유권; 소유물
metamorphose v. 변형되다
multifaceted a. 다면적인
transition n. 이행부, 과도기
temporal a. 시간의
commodify v. 상품화하다
expertise n. 전문적 지식(기술)
shed v. 없애다, 버리다

01 ▶ '상품은 점점 더 정보 집약적이고 상호 작용적으로 변한다', '각자의 삶이 사실상 상업적 시장이 된다', '타인의 시간과 전문 기술을 제한된 시간만큼 빌린다', '자본주의는 자신의 물질적 기원들을 버리고 점점 더 시간적인 것으로 변해가고 있다.'는 내용을 바탕으로 (C)의 진술은 본문과 일치함을 알 수 있다.

02 ▶ temporal은 '시간의, 시간의 제약을 받는'이라는 뜻이므로, (A)의 time-related(시간과 관련된)가 정답이다.

≫ 정답 01 (C) 02 (A)

중동(中東)은 사라져 버린 영광, 현재의 편견, 그리고 미래의 두려움 속에 살아가고 있다. 괭이로 그 땅을 긁어 보라, 그러면 오래 아주 오래 전에 사라진 제국들, 즉 흥망성쇠를 거듭해 온 문명의 발상지의 유물들과 기록된 역사만큼이나 오래된 종교들의 기념물들을 발견하게 될 것이다.

나일 강에서 유프라테스 강에 이르기까지, 과거 낙타 대상(隊商)들이 터벅터벅 걸었던 것과 거의 똑같은 길을 오늘날에는 세계를 연결하고 있는 항공망이 뒤얽힌 지역에서, 완강하고 성미 급하며 편견에 사로잡힌 인간은 인간 드라마의 해묵은 줄거리를 계속 답습하고 있다. 거의 모든 것이 변했지만, 중동에서는 기원전부터 아무 것도 변한 것이 없다.

대상(隊商)들이 모여들던 도시 퀸 제노비아(Queen Zenobia)의 팔미라(Palmyra)는 장엄하지만 이제는 우울한 도시가 되어 오래 전에 죽은 사람들의 꿈을 상기시켜 주는 곳이다. 지난날의 신들마저도 죽어 버린 바알베크(Baalbek)는 단지 관광객의 관심을 끄는 곳에 지나지 않으며, 그나마 요즈음에는 찾는 관광객들이 없다. 인간의 불멸에 대한 영원한 희망을 나타낸 장엄한 기념탑인 피라미드들조차 닳고 주름져 이제는 세월의 잔인함을 감추고자 화장하듯이 땜질했다.

하지만, 근본적으로 아무 것도 변한 것이 없다. 인간과 인간의 감정, 인간과 인간의 무지와 지식, 오만에 찬 인간, 다른 인간과 전쟁을 벌이고 있는 인간 등이 무대를 준비하고 격동의 중동이라는 무대를 지배하고 있다.

---

scrabble v. 휘갈겨 쓰다
hoe n. 괭이
relic n. 유적, 유물
wax v. 커지다; 증대하다
wane v. 작아지다
monument n. 기념비, 기념탑
trail n. 자국, 지나간 흔적; 오솔길
plodding a. 터벅터벅 걷는; 단조로운
persistent a. 고집하는, 완고한; 영속하는
melancholy a. 우울한
grandiose a. 웅장한, 웅대한
immortality n. 불사, 불멸
scuff v. 상하게 하다, 닳게 하다
cosmetically ad. 화장용으로, 미용으로

01 ▶ 오랜 세월이 흘러도 여전히 투쟁이 종식되지 않는 중동지역의 문제는 서로 투쟁하는 인간의 본성 때문이다. 그리고 persistent, passionate, prejudiced로 요약되어 있는 인간의 근본적인 성격들이 인간의 약점을 지적하고 있다.

02 ▶ '인간의 본성에는 변함이 없다'고 했으며, 오늘날 중동 사람들을 '자만심에 빠진 인간(Man in his pride)'이라 했다. 따라서 고대 중동 사람들도 (A)의 '자만심이 강한, 헛된 욕망에 사로잡혀' 있었다고 할 수 있다.

03 ▶ '역사만큼 종교가 오래되었다'와 '기원전부터 아무 것도 변한 게 없다'로 미루어 중동의 고대 문명은 '기독교 이전에 존재했다'고 할 수 있다.

》 정답 01 (D) 02 (A) 03 (B)

176

대부분의 동물은 하나 이상의 종(種)을 먹이로 먹고 살아간다. 따라서 "먹이망"이라는 용어가 "먹이사슬"보다 먹이 관계를 더 잘 설명해준다. 먹이망은 많은 먹이사슬을 포함한 복잡한 먹이공급 체계이다. 예를 들어, 산토끼와 사슴은 식물을 먹는다. 올빼미는 산토끼를 먹고 마운틴라이언은 산토끼와 사슴을 먹는다. 이 네 종은 모두 함께 하나의 먹이망을 이루는 먹이사슬 부분들이다.

먹이사슬의 첫 고리는 언제나 녹색식물이다. 녹색식물 같이 엽록소를 가진 유기체(생물)만이 먹이를 만들 수 있다. 예를 들어, 수상 먹이사슬의 첫 고리는 조류(藻類)이다. 대부분의 조류는 광합성으로 먹이를 만드는 미세한 녹색식물이다. 광합성에서는 햇빛에너지가 이산화탄소와 물을 당분으로 바꾼다. 호수나 바다의 작은 물고기가 조류를 먹는다. 이번에는 또 이 작은 물고기가 더 큰 물고기에게 잡아먹힌다. 큰 물고기는 또 더 큰 물고기에게 잡아먹힌다. 물고기의 먹이공급은 조류에 의해 이루어진다. 이 먹이가 그 다음 동물이 다른 동물을 먹을 때 먹이사슬을 통해 전해지는 것이다.

생물은 먹이를 얻는 방법에 기초하여 세 부류로 나뉠 수 있다. 즉, 생산자와 분해자와 소비자이다. 엽록소를 가진 생물이 생산자이다. 그래서 녹색식물은 생산자이다. 다른 동물과 식물을 먹는 동물은 소비자이다. 죽은 동식물을 부패시키는 단세포 생물인 미생물은 분해자이다. 분해자도 또한 자신의 먹이를 만들 수 없기 때문에 소비자이다.

prey on ~을 먹이로 하다, ~을 먹고 살다
chlorophyll n. 엽록소
aquatic a. 수생의, 물의
algae n. 조류, 말무리
photosynthesis n. 광합성
carbon dioxide 이산화탄소
decomposer n. 분해자
decay n. 부패

01 ▶ 서로 얽혀 있는 생물의 먹이망을 설명하는 목적의 글이다.
02 ▶ 문맥상 앞 문장의 algae를 가리킨다.
03 ▶ 본문 마지막 문장 참고

≫ 정답 01 (A) 02 (C) 03 (B)

177

1912년 프레데릭 G. 홉킨스와 캐스미어 펑크는 각기병, 구루병, 괴혈병과 같은 인간의 특정 질병이 식단에 특정 영양소가 없기 때문에 생긴다고 했다. 이 영양소에 비타민(필수 아민)이라는 이름이 붙여졌는데, 그것은 그러한 물질로 처음으로 분리해낸 티아민(비타민 B1)이 아민(아미노기를 포함하고 있는 화합물)이기 때문이었다. 다른 필수 물질들을 분리하고 분석했을 때 그것들은 아민이 아닌 것으로 판명되었지만, 비타민이라는 용어는 그대로 남아 소량으로 필요한 필수 성장 요소를 가리키게 되었다. 그 이후로 여러 가지 비타민이 발견되었다. 몇몇 비타민의 역할은 알려져 있지 않지만, 상당수의 비타민들은 조효소인 것으로 드러났다.

처음에는 원인을 밝혀내지 못한 영양 요소를 표시하는 데 알파벳 글자를 썼다. 이러한 알파벳 글자들(A, B, C, D, E, K 등)이 계속 이어져 왔으나, 몇몇 요소가 실제로는 한 가지 물질 이상으로 구성돼 있다는 사실이 밝혀졌다. 비타민 B의 경우 12개 이상으로 구성돼 있는 것으로 드러났다. 이러한 요소들은 이제 특정 물질, 가령 티아민(B1), 리보플라빈(B2), 판토텐산(B3), 그리고 세 가지 연관 물질, 그리고 니아신으로 명명되었다. 이러한 것들은 종종 함께 나타나기 때문에, 비타민 B 복합체로 불린다.

beriberi n. 각기병
rickets n. 구루병
scurvy n. 괴혈병
compound n. 합성물, 혼합물
retain v. 보류하다, 보유하다
factor n. 요소, 요인
persist v. 지속하다, 존속하다
entity n. 실재, 존재
designate v. 지정하다; 명명하다

01 ▶ 비타민이라는 물질의 정의와 그 명칭의 유래, 그리고 현재까지의 경과에 대한 내용을 담고 있다. 따라서 글쓴이의 주된 목적은 (B)가 된다.

02 ▶ '일부 비타민의 역할은 알려져 있지 않다'고 했다.

03 ▶ 일반적인 개념을 먼저 말한 후에 그에 대한 예를 들고 있는 구조이다.

》 정답 01 (B) 02 (D) 03 (A)

178

여성들은 대부분 경제적인 이유로 일을 하게 된다. 오늘날 그들은 과거 그 어느 때보다 더 직업 선택의 폭이 넓어졌다. 여성들은 좋은 교육을 받고, 자신감이 넘치며, 기술 분야에 대해서도 알아야 할 것을 알고 있고, 그래서 여전히 그들을 절실히 필요로 하고 있는 노동시장으로도 진입하고 있다. 인구 조사국에 따르면, 1998년에 16세 이상의 여성 중 거의 60%가 일을 하고 있었는데, 이는 1970년의 43%와 비교되는 수치이다. 출산 여성들도 평균적으로 더 빨리 일에 복귀한다. 1998년에는 한 살 미만의 아이를 둔 여성의 거의 62%가 일을 했는데, 이것은 1975년의 31%에서 크게 늘어난 것이다. 여성들은 이른 나이에 아이를 가지며, 적어도 가질 계획을 한다. 27세의 안드레아 트런칼리는 늦은 나이에 엄마가 되는 위험에 대해서 배우고 나서 의과대학원 1학년 재학 중에 아이를 가질 생각을 했다고 한다. 사실 신세대는 그들의 가족을 구성하는 일을 대단히 중요하게 생각한다. "이 젊은이들은 대체로 이혼 가정에서 자라났어요."라고 쉴라 워싱턴은 말한다. "그래서 가족의 가치를 더 중요시하는지도 모르지요."

maternal a. 어머니의; 모성의
establish v. 확립하다, 설치하다; 입증하다
salient a. 현저한, 두드러진
saline a. 소금의; 염분이 있는
converse a. 역(逆)의, 거꾸로의
imbecile a. 저능한, 우둔한

01 ▶ savvy a. 사리를 이해한, 정통한(= versed)

02 ▶ 전후반부의 내용을 종합하면, (D)가 정답이다.

03 ▶ '이른 나이에 아이를 가지거나, 적어도 가질 계획을 갖는다'고 했다.

》 정답 01 (E) 02 (D) 03 (C)

자기 자신을 심리학자로 소개하게 되면, 다음과 같은 질문을 받게 된다. "심리학이 무엇인가요?" 혹은 "어떤 일을 하세요?" 심리학은 많은 사람들에게 익숙하지만 별로 아는 사람들이 없는 그런 부류의 용어에 속한다.

일반적인 심리학 교재를 보면, 심리학은 인간의 정신과 행동을 연구하는 과학적 학문이라고 되어 있다. 그러나 이러한 정의는 더 많은 질문을 양산한다. 우선, 많은 양의 심리학 자료들이 '동물 심리학'이란 이름 아래 명시되어 있는 것을 발견할 것이다. 동물의 행동과 정신 상태를 연구하고 또 이것을 인간과 비교함으로써 인간 정신에 대한 이해의 폭이 넓어지게 된다. 인간과 그들의 친구인 동물의 관계를 연구함으로써 인간의 행동학적 복지를 증진시키는 것을 돕는 더 많은 방식을 찾을 수 있다. 심리학은 과거 틀에 박힌 정의를 넘어서고 있다. 지금까지 그랬듯이 앞으로도 계속 과학의 미개척 지대에 있는 많은 통합적 분야로 진출하게 될 것이다.

심리학이란 인간의 정신과 행동을 연구하는 과학적 학문이지만 인간에게만 국한되지는 않는다고 말하는 것이 옳을 것이다. 이러한 포괄적인 정의는 심리학의 다양한 부속 분야들을 포함한다. 물론 이보다 더 많이 있지만, 임상 심리학, 발달 심리학, 인지 심리학, 그리고 사회 심리학 등이 바로 잘 알려진 몇몇 예들이다. 사실, 미국 심리학회에는 현재까지 53개의 분과가 있다. 또한 심리학과 친척 관계에 있는 학문들도 있다. 그 중에는 사회학, 인류학, 생물학, 정신의학이 있다. 마지막에서 언급한 정신의학은 심리학자의 역할과 정체성을 이해하는 데 있어서 또 다른 종류의 혼란을 가져온다.

---

psychologist n. 심리학자
psyche n. 정신
companion n. 동료
ethological a. 행동학의
outgrow v. 성장하다; 벗어나다
frontier n. 변경(邊境), 미개척 분야
anthropology n. 인류학
psychiatry n. 정신의학

01 ▶ 이 글은 심리학의 포괄적 정의와 다양한 분야(영역)에 대해 설명하고 있다.

02 ▶ 심리학의 부속분야로서 임상심리학, 발달심리학, 사회심리학, 인지심리학이 예로 제시되었다. "정신의학(psychiatry)은 심리학과는 친척관계의 학문이며 심리학의 정의와 역할을 정의하는데 혼란을 겪게 한다"고 했으므로, 심리학의 부속분야라고 하기 어렵다.

03 ▶ 이 글에서 심리학의 광범위함을 언급하며, 학문에 있어서 여러 종류의 다른 학문과 결합할 수 있는 가능성에 대해 언급한 내용을 찾을 수 있다.

》 정답 01 (A) 02 (E) 03 (C)

로봇이 제조업 분야 노동력의 일부를 차지한 지도 수십 년이 되었다. 예를 들어, 현재 자동차 제조업체 근로자 열 명 중 한 명은 금속과 전자부품으로 만들어진 근로자(로봇)이다. 가정용 로봇이 세상에 나온 것은 이보다 더뎠다. 가사 일은 공장의 조립생산 라인 일보다 예측하기가 더 어렵고 덜 반복적이어서 간단한 기계언어로 설명하기가 어렵기 때문이다. 한 가지 해결책은 진공청소 같은 개별적인 과제에 적응할 수 있는 로봇을 설계하는 것이며, 또 하나의 해결책은 보통사람들이 여러 부품으로 자신의 로봇을 만들어 자신이 원하는 일을 그 로봇이 하도록 프로그래밍 하면 될 만큼 간단하고 저렴한 로봇을 만드는 법을 알아내는 것이다. 피츠버그에 있는 카네기 멜론(Carnegie Mellon) 대학의 과학자들은 그들이 TeRK라 부르는 교육개발 프로젝트를 추진하면서 바로 이 방침을 취하고 있다. 구글과 인텔과 마이크로소프트로부터 자금 지원을 받아 그들은 일련의 자가 제작 로봇들을 만들었는데, 거의 누구나 만들 수 있을 만큼 간단하고 저렴하다고 한다. 그것은 카네기 멜론 대학이 만들었고 같은 대학 웹사이트에서 349달러에 팔리고 있는 로봇 '두뇌'에 해당하는 Qwerk라 불리는 블랙박스로 시동된다. 가게에서 파는 부품들과 몇 가지 간단한 지시사항을 이용하면 누구든 키가 10센티미터인 로봇을 만들어 거기에 Qwerk 두뇌를 프로그래밍 해 넣을 수 있다. 비디오카메라가 장착된 바퀴 달린 로봇을 만들면 이 로봇이 집을 지키면서 침입자가 들어오면 경보를 울릴 수 있고, 아니면 개가 부엌 조리대에서 음식을 훔쳐가지 못하게 할 수도 있다. 한 곳에 고정된 로봇이라면 공기 냄새를 맡고 오염물질을 감지해낼 수도 있을 것이다.

auto-worker n. 자동차 제조 근로자
household chore 가사 일
assembly line 조립생산라인
vacuum v. 진공청소기로 청소하다
tack n. 방침, 정책(= policy)
building-it-yourself a. 손수 만드는, 자가제작의
off-the-shelf a. 출하대기의, 기성품인
Fido n. 개의 이름; 개
stationary a. 정지된, 고정된
sniff v. 코를 킁킁거리다, 냄새를 맡다

01 ▶ (D) 가정용 로봇과 (E) 자가 제작 로봇을 구별해야 한다. 본문은 주로 후자에 대한 글이다.

02 ▶ (C) program them의 them은 their own robots를 가리키고 ③의 they는 ordinary people을 가리킨다.

03 ▶ 개별 과제에 적응할 수 있는 로봇을 설계하는 것이 하나의 해결책이라고 했을 뿐 설계하는 방법에 대해서는 언급이 없다.

》 정답 01 (E) 02 (C) 03 (B)

당신은 감정이 의사 결정의 적이라고 생각할지 모르지만, 사실 감정은 의사 결정의 필수 요소이다. 마음을 정할 때마다 뇌의 감정 중추인 대뇌 변연계가 작동하는 것이다. 한 신경학자가 뇌의 감정 부위만 손상된 사람들을 연구해본 결과 그들은 무엇을 입을지, 무엇을 먹을지에 대한 기본적인 결정도 할 수 없는 것으로 밝혀졌다. 그는 이것이 과거의 선택에 대한 기억이 뇌에 저장되는데 우리가 이 기억을 이용해 현재의 결정을 특징짓기 때문일지 모른다고 추측한다. 그러나 감정의 영향 하에서 선택을 하는 것은 결과에 중대한 영향을 미칠 수 있다. 화를 예로 들어보면, 화가 난 소비자들은 여러 대안들을 고려해보지 않고 제일 먼저 내놓는 것을 선택해버릴 가능성이 더 높다. 화가 우리를 성급하고 이기적이며 위험에 빠지기 쉽도록 만들 수 있는 것 같다. 모든 감정이 우리의 생각과 동기부여에 영향을 미친다. 그래서 감정의 영향 하에서는 중요한 결정을 하지 않는 것이 가장 좋을지도 모른다. 그러나 좋은 선택을 하는 데 도움을 주는 것 같은 감정이 하나 있다. 미국의 학자들은 슬픈 사람들이 시간적 여유를 갖고 제시된 대안들을 고려해보고난 후 가장 좋은 선택을 한다는 것을 발견했다. 사실 많은 연구가 보여주는 바로는, 우울한 사람들이 가장 현실적인 세계관을 갖고 있다. 심리학자들은 이것을 가리켜 '우울한 현실주의'라는 용어를 만들어내기까지 했다.

integral a. 필수적인
limbic system 대뇌 변연계
neurologist n. 신경학자, 신경과의사
speculate v. 추측하다
inform v. 특징짓다
opt for 선택하다
risk-prone a. 위험에 빠지기 쉬운
on offer 매물(賣物)로 나온
take on the world 세계관
coin v. (용어를) 만들어내다

01 ▶ impetuous a. 충동적인, 성급한 (= rash)
02 ▶ 이 글은 전반부에서 감정 자체는 의사 결정의 필수 요소임을 말하고 이어서 개별 감정은 의사 결정 결과에 영향을 미칠 수 있는 것임을 말하고 있으므로 (C)가 요지로 적절하다. (A)와 (B)는 지엽적인 사실이고 (D)는 이 글의 내용과 무관하다.
03 ▶ 바로 앞 문장에 설명되어 있다.

》 정답 01 (A) 02 (C) 03 (D)

비즈니스가 변하고 있다. 회사는 오로지 실리적인 일에만 중점을 두어야 한다는 오랜 개념이 잘하는 것과 좋은 일을 하는 것은 풀어질 수 없이 연결되어 있다고 믿는 사회적인 기업가로 구성된 새로운 세대들에 의해 도전받고 있다. 빈곤, 질병, 교육의 부족과 오염과 같이 다양한 전 세계 문제는 역사적으로 정치 및 사회 운동가에 의해 다루어졌지만 지금은 기업들에 의해 다루어지고 있다.

사회적 참여에 대한 외침은 CEO들과 직원들로 이끌어지는 회사 내로부터 들려오고 있다. 그들은 사회적 책임은 모든 기관의 임무에 있어 빠뜨릴 수 없는 부분이라고 믿는다. 많은 회사들은 신입사원들이 봉급과 혜택뿐만 아니라 직업을 통해서 사회적 기여를 할 수 있도록 하는 기회에 대해 묻고 있다고 말한다. 향후 예상된 주요 인재 부족에 직면한 기업들은 사회를 보살피는 기업 문화가 가장 뛰어나고 충실한 인재를 끌어올 수 있다고 생각할지 모른다.

개발도상국의 많은 어린이들을 빈곤으로 전락하게 만드는 교육의 부족을 타파하는 것과 같이 기술 또한 변화에 주요한 역할을 할 것이다. 상당수 기술 관련 기업들이 비영리로 진행되는 '어린이 1명당 컴퓨터 한 대씩' 운동에 각 기업 당 2백만 달러를 기부했는데, 이 운동은 가난한 국가들의 정부에 판매되고 어린이들에게 제공될 100달러 가격의 휴대용 컴퓨터를 제조할 계획이다. 5억여 명의 어린이들이 전기를 공급받지 못하기 때문에 그 컴퓨터의 배터리는 크랭크, 발판 또는 풀 코드를 이용해 충전될 수 있다.

bottom line 순익[손실]
inextricably ad. 풀 수 없이, 해결할 수 없이
tackle v. 달려들다; 논쟁하다
involvement n. 관련; 연루
integral a. 완전한; 필수의
contribution n. 기부; 기여, 공헌
battle v. 싸우다; 그럭저럭 생활하다
apiece ad. 하나에[한 사람]에 대하여; 각각

01 ▶ 본문은 전과 달리 사회적 기여에 대단한 관심을 보이고 있는 기업들의 모습을 설명하고 있으므로 (D) '기업들이 사회에 대한 의무를 느끼는 새로운 풍조'가 정답이다.

02 ▶ ①은 'doing good(선한 일을 하는 것)'과 비교되는 표현으로 앞서 언급된 실리적인 일에 중점을 두는 일을 의미한다. 나머지 보기는 모두 '사회에 대한 의무'를 가리키고 있다.

03 ▶ 세 번째 문단에서 전기와 같은 자원이 부족한 곳의 어린이들에게 교육의 기회를 주기 위해 기술을 이용하여 수동 배터리를 사용할 수 있는 컴퓨터를 만들었다고 하였다.

≫ 정답 01 (D) 02 (A) 03 (D)

21세기로 넘어오고 난 후 이제 디지털기술이 세계를 정복했다. DVD의 판매량이 비디오테이프의 판매량을 훨씬 앞지르고, 소비자나 전문가 모두 디지털 카메라를 더 좋아한다. 그러나 디지털기술은 아직도 적들이 있는데 가장 큰 적이 영화산업일지 모른다. 극장 상영용으로 제작되는 대다수의 영화가 아직도 전통적인 16미리 내지 35미리 필름 카메라로 촬영이 되며, 마틴 스콜세지와 스티븐 스필버그 같은 유명 감독들도 새로운 형식으로 넘어가기를 거부하고 있다.

할리우드는 왜 (디지털기술을) 거부하고 있나? 디지털기술이 더 저렴해서 고군분투하는 어려운 영화 제작자에게는 저예산의 디지털카메라 방식을 사용하는 것이 여러 가지로 사정이 달라짐을 의미할 수 있다는 것에 이제는 대부분의 사람들이 동의한다. 그러나 일부에서는 아직도 디지털기술이 미학적인 면에서 좀 떨어진다고 생각하며 또 더러는 디지털기술이 사용하는데 유연성이 있어 보이지만 사실은 그렇지 않다고 이의를 제기하기도 한다. 그것은 사진 찍는 소형 디지털카메라와는 달리 디지털 영화촬영 장비는 부피가 클 수도 있기 때문이다. 그리고 만일 감독이 디지털장비의 작동법에 대해 잘 모르면 그것으로 촬영한 결과가 어떨지 짐작하기가 어려울 수 있다. "어떤 일이든 분명히 알고 있다는 확신을 갖고 해나가야 하는데, 촬영기사들 중에는 (디지털기술로는) 아직도 옳은 촬영법을 찾아 끙끙대고 있는 사람이 많습니다."라고 영국의 영화촬영기사 닉 모리스(Nic Morris)는 말한다. 그래도 (디지털기술 사용을) 주저하는 가장 그럴듯한 이유는 스콜시지와 스필버그 같은 유명 감독들이 관심 없어 하기 때문이다. 이들은 일반적으로 전통적인 필름이 아직도 디지털기술보다 더 선명한 영상을 제공해 준다고 생각하는데, 이것은 필름이 비용이 더 많이 든다는 점을 메우고도 남는다. 비용을 아끼는 것은 젊고 어려운 형편의 영화 제작자들에게는 중요할지 모르지만, 할리우드의 명감독들에게는 문제가 되지 않는 것이다.

---

cinematic a. 영화의
release n. 상영
format n. 형식, 체제
flexibility n. 유연성, 융통성
bulky a. 부피가 큰
cinematographer n. 영화촬영기사
find one's way 길을 찾아가다, 애써 나아가다
rich a. 선명한

01 ▶ 새로운 형식으로 넘어간다는 것은 새로운 기술인 디지털카메라로 영화를 만드는 것을 의미한다.

02 ▶ 디지털 장비에 대해 아직 모르는 게 많아 자신 있게 촬영할 수 없다는 뜻으로 한 말이다.

03 ▶ (A) 21세기로 넘어올 무렵 이후니까 100년 넘은 것이 아니라 아주 짧은 역사이다. (B) 스티븐 스필버그도 이 글 마지막의 Hollywood's elite에 속하는 사람이다. (C) 미학적으로 더 낫고 더 선명한 영상은 전통적인 필름에서 얻어진다. (D) 낮은 비용 때문에 젊은 감독들이 디지털카메라를 사용할 것으로는 생각되지만 이들이 만든 영화가 대부분에 해당하는지는 모른다.

》 정답 01 (A) 02 (C) 03 (B)

문학 분야의 낭만주의 혁명을 따라 음악 분야에도 유사한 혁명이 일어났다. 1820년경 베토벤(Beethoven)은 자신이 작곡 양식으로 이용했던 고전주의 형식들을 종종 산산이 부숴버릴 정도로 위협했던 열정적인 악곡들을 쓰기 시작했다. 베토벤이 1824년에 완성한 9번 교향곡은 그 길이와 복잡성뿐 아니라, 마치 고전주의 교향곡의 순수 기악 형식은 자신이 느낀 모든 것을 표현할 수 없다는 듯이 그가 성악 독창자들과 합창단을 마지막 악장에 도입했다는 사실로도 유명하다. <전통으로부터의 이러한 급진적 이탈 이후에, 많은 작곡가들이 자유로이 실험을 했다.>

베토벤은 또한 교회나 귀족의 후원 없이 스스로 일하여 생활비를 벌었던 최초의 작곡가로 음악사에서 중요하다. 하이든(Haydn)이 에스테르하지(Esterhazy) 왕자의 후원을 받았던 것 같이 작곡가에게 급료를 줄 수는 없었지만 베토벤의 연주회 티켓을 기꺼이 구입했던 새로운 부르주아 청중의 등장으로 인해 그는 혜택을 받았다. 레슨을 하고 곡을 판매하고 연주회를 열면서 번 돈으로 베토벤은 아주 부유하게 살지는 못했어도 먹고 살 수는 있었다. 이는 베토벤이 하이든과 모차르트와 같은 거장들조차도 벗어나지 못했던 예술가 하인의 역할을 거부하며 자신의 궁극적 개인주의를 표현할 수 있게 해준 결정적인 요인이었다. 그는 자신이 하고 싶은 대로 작곡할 수 있었으며 대중에게 자신을 따라오라고 촉구할 수도 있었다.

신흥 중산층의 대두는 신선한 감동을 추구하는 새로운 청중을 만들어냈다. 이 새로운 청중은 또한 예술적 감정에 강력하게 이끌린 청중이었으며, 음악은 다른 어떠한 예술보다도 강력한 감정을 끌어낼 수 있는 능력을 가지고 있다. 비록 낭만주의 작곡가들이 소나타와 같은 형식들을 계속해서 사용하기는 했지만, 새로운 청중들은 주제의 발전에 관한 세부 사항들을 이해하기보다는 멜로디, 하모니, 리듬의 파도에 몸을 맡겼다.

---

in the wake of ~을 본떠서, ~의 결과로서
composition n. 악곡
asunder ad. 산산이, 조각조각으로
symphony n. 교향곡
notable a. 유명한, 뛰어난
soloist n. 독주자, 독창자
movement n. (교향곡의) 악장
instrumental a. 악기의
earn one's living 생활비를 벌다, 밥벌이를 하다
subsidize v. 장려금을 지급하다, 출자하다
aristocrat n. 귀족
emergence n. 출현
afford v. ~할 수 있다, ~할 여유가 있다
retain v. 보유하다, 고용하다
prosper v. 번영하다, 성공하다
confine v. 가두다, 감금하다
elicit v. 이끌어내다, 도출하다

01 ▶ 본문은 문학 분야에 이어 음악 분야에도 낭만주의 혁명이 일어났다며, 고전주의 전통에서 이탈하고 스스로 일한 것으로 생활비를 벌었던 최초의 낭만주의 작곡가인 베토벤에 대해 소개하고 있다. 글의 제목은 글의 중심 내용을 직간접적으로 함축해야 하므로 (D)가 정답으로 적절하다.

02 ▶ 본문에서 After this radical departure from classical tradition과 연관된 부분을 찾고 그 부분이 many composers felt free to experiment와 자연스럽게 연결되면 정답이다. 첫 번째 문단의 the fact that he experimentally introduced vocal soloists and a chorus into the final movement는 this radical departure from classical tradition을 지칭하며 베토벤의 이러한 시도 이후로 많은 작곡가들이 자유로이 실험을 할 수 있었다.

03 ▶ This는 바로 앞문장인 With the money he received from lessons, from the sale of his compositions, and from his public performances, Beethoven was able to survive if not to prosper.를 가리킨다.

» 정답 01 (D) 02 (A) 03 (C)

인생에서 변화만큼 사람의 마음이 더 열광적으로 환영하거나 혹은 몹시 두려워하는 것은 거의 없다. 서른을 넘긴 사람들은 크든 작든 변화에 적응을 잘하지 못하거나 덜 개방적이라고 오랫동안 생각돼 왔다. 그러한 인식은 현(現)세대를 반영하지 않는데, 나이 든 사람들은 정체되어 있으며 보수적이라고 널리 알려진 생각을 어떻게 하면 갱신할 수 있을까? 간디(Mohandas Gandhi)는 "당신은 세상에서 당신이 보고 싶어 하는 변화 자체가 돼야 한다."고 말했다. 간디는 말로만 하지 말고 행동으로 보이라고 말했음이 분명하다.

나는 대개 모든 연령대의 사람들이 온당한 변화에 개방적이라고 생각한다. 각 연령 집단이 어떻게 '온당한'의 의미를 정의하느냐가 세대 간의 차이점일지 모른다. 당신은 어떠한 변화를 추구하고 있는가? 아니면, 어떠한 변화를 받아들일 수 있는가? 당신이 추구하는 변화를 위해 하고 싶거나 하고 싶지 않은 것은 무엇인가? 변화를 일으키기에는 당신은 너무 나이가 들고 지쳤고 돈이 없거나 미미한 존재라고 마음속으로 말해 본 적이 있는가? 친구나 동료, 국가의 지도자로부터 이러한 핑계들을 받아들일 것인가?

변화는 단지 삶에 있어 필수적인 것이 아니라 삶 그 자체이다. 또한 우리를 변화시키기 위해 (변화의) 규모가 클 필요는 없다. 즉, 어떤 사람의 일상생활에서의 변화 같은 간단한 것들이 한 사람의 기분을 뒤틀리게 할 수 있으며, 세계적 규모의 변화보다 아마 더욱 그렇게 만들지도 모른다. 다시 말해, 일상생활에서 변화에 대한 반응에 영향을 미치는 것은 변화 자체에 대한 개인의 태도이다. 변화는 확실히 일어나며 계속 일어나게 된다는 점을 이해할 필요가 있다.

psyche n. 영혼, 정신
dread v. 몹시 두려워하다; 걱정하다
profoundly ad. 깊이, 심원하게; 간절히
adaptable a. 적응할 수 있는; 융통성 있는
stagnant a. 흐르지 않는; 불경기의; 정체된
go about 돌아다니다; ~하려고 애쓰다, 끊임없이 ~하다
notoriously ad. 널리 알려져서
conservative a. 보수적인
scale n. 눈금; 크기
routine n. 판에 박힌 일; 일상의 과정
out of sorts 기분이 좋지 않은; 화가 난
proportion n. 비율; 조화; 균형

01 ▶ 본문에서 작가는 변화가 불가피하게 일어나는 것이라고 하면서, 첫 번째 문단에서 변화를 받아들여 행동으로 옮기라고 한 간디의 말을 인용하였다. 또한 두 번째 문단에서는 변화에 소극적인 사람들을 언급하며 변하지 않으려고 하는 사람들을 우회적으로 비판하고 있다. 따라서 '변화에 대한 적극적인 자세를 권하기 위해'가 글의 목적으로 가장 타당하다.

02 ▶ 변화 그 자체가 되어야 한다는 간디의 말을 풀이하고 있는데, 이는 변화를 행동으로 옮겨야 한다는 의미이다. 밑줄 친 문장은 말보다 행동으로 보이는 실천의 중요성을 강조하는 어구로 "우리의 행동을 통해 우리의 믿음을 보여주어야 한다"는 뜻이 된다.

03 ▶ 두 번째 문단에서 모든 세대는 온당한 변화에 개방적이며 글쓴이의 생각으로 온당함의 정의는 각 세대마다 다르다고 하였으므로, "각 세대마다 무엇을 변화시켜야 하는가에 대한 나름의 기준이 있다"가 글쓴이의 의견과 부합한다.

» 정답 01 (D) 02 (B) 03 (C)

일의 속성과 일하는 사람의 능력에 따라 단지 지루함의 해소에서부터 가장 심원한 기쁨에 이르기까지 일에는 많은 등급이 있다. 대부분의 사람들이 해야 하는 대부분의 일은 그 자체로는 흥미롭지 못하지만 그러나 이러한 일일지라도 어떤 큰 이점은 있다.

자신의 판단에 의해 자신의 시간을 자유롭게 채우도록 내버려두면 대부분의 사람들은 할 만한 가치가 있는 충분히 즐거운 어떠한 것을 할 것인가 생각하는 것으로 난처해한다. 그리고 결정하는 것이 어떤 것인지 간에 다른 일이 더 즐거웠을 것이라는 느낌으로 불안해한다.

여가를 현명하게 채우는 것이 문명의 마지막 성과이며, 그리고 현재 이 수준에 이른 사람은 극히 드물다. 게다가 선택의 행사는 그 자체로 피곤한 일이다. 비범한 진취성을 가진 사람을 제외하면, 명령이 그리 불쾌하지 않은 경우에 하루 매 시간에 무엇을 해야 되는 지를 듣는 것은 확실히 기분 좋은 일이다. 한가한 부유층의 대부분은 고된 일로부터의 자유의 대가로서 말도 못할 지루함을 겪는다. 때로는 아프리카에서 큰 동물을 사냥함으로써 또는 세계 일주를 하면서 기분전환을 하겠지만 그러한 대단한 일들은 제한돼 있다.

---

relief n. 경감, 제거
tedium n. 싫증, 지루함
profound a. 깊은, 심원한
sufficiently ad. 충분히, 족히
positively ad. 확실히, 절대적으로; 긍정적으로
boredom n. 권태
drudgery n. 고된 일, 단조롭고 고된 일
game n. 사냥감

01 ▶ initiative n. 주도권; 진취성, 진취적 기상(= drive)

02 ▶ 힘든 일을 하지 않아도 되는 '대가(price)'로 지루함을 견뎌내어야 하기에 값비싼 레저 활동을 즐기기도 한다는 문맥이 가장 자연스럽다.

03 ▶ 글쓴이는 일 자체가 흥미롭지 않을지 모르지만 큰 이점이 있다고 언급하며, 일을 할 필요가 없는 여가 시간을 어떻게 보내야 할지 고민하는 사람들에 대해 설명하고 있다. 따라서 글쓴이는 "하루의 대다수의 시간들을 채워 주는 일은 우리가 무엇을 해야 하는지를 결정하는 수고를 덜어준다"는 의견에 동의할 것이다.

》 정답 01 (D) 02 (C) 03 (D)

변형된 미생물을 만드는 것을 목표로 하는 신세틱 지노믹스(Synthetic Genomics)사(社)는 크레이그 벤터(Craig Venter)에 의해 설립되었다. 벤터와 그의 동료들은 한 박테리아의 유기체가 새롭고 흥미로운 일을 하도록 결정적인 변형을 일으켜 그 박테리아의 모든 DNA 염기배열을 합성하고자 하며, 인공 염색체가 살아나기를 바라며 박테리아의 세포에 이식시키려 한다. 벤터는 이러한 프로젝트에 대해 "이 일은 소프트웨어를 설치하는 것입니다. 다시 말해, 우리는 기본적으로 게놈을 시동하고 작동하도록 하는 것입니다."라고 컴퓨터 용어로 설명한다.

생명이 유전자 정보에 불과하다는 생각은 정신이 번쩍 들게 한다. 우리가 숙고해야 할 점은 인공 생물체를 만드는 데 있어 잠재적인 혜택과 장차 일어날 수도 있는 위험요소간의 균형을 잡는 것이다. 신세틱 지노믹스의 의도는 존경할 만하다. 그들은 박테리아를 변형시켜 대기에서 이산화탄소를 잡아내거나 오염이 없는 새로운 연료를 생산하고자 한다. 하지만 여기에는 우려할 만한 이유가 있다. 공개적으로 이용 가능한 염기배열로부터 얻은 DNA를 합성하는 기술은 보다 저렴해지고 간단해지고 있다. 유전자 정보, 예를 들어 조류독감 바이러스의 염기배열은 인터넷에서 접할 수 있다. 이는 과학을 위해서는 바람직하지만, DNA를 합성할 수 있는 능력을 지니고 벤터와 그의 동료들보다 선하지 않은 동기를 가지고 있는 누군가가 치명적인 새로운 전염성의 미생물을 만들기 위해 유전자 정보를 악의적으로 사용할 수도 있다.

microbe n. 세균; 미생물
synthesize v. 종합하다; 합성하다
sequence n. 연속; 전후 관련
modification n. 수정; 변경; 변형
chromosome n. 염색체
jargon n. 뜻을 알 수 없는 말; 특수 용어
sobering a. 정신이 번쩍 들게 하는
carbon dioxide 이산화탄소
colleague n. 동료, 동업자
infectious a. 전염성의, 전염하는

01 ▶ (D) '변형시킬 박테리아를 고르는 기준'에 대해서는 언급되어 있지 않다.

02 ▶ 벤터는 추진하고 있는 프로젝트를 컴퓨터 용어로 설명하며, 전혀 다른 두 가지 내용을 같은 성질로써 연결시키고 있으므로 '은유법'이 정답이 된다. (A) 직유법 (B) 역설법 (D) 모순어법

03 ▶ 벤터와 같이 좋은 의도를 가지고 혜택을 제공하려는 목적으로 프로젝트를 추진한다는 내용과 상반된 내용이 연결되어야 한다.

▶ 정답 01 (D) 02 (C) 03 (B)

인생을 쇼핑센터에서 쇼핑하며 보내는 어느 날의 긴 오후라고 생각해 봐라. 우리 모두는 가치를 심사숙고하며 많은 시간을 보낸다. 저 모카라테는 정말로 4달러의 가치가 있는 것일까? 당신이 선택한 상품을 위해 결국 200달러 수표를 쓸 것인가? "그럼 그것은 얼마만큼 가치가 있는 걸까?"라고 우리가 자문하지 않는 날이 없다. 물론 이 질문에 대한 절대적이며 보편적인 정답은 없다. 가치와 값을 판단하는 것은 돈과, 그리고 비교하기 힘든 수많은 상품 모두에 대한 태도와 느낌이 복잡하게 뒤섞여있는 것이다.

심리학자들을 포함해 많은 사람들은 어떻게 우리가 사물에 가치를 매기는지에 대단한 관심을 가지고 있다. 어떻게 뇌는 불가능할 정도로 혼란스러운 일상시장의 여러 가지를 서로 구별하여 선택에 도달하는 것일까? 프린스턴(Princeton) 대학의 두 과학자는 이 문제에 대해 연구해 왔으며 이러한 일상적인 결정의 난해하면서도 놀라운 속성에 대한 몇 가지 실마리를 얻었다. 그들은 우리가 도달하는 많은 경제적인 결정은 객관적인 가치와는 거의 연관성이 없다고 생각한다. 시장에서의 선택은 뇌가 갖고 있는 세계에 대한 기초적이며 내부적인 지각과 이런 지각이 우리의 편안하고 안심하는 감정을 형성하는 방법과 훨씬 더 많이 관련이 있다. 이러한 시각에서 보면 화폐조차도 명확하고 절대적인 가치를 지니고 있지 않은데, 지폐와 동전에 새겨져 있는 숫자와는 상관없이 그것들은 개인의 마음으로부터 진정한 가치를 얻는다.

---

contemplate v. 심사숙고하다
candidate n. 후보자; 지원자
attitude n. 태도, 마음가짐
commodity n. 일용품, 필수품
defy v. 문제 삼지 않다; ~을 허용하지 않다
subtle a. 미묘한
have to do with ~와 관련이 있다
objective a. 객관적인
perception n. 지각; 인식
currency n. 통화, 화폐

01 ▶ 글의 전반적인 내용을 물어보는 문제이다. 첫 문단에서 우리가 매일 사물의 가치에 대해 자문하며 살아간다고 기술하고 있으며 두 번째 문단에서는 무엇이 가치를 결정하여 사람들이 시장에서의 선택을 하게 만드는지 연구한 심리학자들의 이야기가 소개되어 있다. 두 번째 단락 둘째 문장 이하는 무엇을 가치 있게 여기는가가 아니라 가치를 어떻게 매기는가에 대한 내용이다. 따라서 (A)가 아니라 (C)가 적절하다.

02 ▶ (A) 돈은 명확하고 절대적인 가치를 지닌 것이 아니라고 하였다. (B) 우리는 사물의 가치에 대해 매일 자문한다고 하였다. (C) 보편적인 가치와 관련된 내용은 언급되지 않았다. (D) 시장선택과 객관적인 가치는 관련성이 적긴 하지만 전혀 관련이 없다고는 할 수 없다.

03 ▶ 여기서 they가 가리키는 것은 bills and coins, 즉 돈이다. 앞에서 가치라는 것이 사람의 내부 인식 작용에 의해 결정된다고 하였으므로, 이와 부합하는 내용이 와야 한다. 이러한 관점에서 보면 돈도 결국 사람의 마음속에서 그 가치가 인식되는 것이므로 사람의 마음으로부터 돈의 가치가 결정된다는 내용의 (A)가 정답이다.

» 정답 01 (C) 02 (B) 03 (A)

한 우연한 발견이 지질학자들이 지진을 예측할 수 있는 길에 한 걸음 더 가까이 다가가도록 만들었다. 기압의 압력 변화로 일어나는 지하의 변화를 측정하는 지진과 관련 없는 노력의 일부로서 연구팀은 샌 안드레아스(San Andreas) 단층에서 일어난 지진보다 10시간이나 앞서 지하의 압력이 상승하는 것을 발견했다. 만약 속행되는 실험이 이 발견을 더욱 발전시킨다면, 언젠가는 지질학자들이 지진이 일어나기 몇 시간 전에 안전한 피난처를 찾도록 사람들에게 알릴 수 있게 될지도 모른다.

연구원들은 캘리포니아의 파크필드(Parkfield) 근처에 있는 깊이가 0.5마일이고 측정 장치에서 5야드 떨어진 시추공 안에 최첨단기술의 입체음향 스피커를 내려서 사용했다. 두 달 동안 연구원들은 스피커에서 측정 장치까지 초 당 세 번의 진동 신호를 전송하여 두 장치 사이에서 오가는 시간을 계산했다. 과학자들은 진동파가 단지 두 경우에, 즉 진도 1의 지진이 일어나기 2시간 전과 놀랍게도 진도 3의 지진이 일어나기 10시간 전에만 극적으로 느려진다는 사실을 알았다.

연구팀은 단층대를 따라 형성되는 엄청난 양의 압력이 지진이 일어나기 전의 마지막 시간 동안 바위 안에 작은 틈들을 만들어 바위의 밀도를 증가시키고 전송 신호를 느리게 하는 것이라는 이론을 세웠다. "갈라진 틈이 많을수록 진동 전송 속도도 더욱 느려집니다."라고 연구의 공동 저자인 폴 실버(Paul Silver)는 말한다. 여전히 알 수 없는 것은 진도 3의 지진이 낮은 진도의 지진보다 훨씬 더 오래 지진 전(前) 신호가 나타나는 것이 중요한 의미가 있는지, 아니면 이것이 단지 진도가 더 크고 진앙이 감지장치에서 더 가까웠기 때문에 발생한 것인지 하는 문제이다.

---

seismologist n. 지진학자
barometric a. 기압의
subterranean a. 지하의
precede v. ~에 선행하다, ~보다 앞서다
fault n. 단층
equivalent n. 동등한 것, 등가물
lower v. 낮추다, 내리다
device n. 장치
transmit v. 보내다
pulse n. 파동, 진동
calculate v. 계산하다
magnitude n. 진도(震度)
temblor n. 지진
immense a. 막대한
crack n. 틈, 균열
velocity n. 속도
significance n. 의미; 중요성
epicenter n. 진앙(震央)

01 ▶ 이 글은 지진이 시작되기 전에 지하의 압력이 변화한다는 것을 우연히 다른 실험을 하다 발견했다는 내용이다. 아직은 의문투성이지만 실험이 진척된다면 지진을 미리 예고할 수 있을지도 모른다고 하면서 실험의 내용에 대해 상세하게 기술하고 있다. 따라서 제목으로는 '지진을 예측하는 새로운 단서'가 가장 알맞다.

02 ▶ 첫 번째 문단 두 번째 문장의 an unrelated effort가 힌트이다. 지진과는 전혀 상관없는 기압 변화에 따른 지하의 변화를 연구하다 우연하게도 지진이 일어나기 몇 시간 전에는 진동파가 느려진다는 사실을 발견한 것이다. 따라서 빈칸에 들어갈 말로는 '우연한 발견'이 가장 알맞다.

03 ▶ (A) 첫 번째 문단 마지막 문장에서 계속되는 실험이 발견을 발전시킨다면 언젠가는 지진이 일어나는 것을 미리 경고할 수 있을 것이라고 하였다. (B) 두 번째 문단 마지막 문장에서 진도 1과 진도 3의 지진이 일어날 때 진동파가 극적으로 느려졌다고 언급하고 있다. (C) 마지막 문단 첫 번째 문장에서 압력이 바위 안에 틈을 만들고 전송 신호를 느리게 한다고 주장한 연구원들의 이론을 소개하고 있다. (D) 진도 3의 지진 전 신호가 더 긴 것이 진도가 더 크기 때문이라는 것은 아직 알 수 없는(unknown) 것이다.

》 정답 01 (B) 02 (B) 03 (D)

현대에서 정보 기술과 그것과 관련된 시스템들이 세상을 자료들로 넘치게 했다. 조직의 정보/지식 구성요소는 군대, 기업체, 국가 그리고 개인의 성공을 결정한다. 사실, 단지 정보를 가지는 것보다 더 중요한 것은 정보를 입수하고 처리하고 사용하는 속도이다. 그것은 조직의 생존을 위한 근본적이고 중요한 성공 요인들 중의 하나가 되었다. 이렇기 때문에, 그것은 그 어떤 경쟁적이며 적대적인 상황에서도 전투원의 가장 중요한 목표가 되었다. 정보는 이제 전략적, 전술적, 작전 차원 등 모든 수준에서 힘일 뿐만 아니라 무기이다. 사실, 데이터 생산의 속도와 정보 구성요소에 대한 강조가 전략과 작전을 똑같은 것이 되게 하기 때문에 정보화시대는 이런 용어들을 불분명하게 했다. 모든 주요한 무기처럼, 정보는 방어되어야 할 필요가 있다. 따라서 정보는 물질적 자산만큼 보호되어야 한다. 사실, 물질적 자산을 유지 관리하는 것보다 정보와 그와 관련된 시스템의 완전무결과 타당성을 유지 관리하는 것이 더 중요하다고 주장할 수도 있다. 이 책은 정보 전쟁의 세계와 관련된 개념을 논의할 것이다. 그것은 긍정적인 자신들의 이미지를 구축하고 경쟁자 혹은 적대자의 부정적인 이미지를 구축하기 위해 정보를 이용하는 세계에 관한 것이다. 해커들이 시스템을 침해하고자 하는 상황이 현대의 풍조이다. 경영자들이 무시하다가는 위험하게 될 세계이다.

---

antagonistic a. 적대의; 상반[모순, 대립]되는
tactical a. 전술상의, 전술적인
blur v. (눈, 시계 등을) 희미하게 [흐리게] 하다
component n. 성분, 구성 요소[부분], 부품
integrity n. 성실, 정직, 고결
beneficial a. 유익한, 이익을 가져오는(to)
the order of the day 당시[시대]의 풍조, 요즘의 유행
at one's peril 위험을 각오하고

01 ▶ "정보는 물질적 자산만큼 보호되어야 한다. 사실 물질적 자산을 유지 관리하는 것보다 정보와 그와 관련된 시스템의 완전무결, 타당성을 유지 관리하는 것이 더 중요하다"라는 내용을 통해 (D)가 정답으로 적절함을 알 수 있다.

02 ▶ "부정적인 경쟁자 혹은 적대자의 이미지와 긍정적인 그들의 이미지를 구축하기 위해 정보를 이용하는 세계"를 통해 (D)가 본문의 내용과 일치함을 알 수 있다.

03 ▶ "이 책은 정보 전쟁의 세계와 관련된 개념을 논의할 것이다"라는 것을 통해 책의 머리말 부분임을 알 수 있다.

》 정답 01 (D) 02 (D) 03 (B)

[1] 어느 대기업의 사장이 다른 면으로는 자격이 있지만 너무 꼼꼼하게 치장을 하고 와서 퇴짜를 놓았던 한 구직자에 대해 말해주었다. "치장을 잘 하는 것은 중요하다고 생각합니다," 그 사장이 설명했다. "하지만, 이 사람은 너무 완벽해서 무서울 정도였어요. 옷도 완벽하고, 머리도 완벽하고, 손톱도 완벽하고, 심지어 치아도 완벽했지요. 그는 너무 인공적이었고, 난 그걸 신뢰할 수 없었지요. 완벽한 사람은 아무도 없지요." 너무 많은 사람들이 만약 상사가 몇 가지 불완전한 점을 보게 되면 그들에겐 기회가 주어지지 않을 거라고 생각한다. 그들은 말을 조심하고, 말실수를 하여 그만 끔찍한 비밀, 즉 자신들이 불완전하다는 사실을 드러낼까봐 무서워 회의에서 뒷줄에 앉아 될 수 있는 대로 눈에 띄지 않으려 한다.

실수를 피할 유일한 방법은 결코 어떤 것이건 새로운 일을 하지 않는 것이다. 내 생각에, 절대로 실수를 하지 않는 직원은 그의 창조성이 답보 상태에 있다는 것을, 그가 하루하루의 사소한 일에 몰두하느라 미래를 생각하지 않는다는 것을 보여준다. 몸을 사리는 직원은 아무것도 이룰 수가 없다.

[2] 우리는 종종 취업 면접에 완벽을 기할 필요가 있다고 생각한다. 그러나, 완벽하려고 노력하는 것은 잘못된 노력일 뿐만 아니라 부정확한 전략이다. 구직 면접은 완벽한 차림새, 기능이나 이력서 작성 요령에 대한 것이 아니다. 그것은 인간관계, 지원자의 인성을 알아내고, "이 사람과 같이 일하고 싶은가?"와 같은 질문에 답하는 것에 관한 것이다. 그리고 대부분의 직장에서 변하지 않는 한 가지가 있다. 사람들은 생산적이고 재미있는 동료가 되어줄 지원자를 고용한다는 것이다. 이상하게도 우리에게서 뭔가가 부족할 때 우리는 더욱 완전하다는 것을 기억하라. 그리고 우리가 가진 그 한계들 때문에 우리는 갈망하고, 노력하고, 희망하고, 더 나은 무언가에 대한 꿈으로 우리의 영혼을 살찌운다. 그러니, 너무 완벽하려고 애쓰지 마라. 결점을 인정해라 그러면 그것이 당신을 더욱 인간적이고 진실 되게 만든다.

---

qualified a. 자격을 갖춘
turn down 거절하다, 퇴짜 놓다
groom v. 단장하다
meticulously ad. 꼼꼼하게, 깐깐하게
evaporate v. 사라지다, 증발하다
inconspicuous a. 눈에 띄지 않는
slip v. 미끄러지다, 실수하다
at a standstill 답보 상태에 있는, 정체된
be immersed in ~에 몰두하다
misguided a. 잘못된
attire n. 복장
resume trick 이력서 (작성) 요령
flaw n. 결점

01 ▶ 앞의 내용이 지나치게 완벽한 모습을 한 지원자에 대한 거부감을 나타내고, Nobody is perfect.로 연결되기 때문에 ①의 plastic은 '꾸민, 인공적인'의 의미를 갖는다. ②의 go nowhere는 '실패하다, 성공하지 못하다'의 일반적인 의미 그대로 쓰이고 있다

02 ▶ 지문 [1]은 사소한 세부에 완벽을 기하는 지나치게 조심하는 자세가 아니라, 다소 실수가 있더라도 새로운 시도를 통해 발전하고 성취하는 창조적인 인재의 중요성을, 지문 [2] 역시 완벽함보다는 진솔하고 사교적인 인성이 구직자에게서 가장 바람직한 특성임을 강조하고 있다.

» 정답 01 (C) 02 (B)

고등학교 영어교사인 아이린 멘데빌(Irene Mendevil)은 그녀의 학생들에게 고함을 지를 때, 목이 아프다고 이야기한다. 그래서 그녀는 확성기를 사용하기 시작했다. "저는 제 목소리를 완전히 잃어버린 경험이 있어요."라고 그녀가 끊임없이 고함을 지르는 것에 대해 말했다. "아무 소리도 제 입에서 나오지 않았어요. 저는 학생들에게 무엇을 해야 하는지를 말하기 위해 종이에 적어야만 했어요." 멘데빌 씨는 올해 33세로 그녀의 반이 너무 커서 학생들에게 자신의 목소리를 듣게 하는 것만도 큰 문제일 정도여서 고함을 지른다. 그리고 9200만 명의 인구가 빠른 속도로 증가하고 교육예산은 너무나 작아서 아이들을 가르칠 공간을 찾을 수 없는 국가에서는 이런 학교가 특별한 것도 아니다. 경제가 갈수록 힘들어지고, 가족들은 학생 수가 더 적은 학급으로 되어 있는 사립학교를 감당할 수 없어서 더 많은 아이들이 공립학교에 들어온다. 초등학교부터 고등학교까지 전국적으로 2100만 명의 학생들이 등록한 채로 이번 학년은 시작되었는데, 이는 작년 대비 거의 정확하게 100만 명이 더 늘어난 수치이다. 정부가 3년 전에 교실 짓기 운동을 시작했지만, 여전히 27,124개의 교실이 부족하다고 교육정책 개선을 옹호하는 국립정책연구소(NIPS)에서 일하고 있는 전(前) 교육부 차관 후안 미구엘 루즈(Juan Miguel Luz)가 말했다. 모든 학생들을 다 쑤셔 넣기 위해, 많은 교실들은 칸막이로 둘로 나누어져 있다. 계단통과 복도는 미니교실로 전환되었다. 2016년에 이러한 압박 중 일부를 덜어내고자 오전·오후반 수업이 도입되었다.

amplifier n. 확성기
explode v. 폭발적으로 증가하다
tighten v. 절박해지다, 궁해지다
haven n. 피난처, 안식처
enrollment n. 등록, 입학
elementary a. 기본이 되는, 초보의
under secretary 차관
stairwell n. 계단통
corridor n. 복도
miniature a. 소형의, 소규모의
session n. 수업
take off ~을 제거하다, 없애다

01 ▶ get a sore throat은 '목이 아프다'는 뜻이다. '목이 쉬다, 가래가 끓다'는 뜻의 숙어인 (B)가 가장 이와 뜻이 가깝다.

02 ▶ 시종일관 열악한 교육환경에 관한 글이다. 교실이 부족하다고 했으므로, 학생을 모두 수용하기 위해서는 '쑤셔 넣다'는 (B)의 squeeze in이 나와야 자연스럽다.

03 ▶ 그 나라는 3년 전에 교실 짓기 운동을 시작했지만, 여전히 교실이 부족하다고 했다. 따라서 (C)의 내용과는 거리가 멀다.

» 정답 01 (B) 02 (B) 03 (C)

지친 여행자에게 뉴저지(New Jersey)의 링컨(Lincoln) 터널 입구에 있는 아르데코(Art Deco) 아치는 8달러의 통행료를 내고 가면 맨해튼(Manhattan) 중심가를 즐길 수 있다는 신호이다. 1997년 10월 전에는 그 아치를 통과하는 데 지금보다 시간이 훨씬 더 오래 걸렸다. 그러나 그 후에 미국 북동부 전 지역에서 사용되는 자동 통행료 지불 시스템인 E-ZPass가 터널의 일부 통행료 차선에 설치되었다.

E-ZPass의 도입으로 인해 터널과 다른 통행료 부스에서의 지체가 거의 85% 정도 감소한 것으로 추정된다. 이것은 운전자들이 통행료를 지불하기 위해 공회전 상태로 기다리는 동안, 낭비되는 시간과 연료가 줄어드는 것을 의미했다. 그러나 통행료 부스를 빨리 통과하는 것은 또한 지역의 공해가 줄어든다는 것을 의미했다. 콜롬비아 대학의 자넷 커리(Janet Currie)와 리드 워커(Reed Walker)가 실시한 연구는 이것이 예기치 않은 결과를 낳았다는 것을 발견한다.

많은 미국인들은 붐비는 대로변 가까이에 산다. 연구원들은 대부분의 통행료 부스에 E-ZPass가 설치된 기간 동안 고속도로에서 2km 이내에 살았던 뉴저지와 펜실베니아(Pennsylvania)의 여성들에게서 태어난 모든 아이들에 관한 의학 자료들을 살펴보았다. 그들은 E-ZPass가 도입된 이후에 거의 12퍼센트 적은 수의 비정상적으로 낮은 출생체중의 아이가 통행료 부스의 2km 이내에서 살았던 여성에게서 태어났다는 것을 알았다. 통행료 부스에서 멀리 떨어진 곳에 살았던 엄마에게서 태어난 아이들에게는 변화가 없었다. 조산(早産)에서도 유사한 결과가 나왔다. 교통 혼잡의 감소가 성질을 잘 내는 운전자들을 달래는 것 이상의 훨씬 많은 일을 하는 것 같다. E-ZPass를 등록했던 사람들은 의도하지 않게 많은 아이들에게 은혜를 베푼 것이다.

weary a. 피곤한, 지친
toll n. 통행료
reckon v. 세다, 합산하다; 간주하다, 판단하다
booth n. 노점, 매점; 부스
premature a. 조숙한; 시기상조의
congestion n. 교통 혼잡
soothe v. 달래다
ratty a. 성질 잘 내는; 쥐 같은

01 ▶ E-ZPass의 도입으로 인한 교통 혼잡의 감소가 아이들의 건강을 향상시키는 결과를 나왔다는 내용이므로 (C)가 글의 주제로 적절하다.

02 ▶ E-ZPass가 아이들의 건강에 의도치 않은 좋은 영향을 미쳤으므로, (D)가 정답으로 적절하다.

03 ▶ E-ZPass의 도입으로 건강이 향상되는 의도하지 않은 결과를 나왔으므로 (C)를 유추할 수 있다.

》 정답 01 (C) 02 (D) 03 (C)

북극 툰드라는 세계에서 가장 광대한 생태계이며 그 아래에 놓인 영구 동토층이라고 알려진 동결 지반의 깊이는 수백 미터에 이른다. 그러나 매년 대기에 뿜어지는 수백만 톤의 이산화탄소와 다른 온실 가스에 반응하여 지구의 온도가 올라감에 따라, 영구 동토층도 온도가 오르고 있다. 영구 동토층이 해빙되면서, 박테리아가 영구 동토층에 있는 유기물질을 파괴하기 시작한다. 이것은 또 다른 온실 가스로 이산화탄소의 온난화 잠재 가능성의 25배인 메탄뿐 아니라 이산화탄소 또한 더 많이 방출한다. 지구의 영구 동토층은 지구 대기의 탄소량의 2배 정도를 함유하고 있는 것으로 추정된다. 이것이 전부가 아니다. 또한 영구 동토층이 해빙되면서 질산염와 인산염이 툰드라로 새어 나오고 있으며, 처음에는 상당히 척박한 서식지였던 곳에 새로운 식물 종이 기반을 마련할 수 있도록 해주고 있다. 이것은 또한 지구의 지표면을 해치고 있고, 세계의 석회암이 풍부한 지역의 카르스트 지형과 닮아서 열카르스트라고 알려진 둥근 지붕과 팬 곳이 있는 풍경을 만들고 있다. 영구 동토층은 또한 그 위에 놓인 건물, 도로, 그리고 수송 관로와 같은 인간 시설을 파괴하고 있다. 그래서 이러한 모든 이유로 이 얼음지역에 대한 더 많은 연구가 필요하다. 그리고 그것이 벌링턴(Burlington)의 버몬트 대학(University of Vermont)의 브렉 보든(Breck Bowden)이 지휘하고 미국과 캐나다의 17개 리서치 그룹을 포함한 프로젝트의 목표이다. 프로젝트는 어떻게 영구 동토층의 해빙이 북극의 수많은 개울, 강, 그리고 호수에 영향을 미치는지 알아내려고 노력할 것이다. 물이 영향을 받은 지역을 지나면서, 그렇지 않으면 영구 동토층의 언 흙속에 갇혀 있을 영양분과 침전물이 나오게 한다. 역설적이게도 이러한 것들은 조류의 성장에 서로 상반되는 영향을 미친다. 인산염과 질산염은 조류의 성장을 촉진하는 반면 여분의 침전물은 수역의 바닥에 영양분을 잡아둠으로써 조류의 성장을 억제한다.

permafrost n. 영구 동토층
underlie v. ~의 밑에 있다
thaw v. (눈, 서리, 얼음 따위가) 녹다
leak v. 새다; 누설하다
nitrate n. 질산염
phosphate n. 인산염
foothold n. 발판, 기반
limestone n. 석회암
karstic a. 카르스트 지형의
sediment n. 침전물, 퇴적물
stimulate v. 자극하다, 활발하게 하다

01 ▶ ⓒ its는 a landscape of domes and pits를 지칭한다.
02 ▶ (A) 영양분이 영구동토층에 얼어 있다고 했지 없다고 하지 않았으며, (B) 영양분은 조류의 성장을 촉진하는 역할을 하며, (D) 열크라스트가 석회암이 풍부한 지역은 아니다.
03 ▶ 영양분과 침전물은 모두 조류의 먹이가 되어 성장에 도움이 될 것으로 추측되나, 영양분은 조류 성장을 촉진하는 반면, 침전물은 이것을 억제하는 상반된 역할을 하므로 (D)가 빈칸에 적절하다.

» 정답 01 (C) 02 (C) 03 (D)

사실 지구 온난화는 반드시 해결되어야 하며, 우리는 화석 연료에서 벗어나 친환경 에너지로 나아가야 한다. 그러나 이와 관련하여 현재의 접근법이 그 어떤 성과라도 거두고 있다고 생각하는 것은 잘못이다.

유럽연합(EU)은 온실가스 배출량을 2040년까지 25% 줄이고 같은 양만큼 친환경 에너지를 늘이게 될 엄중한 목표를 이행하여 많은 사람들의 칭찬을 받고 있다. 그러나 그 정책은 2100년의 기온을 (지금에 비해) 화씨 0.1도만큼만 낮출 것인 반면에 그때까지 남은 기간 동안 매년 약 3,800억 달러의 비용이 들게 할 것이다. 이렇게 어마어마한 비용이 드는 것은 화석 연료를 대체할 저렴한 대체 연료가 없기 때문이다. 현재의 친환경 기술은 너무나 비효율적이어서, 한 가지만 예를 들자면, 만일 풍력을 (대체 에너지원으로 개발할 것을) 진지하게 생각한다면 (그것으로) 충분한 에너지를 발생시키려면 대부분의 나라를 풍력발전 터빈으로 뒤덮어야 할 것이다. 그리고 여전히 저장이라는 큰 문제를 갖게 될 것이다. 바람이 불지 않을 때는 발전을 전혀 하지 못할 테니까.

현명한 에너지 정책은 먼저 인간의 창의적 재능을 발휘케 하여 우리 앞에 놓인 큰 기술적 난제를 해결하는 데 집중해야 한다. 공공투자와 민간투자가 모두 필요한데, 여기에는 더욱 저렴한 저탄소 신기술 개발을 목표로 한 정부의 상당한 규모의 연구개발비 지출이 포함된다.

화석 연료의 가격을 크게 올려 사용하기를 원하는 사람이 없게 만들려는 것은 대단히 어리석은 짓이다. 대신에, 친환경 에너지 가격이 내려가고 대체 에너지가 개발도상국을 포함한 모든 사람이 사게 될 정도로 급속히 저렴해지도록 기술혁신을 촉진해야 한다. 그런 정책이 우리의 현재 접근법보다 더 똑똑한 정책일 것이며 장차 어디서나 친환경 에너지가 개발 사용되는 결과를 실제로 초래할 것이다.

---

applaud v. 박수갈채하다, 칭찬하다
implement v. 이행하다
stringent a. 절박한, 엄중한
emission n. (온실가스) 배출량
price tag 정가표
affordable a. (값이) 알맞은
blanket v. 덮다
unleash v. 풀어놓다; (감정이나 반응을) 불러일으키다

01 ▶ 콜론 다음에서 '바람이 불지 않을 때는 발전을 전혀 하지 못할 테니까'라고 했으므로, 바람이 불 때 발전한 것 중 일부를 바람이 불지 않을 때를 위해 저장 비축해두어야 하는 문제가 생길 것이다.

02 ▶ 비효율적인 현재의 에너지 정책 대신, 인간의 창의적 재능을 발휘케 하여 대체에너지의 가격을 낮출 수 있도록 기술 혁신을 이루는 데 정책의 초점을 맞추어야 한다는 취지의 글이므로 (C)가 글의 요지로 적절하다.

03 ▶ 본문에서 ingenuity는 '창의적 재능, 창의력'이라는 뜻으로 쓰였으므로, (B)의 inventiveness가 정답이다.

» 정답 01 (A) 02 (C) 03 (B)

농담처럼 들릴지 모르지만 지미 킴멜(Jimmy Kimmel)은 전국 친구삭제의 날(NUD)을 제안할 때 무언가 알고 있었는지도 모른다. 페이스북 덕택에 우리들 중 많은 사람들에게 너무나 많은 친구가 생겼다. 그런데 사실은 대부분의 경우, 그들은 전혀 진짜 친구가 아니다.

보통 페이스북 사용자에게는 약 120명의 친구가 있다. 인류학자인 로빈 던바(Robin Dunbar)는 인간은 평균적으로 약 150명의 친구가 있으며, 인간의 뇌는 그 이상의 친구를 실제로 수용하지 못한다고 주장한다. 던바는 당신에게 약 5명의 핵심친구가 있고 또 10명의 가까운 친구가 있으며 10명의 친구 범주 밖에 또 35명의 친구가 있으며, 이들 외에도 소위 '우정의 의무'가 있는 약 100명의 친구가 있다고 한다. 그럼 수천 명의 '친구'를 가진 페이스북 사람들은 어떤가? 글쎄, 그들의 변명을 듣자면, 그 수천 명의 사람들을 친구라고 지칭하는 것이 당신이 아니라 페이스북이라는 것이다. 많은 경우 사람들은 오직 인원수만 많기를 원하는 사람들도 많지만, 사람들은 (보통) 사회적으로나 직업적으로 서로 연락을 주고받기 위해 친구가 된다. <내가 처음에는 알지 못했지만 나를 어떤 이유로 친구로 삼았던 많은 사람들이 친구들이 되었는데, 내가 지금 관심을 가지고 계속되는 사회적 의무를 추구하는 데 있어 흥미 있어 하는 사람들이다.>

그래서 전국 친구삭제의 날인 11월 17일 수요일에, 오직 좋은 사람이고 싶은 마음에 받아들인 성가신 페이스북 친구들을 삭제하기 전에 당신은 재고할지도 모른다. 왜냐하면 그들은 더 알아갈 정도로 아주 흥미로운 사람들일 뿐만 아니라 당신에게 친구가 많을수록, 당신이 더 부자가 된다고 보도한 연구도 있기 때문이다.

anthropologist n. 인류학자
complement v. 보충하다, 보완하다
obligation n. 의무, 책임
get rid of ~을 제거하다
annoying a. 성가신, 귀찮은

01 ▶ (A) 페이스북 친구를 삭제하는 것이 꼭 바람직한 것은 아니라는 뜻에서 친구들이 많을수록 부자가 된다는 연구를 인용했을 뿐이지, 실제로 친구가 많다고 해서 꼭 우리가 부자 되는 것을 보장해 주는 것은 아니다. (B) 로빈 던바에 따르면, 우리는 친구를 핵심친구, 가까운 친구, 그 밖의 친구로 나눈다고 했다. (C) 페이스북에서 많은 친구들을 삭제하는 것이 쉬운지 어려운지는 글에서 알 수 없다. (D) 인원수만 많기를 원하는 사람들이 많다고 했으므로 오직 자신의 페이스북 인기만을 원하는 사람들이 꽤 있음을 알 수 있다. 따라서 (D)가 정답이다.

02 ▶ 제시된 문장에서 '페이스북에서 어떠한 이유로 나를 친구로 맺었던 사람들을 처음에는 알지 못했지만, 친구가 되었고 지금은 내가 관심 있어 하는 사람'이라고 하였다. 따라서 이는 본문의 처음에서부터 줄곧 페이스북 친구에 대해 회의적인 입장을 취해온 저자가 새로운 의견을 말하고 있는 것이므로 페이스북 친구삭제 전 재고를 권하는 내용인 마지막 단락 앞, 즉 [IV]에 주어진 문장이 오는 것이 적절하다.

03 ▶ 실제 친구를 뜻하는 ①, ②, ④와 달리 ③의 friends는 Facebook이 임의로 부르는 용어이다.

≫ 정답 01 (D) 02 (D) 03 (C)

암은 가장 공격적이고 대개 치명적인, 보다 광범위한 종류로 보자면 종양으로 알려져 있는 질병에 대한 비전문적 용어다. 종양은 상대적으로 독립적인 존재로 설명되는데, 이는 그것이 세포 각각의 성장과 신진대사와 살아있는 유기체의 총체적 상호작용을 관장하는 생물학적 메커니즘을 전혀 따르지 않기 때문이다. 어떤 종양들은 그것이 발생한 조직들보다 더 빨리 성장하고, 다른 어떤 종양들은 정상적인 속도로 자라나지만 다른 요인들 때문에 결과적으로는 정상적인 조직이 아니라 비정상적인 종양으로 인식되어지게 된다. 종양에서 보이는 변화들은 이러한 특징들이 각각의 세포에서부터 그 후손에 계속 전달된다는 점에서 유전적이다. 양성 혹은 악성으로서의 종양의 주요 분류는 그것들의 성질과 관련이 있다. 몇몇 상대적인 차이점들은 이러한 두 가지 분류를 특징짓는다. 예를 들면, 양성 종양은 껍질에 싸여있지만 악성 종양은 그렇지 않다. 악성 종양은 양성 종양보다 빨리 자라며 주위에 있는 정상적인 조직에 침범한다. 양성 종양 조직은 그것이 파생되어진 조직과 유사한 방식으로 구축되는 한편, 악성 조직은 비정상적이고 정형화되어 있지 않은 모습을 하고 있다. 사실, 대부분의 악성 종양은 염색체 구조 — 즉, 복제되어 다음 세대의 세포에게 전달되는 유전 물질을 구성하는 DNA 분자 구조에 있어서 비정상적인 면을 보인다. 그러나, 가장 큰 차이점으로는 양성 종양은 전이(轉移)— 즉, 발생 지점 외의 곳에서 성장하기 시작 — 하지 않는 반면에 악성 종양은 전이한다는 것이다.

lay a. 속인의, 평신도의; 전문가가 아닌
neoplasm n. 종양
metabolism n. 물질대사
interaction n. 상호작용
factor n. 인자, 요소
heritable a. 유전성의
classification n. 분류
benign a. 양성의; 온화한
malignant a. 악의 있는; 악성의
encapsulate v. 캡슐로 싸다; 분리하다
tumor n. 종기; 종양
chromosome n. 염색체
duplicate v. 복사하다, 복제하다
metastasize v. 전이(轉移)하다

01 ▶ 글 후반부에서 양성 종양과 악성 종양의 결정적인 차이로 '전이(轉移)'를 들고 있다.

02 ▶ "악성 종양은 양성 종양보다 빨리 자라며, 비정상적이고 정형화되어 있지 않은 모습을 하고 있다"고 했다.

03 ▶ ①에는 '생물학적 메커니즘을 전혀 따르지 않는다'와 호응하는 autonomous 혹은 disobedient가 가능하고, ②에는 '유전적이다'와 호응하는 progeny와 offspring이 가능하다.

04 ▶ ⓐ 이하가 근거에 해당하는 진술이므로 ⓐ에는 in that이 적절하고, ⓑ 바로 뒤에 이어지는 내용은 앞에서 언급한 '전이'에 대한 부연설명이므로 ⓑ에는 that is 혹은 that is to say가 적절하다.

》 정답 01 (B) 02 (B) 03 (A) 04 (B)

198

　자연선택이란 개체군 내의 개체가 가진 차이가 환경 속에서 생존하고 번식하는 능력에 영향을 미치는 생물학적 과정을 일컫는다. 개체에 있어서의 차이는 부모에게서 물려받은 유전 형질에 의한 것이다. 개체군에서, 번식을 방해하는 형질은 그 어떤 것이든 여러 세대에 걸쳐 사라지는 경향이 있다. 오랜 시간에 걸쳐, 적응을 하지 못한 개체들이 사라지기 때문이다. 반대로, 살아남아 번식하는 개체들은 환경에 보다 적합한 개체들을 낳는 경향이 있다. 자연선택은 생물이 환경 속에서 살아남을 수 있는 능력을 증진시키는 적응성을 향상시켜 주는 경향이 있는 것이다.

　자연선택은 돌연변이라고 부르는 새로운 형질이 생겨난 후 환경에 적응하지 못하여 도태되는 경우에 개체군을 안정시키는 역할을 할 수 있다. 개체가 환경에 보다 잘 적응하도록 하는 새로운 형질이 나타나는 경우에는, 반대의 결과가 일어난다. 오랜 세월에 걸쳐, 이러한 돌연변이가 개체군 속에 널리 퍼져감에 따라 그런 종은 변화를 겪게 될 것이다. 인간의 경우, 뇌의 크기가 커짐으로 인해 환경에 더 잘 적응할 수 있게 되었는데, 그리하여 뇌의 크기가 점진적으로 늘어났다. 환경에 있어서의 변화, 특히 심각한 환경 파괴가 일어나는 경우, 개체군의 전체적인 유전자 구성에 변화가 일어나는 것이 정상적이다. 특정 환경에 특별하게 적응하는 경우, 오랜 시간이 지나고 나면 아(亞)개체군이 발전하게 되는데, 이것들은 특정 토양 조건이나 양식 등에 더 잘 적응한 것들이다. 시간이 충분히 주어진다면, 이러한 아개체군들은 서로 다른 환경에서 살고 서로 교배하지 않는 얼룩말과 말처럼 독립된 종으로 발전해 나갈 수도 있다.

natural selection 자연선택, 자연도태
reproduce v. 번식하다
inheritance n. 상속; 유전 형질
die out 멸종되다, 자취를 감추다
stabilize v. 안정시키다, 견고하게 하다
mutation n. 돌연변이
subpopulation n. 부분 모집단, 부차 집단
interbreed v. 이종 교배하다; 잡종 번식하다

01 ▶ 개체에 있어서의 차이는 부모에게서 물려받은 '유전 형질'에 의한 것이다

02 ▶ 환경에 있어서의 변화, 특히 심각한 환경 파괴가 일어나는 경우에는 개체군의 전체적인 유전자적인 구성에 변화가 일어나는 것이 일반적이다

03 ▶ 말과 얼룩말을 개체군과 거기서 새로이 발전한 아(亞)개체군의 관계로 파악하고 있다. 따라서 이 두 종(種)이 한때는 같은 종이었다고 볼 수 있다.

04 ▶ 자연선택이 개체군에 미치는 영향과 역할, 그 결과에 대해 주로 이야기하고 있다.

▶▶ **정답**　01 (C)　02 (D)　03 (A)　04 (B)

착한 행동에 대해서는 용돈을 올려주고 반대의 경우 용돈을 깎는 수법은 부모들이 일반적으로 시도하는 방법이다. 영국 정부는 자국의 청소년들에게 이와 유사한 방법을 적용하고자 하고 있다. 영국 정부의 계획에 따르면, 2008년부터 13세에서 19세의 모든 청소년들은 이른 바 오퍼튜너티 카드(Opportunity Card)를 소지하게 된다. 이 카드는 12파운드 가치의 신용 포인트가 적립된 형태로 발급된다. 빈곤 가정의 청소년들이나 유용한 활동에 참여 하는 학생들(자원 봉사를 하는 청소년들 또는 정기적인 학교 출석률을 보이는 청소년들)은 더 많은 포인트를 적립할 수 있게 되는데, 이는 대략 한 달에 12파운드 정도가 될 전망이다. 이와는 반대로, (무단결석이나 공공 기물 파괴와 같은) 비행을 일삼는 청소년들은 상대적으로 적은 포인트를 받거나 아예 포인트 적립을 할 수 없게 된다. 이러한 적립 포인트는 스포츠 센터의 강의나 댄스 교습 또는 다른 형태의 건전한 여가 활동 시 현금처럼 사용할 수 있다.

이러한 계획은 공공정책에 있어 영국 정부가 가장 선호하는 방식을 극명하게 보여주는 좋은 사례라 할 수 있겠다. 영국 정부의 공공 정책은 기본적으로 중앙개입적이거나 시장의 원리에 충실한 모습을 보인다. 사실 이러한 방식은 참여하는 학생들에게도 득이 되고 또한 학생들의 비행을 억제함으로써 다른 모두에게도 득이 된다는 점에서 누이 좋고 매부 좋은 정책처럼 비칠 수도 있다. 영국 정부는 건전한 활동에 참여하지 않는 학생들이 비행을 저지를 가능성이 높다는 상관관계를 보여주는 학문적 연구를 인용하고 있다. 운동, 음악 또는 미술과 같은 건전한 활동은 이와는 대비되게 청소년들에게 목적의식을 부여한다는 것이다.

그러나 이러한 방식에는 여러 결함들이 내재돼 있다. 선행을 유도하기 위한 인센티브가 단순한 "대가의 지불"로 변질된다면 선의(善意) 자체를 퇴색시킬 수 있는 위험이 발생할 수 있다. 선행과 즉각적인 물질적 보상을 긴밀히 연계한다는 것은 공동체 정신을 약화시키는 결과를 초래할 수도 있는 것이다. 많은 부모들이 경험하듯이, 선행에 대한 대가로 물질적 보상을 받는 아이는 모든 것에 대해 물질적 보상을 기대하게 된다. 더욱이 물질적 유혹을 통해 청소년들을 교육으로 유도한다는 것은 그 자체가 매우 생경해 보인다. 출석을 한다는 것은 그 자체로서 바람직한 행위이지 물질적 보상이 따라야 할 것은 아니다. 영국보다 빈곤한 국가의 수백만의 청소년들이 단지 학교에 가기 위해 엄청난 희생을 감수한다는 점을 명심해야 할 것이다. 영국의 교육에 문제가 있다면 그것은 수요 측면의 문제라기보다는 공급 측면의 문제라고 보는 것이 맞을 것이다.

---

scheme n. 계획, 기획
truancy n. 태만, 무단결석
vandalism n. 공공기물 파손죄
interventionist n. 개재, 조정; 중재
correlation n. 상호관계
blunt v. 무디게 하다, 둔감하게 하다
goodwill n. 호의, 친절
sacrifice n. 희생
demand n. 수요

01 ▶ 첫 번째 빈칸에는 현금처럼 사용 할 수 있다는 의미의 redeemable이 와야 적절하다. 두 번째 빈칸에는 공동체 정신을 약화시키거나 퇴색시킨다는 의미가 와야 하므로 corrode나 erode가 올 수 있다.

02 ▶ 저자는 세 번째 단락부터 영국 정부의 새로운 제도(Opportunity Card)에 대해 문제점을 제기하고 있다.

03 ▶ 이 글은 영국 청소년들을 위한 새로운 계획에 대해 소개하고 있다. 선행, 유용한 활동 등을 통한 포인트 적립, 선행을 유도하기 위한 인센티브, 교육의 문제점에 대해 다루고 있지만 이 글에서 주가 되는 내용은 아니다.

04 ▶ 오퍼튜니티 카드의 발급을 고려하고 있는 곳은 영국이다.

▶ 정답 01 (B) 02 (C) 03 (A) 04 (D)

카타르의 Abd Allah bin Hamad al-Attiyah 산업에너지부 장관은 OPEC의 중추적인 역할을 하고 있는 사우디아라비아의 일일 당 OPEC의 생산 상한선을 150만 배럴로 늘리자는 요청에 대한 지지를 발표했다. 그는 "이것은 OPEC이 석유 가격 인상을 억제하기 위해 최선을 다하고 있다는 것을 보여 주고 있는 훌륭한 지표입니다."라고 말했다. 석유 가격은 최근 들어 급격히 상승해 왔고, 금요일에는 뉴욕에서 1배럴 당 유례없는 가격인 41.56 달러에 팔렸다.

하지만 Attiyah는 이러한 고유가는 정치적 두려움에서 야기된 것이지 시장에서의 석유 부족 때문은 아니라고 말했다. "두려움이라는 요소가 8달러를 더 부담하게 만들고 있습니다. 나는 우리의 모든 최종 소비자들을 점검하며 그들에게 하나의 질문을 던졌습니다. '석유가 부족하다고 생각하십니까?' 그들의 대답은 '아니오'였습니다." 분석가들은 이라크와 사우디아라비아에서의 테러리스트의 공격과 관련된 안전에 대한 두려움을 가격 상승의 주된 이유로 들었다.

Attiyah는 OPEC이 이미 일일 당 공식 상한선인 2,350만 배럴에 150만 배럴 이상을 초과하여 생산하고 있다고 말했다. 하지만 그는 OPEC이 암스텔담이나 베이루트에서 개최될 회의에서 얼마만큼 증산에 대한 합의가 이루어질지 정확한 수치를 알려주지는 않았다.

---

voice v. 목소리로 내다, 말로 나타내다[표현하다]
indication n. 지시, 지적; 암시
check v. 억제하다, 저지하다
all-time high 사상 최고치
end user 최종 소비자
petroleum n. 석유
put a figure on ~의 수치를 정확하게 말하다
canopy n. (침대 위에 지붕처럼 늘어뜨린) 덮개

01 ▶ 이 글은 '현재 증산 정책에도 불구하고 최근 석유 값이 계속 치솟는 이유와 OPEC 회원국의 대응책'을 논하고 있다.

02 ▶ kingpin n. 중추적 인물(= leader)

03 ▶ 둘째 문단에 카타르 에너지 장관은 '현재의 고유가는 정치적 두려움에서 야기된 것이지 석유부족 때문이 아니다'라고 했다. 또 석유 분석가들도 이를 주된 이유를 들고 있다. 마지막에서 그는 'OPEC 회의에서 얼마만큼 증산에 합의가 이루어질지 정확한 수치를 알려주지 않았다'고 했다. 즉 석유부족이 아니라 정치적 두려움 때문에 이런 현상이 일어나고 있으므로 가격을 낮추기 위해 필요한 석유 증산량은 결국 (D)의 '아무도 모른다'가 가장 적절한 답이다.

04 ▶ ceiling n. 최고 한도(= top limit)

▶▶ 정답 01 (A) 02 (A) 03 (D) 04 (C)

동물의 몸은 무한정으로 작을 수 없다. (몸의 크기에 대한) 많은 제약은 그 어떤 형태에서나 몸의 크기가 작아짐에 따라 몸의 부피에 대한 표면적의 비율이 커진다는 사실에서 비롯된다. 이것은 온혈동물인 조류와 포유류에게는 중대한 문제인데, 이들은 크기가 작아질수록 열을 더 빨리 잃고, 이를 보충하기 위해 열을 더 빨리 발생시켜야 하기 때문이다. 작은 조류와 포유류는 몸의 신진대사를 절대한계까지(최대한으로) 실행한다. 크기에 대한 이런 한계의 전형적인 증거는 가장 작은 뾰족뒤쥐들에게 있는데, 이들은 피부를 통해 급속히 잃고 있는 에너지를 보충하기 위해 끊임없이 먹고 있다. 바로 이런 이유로 해서, 기록된 가장 작은 조류로 길이가 30mm인 쿠바의 벌새와 알려진 가장 작은 포유류로 유럽, 북아프리카, 동남아시아 전역에서 발견되는 40mm 길이의 에트루리아 피그미 뒤쥐는 알려진 가장 작은 파충류로 주둥이에서 항문까지의 길이가 단 14mm인 카리브해의 드와프 게코보다 훨씬 더 크다. 그러나 냉혈동물에게 열손실은 문제가 되지 않지만 수분손실은 문제가 된다. 이것은 양서류에게 특별한 문제이다. 만일 작은 개구리가 건조한 대기 속으로 나가면 금방 말라버릴 수 있다. 어류는 상황이 더 쉬워 보일 것이다. 냉혈동물인데다가 수상생활을 하니 열손실과 탈수는 문제가 아니다. 그러나 그런 동물의 크기에 작용하는 또 다른 제약이 있다. 몸 여기저기에 뼈가 몇 개 없어져도 아주 작은 동물에게는 그다지 차이가 없을 지도 모르지만, 그래도 모든 신체부위들은 제 기능을 해야 한다. 그리고 신체기관의 크기를 어느 정도로까지 작아지게 할 수 있는가 하는 것에는 근본적인 한계가 있다. 한 가지 한계는 신체기관은 세포로 만들어져 있는데 뇌와 눈 같은 복잡한 기관을 만드는 데는 일정 수의 세포가 필요하다는 것이다. 결국, 작은 동물의 기관이 큰 동물의 기관보다 몸 크기에 비해 상대적으로 더 큰 셈이다.

constraint n. 제약
ratio n. 비율
compensate v. 보충하다
metabolism n. 신진대사
shrew n. 뾰족뒤쥐
renew v. 갱신하다, 보충하다
hummingbird n. 벌새
reptile n. 파충류
snout n. 주둥이
anus n. 항문
amphibian n. 양서류
in a matter of minutes 곧, 금방
desiccation n. 건조, 탈수
kick in 효과를 내다, 작용하다
scale down 축소하다
upshot n. 결과, 결말, 결론

01 ▶ 마지막 문장의 upshot이 '결과, 결론'의 뜻이므로 빈칸은 앞의 내용을 결론짓도록 채워져야 한다. 앞 문장은 몸 크기를 아무리 작게 해도 신체기관은 일정 수의 세포가 필요하니 더 이상 작게 할 수 없다는 말이다. 따라서 작은 동물의 기관은 큰 동물의 기관보다 절대적으로는 더 작겠지만 몸 크기에 비해 상대적으로는 더 클 것이다.

02 ▶ '하루 중 활동하는 시간'은 주행성(diurnal)이냐 야행성(nocturnal)이냐 하는 문제로 몸 크기와는 무관하다.

03 ▶ 끝에서 아홉 번째 문장과 여덟 번째 문장에서 (C)의 '개구리는 양서류에 속하는 냉혈동물임'을 추론할 수 있다. (A) 부피(크기)가 같을 경우, 긴 동물이 표면적이 커서 체열을 더 빨리 잃는다. 구(球)의 표면적이 가장 작다(추울 때 몸을 웅크리는 이유). (B) 작을수록 체열을 더 빨리 잃고 그러면 열을 보충하기 위한 신진대사는 더 빨라야 할 것이다. (D) 뇌와 눈 같은 복잡한 기관을 만드는 데 일정 수의 세포가 필요하다고 했을 뿐 뇌와 눈의 세포 수가 같다는 말은 아니다.

04 ▶ 이 글은 동물의 몸이 왜 무한정으로 작아질 수는 없는지를 주관적인 생각이나 주장을 배제하고 객관적인 사실과 정보를 기초로 하여 설명한 글이므로 (D)가 적절하다.

» 정답 01 (B) 02 (A) 03 (C) 04 (D)

202   무자퍼 샤리프(Muzafer Sharif)는 집단 충성을 보여주기 위해 11세 소년들의 집단을 대상으로 아주 흥미로운 실험을 실시했다. 이 소년들은 성장배경이 상당히 유사했으며, 실험초기에는 누가 누구인지 전혀 몰랐다. 소년들은 샤리프의 감독 하에 실험계획에 참가하기 위해 여름캠프에 갔다.

보통 때와 마찬가지로 소년들은 자발적으로 우애집단을 신속하게 형성했다. 그리고 나서 샤리프는 소년들을 두 집단으로 임의 분할하고 각 집단이 비교적 멀리 떨어져서 지내도록 했다. 이 목적은 소년들이 형성한 유대감을 깨는 것이었다. 소년들은 곧 새 집단에서 새로운 유대를 형성했다. 그러자 샤리프는 두 집단을 운동과 게임으로 서로 경쟁하도록 했다. 소년들은 자신이 소속된 집단 내에서는 협동했으며 타 집단에는 적대적이었는데, 이런 타 집단에는 물론 이전 친구들이 몇 명 있었다. 실험을 절정에 이르게 하기 위해 샤리프는 비상상황을 연출했다. 즉, 급수를 중단했던 것이다. 이 집단들은 서로 협동하지 않을 수 없었고, 이 상황은 소년들이 최근에 서로에 대해 형성한 적대감을 잊게 하는 데 특히 성공적이었다. 한 집단에서 배척당했던 소년들은 바로 그 집단에 의해 갑작스럽게 환영받았다. 샤리프는 이 실험으로 집단체계의 형성에 기여할 수 있는 다른 요인들보다도 상황이 우선함을 평가할 수 있는 기회를 갖게 되었다. 그 영향력을 양으로 측정하는 것은 불가능하다고 하지만 상황이 집단 역학과 아무런 상관이 없다고 주장하는 것은 그야말로 어리석은 짓이 될 것이다.

demonstrate v. 증명하다
homogeneous a. 동종[동질]의
supervision n. 관리, 감독
norm n. 기준; 규범
spontaneously ad. 자발적으로
randomly ad. 닥치는 대로, 임의로
culminate v. 완결시키다; 절정을 이루게 하다
oblige v. 강요하다, 억지로 시키다
banish v. 내쫓다(from)
dominion n. 지배권; 통제
quantify v. 양을 정하다; 양을 재다
utter a. 전적인, 완전한
stupidity n. 우둔, 어리석음
group dynamics 집단 역학

01 ▶ 특정한 상황을 의도적으로 일으켜 집단 내 구성원들의 반응을 보고 있으므로 '상황이 집단 역학에 미치는 영향'이 정답이 된다.

02 ▶ cut off는 '수도나 전기 공급을 끊는다'라는 의미이며 앞문장의 부가 설명인 응급상황 중의 하나가 된다. banish는 전치사 from[out of]과 함께 쓰이며 '추방하다', '배척하다'등의 뜻으로 쓰인다.

03 ▶ 샤리프는 이 실험을 통해 양으로 측정할 수는 없지만, 다른 요인들보다 상황이 집단 체계 형성에 우선적으로 작용한다는 것을 알게 되었다고 했으므로, '상황이 집단 역학과 아무런 상관이 없다'는 언급은 완전히 생각 없는(utter stupidity) 주장이 될 것이다.

04 ▶ 집단 내 소년들은 주어지는 다양한 상황에 따라 유대를 형성하다가도 깨어버리기도 하는 등 환경에 잘 적응하고 있다는 것을 알 수 있다.

▶▶ 정답 01 (C) 02 (D) 03 (D) 04 (C)

최근 발견된 행성 글리제(Gliese) 581c는 항성으로부터 액체 상태의 물을 가질 수 있는 알맞은 거리에 떨어져 있기 때문에 외계인을 찾아 나서는 사람들에게 가장 큰 희망이 될지 모른다. 제네바 관측소의 스위스 팀이 내린 결론들 중 하나는 지구와 같은 작은 행성들은 아마도 흔히 존재하고 있을 것이라는 것이다. 그렇다면 항성들 사이에 생명체 또한 흔히 있다는 것인가? 또한 이것이 우리에게 중요한 것일까?

문명이 발생된 이래로, 하늘의 지위는 우주 속에서 자신의 위치에 대해 인류가 갖고 있던 개념에서 중추적인 역할을 했다. 중세 시대의 "세상", 즉 우주는 달, 그 밖의 여러 행성들, 태양 및 그 가장 멀리 바깥쪽 하늘에 박혀 있는 별들이 있는 일련의 동심원의 천구(天球) 내에 지구의 천구가 에워싸여 있는 채로 이루어져 있는 것으로 여겨졌다. 그 너머는 신의 영역이었다. 별들이 있는 천구는 밤하늘에서 별자리가 회전하는 것을 설명하기 위해 생각해 낸 것이었다. 이것은 인류가 중심을 장악하고 있는 벽으로 둘러싸인 아늑한 세상이었던 것이다. 하지만 코페르니쿠스는 태양이 중심에 있는 태양계가 지구로 하여금 태양을 공전하게 한다고 하여 중세시대 우주의 개념을 뒤엎어버렸다. 코페르니쿠스의 주장처럼 항성들이 아닌 지구가 돌고 있는 것이면 중세시대의 그 모든 천구들은 필요가 없었다. 현재 지구가 중심인 우주를 옹호할 사람은 거의 없을 것이지만, 많은 사람들에게 있어 인류는 신의 중심적인 관심사로 남아 있다. 글리제 581c와 그 밖의 다른 세계가 생명체로 넘쳐나고 있다면, 이러한 믿음은 지켜지기 어려울 지도 모른다. 그러나 우주에 산다는 것이 더욱 흥미로운 일이 될 것이다.

harbour v. 감추다; 숨기다
dawn n. 새벽; 처음, 시작
concentric a. 중심이 같은
outermost a. 가장 바깥쪽의
firmament n. 하늘; 창공
sphere n. 천체; 영역
nocturnal a. 밤의; 야간의
revolution n. 회전, 공전
teem v. 충만하다(with)

01 ▶ 'cocoon(고치로 둘러싸다, 둘러싸서 호위하다)'은 protect(보호하다)와 일맥상통한다. 이 단어가 제시된 후의 문장 This was ~ the centre에서 a cosy walled-in이 단어의 의미를 유추하는 데 단서가 된다.

02 ▶ 코페르니쿠스의 이론에는 천구라는 개념이 필요하지 않다.

03 ▶ 중세에 믿었던 기존 이론과 다른 이론을 제시한 내용이 바로 이어져 나오므로 중세의 이론을 뒤집었다는 문장이 들어가야 한다.

04 ▶ "외계에 생명체가 존재한다면 이 우주에 사는 것이 흥미로운 일이 될지 모른다"로부터 외계 생명체에 대해 '기대를 가지고 있다(hopeful)'는 것을 알 수 있다.

» 정답 01 (B) 02 (C) 03 (A) 04 (C)

소비자들이 불경기를 헤쳐 나가기 위해 잔뜩 벼르고 있는 상황에서 어느 환경 단체가 한 가지 제안을 했다. 생수가 아닌 수돗물을 마시라는 것이다. 미국 환경 운동 단체(EWG)는 일부 생수가 "수돗물과 전혀 차이가 없다"고 비난하는 보고서를 발표했다. 그리고 그 단체는 일부 유명 상표에서 비료 찌꺼기, 진통제, 그리고 그 밖의 다른 화학물질들을 발견했다.

많은 생수가 매혹적인 광고에서 장담하는 만큼 깨끗할지도 모르지만, 진짜 문제는 깨끗한 생수와 그렇지 못한 생수를 구별하는 것이다. 공공 상수도는 연방 정부에 의해 규제되지만, 생수는 그렇지 않다. 대부분의 업체를 대표하는 미국 생수 협회(IBWA)는 오염물질이 없도록 하는 자발적인 기준을 가지고 있다. 협회는 제조업자들에게 소비자가 전화해서 문의했을 때 물 안에 무엇이 들어있는지에 관한 적절한 정보를 공개하기를 권하고 있다.(그러나 강제 사항은 아니다.)

연방 정부는 모든 상수도 회사로 하여금 1년에 한 번씩 물 안에 무엇이 들어 있으며 그것이 연방 기준과 부합하는지 소비자에게 알리도록 하고 있다. 이런 공공 보고서는 항상 마땅히 유용해야하는 만큼 유용하지는 않다. 어떤 보고서는 깨알만한 크기로 인쇄되어 있고 화학자들이나 가장 잘 이해할 수준으로 돼 있다. 하지만 적어도 그것들은 쉽사리 입수가 가능하며, 생수의 세부사항도 마찬가지로 공적으로 이용할 수 있도록 해야 한다. 여분의 비용이 지불되는데다 더욱 깨끗하다는 보증이 있으므로, 생수는 수도꼭지에서 나오는 덜 비싼 물만큼 좋거나 그보다 더욱 좋아야 한다. 그리고 소비자들은 이를 증명하는 공인된 데이터를 볼 수 있어야 한다.

hunker down 단단히 벼르다
cope with 대처하다
tap water 수돗물
fertilizer n. 비료
residue n. 찌꺼기
medication n. 약물
alluring a. 매혹적인
commercial n. 광고
contaminant n. 오염물질
pertinent a. 적절한
certified a. 공인된

01 ▶ 앞에서 필자는 생수의 깨끗함에 의문을 제기하면서 공공 상수도는 정보를 공적으로 제공하지만 생수는 그렇지 않다고 설명하고 있다. 이와 함께 마지막 문단에서 생수가 깨끗해야할 뿐만 아니라 거기에 대한 정보 역시 공개되어야 한다고 주장하고 있다. 따라서 이 글의 의도는 "생수의 깨끗함에 대한 정보가 제공되어야 한다고 주장하기 위해서"이다.

02 ▶ 모든 수도 회사가 연방 정부에 의해 독점되어야 한다는 것은 본문에서 추론할 수 없다.

03 ▶ 경제 위기라는 상황 속에서 소비자들에게 제안했으므로 돈을 아낄 수 있는 제안을 했을 것이다. 또한 미국 환경 단체가 생수와 수돗물이 별반 차이가 없음을 확인했으므로 물을 사먹는 대신 수돗물을 마시라고 제안했을 것이다.

04 ▶ 너무 작은 글씨로 어렵게 써서 "평범한 사람들(mediocrities)이 이해하기 어렵다"는 뜻으로 볼 수 있다.

» 정답   01 (D)   02 (C)   03 (C)   04 (B)

나는 센트럴 파크에서 뉴욕을 여름에도 잠시 살기 좋은 장소로 만드는 어느 멋진 서늘한 저녁 시간에 사내 소프트볼 경기를 하고 있었다. 나는 멀리 우익수로 위치하였기에 자연스럽게 눈앞에 있는 경기보다는 다른 생각을 하게 되었다. 나는 산들바람에 흔들거리는 큰 나무들을 바라보았고 갑자기 두려움에 사로잡혔다. 재앙이 오고 있고 이것은 눈에 보이는 모든 것을 파괴해 버린 나무들의 탓이다. 다른 것과 마찬가지로 이렇게 생각하게 된 이유는 나이트 샤말란(M. Night Shyamalan) 때문인데, 인류에게 큰 위협을 가하는 자연 재해를 피해 다니는 어느 가족에 대한 공포스릴러물인 그의 가장 최신 영화 <해프닝>을 본 사람이라면 그 이유를 알 것이다.

내가 보는 영화들만이 나의 생각을 음울하게 만드는 것은 아니다. 환경에 관한 보도가 당신에게 종말론적인 사고방식을 갖게 한다. 녹고 있는 남극의 빙하와 상승하는 해수면, 불타고 있는 우림, 오염된 중국의 대도시들, 지난 6천만년 동안 예상했던 비율보다 최대 1만 배까지 빠른 비율로 멸종되고 있는 동물들이 그것이다. 기후변화에 대해 말하자면 단순히 기온 상승이나 변화된 풍경만을 이야기하는 것이 아니다. 우리가 모두 알고 있는 인류 문명의 종말을 이야기하고 있는 것이다. 우리는 일상 속 소비생활을 통해 우리 스스로 종말을 불러오는 상황을 만들고 있다고 두려워하고 있다. <간단히 말해, 차를 움직이고 에어컨을 켤 때마다 우리 모두 자기 무덤을 파고 있다는 것이다.> 지구 온난화가 제대로 시작되면 결국에는 막을 도리가 없기 때문에 매우 끔찍하다. 그러나 두려움은 좋은 동기부여가 되지 않는데, 특히 기후 변화를 늦추기 위해 만들어야 할 수십 년이 걸릴 사회적 변화에 관해서는 더욱 그러하다. 우리가 필요한 것은 이산화탄소가 적은 세계가 단순한 생존을 넘어서 우리에게 이익을 가져다 줄 것이라는 적극성이며, 우리에게 전해져야 할 메시지는 바로 이런 것이다.

---

temporarily ad. 일시적으로
station v. 배치하다
sway v. 흔들리다
instantly ad. 당장에, 즉시
grip v. 꽉 쥐다; 마음을 사로잡다
dread n. 공포; 불안
on the run 달려서, 도주하여; 부산을 떠는
paranoid a. 편집성의; 편협한
cinematic a. 영화의
torch v. 태우다; 방화하다
megalopolis n. 거대도시; 인구 과밀지대
extinct a. 꺼진; 멸종한
alter v. 바꾸다
sin n. 죄; 죄악; 과실
dig v. 파다; 채굴하다

01 ▶ 끔찍한 자연재해를 다룬 영화에 관한 자신의 일화를 소개하며 '일어날지 모르는 종말에 대해 두려워하는 개인적 모습'을 예로 나타내고 있다.

02 ▶ 두 번째 문단 다섯 번째 문장을 참고한다. 지구에서 일어나는 현상들에 대한 보고서로 인해 사람들이 '종말론적인 사고'를 가지게 된다는 것을 알 수 있다.

03 ▶ Put it simply에서 앞서 언급한 내용을 다시 설명하고자 하는 것을 알 수 있다. 자동차 운전과 에어컨 사용에 대해 언급하며 스스로의 무덤을 파고 있다고 한 것은 일상생활을 통해 최후를 맞이할 조건을 만들고 있다는 내용과 유사하다. 자동차 운전과 에어컨 사용은 일상생활이며, digging our own graves는 the end of human civilization을 가리킨다. 따라서 (B)가 정답으로 적절하다.

04 ▶ 두 번째 문단 마지막 부분에서 '현재 일어나고 있는 현상들에 대해 두려워하는 것은 좋은 해결 방안을 제시할 수 없으므로 희망을 가지고 방안을 제시하자'고 하였다. 따라서 글쓴이의 의견으로는 "두려움이 희망을 가로막게 해서는 안 된다"가 가장 적절하다.

» 정답 01 (A) 02 (D) 03 (B) 04 (C)

206	그것은 세계 불가사의의 하나로 널리 여겨지며 연간 수백만 명의 관광객들을 끌어들이고 있지만 베니스 시는 수면 위에 떠있을 수 있는 능력을 위협하는 계속되는 문제에 직면하고 있다. 도시의 범람문제는 잘 알려져 있다. 매년 물이 도시의 유명한 거리로 들이닥치면서 역사적 건물에 엄청난 손실을 가하고 종종 귀중한 예술품에 피해를 입힌다. 그러나 베니스는 또한 점차 감소하는 지역주민 인구와 그들이 보조를 맞출 수 없다고 주장하는 증가하는 관광객의 유입 문제를 겪고 있다. 위기에 처한 베니스는 지역주민 인구의 두 배가 되는 6만 명까지 관광객들이 언제든 그 도시에 들어올 수 있다고 말한다. <이 숫자는 비엔날레나 도시의 유명 영화축제와 같은 대규모 문화 행사기간 동안 훨씬 증가할 수 있다.> "더 이상의 지역주민들은 없고, 더 이상의 지역 문화는 없다, 베니스(베네치아풍)의 삶의 방식은 없다, 도시 전체가 (도시라기보다는) 매일 더 박물관과 같다."고 지역단체의 대변인인 마테오 세키(Matteo Secchi)가 말했다. 세키와 그의 지지자들은 지역인구가 17만 5천도 안되었던 1951년 이후 급격하게 감소한 베니스의 인구를 유지하기 위해 투쟁하고 있다. 인구가 6만 명 이하로 감소한 것으로 추정된 2009년에 세키와 다른 지역 주민들은 도시가 죽었다고 느껴 상징적인 장례 행렬을 연출했다. 그러나 세키는 관광객들을 비난하지 않는다. 그는 도시가 살아남기 위해서 관광객이 필요하다는 점을 인식하고 있다. 그와 그의 지지자들은 도시의 산업을 관광으로부터 벗어나 다양화함으로써 보다 소수의 주민들만 유럽본토의 일자리를 얻기 위해 베니스를 떠나도록 조르지오 오르소니(Giorgio Orsoni) 베니스 시장에게 로비를 하고 있다.

wonder n. 불가사의한 것
flooding n. 범람
surge v. 밀어닥치다
dwindle v. 점차 감소하다
influx n. 유입
keep up with ~을 따라가다
swell v. 증가하다
biennale n. 격년행사; 비엔날레
spokesman n. 대변인
funeral procession 장례 행렬
diversify v. 다양화하다
mock a. 거짓된, 가짜의; 모의의
job-seeker n. 구직자
in jeopardy 위기에 처한
restore v. 복원하다; 회복시키다
preserve v. 보존하다

01 ▶ 주어진 문장의 Those numbers는 내용상 대규모 문화 행사를 보기 위해 베니스를 방문하는 관광객의 숫자를 지칭한다. 따라서 일반적인 관광객 수에 대해 언급하고 있는 문장의 뒤인 [II]에 오는 것이 가장 적절하다.

02 ▶ 본문의 끝 부분에서 관광객을 비난하지는 않으며 도시의 생존을 위해 그들이 필요하다는 점을 인식하고 있다 했으므로 (D)는 잘못된 진술이다. 상징적인 장례 행렬을 연출했다고 했으므로 (A)는 사실이며, 지역주민 인구의 두 배가 되는 6만 명까지 관광객들이 베니스를 방문할 수 있다고 했으므로 (B)도 사실이다. 또한 관광업을 제외한 다양하지 않은 도시의 산업으로 인해 사람들이 유럽본토로 일을 구하기 위해 떠난다고 했으므로 (C)도 올바른 진술이다.

03 ▶ 본문에서는 '수면 상승'과 '지역주민과 관광객 수의 불균형으로 인한 도시 몰락위기'라는 베니스가 처한 두 가지 문제점에 대해 얘기했다. 따라서 제목으로는 이 두 문제점을 모두 포괄하는 (C)가 적절하다. (C)에서 Real Venice는 베니스의 문화와 삶의 방식이 보존돼야 한다는 점을, Afloat는 수면상승 문제가 해결돼야 한다는 점을 의미한다.

04 ▶ wreak havoc on ~에 엄청난 피해[손실]를 입히다(= ravage)

》 정답 01 (B) 02 (D) 03 (C) 04 (A)

옛날 옛적에 우리는 소수의 사람들이 다수의 사람들에게 정보를 전달하는 방송 사회에서 살았다. 그 정보는 우리가 무엇을 보고 읽거나 듣는지와 우리가 무엇을 보고 읽거나 듣지 말아야 하는지를 결정하는 라디오 방송국, 신문사, TV 방송국과 같은 정보의 누설을 통제하는 사람들에 의해 규제되었다. 과거에는 (사상·견해 등의) 주류가 있었지 소수 비주류는 없었다. 하지만 그리고 나서 월드 와이드 웹이 등장했고 그러한 정보통제자들을 날려 보냈다. 갑자기 컴퓨터와 인터넷 연결을 갖춘 누구나 대화에 참여할 수 있게 되었다. 셀 수 없는 견해들이 꽃피었다. 더 이상 주류는 존재하지 않았고 대신 인터넷 사용자들이 자유롭게 헤엄칠 수 있는 정보의 바다가 생겨났다. 그것은 일라이 파리서(Eli Pariser)가 그의 신간서적『The Filter Bubble(펭귄 출판사)』에서 주장하듯이 그것이 더 이상 사실이 아니라는 점을 제외하면 훌륭한 생각이다. 눈에 보이지 않게 지난 몇 년 동안 인터넷 거인 페이스북과 구글의 주도 하에 주요 소셜 네트워크들과 검색 엔진들이 그들의 검색 결과를 개별 인터넷 사용자에 맞춰 조정하기 시작했다. 이는 개인화라고 불리는데 겉으로 보기에는 마치 좋은 것처럼 들린다. 한때 구글이 모든 사람에게 동일한 알고리즘에 기초해 검색 결과를 전달했던 것이, 이제는 우리가 큰 (검색) 박스에 어구를 입력할 때 보게 되는 것은 우리가 누구인지, 우리가 어디에 있는지 그리고 우리가 무엇인지에 의해 좌우된다. 페이스북은 페이스북의 모든 중요 뉴스 피드(투고된 뉴스의 내용을 한 뉴스 서버에서 다른 뉴스 서버로 전달하는 것)에 대해 오래전부터 구글과 같이 해왔다. 당신은 마크 주커버그(Mark Zuckerberg)와 그의 회사가 당신에 대해 가지고 있는 자료를 토대로 상이한 상태 업데이트와 이야기들이 (검색 결과의) 최상위로 올라가는 것을 보게 될 것이다.

---

gatekeeper n. 문지기; 정보통제자
transmit v. (지식 등을) 전하다, 전파시키다
viewpoint n. 관점, 견해
mainstream n. 주류; 대세
blow away ~을 날려 보내다
invisibly ad. 눈에 보이지 않게
behemoth n. 거인, 거대한 짐승; (기계 등의) 강력한 것
personalization n. 개인화
algorithm n. 알고리즘, 연산
identical a. 동일한
term n. 용어
status n. 상태, 지위
flourish v. 번창하다, 잘 자라다
dwindle v. (점점) 줄어들다
manipulate v. 조작하다
shrivel v. 쪼글쪼글해지다, 쪼글쪼글하게 만들다
conceal v. 감추다, 숨기다

01 ▶ 본문을 크게 두 부분으로 나눌 경우, 과거 방송 사회에 살던 시절 월드 와이드 웹의 등장으로 인터넷 사용자들이 자유롭게 정보의 바다를 헤엄칠 수 있던 긍정적 내용의 부분과 일라이 파리서의『필터 버블』을 중심으로 앞서 나온 긍정적 내용을 반박하며 개인화된 맞춤형 검색을 이야기 하는 부분으로 나눌 수 있다. 따라서 ④를 기준으로 나누는 것이 적절하다.

02 ▶ 이 글에서는 맞춤형 검색(customized search)에 대해 부정적인 시각을 보이고 있으므로 (A)가 정답으로 적절하다.

03 ▶ 첫째 빈칸 앞의 문장에서 컴퓨터와 인터넷 연결만 갖추면 누구나 대화에 참여할 수 있게 되었다고 했으므로 셀 수 없이 많은 견해들이 '꽃피었다(번영했다)'고 하는 것이 자연스럽다. 또한 소셜 네트워크들과 검색 엔진들이 검색 결과를 개별 인터넷 사용자에 '맞춰 ~하기' 시작했는데 이를 개인화라 부르며 구글과 페이스북이 개별 이용자의 정보에 따라 다른 검색 결과를 보여주는 예를 들어주고 있다. 따라서 둘째 빈칸에는 '(남에게) 맞추다'를 뜻하는 단어가 적절하다.

04 ▶ 일라이 파리서는 구글과 페이스북의 예를 들며 개인화라고 불리는 맞춤형 검색이 겉으로 보기에만 좋은 것이라고 했다. 그렇다면 본문의 다음 단락에 이어질 내용으로는 이러한 개인화된 검색이 좋지 않다는 주장에 대한 근거로 맞춤형 검색, 즉 검색 정보를 개인에 따라 여과해서 보여주는 시스템의 부정적 영향이 자연스럽다.

》 정답 01 (B) 02 (A) 03 (D) 04 (C)

208   영국의 낭만주의 예술은 풍경화에서 가장 큰 성공을 거두었다. 존 크롬(John Crome)은 빛과 공기를 강조함으로써 영국식 스타일의 토대를 마련했다. 그러나 이 시기에 있어 가장 유명한 두 명의 영국 풍경화가는 존 콘스터블(John Constable)과 터너(J. M Turner)였다. 그들은 안개가 자욱한 영국의 분위기를 그리는 데 있어 대가(大家)들이었다. 콘스터블은 색채가 풍부하고 그윽했다. 그는 점묘 화법으로 그림을 그린 최초의 화가였다. 이러한 기법 덕분에 그의 그림은 유난히 밝다. 드라크로아(Delacroix)는 이러한 기술에 크게 감탄했으며, 이것은 나중에 프랑스 인상파 화가들이 비슷한 효과를 만들어내는 데 사용되었다. 자신의 색채 이용으로 가장 잘 알려져 있긴 하지만, 콘스터블은 또한 형태와 구성에 대한 해박한 지식으로도 높이 평가되고 있다. 터너는 많은 풍경화의 옛 대가들을 연구했다. 그가 가장 큰 영향을 받은 것은 17세기 프랑스의 풍경화가인 끌로드 로라잉(Claude Lorrain)에게서였다. 그는 시원하고 청명한 하늘을 자주 그렸는데, 이것이 터너에게 깊은 인상을 주었다. 터너는 그러한 하늘을 색과 빛이 그림 전체에 퍼져 있는 극적인 열기로 승화시켰다. 터너의 그림에서 소용돌이치는 움직임 속에 있는 습기를 머금은 구름, 물, 그리고 채색된 빛은 자연의 거대한 힘을 나타내는 상징이 되었다.

---

emphasis n. 강조
portray v. 그리다; 묘사하다
daub n. 칠, 칠하기
broken color 점묘 (화법)
luminous a. 빛을 내는, 빛나는
intensify v. 강렬하게 하다
fever n. 열병; 열중, 열광
swirl v. 소용돌이치다

01 ▶ 존 크롬이 영국식 스타일의 토대를 마련했다.

02 ▶ '콘스터블은 점묘화법으로 그림을 그린 최초의 화가였으며, 이 기법은 나중에 프랑스 인상파 화가들이 비슷한 효과를 만들어내는데 사용되었다'고 돼 있다.

03 ▶ vaporous a. 증기 비슷한, 증발기가 많은, 안개 자욱한(= misty)

04 ▶ '터너의 그림에서 소용돌이치는 움직임 속에 있는 습기를 머금은 구름, 물, 그리고 채색된 빛은 자연의 거대한 힘을 나타내는 상징이 되었다'고 했다. 이는 그의 그림이 움직임을 내포하고 있는 역동적인 그림이었다는 의미로 해석할 수 있다.

》 정답 01 (B) 02 (C) 03 (B) 04 (D)

녹아가는 눈과 합쳐져서 지난달 미(美) 중서부 지방 전역을 찢어놓았던 엄청난 토네이도와 폭풍우는 미시시피 강을 터질 듯이 가득 차게 만들어 놓았다. 대피 소동과 강을 따라 발생한 대규모 범람 속에서, 전문가들은 기록이 계속 깨지고 있다는 것은 알고 있지만, 사태가 진정될 때까지는 얼마나 많은 강물이 실질적으로 강둑을 터지게 했는지와 같은 이번 홍수(범람)의 총규모를 알 수는 없을 것이라고 말한다.

"미시시피 강 유역 전역에는 언제나 비가 오는데, 비가 시간적으로 분산돼서 내리면 아무런 문제가 생기지 않는다. 문제가 생기게 되는 것은 바로 비가 동시에 내리고 여러 강줄기들이 전체 하천계의 총수량을 증가시킬 때이다."라고 테네시 주 멤피스에 있는 미 국립기상청의 과학운영책임자인 톰 살렘(Tom Salem)이 말했다.

미시시피 강을 따라 위치해 있는 일부 지역들에서는 지난 4월 (한 달) 동안 10~20인치(25.4~50.8센티미터)의 강우가 관측됐다고 미 국립기상청의 수문학자(水文學者) 로이스 폰테노트(Royce Fontenot)가 말했다. 강의 수위가 현재 기록적인 수준에 다다르고 있는 반면, 피해 규모(정도)는 범람이 그친 이후까지는 알 수 없는데, 그 시기는 6월이 넘어갈 수 있을 것이라고 폰테노트는 말했다. 우리는 얼마나 많은 강물이 미시시피 강으로부터 육지로 넘쳐흘렀는지 알 수 없다. 이것은 우리가 실시간으로(즉시) 알 수 있는 것이 아니다. 우리는 사후에 범람 지역을 조사할 필요가 있을 것이다.

---

deadly a. 치명적인; 심한
rainstorm n. 폭풍우
burst at the seams ~이 터질 듯이 가득 차다
evacuation n. 피난, 대피; 철수
breach v. (성벽·방어선 등을) 돌파하다
quiet v. 잠잠해지다, 진정되다
river basin (강의) 유역
hydrologist n. 수문학자(水文學者)
overflow v. 넘치다, 범람하다
survey v. 개관하다; 측량하다; 조사하다
after the fact 사후에

01 ▶ 첫째, 셋째 단락에서 기록들이 계속해서 깨지고 있으며 기록적인 수준에 다다르고 있다 했으므로, 홍수가 예상되는 지역의 사람들이 대피계획을 마련할 것임을 추론할 수 있다.

02 ▶ ④의 경우, 관계부사 다음에 불완전한 문장이 제시돼 있는 점이 옳지 않다. 이것을 계속적 용법의 관계대명사 which로 고친다.

03 ▶ 둘째 단락에서 알 수 있듯이 미시시피 강 범람의 원인은 단순히 비가 많이 와서가 아니라 (동시다발적인) 호우의 집중 때문이다. 따라서 빈칸에는 '대량, 과다'를 뜻하는 (D)의 abundance가 아닌 '집결, 집중'을 뜻하는 (B)의 concentration이 적절하다.

04 ▶ 빈칸 앞의 내용이 미시시피 강의 범람에 관한 것이므로 빈칸에는 강물이 강둑을 비유적으로 (넘지 말아야 될 선을 위반하고) '넘어섰다, 돌파했다'고 하는 것이 자연스럽다. 따라서 (A)가 정답으로 적절하며 나머지 보기에 대한 근거는 본문에서 찾을 수 없다.

» 정답 01 (C) 02 (D) 03 (B) 04 (A)

그 메시지는 일본에서 늘상 인터넷에 올려지는 다른 많은 솔로들의 광고만큼이나 해롭지 않게 시작되었다. 도쿄 출신의 그 외로운 남자 대학생은 "동반자를 찾습니다."라고 썼던 것이다. 그런데 그는 꿈의 데이트 상대를 찾고 있는 게 아니었다. "모든 걸 다 준비해두었고 이제 수면제만 구하면 돼요."라고 게시된 글은 끝맺었던 것이다. 2주일 후인 5월 21일에 그 대학생은 군마 현의 어느 숲길의 차 안에서 죽은 채로 발견되었다. 그와 함께 다른 두 젊은이의 시체도 있었는데, 그들은 그가 인터넷으로 초대한 데 대해 분명한 답을 보낸 후 일산화탄소 중독으로 집단자살을 벌였던 것이다.

매년 자살하는 3만 명의 일본인 가운데는 실직한 중년 샐러리맨이라는 지금까지의 전형에 더 이상 맞지 않는 예가 많이 있다. 남녀 젊은이들 사이에서 자살이 늘고 있으며, 인구통계상의 변화와 더불어 새로운 자기파멸의 방식이 찾아오고 있다. 젊은이들은 그들의 쓸쓸한 여정에 기꺼이 동행해줄 자포자기한 동조자들과 접속하기 위해 자살 사이트라는 기이한 인터넷 탈선 수단을 이용하고 있다. 2월에는 모두 20대인 두 명의 여자와 한 명의 남자가 자살 사이트에서 만나 사이타마에 있는 한 아파트에서 자살했다. 그 후 지금까지 유사한 사건이 일곱 차례 있었고 14명이 사망했다.

사이타마에서의 자살 희생자들이 만났던 웹사이트인 신쥬 게이지반(자살 계약 게시판 서비스)는 폐쇄되었지만 다른 많은 사이트들은 그대로 남아있다. "젊은이들이 인간관계를 구축하기 위해 사용하는 방법이 달라졌어요."라고 Chubu Gakuin 대학 정신의학 교수인 타케히코 키까와는 말한다. 그리고 그것은 그 관계가 필경 오래가지 않을 관계인 경우도 마찬가지이다. 일부 자살 희생자들은 운명의 날까지도 결코 직접 만나지 않는다. 그럼에도 불구하고 그들은 모두 서로를 묶어주는 강력한 끈을 공유하고 있는데, 그것은 혼자 죽는 것에 대한 두려움인 것이다.

---

routinely ad. 일상적으로
companion n. 동료, 동반자
undergrad n. 대학생, 학부 재학생
sleeping pill 수면제
collective suicide 집단 자살
carbon monoxide 일산화탄소
poisoning n. 독살; 중독
stereotype n. 고정관념, 판에 박힌 문구
demographics n. 인구 통계
aberration n. 상궤를 벗어남, 탈선
desperate a. 필사적인; 자포자기의, 절망적인
bleak a. 쓸쓸한
bulletin board 게시판
psychiatry n. 정신병학, 정신의학

01 ▶ 인터넷을 통해 동반자살을 할 사람을 구하는 새로운 풍조에 대해 이야기하고 있다.

02 ▶ 혼자 사는 사람이 동반자를 찾는 것은 불순한 의도가 전혀 없다고 할 수 있다.

03 ▶ ㉮, ㉯, ㉰는 모두 동반자살을 의미하는 반면, ㉱는 혼자 죽는 것에 대한 두려움을 의미한다.

04 ▶ 집단 자살이 서로 아는 사람들 사이에서 이루어지는지의 여부는 본문을 통해 추론할 수 없다. 본문에서는 오히려 서로 모르는 사람들의 동반자살을 이야기하고 있다.

》 정답 01 (B) 02 (C) 03 (D) 04 (B)

사회에 노출되고 그 경험을 흡수하는 과정 전체를 '사회화'라고 한다. 물론, 어떤 특정 개인의 사회화는 그들 가족의 사회경제적 계층과 종교적 신념, 정치적 견해 그리고 다른 요소들에 의해 크게 영향을 받지만, 아마 현대 사회에서 가장 중요한 신념을 만드는 것은 — 그리고 긍정적인 면이 거의 없는 것은 — 텔레비전일 것이다. 보통의 미국인들이 고등학교를 졸업할 때까지, 그들은 학교에서 11,000시간을 보내는 데 반해 텔레비전을 보는 데는 22,000시간 이상을 보낸다. 텔레비전은 시청자들 특히 나이가 어린 시청자들에게 여러 측면에서 부정적인 영향을 미친다. 첫째로, 그들을 방관자의 입장에 둠으로써, 텔레비전은 비활동성을 조장한다. 즉, 만족과 재미가 단지 수동적으로 받아들여지는 것이라는 걸 암시한다. 둘째로, 나이가 어린 사람들에게 18살까지 대략 평균 750,000편의 광고를 퍼부음으로써 텔레비전 시청이 소비자 가치를 무비판적으로 받아들이는 것을 촉진한다. 텔레비전을 시청하는 것은 또한 자기방종, 충동성을 촉진하며, 일시적인 만족감을 추구하도록 만든다. 세 번째로, 빈번한 장면 전환과 프로그램을 방해하는 광고를 함으로써, 텔레비전은 나이가 어린 사람들이 집중 기간을 발달시키는 것을 방해한다. 마지막으로, 토크쇼 사회자와 다른 유명 연예인들을 권위자로 제시함으로써, 텔레비전은 법적인 전문가와 단순한 매체 인사를 구분할 줄 아는 사람들의 능력을 손상시킨다.

acculturation n. 사회화, 문화적 적응
socioeconomic a. 사회 경제적인
spectator n. 방관자; 관찰자
passively ad. 수동적으로
bombard v. (질문·비난 등을) 퍼붓다[쏟아 붓다]
uncritical a. 무비판적인
self-indulgence n. 자기방종
impulsiveness n. 충동성
gratification n. 만족
undermine v. 몰래 손상시키다, 서서히 해치다
complimentary a. 무료의; 칭찬하는

01 ▶ 첫 번째 문장 The whole process of being exposed to society — and of absorbing that experience — is called "acculturation" 참고. acculturation은 사회에 노출되고 그 경험을 흡수하는 과정 전체라고 했으므로 정답은 (B)이다.

02 ▶ (A), (D) 본문 14번째 줄에 Second, by bombarding young people … uncritical acceptance of consumer values 참고. (B) 끝에서 5번째 줄 television prevents the development of young people's attention spans 참고.

03 ▶ 이 글은 텔레비전이 나이가 어린 시청자들에게 끼치는 부정적인 영향을 네 가지로 나누어 설명하고 있는 글로 어조는 논쟁적이다.

04 ▶ 필자는 미국 학생들이 텔레비전을 너무 많이 시청한다고 이야기하였으므로 미국 학생들이 텔레비전을 덜 보고 공부를 더 많이 해야 한다는 의견에 동의할 것이다.

》 정답 01 (B) 02 (C) 03 (A) 04 (C)

'거짓말 탐지기'는 진실을 탐지할 수 있는 확실한 방법을 원하는 정부, 경찰서, 사업체에 의해 사용되고 있지만 그 결과가 항상 정확한 것은 아니다. 거짓말 탐지기는 감정 탐지기라 부르는 것이 적절한데, 왜냐하면 말하고 있는 것과 상반되는 신체적 변화를 측정하는 데 그 목적을 두고 있기 때문이다. 거짓말탐지기는 심장 박동수, 호흡, 혈압, 피부의 전기 활성도(전기 피부 반응, GSR) 등을 기록한다. 거짓말 탐지검사의 첫 단계에서는, 몸을 기계와 전기선으로 연결하고서 몇 가지 중립적인 질문을 (이름이 무엇입니까? 어디에 살고 있습니까? 등) 받게 된다. 이 때의 신체 반응이 다음에 실시되는 검사를 평가하는 기준이 된다. 그런 다음, 중립적인 질문들 사이에 몇 가지 중대한 질문(언제 은행을 털었습니까?)을 하게 된다. 그것은 만약 당신이 유죄라면 아무리 부인하려 하더라도 몸이 사실을 밝혀줄 거라는 가정을 전제로 하고 있다. 당신의 심장 박동수, 호흡, 피부 전기활성도가 죄를 캐묻는 질문에 대답할 때 급작스레 변하게 될 것이다.

이론상은 그러하다. 하지만 심리학자들은 거짓말 탐지기가 전혀 신뢰할만하지 않다는 것을 알게 되었다. 대부분의 신체 변화는 모든 감정에 걸쳐 동일하게 나타나기 때문에, 기계는 당신이 죄의식을 느끼고 있는지, 화가 났는지, 신경이 곤두서 있는지, 스릴을 느끼고 있는지, 혹은 활기찬 하루를 보낸 뒤 기분이 좋아졌는지를 구별하지 못한다. 결백한 사람들도 거짓말 탐지기 조사를 받는 모든 절차에 대해서도 긴장하고 예민한 반응을 보일 수도 있다. 그들이 '은행'이라는 특정 단어에 대해, 꼭 은행을 털었기 때문이 아니라 최근에 부도수표를 발행했기 때문에 생리적 반응을 보일 수도 있다는 것이다. 두 경우 모두에 있어서, 기계는 '거짓말'로 기록을 한다. 정반대의 실수 역시 흔하다. 거짓말이 습관이 돼 있는 사람들은 아무렇지 않은 듯 거짓말을 할 수 있고, 어떤 사람들은 중립적인 질문을 받는 동안 흥미진진한 경험에 대해 생각하거나 근육을 긴장시킴으로써 기계를 속이는 법을 터득한다.

detect v. 발견하다, 간파하다
contradict v. 부정하다, 반박하다; ~와 모순되다
polygraph n. 거짓말 탐지기
galvanic a. 전기의, 전류의
neutral a. 중립의; 불편부당의; 중간의
assumption n. 가정, 억측; 가설
respiration n. 호흡
abruptly ad. 갑자기
incriminate v. ~에게 죄를 씌우다
physiologically ad. 생리학적으로
flinch v. 주춤하다, 움찔하다

01 ▶ 본문은 거짓말 탐지기가 이론상으로는 훌륭하지만 실제 사용에는 문제가 있다는 내용이다.
02 ▶ 본문은 거짓말 탐지기의 사용을 비판하고 있다.
03 ▶ 저자는 유죄에 대한 근거자료로 거짓말탐지기만을 사용하는 것은 옳지 않다고 보고 있다.
04 ▶ 거짓말 탐지기에 관한 일반적인 통념을 반박하고자 설득적인 어투를 사용하고 있다.

》 정답 01 (C) 02 (B) 03 (D) 04 (D)

데이비드 배니거스는 눈에 띄지 않을 대규모 강의에 편중하여 수업을 들었다. 식사시간에는 사용할 수 있는 학생증을 갖고 있지 않은 듯했으며 친구들에게 의존하여 식당에 들어갔다. 저녁에는 친구들을 설득해 친구들의 기숙사 방에서 밤을 보냈다. 그러나 그의 학교친구들은 그에게서 몇 가지 이상한 점을 발견하게 되었는데 바로 그는 아무 숙제가 없어 보였다는 것이다. 그리고 나서 라이스 대학교에 온 지 2년이 지난 9월에 한 친구는 배니거스가 학생용 페이스북 페이지를 만들기 위해 다른 사람의 이메일 주소를 사용하였다는 것을 알게 되었고 배니거스에게 학생이라는 것을 증명하라고 다그쳤다. 배니거스는 증명해내지 못했다.

가짜 학생은 드물지만 이들은 최근 프린스턴, 예일, USC 대학 등 미국 전역에서 모습을 드러내고 있다. 그 동기가 무엇이든 배니거스와 같은 가짜 대학생들은 어린 학생들이 새로 만난 사람들에 둘러싸여 난생 처음 혼자 생활하는 대학의 자유로운 분위기를 이용한다. 기숙사에서 하룻밤에 오고가는 손님들은 흔히 볼 수 있다. 때로는 낙제한 학생들이 집으로 돌아가기 두려워 캠퍼스에 머무르기도 한다. 하지만 수개월 혹은 수년 동안 학생인 체 하는 것은 속이기 위한 특별한 재능과 운을 필요로 한다.

"가난한 집안에서 자란 배니거스는 다른 이에게 피해를 줄 의도는 없었다"고 배니거스의 변호인 엔리케 고메즈는 말했다. "그는 단지 그의 어머니가 자랑스러워하길 원했고 라이스 대학의 학생들과도 잘 어울렸다"고 말한 고메즈는 "어쩌면 그는 바람직하지 않은 판단을 내렸을지 모르지만 나쁜 의도는 없었다"고 하였다.

gravitate v. (중력에) 끌리다; 가라앉다
stand out 튀어 나오다; 눈에 띄다
handy a. 곁에 있는, 바로 쓸 수 있는
dining hall (대학 구내의) 대식당
dorm n. 기숙사
odd a. 우연한; 기묘한; 이상한
impostor n. 협잡꾼; 사기꾼
exploit v. (부당하게) 이용하다
live on one's own 혼자 살다
flunk out 성적 불량으로 퇴학당하다
deceit n. 속임수; 사기
socialize with ~와 격의 없이 교제하다

01 ▶ 본문은 학생으로 가장한 데이비드 배니거스란 사람이 생활한 모습과 가짜 학생으로 드러나게 된 경위를 객관적으로 설명하고 있다.

02 ▶ 배니거스에게 신분확인을 종용한 사람은 다른 사람의 이메일 주소를 이용해 페이스북 페이지를 만든 배니거스의 의심스러운 행동을 알아챈 것이다. 이로부터 그와 배니거스의 사이가 좋지 않았다는 점을 추론할 수 없다.

03 ▶ pop up 갑자기 나타나다(= appear suddenly)

04 ▶ 어머니가 자랑스러워하길 바라서 학생인 체 하였고 해를 끼칠 의도는 없었다고 배니거스의 변호인은 말하고 있다. 이는 학생으로 위장하기로 한 바람직하지 않은 판단을 내렸지만 누군가에게 피해를 줄 'ill intent(나쁜 의도)'는 없다고 말할 수 있다.

▶ 정답 01 (C) 02 (C) 03 (D) 04 (A)

이스트 앵글리아(East Anglia) 대학이 실시한 새로운 연구는 문명이 어떻게 그리고 왜 발생하게 되었는가에 대한 기존의 견해에 도전하게 될 것이다. 문명은 대개 재앙적인 기후 변화에 계획되지 않던 적응을 하면서 생겨난 우연적인 부산물이었다. 문명은 마지막 수단이었다. 즉, 악화되는 환경 조건에 대항하여 사회와 식량 생산 및 분배를 조직하는 수단이었던 것이다. 대부분의 사람에게는 아닐지라도 많은 이들에게 문명의 발달은 더 고된 삶과 더 적은 자유, 더 많은 불평등을 의미했다. 도시 생활로의 전환은 대부분의 사람들이 살아남기 위해 더욱 열심히 일하는 것을 의미했고 전염병에 더 심하게 노출되었다. 많은 사람들에게 건강과 영양 상태는 개선되기보다는 더 악화되었을 가능성이 있다. 이 연구는 또한 인류의 진보와 문명의 본질 그리고 오늘날까지 이어져 오고 있는 정치적, 종교적 체계의 기원에 대해 지금껏 깊이 간직해 왔던 믿음과 상충되기 때문에 심오한 철학적 의미를 내포하고 있다. 이 연구는 문명은 자연스러운 상태가 아니라 기후 악화의 적응 즉, '극단적인 상황' 속 인간성의 상태에 따른 의도되지 않은 결과라는 점을 암시하고 있다. 사람들은 그들의 지위를 강화하기 위해 종교적 권위와 정치적 이데올로기를 사용했던 스스로 임명한 엘리트들에게 지배되어 증가된 사회적 불평등과 조직적 갈등의 형태를 지닌 더 거대한 폭력을 경험하였다. 이러한 정부 모형들은 오늘날에도 여전히 우리에게 남아 있으며 우리는 최후의 가장 거대한 전 세계적 기후의 변동의 결과로 어떻게 우연히 문명이 발생되었는가를 이해함으로써 그것들을 더 잘 이해할지 모른다.

---

by-product n. 부산물
last resort 마지막 수단
adaptation n. 적응; 순응
catastrophic a. 대변동의
distribution n. 분배; 배분
deteriorate v. 악화되다
transition n. 변이; 추이; 과도기
profound a. 뿌리 깊은; 심한; 정중한
implication n. 내포; 함축; 연루
persist v. 고집하다; 지속하다
upheaval n. 대변동

01 ▶ '기존의 견해와 달리, 문명의 발달은 심각한 기후 변화가 주요인이다' 라는 주장에 대해 설명한 글이다.

02 ▶ "문명은 마지막 수단이었다"는 것은 "결국에는 문명을 발전시킬 수밖에 없었다"는 의미이다.

03 ▶ 앞서 언급한 정부의 특징으로 엘리트들이 지위를 유지하기 위해 불평등 및 조직화된 폭력이 악화된 점을 언급하고 있다. 이는 정부의 형태 중에서 '부정(不正)함'을 나타내고 있는 것이다.

04 ▶ 문명으로 인한 생활의 변화로 인해 건강이나 영양 상태가 더욱 악화되고 더 많은 불평등을 겪게 되었다고 하였으므로 (B) "문명으로 인한 생활 방식의 변화는 더 좋은 생활조건을 이끌었다"는 사실이 아니다.

≫ **정답** 01 (B) 02 (A) 03 (C) 04 (B)

215

아마존이 불타오르고 동남아시아의 숲이 조직적으로 베어지고 있었을 때, 생물학자들은 무엇이 세계 야생동물에게 가장 큰 위협인지에 대해 명확히 알게 되는데, 그것은 총을 든 인간이 아니었다. 수십 년 동안 주된 위협요소는 서식지의 파괴였다. 가축을 기르기 위해 숲을 태우는 빈곤한 현지인들에 의해서든 아니면 나무로 가득 찬 말레이시아의 언덕을 깎는 다국적기업에 의해서든, 야생동물들은 보금자리를 빼앗겨 죽어가고 있었다. 그러나 이제는 상황이 변했다. 오늘날의 문제는 사냥이다. 사냥이 주는 위협은 지난 10년 동안 급격히 증가하고 있는데, 대체로 그렇게 된 원인은 벌목이나 탄광을 위해 숲을 개방하면서 도로가 전에는 닿을 수 없던 곳을 마을로 연결하기 때문이다. 야생동물이 있는 곳에 접근한 다음 시장에 내놓기가 수월해졌다. 경제적 힘 역시 작용한다. 국제화 덕분에 육류, 모피, 가죽 그리고 그 밖의 다른 부위들이 전 세계적으로 대규모로 팔리고 있다. 하노이와 광저우의 미식가들이 인도네시아산(産) 거북이와 천산갑을 마음껏 즐기는 한편, 가나의 훈제 원숭이 몸통은 뉴욕과 런던으로 나간다. 야생동물 고기를 먹는 것은 이제 지위를 상징하는 것이 되었다. 동남아시아의 절반의 보호구역에서 사냥으로 인해 몸집이 큰 포유동물 중 최소한 한 개의 종(種)이 소멸되었고, 대부분의 지역에서 다른 더 많은 종들이 사라졌다. 주말에 유네스코(UNESCO)는 야생동물의 도살 상황을 조사하기 위해 팀을 보낼 예정이라고 밝혔다.

aflame a. 불타올라; 이글이글 타올라
systematically ad. 조직적으로
destitute a. 빈곤한
cattle n. 소; 가축
escalate v. 급등하다
logging n. 벌목
mining n. 광업, 채광
impenetrable a. 뚫을 수 없는; 발을 들여 놓을 수 없는
have access to ~에게 접근할 수 있다
carcass n. 시체; 잔해
gourmet n. 미식가
pangolin n. 천산갑
scaly anteater 천산갑
bushmeat n. 야생동물 고기
mammal n. 포유동물

01 ▶ 서식지를 잃거나 사냥으로 학살당하는 야생동물의 상황을 설명하고 있다.

02 ▶ 빈칸 바로 다음 문장(Whether it ~ wildlife was dying because species were being driven from their homes)을 참고한다. 산에 불을 지르고 산림을 파괴하면서 야생 동물이 서식지에서 쫓겨난다는 것은 '서식지의 파괴'를 의미한다.

03 ▶ That threat has been ~ once impenetrable places to towns에서 (B)를 유추할 수 있다.

04 ▶ 앞서 국제화와 경제적인 요인으로 야생동물 고기 등이 전 세계적으로 방대한 물량으로 거래되고 있다고 언급하였으며 이에 대한 예시로 뉴욕이나 런던에서 가나산 원숭이를 먹고 하노이와 광저우에서 인도네시아산 천산갑을 즐긴다는 사실을 든 것이다.

≫ 정답 01 (C) 02 (C) 03 (B) 04 (B)

국제 관계에 대한 토마스 프리드만(Thomas Friedman)의 맥도날드 이론을 기억하는가? 그 이론은 만약 두 나라가 풍요로운 대중소비사회로 발전해서 중산층이 빅맥을 먹을 수 있을 여유를 갖게 되면, 그들은 분쟁을 해결하는 데 있어서 일반적으로 평화로운 수단을 찾을 거라는 것이다. 그들은 문제를 해결하기 위해 박격포를 사용하기보다는 앉아서 해피밀을 즐길 것이다. 맥도날드의 매장이 있는 이스라엘과 레바논 간의 최근의 불쾌한 사건이 그 이론을 종식시켰다. 그러나 현실정치에 대한 황금색 아치(맥도날드의 로고) 이론은 존속하는 동안 상당한 위력을 발휘했다.

이와 비슷하게, 나는 국제 경제학의 스타벅스 이론을 제안한다. 한 나라의 금융 수도 안에 비싸고, 항해를 테마로 한 가짜 이탈리아 이름의 프라푸치노 매장의 수가 많으면 많을수록 그 도시는 큰 경제적 손실의 고통을 받았을 가능성이 더 높다는 것이다.

그것이 다소 과장된 것처럼 들릴지도 모르겠지만, 나와 함께 살펴보자. 최근의 위기는 캘리포니아, 라스베이거스, 플로리다를 중심으로 전국에 걸쳐 광적으로 달아올랐던 부동산 시장과 뉴욕을 중심으로 불어닥친 전국적인 신용거래 광풍이 불행하게 합쳐진 것이 원인이다. 이 두 개의 거품을 의인화한 브랜드를 하나 고르라면 그것은 스타벅스일 것이다. 시애틀에 본사를 둔 이 커피 체인점은 새로운 주택개발 사업을 따라 교외와 근교로 확장했고, 거기서 부동산 중개인과 그들의 고객의 휴식장소가 되었다. 또한 대도시의 경제 구역, 특히 경제 중심지에 융단 폭격을 하듯이 매장을 넓혀갔는데, 맨해튼에만 약 200개가 된다. 스타벅스의 거품이 가득한 음료는 거래인들이 부채담보부증권(CDO)을 주고받으며 몇 시간이고 버틸 수 있도록 해주는 카페인으로서 부동산 붐의 원료가 되어 주었고, 미심쩍은 대출 서류를 처리하기 위해 시간 외 업무를 한 모기지 브로커들에게 힘이 되어 주었다.

---

evolve v. 서서히 발전[전개]하다; 진화하다
prosperous a. 번창하는; 부유한
adjudicate v. 판결하다, 재결하다
mortar n. 박격포
put an end to ~을 끝내다, 그만두게 하다
realpolitik n. 현실 정책; 정치적 현실주의
faux a. 인조의, 가짜의
doppio n. 에스프레소 2잔
frenzied a. 열광적인, 광포한
personify v. 인격화[의인화]하다
pitstop n. (자동차 여행 중 식사나 휴식을 위한) 정차

01 ▶ 서로 전쟁을 할 가능성이 적다는 의미이다.
02 ▶ 첫 문단에서 맥도날드 이론을 제시한 후 그와 같은 맥락에서 자신의 이론인 스타벅스 이론을 제시하고 있다.
03 ▶ 스타벅스가 많으면 많을수록 경제가 어렵다고 했는데, 이와 같은 맥락에서 보면 스타벅스가 없으면 경제위기의 고통을 겪을 가능성은 줄어든다고 추론할 수 있다.
04 ▶ 스타벅스가 많으면 많을수록 그 도시는 금융이나 재정 분야에서 문제를 겪고 있을 가능성이 크다는 이론을 소개하고 있는 글로 볼 수 있다.

» 정답 01 (A) 02 (C) 03 (B) 04 (A)

리더가 되는 것은 "잘못 될 수 있는 일은 잘못되기 마련이다"라는 머피의 법칙의 정당성을 발견하는 데 좋은 방법이 된다. 리더는 사람과 온갖 일들이 엮여 있는 수많은 문제들을 해결하도록 끊임없이 요구받는다. 이러한 문제들과 그 문제들을 해결하는 데 수반되는 어려움 때문에 많은 사람들은 리더의 위치는 스트레스가 많은 일이라고 생각한다. 또한 관리자의 위치에 있는 사람들은 그들이 통제권을 가지고 있지 않는 부분들에 대한 책임을 지고 있어야 한다는 사실에 불만을 토로하는 경우가 많다. 예를 들어, 리더로서 당신은 일을 잘 하지 못하는 팀원과 근무를 하게 되지만, 그 사람을 해고할 권한이 없을지 모른다. 당신은 또한 일을 효율적으로 처리하기 위한 직원과 자금이 주어져 있지 않은 상황에서, 우수한 서비스나 상품을 만들어 내도록 주문을 받을지 모른다.

게다가 리더십은 당신이 마음을 터놓을 사람들의 수를 제한한다. 어떤 동료들에 대해 다른 동료에게 불평을 하는 것은 전문가답지 않을뿐더러 경망스러운 것이다. 그러면 또한 당신은 상관에게 당신의 부하 직원에 대한 불만사항을 발언하는 것을 신중히 해야 한다. 그러한 불만 사항은 사기에도 악영향을 준다. 더욱 심하게는, 당신의 자리보전을 위협할 수도 있다. 당연하게도, 리더의 위치에 있는 사람들은 '한 패거리의 일원'이 되지 못하는 것에 대하여 불만을 가지고 있다.

사무 보조원에서 이사회 의장에 이르기까지 조직의 모든 직급에 속한 사람들은 정치적 요소를 인식해야만 한다. 그러나 개인의 한사람으로서 기여하는 것이 리더보다 정치를 더 쉽사리 피할 수 있다. 당신은 리더로서 아래, 양옆, 위 세 가지 방향으로 정치력을 행사해야 한다. 동맹과 연합을 형성하는 것과 같은 정치적 책략들은 리더의 역할 중 필수적인 부분이다.

validity n. 정당성; 타당성
numerous a. 다수의; 수많은
enormously ad. 터무니없이; 대단히
managerial a. 경영의, 관리의
in charge of ~을 맡아서; 담당해서
confide v. 털어 놓다; 신용하다, 신뢰하다
wary a. 경계하는; 주의 깊은, 신중한
voice v. 목소리로 내다; 표현하다
superior n. 윗사람; 상관; 선배
byplay n. 부수적인 연기
alliance n. 동맹; 협력
coalition n. 연합; 합동

01 ▶ attendant on 수반하는(= accompanying)

02 ▶ 본문은 리더들이 겪는 고충을 설명하고 있으므로, 글의 목적은 (A) '리더들이 겪는 어려움을 설명하기 위해'가 된다.

03 ▶ 많은 양의 업무를 소화해 내기 위한 (A) '인내심', 다른 사람들에 대한 불만 사항을 이야기하는 것에 신중을 기하는 (B) '신중함', 정치력을 발휘해야 하는 (D) '정치 수완'이 필요하다. (C) '우유부단함'에 대한 부분은 소개되지 않았다.

04 ▶ 두 번째 단락에서 속마음을 털어 놓을 사람이 적어지고, 집단의 무리가 되지 못하는 고충을 설명하고 있으므로 (B) '고독한'이 정답이 된다.

▶ 정답 01 (B) 02 (A) 03 (C) 04 (B)

역사가들은 진화의 진행이 먼 과거에 서서히 멈추어 버렸기 때문에 인류 진화론에 관심을 기울일 필요가 없다고 종종 생각한다. 그러한 생각은 인간 유전자 분석에 기초한 새로운 발견들을 비추어 볼 때 확실성이 점차 떨어진다. 인류는 5만 년 전에 아프리카 북동부에 있는 조상의 고향을 떠난 후로 유전적 부동(浮動)이라고 알려진 무작위적인 과정과 자연 선택을 통해 계속 진화해 왔다.

대부분의 사례에서 선택압, 즉 어떤 부류들이 번식의 측면에서 성공적이며 더 많은 유전자를 다음 세대에 전해주는지를 결정하는 집단에 작용하는 힘의 원천은 알려져 있지 않다. 하지만 과학자들은 다양한 대륙의 사람들이 새로운 질병, 변화하는 기후 및 변경된 식단과 같은 압력에 적응하였다는 것을 밝혔다. <이러한 변화들의 놀라운 특징은 그러한 변화들이 지역마다 다르다는 것이다.> 이와 같이, 단일 대륙에 기초한 인구 또는 인종에서 발견된 선택압이 작용하는 유전자는 다른 지역에서 발견된 것들과 대개 차이가 난다.

유전자 변화에 대한 목록의 등장이 역사와 유전자간의 상호작용에 대해 새로운 통찰력을 열어줄지도 모른다. 지난 5천년 동안 가장 중요한 진화론적 사건이 무엇이냐고 묻는다면, 그것은 식단의 변화를 가져온 농사의 확산 또는 전쟁이나 질병을 통한 어느 인구의 절멸과 같은 문화적인 것이다. 이러한 문화적 사건이 인간의 게놈에 깊은 흔적을 남겼을 가능성이 있다.

---

pay attention to ~에 유의하다
grind to a halt 끼익 소리 내며 서다, 천천히 멈추다
in light of ~에 비추어, ~을 고려하면
decode v. 해독하다; 설명하다
ancestral a. 조상의
genetic drift 유전적 부동
natural selection 자연선택
selective pressure 선택압
reproductive a. 생식의; 재생의
contribute v. 기여하다; ~의 원인이 되다
subsequent a. 차후의; 다음의
extinction n. 사멸, 절멸

01 ▶ 인류는 질병의 발생 및 식단의 변화와 같은 환경 및 문화적 요소에 영향을 받아 진화를 계속해 왔다는 내용의 연구 결과를 소개하고 있는 글이다.

02 ▶ 먼 과거에 이미 멈추었다는 의미이므로 (B)가 가장 적절하다.

03 ▶ these changes는 사람들이 새로운 질병, 변화하는 기후, 변경된 식단으로 변화한 점을 의미한다. 또한 지역마다 다르다는 특징은 Likewise(이와 같이) 이후에 부연 설명된 점을 확인한다.

04 ▶ 문화적 변화가 인간 게놈 내에 유전적 변화를 남겼다는 문맥을 이루어야 한다.

》 정답 01 (A) 02 (B) 03 (C) 04 (A)

사이코패스는 인간이 접하는 가장 흥미진진하면서도 골치 아픈 문제들 중 하나다. 대개 사이코패스는 어떤 사람이나 어떤 물건에도 애착을 느끼지 않는다. 이들은 '약탈자적인' 방식으로 살아간다. 이들은 자신들이 잡혔을 때를 제외하고는 후회나 양심의 가책의 감정을 거의 느끼지 못하거나 아예 느끼지 못한다. 이들은 사람들과의 관계를 필요로 하긴 하지만 사람들을 정복하거나 제거해야 할 장애물로 본다. 그게 아니라면, 이들은 사람들을 이용 대상으로 생각한다. 이들은 사람들을 자신을 자극하고 자기 자존감을 높이는 수단으로 이용하며, 항상 물질적인 잣대(돈, 재산 등)로 사람들을 평가한다.

사이코패스는 언어지능이 높을 수도 있지만, 이들에게는 전형적으로 '감정지능'이 결여되어 있다. 이들은 다른 사람들의 감정을 가지고 놀면서 타인을 조종하는 데 전문가가 될 수 있다. 이들이 하는 이야기의 감정적인 부분(예를 들어, 이들이 어떤 감정을 느꼈고 왜 그렇게 느꼈는지)은 질적으로 천박하다. 사이코패스에게서 발견할 수 있는 가장 확실한 징후는 감정지능의 결여이다. 두 번째 징후로는 이들의 범죄 행태 이력을 들 수 있는데, 이들은 과거 경험에서 교훈을 얻는 것이 아니라 단지 잡히지 않을 방법만을 생각한다.

---

distressing a. 괴롭히는, 비참한
attach v. 애착심을 갖게 하다, 사모하다
predatory a. 약탈하는
remorse n. 후회, 양심의 가책
obstacle n. 장애물, 방해물
eliminate v. 제거하다, 없애다
stimulation n. 자극; 격려
self-esteem n. 자부심, 자만심
invariably ad. 변함없이, 항상
in terms of ~의 관점에서, ~에 의해
property n. 재산; 속성
verbal a. 말의; 구두의, 구술의
typically ad. 전형적으로
manipulate v. (부정하게) 조종하다; 조작하다
shallow a. 얕은; 피상적인, 천박한
aspect n. 양상; 국면

01 ▶ 본문에서 사이코패스가 잘못을 뉘우치지 않는다고 기술했으나 except when they are caught라는 예외 상황을 주목한다. 물론 이 경우에 사이코패스가 느끼는 regret은 보통 사람들이 느끼는 도덕적인 양심의 가책과는 다른, 본인이 잡힌 데 대한 유감 정도의 감정이다.

02 ▶ 빈칸 바로 앞 문장을 보면 사이코패스가 사람들을 정복하거나 제거해야 할 장애물로 생각한다고 기술되어 있다. 빈칸 바로 뒤에는 사이코패스가 사람들을 이용 대상으로 본다고 기술된 것으로 보아, Or(사이코패스가 사람들을 정복하거나 제거해야 할 장애물로 생각하는 것이 아니라면)이 타당한 연결어임을 알 수 있다.

03 ▶ The lack of emotional intelligence is the first good sign you may be dealing with a psychopath에 나와 있듯이 본문에서는 사이코패스의 가장 대표적인 특징을 감정지능의 결여로 보고 있다.

04 ▶ 밑줄 친 부분을 직역하면 "사이코패스가 하는 이야기의 감정적인 면(예를 들어, 사이코패스가 어떤 감정을 느꼈고 왜 그런 감정을 느꼈는지)은 질적으로 천박하다"이다. 따라서 밑줄 친 부분의 의미는 "사이코패스의 이야기는 그들의 감정적인 저속성을 보여 준다"는 것이다.

» 정답 01 (B) 02 (C) 03 (D) 04 (B)

편견은 다른 사람이나 다른 집단에 대해 부정적으로 예단하는 것으로 정의될 수 있다. 법적으로는 한 사람은 '유죄가 입증될 때까지 무죄'이지만, 편견을 가진 사람은 그 편견이 틀린 것으로 판명될 때까지 그 편견을 믿으므로, 편견은 반대 방향으로 작용하는 경향이 있다. 편견은 억압될 수 있지만, 특히 압박을 받을 때에는 밑에 깔려 있는 태도, 견해, 신념으로 자주 드러날 수 있다. 우리의 편견은 종종 사회의 다른 집단에 대한 지식의 공백을 메꾸기 위해 우리가 '준거 틀'에 의존하는 데서 비롯된다. 이것은 정형화라고 불리며 공동체나 개인에 관한 것일 수 있다. 정형화란 단지 어떤 사람들이 특정 집단의 구성원이거나 특정 공동체에서 산다고 해서 그 집단의 특징이라고 생각하는 특정한 특성을 공유해야 한다고 믿는, 사람들의 집단에 관한 전면적인 일반화를 가리킨다.

고든 올포트(Gordon Allport)는 다섯 단계의 편견을 확인했다. 그는 특히 자신의 척도를 나치 독일 하의 유대인들의 경험과 연관시켰다. 이러한 접근방식은 비록 비판에 <저항하지만>, 여전히 특정 공동체 또는 특정 공동체 소속의 개인에 대한 편견의 본질을 이해하는 데 도움이 되는 유용한 도구다. 올포트 모델의 다양한 척도는 다음과 같다.

부정적 언사 — 흰색을 순수와, 검은색을 열악 또는 사악과 동일시하는 색깔의 표현에서 드러난다. 다른 예로는 정형화된 표현 또는 민족에 관한 농담이 있다.

회피 — 이것은 아주 간단하게 다른 개인이나 그룹을 피한다는 것을 의미한다.

차별 — 불평등한 대우를 의미한다. 이러한 불평등한 처사는 지배적인 집단의 힘을 강화시키고 소수 집단에 불이익을 준다. 종교, 성별, 성적 성향, 장애, 나이를 이유로 한 차별은 불법이다. 차별의 과정에는 고용을 거부하거나 공공 기관이 덜 전문적인 서비스를 제공하는 것을 포함할 수 있다.

물리적 공격 — 개인의 재산에 대한 공격에서부터 직접적인 물리적 공격에 이르기까지 다양할 수 있다.

말살 — 이것은 편견의 궁극적인 폭력적 표현이다. 극단적으로 이것은 전체 공동체에 대한 인종 청소로 드러날 수 있다.

---

prejudgment n. 예단
guilty a. 유죄의
underlie v. 기저를 이루다
frame of reference 준거 틀
stereotype v. 정형화하다
sweeping a. 광범위한
scale n. 척도
locution n. 말투
equate v. 동일시하다
extermination n. 절멸, 말살

01 ▶ ⓒ는 While이 이끄는 양보절 속에 있는데, 주절에서 이 접근법이 '여전히 유용하다'고 하였으므로 양보절 내에는 그 접근법이 '비판을 받는다'는 표현이 들어가는 것이 맞다. 따라서 ⓒ는 resistant가 아니라 open으로 고치는 것이 적절하다.

02 ▶ 문맥상 '형사적 범죄는 그것이 입증될(proved) 때까지 무죄로 추정되는' 반면, '편견은 그 편견이 틀린 것으로 판명될(disproved) 때까지 그 편견이 유지되므로' 반대 관계에 있다고 추론할 수 있다.

》 정답 01 (C) 02 (B)

시간이 시작된 이래로, 우리의 생각이 어떻게 우리의 성취를 궁극적으로 이루어내는가에 대해 많은 글이 써졌다. 우리의 생각이 결실을 맺을 것이라고 아무 의심 없이 믿기만 하면 되고 그래서 우리의 생각은 그렇게 된다(결실을 맺게 된다)는 말이 있다. 어려운 부분은 아무 의심 없이 믿어야 한다는 것이다. 대부분의 경우 우리는 언제 어떻게 우리의 생각이 결실을 맺을지 알지 못한다. 그것은 우리들 대부분이 갖고 있지 않은 어느 정도의 믿음을 요구한다.

그것은 머리빗을 가짜 마이크로 사용하면서 유명 가수인 척하는 아이가 갖고 있는 그런 종류의 믿음이다. 그 아이는 자기가 확실히 유명 가수가 될 것이라는 것을 (그냥 믿는 것이 아니라) 알고 있다. 사실, 그 아이는 어린 마음속에 이미 유명 가수가 되어있고 단지 시간이 조금 지나면 세상 사람들이 그 아이를 발견하게 되는 것이다. 자신의 운명이라는 것을 알고 있었기 때문에 자라서 존경받는 과학자가 된 초등학생 나이의 남자아이도 있고, 어렸을 때 자신의 골프 우상의 성적을 자신도 이루고 어쩌면 언젠가는 그 성적을 능가하는 것에 집중하여 역사상 가장 우수한 골퍼 중 하나가 된 골퍼도 있으며, 자신의 운명으로 알았기 때문에 결국 세계에서 가장 크고 가장 성공적인 상장기업을 이끈 대학생 나이의 젊은 여성도 있다.

이 모든 사람들의 공통점은 그들은 시간만 좀 지나면 꿈이 이루어진다고 믿었다는 것이다. 사실, 그들은 미래의 자신의 모습에 대한 긍정적이고 변치 않는 생각에 집중했으며 이 생각이 하루 종일 하는 생각 중에 가장 절실한 부분이 되었던 것이다.

---

dawn n. 새벽; 시작
drive v. 몰다, 가동하다, 성립시키다
come to fruition 결실을 맺다
mock a. 가짜의; 모의의
esteemed a. 존경받는
destiny n. 운명
surpass v. 능가하다
idol n. 우상
immutable a. 불변의, 변치 않는
consuming a. 통절한, 절실한

01 ▶ ① 앞의 his나 her는 꿈을 반드시 성취시키는 사람을 가리키고 it은 자라서 존경받는 과학자가 되는 것이나 CEO가 되는 것을 의미하므로 그렇게 되는 것을 자신의 운명으로 알고 있었기 때문에 그렇게 되었을 것이다. 따라서 (C) '(운명)'가 정답으로 적절하다. (A) 특기, 장기 (B) 꿈같은 계획, 허황된 생각 (D) 희망적 해석(희망사항일 뿐인 생각)

02 ▶ 이들은 자신의 꿈이 이루어지고 노력이 결실을 맺을 것이라는 것을 의심 없이 믿었다고 했으므로 (B)가 사실이 아니다.

≫ 정답 01 (C) 02 (B)

대중음악은 본질적으로 장기적인 논리적 연관을 결여하고 있고, 따라서 클래식보다 못하다는 생각을 크래머(Kramer)가 처음 했던 것은 아니다. 실제로 이 주장은 크래머보다 훨씬 이전, 소위 '고급'/'저급'이라는 구분을 낳았던 테오도르 아도르노(Theodor W. Adorno)의 1941년 『대중음악에 대하여』라는 논문에서도 중요한 주장이었다. 크래머와 마찬가지로 아도르노도 음악 현상에 대해 설득력 있는 주장을 펼치는 장인이다. 그는 사회철학자로 이해되고 있지만, 그의 글의 절반 이상은 음악에 대한 것이다. 아도르노가 보기에 음악은 사회에 대해 생각하고, 사회를 이해하는 데 엄청난 도움을 줄 수 있는 비옥한 땅이다. 그가 보기에 음악의 구조는 그 음악이 만들어지고 작동하는 사회 구조와 뗄 수 없는 관계를 가지고 있고, 비판적인 대화를 나눈다. 음악은 예술을 위한 예술로서가 아니라 사회와의 복잡하면서 잠재적으로 모순적인 관계 속에서 가장 잘 이해된다는 그의 견해는 대중음악에 대한 연구들에도 근간이 되고 있다.

하지만 아이러니컬하게도 아도르노의 대중음악에 대한 견해가 대단히 부정적이라는 점은 널리 알려져 있다. 물론 클래식 음악 분야에도 비판적인 요소는 많다. 아도르노의 핵심적인 믿음은 사회는 근본적으로 파괴되었고, 후기 베토벤(Beethoven) 이후 좋은 음악이란 모름지기 그 구조를 통해 이렇게 파괴된 세계의 상태를 반영해야 된다는 것이었다.

---

by no means 절대 ~하지 않다
assertion n. 주장
fertile a. 비옥한
art for art's sake 예술을 위한 예술
potentially ad. 잠재적으로
contradictory a. 모순적인
infamous a. 악명 높은
realm n. 영역
derision n. 조롱

01 ▶ 아도르노는 음악은 사회를 반영해야 한다고 하였으므로, 사회와 아무 관련 없이 평가되어야 한다는 내용의 (E)가 정답이다.

02 ▶ 첫 단락 마지막 문장에서 아도르노의 견해가 많은 대중음악 연구의 근간이 되고 있다고 한 다음 접속부사 though에 의해 다음 단락이 연결되므로, 많은 연구가들이 그의 견해를 중요시하는데도 정작 본인은 대중음악을 '부정적'으로 보고 있다는 것은 아이러니컬하다는 내용이다.

» 정답 01 (E) 02 (D)

공생(共生)은 밀접한 상호의존 관계에 있는 두 개의 종(種)을 설명하는 데 쓰는 생물학 용어이다. 공생 관계에서, 한 쪽은 항상 이득을 보는 반면, 다른 쪽(숙주(宿主)라고 한다)은 그 관계로 인해 해를 입을 수도 있고, 이득을 볼 수도 있고, 아무 영향을 받지 않을 수도 있다. 공생관계는 한 쪽이 다른 한 쪽에게 해를 입히는 경우 기생하는 관계다. 기생충은 숙주의 목숨을 앗아갈 수도 있다. 사람과 다른 동물의 내장에 살면서 필요한 양분과 영양분을 숙주로부터 훔쳐 먹는 십이지장충이 한 예에 해당한다. 숙주가 영향을 받지 않는 경우에는 편리공생(片利共生)이라고 한다. 숙주에게 아무런 해를 끼치지 않으면서 소라게의 껍질 속에 사는 작은 벌레 종(種)이 거기에 해당한다. 수많은 작은 동식물들이 크기가 큰 숙주, 특히 나무와 편리공생 관계에 있으면서, 보호를 받는 한편 해를 주진 않는다. 상리공생(相利共生)은 숙주와 기생생물 양자 모두가 이득을 얻는 상호의존적 관계다. 예를 들어, 큰 반추(反芻)동물(소, 염소, 양, 낙타와 같은 동물들)의 내장 속에는 모두 공생하는 박테리아가 있다. 이들 박테리아는 반추동물이 먹는 식물 물질을 소화시켜 그것을 큰 동물이 살아가는 데 필요한 비타민과 단백질로 바꾼다. 상리공생에서는 숙주가 다른 종(種)의 도움 없이는 특정 물질을 소화하지 못하는 경우가 흔하다. 또 다른 종류의 상리공생은 지의류(地衣類)의 경우다. 지의류는 사실상 협력관계에 있다. 한쪽은 이끼가 필요로 하는 수분과 조직을 제공해주는 균류(菌類)다. 나머지 한쪽은 조류(藻類)인데, 이것은 광합성 과정을 통해 두 유기체 모두가 쓰는 양분을 만들어낸다.

symbiosis n. 공생, 공동생활
species n. 종류, 종(種)
parasite n. 기생동물, 기생충
intestine n. 장(腸)
commensalism n. 편리공생, 공생, 친교
ruminant n. 반추동물
lichen n. 지의류; 이끼
photosynthesis n. 광합성

01 ▶ '숙주가 아무런 영향을 받지 않는 경우에는 편리공생(片利共生)이라고 한다'고 했다.

02 ▶ '상리공생(相利共生)은 숙주와 기생생물 양자 모두가 이득을 얻는 상호의존적인 관계이다'고 돼 있다.

03 ▶ 여러 공생 관계의 구체적인 내용을 모두 아우르는 진술은 (A)이다.

04 ▶ 생물들의 상호관계에 관한 내용이므로 (A)가 정답이다.

▶ 정답 01 (D) 02 (C) 03 (A) 04 (A)

224

자기기만이란 거짓을 사실이라고 스스로 받아들이게끔 하는 과정이다. 간단히 말해, 자기기만이란 잘못된 믿음을 스스로에게 정당화시키는 방식인 것이다. 자기기만이 어떻게 작용하는가를 설명하기 위해 철학자들과 심리학자들은 믿으려는 의지에 부정적인 방식으로 무의식적으로 영향을 미치는 이기심, 편견, 욕망, 불안감 그리고 다른 심리적 요인들에 초점을 맞춘다. 그 흔한 예는 아이가 거짓말을 하고 있다는 점을 강력하게 뒷받침해 주는 객관적인 증거가 있음에도 본인의 아이가 진실을 말하고 있다고 믿는 부모일 것이다. <그들은 자신의 아이가 진실을 말하기를 바라기 때문에 스스로를 아이를 믿도록 속인다.> 그렇게 유발된 믿음은 증거를 올바르게 평가하는 능력의 부족으로 생겨난 믿음보다 더 많은 결함이 있는 것으로 여겨진다. 전자의 경우 부정직함과 비이성적인 것과 같은 도덕적 결함으로 여겨진다. 후자는 운명의 문제로 간주되는데, 예를 들어, 어떤 사람들은 인지와 경험적 정보로부터 올바른 추론을 해낼 만큼의 능력을 그저 타고 나지 않았다.

그러나 위의 예의 부모가 자기 아이를 비난하는 사람보다 자신의 아이와 함께 한 친밀하고 폭넓은 경험이 있기 때문에 자신의 아이를 믿는 것도 가능한 일이다. 그 부모는 무의식적 욕망에 영향 받지 않을 수 있으며, 연루된 다른 사람들에 대해선 모르지만 자신의 아이에 대해 알고 있는 것을 토대로 판단을 내리고 있을지도 모른다. 부모는 자식을 신뢰하고 자식을 매도하는 사람들을 신뢰하지 않는 매우 타당한 근거를 가지고 있을지 모른다는 것이다. 간단히 말해, 자기기만의 명백한 소행은 무의식적인 동기나 비이성적 요인에 아무 관련 없이 그저 인식의 관점에서 설명될 수 있을 것이다. 자기기만은 도덕적이거나 지적인 결함이 아닐는지 모른다. 이것은 자신의 아이에 대해 매우 잘 알고 있고, 사실이 보이는 것과 다를 수 있다고 생각하고 본인 아이를 비난하는 사람들에 대해 거의 알지 못해 자신의 아이를 의심할 충분한 이유가 없는 그런 기본적으로 정직하고 지적인 사람이 판단하는 필연적으로 있을 수밖에 없는 결론일 수 있다. 독립된 제삼자가 상황을 판단하여 아이가 거짓말을 하고 있다는 증거가 압도적이라고 동의할 수 있다. 그러나 제삼자가 판단을 잘못한 것이라면 우리는 그가 자기기만을 한 것이 아니라 그저 혼동 한 것이라 말할 수 있겠다. 우리는 부모들이 단지 혼동한 것이 아니라 비이성적으로 행동한다고 가정하기 때문에 자기기만을 하는 것이라 생각한다. 어떻게 우리는 이것을 확신할 수 있을까?

---

self-deception n. 자기기만
mislead v. 그릇 인도하다
prejudice n. 편견, 선입관
motivate v. ~에게 동기를 주다; 유발하다
inference n. 추측; 추론
flaw n. 결점; 흠
intimate a. 친밀한; 정통한
on the basis of ~의 기반으로, ~에 근거하여
unconscious a. 무의식의; 모르는
perception n. 지각; 인식
cognitive a. 인식의; 인식력이 있는
accuser n. 고소인; 비난자

01 ▶ 주어진 문장의 they는 본인의 아이가 진실을 말하고 있다고 믿는 '부모'를 가리킨다. A common example에서 아이를 믿어 버리는 부모의 사례를 들고 있으므로, 이 문장 다음인 [Ⅲ]에 주어진 문장이 들어가는 것이 적절하다.

02 ▶ 어떤 사람들은 주어진 정보를 통해 추론할 수 있는 능력이 주어져 있지 않다는 것은 태어날 때 그러하지 않게 정해졌다는 뜻으로 '운명(fate)'에 의해 좌우된다는 것이다.

03 ▶ overwhelming은 본문에서 증거가 '압도적인'이라는 뜻으로, (D)의 undeniable(부인할 수 없는)이 정답이다.

04 ▶ 마지막 문장에서 부모들은 단순히 혼동한 것이 아니라 비이성적으로 생각을 하고 있다고 가정한다고 하였으며 이를 어떻게 확인할 수 있는지를 묻고 있다. 따라서 이어질 내용으로 '부모들이 논리적으로 행동하는가의 여부를 확인하는 방법'이 가장 적절하다.

» 정답 01 (C) 02 (B) 03 (D) 04 (D)

예술작품은 다양한 수준에서 수용되고 평가받는다. 양극단의 두 유형이 두드러지는데 하나는 숭배적 가치를 강조하는 것이고, 다른 하나는 예술품의 전시적 가치를 중시하는 것이다. 예술적 생산은 숭배를 위해 기능하는 의식적 물건들을 제작함으로써 시작된다. 이때 중요한 것은 그들의 존재이지 보여주기 위한 것이 아니라는 것을 추측할 수 있다. 구석기 시대 인류가 자신들 동굴 벽에 엘크를 그렸을 때 그것은 마법의 도구였다. 그 그림을 동료들에게도 보여줬겠지만 보여주려고 한 주된 대상은 정령들이었다. 오늘날 숭배적 가치는 예술작품이 덮여있을 것을 요구한다. 신상 안치소에 놓인 신상들에 대한 접근은 오직 그곳을 담당하는 사제에게만 한정된다. 어떤 성모 마리아상은 연중 내내 덮어둔다. 중세시대 대성당의 어떤 조각상들은 1층에 있는 관람객에게 보이지 않는다.

다양한 예술 관행들이 의식으로부터 해방됨에 따라 예술작품의 전시 기회는 증가하게 된다. 사원 내부에 정해진 장소가 있는 신상보다 여기저기로 보낼 수 있는 인물 흉상의 전시가 더 쉽다. 그림의 경우도 마찬가지여서 그림은 앞서 있었던 모자이크나 프레스코보다 전시가 더 쉽다. 그리고 원래 미사를 대중들 앞에서 시연할 때의 멋스러움은 교향곡의 멋스러움만큼 큰 것이었지만, 후자는 미사의 멋스러움을 능가할 수 있다는 것을 약속한 그때 출현하였다.

예술작품을 기술적으로 복제 생산하는 다양한 방법들이 등장하면서, 예술품의 전시 적합성의 증가는 예술의 두 기둥 간의 양적 변동이 예술 본성의 질적 변동으로 이어지는 결과를 초래할 정도가 되었다. 이것은 선사 시대, 예술의 숭배적 가치를 절대적으로 강조함으로써 예술이 다른 무엇보다도 마법의 도구였던 시절의 상황에 비견될 만하다. 시간이 흐른 뒤에야 비로소 예술품의 가치가 인정되기에 이르렀다. 마찬가지로, 오늘날에도 전시적 가치를 절대적으로 강조함으로써 예술품은 완전히 새로운 기능들을 가진 창작품이 되었는데, 그 기능들 중의 하나로 우리가 인식하고 있는 예술적 기능은 언젠가는 부수적인 기능으로 치부될지도 모른다. 이것은 거의 분명하다. 오늘날 사진술과 영화는 이처럼 새로운 기능을 실증하는 유용한 사례들이다.

cult n. 숭배, 추종
cella n. 신상 안치소
medieval a. 중세의
cathedral n. 대성당
bust n. 흉상, 반신상
divinity n. 신성, 신
incidental a. 부수적인
serviceable a. 쓸 만한
exemplification n. 예증, 실례
mimesis n. 모방

01 ▶ 필자는 예술품의 '전시적 가치'가 '숭배적 가치'를 능가하는 양적 변화가 결국에는 예술의 본질, 예술의 기능에 대한 사람들의 인식까지 바꾸어 놓을 것이라고 말하고 있다. 빈칸에는 '전시적 가치'를 달리 표현하는 말이 들어가는 것이 적절하다.

02 ▶ 세 번째 단락의 첫 문장에서 "예술품의 전시 적합성의 증가는 예술의 두 기둥 간의 양적 변동이 예술 본성의 질적 변동으로 이어지는 결과를 초래할 정도가 되었다."고 하였고, 마지막 두 문장에서 "우리가 인식하고 있는 예술적 기능은 언젠가는 부수적인 기능으로 치부될지도 모른다. 이것은 거의 분명하다."고 말하고 있음을 볼 때 (D)의 진술이 필자의 주장과 가장 일치한다.

》 정답 01 (B) 02 (D)

대서양의 양쪽 해안선들은 뚜렷하게 상호 대응한다. 페르남부코에 있는 브라질의 동쪽 끝 지역은 기니의 아프리카만의 움푹 들어간 요면(凹面)과 거의 완전히 일치하는 불쑥 나온 철면(凸面)을 가지고 있는가 하면, 리오 데 오로와 리베리아 사이의 아프리카 해안의 지형들은 카리브해의 지형들과 마찬가지로 유사하게 거의 들어맞을 것이다.

이와 유사한 대응들이 지구의 다른 많은 지역들에서도 관측된다. 이러한 관측의 결과는 약 60년 전에 과학적인 관심을 일깨우기 시작했는데, 그 때 함부르크 대학의 교수였던 알프레드 베게너가 그 관측을 지질학사에 있어서 혁명적인 이론을 공식화하는 기초로 사용했다. 베게너에 의하면, 원래는 단 하나의 대륙 혹은 땅 덩어리밖에 없었다는 것인데, 그는 이 대륙을 판게아라고 불렀다. 그는 대륙의 땅 덩어리들이 (그것이) 얹혀 있는 바닥보다 더 가볍기 때문에, 그 덩어리들은 틀림없이 빙원(氷原)들이 바다 위에 떠다니는 것처럼 '시마(sima)'로 알려진 화성암 하층부 위를 떠다니고 있을 것이라 추론했다. 그 때 그는 대륙들이 당연히 표류하고 있지 않을까 하는 의문을 가졌다. 지구는 자전과 그 밖의 다른 힘으로 인해 금이 가게 되어서 마침내 본래의 '판게아'가 대서양의 중심에 세로로 가라앉은 산맥들로 오늘날 나타나 있는 광범한 선을 따라 산산이 흩어지게 될 것이라고 그는 생각하게 되었다. 아프리카는 정지해 있어왔던 것처럼 보이지만, 아메리카 대륙들은 분명히 1억 년 이상이나 현재의 위치에 도달할 때까지 서쪽으로 표류해온 것 같다. 우리는 대륙이 움직이지 않고 고정돼 있다는 생각에 익숙해져 있기 때문에 그 현상이 근거 없는 것처럼 보이지만, 그 대륙들이 서로 떨어져 있는 거리에 근거하여 생각해 보면 대륙의 표류는 1년에 2인치에 불과했으리라는 계산이 가능하다.

---

parallelism n. 평행; 대응
convexity n. 볼록함, 볼록한 모양; 볼록면
correspond v. (양 등이) 같다; 일치하다
concavity n. 오목함, 오목한 모양
contour n. 윤곽; 지형선
approximation n. 근사(近似), 비슷한 것
substratum n. 하층; 토대, 기초
igneous a. 불의, 불 같은; <지질학> 화성(火成)의
longitudinal a. 경도의, 세로의
submerge v. 물속에 잠그다[가라앉히다]
fantastic a. 근거 없는
immobility n. 움직일 수 없음

01 ▶ 서로 들어맞는 많은 지역의 해안선을 근거로 '하나의 대륙에서 떨어져 나감으로써 오늘날의 대륙이 만들어졌음'을 주장한 새로운 이론, 즉 대륙이동설에 관한 내용이다.

02 ▶ 두 번째 문단의 두 번째 문장 중 'when Alfred Wegner ~ used it as a basis for formulating a revolutionary theory ~'에서 착안한다.

03 ▶ 둘째 문단 중, 'they(continental masses) must float on the substratum of igneous rock, known as sima'에서 정답을 추론할 수 있다.

» 정답 01 (A) 02 (D) 03 (D)

227

우리는 날마다 언론에서 과거에는 상상도 할 수 없었던 과학 기사를 보게 된다. 주로 백신을 거부하는 사람들 때문에, 미국의 22개 주에 걸쳐 홍역이 700건 이상 발생했다. 기후 변화 법안은 미국 상원에서 교착 상태에 빠져 있는데, 이는 주로 일상적으로 기후와 날씨를 혼동하는 당파적인 정치인들 때문인데, 심지어 과학자들은 우리가 2030년까지 전 세계의 탄소 배출을 절반으로 줄이고 2050년까지 탄소 배출을 제로로 만들어야 한다고 말한다. 그리고 내 인생에서 가장 믿기 어려운 사실 중 하나는 평평한 지구 운동이 증가하고 있다는 것이다. 설상가상으로 과학자들(그리고 그 밖에 과학에 관심 있는 사람들)은 과학을 부정하는 것에 대해 맞서 싸울 효과적인 방법을 사실상 찾지 못했다. "사실이 우리의 마음을 바꾸지 못하는 이유"와 같은 제목이 주요 뉴스로 다뤄지는 '탈진실' 시대에 과학에서 뿐만 아니라 다수의 다른 사실의 문제에서도 증거를 거부하는 사람들을 설득하는 방법은 미해결 문제이다. 실증적인 영역에서 과학자들은 종종 증거를 제시하는 대응방식을 선택하고, 그 후에 자신들의 자료가 받아들여지지 않거나 그들의 신뢰성이 의심을 받으면 화를 내고 더 관여하지 않는다. 아마도 이것은 이해할만한 일이지만, 나는 또한 과학을 부정하는 사람들을 외면하고 비이성적이라고(그들이 실제로 비이성적일 수 있지만) 묵살해버리는 것은 위험하다고 생각한다. 심지어 더 나쁜 것은 지구 온난화에 관한 '100% 의견 일치'가 있는지 혹은 백신이 자폐증을 일으키지 않는다고 우리가 '확신' 하는지에 대한 문제로 그들이 괴롭힐 때 '증거'에 대해 고함을 치며 대응하는 것이다. 이것은 과학과 관련한 해로운 근거 없는 믿음들 중 하나에 위안과 도움을 줄 뿐이다.

그러나 우리는 사실상 더 이상 이렇게 할 여력이 없고 과학의 성공에 대해 이야기함으로써 과학을 방어할 여력 또한 없다. 기후 변화에 대한 '회의론자들'은 또한 화학 요법의 경이로운 업적을 이미 알고 있지만 그것이 1998년도 지구 온도의 급상승과 무슨 관계가 있는가? 그리고 과학 철학자들은 지난 백 년 동안 과학과 비과학 사이를 확실히 구분할 수 있는 논리적 기준을 찾고자 했으나 소용이 없었다. 더 나은 대응방식은 증거, 확실성, 논리에 대한 방식에 대해서 이야기하는 것을 중단하고 과학적 '가치'에 대해 더 많은 것을 이야기 하는 것이다. 과학이 가진 독특한 점은 방법이 아니라 과학의 '태도'라는 생각을 나는 지지한다. 이 생각은 과학자들이 증거를 중시하고 새로운 증거를 근거로 하여 관점을 기꺼이 바꾸고자 한다는 것이다. 이것이 과학자들을 과학을 부정하는 사람들 및 모방자들과 진정으로 구분시키는 것이다.

---

measles n. 홍역
stall v. 교착 상태에 빠지다, 지연되다
to make matters worse 설상가상으로
open question 미해결 문제, 미결 안건
empirical a. 경험[실험]에 의거한, 실증적인
integrity n. 진실성; 온전함
walk away (힘든 상황·관계를 외면하고) 떠나 버리다
hector v. 호통을 치다, 위협하다, 괴롭히다
consensus n. 의견 일치, 합의
bluster v. 고함치다, 엄포를 놓다
demarcation n. 경계; 구분

01 ▶ 이 글은 백신을 거부하는 사람, 기후 변화를 믿지 않는 사람, 평평한 지구를 주장하는 사람 등 과학을 부정하는 사람들이 증가하는 탈진실 시대에 이들을 어떻게 다루어야 하는지에 대해서 설명하고 있으므로 (B)가 글의 제목으로 적절하다.

02 ▶ this는 앞 문장의 "과학자들이 증거를 중시하고 새로운 증거를 근거로 하여 관점을 바꾸고자 한다는 생각"을 가리킨다. 이것은 새로운 증거가 나오면 기존의 것을 바꾸고 새로운 것의 가능성을 수용하는 것이라고 볼 수 있으므로 (E)가 정답이다.

》 정답 01 (B) 02 (E)

228 현대 오염 문제의 역사는 대부분의 오염이 과실(過失)과 무지(無知)에서 비롯되었다는 사실을 보여주고 있다. 우리는 우리의 활동으로 인해 발생하는 모든 가능한 결과를 깊이 연구하지 않고서 자연을 간섭하고자 하는 끔찍한 성향을 갖고 있다. 우리는 살아있는 유기체에 방사성 물질, 합성 화학약품, 또 많은 여타 강력한 화합물이 끼치는 영향을 완전히 이해하기도 전에 그것들을 만들어 퍼뜨리고 있다. 우리의 교육은 위험할 정도로 불완전하다.

사람들은 종종 과학의 목적이 미지의 영역으로 가서, 탐험하고, 발견하는 것이라고 주장하고 있다. 이전에도 유사한 위험을 무릅썼고, 이러한 위험은 기술적 진보에 필수적이라고 말할 수도 있을 것이다.

이러한 주장은 하나의 중요한 요소를 간과하고 있다. 과거에는, 과학의 진보라는 이름으로 감수했던 위험들은 좁은 장소와 짧은 기간에 국한되었다. 그러나 우리가 현재 달성하고자 하는 발전의 영향은 결코 한 지역에 국한되지도 일시적이지도 않다. 대기오염은 도시의 광범위한 지역을 덮고 있다. 바다의 오염물질은 전 세계의 거의 모든 지역에서 발견되고 있다. 막대한 삼림과 농경지에 퍼져있는 합성 화학물질은 수십 년 동안 토양 속에 잔류할지 모른다. 방사성 오염물질은 여러 세대에 걸쳐 생물권에서 발견될 것이다. 이러한 문제들은 현대 과학의 힘이 확대됨에 따라 점점 커지고 지속적인 것이 되었다.

어떤 사람은 현대의 오염물질이 가져다주는 위험은 여타 인간 활동과 관련해서 생기는 위험과 비교해서 사소한 것이라고 주장할지 모른다. 스모그, 낙진, 혹은 화학 잔류물이 끼치는 실질적인 피해에 대한 추산이 위험을 충분히 이해하기도 전에 위험이 가해지고 있는 현실을 희석시키지는 않는다.

이러한 논쟁의 중요성은 과학이 자연의 과정에 대한 인간의 간섭을 예측하고 통제하지 못한데 있다. 환경에 대한 우리의 책임을 먼저 생각하지 않고 기술이라는 새로운 시대를 맞이한다면, 우리는 앞으로 여러 위험 요소로 인해 가공할 위험에 직면하게 될 것이다.

---

negligence n. 태만; 부주의
appalling a. 섬뜩하게 하는; 지독한
radioactive a. 방사성의, 방사능의
potent a. 세력 있는; 효능 있는
compound n. 혼합물, 화합물
overlook v. 너그럽게 봐주다
localize v. 한 지방에 그치게 하다, 국한하다
persistence n. 영속, 지속
fallout n. 낙진; 부산물, 부수적인 결과
residue n. 나머지, 찌꺼기
obscure v. 어둡게 하다; (명성 등을) 가리다

01 ▶ '대부분의 오염이 과실과 무지에서 비롯되었으며, 우리는 우리의 활동으로 인해 발생하는 모든 가능한 결과를 깊이 연구하지 않고서 자연을 간섭하고자하는 성향을 갖고 있다'는 내용을 통해 글쓴이는 과학자들이 오염의 문제에 대해 '무관심하다고(nonchalant)' 생각함을 알 수 있다.

02 ▶ synthetic a. 종합의; 합성의, 인조의(man-made)

03 ▶ '우리가 현재 달성하고자 하는 발전의 영향은 결코 한 지역에 국한되지도 일시적이지도 않다'고 믿고 있기 때문이다.

》 정답 01 (C) 02 (D) 03 (A)

1665년에 영국의 과학자 로버트 후크는 현미경으로 코르크의 얇은 조각을 관찰했다. 그의 눈에 많은 빈 공간이 보였다. 그는 이것을 세포라고 명명했다. 19세기에 과학자들은 개량된 현미경으로 세포들을 더 명확하게 보기 시작했다. 1831년 영국 식물학자인 로버트 브라운은 세포의 중심부, 즉 핵을 발견했다. 수년 후 독일 생물학자 매튜 슐라이덴과 테오도르 슈반은 어떤 종류의 생물들이 세포를 가지고 있나 알아보려고 실험을 했다. 후에 생물학자들은 세포가 번식하여 새로운 세포가 만들어진다고 결론을 내렸다. 그들의 실험과 연구가 오늘날 다음의 세포설을 인정받도록 하였다.

(1) 모든 생물체는 하나 또는 그 이상의 세포로 구성되어 있다.

(2) 세포는 조직체의 기본 단위이며 생물체 내에서 작용한다.

(3) 모든 세포는 다른 세포로부터 만들어진다.

세포는 다양한 부분과 기능을 가지고 있다. 동물 세포의 주요 부분은 핵, 소포체, 미토콘드리아, 골지 복합체, 페록시솜, 중심립, 리보솜 등이다. 핵의 기능은 모든 세포 활동을 통제한다. 소포체는 핵막을 세포막과 연결하여, 세포내의 물질을 이동시키는 역할을 한다. 미토콘드리아는 "세포 안의 발전소"로, 음식물이 분해될 때 에너지를 생산한다. 골지 복합체는 세포 내의 한곳에서 합성되는 분자들을 모으고 꾸려서 다른 곳으로 분배한다. 페록시솜는 효소를 운반한다. 중심립은 세포의 복제를 돕는다. 세포가 복제되면, 1개의 세포가 2개가 되며 각각의 세포는 일련의 염색체를 받아야 한다. 리보솜은 세포에서 단백질이 만들어지는 부분이다.

식물 세포의 주요 부분은 세포벽, 액포, 엽록체, 핵, 미토콘드리아, 골지 복합체, 그리고 리보솜이 있다. 세포벽은 세포 안에 산소, 물, 광물질이 들어올 수 있게 하면서, 식물을 부양한다. 액포는 세포가 사용할 준비가 될 때까지 양분, 물, 광물질을 저장한다. 엽록체는 태양으로부터 오는 에너지를 붙잡는데, 식물은 이 에너지로 양분을 만든다. 다른 부분들, 핵, 미토콘드리아, 골지 복합체, 리보솜은 동물 세포에서와 비슷한 기능을 갖고 있다.

---

membrane n. 세포의 막
endoplasmic reticulum n. 소포체
centriole n. 중심립
mitochondrion n. 미토콘드리아
golgi complex n. 골지 복합체
ribosome n. 리보솜
chromosome n. 염색체
vacuole n. 액포
enzyme n. 효소
chloroplast n. 엽록체

01 ▶ 동식물의 세포에 대해 전반적인 사항들을 다루고 있다.
02 ▶ 엽록체는 식물 세포에 존재한다.
03 ▶ 중심립이 세포의 복제를 돕는 역할을 한다.
04 ▶ membrane n. 얇은 막(膜)(= thin piece of skin), (세포 생물의) 세포막

》 정답 01 (D) 02 (B) 03 (D) 04 (A)

그러나 어느 날 그는 잠시 동안 머리가 명료해졌다. 그 날은 두 아들이 와서 그에게 공손히 인사했고, 왕룽은 그들 뒤를 말없이 따라갔다. 그들은 발걸음을 멈추었고, 왕룽은 둘째 아들이 으스대며 말하는 소리를 들었다.

"우리 이 밭과 저 밭을 팝시다. 그리고 그 돈을 우리 둘이 공평하게 나눕시다. 형 몫은 내가 높은 이자로 빌리겠어요. 왜냐하면 철도가 똑바로 뚫려서 쌀을 바다로 수송하면 내가…" 그러나 노인의 귀에는 '땅을 판다'는 말만 들렸다. 그는 소리를 질렀다. 그는 화가 나서 목소리가 갈라지고 떨리는 것을 어쩔 수가 없었다.

"아니, 이 못된 게으른 자식들 같으니! 땅을 판다고?" 그는 숨이 막혀서 넘어질 뻔했다. 아들들이 붙잡고 부축하여 일으켰다. 그는 울기 시작했다. 그들은 아버지를 달래며 말했다. "아닙니다, 아니에요. 절대 땅을 팔지 않겠습니다." "땅을 팔기 시작하면 그 집안은 끝나는 법이니라." 그는 또박또박 말했다. "사람은 땅에서 태어나 땅으로 돌아가는 게 운명이니라. 그러니 너희들이 살 수 있는 땅이 있다면, 어느 누구도 너희들에게서 삶의 터전을 빼앗아 갈 수 없느니라." 노인은 뺨에 묻은 눈물을 닦지 않아 그대로 말라 소금 얼룩이 되었다. 그는 허리를 굽혀 한 줌의 흙을 집어 올리든 채 중얼거렸다. "땅을 팔면 끝장이다." 두 아들이 그를 양 쪽에서 부축하고 그의 팔을 잡았다. 노인은 손 안에서 부드럽고 따뜻한 그 흙을 꼭 쥐고 있었다. "안심하십시오, 아버지, 믿고 안심하세요. 땅을 팔지 않겠어요." 그러나 그들은 노인의 머리 위에서 서로 쳐다보며 미소를 지었다.

---

mincing a. 뽐내는, 으스대는, 거드름피우는
interest n. 이자
choke v. 목이 막히다, 질식시키다
soothe v. 위로하다, 달래다
brokenly ad. 또박또박, 띄엄띄엄
stain n. 얼룩, 오점
stoop v. 허리를 구부리다, 머리 숙이다
mutter v. 작은 소리로 투덜거리다

01 ▶ soothe v. 달래다, 진정시키다(↔agitate 동요시키다)
02 ▶ '땅에서 태어나 땅으로 돌아간다'는 땅이 삶과 죽음의 근원이라는 것이다.
03 ▶ 아버지에게 절대로 땅을 팔지 않겠다고 다짐했지만, 실제로는 그렇게 하지 않을 것임을 암시하는 행동이다.
04 ▶ 땅을 절대 포기해선 안 될 삶의 터전으로 여기고 있는 아버지의 생각이 테마가 될 수 있을 것이다.

» 정답 01 (A) 02 (B) 03 (D) 04 (D)

당신은 체육관에 갈 때, 운동기구를 사용한 전후에 손을 씻는가? 정기적으로 세척한 마루운동용 매트를 가져오는가? 항균성 비누로 샤워하며, 운동 직후엔 깨끗한 옷으로 갈아입는가? 당신은 당신 혼자 쓰는 수건, 면도기, 비누, 물병을 사용하는가?

만약 당신이 위에 열거된 질문들 중에 하나라도 '아니오'라고 대답한다면, 당신은 운동경기가 이뤄지는 환경에서 들불처럼 번질 수 있는 많은 피부병 중의 하나에 걸릴 수 있다. 6월, 미국 운동 트레이너협회(NATA)는 학교가 되었든 영리목적의 체육관이 되었든, 어떤 공동 운동시설에서 운동하는 사람 누구에게나 적용될 수 있는 운동선수들이 걸리는 피부병의 원인, 예방책, 그리고 치료책에 관한 성명서를 발표하였다.

그 성명서를 작성한 사람들은 '운동선수들의 피부병이 아주 흔한 것'이며, 경쟁종목 스포츠에 참가하는 사람들 사이에 발생하는 전염병의 절반 이상을 차지한다고 지적했다. 그런데 만약 당신이 피부문제를 대수롭지 않게 생각한다면, 필라델피아 소재 Drexel 대학교의 레슬링선수이자 올해 21살로 대학교 3학년인 카일 프레이(Kyle Frey)에게 무슨 일이 일어나는지를 살펴보자.

프레이씨는 지난 겨울 자신의 팔에 여드름이 난 것을 알아차렸으나 이를 아무렇지도 않게 여겼다. 프레이씨는 토요일 한 경기에서 다른 선수와 시합을 벌였는데, 다음 날 아침 여드름이 그의 이두근 크기로 커졌고 매우 고통스러웠다.

그의 운동 트레이너는 프레이씨를 바로 응급실로 보냈으며, 응급실에서 상처를 절개하였다. 이틀 뒤, 프레이씨는 자신의 몸에 대부분의 항생제에 내성이 있는 잠재적으로 치명적인 포도구균인 MRSA가 있다는 것을 알게 되었다. 프레이씨는 병원에서 5일을 보내며, 그곳에서 상처를 수술해서 소독하고 봉합한 후 그 감염이 제거된 항생물질로 치료를 받았다. 그는 인터뷰에서 어떻게 그가 MRSA에 걸리게 되었는지를 알지 못한다고 말했다. "레슬링 매트가 아마도 오염되었던 것 같아요, 아니면 제가 감염된 누군가와 레슬링을 했을 수도 있죠."

이런 일이 항상 체육관에서 건강에 신경을 쓰며 다른 사람들과 자신의 소지품을 공유하지 않는다고 이야기한 프레이씨에게 일어난다면, 이런 일은 당신에게도 일어날 수 있다.

---

antibacterial a. 항균성의
wind up with 결국 ~로 끝나다
gym n. 체육관
infection n. 전염; 전염병
outbreak n. 발병
pimple n. 여드름
think little of ~을 아무렇지 않게 여기다
biceps n. 이두근
lesion n. 부상, 상해
lance v. 절개하다
MRSA n. 메티실린 내성 황색 포도구균
deadly a. 치명적인, 생명에 관계되는
staphylococcus n. 포도구균
stitch v. 꿰매다, 봉합하다
antibiotic n. 항생물질
contaminate v. 오염시키다

01 ▶ 이 글은 체육관에서 위생을 철저히 하지 않으면 피부병이 크게 번진다는 경고성 글이므로 '운동을 할 때도 위생을 최우선시 하라'는 (C)가 정답이다.

02 ▶ (A) 경쟁종목 스포츠를 하는 운동선수들은 다른 운동선수들보다 피부병 등 전염병에 걸릴 확률이 더 높을 것이다. (B) 프레이씨가 걸린 병은 마지막 문장에서 당신에게도 나타날 수도 있다고 했다. (D) 팔에 난 여드름이 이두근 크기로 커져서 매우 고통스러운 상태로 변했다고 했으므로 작은 피부트러블도 걷잡을 수 없는 상태로 갈 수 있음을 알 수 있다. (C) 피부병이 들불처럼 번진다고 했으므로 전염병임을 알 수 있지만, 전염병에 걸린 사람을 격리시켜야 한다는 말은 이 글만으로는 알 수 없으므로 (C)가 정답이다.

03 ▶ 운동과 관련해 인용된 미국 운동 트레이너협회의 성명서와 카일 프레이의 인터뷰를 통해 '신문의 건강 특집기사'에서 발견할 수 있을 것이다.

04 ▶ position paper는 '의견서'나 '성명서'를 의미하며, 뒤에 피부병의 원인, 예방책, 그리고 치료책에 관한 것이라고 했으므로 (B)가 정답이다.

» 정답 01 (C) 02 (C) 03 (D) 04 (B)

소셜 미디어가 급격히 증가한 이래로 피츠버그 대학의 매체기술건강 연구센터의 소장인 브라이언 프리맥(Brian Primack)은 그것이 사회에 미치는 영향에 관심을 가져왔다. 제시카 레벤슨(Jessica Levenson)과 함께 그는 좋은 점과 나쁜 점을 살펴보며 기술과 정신건강 사이의 관계를 연구하고 있다. 소셜 미디어와 우울증 사이의 연관성을 연구하면서 그들은 이중적 효과가 있을 것이라고 예상하였다. 즉 소셜 미디어가 때로는 우울증을 완화시키고, 때로는 악화시켜 그래프상에서 매끄럽게 "U" 모양의 곡선이 나타나는 결과를 예상하였다. 그러나, 거의 2천 명에 달하는 사람들을 조사한 결과 좀 더 놀라운 사실이 드러났다. 곡선은 전혀 나타나지 않았고, 바람직하지 않은 방향으로 직선이 나타난 것이었다. 달리 말해, 소셜 미디어의 증가는 우울증, 불안감 및 사회적 고립감의 증가 가능성과 관련이 있다. "객관적으로 이렇게 말할 수 있을 것입니다. 어떤 사람이 친구들과 교류하면서 '좋아요'를 누르고 이모티콘들을 달 때 그 사람은 많은 사회적 자본을 소유하고, 인간관계가 매우 넓다고 말할 수 있을 것입니다. 그러나 우리는 그런 사람들이 더 많은 사회적 고립감들을 느낀다는 것을 발견했습니다."라고 프리맥은 말한다.

그러나, 정확한 인과적 방향은 불분명하다. 우울증이 소셜 미디어 사용을 증가시키는 것인가, 아니면 소셜 미디어의 사용이 우울증을 증가시키는 것인가? 양방향으로 모두 작용해 "악순환의 가능성이 잠재되어 있다."는 것이 이를 한층 더 심각한 문제로 만드는 것이라고 프리맥은 말한다. 우울증이 깊을수록 소셜 미디어를 더 많이 사용하고, 이것이 다시 그들의 정신건강을 악화시키는 것이다. 그러나 또 다른 우려할 만한 영향이 있다. 2017년 9월 1,700여 명 이상의 젊은이들을 대상으로 한 연구에서, 프리맥과 그의 동료들은 소셜 미디어 활동에 관한 한 하루 중 언제 하느냐가 근본적인 역할을 한다는 사실을 발견했다. 잠들기 전 30분 동안의 소셜 미디어 활동은 잠을 제대로 못 자는 데 가장 결정적 역할을 하는 지표라는 사실이 발견되었다. "하루에 총 사용시간과는 전혀 무관하였습니다."라고 프리맥은 말한다. 잠들기 직전 30분 동안은 디지털 기기를 멀리하는 것의 그 어떤 점이 평온한 잠을 위해 결정적으로 중요한 것으로 보인다. 이를 설명할 수 있는 요인들은 몇 가지가 있다. 잘 알려진 경고는 화면에서 뿜어져 나오는 파란빛이 우리의 멜라토닌 수준을 억제한다는 것이다. 멜라토닌은 잠들어야 할 때를 우리에게 효과적으로 알려주는 화학물질이다. 소셜 미디어 사용은 하루의 시간이 흐를수록 사용자의 불안감을 증가시켜 잠들 때가 돼도 끄지 못하게 되는 것일 수도 있다. "잠들려 애를 써도 생각과 감정들이 계속 일어나 우리를 괴롭히는 것이죠."라고 프리맥은 말한다. 혹은 좀 더 명백한 이유는 소셜 미디어가 너무 매력적이어서 우리가 잠자야 하는 시간을 단지 빼앗는 것인지도 모른다.

---

meteoric a. 유성과 같은; 급격한
dual a. 이중의
alleviate v. 경감하다, 완화시키다
exacerbate v. 악화시키다
plot v. (좌표를) 나타내다
likelihood n. 가능성
emoji n. 이모티콘
vicious cycle 악순환
slumber n. 잠
haunt v. 늘 붙어 다니며 괴롭히다
alluring a. 매혹적인

01 ▶ 빈칸 ① 다음의 진술 "우울증이 깊을수록 소셜 미디어를 더 많이 사용하고, 이것이 다시 그들의 정신건강을 악화시키는 것이다."를 참조하면 '악순환'이라는 말을 추론할 수 있다. 한편, 빈칸 ②의 경우, "잠들기 전 30분 동안의 소셜 미디어 활동은 잠을 제대로 자지 못하는 데 가장 결정적 역할을 한다."고 하였으므로 평온한 잠을 위해서는 '디지털 기기를 멀리하는 것'이 관건임을 알 수 있다.

02 ▶ 첫째 단락의 마지막 부분에서 "소셜 미디어를 많이 사용하는 사람들일수록 더 많은 사회적 고립감들을 느낀다는 것을 발견했다."는 내용이 있다.

» 정답 01 (D) 02 (B)

19세기 중반 이후까지, 암은 은밀히 살인을 저지르는 것으로 인식되었다. 암의 숨어 있는 힘은 조용한 어두움으로 위장하고 있었고 그것이 찌르는 첫 고통은 살인적인 침투가 너무 많은 정상 조직을 억눌러 제압당한 주세포의 방어 능력이 복구될 수 없었을 때가 돼서야 비로소 느껴졌었다. 그 범죄자(암)는 그것이 소리 없이 씹어 먹었던 생명을 악성 괴저로 토해냈다.

오늘날 우리는 더 잘 알고 있다. 왜냐하면 우리는 현대 과학의 산물인 현미경을 통해 우리의 오랜 적을 관찰했을 때 다른 성격을 인식하게 되었기 때문이다. 암은 결코 은밀한 적이 아니고 사실은 악의에 찬 엄청난 살인 행위를 광포하게 저지르고 있다.

이 병은 지속적이며 무제한적이고, 주변을 떠나지 않고, 불을 질러 대는 과격한 파괴의 원정(遠征)을 추구한다. 이런 가운데 암은 규칙을 무시하고, 명령을 따르지 않으며, 살인적인 파괴적 폭동으로 모든 저항을 파괴한다. 암세포는 야만인 집단처럼 미쳐 날뛴다. 지도자가 없고 지휘도 받지 않으며 손에 닿는 모든 것을 약탈하는 것만 초지일관 추구한다.

의학자들이 '자발성(autonomy)'이라는 단어를 사용하여 의미하는 것이 바로 이것이다. 살인 세포들이 증식하는 형태와 속도는 살아 있는 동물 내에서 지켜지는 예의범절을 어기고 있다. 주요한 영양분들은 동물에 영양분을 제공하지만 동물 자신의 원형질에서 새로 생겨났던 이 덩치가 커져 가는 잔혹한 것에 의해 죽고 마는 것이다.

이런 의미에서 암은 기생충이 아니다. 갈렌이 그것을 *praeter naturam*, 즉 '자연에서 벗어난 것'이라고 부른 것은 틀렸다. 맨 처음의 암세포들은 전혀 의심하지 않는 부모에게서 나온 서자이지만 그 부모들은 마지막에 암세포를 버리게 된다. 왜냐하면 그들이 못생겼고, 기형이며 제멋대로 굴기 때문이다. 살아 있는 조직체들의 사회에 적응할 수 없는 자들로 구성된 통제 불능의 폭도가 바로 암이며 그들의 행동 모습은 마치 끊임없이 못된 짓만 골라서 하는 청소년 폭력배들과 비슷하다. 그들은 세포 사회의 청소년 범죄자들이다.

---

strangle v. 교살하다, 질식사시키다; 억압하다
perpetrator n. 가해자, 나쁜 짓을 하는 사람
regurgitate v. ~을 토해내다, 역류시키다
gangrene n. (병의) 회저; 부패[타락]의 근원
berserk a. 광포한
exuberance n. 풍부
circumferential a. 원주의; 주변을 빙빙 둘러싸는
barn-burning a. 과격한, 굉장한
homicide n. 살인(행위)
run amok 미쳐 날뛰다
decorum n. 예의 바름, 예절
bastard offspring 서출의 자식
juvenile delinquent 청소년 범죄자

01 ▶ 첫 문단에서 '19세기 중반 이후까지 암은 은밀히 살인을 저지르는 것으로 인식되었다'고 했다.

02 ▶ 둘째 문단에서 '현미경을 통해 잘 관찰 할 수 있다'고 했다.

03 ▶ 다섯째 문단의 첫 문장에 'In this sense, cancer is not a parasite.'라고 했다. 따라서 (B)가 '암의 성격'으로 적절치 못하다 할 수 있다. 다섯째 문단에서 암을 'the bastard offspring'으로, 셋째 문단에서 'a barbarian horde'으로, 그리고 마지막 문장에서는 'the juvenile delinquents'라고 비유하고 있다.

04 ▶ 이 글은 전체적으로 암의 해로운 성격을 지적하는 글이라 할 수 있다.

» 정답 01 (A) 02 (C) 03 (B) 04 (A)

그녀의 이런 편견이 강렬히 되살아나자, 키블(Keeble)은 말을 하다 멈춰 섰다. 그리고 계속해서 말하는 데 필요한 용기를 얻으려고 자신의 주머니 속에 있는 열쇠를 만지작거려야만 했다. 그는 자신의 아내를 응시하고 있지는 않았지만 그녀가 얼마나 험상궂은 표정을 지었는지 알고 있었다. 이 일은 그에게 상쾌한 여름 아침에 편안하고 즐거운 일이 아니었다.

키블은 카펫에 자신의 눈을 고정시키고 진한 핑크빛 얼굴을 띤 채 말을 이어갔다. "그녀는 자신의 편지에서 젊은 잭슨이 대농장을 구입할 기회를 얻게 되었다고 했어... 링컨셔에 있는, 내 생각엔 그녀가 말했는데... 만약 그가 3천 파운드를 구할 수만 있다면."

그는 잠시 말을 멈추고 그의 아내를 훔쳐보았다. 그가 우려했던 대로 그녀의 표정은 굳어 있었다. 마치 마법에 걸린 것처럼 그 이름은 분명 그녀를 대리석으로 만들어 놓았다. 아마도 그녀는 한숨을 쉬고 있을 테지만 그것에 대해 어떤 내색도 보이지 않았다.

키블은 또 다시 열쇠를 만지작거리는 소리를 내면서 말하였다. "그래서 나는 단지 생각중이야. 여러 생각들이 떠오르는데... 이 일은 투기행위처럼 보이진 않아... 그곳은 분명 많은 돈을 가져다 줄 거야... 현재 농장소유주는 해외로 나가고 싶어 하기 때문에 땅을 판 거야... 그리고 그들은 빌려준 돈에 대해 이자를 지급할 거야..." (얼어붙은 조각상이) 소생하듯 그의 아내(조각상)는 쌀쌀맞게 물었다. "도대체 무슨 돈을 빌려준다는 거야?"

---

rattle v. 덜걱덜걱 소리 내다
forbidding a. 가까이 하기 어려운, 험악한
congenial a. 마음이 맞는; 즐거운
steal a glance 훔쳐보다
congeal v. 경직시키다
spell n. 주문, 마법; 매력
obbligato n. 오블리가토; 반주음, 배경음
cross one's mind 생각이 떠오르다
speculation n. 사색; 추측; 투기
coin money 돈을 마구 벌다
disjointed a. 뒤죽박죽의
metaphor n. 은유; 비유
manifestation n. 표현, 표시, 명시

01 ▶ 키블이 중간 중간 말을 멈춘 이유는 그의 아내의 눈치를 살폈던 것이다. 즉 그의 아내에게 접근하는 데 주저함을 보여준다고 할 수 있다.

02 ▶ 은유 내지는 비유로 표현된 것이 아닌 것을 찾는 문제이다. (D)는 '키블의 아내가 한숨을 쉬고 있다'는 사실적인 표현이므로 (D)가 정답이다.

03 ▶ 키블의 초조하고 불안한 모습은 열쇠를 만지작거리고, 그의 아내를 바라보지 않고 카펫을 응시하는 모습에서 찾아볼 수 있다.

04 ▶ 글의 전체적인 내용을 보면 남편이 대부(loan)에 관해 아내에게 자세하게 이야기 하고 있음에도 불구하고 아내는 아무런 반응을 보이지 않고 있다가 마지막에 '무슨 대부이냐'고 다시 되묻고 있다. 이것은 아내가 남편의 이야기에는 귀를 기울이지 않았다는 것이며 돈을 빌려주는 것에 반대하거나 관심을 갖고 있지 않았다는 것을 짐작할 수 있다.

» 정답 01 (C) 02 (D) 03 (C) 04 (A)

1850년 이전, 미국에서 도시가 성장하고 수백 개의 새로운 공장이 건설되고 또한 철도가 확장됨에 따라, 좀 더 나은 조명의 필요성이 크게 대두되었다. 그러나 미국 가정에서 조명은 옛날에 비해 거의 나아진 게 없었다. 식민지 시대 내내, 가정에서는 수지 양초 혹은 고대 로마에서 사용한 종류의 램프로 불을 밝혔는데, 이것은 물고기나 다른 동물의 기름 또는 식물의 기름이 담긴 접시에 심지 역할을 하는 천 조각을 말아 넣은 것이었다. 돼지기름을 쓰는 사람들도 있었으나, 그것을 부드럽게 유지시키고 불에 탈 수 있게 하기 위해서는 밑에서 숯을 가열해주어야 했다. 향유고래에서 질 좋은 기름을 얻을 수 있었으나, 이것은 값이 비쌌다. 1830년에 "용뇌유(龍腦油)"라는 새로운 물질이 특허를 얻었는데, 그것은 매우 훌륭한 발광체임이 밝혀졌다. 그러나 용뇌유가 밝은 빛을 내긴 했지만, 그 역시 값이 비쌌고, 나쁜 냄새가 났으며, 또한 위험할 정도로 폭발성이 강했다.

1830년에서 1850년 사이에, 미국에서 보다 싸게 불을 밝힐 수 있는 유일한 희망은 가스를 보다 널리 사용하는 것인 듯 보였다. 1840년대에 미국의 가스 제조업체들은 석탄에서 조명용 가스를 생산하는 데 있어서, 보다 향상된 영국의 기술을 채택했다. 그러나 가스 파이프라인을 소비자에게까지 연결하는 비용이 매우 비쌌기 때문에 19세기 중반까지 가스를 이용해 불을 켜는 것은 도시 지역이나 공공 건물 혹은 부유한 사람들만 가능했다.

1854년에 캐나다인 의사 에이브러햄 게즈너(Abraham Gesner)가 뉴 브룬스윅과 노바 스코셔에서 발견한 송진같은 광물을 증류하는 과정에 대해 특허를 얻었는데, 이 과정을 통해 조명용 가스와 '등유'라고 이름붙인 기름을 얻었다. 등유는 용뇌유보다 값이 저렴했지만, 냄새가 좋지 않았고, 그래서 게즈너는 등유로 큰 돈을 벌진 못했다. 그러나 게즈너는 북아메리카의 광산에서 얻은 물질로 조명용 기름을 만드는 새로운 희망을 불러일으켰다.

---

wick n. (양초의) 심지
tallow n. 쇠기름, 수지
lard n. 라드, 돼지기름
charcoal n. 숯, 목탄
camphene n. 용뇌유
illuminant n. 발광체, 광원
feasible a. 실행할 수 있는, 가능한
odor n. 냄새
kerosene n. 등유

01 ▶ '더 나은 의료시설에 대한 수요'는 언급되지 않았다.
02 ▶ '19세기 중반까지 가스를 이용해 불을 켜는 것은 도시 지역이나 공공 건물 혹은 부유한 사람들만 가능했다'고 했으므로, (C)가 정답이다.
03 ▶ '값이 저렴했다'고 돼 있다.
04 ▶ 글의 구성 방식을 묻고 있다. 본문에서는 시간의 순서에 따라 기술하고 있다.

» 정답 01 (B) 02 (C) 03 (B) 04 (A)

미국 헌법에는 대통령 후보 지명에 대해 아무런 규정이 없다. 헌법의 골격을 만든 사람들이 그러한 체제로 헌법을 만들었기 때문에, 선거권을 가진 사람들이 자신의 판단 아래 '가장 현명하고 뛰어난' 사람들을 대통령으로 뽑곤 했다. 그러나 정당의 등장과 더불어, 그러한 체제에도 급격한 변화가 생겼으며, 그 변화로 인해 후보 지명의 필요성도 제기되었다.

대통령 후보를 지명하기 위해 정당이 고안해 낸 최초의 방법은 소규모 의원단체인 정당간부회의를 통하는 것이었다. 그 방법은 1800년에서 1824년 사이에 치러진 선거에서 빠지지 않고 이용되었다. 그러나 그 폐쇄적인 특성 탓에 1820년대 중반에 더 이상 쓰이지 않게 되었다. 1832년의 선거에서, 양대 정당은 후보 지명을 위한 방안으로 전당대회를 활용했다. 이후로는 전당대회가 계속하여 그 역할을 맡았다.

전당대회를 거침으로써, 대통령으로 누굴 뽑을 지는 사실상 공화당과 민주당의 지명자 둘 중의 한 사람으로 좁혀진다. 그렇지만 그 중요한 절차를 법으로 구속하고 있지는 않았다.

헌법에는 대통령으로 지명이 되는 대상에 대해 아무 것도 기록되어 있지 않다. 당연히 그 문제에 관한 법령도 없다. 연방법의 유일한 조항은 전당대회의 자금조성과 관련한 것이다. 또 각각의 주(州)에도 대표를 뽑고 투표를 하는 방법 등과 같이 전당대회와 관련한 문제들을 다루는 조문이 아주 조금 있을 따름이다. 요컨대, 전당대회는 정당의 창조물인 동시에 의무이기도 한 것이다.

공화당과 민주당 모두 전당대회의 계획과 준비를 전국 위원회에서 맡고 있다. 전당대회가 개최되기 1년 정도 전에, 전국 위원회 위원들이 (대개 워싱턴 DC에서) 만나 장소와 시간을 정한다. 전통적으로 7월을 선호했으나, 각 당은 빠르게는 6월 중순에, 늦게는 8월 하순에 모이기도 했다.

전당대회가 개최되는 곳은 가장 중요한 문제이다. 전당대회를 치를 수 있는 적절한 집회장소가 있어야 하고, 호텔 등의 숙박시설이 충분해야 하며, 많은 오락 시설, 끝으로 효율적인 교통 편의시설이 있어야 한다.

---

constitution n. 헌법
provision n. 준비; 규정
nomination n. 지명; 추천
caucus n. (정당 등의) 간부회의
downfall n. 몰락, 몰락의 원인
convention n. 집회; 전당대회
nominee n. 지명된 사람, 후보
statutory a. 법령의
have to do with ~와 관계가 있다
delegate n. 대표자, 대리인
transportation n. 교통

01 ▶ 정당의 등장과 함께 대통령 후보를 지명해야 할 필요성이 제기되었다고 돼 있다.

02 ▶ '폐쇄적인' 특성 탓에 1820년대에 더 이상 쓰이지 않게 되었다고 돼 있다. 이것은 곧 많은 사람들에게 개방되어 있지 않았다고 바꿔 설명할 수 있으므로, 결국 많은 시민이 참여하지 않는 탓에 폐용되었다고 볼 수 있다.

03 ▶ '헌법에는 대통령으로 지명이 되는 대상에 대해 아무 것도 기록되어 있지 않았으며, 연방법의 유일한 조항은 전당대회의 자금조성과 관련한 것이다'고 돼 있다.

04 ▶ 대통령 지명에 관한 조문과 관련하여 연방법과 주 법을 비교하고 있다.

05 ▶ 마지막 문단 참조

» **정답** 01 (C) 02 (D) 03 (D) 04 (D) 05 (B)

동시대를 살았던 어니스트 헤밍웨이와 윌리엄 포크너는 미국이 배출한 2명의 가장 뛰어난 20세기 소설가였다. 두 사람 모두 현대 세계를 뚜렷하게 대표하고 있고, 또 의견을 같이하는 공동 관심사도 있긴 하지만, 그럼에도 각자는 보다 의미 있는 면에서는 서로 전혀 다르다고 할 수 있다. 헤밍웨이의 소설들은 개인주의를 바탕으로 하고 있어서, 인간을 표류하는 외로운 존재로 그리고 있다. 그래서 헤밍웨이가 그리는 작품세계에는 거대한 적(敵) — 대개 무의미와 현대성과 같은 것들이다 — 과 용감히 맞서는 주인공이 전형적으로 등장한다. 이와 대조적으로, 포크너는 다른 피부색과 계급의 사람을 포용한 사회 전체를 그렸다. 헤밍웨이의 작품이 대체로 서로 연결되지 않는 독립된 소설들로 이루어져 있는데 반해, 포크너의 작품은 그의 고향인 미시시피 주의 생활을 바탕으로 한 서로 융화된 남부의 서사시로 이루어져 있다. 포크너의 작품에서는 같은 인물들 상당수가 다시 등장한다.

물론 두 작가 모두 도덕적 가치에 관심이 있었다. 헤밍웨이에게는 개인의 용기와 인내가 가장 중요한 가치였다. 대부분의 경우, 가령 자연이나 사회와 싸울 때와 같은 경우에 있어, 인간은 자신이 반드시 겪어야 하는 싸움에서 승리하지 못 한다. 그렇기 때문에, 가장 중요한 질문은 바로 어떻게 싸우는가 하는 것이다. 비록 패배하더라도 꽁무니를 빼는 일이 없었다면, "고난 중에 영광"을 얻는 것이며, 이는 자신의 삶에 의미와 위엄을 부여할 수 있는 일종의 승리라고 할 수 있다는 것이다.

그와는 대조적으로, 포크너가 중시한 도덕적 가치는 개인보다는 사회에 바탕을 둔 것이었다. 포크너가 살았던 남부는 노예제라는 악습이 전해오고 있었고, 이로 인해 후대에까지 큰 영향을 미친 뿌리 깊은 문제들이 독립전쟁 전후에 생겨났던 곳이다. 그렇기 때문에 포크너는 인간의 본성에 대해 사뭇 다른 견해를 갖고 있었다. 그는 자신들보다 큰 사회적 힘에 대항하여 싸우는 "선한 사람들" — 백인, 흑인, 인디언들 — 을 그리고 있다. 옳은 바를 행하려고 하지만, 그들은 자신들의 삶을 지배하고 있는 비양심적이고 나쁜 일을 꾸미는 사람들 앞에선 종종 무기력한 사람들이다.

문체의 관점에서 보면, 헤밍웨이가 쓴 문장들은 짧고 치밀하고, 주로 명사와 동사로 이루어져 있으며, 형용사와 부사는 가급적 피했다. 그 결과, 힘 있고 간결한 효과를 얻을 수 있었다. 헤밍웨이는 또한 소설의 힘은 소설의 이면 곧, 소설 속에서 직접 말하지 않았지만 함축되고 있는 바에 있다고 믿었다. 포크너의 필체는 이와는 완전히 정반대였다. 그의 산문은 화려하고 복잡하며, 또한 뒤얽혀 있다. 그가 쓴 글의 문장은 매우 길고 — 때로는 한 문장이 한 페이지의 절반에 이를 정도가 되었다 — 형용사와 부사를 많이 쓴다. 그는 자신이 말하고자 하는 테마와 이야기들을 충분히 그리고 숨김없이 전개한다. 실로, 그의 작품들은 생각과 감정들로 넘쳐나고 있다고 할 만하다.

---

contemporary a. 동시대의
fortitude n. 용기, 불굴의 정신
flinch v. 주춤하다, 꽁무니 빼다
connive v. 묵인하다, 공모하다, 눈감아주다
unscrupulous a. 부도덕한
noun n. 명사
verb n. 동사
adjective n. 형용사
adverb n. 부사
compression n. 압축; 간결, 요약
convoluted a. 뒤얽힌, 매우 복잡한

01 ▶ 헤밍웨이와 포크너의 작품과 문체, 가치관 등의 차이에 관해 주로 이야기하고 있다.

02 ▶ 두 번째 문단 참조.

03 ▶ 헤밍웨이가 개인에 초점을 둔 반면, 포크너는 사회에 초점과 관심을 갖고 작품을 썼다고 할 수 있다. 따라서 인물을 그리는 데 있어, 포크너의 시야와 범위가 헤밍웨이에 비해 넓었다고 할 수 있다.

04 ▶ 두 작가에 대한 독자들의 견해는 언급돼 있지 않다.

05 ▶ 헤밍웨이와 포크너가 서로 다른 점이 있긴 했지만, 둘 다 20세기의 위대한 소설가였다는 것이 본문에서 말하고자 하는 바이다.

》 정답 01 (C) 02 (C) 03 (B) 04 (C) 05 (D)

의학에서 신체는 평형, 즉, 불변한 상태를 추구한다는 것이 지금까지의 지배적인 생물학적 개념이 되어왔다. 예를 들어, 열을 내며 아플 때 신체는 땀을 내거나 아니면 몸을 식히는 다른 방법으로 건강을 회복하고자 한다. 이것이 항상성(恒常性)의 관점에서 본 견해이다. 항상성에 의하면 각 신체기능에는 이상적인 중수(中數)가 있으며, 건강한 사람의 기능은 그 중수 주위에 무작위적으로 산재(散在)한다는 것이다.

시생물학(時生物學) 분과에 의하면 이러한 접근법은 잘못된 것이거나 아니면 적어도 불완전하다. 신체기능들이 기복을 이루는 것은 사실이지만 무작위적으로 그렇게 하는 것은 아니다. 신체기능들은 아주 규칙적으로 상하로 움직인다. 이들 기능들은 그것들 간에 질서를 유지하며 이것들이 만들어 내는 가지각색 수치들은 이러한 폭넓고 정서적인 변화를 모르는 의사들이 각기 다른 해석을 내리게 할지도 모른다.

신체의 화학 및 생물학적 기능의 대부분이 매일 심지어 10배까지도 변하기 때문에 생물학자들은 동물은 — 사람이든 모르모트든 — 하루 중 시간에 따라 사실상 신체적으로나 화학적으로나 다른 생물이라는 사실을 점차적으로 이해하게 되었다.

시생물학은 생물학적 연구를 수행하는 방법을 이미 변화시키기 시작했으며 의학 전(全)분야에도 중대한 영향을 미칠 것으로 기대된다. 그것은 시간과 관련된 질병의 예방에서부터 진찰을 개선하는 일과 치료를 개선하는 일에 이르는 시술(施術)의 각 단계에 이르는 결과들을 변화시킬 수 있다. 일부 재래적인 의학상식들은 포기해야 할지 모른다. 예를 들어 오늘날은 시간이 다르면 효과가 다르다는 사실을 전혀 고려하지 않고 하루 약을 세 번 또는 네 번 투약하고 있을 것이다.

prevailing a. 지배적인
equilibrium n. 균형, 평형
homeostatic a. 항상성(恒常性)을 나타내는
mean n. 중간, 중수(中數)
flutter v. 펄럭이다, 퍼덕거리다
discipline n. 학문의 분야
chronobiology n. 시생물학(바이오리듬 연구)
fluctuate v. 기복을 이루다, 오르내리다
keep in order 질서를 유지하다
tenfold a. 10배의
diagnosis n. 진단
without regard for ~을 고려하지 않고

01 ▶ 시생물학의 발달로 신체는 하루를 두고도 수치가 현저한 차이를 나타내기 때문에 시간대마다 그 효과가 달리 나타난다는 사실을 고려하지 않고 일률적으로 하루 3~4회 투약하는 재래적 의학 상식을 버려야 한다는 취지의 글이다. 즉, 신체의 자연 리듬의 중요성을 지적하고 있다.

02 ▶ 두 번째 문단 두 번째, 세 번째 문장을 보면 신체 기능이 규칙적으로 변한다는 것을 알 수 있다.

03 ▶ 두 번째 문단 마지막 문장 They keep in order among themselves, … unaware of this wide, normal variation을 보면 저자는 많은 의사들이 신체 리듬에 관하여 알지 못했다고 생각하고 있다.

04 ▶ 시생물학적 관점에서는 투약시간대가 다르면 결과가 다르다고 지적한다. 즉 언제 투약하는가를 중요시하고 있다.

05 ▶ rules of thumb는 '경험적 법칙, 주먹구구'라는 뜻이다. '인습적인 관행'의 뜻인 (B) customary practices가 의미가 가장 가깝다.

》 정답 01 (D) 02 (B) 03 (C) 04 (B) 05 (B)

기후 조건은 지구 대기권의 성분에 따라 미묘하게 조절된다. 만약 대기에 변화가 있다면, 예를 들어, 대기 중 기체의 상대적인 비율에 있어서 변화가 있다면, 아마 기후 역시 변할 것이다. 또한 가령, 수증기가 약간 증가하는 경우 대기권의 열 보유력이 증가하여 지구 온도의 상승을 가져올 것이다. 이와는 대조적으로, 수증기가 크게 증가한다면, 구름층의 두께와 범위가 늘어나서 지구표면에 이르는 태양에너지의 양을 감소시킬 것이다.

대기 중 이산화탄소의 양은 기후변화에 중요한 영향을 미친다. 지구로 유입되는 에너지의 대부분은 대기 중의 이산화탄소를 잘 뚫고 나가는 단파장 방사선이다. 그러나 지구는 받아들인 에너지의 상당량을 장파장 방사선의 형태로 방출하며, 이산화탄소는 이것을 흡수했다가 지구로 되돌려 보낸다. 온실효과로 알려져 있는 이러한 현상은 행성의 표면온도를 증가시킬 수 있다. 온실효과의 극단적인 예는 대부분이 이산화탄소로 구성된 두꺼운 구름으로 덮인 행성인 금성이다. 금성의 표면 온도는 430℃로 측정되고 있다. 만약 대기권의 이산화탄소 함유량이 줄어든다면 온도는 떨어진다. 어떤 믿을만한 이론에 따르면, 만약 대기권의 이산화탄소 농도가 반감된다면 지구는 완전히 얼음으로 덮일 것이다. 그러나 또 다른 믿을만한 이론은 이산화탄소 농도의 반감이 단지 지구온도의 3℃ 하락을 가져올 것이라고 설명하고 있다.

만약 화산이나 산불의 증가 때문에 대기권의 이산화탄소 양이 증가한다면, 기후가 더 따뜻해질 것이다. 따뜻한 기온과 이산화탄소에 크게 좌우되는 식물의 성장은 아마 증가될 것이다. 결과적으로 식물은 더욱더 이산화탄소를 소모할 것이며, 궁극적으로는 이산화탄소의 양은 감소하고 이어서 온도는 내려갈 것이다. 온도가 떨어진다면 많은 식물이 죽을 것이다. 그 때문에 이산화탄소가 대기권에 되돌아오고 점차로 온도는 다시 상승할 것이다. 그래서 만약 이런 과정이 일어난다면, 일정한 정도의 일상 온도 증감으로 대기권의 이산화탄소 양에 장기간 변동이 있을 것이다.

일부 기상학자들은 화석연료의 연소가 대기 중의 이산화탄소의 양을 증가시켜왔고 적어도 지구 기온을 1℃ 증가시켰다고 주장했다. 그러나 가정된 1℃의 지구 온도 증가는 실제로 단지 몇몇 지역의 온도 상승이고, 수많은 기상대가 있는 지역에 국한된 것이며 단지 대기순환의 형태의 변화에 있어서 야기되었을 수도 있다. 예를 들면, 남반구 오세아니아 지역 같은 다른 지역들은 기상 기록소의 부족 때문에 알려지지 않은 동등한 온도 감소를 겪었을 수도 있는 것이다.

---

delicately ad. 섬세하게, 미묘하게
composition n. 구성; 성분
proportion n. 비율
radiation n. 방사선, 발산, 복사열
wavelength n. 파장
concentration n. 농도
oscillation n. 진동, 변동, 진폭
climatologist n. 기상학자
hemisphere n. 반구(半球)
meteorological a. 기상학상의
equivalent a. 동등한, 같은

01 ▶ 세 번째 단락에 (D)의 질문에 답할 수 있는 내용이 있다.

02 ▶ 금성은 온실효과의 대표적인 예로서 대기 중 이산화탄소 함유량이 행성의 표면온도를 증가시킬 수 있다는 주장을 지지해준다.

03 ▶ 본문의 If the CO₂ content of the atmosphere is reduced, the temperature falls 참조. 만약 대기권의 이산화탄소 함유량이 줄어든다면 대기권의 온도는 떨어진다고 하였다.

04 ▶ (B) '기상 기록소의 효율성에 관한 일반화'는 본문에 없는 내용이다.

》 정답 01 (D) 02 (D) 03 (A) 04 (B)

240

오늘날 미국 정부가 모든 시민들에게 의료보건을 제공하지 않는다고 비판하는 사람들은 의료보건 정책을 의료보험과 같다고 생각하는 것과 마찬가지다. 이러한 기준으로 보면, 17세기와 18세기의 미국은 이렇다 할 공중보건법의 개념조차 없었던 것이 된다. 그러나 실제로는 비록 산업화 이전의 미국에 관료조직을 갖춘 조직 체계가 전반적으로 부족했긴 했어도, 광범위한 보건 규정은 두드러진다고 할 수 있다.

물론, 18세기 공중보건에서 정부의 역할은 오늘날과는 꽤 다르게 실행되었다. 보건규정을 담당하는 기구가 현대의 관료제도 보다 덜 안정적이어서, 위기 때는 생겨났다가 위기가 진정되고 나면 사라지는 일을 반복하곤 했다. 초점 역시 흔한 전염병이나 일상생활에서 본질적으로 수반되는 만성 풍토병이 아닌, 대단히 특이하고 대처가 절실한 전염병에 맞추어졌다. 게다가, 특히 17세기에는 종교적 영향이 상당하였다. 끝으로, 민간 기구와 정부 기관의 경계가 명확하지 않던 시대에는 정부가 책임져야 할 많은 일들을 오늘날의 시각에서는 민간기구라 여겨질 만한 곳에서 수행했다. 그럼에도 불구하고, 복지국가로 시작되기 한참 전이었던 당시 보건규정의 범위는 놀랄 만하며, 그 규정을 탄생시킨 사람들이 가진 정부와 보건의 관계에 대한 생각이 일반적으로 추정되는 것보다 복잡했다는 점을 시사해주고 있다.

equate v. 같다고 생각하다
paucity n. 소수; 소량; 결핍
bureaucratic a. 관료정치의; 관료식의
stand out 튀어 나오다; 눈에 띄다
wither v. 시들다; 쇠퇴하다
epidemic n. 유행병, 전염병
endemic a. (병이) 한 지방에 특유한, 풍토성의
chronic a. 만성적인, 고질적인
demarcation n. 경계(선); 한계
assume v. 추정하다, 가정하다
tedious a. 지루한, 싫증나는
insoluble a. 풀[설명할] 수 없는; 용해되지 않은

01 ▶ '현재 보건 정책을 비판하는 사람들은 보건 정책을 보험과 동일시하고 있으며, 그러한 기준으로 보면 과거에는 보건 정책이라는 것은 존재하지 않는 것이나 마찬가지겠지만, 실제로는 당시 보건 정책이 제법 훌륭하다'고 하였다. 따라서 작가는 비판가들은 보건 규정에 대해 편협한 판단 기준을 가졌다고 생각할 것이다.

02 ▶ wither away(사라지다)는 appear와 함께 tending to에 연결되는 것이므로 appear와 병치구조를 이루어야 한다. 따라서 (to) wither away가 정답이 된다.

03 ▶ part and parcel 본질적인 부분(= an essential and unavoidable part)

04 ▶ 작가는 미국 정부의 보건 정책을 비판하는 사람들을 반박하는 것으로 글을 시작하고 있으며, 마지막 부분에서 우리가 생각하는 것보다 보건 정책을 탄생시킨 세대(the founding generation)의 보건정책 수행 등이 나쁘지 않았다는 것을 언급하고 있으므로 정답은 (B)가 된다.

» 정답 01 (A) 02 (C) 03 (D) 04 (B)

대중매체와 정부 관리들이 갖고 있는 사람들을 혼동시키는 경향 중 하나는 거짓은 아니지만 단지 부분적으로만 정확한 나쁜 정보를 내보내는 점이다. 그들은 불충분하고, 또한 전체 가운데 일부만 뚝 떼어낸 정보를 퍼뜨리는데, 이것은 잘못된 과장이나 검증되지 않은 억측을 이끌어 낸다. 사람들은 무엇인가 잘못되었다고 느끼기 시작하며, 이 새로운 느낌은 부정할 수 없는 사실이 되거나 더 심하게는 그릇된 정책의 바탕이 된다. 범죄는 그런 정보로 가득 찬 영역이다. 대부분의 사람들은 범죄가 너무 많이 발생한다는 데 동의하겠지만, 가장 잘 이루어진 조사에 의하면 범죄율은 악화되지 않았다. 사실, 일부 범죄 피해율은 줄어들기까지 했다. 예를 들어 1980년 이래로 매해 발생하는 살인사건의 수는 증가되지 않았다. 더군다나, 86퍼센트의 국민은 폭력 범죄를 단 한번도 경험하지 않았다. 하지만 우리는 우리의 집과 자가용을 위해 안전장치들을 계속하여 구매하고, 더 많은 감옥을 짓기 위해 채권을 발행한다. 반대사실을 보여주는 증거에도 불구하고 우리는 덜 안전하다고 느끼는 것이다. <우리는 또한 여러 해에 걸쳐 미국의 생활수준이 떨어지고 있다는 이야기를 들어왔다. 그러나 지난 25년 동안 가구의 평균 수입은 20%가 올라갔다. 그러나 그 증가폭이 우리가 기대했던 것보다 훨씬 더디고 너무 느려서 1년만에는 거의 느끼지 못한다. 다시금 우리는 늘어난 대신 줄어들었다고 느끼는 것이다.> 모든 위험이나 악한 사회추세가 보이는 것처럼 끔찍한 정도는 아니다. 의식적으로 너무 주목하면 진실을 깎아내릴 수도 있다. 우리는 거짓 없는 증거와 대중의 편견 및 불안을 혼합하여 인위적인 사실을 지어낸다. 만일 매체가 공정하게 자료를 제시하지 않는다면, 우리는 판단을 내리기 전에 분별력을 가져야 할 것이다.

---

disturbing a. 불안케 하는
dispense v. 분배하다
inference n. 추리, 추측; 결론
sensation n. 감각; 기분; 물의
abound v. 많이 있다; 풍부하다
initiative n. 발의; 솔선; 주도
adverse a. 거스르는; 불리한; 해로운
consciousness-raising n. 자기 발견(법)
synthetic a. 종합적인; 인조의
prejudice n. 편견; 선입관
unbiased a. 선입견이 없는, 공평한
discerning a. 통찰력(식별력) 있는

01 ▶ 본문은 어떻게 사실이 왜곡되어 사람들에게 전달되고 영향을 미치는가에 대해 설명하고 있다.

02 ▶ unwarranted a. 보증되지 않은, 부당한(= groundless) irrefutable a. 반박할 수 없는(= unquestionable)

03 ▶ 제시된 문장은 사람들에게 잘못 알려진 사실과 그로 인한 사람들의 반응의 예가 된다. also로 연결되어 있는 점, 마지막 문장에 again이 있는 점 등을 감안하면, 앞에 먼저 제시된 범죄율에 대한 예에 뒤이어 오는 것이 자연스럽다.

04 ▶ 대중매체와 (일부) 정부 관리들이 퍼뜨리는 disturbing news는 실제로는 그러하지 않은데 나쁜 쪽으로 해석되어 나오는 정보를 말한다.

▶ 정답 01 (A) 02 (D) 03 (C) 04 (B)

오웬이 런던에 도착했을 때 오드리는 다른 도시에 있었고 일주일 후에야 돌아왔다. 전화기를 통해 들려오는 그녀의 목소리는 휴가가 끝난 후 안정을 찾지 못했던 그를 진정시키는 데 충분하였다. 그러나 그는 가까이 있어도 그녀를 만날 수 없다는 생각에 개이지 않을 구름처럼 그를 뒤 엎어버린 명상적인 우울함에 잠겼다. 그는 넋이 나간 채 행동하였고 살도 빠졌다.

만약 고객들이 그의 우울하고 창백한 얼굴이 어쩐지 걱정되지 않는다면, 그 이유는 영리를 추구하며 바쁘게 돌아가는 현대의 생활이 비즈니스맨들에게 은행원의 창백한 얼굴을 살펴 볼 여유를 주지 않기 때문일 것이다. 그들을 정말 성가시게 한 것은 그가 부드러운 공상에 빠져 업무를 하는 점이었다. 그는 수입어음 관리 부서에 있었는데, 그 부서의 특징 중의 하나는 오후가 끝날 무렵 모자를 쓰지 않고 왼쪽 팔에 끈을 단 가죽 가방을 맨 활기 넘치는 젊은 남자들이 핀으로 단단히 고정된 알 수 없는 서류들을 시끄럽게 요구하며 쇄도한다는 것이다. 오웬은 이제껏 이러한 젊은 남자 고객들이 원하는 것이 무엇인지 잘 알지 못했으며, 지금 업무에 초연한 그의 마음은 이 문제를 해결하는 것을 더욱 단호히 거부하였다. 그는 군중에게 아낌없이 금품을 나누어 주는 데 여념 없는 왕과 같은 태도로 마구잡이로 서류를 주었으며, 이에 따른 혼란은 화가 잔뜩 난 부장이 직접 나서서 해결해야만 했다.

사람의 인내심은 한계가 있다. 그 일이 있고 2주가 지날 무렵 과로에 시달린 부장은 그를 교체해 줄 것을 요청했고, 오웬은 우편 요금 부서로 옮겨졌는데 그곳에서 그는 오드리와 전화통화를 하지 않는 시간에는 큰 장부에다가 우편물 주소를 기록하여 우체국으로 가지고 갔다. 우편물에 소인을 찍어야 했지만 사랑에 빠진 남자는 만사를 다 생각할 수는 없기에 종종 이 절차를 무시하기 일쑤였다.

---

restlessness n. 침착하지 못함, 불안
envelop v. 싸다, 봉하다
distrait a. 멍한, 방심한
pallor n. (얼굴의) 창백
inrush n. 침입; 쇄도
strap v. 끈으로 매다
clamour v. 극성스럽게 요구하다
cracking a. 몹시 빠른; 맹렬한
emphatically ad. 강조하여, 단호히
grapple with 해결하려고 애쓰다
air n. 모양; 태도
largess n. 증여; 선물
wrathful a. 격노한
formality n. 형식적인 것, 절차
musing n. 심사숙고, 묵상

---

01 ▶ 오드리의 목소리로 안정을 다시 찾았지만 그녀를 직접 만날 수 없다고 생각하는 오웬의 기분을 추론하는 문제이다. 이어서 이 기분은 '개이지 않을 구름처럼 그를 뒤 엎어 버리고', 오웬은 '넋이 나가고', '살도 빠졌다'는 등의 내용으로 미루어, '우울함에 빠진(a meditative melancholy)' 그의 기분을 추론할 수 있다.

02 ▶ 가까이 있어도 직접 그녀를 만날 수 없다는 생각이 들었다고 하였다.

03 ▶ What did pain ~ duties에서 업무를 할 때 오드리 생각으로 공상에 빠진 오웬의 모습을 알 수 있으며 이에 따라 고객이 주문을 할 때 업무에 초연한 상태(his detached mind)로 임하였기에 혼란을 초래하였다.

04 ▶ 작가는 오드리 생각에만 빠져 있는 오웬의 행동과 감정을 묘사하고 있다. 두 번째 문단에서 업무를 경솔히 처리하고 있는 오웬을 '군중에게 아낌없이 금품을 나누어 주는데 여념 없는 왕'으로 빗대어 풍자적으로 표현하고 있다. 또한 마지막 문장 He was supposed also to stamp ~ this formality에서 스탬프를 찍어야 하는 중요한 과정을 잊은 오웬을 '사랑에 빠진 남자가 만사를 다 기억할 수는 없다'며 다소 빈정거리는 태도를 드러내고 있다.

》 정답 01 (B) 02 (C) 03 (A) 04 (C)

1950년대 초에 리우 빈얀은 키 크고 말 잘하는 청년으로 사회주의 이상에 매우 헌신적이며 중화인민공화국에서 혁혁한 경력을 쌓을 준비가 되어있었다. 부패에 관한 글을 쓴 혐의로 1957년에 공산당에서 숙청되어 가난한 산간 지방으로 추방되었을 때 그는 중국에는 "두 가지 정반대되는 종류의 진리"가 있다는 것을 문득 알게 되었다. "소작농들의 염원"이 한 가지 종류의 진리였고 "고위층의 정책"이 또 다른 진리였다. 리우의 나머지 인생은 — 뛰어난 성취 뿐 아니라 고통마저도 — 첫 번째 종류의 진리 편에 서기로 한 그의 선택의 결과였다. 많은 중국인들은 사회주의의 선전어구와 힘들고 때로는 파국적이기까지 한 일상생활의 현실 사이에 간격이 점점 벌어지는 것을 목격했다. 일부 사람들은 몸을 낮추고 타협하는 쪽을 택했지만 리우는 고집스럽게도 자신이 목격한 바에 대해 글을 써나갔다. 약한 자를 괴롭히는 일이 있으면 있다고 말하고 부패가 있으면 그 실상을 낱낱이 파헤치고 신문이 거짓을 전해도 그것이 또 다른 종류의 진리인 양 꾸미지 말라는 것이었다.

그의 글이 거둔 카타르시스 효과로 인해 리우는 두 차례 거대한 인기를 누렸는데, 한 번은 1956년이었고 또 한 번은 1980년대 초였다. 그러나 진실을 말한 결과 값비싼 대가를 치르게 되었다. 그는 80 평생 중 22년(1957-1979)을 국내에서 추방 생활을 했고 또 17년(1988-2005)을 해외로 강제 추방되어 살았다. 말년에 귀국하게 해달라는 그의 요청을 중국의 지도자들은 무시해버렸다. 왜 그는 그러한 삶을 택했는가? 1979년 어느 연설에서 리우는 이렇게 말했다. "나는 부동의 사실을 하나 깨달았어요. 그것은 오늘날 중국에서는 누군가가 말을 하거나 글을 썼는데 아무런 반대가 없으면 그 사람은 괜한 말을 한 셈이라는 거지요.(조금이라도 중요한 말을 하면 비판받는다는 뜻) 유일한 대안은 구석에 웅크리고 앉아 침묵을 지키는 건데, 그러나 그러려면 왜 삽니까?" 그의 뛰어난 미덕은 정직뿐이 아니었다. 그는 아주 세심한 글을 썼으며 날카로운 분석력의 소유자였다. 중국 사회에 대한 이해도나 중국인민에 대한 변치 않는 애정 면에서 그에 필적할 사람은 아마도 거의 없을 것이다.

purge v. (몸, 마음을) 깨끗이 하다; 추방하다, 숙청하다
diametrically ad. 정반대로; 전혀
lie low 엎드리다, 웅크리다, 때를 기다리다
cathartic a. 카타르시스를 일으키는
wane v. 달이 이지러지다, 쇠약해지다
a hard fact 움직일 수 없는 사실
cower v. 움츠리다, 위축되다
abiding a. 지속적인, 변치 않는

01 ▶ 이 글은 리우 빈얀 개인의 삶에 대한 글이지 중국의 민주화, 표현의 자유 등에 대한 글이 아니다.
02 ▶ 사실을 사실대로 말하는 것은 '정직'이라는 덕목이다.
03 ▶ 마지막 문장으로 보아, 하층민들에 대한 애정도 있었다고 봐야 한다.

》 정답 01 (C) 02 (B) 03 (D)

80%의 여성이 임신 중에 인지기능의 손상을 경험하는 상황이어서, 이제 "임신 뇌"라는 개념이 확립된 것도 놀랄 일이 아니다. 그러나 최근의 한 논문은 출산 전의 기억력 상실, 스트레스, 그리고 머리가 멍해지는 것은 사실은 여성에게 어머니가 되는 준비를 시키는 데에 아주 중요한 역할을 하는 것일지 모른다는 점을 시사한다.

1940년대 이후로 의사들은 임신 중의 왕성한 호르몬 분비가 여성이 어머니 역할에 필요한 것을 갖추도록 도와주는 것이 아닌가 생각해왔다. 그러나 호르몬이 십대의 뇌와 폐경기의 뇌에 어떤 영향을 미치는가에 대해서는 많이 알려져 있는 반면, 인간에게 있어서 임신 뇌에 대한 이해와 연구는 미미하다. 최근의 연구는 대체로 임신한 설치류에 대해 행해져왔고 연구 결과 임신 중의 왕성한 호르몬 분비가 대담성을 증가시키고 불안을 감소시킬 뿐 아니라 (먹이를 더 빨리 더 잘 찾게 해주는) 공간능력과 다중작업수행능력을 향상시킨 것으로 밝혀졌다. 이 쥐들은 살아있는 내내, 새끼가 다 큰 후에도 오랫동안, 임신의 긍정적 효과를 누렸다.

지금 과학자들은 동물에서 발견한 사실들을 사람에게 적용하려 하고 있다. 채프맨 대학의 심리학 교수인 로라 M. 글린은 새 논문에서 임신한 여성의 호르몬에 흠뻑 젖은 뇌가 부모로서 아기를 키우는 힘든 일을 위해 준비해가는 과정인 "모성 프로그래밍"의 존재를 주장한다. 알고 보면, 임신과 관련한 가장 불편한 몇 가지 점들, 이를테면 가상의 것이나 스트레스에 불과한 것으로 종종 일축되어버리는 막연하지만 성가신 인지능력과 기억력의 쇠퇴 같은 것들이 사실은 여성이 어머니가 되면서 일어나는 정신 전환의 부작용일 수도 있는 것이다. 달리 말하면, 아기와 하나가 되어 아기를 돌보는 새로운 능력을 얻음과 동시에 기억력을 잃어가고 있는 것일지도 모른다.

---

take hold 확립되다, 효력이 있다
fuzzy-headed a. 머리가 멍한, 멍청한
prenatal a. 태아기의
hormonal bath 왕성한 호르몬 분비
menopausal a. 폐경기의
rodent n. 설치류(쥐, 토끼 등)
forage v. 찾아다니다, 뒤적여 찾다
multitasking n. 다중업무처리, 다중작업수행
pup n. 강아지, (동물의) 새끼
mental shift 정신 전환

01 ▶ 달리 말한 마지막 문장에서 기억력을 잃어가는 한편으로 육아에 필요한 새로운 능력을 얻게 되는 것일지 모른다고 했으므로 빈칸에는 지적 능력의 내용이 바뀌는 (C)의 '정신전환'이 적절하다.

02 ▶ 이 글은 임신 뇌에 대한 이야기이므로 '임신이 뇌를 어떻게 변화시키는가'가 제목으로 가장 적절하다.

03 ▶ (A)는 셋째 단락 둘째 문장에 the pregnant woman's hormone-soaked brain으로 나와 있고, (B)는 첫 단락 첫 문장에 나와 있으며, (C)는 마지막 문장에 capacities to bond with and care for an infant로 나와 있으나, (D)의 memory lapses는 마지막 단락 끝에서 두 번째 문장에서 '가상의 것이거나 스트레스에 불과한 것으로 종종 일축되어버린다'고 했을 뿐이므로 실제로는 진짜 기억력 쇠퇴이지 가상의 기억력 쇠퇴가 아닌 것이다.

04 ▶ 마지막 단락에 나온 글린의 "모성 프로그래밍" 주장과 일치하는 말을 필자는 그 다음 문장 이하에서 하고 있으므로 (A)가 정답이다.

» 정답 01 (C) 02 (B) 03 (D) 04 (A)

북아메리카에 온 초기 영국인 식민지 개척자들의 보수주의, 즉 영국식 방법으로 일을 하고자 하는 강한 애착은 뉴잉글랜드 지방에서 만든 가구에 있어서도 중요한 역할을 하곤 했다. 뉴잉글랜드 지방 최초의 가구제작자들이 이용하던 도구는 수백 년 심지어는 수천 년 동안 사용되어 온 도구와 결국 크게 다르지 않았는데, 이러한 도구들은 장도리, 톱, 끌, 대패, 송곳, 나침반, 자와 같은 것들이었다. 이 도구들은 대체로 목수, 통 제작자, 조선공 등, 나무를 가지고 일 하는 모든 사람들이 사용했던 도구였다. 당시 가구 제작자들은 기껏해야 특별한 날이 있는 대패나 좀 더 정교한 끌을 가지고 있었을지 모르나, 식민지 초기에는 전문화가 많이 이루어질 수 없었을 것이다.

1600년대 초기 수십 년 동안의 가구 제작자들은 "이음장이"로 알려졌는데, 그것은 적어도 이 시기의 영국 사람들 사이에서는 가구를 제작하는 주된 방법이 장부촉 이음이었기 때문이었다. 장붓구멍은 한 조각의 나무에 끌로 파서 깎아 낸 구멍이며, 장부는 장붓구멍에 들어맞도록 다른 나무 조각으로 모양을 낸 돌기이다. 그리고 (송곳으로) 장붓구멍의 끝과 장부 사이를 뚫어 작은 구멍을 내고, 거기에 뾰족하게 깎아낸 나무못을 박아 그 이음매 부분을 튼튼히 채워놓을 수 있다. 여기에서 "이음장이"라는 용어가 나오게 되었다. 판자 같은 것들도 기본 구조물의 홈에 딱 들어맞게 했다. 이러한 종류의 제작 방법은 집을 만드는 데서부터 상자를 만드는 데 이르기까지 온갖 것들에 사용되었다.

상대적으로 이 시기에는 철물이 거의 사용되지 않았다. 수작업으로 쇠붙이를 주조하여 만들어낸 못 몇 개가 사용되긴 했지만, 나사나 아교는 없었다. 경첩은 종종 가죽으로 만들었으나, 금속으로 된 경첩 또한 사용되었다. 조잡한 수준의 여러 잡동사니들은 식민지의 대장장이들이 만들어냈지만, 좀 더 세련된 것들은 수입을 했다. 자물쇠와 금속키로부터 나무를 보호하기 위한 열쇠구멍 가리개는 종종 수입되었다.

무엇보다도, 초기 영국인 식민지 개척자들이 수입했던 것은 그들이 영국에 있을 때 알고 있던 가구의 전통적 형태나 디자인에 대한 지식과 정통함, 또한 그것을 유지하려는 헌신이었다.

---

colonist n. 식민지 개척자, 이주자
chisel n. 끌, 조각칼, 정
plane n. 대패
auger n. (나사) 송곳
carpenter n. 목수, 목공
shipwright n. 배를 만드는 목수
mortise n. 장붓구멍
tenon n. 장부
protrude v. 내밀다, 불쑥 나오다
whittle v. 나무를 조금씩 깎다
peg n. 나무못, 쐐기
chest n. 대형 상자, 궤
hinge n. 경첩, 돌쩌귀
escutcheon plate 열쇠 구멍 가리개

01 ▶ 장붓구멍에 장부를 끼워놓은 후 고정하는 방식이므로, 그 방식이 '자물쇠와 열쇠'와 유사하다고 하겠다.

02 ▶ 장붓구멍의 끝과 장부 사이를 관통해 구멍을 내는 데 송곳을 사용했다.

03 ▶ '투박하고 조잡한 수준의 것들은 직접 제작한 데 반해, 보다 세련된 것들은 수입했다'는 내용을 통해, 식민지의 대장장이들이 정교한 것을 만드는 데는 능하지 않았음을 알 수 있다.

04 ▶ (A), (D)는 본문의 내용을 통해서는 알 수 없는 것들이고, (C)의 경우, '당시 가구 제작자들은 기껏해야 특별한 날이 있는 대패나 좀 더 정교한 끌을 가지고 있었을지 모르나, 식민지 초기에는 전문화가 많이 이루어질 수 없었을 것이다'는 내용을 통해 정답이 될 수 없음을 알 수 있다.

▶ 정답 01 (A) 02 (C) 03 (A) 04 (B)

눈송이는 처음에 산소원자와 수소원자의 약한 결합력 때문에 작은 무리로 생겨나게 되는 무수히 많은 물 분자로부터 만들어진다. 산소원자와 수소원자의 결합력은 이어서 그 물 분자 무리를 결빙한 상태의 분자결정으로 만드는데, 이것은 분자가 완벽하게 격자구조를 이룬 것이다. 마침내 이러한 분자결정이 여러 개가 모여서 한 개의 눈송이가 된다. 과학자들은 분자들을 자연적인 결정으로 모이게 하는 힘을 여러 가지 주요 물질을 만들어 내는 데 이용할 수 있다는 것을 오랜 세월에 걸쳐 깨달아 왔다. 과학자들은 90,000개 이상의 분자결정 구조를 밝혀냈는데, 이 중 가장 잘 알려진 것이 아스피린과 방충제이다.

최근에는, 연구원들이 어떤 종류의 분자와 어떤 조건이 독특하고 유용한 성질을 가진 분자결정을 만들어내는지를 더 잘 이해하고자 분자가 결정을 이루는 방법을 연구했다. 과학자들은 결정의 물질적 특성이 대체로 결정 속의 분자의 구성에 좌우된다는 사실을 알고 있지만, 그러한 결정의 집합체를 제어하는 요인에 대해서는 거의 알고 있지 못하다.

분자결정을 인위적으로 합성하는 것은 건물을 디자인하는 것과 유사하다. 건물의 건축이 시작되기 전에, 건축가는 대들보의 크기와 모양과 리벳의 위치나 개수를 구체적으로 밝혀야 한다. 이와 유사하게, 새로운 분자 결정을 만들어내기 위해 화학자들은 적절한 크기와 모양의 분자를 택해야 하며 또한 그 결정을 계속 결합시킬 분자간의 힘을 택해야 한다. 화학자는 대개 다양한 모양과 크기의 분자를 많이 발견할 수 있지만, 예상할 수 있는 방법으로 결합하는 분자를 발견하는 것은 쉽지 않다.

---

originate v. 시작하다, 근원이 되다
countless a. 셀 수 없는, 셀 수 없을 정도로 많은
molecule n. 분자
oxygen n. 산소
hydrogen n. 수소
assemble v. 모으다, 집합시키다
mothball n. (나프탈렌 따위의) 둥근 방충제
property n. 재산, 자산; 성질, 특성; 고유성
synthesize v. 종합하다; 합성하다
specify v. 자세히 쓰다; 일일이 이름을 들어 말하다
girder n. 대들보
appropriate a. 적합한, 적절한; 특유의
predictable a. 예상할 수 있는, 예언할 수 있는

01 ▶ '과학자들은 분자들을 자연적인 결정으로 모이게 하는 힘을 여러 가지 주요 물질을 만들어 내는 데 이용할 수 있다는 것을 오랜 세월에 걸쳐 깨달아 왔다'고 했다.

02 ▶ 인위적으로 분자결정을 합성해 내기 위함이다.

03 ▶ 마지막 문단에서 '적절한 크기와 모양의 분자를 택해야 하며 또한 그 결정을 계속 결합시킬 분자간의 힘을 택해야 한다'고 했다. (C)는 언급하지 않았다.

04 ▶ ⓑ는 접속사 없이 두 문장이 나열되어 있다. 따라서 them을 관계대명사 which로 바꿔야 한다.

》 정답 01 (D)   02 (B)   03 (C)   04 (B)

미국 식품의약국은 최근에 식용동물의 건강상태와 성장을 향상시키기 위한 항생물질 사용에 대해 엄격한 제재조치를 계획하고 있다. 사료에 첨가한 약물은 많은 미생물을 죽이지만 또한 항전염성 약품에 내성이 있는 세균변종의 출현을 조장하기도 한다. 예를 들면, 이미 페니실린과 테트라사이클린은 치료법상으로 예전의 효과만큼 못하다. 약품 저항성은 세균의 다른 변종과 심지어 다른 종 사이에서도 교환될 수 있는 플라즈미드라 불리는 작은 유전자 고리에 의해 주로 전달된다. 플라즈미드는 또한 분자 생물학자들이 유전자 이식실험을 할 때 사용하는 두 종류의 매개체들 중 하나이다(다른 하나는 바이러스다). 현재의 방침은 항생물질에 내성 있는 유전자를 가진 플라즈미드를 실험실에서 사용하는 것을 금지하고 있다. 그러나 실험실의 과학자들에 대한 이러한 규제를 강화해야 할 것인지 아닌지를 둘러싸고 의회의 논쟁이 격렬해진 동안, 일련의 해로운 결과를 야기시키는 무분별한 농사 관행에 대해서는 의회의 관심이 거의 집중되지 않고 있다.

antibiotic n. 항생물질
medication n. 약물치료, 투약(법)
microorganism n. 미생물
strain n. 종족, 혈통, 계통; 품종; 변종
therapeutically ad. 치료법상으로, 치료법으로
confer v. 수여하다; 베풀다; 의논하다
molecular a. 분자의; 분자로 된
rage v. 격노하다; 날뛰다; 한창이 되다
ill-advised a. 무분별한, 경솔한

01 ▶ 약품이 첨가된 사료를 사용하는 관행과 이에 따라 나타날 수 있는 여러 부작용에 대해 우려를 표하고 있다.

02 ▶ 플라즈미드는 약품저항성을 전달하는 작은 유전자 고리라고 나와 있으므로, 다른 박테리아 종 사이에서도 교환될 수 있는 플라즈미드로 인해 약품에 내성이 있는 미생물이 형성된다는 것을 알 수 있다.

03 ▶ 항생제의 효과를 떨어뜨리는 등 부작용을 일으킬 수 있는 세균변종에 대해 우려(apprehensive)하고 있다.

04 ▶ **deleterious a.** 심신에 해로운, 유독한(= harmful)

》 정답   01 (C)   02 (A)   03 (D)   04 (D)

10년마다 실시되는 미(美) 인구조사에 의해 제공된 여성의 직업에 관한 정보는 사회 변화를 반영하여 19세기 동안 더욱 자세하고 정확해졌다. 1840년까지 가구(家口)의 수로 셈하는 단순한 계산 방식은 가내 기반의 농업 경제와 계층적 사회 질서를 반영하고 있었다. 즉, 나머지 가족 구성원들은 직업 부류 등 여러 범주에서 계산된 총 인원수로 표시되는 반면에, 가장(남성이거나 부재로 추정하였음)은 이름으로 명시되었던 것이다. 농업분야와 마찬가지로, 대부분의 기업은 일가가 경영하는 방식이었으므로, 인구조사는 각 개인의 특징보다는 전체 한 가구의 특성으로서의 경제 활동을 측정하는 것이었다.

1850년의 인구조사는 반(反)노예제와 여성 인권 운동에 어느 정도 반응을 보이며, 가구에 속한 각 구성원들에 대한 구체적인 정보를 수집하기 시작하였다. 1870년이 되어서야 성별에 따른 직종이 분석되었다. 그 당시 인구조사 국장은 180만 명의 여성들이 가정 밖에서 "수입과 평판이 좋은 직업"에 고용되었다고 보고했다. 더군다나 그는 임의로 "집안일을 하는" 여성이 한 가정에 한명씩 존재하는 것으로 보았다. 이 두 부류의 여성 그룹 사이에서 중복된 부분은, 유급 노동인구로의 여성의 빠른 유입과 산업화로부터 야기된 사회문제들로 인해 여성인권 옹호자와 여성 통계학자들이 보다 철저하고 정확한 여성의 직업과 임금의 통계를 요구하였던 1890년이 지나서야 산정되었다.

---

census n. (통계)조사; 인구[국세]조사
enumeration n. 셈, 계산, 열거
household n. 가족; 세대
specify v. 상술하다, 자세히 쓰다
enterprise n. 기획; 기업(체); 모험심
attribute n. 속성, 특질; 상징
antislavery n. 노예 제도 반대
superintendent n. 감독자, 지휘자
arbitrarily ad. 임의로; 독단적으로
industrialization n. 산업화
statistician n. 통계학자

01 ▶ 서로 상반된 내용으로 이루어진 두 문장은 '그러나, 한편'의 뜻인 whereas(= while)로 자연스럽게 연결될 수 있다.

02 ▶ 앞에서 당시 인구조사는 가장을 제외하고는 각 구성원에 대한 특징을 제대로 반영하지 않았다고 하였고, 문제의 문장 뒤에 1850년의 인구조사에는 개인의 정보를 수집하기 시작하였다는 내용이 이어지는 점에 미루어 정답을 알 수 있다.

03 ▶ 여성의 소득 수준(income level)과 학력(educational background)에 의한 인구 조사는 본문에 언급되어 있지 않다.

04 ▶ 1840년의 인구조사에서 개인은 단지 직업별 총인원수로 표시되었다고 하였으므로 (B) '농업에 종사하지 않는 사람들의 수'를 제공했을 것이다. 성별에 따라 직업을 정리한 것은 1870년이 지나서이며, social movements는 직업이라고 규정하기 어려우므로 나머지 보기는 답이 될 수 없다.

05 ▶ 마지막 문장에서 여성의 증가된 사회 진출로 인해 여성인권 옹호자와 여성 통계학자들은 좀 더 명확한 여성의 직업과 임금에 대한 정보를 요구하였다고 했으므로, 그들은 이전 통계는 불충분하며 미국 내 경제 변화를 제대로 반영하지 않는다고 생각했을 것이다.

》 **정답** 01 (C) 02 (B) 03 (C) 04 (B) 05 (B)

알래스카의 중앙 산맥에 위치한 데날리(Denali)라고 이름 붙여진 한 봉우리는 해수면 위로 20,320 피트 솟아있다. 그것은 북미에서 가장 높은 봉우리이자 데날리 국립공원의 중심부이다. 미국에서 가장 큰 황야 지역 중의 하나인 그 공원은 방문객들의 접근을 제한하고 있다. 그러나 이러한 제한에도 불구하고 관광객은 1950년 6,000명 미만에서 1990년 546,000명 이상으로 증가했다. 이 공원이 점점 유명해지면서 일반적으로 야생 지역을 보전하는 방법뿐만 아니라 데날리의 앞으로의 이용에 대한 진지한 토론이 촉진되고 있다.

국립공원의 일부를 개인이 소유하면 그 땅을 사용하는 데 한 가지 중요한 문제가 발생한다. 데날리에서, 백만 에이커 이상의 방대한 면적의 대부분의 땅을 국립공원 관리청이 소유하고 있지만, 일부 천 에이커의 땅은 광산지대로 여전히 개인이 소유하고 있다. 데날리의 이러한 광산 지대는 한 때 금과 같은 자원이 풍족하였지만, 그것은 강과 시내를 오염시킨 비소, 납과 같은 중금속의 원천이기도 했다. 환경보호론자들은 정부가 광산 회사들이 광산 사업을 시작하는 것이 허용되기 전에 광산 사업을 하면 일어날 수 있는 가능한 영향들을 보여주는 성명서를 제출하도록 요구하도록 하는 데 성공하였다. 이러한 필요조건 때문에 많은 개인들은 그들의 광산을 닫았고, 일부는 그들의 땅을 국립공원 관리청에 팔았다. 그러나 땅 소유주들의 일부는 자신의 땅을 정부에 파는 것이 좋은지 미래에 사용이 가능하도록 보유하는 것이 좋은지 궁금해 하고 있다. 더 많은 도로가 공원에 접근을 쉽게 하기 위해 건설됨에 따라 이전에는 멀기만 했던 이 지역에서 관광객들이 증가하게 되었다. 방문객들 수의 이러한 증가로 호텔과 다른 부동산의 개발을 위한 수요가 생겼다. 이것과 경제의 밀접한 관련은 토지 소유자들에게 흥미를 갖게 했지만, 그러나 황야를 보전하는 데 관심이 있는 사람들을 당황스럽게 하였다.

wilderness n. 황야, 황무지, 사막
tourism n. 관광 사업; 관광객
preserve v. 보전하다, 보호하다
tract n. 넓이, 넓은 면적; 지역
privately ad. 개인으로서; 남몰래
abundant a. 풍부한; (자원 등이) 풍족한
arsenic n. 비소
environmentalist n. 환경보호론자
implication n. 함축; 밀접한 관계
dismay v. 당황케 하다; 실망시키다

01 ▶ 첫 번째 빈칸은 진지한 토론이 시작되게 했다는 의미로 prompting이 적절하고, 두 번째 빈칸은 토지 사용에 대한 중요한 문제가 발생하였다는 의미로 arises가 와야 한다.

02 ▶ 황야 지역을 보전하는 방법뿐만 아니라 데날리의 앞으로의 이용에 대한 진지한 토론이 있다고 했으므로 (B)가 적절하다.

03 ▶ 도로가 건설되면서 관광객의 수가 증가하고 이러한 증가는 호텔과 다른 부동산의 개발을 위한 수요가 있으므로 광산 소유자들은 더 많은 돈을 받고 팔 수 있을 것이다.

» 정답 01 (C) 02 (B) 03 (C)

250

인간의 이상적인 모습은 다수의 관심사와 재능을 가진 다재다능한 사람, 즉 "르네상스적 교양인"으로 종종 특징지어져 왔다. 이 아부적인 용어는 풍부하고 다양한 관심사를 가진 사람을 설명할 때 오랫동안 사용되어 왔다. 르네상스인이라는 개념은 카스틸리오네(B. Castiglione)의 1518년 작품인 『정신(廷臣)의 책』으로부터 유래하는지도 모른다. 정신(廷臣)들은 개인적, 문화적 우아함을 추구하는 수단을 가지고 있었던 귀족인들이었다. 카스틸리오네는 이상적인 남성 정신은 작문과 웅변에서 뿐만 아니라 예술, 체육, 무기 사용에 있어서도 능숙해야 한다고 생각했다. 정신은 어느 상황이라도 지배하며 모든 일에 소신 있고 온화해야했다. 이상적인 여성 정신은 문학과 예술에 정통해야 했고, 최고의 품격을 지니고 있어야 하며, 항상 여성스럽게 행동해야 했다.

르네상스인을 구현시킨다면, 그것은 의심할 바 없이 레오나르도 다빈치가 될 것이다. 다빈치는 모나리자를 만들어낸 그 유명한 예술적 능력뿐만 아니라 해부학, 천문학, 식물학, 지리학을 공부했으며 수백 가지 기계 발명품의 설계도를 그렸다. 다빈치에 버금가는 미국인으로는 뛰어난 작가, 발명가, 정치인이었던 벤자민 프랭클린(Benjamin Franklin)을 꼽을 수 있을 것이다. 그러나 현대에는 다빈치나 프랭클린이 보여준 학식과 업적에 근접할 수 있는 사람은 거의 없다. 기술이 발전하고 전문화되고 있는 시대에, 르네상스인은 불행히도 멸종 위기에 놓여버린 하나의 종(種)인 것이다.

---

courtier n. (왕을 보필하던) 조신(朝臣), 정신(廷臣)
refinement n. 정제; 세련; 정밀
oratory n. 웅변(술); 수사
suave a. 기분 좋은; 유순한
anatomy n. 해부학
counterpart n. 상대물, 대응물
endangered a. 멸종 위기에 처한

01 ▶ 박식한 르네상스시대 인물에 대해 설명하고 있으므로 '다재 다능'이라는 의미임을 유추할 수 있다.

02 ▶ 뒤 이어 나오는 also로 보아 ①에는 부연 설명을 나타내는 전치사(구)가 나와야 하며, 앞 문장과 대조를 이루는 내용으로 시작하고 있는 ②에는 역접의 접속사가 나와야 하므로 (C)가 정답이 된다.

03 ▶ 글쓴이는 다방면에서 두각을 나타내고자 했고 또 실제 그러했던 르네상스 인물들에 대해 감탄을 드러내고 있다. 한편, 글쓴이가 그 이상적인 모습에 감탄하긴 했으나 다시 르네상스 시대가 부활하기를 희망하는 언급은 없으므로 (C)는 답이 될 수 없다.

04 ▶ 본문 마지막 문장에서 "현대의 기술 발달과 전문화로 인해 요즘에는 르네상스시대처럼 다재다능한 인물을 거의 찾아 볼 수 없다"고 하였다.

» 정답 01 (A) 02 (C) 03 (A) 04 (D)

월등한 서비스 제공이 회사에 경쟁력 있는 강점을 낳는다는 사실이 서비스를 개선하려는 모든 노력이 그러한 이점을 만들어 낸다는 것을 의미하지는 않는다. 서비스 분야의 투자는 생산과 유통 분야에서의 투자와 같이, 비용절감과 수익증대와 같이 직접적이고 실체적인 이익을 토대로 하여 다른 방식의 투자와 비교하여 고려되어야 한다. 회사의 명성에 타격을 주지 않으며 용납 못할 정도의 속도로 고객이 빠져나가지 않게끔 서비스를 제공하여 이미 경쟁사와 사실상 동등한 위치에 있다면, 서비스는 극히 심한 경우가 아니고서야 결정적으로 작용하지 않으므로, 더 높은 수준의 서비스를 위한 투자는 헛되이 될지 모른다.

이러한 사실이 한 은행의 경영진들에게는 분명치 않았는데, 그 은행은 은행원을 기다리는 고객의 시간을 줄이는 투자에도 불구하고 경쟁적 위치를 개선하는 데 실패하였다. 그들은 은행 업계에서 거래 은행을 옮기는 불편함으로 야기되는 고객의 미비한 이동 수준을 인지하지 못했다. 또한 해당 서비스가 새로운 고객을 이끌어 낼지 결정하기 위해 고객의 흥미를 자아낼 새로운 기준의 서비스를 만들거나, 경쟁사가 모방하기 어렵다는 것을 입증하는 식으로 서비스 개선을 분석하지도 않았다. 그 서비스 개선의 유일한 가치는 고객에게 개선된 부분이 쉽게 설명될 수 있다는 것이었다.

---

generate v. 발생시키다
competitive advantage 경쟁우위
distribution n. 분배; 유통
revenue n. 소득; (pl.) 총수입
be on a par with ~동등하다
teller n. (은행의) 금전 출납 계원
inertia n. 불활동, 불활발; 관성
sustaining a. 떠받치는, 지탱하는; 유지하는
exuberant a. 활기[생동감] 넘치는
negligible a. 무시해도 될 정도의
prospective a. 장래의, 유망한

01 ▶ 도입부에서 우수한 서비스 제공이 회사의 경쟁력을 항상 높이는 것은 아님을 언급하면서 회사의 경쟁력을 높일 수 있는 다른 투자 방식과 비교하여 결정되어야 한다고 했다. 따라서 투자에 대한 좀 더 신중한 평가를 제안하는 것이 이 글의 목적이 된다.

02 ▶ 경쟁적 위치에 서는 데 실패한 은행(the regional bank)은 타사가 그들이 제공하는 서비스를 모방하지 못하도록 서비스 개선을 분석한 것이 아니라고 하였다. 따라서 그 은행 경영진들은 그들이 제공하는 서비스를 경쟁사가 모방할 수 있는지에 대한 여부를 고려하지 않았다는 점을 유추할 수 있다.

03 ▶ tangible a. 만져서 알 수 있는, 실체적인(= concrete)

04 ▶ 이 문장에 앞서 서비스 개선에 노력했음에도 불구하고 경쟁적 입지를 얻는 데 실패한 은행을 사례로 들었다. only는 그 노력에 비해 얻은 유일한 이점을 수식하고 있으므로 상대적으로 적은 서비스 투자의 가치를 강조한다.

▶ 정답 01 (B) 02 (C) 03 (A) 04 (B)

내가 미국에서 잘 적응해 나갈 때마다, 아버지는 내가 서구 생활 방식을 받아들이는 것에 대해 불쾌해 하시며 경멸적으로 받아들이시는 반면, 오빠들은 그런 나의 편이 되어 주었다. 나는 나의 백인 친구들처럼 되고 싶었다. 그들처럼 보이고 싶을 뿐만 아니라, 그들처럼 행동하고 싶었다. 나는 내 또래의 여자친구들처럼 밖에서 사람들과 잘 어울리고 당당하게 행동하려 부단히 노력했다. 집에서는 이런 나의 성격을 아버지에게 보이지 않으려 조심스러워 했다. 나는 체구가 큰 편이며 걸을 때도 씩씩했는데 아버지는 내가 일본 여성처럼 보이지 않는다는 점조차 충분히 못마땅하게 여기셨다. 집에서 나는 조용하거나 차분하게 행동하지 않았지만, 아버지 앞에서는 여전히 할 수 있는 한 일본 여성처럼 행동하려 노력했다.

사춘기가 지나고 남자들에 대한 관심이 더해가면서, 동양 여성이 남자들에게 어떤 흥미를 일으킨다는 것을 알게 되었다. 나는 너무 어려서 어떻게 그리고 왜 동양 여성이 서양 남자들을 매료시키는지 이해할 수 없었으며, 당연히 그것이 "진정한 나의 모습을 보는 것이 아니라는"것을 알기에는 정말 너무 어렸다. 오빠들은 "서양 남자들을 믿지 마"라고 경고하곤 하였다. "그들이 바라는 것은 단 한 가지다. 그들은 너를 하인처럼 취급할 것이며 자신들을 떠받들어 주길 바란다. 너한테 잘 대해 주는 방법조차 모른다"라는 것이다. 오빠들은 백인 여자와 절대 데이트를 하지 않았다. 사실, 나는 대학에 들어가기 전에는 백인 남자들과 데이트다운 데이트를 한 적이 없었다. 고등학교 때엔, 백인 남자들을 만날 수 있는 사교장에 몰래 나가곤 하였다. 아버지가 아시면 어떻게 하셨을지 감히 상상조차 못했다.

오빠들은 내가 전에 그들을 대했던 것처럼 백인 남자들을 대해서는 안 된다고 하였다. 백인 남자들은 이런 행동을 이해하지 못하므로 그들에게 "시중들거나" 내가 그렇게 할 거라고 생각하게 놔두어선 안 된다는 것이었다. 다시 말해, 일본 남자들에게는 일본 여자가 되어야 하고 백인 남자들에겐 백인 여자가 되어야 한다는 것이다. "이중 잣대" 속에서의 이중 정체성은 나 스스로의 역할과 여자로서의 역할의 혼란을 일으킬 뿐만 아니라, 내가 민족적으로 어디에 속하는 지에 대한 혼동을 초래하였다. 나의 의식 깊은 곳에서 오빠들의 경고가 잠재한 채, 나는 백인 남자들에게 적극적이며 확고하고 "위압적으로" 대하려 애쓰곤 하였다. 그들이 나를 순정적이고 소극적이며 나비부인처럼 모든 걸 다 주는 사람으로 생각하게 해선 안 되었다. 동양 남자들에게는 나의 천성적인 열정을 가라앉히고 어머니와 언니들이 보여준 모델을 통해 스며든 행동양식에 정착했다. 이 두 역할 어느 것도 편하지 않았다.

Caucasian n. 백인
disdainful a. 경멸적인; 무시하는
undermine v. (명성 따위를) 손상시키다
capitulation n. (조건부) 항복
assertively ad. 단호하게
serene a. 고요한; 차분한
puberty n. 사춘기
evoke v. 불러일으키다
wait on hand and foot 최선을 다해 섬기다
admonition n. 훈계; 충고
lurk v. 숨다, 잠복하다
tone down 부드럽게 하다
instill v. 스며들게 하다; 서서히 가르쳐 주다

01 ▶ 그녀의 아버지는 그녀가 서구식으로 행동하는 것에 명예가 손상되어(undermined) 불쾌하게 느꼈다고 하는 점으로 미루어 그(her father)의 권위를 잃어버린다고 느낀다는 것을 알 수 있다.

02 ▶ 백인 남자들은 그녀를 아버지의 보수적 성향과 백인 친구들처럼 되고 싶어 하는 마음 사이에서 갈등하고 있는 모습보다 전형적인 일본여성으로만 보고 관심을 가지고 있으므로 "not seeing"은 "진정한 그녀의 모습을 볼 수 없는 무능력"을 말하고 있다.

03 ▶ 일본 남자에겐 일본 여자가 되고 백인 남자에겐 백인 여자가 되어야 하는 사실은 이중 잣대(double standard)속에 이중 정체성(double identity)을 지녀야 한다는 것을 의미한다.

04 ▶ 백인 남자들이 기대하는 전형적인 일본인 여성을 지칭하는 것이다.

» 정답 01 (D) 02 (B) 03 (B) 04 (D)

옛날에 미국 이민자들은 근면함, 용기, 결단력으로 누구든지 부(富)를 성취할 수 있다는 개념인 아메리칸 드림을 믿었다. 아메리칸 드림은 대부분의 이민자들에게 즉시 실현되지는 않았지만 근면함과 가족을 위해 기꺼이 희생하는 의지가 다음 세대에서 이익을 창출하는 투자가 되었다. 삶은 그들의 자녀, 손자, 증손자들에게 훨씬 수월해졌는데 그들은 (부모세대 덕분으로) 대학 학위를 획득하여 성공적인 직업을 추구할 수 있게 되었다. 한때 모든 신세대들이 그들의 부모세대들보다 더 나은 삶을 열망하는 것은 일반적이었다. 미국인이 된다는 것은 (그들 언어가 아닌) 다른 언어를 배우고, 이 땅의 법과 관습을 배우며 준수하고, 본국보다 미국을 신봉하고, 전쟁에서 미국의 편에 서는 것을 의미했다. 오늘날 아메리칸 드림은 급격히 변하였는데, 어떤 이들은 산산이 부서졌다고 주장할 것이다. 많은 이민자들은 더 나은 삶을 위해 미국으로 오고, 반면에 다른 이들은 임금을 고국에 있는 가족들에게 보내며 단지 직업 때문에 미국으로 온다. 미국으로 오는 외국인들은 '미국화' 되어 미국인이 되려고 온 것이었다. 그들은 사회의 일부분이 되어감에 따라 이러한 열망을 그들의 자녀들에게 심어주었다. 그들의 문화는 더 큰 미국 문화로 융합되었는데, 이것은 문화가 동화되는 큰 도가니(the Great Melting Pot)와 같은 장소가 된 것이다. 그리고 바로 그것이, 많은 사람들이 주장하기를, 정확히 말해 미국으로 오는 너무나 많은 사람들이 이제는 더 이상 동화되기를 바라지 않는 이유이다. 그들은 고국의 문화, 전통 및 정체성을 잃는 것을 두려워한다. 그리하여 그들의 언어와 관습을 고수하여, 심지어 거리 표시판과 운전면허 시험 그리고 정부 문서가 그들 본국의 언어로 이루어져야 한다고 주장하는 정도에 이르기도 한다. 한때 아메리칸 드림을 실현하는 데 필수적으로 여겨졌던 영어로 말하고 읽고 쓰는 일은 진부하고 방해가 되며, 심지어는 자신이 택하는 방식으로 살아갈 권리를 침해하는 것으로 여겨지고 있다. 상반된 이데올로기의 문화전쟁이 벌어져 정부를 양극화시키고 국가를 분열시키고 있다.

turn out 결국 ~임이 밝혀지다
yield v. 산출(産出)하다; 양보하다
dividend n. 배당금; 이익 배당
aspire v. 열망하다; 대망을 품다
embrace v. 포옹하다; 환영하다
side v. 찬성하다; 편들다
shatter v. 부서지다; 산산조각 나다
instill v. 스며들게 하다; 주입시키다
cling vi. 고착하다; 매달리다
obsolete a. 쓸모없게 된; 쇠퇴한
intrusive a. 강제하는; 침입하는; 주제넘게 나서는
infringement n. (법규)위반; 침해
wage v. (전쟁 따위를) 수행하다
polarize v. 양극화하다

01 ▶ [IV] 이후 과거에 비해 달라진 오늘날의 이민자들에 대한 언급이 시작되고 있다.

02 ▶ 불법 이민자들에 대한 (미국)정부의 반응은 언급되지 않았다.

03 ▶ '미국화 되기(Americanized)'위해 노력했던 과거의 이민자들과 달리 오늘날 이민자들은 본국의 전통 및 문화를 잃지 않기 위해 더 이상 '미국화하지' 않으려 하기에 그들의 문화 또한 미국 문화로 융화되지(fused into) 않을 것이다. Americanized 또는 fused into는 assimilate(동화되다)로 표현할 수 있다.

04 ▶ the Great Melting Pot은 앞 문장을 통해 보면 이민자들의 서로 다른 문화가 미국 문화로 융화되는 현상을 비유적으로 표현한 것임을 알 수 있다. 따라서 (C) '미국인이라는 정체성을 가지고 미국식으로 살아가는 서로 다른 문화배경을 지닌 이민자들이 the Great Melting Pot을 가장 잘 나타내는 예가 된다.

05 ▶ 과거와 달리 아메리칸 드림에 대해 냉소적인 현재 이민자들의 모습에 대해 설명하고 있으며, 마지막 문장에 정부를 양극화시키고(polarizing) 국가를 분열한다(dividing)고 했으므로 (C) "미국 이민자들은 아메리칸 드림을 더 이상 환영하지 않으며 이는 국가를 불안정하게 한다"가 정답이다.

» 정답   01 (D)   02 (B)   03 (D)   04 (C)   05 (C)

도덕성은 이해하기 힘든 개념일지 모르지만 우리는 도덕성을 빠르게 습득한다. 하버드 대학의 심리학 교수인 마크 하우서(Marc Hauser)는 대부분의 언어학자들이 믿고 있는 우리가 태어날 때부터 갖춘 기본적인 언어 습득에 상당하는 것, 소위 도덕 문법 감각을 우리 모두가 가지고 있다고 믿는다. 그러나 우리가 태어날 때부터 도덕 프로그램을 단지 갖추고 있다고 해서 도덕적 행동을 실행에 옮기는 것은 아니다. 무엇인가 그 소프트웨어를 작동시키고 적절하게 배열해야 한다. 단어들이 모여 문장을 이루기 전까지 문장론이 아무것도 아니듯, 옳고 그름 또한 누군가가 어떻게 그것을 적용하는지 가르쳐주기 전까지 소용이 없다. 그러한 가르침을 주는 사람은 우리 주변에 있다. 인간은 누군가는 도와야 하고 누군가는 돕지 말아야 할 상황에서 아주 갈등을 느끼게 되는데, 이에 대한 일반적인 규칙은 "집에서 가까운 사람은 도우며 멀리 사는 사람은 내버려 두라"는 것이다. 그것은 부분적으로 어떤 이의 고통을 당신이 직접 볼 수 있을 때가 단지 누군가의 고통이 설명으로 전해질 때 보다 더 현실로 와 닿기 때문이다. 하지만 부분적으로는 당신이 속한 지역의 번영이 당신의 생존에 필수적이고 상대 지역의 번창은 당신과 무관했을 때도 그러하다. 집단의 도덕을 강제하는 가장 강력한 도구들 중의 하나는 배척을 하는 것이다. 한 집단의 구성원이 되는 것이 자신의 식량 및 가족 그리고 약탈자로부터의 보호를 보장하는 길이라면, 배척을 당하는 것은 끔찍한 일이 될 수 있다. 클럽, 사회단체 그리고 우애단체에서는 바람직하지 않은 구성원들을 탈퇴시키고, 미 군부는 징계도구로써 강제 전역시키겠다는 위협을 가하다가 심지어 '불명예'라는 처분을 내려 전직군인에게 평생 따라다닐 기록을 더럽히기도 한다. 인간은 약하고 무방비상태에 있으며 약탈자에게 공격받기 쉽다. 추방당하지 않는 것은 우리에게 중요하다.

grasp v. 붙잡다; 이해하다
linguist n. 어학자; 언어학자
syntax n. 구문론
plight n. 곤경; 어려운 입장
shun v. 피하다
fraternity n. 동포애; 우애 단체
disciplinary a. 훈련 상의; 규율의
defenseless a. 무방비의
predator n. 약탈자; 육식동물
banishment n. 추방

01 ▶ 우리는 도덕성을 빨리 습득하며, 하우서는 이를 도덕 문법이라고 칭하며 우리에게 주어져있는 것이라고 주장한다. 이에 대한 부연 설명으로, 태어날 때부터 주어져 있는 기본적인 언어습득에 상당하는 것이므로 ①에는 'equivalent(동등한 것, 상당하는 것)'가 들어간다. 또한 도덕프로그램이 주어져 있어도 누군가 어떻게 적용할 것인지 가르쳐주기 전까지는 아무 소용이 없는 것이라고 하였다. 따라서 이러한 도덕 프로그램이 있다고 해서 도덕적 행동을 실행에 옮기는 것이 아니므로 ②에는 'practice(실행하다, 실천하다)'가 들어가야 한다.

02 ▶ 문장 ③은 하나하나도 중요하지만 완성과 실행의 중요성을 강조하는 말이다. (A) "구슬이 서 말이라도 꿰어야 보배다"가 정답이다. (B) "티끌 모아 태산"은 꾸준한 노력을 강조한다. (C) "호미로 막을 것을 가래로 막는다" (D) "행동과 말은 맞아야 한다"

03 ▶ blackball v. 반대투표하다, 배척하다(= exclude)

04 ▶ 도덕성을 자신의 안전을 보장하기 위한 수단의 측면에서 설명하고 있다.

» 정답 01 (B) 02 (A) 03 (B) 04 (C)

연금술은 1317년에 교황 요한 22세가 내린 교서에 의해 금지됐다. 이 금지령은 연금술이 꽤 널리 퍼져 있었음을 반증해 주고 있다. 중세의 연금술사들의 이론에는 새로운 것이 그다지 많지 않았다. 금속은 유황의 남성적인 원리와 수은의 여성적인 원리와의 결합으로 생겨나고, 비금속은 죽음과 소생의 과정을 거쳐 귀금속으로 만들어진다고 그들은 믿었다. 일반적으로 무기물은 살아 있는 것으로서, 육체와 영혼, 또는 물질과 정신으로 이루어져 있었다. 물체의 구성요소는 열을 가함으로써 분해될 수 있고, 그 때 정신은 증기로 떨어져 나오는데, 그 증기는 때에 따라서는 액체로 응축될 수가 있다. 물체의 성질과 특징은 그 정신에 의해 결정된다. 그러므로 증류를 해서 얻은 액체에는 그것이 생겨난 물질의 농축된 정수가 포함돼 있다.

이러한 액체는 매우 활성적이고 유력한 작용제인 까닭에 늙은 육체에다 새로운 생명을 넣어 주고 비금속물질에다 귀금속의 특성을 부여한다. 이리하여 이론적으로는, 변성(비금속의 귀금속화)은 비금속의 물질에 귀금속의 정신을 불어 넣음으로써 이룩할 수가 있다. 그러나 갖가지 금속 가운데서, 수은만이 증류되어 유리(遊離)시킬 수 있는 '정신'을 나타낸다. 수은의 증기는 연금술사의 이론에 따라 비금속의 표면을 은빛이 되게 했으므로, 수은은 은의 정신이며 금속의 조상으로 간주되었을 뿐더러, 만물의 기원이라 여겨졌다.

---

bull n. (로마 교황의) 교서
medieval a. 중세의, 중세풍의
sulphur n. 유황
mercury n. 수은
ennoble v. 귀금속(부식하지 않는 금속)으로 만들다
resuscitation n. 소생, 부활
constituent n. 구성요소, 성분
transmutation n. 변형, 변성(비금속의 귀금속화)
in accordance with ~에 따라, ~와 일치하여
progenitor n. (사람, 동식물의) 조상; 선배, 원본

01 ▶ 첫 번째 문장에서 정답을 찾을 수 있다.
02 ▶ 바로 앞 문장에서 essential이 물체의 성질과 특징을 결정할 수 있다는 내용을 찾을 수 있으므로, essential은 '정신'을 나타냄을 알 수 있다.
03 ▶ 많은 금속 중 수은만이 증류되어 유리시킬 수 있는 정신을 나타낸다고 했다.

》 정답 01 (A) 02 (C) 03 (C)

사회학자 멜빈 칸(Melvin H. Kohn)은 중산층과 노동 계층 부모들 사이에서 가장 중요한 가치 차이 중 하나로 교육을 예를 들며 "중산층 부모들은 자녀의 내면적인 원동력을 좀 더 주의 깊게 생각하는 반면에 노동 계층 부모들은 그들의 자녀가 외부로부터 주어지는 기준에 순응하기를 원한다."라고 말한다. 그러므로 중산층 부모들은 의도를 더 강조하는 반면 노동 계층 부모들은 자녀들의 행동의 결과를 강조하는 경향이 있다. 예를 들어, 중산층 엄마들은 아이들이 '거친 놀이'를 할 때 보다 '흥분하며 화를 낼 때' 훨씬 더 벌을 주는 것 같다. 그들은 '짜증내는 기질'을 관찰하는 것이지 자기 제어와 내면 절제로 볼 수 있는 거친 놀이를 관찰하는 것이 아니다. 이와는 다르게 노동계층 엄마들은 파괴적인 행동의 결과를 걱정하기 때문에 양쪽 상황 모두에 대해 자녀들을 체벌한다. 칸은 이러한 가치의 차이들과 육아 활동은 직업 상태의 차이에서 많은 부분이 유래한다고 추측한다. 노동 계층 부모들은 성인으로서의 준수와 복종이 높이 평가받는 특징이 될 것이라고 예상한다. 중산층 부모는 독창성과 자제력으로 성공을 할 수 있다고 생각되는, 전문적인 직업을 가진 아이들을 그려보곤 한다. 최근에 제임스(James D.)와 소냐 라이트(Sonia R. Wright)는 칸의 연구에서 부분적인 반복 실험을 수행했고 사회 계층에 따라 자기 훈련의 가치가 증가하는 경향을 찾았다는 것을 확인했다. 그러나 라이트는 칸은 부모들이 그들의 자녀들에게 전하는 가치와 사회 계층 사이의 연결고리의 근원으로서 교육 수준 교육자로서의 아버지를 좀 더 입증하는 대신 직업의 중요성을 과장한다고 주장한다.

사회 계층의 차이점들은 육아활동 뿐만 아니라 부모가 자기 자식들과 형성하는 관계도 드러낸다. 예를 들면 중산층 부모들은 자녀의 심리적인 욕구에 반응하도록 기대된다. 결과적으로 중산층 부모들의 육아법칙 — 그들의 활동력 집중과 자녀의 내적인 발전에 대한 노력 둘 다 크게 다르지 않다.

그러나 여성 운동이나 교육 수준의 향상, 여성과 소수민족에게 더욱 확대된 교육기회는 젊은 노동계층 사람들에게 영향력을 주기 시작해서 육아에 관해서, 계층과 노동 분담 사이의 전통적인 상관관계를 약화시킴에도 불구하고 사회화가 구속과 복종에 집중되어 행해지는 노동계층 가정에서는 어머니는 엄격한 교육자로서 아버지를 보조하는 역할을 하는 것 같다.

---

attentive a. 주의 깊은, 세심한
dynamics n. 원동력, 힘
temper n. 천성, 기질
tantrum n. 발끈, 울화통
disruptive a. 파괴적인
conformity n. 순응, 적합, 일치
initiative n. 독창력
replication n. 응답, 반향
transmit v. 전하다
constraint n. 강제, 압박, 구속
disciplinarian n. 훈련자
blurring a. 흐리게 하는, 희미하게 하는

01 ▶ 이 글은 전체적으로 사회계층과 부모와 자녀의 관계는 밀접하게 관계되어 있다고 설명하고 있다.

02 ▶ 첫 번째 문단에 노동 계층 부모들은 그들의 자녀가 외부로부터 주어지는 기준에 순응하기를 원한다고 했다.

03 ▶ 글쓴이는 어느 한 연구를 옹호하는 것이 아닌 중립적인 관점에서 이야기하고 있다.

》 정답 01 (C) 02 (D) 03 (C)

1906년 독일의 신경학자 알로이스 알츠하이머는 최근 사망한 한 여성 환자에게서 자신이 목격한 바를 설명했다. 그 여성 환자는 51세의 나이에 옆에서 불러주지 않으면 자신의 이름을 더 이상 쓸 수 없었고, 집안일도 할 수 없었으며, 방향감각을 잃어버리는 일이 많아지는 징후와 기억력과 판단력과 의사결정능력과 언어능력과 신체적 능력이 점차적으로 손상되는 징후를 보였다.

[Ⅲ] 알츠하이머가 보기에는 노쇠현상이 너무 일찍 찾아온 것 같았다. 그녀는 그 당시에는 정상적인 노화의 일부로 여겨진 치매의 증세를 보일 정도의 나이는 아직 아니었다. 그래서 그는 그것을 초로성 치매라 불렀다. 증세가 악화되어 그녀는 마침내 혼수상태에 빠졌다. 55세의 나이로 그녀가 사망하자, 알츠하이머는 그녀의 뇌를 검사해 보았다.

[Ⅰ] 얇게 썬 뇌의 조각들을 현미경으로 관찰했을 때, 세 가지 특징이 두드러졌다. 뇌 자체가 심하게 쭈그러들어 있었으며, 두 번째로는 뇌 조직에 특이한 물질이 이상하게 축적되어 있었다. 세 번째로는 뇌의 신경신호 전달체인 뉴런 내부에 또 다른 물질이 마디가 많은 실타래를 꼬아놓은 것처럼 마구 뒤엉켜 있었다. 플라크와 탱글이라 부르는 이 물질들이 지금에 와서는 알츠하이머병을 다른 신경질환과 구별지어주는 두 가지 필수적인 특징으로 여겨진다.

[Ⅳ] 그러나 50년 이상 동안 알츠하이머병의 증세는 정상적인 노화의 일부이며 65세 미만의 사람들에게 나타날 경우에만 진정한 질병인 것으로 생각되었다. 그런 환자들은 전체의 5% 내지 7%에 이르며 알츠하이머병의 가족력을 갖고 있다고 맥마스터 대학 교수이자 캐나다 알츠하이머 학회의 과학이사인 잭 다이아몬드 박사는 설명한다.

[Ⅱ] 그러나 1960년대에는 이미 학자들은 플라크와 탱글이 노인들에게조차도 정상적인 것이 아니며 하나의 잠행성 질병이 진행되고 있는 것이라는 것을 깨닫기 시작했다.

---

deceased a. 사망한
prompting n. (연극) 대사 일러주기
household n. 가족, 한 집안
disorientation n. 방향감각의 상실
prematurely ad. 너무 때 이르게
senile a. 노쇠한
dementia n. 치매
comatose a. 혼수상태의
strike v. (눈에) 띄다, (주의를) 끌다
tangle n. 엉킴, 얽힘
gnarled a. 마디가 많은
twine n. 꼰 실, 뒤엉킴
familial a. (병이) 한 가족에 특유한
insidious a. (병이) 잠행성인(모르는 사이에 진행하는)

01 ▶ 이 글은 알츠하이머병이 처음에는 정상적인 노화의 일부로 오해되었다가 나중에 하나의 질병으로 인식된 연유를 설명한 글이므로 (B)가 제목으로 가장 적절하다.

02 ▶ 첫 단락에 나온 여성 환자의 증세에 뒤이어 [Ⅲ] 이 증세에 대한 알츠하이머의 판단, [Ⅰ] 사망한 여성 환자의 뇌 검사의 결과, [Ⅳ] 이 결과를 처음에는 정상적인 노화의 일부로 본 것, [Ⅱ] 1960년대에 와서 하나의 질병으로 보게 된 것의 순서가 적절하다.

03 ▶ (A)는 본문 속의 without prompting에, (B)는 disorientation에, (C)는 familial Alzheimer's와 an insidious disease에 각각 해당한다. (D)는 과거 50년 이상 동안의 잘못된 생각일 뿐이다.

» 정답 01 (B) 02 (C) 03 (D)

"당신은 눈꺼풀이 무거워지고 잠들게 됩니다." 최면학자들은 최면이라고 불리는 몽환의 경지를 이끌어 내기 위해 이러한 비슷한 구절을 사용한다. 오랫동안 최면은 속임수로 여겨졌다. 일부 최면에 열광하는 사람들은 최면이 아픈 사람들을 치료하는 데 쓰일 수 있다고 믿지만, 대부분의 의사들은 그러한 생각을 비웃었다. 의사들은 최면을 '심리조작'으로 부르며 전혀 믿지 않았다. 하지만 오늘날 시대가 변화했다. 의사들은 정신과 몸의 관계의 중요성을 이해하여 최면에 대해 기꺼이 다시 한 번 생각해 보고자 한다.

최면이란 도대체 무엇인가? 대부분의 참고 문헌에서는 최면을 의식이 전환된 상태라고 정의한다. 어떤 사람들은 이 정의가 정확하다고 한다. 다른 이들은 맞지 않다고 한다. 로버트 베이커(Robert Baker) 박사는 20년 넘게 최면술을 해왔지만 최면이 전환된 상태를 일으킨다고는 생각하지 않는다. 베이커 박사는 "아무리 우리가 오래 살펴보아도 전환된 의식 상태는 찾아 볼 수 없을 때 최면이 어떤 종류의 특정한 상태를 수반한다고 주장하는 것은 터무니없다."라고 말한다. 실제로 조사자들은 최면에 빠진 동안 뇌가 변화한다는 증거는 찾지 못했다. 베이커 박사와 같은 사람들은 최면에 빠진 마음이 그 마음 자체에 속임수를 쓰는 것이라고 생각한다. 사람들이 말하기를 최면은 뇌의 한 부분이 정지되고 다른 한 부분은 고도로 집중된 상태에서 일어난다고 한다.

다른 사람들은 최면을 수면상태로 정의한다. 몸에 긴장이 풀리고 마음 상태가 좀 더 한가로워지며 집중되고 호흡이 더욱 규칙적이게 된다는 것이다. 정신병학자 로버트 피셔(Robert Fisher) 박사는 최면이 영화관에 가는 것과 같다고 말한다. 영화관에 들어갈 때는 모든 것을 의식한다. 사탕 포장지가 바스락거리는 소리를 들을 수 있다. 바로 앞에 앉아 있는 사람의 머리를 인지할 수 있다. 발밑에 엎질러진 팝콘을 느낄 수도 있다. 그러나 피셔는 "화면이 영화로 채워지면 영화에 점점 빠져들어 당신은 초점이 맞추어진 집중된 상태가 된다"고 말한다.

대부분의 사람들은 최면이 의식의 전환인가 하는 여부에 대해 신경 쓰지 않는다. 그들은 최면의 정확한 정의를 찾고 있지 않다. 그들은 오로지 "최면이 나에게도 효과가 있을까? 최면이 담배를 끊거나 살을 빼는 데 도움을 줄 수 있을까?"라고 묻는다.

이러한 실제로 이용할 수 있는 수준에서 최면이 효과가 있다는 증거가 많이 있다. 최면이 어떤 행동을 변화시킬 수 있다는 증거가 있다. 흡연이 하나의 예이다. 정신요법학자 로라 포스터 콜린즈(Laura Foster Collins)는 그녀의 환자들이 나쁜 습관을 버릴 수 있게 도와주고 있다. 어떤 환자들은 담배를 완전히 끊었으며 담배를 피우고 싶은 충동을 없애기조차 하였다. 하지만 최면술의 결과 오직 다섯 명 중 한명만이 완전히 담배를 끊었다. 담배를 피워 본 사람이라면 담배를 끊는 것이 얼마나 어려운 일인지 안다. 최면은 도움이 되지만 담배를 끊으려는 강한 욕구가 결합되어야만 하는 것이다.

---

hypnotist n. 최면학자
hypnosis n. 최면(상태); 최면술
induce v. 꾀다; 야기하다
trance n. 몽환의 경지; 황홀
enthusiast n. 열광자, 팬
scoff at 비웃다; 조롱하다
alter v. 바꾸다; 변경하다
practice v. 실행하다; 연습하다
psychiatrist n. 정신병학
crackle n. 딱딱[바삭 바삭]하는 소리
wrapper n. 포장지
absorb v. 흡수하다; 열중케 하다
consciousness n. 자각, 의식
psychotherapist n. 정신[심리] 요법 의사
urge n. 충동
kick the habit of ~하는 습관을 버리다

01 ▶ 베이커 박사는 최면이 의식을 전환한다고 믿지 않는다고 하였으며, 어떤 증거도 찾지 못하였다고 하였다. 따라서 최면이 의식을 전환하는 것과 같은 어떤 특정한 상태를 수반한다는 것을 믿는 것은 '터무니없는(absurd)' 일이라고 말할 것이다.

02 ▶ 어떤 이들은 뇌의 한 부분이 정지하고 다른 한 부분이 고도로 집중되어 있는 상태에 최면이 일어난다고 했다.

03 ▶ 마지막 문단 마지막 줄에서 담배를 끊는 것은 어렵기 때문에 담배를 끊는다는 강한 의지를 가져야 한다고 했다.

04 ▶ 작가는 최면이 실제 이용 가능한 수준에서는 효과가 있다고 언급하고 있으며 그 증거를 제시하고 있다. (C) '희망이 있는'이 가장 적절하다. 실제로 최면이 효과가 있어도 담배를 끊는 데 모두가 성공한 것이 아니라 의지를 가지고 최면에 임한 사람만이 끊을 수 있다고 하였다.

» 정답 01 (A) 02 (B) 03 (D) 04 (C)

마하트마 간디가 옷을 통일, 능력, 그리고 제국주의 정복으로부터의 해방의 은유로 사용한 것을 연구한 살레지오 교육커뮤니케이터 피터 곤잘브스의 최근 작품인 『카디: 간디의 초대형 체제전복 상징』은 사회를 질적으로 변화시킬 수 있는 상징의 힘을 연구한다.

간디의 대단히 양극화된 환경에서의 복잡한 문제(도전)들을 논의하여 역사적 증거를 함께 섞어 넣으면서, 곤잘브스는 독립을 이루기 위한 전략적 사업으로서의 카디를 통한 변화의 상징적 가능성을 고찰한다. 이 책은 그의 이전 작품인 『해방을 위한 옷』과 긴밀히 연관되어 있다. 두 작품 모두 출발점이 간디의 옷을 통한 커뮤니케이션으로 동일한데, 이 선택은 푸르나 스와라지(완전 자치)를 추구함에 있어 불의한 권위적 체제를 동요시키려는 의도의 대단히 용기 있는 전략이었다고 곤잘브스는 주장한다. 그러나 현재의 작품은 그 접근법의 독창성과 풍부한 문서자료 제시와 간디의 사상과 행동의 적절성과 깊이를 명확히 보여주는 점 등이 주목할 만하다.

저자는 간디가 개인적 성실과 사회정치적 변화를 추구함에 있어 옷의 기호학을 모색했다는 역사적 증거를 모으기 위해 다학제적 접근법을 채택하고, 간디의 옷을 통한 커뮤니케이션의 기저에 깔려있는 체제 전복적 요소를 면밀히 조사한다. 그는 또한 대영제국과 인도국민회의 사이의 갈등, 힌두교도와 이슬람교도 사이의 긴장, 시골과 도시의 분리, 힌두교도(인도인)의 정체성 분열에서의 카스트의 역할 등과 같은, 간디의 대단히 양극화된 환경에서의 복잡한 문제(도전)들도 논의한다.

---

empowerment n. 권한[능력]부여
subjugation n. 정복, 종속
subversion n. 전복, 타도
thread together 함께 섞어 짜다
polarize v. 양극화하다, 분열[편향, 대립]시키다
ploy n. 일, 책략, 계획
destabilize v. 불안정하게 하다, 동요시키다
noteworthy a. 주목할 만한
relevance n. 적절성
multi-disciplinary a. 다학제적(多學齊的)인
semiotics n. 기호학
attire n. 옷, 의복
quest n. 탐구, 추구
personal integrity 개인적 성실, 전인적 품성
sartorial a. 바느질의, 옷의
divide n. 분리
caste n. 카스트(인도의 세습적 계급)
fragmentation n. 분열

01 ▶ (A) 이 글은 Peter Gonsalves가 쓴 "Khadi: Gandhi's Mega Symbol of Subversion"이라는 책에 대한 서평(book review)이다. (B) 마지막의 Indian textile industry를 Indian independence movement 정도로 고쳐야 한다. (C) 간디가 카디를 신체적 속박(bodily bondage)의 상징으로 본 것은 아니다. (D) 마지막 문장에서 식민지 인도는 계층, 인종, 종교 면에서 분열된 상호 적대적인 사회였음을 알 수 있다.

02 ▶ 첫 단락 첫 문장에서 khadi가 cloth(clothing)임을 알 수 있고, 둘째 단락 첫 문장에서 khadi는 a strategic ploy to achieve independence라고 한 다음, 그 다음 다음 문장에서 Gandhi's communication through clothing을 an .... strategy .... in the pursuit of ①의 purna swaraj라 했으므로 ①은 (B)임을 알 수 있다.

03 ▶ Gandhi's search for ②<u>a semiotics of attire</u> in his quest for personal integrity and socio-political change는 첫 단락의 Gandhi's use of clothing as a metaphor for unity, empowerment and liberation from imperial subjugation과 내용이 일치하는 구절이다. 따라서 (A)가 가장 가까운 의미이다.

04 ▶ 둘째 단락에서 Gandhi's communication through clothing이라 했고, 마지막 단락에서 Gandhi's search for ②<u>a semiotics of attire</u>라고 했으므로 빈칸 ③에는 clothing, attire와 관계된, '옷의, 바느질의'라는 뜻인 (C)가 적절하다.

» 정답 01 (D) 02 (B) 03 (A) 04 (C)

대부분의 사회, 특히 민족국가는 사회 계급에 대한 의식이 있어 보인다. 그러나 계급이 보편적인 현상은 아니다. 많은 수렵 채집사회는 사회 계급이 없고, 종종 항구적인 지도자가 없으며, 그들의 구성원을 수직적인 권력 구조로 세분화하는 것을 적극적으로 피한다.

계급을 결정하는 요소는 사회마다 다르다. 심지어 한 사회 내에서도, 어떤 구성원을 사회 계급제도 속에서 더 높거나 더 낮게 만드는 것에 대한 생각은 사람이나 집단마다 매우 다를 수 있다. 계급을 정의할 때 흔히 제기되는 일부 의문점들은 1) 계급을 구분할 때 가장 중요한 기준, 2) 존재하는 계급 구분의 수, 3) 의미를 갖기 위해 개인들이 이 구분을 인식하는 정도, 그리고 4) 계급 구분이 미국과 다른 산업사회에서 존재하는지의 여부 등이다.

계급의 정의에 대한 이론적 논란은 오늘날 중요한 것으로 남아있다. 사회학자인 데니스 롱(Dennis Wrong)은 계급을 현실주의와 명목주의의 두 가지 방식으로 정의한다. 현실주의적 정의는 사회 집단을 형성하기 위해 사람들이 지키는 계급에 대한 명확한 영역에 의존한다. 그들은 자신들을 특별한 계급으로 인식하고 이러한 계급의 사람들과 주로 상호작용한다. 계급의 명목주의적 정의는 교육과 직업 등, 특정한 집단에서 사람들이 공유하는 특성에 초점을 맞춘다. 그러므로 계급은 당신이 당신 자신을 위치시키는 집단이나 그 속에서 상호작용하는 사람들에 의해서가 아니라 이러한 공통적인 특징에 의해서 결정된다.

가장 기본적인 두 집단 간의 구별은 권력층과 비권력층의 구별이다. 사회 계급 내의 더 힘 있는 사람들은 사회 내에서의 그들의 위치를 굳히려고 하고 사회 구조 내에서 더 낮은 사회 계급보다 상위에 그들의 지위를 유지하려고 한다. 많은 권력을 가진 사회 계급은 최소한 그들의 사회 내에서 대개 엘리트로 간주된다. 덜 복잡한 사회에서는 권력/계급 구조는 존재할 수도 있고, 그렇지 않을 수도 있다.

---

nation state (단일) 민족국가
notion n. 생각, 의식
phenomenon n. 현상
permanent a. 영원한, 영구적인
hierarchical a. 수직적인, 상하구조의
criteria n. 기준
adhere v. 지키다, 고수하다
cement v. 굳히다, 시멘트로 접합하다

01 ▶ avoid는 '피하다, 회피하다'의 의미로 evade, avert, shun 등이 그 동의어가 된다. 하지만 convert는 '변환하다, 바꾸다'의 의미다.

02 ▶ 두 번째 문단에서 나열되지 않은 것은 '계급 구분의 역사'이다.

03 ▶ 주어진 문장은 집단의 사람들을 중시하므로 본문에서 언급하는 현실주의와 명목주의 중 현실주의에 해당한다.

04 ▶ 사회 계급이 보편적인 현상은 아니라고 했으므로 (A)는 부적절하고, 사회마다 계급 기준이 다르다고 했으므로 (B)도 옳지 않으며, (D)는 현실주의적 정의에 해당한다.

» **정답** 01 (A) 02 (D) 03 (A) 04 (C)

미국 북동부 지역에서 동물의 종말적 대참사가 일어나고 있다. 미국 어류 및 야생동식물 보호국 관리들에 따르면, 미국의 16개 주와 캐나다에서 코 주위 잔털이 쉽게 알아볼 수 있게 희어지는 것을 특징으로 하는 전염병인 흰 코 균상종으로 2006년 이후 570만 내지 670만 마리의 박쥐가 죽은 것으로 추산된다고 한다. 새로운 추산 결과, 사망한 개체 수는 야생동물 생물학자들이 생각한 것보다 훨씬 더 심각하여, 어쩌면 전번 2009년 추산치의 5 내지 6배에 이르는 것으로 밝혀졌는데, 그것은 동물 뿐 아니라 인간에게도 재난을 초래할 수 있을 것이다.

치명적인 균상종은 북동부 지역에서 모든 종의 박쥐를 말살할 수 있는 잠재력을 갖고 있다. 뉴욕 주 올버니 근처의 한 동굴에서 5년여 전에 처음으로 이 전염병이 발견된 후 매년 겨울마다 광산과 동굴에서 죽은 박쥐 시체의 수를 수고스럽게 헤아려온 생물학자들은 감염된 일부 동굴에서는 박쥐가 한 마리도 남아있지 않다는 것을 발견했다. 가장 취약한 박쥐 종에는 작은 갈색 박쥐와 삼색 박쥐와 이들과 유사한 북부의 귀가 긴 박쥐가 포함되는데, 모두가 대개 장수하는 종이라고 과학자들은 말한다.

이들 박쥐 종들의 있을 수 있는 멸종도 놀랍긴 하지만, 훨씬 더 걱정스러운 것은 생태계의 중요한 일부가 상실될 수 있다는 점이다. 가임(번식) 연령의 암컷 박쥐 한 마리는 매년 자신의 체중과 맞먹는 양의 곤충을 잡아먹을 수 있다. 만일 박쥐가 전멸되면, 여름철 바비큐 파티를 성가시게 하고 인간에게 질병을 확산시키는 곤충들은 말할 것도 없고 식량 및 농업 생산량을 격감시키고 숲에 만연할 수 있는 해충을 포함한 곤충의 개체 수가 폭발적으로 증가할 수 있을 것이다.

지금까지 미국 서부지역의 박쥐 개체군들은 균상종에 감염되지 않은 것으로 여겨지지만, 생물학자들은 균상종이 확산될 기세임을 우려한다. 140명이 넘는 정부기관 및 대학 소속 연구원들이 흰 코 증후군에 대한 대응책을 마련하기 위해 최근 모임을 가졌지만, 지금으로써는 아무 치료책이 없다. 과학자들은 바라건대 너무 늦기 전에 치료법을 찾기 위해 이 병을 앓은 박쥐의 시체를 연구하고 있다.

apocalypse n. 계시, 세상의 종말, 전면적 파괴, 참사
fungus n. 균류, 균상종(菌狀腫)
infection n. 감염, 전염병
telltale a. 숨길 수 없는, 금방 알아보는
fuzz n. 솜털, 잔털, 보풀
death toll 사망자 수
spell v. 의미하다; ~한 결과가 되다; 초래하다
painstakingly ad. 수고스럽게, 정성들여
carcass n. 시체
worrisome a. 걱정되는
reproductive age 번식 연령, 가임 연령
wipe out 닦아내다; 죽이다, 일소하다
decimate v. (전염병 등이) 많은 사람을 죽이다
infest v. 떼 지어 몰려들다, 만연하다, ~에 기생하다
swarm n. (곤충의) 떼, 무리
plague v. 성가시게 하다
be poised to V ~할 태세를 갖추다
be afflicted with (질병을) 앓다
remedy n. 치료법

01 ▶ afoot a. 진행 중인(= happening)

02 ▶ 셋째 단락에서 (B) can decimate food and agriculture yields라 했다. (C) infest forests라 했다. (D) spread disease to humans라 했다. 가임(번식) 연령의 암컷 박쥐 한 마리는 매년 자신의 체중과 맞먹는 양의 곤충을 잡아먹을 수 있는데 박쥐가 전멸되면 곤충(해충)의 수가 늘어날 것이라 했을 뿐 암컷 박쥐의 불임이 늘어난다는 말은 아니므로 (A)는 균상종 확산의 가능한 여파에 해당하지 않는다.

03 ▶ (A) 아직 미국 전역으로 확산되지는 않았고 수그러들지도 않았다. (B) 아직 늦은 것은 아니다. (C) 둘째 단락에서 '북동부 지역에서 모든 종의 박쥐를 말살할 수 있는 잠재력을 갖고 있다'고 했지만 가장 취약한 박쥐 종이 있다는 것은 그렇지 않은 종도 있다는 뜻이고 그러면 모든 종에 같은 정도의 피해를 입히는 것은 아니라는 말이 된다. (D) 첫 단락에서 '사망한 개체 수는 야생동물 생물학자들이 생각한 것보다 훨씬 더 심각하다'고 했으므로 생물학자들은 균상종이 이렇게 많은 박쥐를 죽게 할 것으로 예상하지 못했다는 것을 알 수 있다.

04 ▶ 이 글은 많은 박쥐들이 균상종에 감염되어 죽어가서 생태계를 파괴시키고 인간에게도 재난을 초래할 수 있는 상황을 설명한 글이므로 (B)가 글의 요지로 적절하다.

》 정답 01 (C) 02 (A) 03 (D) 04 (B)

262 　아파르트헤이트(인종분리정책) 시기에 남아프리카공화국의 정치폭력은 언제나 흑인과 백인 사이에서 나타났었다. 그러나 지난 5월 이 나라를 휩쓸었던 이민을 반대하는 살육의 물결 속에서 62명의 살해당한 사람들은 모두 흑인들이었다. 스스로를 낙관적으로 일컬어 '무지개의 나라'라고 불렀던 이 나라를 뒤흔들어놓은 증오와 폭력은 인종차별에 대한 것이 아니라 세계화의 징후였다. "세계화는 가난한 국민을 가진 부유한 나라들을 양산할 것입니다"라고 경제학자 조셉 스티글리치(Joseph Stiglitz)는 주목한다. 이는 남아프리카공화국에서 확연히 나타나는데, 이 나라의 포스트아파르트헤이트 정부는 시장개방경제를 채택하였고 이는 월가(Wall Street)와 국제금융공동체의 갈채를 끌어내는 동시에 연 4퍼센트 내지 5퍼센트의 인상적이고도 꾸준한 경제성장을 달성하는 데 도움을 주었다. 그러나 이러한 성장은 불평등이나 위험할 정도로 높은 실업 수준을 바꾸는 데는 거의 아무것도 하지 못했다. 세계화는 모든 배들을 끌어올리는 흐름이 되어야 했지만 남아프리카공화국에서 나타나는 증거는 수백만 개의 배들이 조류를 타고 있지 못할 뿐 아니라 완전히 다른 바다에 있다는 것을 암시한다. 세계화에 대한 당신의 경험은 당신이 은행에 무엇을 가지고 있느냐에 달려 있다. 사업을 하는 계층에서 세계는 지구촌이며 당신은 전 세계에서 온 사업가들과 연계된다. 트럭을 타고 긴 사막을 통과해야 하거나 망망대해를 건너기 위해 위험한 배를 탄 사람들에게 세계화는 종종 훨씬 더 가혹하다. 매년 수백만 명의 사람들이 합법적으로든 불법적으로든, 가난한 나라에서 산업화된 세계나 남아프리카 공화국처럼 좀 더 잘 사는 개발도상국으로 이민을 가려 한다. 그러나 개발도상국의 가난한 사람들은 결단코 외국의 이민자들과 얼마 되지 않는 자신의 몫을 나눔으로써 그 몫을 감소시키지 않으려 하고 다른 부유한 세계의 사람들과 마찬가지로 자신들 속에 정착하는 외부인들에게 장벽을 세운다.

Apartheid n. 아파르트헤이트(인종차별정책)
era n. 시대
invariably ad. 항상, 반드시, 변함없이
anti-immigrant a. 이민을 반대하는
carnage n. 대학살, 대량살육
sweep v. 휩쓸다
proclaim v. 선언하다, 선포하다
racism n. 인종차별
symptom n. 징후, 증상
globalization n. 세계화
apparent a. 두드러진, 명백한
open-market economy 시장개방경제
cheer n. 갈채, 칭찬
reverse v. 뒤집다, 바꾸다
outsider n. 외부인
two-fold a. 두 부분으로 된, 이중적인; 두 배의
circumspection n. 세심한 주의, 신중; 용의주도
vestige n. 자취, 흔적
commotion n. 소란, 소동

01 ▶ 아파르트헤이트 이후 남아프리카공화국이 시장개방경제를 채택했다. 그 정책이 경제성장의 추동력이 된 것이지 시장개방경제의 추동력이 된 것이 아니다. 따라서 (C)가 정답이다. (A)와 (D)는 세계화가 남아프리카공화국에 미친 명암을 보여준다는 점에서 주제와 관련되어 있으므로 맞는 내용이고, (B)의 경우 본문 세 번째 문장에서 a country that optimistically proclaims itself the Rainbow Nation이라고 했으므로 남아프리카 공화국의 다른 이름이 '무지개의 나라'라는 것을 알 수 있다.

02 ▶ 밑줄 친 부분은 남아프리카공화국의 시장개방경제가 모든 이에게 혜택을 준 것이 아니라는 내용을 담고 있으므로 빈부격차에 대한 내용이 예가 되어야 한다. (A)는 반(反) 이민폭력에 관한 내용이므로 직접적인 관련이 없고, (C)는 하루당 2달러 미만으로 사는 사람의 수가 줄었다고 했으므로 오히려 좋아진 측면이며 (D)는 남아프리카의 경제성장으로 중산층이 잘산다고 했으므로 또한 빈부격차와 관련이 없다. 따라서 정답은 (B)가 되며, 1달러로 사는 사람의 수가 늘었다는 내용이 되어야 한다.

03 ▶ counterpart는 같은 성질을 가지되 다른 장소에 있는 사람들을 가리키므로, 이 문맥에서는 다른 곳에 있는 business class를 가리킨다.

04 ▶ 개발도상국의 빈민들이 자신의 몫을 이민자들과 나누지 않으려 한다고 했으므로 외부인들에게 '장애물'을 세운다는 표현이 맞다.

05 ▶ 본문의 The hatred and violence that has shaken a country that optimistically proclaims itself the Rainbow Nation was not about racism — it was symptom of globalization을 참조하면 '남아프리카의 세계화의 함정'이라는 (B)가 가장 적합한 제목이다. 나머지는 부분적인 내용들을 반영하지만 (B)가 가장 포괄적이면서도 주제를 함축하고 있다고 볼 수 있다.

▶▶ 정답　01 (C)　02 (B)　03 (C)　04 (A)　05 (B)

최근 영향력 있는 한 논문에서는 돈의 단적인 의미는 돈이 돈을 가진 사람이 그가 원하는 것을 얻을 수 있게 해준다는 점에서 도구와 같은 작용을 한다는 것이라고 주장했다. 그러나 그것이 반드시 정확하게 맞는 것은 아니다. 진정한 도구는 직접적으로 당신으로 하여금 무엇인가를 할 수 있도록 한다. 다른 사람들이 도구에 대해 어떻게 생각하는지는 아무런 상관이 없다. 그러나 돈은 전적으로 다른 사람들이 그것을 어떻게 생각하느냐에 따라 결정된다. 사람들이 돈을 특정한 가치가 있는 것으로 인정하기로 동의하지 않는 이상 돈은 그저 쓸모없는 종이와 금속인 것이다. 심리학적으로 말한다면, 돈이란 우리의 정체성에 돈이 어떻게 영향을 미치고, 우리에게 어떤 일이 생기는지, 또한 우리가 다른 사람들이나 스스로에게 어떤 대우를 받을지에 대한 믿음, 기대 그리고 두려움이 동전, 지폐, 은행 계좌 그리고 그 외의 금융 상품으로 구체화한 것이다. 돈은 사회제도를 수단으로 환경을 지배하는 지배력이다. 당신은 사회 제도가 당신이 원하는 것을 당신에게 제공하게끔 하는 지배력을 가지는 것이다.

우리가 스스로를 어떻게 생각하느냐 뿐만 아니라 다른 사람들이 우리를 대하는 태도와 행동이 어떨 것인가에 대한 우리의 믿음이 우리가 돈을 충분히 가지고 있는가의 여부에 따라 결정된다는 점이 주로 우리가 돈에 관심을 가지게 한다. 확실히 돈이 충분한가에 대한 생각은 개인과 대인관계에서 중요한 의미를 지닌. 정신분석학자 오토 페니셀(Otto Fenichel)은 우울증이 종종 강박적인 신경증과 관련이 있으며, 빈곤해질 수 있다는 강박관념적인 두려움이 우울증의 임상적 양상에서 역할을 한다고 지적했다.

straightforward a. 똑바른; 정직한
interpretation n. 해석; 설명
genuine a. 진짜의, 진심에서 우러난
depend on ~에 따라 결정되다
projection n. 발사; 투영; 설계
by means of ~에 의하여, ~을 써서
sufficiency n. 충분(한 상태)
interpersonal a. 사람과 사람사이의, 개인 간의
depression n. 의기소침; 우울
associate v. 연합시키다; 연상하다
compulsion n. 강요; 강박 충동
neurosis n. 신경증; 노이로제
clinical a. 진료소의; 임상의

01 ▶ 첫 번째 문단 일곱 번째 문장(Money, psychologically speaking ~ by ourselves)에서 돈을 심리학적으로 설명하고 있다. 자신에 대한 평가 및 다른 사람들에게 어떠한 대우를 받을지의 여부를 돈을 통해 의식한다고 하였다. 이는 돈은 심리학적 측면에서 '사회적 관계를 위한 심리적 기반'으로 작용한다는 것을 의미한다.

02 ▶ 가난이 직접적으로 우울증에 빠지게 하는 것이 아니라 가난에 대한 두려움이 그렇게 하는 것이다. 따라서 (C)는 추론할 수 없는 진술이다.

03 ▶ 첫 번째 빈칸의 앞 문장에서 돈을 '충분히 가지고 있느냐'에 따라 자신에 대한 평가 및 사람들이 대하는 태도가 결정된다고 하였으므로 빈칸에는 '충분함'을 뜻하는 단어가 들어가야 한다. 또한 돈을 충분히 가지고 있느냐에 따라 스스로에 대한 판단이나 사람들의 대우가 결정된다고 생각한다고 하였으므로, '돈이 충분치 않을 경우'가 우울증에 걸리는 원인이 될 수 있다. 따라서 두 번째 빈칸에는 '빈곤'을 의미하는 단어가 가장 적절하다.

04 ▶ 첫 번째 문단 여섯 번째 문장을 참고한다. '사람들이 돈을 가치가 있는 것으로 인정하기로 동의하지 않는 이상' 돈은 단순한 금속이나 종이에 불과하다고 하였다. 즉, 돈의 실제적인 가치는 '사회 내 사람들의 동의'로 결정된다는 것이다.

≫ 정답 01 (B) 02 (C) 03 (B) 04 (E)

큰 전환점은 내가 13살이었고, 리처드(Richard)가 대학원에 다녔을 때였다. 그는 집에 와 있다가 프린스턴(Princeton)으로 돌아가기 위해 떠났다. 탁자에 한 권의 책이 놓여 있었다. 나는 엄마에게 "리처드가 책을 잊어버리고 놓고 갔어요"라고 말했다. 그 책을 열어보니 안쪽에 리처드의 필체로 쓴 내 이름이 장서표에 적혀 있었다. 그것은 천문학 책으로, 천문학에 대한 대학 교재였다. 그는 프린스턴에서 그 책을 중고로 사서 아무 말도 없이 나에게 준 것이었다.

나는 "어떻게 그 책을 읽어? 아주 어려운데."하고 그에게 물었다. "네가 첫 부분부터 읽고 모르는 데가 나올 때까지 이해되는 한 계속 읽으렴. 그러고 나서 다시 책을 읽기 시작해서 계속 읽으면 마침내 책 전체를 이해할 수 있어"라고 그는 말했다.

여러 해 동안 나의 커다란 꿈은 어떤 남자의 조수가 되어 그저 별을 바라보도록 허락을 받는 것이었다. 학문을 하는 게 아니라, 단지 조력자가 되는 것이 나의 어린 시절 목표였다. 난 그 이상을 상상할 수 없었다. 내 꿈은 다른 누군가가 별을 볼 수 있도록 망원경을 고정시키는 사람이 되는 것이었다.

리처드는 나를 항상 격려했다. 내가 진정으로 원하는 것이 망원경이라는 것을 깨달았을 때, 나는 리처드에게 말해 주었고 그는 나에게 망원경을 사주겠다고 말했다. 나는 망원경 렌즈를 집에서 갈 수 있고 그 다음엔 그가 프린스턴에 있는 기계에서 시험을 해볼 것이다. 나는 신이 났지만, 부모님은 내 방에서 그것을 갈 수 없다고 결정했다. 난 그 이유가 기억나지 않지만, 아마도 렌즈에서 나오는 먼지가 사방에 범벅이 되기 때문이었을 것이다. 그러나 우리는 아파트에 살았기 때문에 지하 계단에 가구 등을 보관하는 창고가 있었는데 거기는 작은 방과 같았다. 그 건물에 사는 남자아이들 중 하나는 지하실에 있는 한 창고에 멋진 화학 실험실을 만들었다. 그래서 나는 때때로 그것을 보러 가곤 했다. 따라서 나도 그곳에 가서 내 렌즈를 갈 수 있을 것이라고 생각했다. 얼마나 멋진가! 부모님께 말했더니 승낙을 안 하셨다. 거절한 이유는 내가 지하실에서 강간당할까봐 두려웠던 것이다. 내가 남자였다면 부모님은 법석을 떨며 내가 렌즈를 갈도록 시켰을 것이다. 결국 난 망원경을 갖지 못했다.

그 책에는 셀리리아 페인 가포쉬킨(Celillia Payne-Gaposhkin)이라는 여성이 언급되었다. 그녀는 하버드에서 재직하며 천문학자로서 책에 나올 정도로 훌륭했다. 부모님의 생각엔 뭔가 잘못이 있었다. 난 누군가가 그것을 할 수 있으면, 나 역시 할 수 있을 것이라고 생각했다. 그래서 난 해냈다. 따라서 그저 상황이 불가능하기 때문에 못할 이유는 없는 것이다.

---

turning point 전환점
astronomy n. 천문학
telescope n. 망원경
basement n. 지하실
raise hell 야단법석을 떨다; 소동을 일으키다
figure v. 마음에 그리다, 상상하다
grind v. 갈아 (가루로) 만들다; (날붙이, 렌즈 등을) 갈다

01 ▶ 리처드는 한 집에 사는 손위 오빠로서 동생이 꿈을 키우는 데 영향을 미쳤다.

02 ▶ 첫머리에서 전환점이라 했고 이 글에서 필자가 꿈을 실현한 과정을 설명했으므로, 이 글 앞에는 어린 시절에 어머니의 반대와 편견으로 꿈이 실현되지 못한 내용이 있을 것이다. (B)와 (D)에서 아버지의 영향력은 오히려 꿈을 꾸게 한 원동력으로 생각할 수 있으므로 답이 될 수 없다.

03 ▶ 위 글은 부모의 반대 등과 같은 장애와 어려움을 딛고 일어난 한 여성의 인간 승리를 다루고 있다. 따라서 제목으로는 '장애물의 극복'이 가장 알맞다.

04 ▶ ①의 this theory는 부모님의 여성에 대한 편견을 일컫는다. 주인공은 결국 꿈을 성취하였으므로 부모의 편견이 잘못된 것임이 드러났다.

» 정답 01 (C) 02 (A) 03 (B) 04 (C)

미국 경제가 재채기를 하면 전 세계가 폐렴에 걸린다는 말은 오래 전부터 있어왔다. 이 증후군에서 벗어나기 위해서 몇몇 외국 지도자들은 미국 금융기관 및 시장과 너무 뒤얽히는 것에 대해 경고해 왔다. 그러나 현재 미국 금융회사들이 유발한 신용위기가 전 세계의 경제를 전염시키고 있는 이상, 워싱턴(미국)에 적개심을 가지고 있는 외국 지도자들마저 미국의 인과응보를 기뻐하지 말아야 할 이유가 있다.

유럽에서 금융긴축은 위기에 대항하여 유럽연합이 광범위한 해결책을 찾아야 한다는 사람들과 자신들의 유로(euro)가 대륙의 다른 곳에 있는 은행들을 구하기 위해 사용되는 것을 원하지 않는 국가들 사이에 숨어있는 불화를 전면으로 표출시켰다. 6개월씩 순환되고 있는 유럽연합의 대통령직을 맡고 있는 프랑스 대통령 니콜라스 사르코지(Nicolas Sarkozy)는 최근에 모든 27개 회원국 은행들을 위한 유럽연합 구제금융 자금을 제안했다. 그러나 독일과 영국은 격렬하게 반대했다.

그러나 설상가상으로, 한때 자신만만했던 독일 관리들은 Hypo Real Estate라고 불리는 그들의 가장 큰 대출회사 중 하나가 700억 달러가 넘는 구제 금융이 필요하다는 것을 지난 며칠 동안 알게 되었다. 이 무기력하게 만드는 사실은 독일의 재무장관이 독일 국민들에게 '미국이 이 위기의 근원이자 중심'이라고 실수로 확언한 지 2주도 채 지나지 않아 발생하였다.

국가의 주권에 대한 유럽연합의 내부 논쟁은 특수한 것이긴 하지만 금융위기에 대한 유럽의 반응은 미국인들에게 중요한 교훈을 준다. 차기 대통령은 테러리즘과 핵 확산뿐만 아니라 더욱 국제화된 경제에 대한 규제와 원칙에도 다각적인 협력을 추구해야 할 것이다. 미국이 파산하기에는 너무 크다면, 또한 미국은 전 세계의 나라들과 너무 연관되어 있어 혼자 힘으로 해결할 수는 없다.

---

sneeze v. 재채기 하다
pneumonia n. 폐렴
syndrome n. 증후군; 일련의 징후
intertwine v. 서로 얽히게 하다, 서로 엮다, 얽어 짜다
contraction n. 수축; (자금·통화 따위의) 제한, 회수
provoke v. (감정 따위를) 일으키다, 일으키게 하다
gloat v. 흡족한[기분 좋은] 듯이 바라보다(on; over)
comeuppance n. 당연한 벌[응보], 인과응보
get one's comeuppance for ~의 당연한 벌을 받다
latent a. 숨어 있는, 보이지 않는; 잠재적인
bailout n. (정부 자금에 의한) 기업 구제(조처)
ardently ad. 열렬하게, 격렬하게
unnerve v. 용기를 잃게 하다, 무기력하게하다
revelation n. 폭로; (비밀의) 누설
sovereignty n. 주권
turmoil n. 소란, 소동

01 ▶ 미국에 의해 촉발된 경제위기가 유럽에 영향을 미쳤음을 이 글을 통해서 말하고 있다. '미국의 경제위기와 유럽에 끼친 영향'이 가장 적절한 제목이다.

02 ▶ this syndrome은 앞에 나온 if the American economy sneezes, the rest of the world gets pneumonia를 말한다.

03 ▶ 독일 장관은 '미국이 이 위기의 근원이자 중심'이라고 말하고 나서 2주도 채 지나지 않아 자신의 나라의 큰 대출 회사 중 하나가 금융구제가 필요한 것을 알게 되었다. 그는 "남을 비난하기 전에 자신을 살펴야 했다."고 할 수 있다. (A) "대접 받으려거든 남을 대접하여라" (B) "김칫국부터 마시지 말라" (D) "말 한마디로 천 냥 빚을 갚는다"

04 ▶ 이 글은 미국의 금융회사에 의해 촉발된 위기가 유럽에 영향을 미쳤으며 이것뿐만 아니라 더 커진 국제화된 경제로 인하여 세계의 모든 나라가 위험에 처해있다는 글이다. "미국이 세계에 대한 경제 의존성으로 벌을 받고 있다"는 것은 이글을 통해 알 수 없다.

» 정답 01 (C) 02 (A) 03 (C) 04 (B)

화이트홀이 물질을 방출하고 블랙홀이 물질을 빨아들인다는 점을 제외하면 화이트홀은 블랙홀과 흡사하다. 시공물질 연속체에 관한 슈바르츠쉴트(Schwarzschild) 거리함수의 음의 제곱근 해(解)는 화이트홀의 존재를 암시한다. 블랙홀과 화이트홀이 물질이나 반물질로 구성될 수 있다는 것을 기억해두는 것이 중요하다.

화이트홀을 연결하는 웜홀은 아인슈타인-로젠 다리로 알려져 있으며, 이론물리학 분야에서 가장 흥미진진한 개념들 중 하나이다. 이론적으로 웜홀은 안정화되어서 물질로 구성된 화이트홀과 반물질로 구성된 화이트홀 사이의 안정적인 균형을 허용할 수 있다. 웜홀을 안정화시키기 위해 특이점 목은 물질로 구성된 화이트홀과 반물질로 구성된 화이트홀을 포함하게 되는데, 이들은 성질상 구체이다. 반물질은 음의 질량을 가지고 있고 양의 표면 압력을 가한다.

아인슈타인-로젠 다리는 물질로 구성된 블랙홀과 반물질로 구성된 블랙홀을 분리시켜준다. 웜홀 양단에 있는 블랙홀들 사이의 진동이 블랙홀을 화이트홀이 되게 하며 이 화이트홀이 물질과 반물질을 서로 반대 방향으로 방출하여 은하 원반 내에서 별들의 나선형 팔들을 형성한다.

반물질의 음의 질량은 웜홀의 목이 보호 영역 외부에 존재하도록 해주고 양의 표면 압력은 웜홀의 목의 완전한 붕괴를 막아준다. <안정된 웜홀을 생성하는 데 있어서 물질과 반물질 속성들은 자의적이거나 순수하게 이론적인 것들이 아니다.> 필요한 형상을 만들어내기 위해서 영역 내에 있어야 할 물질의 에너지-운동량의 크기가 어느 정도의 것인지를 아인슈타인의 방정식들이 명시해준다. 물질로 된 화이트홀과 반물질로 된 화이트홀이 웜홀을 안정화시킬 수 있는 것이다.

---

eject v. 몰아내다, 쫓아내다
square root 제곱근
continuum n. (물질·감각·사건 따위의) 연속[연속체]
antimatter n. <물리> 반물질(反物質)
equilibrium n. 평형상태, 균형
singularity n. 특이성, 특이점
spherical a. 구(球)의, 구면의, 둥근
exert v. (영향력·압력 등을) 지속적으로 행사하다
positive a. 양(陽)의, 플러스의
oscillation n. 진동, 동요
spiral a. 나선[나사] 모양의
galactic a. 은하의; 거대한
equation n. 방정식
specify v. 일일이 열거하다; 자세히 말하다
geometry n. 기하학

01 ▶ 이 글은 화이트홀이 무엇인지 설명한 글로서, 물질과 반물질로 구성된 화이트홀이 웜홀을 안정화시키고 웜홀의 안정화가 두 가지 화이트홀이 안전한 균형을 취하게 해준다고 기술한다. 이 설명 과정에서 블랙홀과 웜홀이 언급된 것이다.

02 ▶ eject의 반의어는 absorb이다.

03 ▶ 물질과 반물질 속성들이 not arbitrary or purely theoretical하다는 기술은 바로 뒷 문장의 아인슈타인의 방정식들이 명시해준다는 기술과 연결된다. 따라서 [IV]가 적절한 위치이다.

04 ▶ 화이트홀의 존재가 이론적으로 "implied(암시)"되었을 뿐이지 실제로 입증되었다는 내용은 없다.

》 정답 01 (C) 02 (D) 03 (D) 04 (B)

미국에서 검열은 도서관 사서들에게 명백한 관심사였지만 교육자들의 근심거리는 거의 아니었다. 2차 대전이 일어나기 전까지 존 스타인벡(John Steinbeck)의 『생쥐와 인간(Of Mice and Men)』과 『분노의 포도(The Grapes of Wrath)』와 같은 작품들이 그 당시 신문에서 심의를 일으키기는 했지만, 검열은 학교 내에서 좀처럼 겉으로 드러나지 않았다. 학생들이 이러한 작품을 읽기 시작했을 때 작품을 둘러싼 열띤 논란이 학교 안으로 흘러들어 갔다. 1949년에 노먼 메일러(Norman Mailer)는 『나자와 사자(The Naked and the Dead)』를 출판하였고, 셀린저(J. D. Salinger)는 1951년에 『호밀밭의 파수꾼(Catcher in the Rye)』을 썼는데, 당시 사회를 지나치게 자유분방하고, 해이하며, 부도덕적이기까지 한 모습으로 그려 보였다. 청소년들은 이러한 묘사에 그대로 휩쓸렸다. 그러한 묘사에 대한 대부분의 항의는 작가와 출판사들을 향하였고, 일부 항의는 물론 이러한 책들을 구비한 서점으로 향하였다. 수년 동안 당시 고등학교 교사들은 논란을 일으킬 그러한 책들을 가르치지 않았으며, 그러한 책을 구비하는 사서들은 더욱이 없었다.

아마 마찬가지로 중요하게도 약 1967년까지 청소년 도서는 청소년들이 폭력, 임신, 술과 마약 등에 일상적으로 마주치는 현실을 결여한 채 일반적으로 건전하고, 순수하며, 단순했다. 그러던 중 1967년, 앤 헤드(Ann Head)의 『Mr. and Mrs. Bo Jo Jones』와 S.E. 힌튼(S.E. Hinton)의 『아웃사이더(The Outsiders)』가 등장하였고, 청소년 문학은 새로운 국면을 맞게 되었다. 이어서 출판된 서적들이 항상 탁월하거나 노골적이지는 않았지만 놀랄 만한 수의 책들이 그러했다. 학생들에게 인기 있는 성인 소설 작가들에 대한 검열을 인정했던 선생님들과 사서들은 이제는 한때 안전했던 청소년 소설이 더 이상 안전하지 않다는 것을 알게 되었다. 검열 공격은 곧 시작되었다. 청소년 도서 중 상당수가 비난받았다.

---

censorship n. 검열
surface v. 나타나다, 표면화하다
furor n. 벅찬 감격; 열광적인 유행; 분노
overly ad. 과도하게, 지나치게
permissive a. 허가하는; 관대한
lax a. 느슨한; 해이한; 방종한
objection n. 반대; 이의
controversial a. 논쟁의 대상인, 물의를 일으키는
devoid of ~이 없는; ~이 결여된
denounce v. 공공연히 비난하다; 고발하다

01 ▶ 당시 사회에 논란을 일으켰던 도서들을 소개하였지만 후에 명작으로 인정받은 여부를 추론할 수는 없다.

02 ▶ 2차 대전이 일어나기 전에는 검열이 거의 일어나지 않았다고 언급하였지만 스타인벡의 작품을 예로 들며 몇 가지 작품이 신문에서 심의를 일으켰다고 하였다. 이는 검열이 실제로 무엇인지에 대한 예를 들기 위해 당시 신문에서 심의를 일으킨 스타인벡의 유명한 작품을 제시한 것이다.

03 ▶ be caught up in은 '~에 휩쓸려 버리다'라는 뜻이며 that description은 당시 사회에 대해 비판적으로 여과 없이 기술한 점을 나타낸다. 따라서 "청소년들은 사회에 대한 거리낌 없는 묘사에 사로잡혔다"와 일맥상통한다.

04 ▶ 두 번째 문단에서 약 1967년까지 청소년 도서는 당시 청소년들의 현실을 반영하지 않고, 그저 건전하고 순수하고 단순하다고 하였다. 따라서 그 당시 청소년 도서는 '면밀하지 않고 피상적이다'라고 여겨질 수 있다.

» 정답 01 (C) 02 (D) 03 (B) 04 (D)

268

　　철학은, 모든 다른 학문들과 마찬가지로, 일차적으로 지식을 목적으로 한다. 철학이 지향하는 지식은 일련의 과학에 통일성과 체계를 부여해주는 지식이며, 우리의 확신, 편견, 믿음의 토대에 대한 비판적 연구에서 나오는 그러한 지식이다. 그러나 철학이 자체의 질문에 대한 명쾌한 대답을 제시하려는 시도에서 커다란 성공을 거두었다고 주장할 수는 없다. 만약에 수학자나 광물학자, 역사학자 혹은 다른 분야의 학자에게 그의 학문에 의해 어떤 명확한 진리들이 규명되었느냐고 묻는다면, 그의 대답은 무궁무진할 것이다. 하지만 당신이 똑같은 질문을 철학자에게 한다면, 그가 솔직하다면 자신의 학문이 다른 과학 분야들에서 얻어진 것과 같은 그런 긍정적 결과를 얻지는 못했다고 인정하지 않을 수 없을 것이다. 사실, 그 이유의 일부는 어떤 주제에 관한 명백한 지식이 가능해지는 순간, 그 주제는 이제 철학이라고 부를 수 없고 하나의 독립된 학문, 즉 과학이 된다는 사실에 의해 설명될 수 있다. 지금은 천문학에 속하는 천체에 관한 전반적인 연구는 한때 철학에 속해 있었다. 마찬가지로, 매우 최근까지도 철학의 한 분야였던 인간의 정신에 대한 연구는 이제 철학에서 분리되어 심리학이라는 과학이 되었다. 그래서 상당할 정도로, 철학의 불확실성은 겉보기에 불확실해 보일 뿐이지 실제는 불확실하지 않다. 다시 말해, 이미 명쾌한 해답을 제시할 수 있는 문제들은 과학에 들어가는 반면, 현재 명쾌한 해답을 제시할 수 없는 문제들만이 남아서 철학이라고 하는 분야를 형성한다.

---

unity n. 통일성, 일관성
conviction n. 신념, 확신
prejudice n. 편견, 선입관
definite a. 뚜렷한, 확실한;
mineralogist n. 광물학자
ascertain v. 확인하다, 규명하다
confess v. 고백하다, 실토하다
positive a. 긍정적인; 적극적인
definite a. 뚜렷한, 확실한
cease v. 그만두다, 멈추다
residue n. 나머지, 찌꺼기

01 ▶ 어떤 지식이 명백해지는 순간 그것은 더 이상 철학이 아니라 과학이 된다고 하였다. 따라서 그 답이 불확실하고 의심스러울 때 철학이 과학의 일부분으로 바뀌는 것이 아니라, 오히려 명확해질 때야 비로소 철학은 과학의 분야로 받아들여지게 되는 것이다.

02 ▶ 일반 과학과 대비되는 철학의 본질적 특성, 즉 철학이 불확실해 보이는 점에 대해 설명하는 글이다.

03 ▶ 과학자들에게 학문에 의해 어떤 명확한 진리들이 규명되었느냐고 묻는다고 했기 때문에 밑줄 친 부분의 his는 과학자들을 의미한다. 따라서 과학을 통해 규명될 수 있는 수많은 대답이 있다는 (D)가 정답으로 가장 알맞다.

04 ▶ 천문학은 본래 철학의 분야였다고 명시하고 있는데, 심리학도 천문학과 '마찬가지로' 철학에서 분리된 학문분야의 한 예로서 제시되고 있다.

» 정답　01 (D)　02 (A)　03 (D)　04 (C)

'맬서스의 붕괴'와 '맬서스의 저주'와 같은 용어의 바로 그 맬서스인 토마스 로버트 맬서스(Thomas Robert Malthus)는 온화한 수학자이자 성직자였으며, 비판자들의 말로는 근본적인 비관론자였다. 일부 계몽 철학자들이 프랑스 혁명의 성공에 들뜬 나머지 인간의 상황이 아무 제약 없이 계속 개선될 것으로 예측하기 시작했을 때, 맬서스는 그들의 예측을 단번에 잠재웠다. 그는 인구는 기하급수적으로 증가하여, 억제되지 않으면 매 약 25년마다 두 배로 증가하는 반면, 농업 생산량은 이보다 훨씬 느리게 산술급수적으로 늘어난다는 것을 알게 되었다. 거기에 인류가 결코 벗어날 수 없는 생물학적 함정이 놓여있는 것이었다.

그는 "언제까지나 인구압은 지구가 인류의 생존에 필요한 식량을 생산할 수 있는 능력보다 더 크다. 이것은 곧 생존의 어려움으로 인해 인구에 대한 강력한 억제가 끊임없이 가해지기 마련이라는 것을 의미한다"라고 1798년에 쓴 『인구론』에서 말했다. 맬서스는 그러한 억제가 산아제한, 금욕, 결혼지연 등과 같이 인간의 의지에 의한 것일 수도 있고 아니면 전쟁, 기근, 질병 등의 재앙을 통한 인간 의지와 무관한 것일 수도 있다고 생각했다. 그는 가장 빈곤한 사람들을 제외하고는 모든 사람들에 대한 식량 구제를 반대했는데, 그런 원조가 비참하게 태어나는 아이들이 더 많아지도록 조장한다고 생각했기 때문이었다. 그런 모진 사랑으로 인해 그는 영국 문학에서도 다름 아닌 바로 찰스 디킨스(Charles Dickens)의 작품에 성미 고약한 특별한 인물로 등장하게 되었다. 『크리스마스 캐롤』에서 가난한 사람들을 위해 적선을 해달라는 부탁을 받자 무정한 은행가인 에베네저 스크루지(Ebenezer Scrooge)는 좋은 일을 하는 사람들에게 가난한 사람들은 구빈원이나 감옥으로 가야 한다고 말한다. 그리고 그런 곳에 갈 바에는 차라리 죽고 싶다면 "그렇게 해서 남아도는 인구를 줄이는 것이 더 낫다"고 말한다.

---

namesake n. 같은 이름의 사람
mild-mannered a. 온화한
glass-half-empty a. 비관적인
enlightenment n. 계몽
giddy a. 어지러운, 경솔한, 들뜬
unfettered a. 구속받지 않는, 자유로운
voluntary a. 자유의지의
involuntary a. 의지와 무관한, 무의식의, 우연의
scourge n. 천벌, 재앙
subsistence n. 생존, 생활
abstinence n. 절제, 금욕, 금주
cameo n. 인상적인 장면; 유명인의 특별출연
alms n. 적선, 의연금
heartless a. 무정한, 냉혹한
do-gooder n. 좋은 일을 하는 사람, 자선가
destitute a. 빈곤한
workhouse n. 구빈원(= poorhouse)

01 ▶ 이 글은 『인구론』을 중심으로 한 맬서스의 사상을 설명한 글이므로 (C)가 제목으로 가장 적절하다.

02 ▶ '맬서스의 붕괴'나 '맬서스의 저주'는 맬서스 본인이 만든 용어가 아니므로 (A)는 사실과 다른 진술이다.

03 ▶ 항상 인구에 비해 식량이 모자라는 상황에서 가난한 사람들은 차라리 죽어서 남아도는 인구를 줄여주는 것이 낫다고 한 것은 열등한 자는 도태되고 적자가 생존한다는 (B) '다윈의 자연선택'을 암시하고 있다. (A) 높은 신분에 따르는 도덕상의 의무로 맬서스의 의견과는 반대된다. (C) 뉴턴의 중력 법칙이다. (D) 처음의 작은 변화(차이)가 나중에 큰 변화(차이)를 가져온다는 데이비드 로렌츠의 나비효과이다.

04 ▶ none이 no one이므로 '다름 아닌 ~(사람)'은 none other than ~이다.

05 ▶ '그들의 무릎을 베어버렸다'는 것은 마치 싹을 자르듯이 더 이상 아무 말 못하게 '침묵시켰다'라는 뜻이다. cut someone off at the knees 크게 망신 주다, 아무 말 못하게 하다

» 정답 01 (C) 02 (A) 03 (B) 04 (B) 05 (D)

현저한 출산율 하락은 브라질만의 현상이 아니다. 지구의 인구증가에 대한 우려에도 불구하고 세계 인구 중 거의 절반이 출산율이 사실상 대체 출산율 이하로 떨어진 나라에서 살고 있는데, 대체 출산율이란 한 부부가 그들 자신을 대체할 만큼만 자녀를 낳는 수준을 말하며 한 가족에 자녀가 두 명을 조금 넘는 정도이다. 출산율은 세계 나머지 대부분 지역에서도 급속히 하락했는데, 사하라 사막 이남의 아프리카는 주목할 만한 예외이다. 그러나 이런 놀라운 추세의 원인과 결과를 이해하려고 노력하는 인구통계학자들에게는 1960년대 이후 브라질에서 일어난 일이 지구상에서 가장 흥미로운 사례연구 중 하나를 제공한다. 브라질은 광대한 땅에 걸쳐있어 지역에 따라 지리, 인종, 문화가 엄청나게 다르지만, 그 인구자료는 지금까지 특히 철저하고 믿을만하다.

브라질의 출산율이 지금 이 정도로까지 그렇게도 급속히 하락한 데에는 많은 이유가 있지만, 그 모든 이유들의 중심에는 수십 년 전에 정부의 장려 없이도 그리고 주교들의 선언을 뛰어넘어 가능한 모든 방법을 동원해 공장을 폐쇄시키기 시작한 강인하고 발랄한 여성들이 있다. 35세가 채 안 되는 나이에 이미 불임수술을 받은 여성들을 만나는 것은 브라질에서 매일 있는 일이며 그들은 그것에 대해 논의하기를 전혀 주저하지 않는 것 같다. "첫 애를 낳았을 때 18살이었어요. 그만 낳고 싶었지만, 어쩌다가 둘째가 태어났어요. 이젠 다 낳았어요."라고 28세의 한 공예품가게 점원이 말했다. 그녀는 26세의 젊은 나이에 영구피임인 난관결찰수술을 받았다. 그리고 브라질에서 자녀를 한 명만 낳는 것은 부유하고 전문직을 가진 여성만이 아니다. 시골과 도시빈민가에는 아기를 연이어 낳는 여성이 아직 수두룩하다는 것이 일반적인 인식이지만 그러나 그것은 사실이 아니다.

---

emphatic a. 두드러진, 현저한
fertility n. 출생률, 출산율
replacement rate 대체 출산율
sub-Saharan a. 사하라 사막 이남의
demographer n. 인구통계학자
implication n. 내포된 의미, 암시, (예상되는) 결과
compelling a. 강력한, 강한 흥미를 돋우는
span v. 걸쳐있다
pronouncement n. 선언, 발표, 의견
resilient a. 탄력 있는, 쾌활한, 발랄한
sterilization surgery 불임 수술
compunction n. 양심의 가책, 주저, 망설임
tubal ligation 난관 결찰 수술(불임수술)
irreversible a. 철회[취소]할 수 없는
contraception n. 피임, 산아제한
slum n. 빈민가

01 ▶ 빈칸 이하, 특히 셋째 문장에서 '출산율은 세계 나머지 대부분 지역에서도 급속히 하락했다'고 했으므로 빈칸에는 (A)가 적절하다.

02 ▶ '공장을 폐쇄한다'는 것은 이 글에서는 (D)의 '아이를 그만 낳는다'는 뜻이다. (A) 파업을 벌이다 (B) 직장을 그만두다 (C) 모성권(출산관련 권리)을 위해 투쟁하다

03 ▶ (A) 급속한 출산율 하락의 예외(exception)라는 말은 출산율이 급속히 (현격히) 하락하지 않았다는 말이다. (B) 첫 단락 마지막 문장에서 '인구자료가 철저하고 믿을만하다'고 한 것은 인구조사를 효과적으로 잘 해왔다는 말이 된다. (C) 둘째 단락에서 '주교들의 선언을 뛰어넘어 공장을 폐쇄시키기(아이를 그만 낳기) 시작했다'고 한 것에서 주교들, 즉 가톨릭 당국은 산아제한에 반대함을 알 수 있다. (D) 마지막 두 문장에서 자녀를 한 명만 낳는 것이 전문직 여성과 시골 여성 모두에 해당됨을 알 수 있을 뿐, 둘을 비교할 수는 없다.

04 ▶ 브라질은 강인한 여성들의 노력으로 출산율이 급속히 하락했다는 것이 이 글의 요지이며 둘째 단락 첫 문장이 주제문이다.

》 정답 01 (A) 02 (D) 03 (B) 04 (C)

사람들은 20세기 후반을 좌뇌형 사고에 지배된 시대였다고 종종 말한다. 교량을 건설하고 컴퓨터를 설계하며 달에 도달하고 새로운 금융 도구를 설계하는 기술은 모두 선형적 사고와 논리를 활용한다. 공학, 법률, 금융 모두 "고전적인" 좌뇌형 활동들이며 이 모든 분야들이 오늘날에도 중요하지만, 어떤 이들은 이 분야들이 변해야 할 필요성을 느끼는데, 특히 전통적으로 좌뇌형 사고의 특징이었던 분석을 컴퓨터가 점점 더 많이 대체해가고 있기 때문에 그렇다. 이와는 대조적으로 전문가들은 미래에는 비선형적이고 직관적이며 시각적인 우뇌형 사고가 지배할 것이라고 주장한다. 다니엘 핑크(Daniel Pink)는 생산단가가 낮아지는 시대에는 디자인이 지배하고, 승자를 결정하는 데 한몫을 한다고 주장한다. 애플의 자산 가치가 마이크로소프트를 능가할 수 있었던 이유는 부분적으로 그들 연구의 핵심에 디자인이 있기 때문이라고 말할 수 있다.

이러한 좌뇌/우뇌 이분법은 노동 인구의 성 역할에 관한 상당한 논란을 불러일으켜왔다. 분석에 의존하는 공학과 금융의 전문직들은 전통적으로 남성들이 지배한 반면, 전형적으로 우뇌형 특징을 지닌 전문직들, 이를테면 예술, 글쓰기, 디자인 등은 여성들에게 더 개방적이었다. 과거의 경우 덧붙이자면, 후자의 직업들과 학과들의 지위는 낮았다. 그러나 지금, 많은 사람들은 분석이 프로그래밍 되고 아웃소싱 될 수 있으므로, 미래에는 이 직업들이 경쟁력을 가질 가능성이 가장 높다고 주장할 수도 있다. 이로 인해 남녀의 사회적 역할이 역전될 수 있고 나아가 남성들의 미래가 절망적이라고 예측하는 사람들까지 나타났다. 『Atlantic』지에서 한나 로진(Hanna Rosin)은 "남성의 종말"이라는 제목의 기사에서 "현대의, 탈공업화 시대의 경제가 남성보다는 여성과 더 잘 맞는다면 어떻게 될까?" 그녀는 "오늘날 유리한 속성들, 즉 사회적 지능, 개방적 의사소통, 가만히 앉아서 집중할 수 있는 능력 등은 최소한 대개 남성적인 것은 아니다."라고 상정한다.

뇌의 서로 다른 영역들과 우뇌와 좌뇌의 활동이 교육과 사회에 미치는 영향을 이해하는 것이 중요하다 할지라도, 규율과 초점은 물론 창의성과 직관력에 의지하여 두 반구를 통합할 수 있는 이들이야말로 궁극적으로 성공할 수 있을 것이다. 난해한 작품을 터득하고자 할 때 피아니스트가 취하는 접근법을 고려해 보자. 음악에 대한 영감을 불러일으키는 통찰에는 우뇌의 종합적 활동이 요구되지만, 음악에 있어 한 번에 한 부분씩 선형적 방식으로 적용되는 힘겹고 엄격한 훈련이 성공적 연주의 기초를 이룬다. 어떤 이들은 "창의성"을 우뇌에 한정하지만, 나는 성공적인 창의적 인간들은 자신들의 뇌 양쪽 반구를 효과적으로 통합한 사람들이라고 주장하고 싶다. 직관력은 논리적 방법과 조화를 이룰 때에만 두드러진 결과를 성취할 수 있다. 다니엘 핑크와는 달리, 나는 우뇌형 인간들이 미래를 지배할 것이라고 생각하지 않는다. 오히려, 완전한 통합형 뇌를 가진 사람들, 혹은 분석과 종합을 함께 융합할 수 있는 서로 다른 강점들을 지닌 사람들의 팀이 성공에 가장 유리한 입지를 차지할 것이라고 생각한다.

linear a. 직선의, 선형의
pundit n. 식자층; 전문가, 권위자
capitalization n. 자본화, 투자; (회사의) 자본 총액
dichotomy n. 이분법
hand-wringing n. 손을 부들부들 떨기
congenial a. 마음이 맞는
posit v. 사실로 상정하다, 받아들이다
predominantly ad. 대개, 대부분
hemisphere n. (뇌·지구의) 반구
underlie v. 기저[기초]를 이루다
analogy n. 비유; 유사점; 유추
hunch n. 예감
congenital a. 선천적인, 성격상의
conducive a. ~에 좋은, ~에 유리한
outstrip v. 앞지르다, 능가하다

01 ▶ 필자는 세 번째 단락에서 21세기의 '성공적인 창의적 인간들은 자신들의 뇌 양쪽 반구를 효과적으로 통합한 사람들', '분석과 종합을 융합할 수 있는 완전한 통합형 뇌를 가진 사람들'이라는 등의 진술을 하고 있다.

02 ▶ 문맥상 여성에게 '더 개방적인, 유리한, 더 잘 어울리는'이라는 의미가 들어가는 것이 적절하다.

03 ▶ '분석과 종합을 함께 융합하는' 존재는 선행사 individuals를 가리키므로 which가 아니라 who가 되어야 한다. 따라서 (e)는 who can, together, blend가 되어야 한다.

04 ▶ 세 번째 단락에서 필자는 '창의성은 우뇌에 한정되지 않고, 뇌 양쪽 반구를 효과적으로 통합한 사람들의 것이다', '직관력은 논리와 조화를 이루어야 한다' 등의 진술을 하고 있으므로, (C)는 본문의 내용과 일치하지 않는다.

》 **정답**   01 (B)   02 (D)   03 (E)   04 (C)

여성들이 왜 공업기술 및 고성장 사업 분야에서 그렇게 저조한지를 더 잘 이해하기 위해, 나는 549명의 성공한 기업인들의 배경과 동기부여에 관한 자료를 분석하는 것을 도와달라고 국립여성정보기술센터(NCWIT)에 요청했다.

여성과 남성 기업가들은 약간은 미묘하게 다르다. 여성들은 그들을 격려해준 비즈니스 파트너에 의해 더 동기부여가 되었다. 여성들은 그들의 직업상/업무상 인맥에 더 큰 가치를 부여했다. 마지막으로, 여성들은 더 조심스러우며 그들 회사의 지적 자본을 보호하는 데 더 많은 우려를 나타냈다. 반면에, 안정된 직장을 유지하기 위한 재정적 압박은 여성들보다 남성들에 의해 더욱 중대하게 받아들여졌다.

그럼에도 불구하고, 남성과 여성 기업가들은 많은 점에서 비슷하다고 연구 결과가 보여주고 있다. 그들은 동등한 수준의 교육을 받았고, 자신만의 사업을 시작하는데 같은 이른 관심 그리고 비슷한 다른 이점들을 갖고 있었다. 남성들과 여성들은 또한 사업을 시작하는 유사한 동기를 갖고 있었다.

남성과 여성 사업가들의 배경과 동기에 있어서의 모든 유사점들과 이제는 대학교에서 여학생의 수가 남학생보다 많다는 사실을 고려해볼 때 우리는 여성 창업 경영인의 부족에 여전히 당황스럽다. 증거 자료는 이것이 여성 쪽의 실패가 아닌 오히려 사회적 실패를 반영하고 있음을 시사한다. 많은 점에서 미국보다 더욱 보수적인 나라인 인도와 대조하는 것을 고려해 보자. 그래도 거기에서는, 여성들이 빠르게 업계의 최고위층 자리까지 올라가고 있다. 인도의 금융업은 더 최근의 것이고 그곳의 여성들은 더 적은 확고히 자리 잡은 금융업 종사자들과 경쟁할지도 모른다고 첨단기술 산업에 있어서의 여성의 역할을 연구해 온 신디 파드노스(Cindy Padnos)가 말한다.

더욱 많은 사람들이 여성을 기업의 경영자로 만드는 것이 사업적으로 이점이 있다는 것을 인식하고 있기 때문에 파드노스는 미국에서의 현 상황이 좋아질 것이라고 낙관하고 있다. 여성이 이끄는 첨단산업 분야의 신생기업들은 투자자본 1달러당 더 높은 수익을 창출하며 남성이 이끄는 신생기업들보다 더 낮은 실패율을 갖고 있다고 그녀의 연구자료가 보여준다.

---

subtle a. 미묘한, 미세한
intellectual capital 지적자본
equivalent a. 동등한, 같은 가치[양]의
startup n. 신생기업, 창업(회사)
perplexed a. 난처한, 어찌할 바를 모르는, 당황한
societal a. 사회(활동)의
conservative a. 보수적인
contend with ~와 다투다, 경쟁하다
optimistic a. 낙관적인, 낙천적인
be at the helm (of~) 키를 잡다, 지도자 입장에 있다
generate v. 산출하다, 창출하다
revenue n. 세입, 수익, 총수입

01 ▶ 두 번째 단락에서 차이점이 소개 된 후 그럼에도 불구하고 유사점도 있다는 내용이 세 번째 단락에서 이어지므로 ⓐ에는 양보와 역접의 의미를 모두 갖은 접속사 Yet이 적절하다. ⓑ에는 문법적으로 전치사가 필요한데, 문맥상 '~을 고려해 볼 때'의 Given이 자연스럽다.

02 ▶ (B)와 (D)는 사실과 반대되는 내용이며, (A)는 주제가 되기에 포괄적이지 못하다.

03 ▶ (B)는 가장 마지막 문장을 통해 확인 가능하며 여성 창업자 부족이 사회적 실패라고 했으므로 (C) 역시 유추 가능하다. (D)는 세 번째 단락을 통해 추론할 수 있다. 반면 마지막 단락의 첫 번째 문장에서 상황이 호전 될 것이라고 낙관했으므로 (A)는 옳지 않다.

04 ▶ **entrenched a.** (깊숙이, 확고히) 자리 잡은(= well-established)

▶ 정답 01 (A) 02 (C) 03 (A) 04 (D)

태양의 신비는 태양표면 폭발의 기묘한 성질이다. 수백만 개의 100메가톤급 수소 폭탄을 동시에 폭파시킨 것에 맞먹는 태양표면 폭발은 우리 태양계에서 일어나는 가장 격렬하고 강력한 폭발이다. 이러한 폭발은 태양의 광구(光球)에서 발생하며, 층의 밝은 빛 방출로 인해 전문 장비로도 보는 것이 쉽지 않다. 태양표면 폭발은 좀 더 쉽게 관찰할 수 있는 또 다른 태양 현상인 태양 흑점과 직접적으로 연관되어 있다. 1608년, 망원경의 발명으로 천문학자들은 마침내 태양의 모습을 들여다볼 수 있었고, 그것이 그들이 예상했던 것처럼 완전하고, 불변하는 노란색의 원반이 아니라 종종 식별할 수 있는 점 또는 흑점으로 인해 흐트러진다는 것을 알게 되었다. 이러한 어두운 지역은 태양 광구에서 가장 차가운 부분이며, 강렬한 자기(磁氣) 활동이 특징이다. 태양 흑점 출현의 빈도는 태양이나 태양 흑점의 11년 주기를 따른다. <우리는 최근까지 2007년 초반 몇 달 안에 끝날 것이라 예상되었던 23번째 태양 주기에 있었다.> 주기의 최소 끝에서는 태양 흑점 활동이 거의 없고, 최대 끝에서는 수백 개의 태양 흑점을 볼 수 있다. 태양 흑점의 증가는 태양표면 폭발 활동의 증가와도 서로 관련이 있음을 나타낸다. 이러한 활동 기간은 인공위성과 우주 비행사들에게 중대한 위험을 안길 수 있다. 한 번의 태양표면 폭발은 인공위성에 심각한 피해를 주거나 인공위성의 궤도를 바꾸기에 충분한 자기 에너지를 방출할 수 있다. 그것은 또한 지구 자기장을 뒤흔들 수 있으며, 넓은 지역에 걸친 정전을 초래하는 전력선의 위험한 동요를 야기할 수 있다. 이러한 위험들과 인공위성에 대한 우리의 의존도가 높아지는 이유 때문에 과학자들이 태양 기상의 성질을 이해하고 태양 활동을 예측하는 보다 정확한 방법을 결정하는 것이 더욱 중요하게 되었다.

---

solar flare n. 태양표면 폭발
equivalent a. 동등한, 대등한
detonate v. 폭발시키다
simultaneously ad. 동시에
photosphere n. (태양, 항성 등의) 광구(光球)
emission n. (빛·열·향기 따위의) 방사, 발산
sunspot n. 태양 흑점
mar v. 손상시키다, 훼손하다
discernable a. 식별할 수 있는, 분간할 수 있는
blemish n. 흠, 오점, 결점
frequency n. 횟수, 빈도, 빈도수
occurrence n. (사건의) 발생
indicate v. 가리키다; 나타내다, ~의 징후이다
correlate v. 서로 관련시키다
pose v. (문제 등을) 제기하다
orbit n. 궤도
surge n. 급상승; 쇄도

01 ▶ 망원경의 발명으로 태양을 볼 수 있게 되었지만 그것이 예상처럼 완벽하거나 모양이 변하지 않는 원형이 아니라는 사실을 강조하기 위해 blemishes라는 단어를 사용하였다. 즉, 태양표면에 반점처럼 보이는 태양 흑점으로 완전한 노란색 원반형 모양이 아니라는 의미에서 blemishes를 언급한 것이다.

02 ▶ 태양 흑점은 11년의 태양 주기나 태양 흑점 주기에 따라 발생하며 주기의 최소 끝에는 태양 흑점 활동이 드문 반면 주기의 최대 끝에서는 매우 활발하다고 했다. 또한 이러한 태양 흑점의 증가가 태양표면 폭발의 증가와도 연관되어 있다고 했으므로 정답은 (B)이다.

03 ▶ 이 문제의 단서는 태양 주기(solar cycle)이다. 즉, 삽입 문장의 앞에는 태양 주기에 관한 내용이 나와야 한다. 그리고 뒤에는 태양 주기의 세부적인 특징들이 나와 있어야 한다. 따라서 삽입된 문장은 [Ⅲ]에 들어가야 한다.

04 ▶ It이 들어있는 문장과 그 앞 문장은 태양표면 폭발의 영향력을 설명하고 있으므로 (D) solar flare가 정답이다.

» 정답 01 (A) 02 (B) 03 (C) 04 (D)

창의성에 대한 인지적 접근은 창조적인 작품이 생성되는 정신적 과정에 초점을 맞춘다. 이러한 과정에는 개념 조합, 개념 확장, 형상화, 은유가 포함된다. 대부분의 심리학자들은 창의성이 전문성, 우연, 직관의 결합을 수반한다고 생각하지만, 이러한 요소들을 강조하는 정도는 다르다. 전문성을 강조하는 이론가들은 창의성이 종종 광범위한 연습과 학습을 통해서만 이룰 수 있다는 증거를 지적한다. 이를 흔히 한 분야에서 10년의 경험이 창의적 성공을 위해 필요하다는 증거에 근거하여, '10년의 법칙'이라고 한다. 전문가들은 초보자들보다 그 분야의 관련 패턴을 발견하고 기억하며 효과적으로 문제를 표현해낼 수 있다. 전문성 이론가들은 창의성이 기억, 계획, 추론, 재구성과 같은 일상적인 사고 과정과 관련되어 있다고 믿는다. 그들은 주어진 분야에 대한 익숙함과 기술을 넘어서는 어떤 특별하거나 무의식적인 사고 과정은 창의성을 위해 요구되지 않는다고 주장한다.

다른 이들은 기존 관점과 접근법에 대한 확고함으로 인해 전문가들이 초보자들보다 기능적으로 고착 및 고정되고, 확증 편향과 같은 현상을 더 잘 드러낸다는 데 주목한다. 어떤 이들은 창조적인 관념 작용으로 이어지는 우연한 만남, 기회 또는 상황의 역할을 강조한다. 또 다른 이들은 창의성을 전문성이나 우연의 문제라기보다는 직관에 귀 기울이면서 잠재력의 불분명한 상태로부터 명확한 구체화의 상태를 향해 직관을 따라가는 것으로 본다. 이러한 관점은 어떻게 연상기반 기억 구조가 직관 현상에 대한 과학적 근거를 제공하는지를 강조하고, 창의적인 사람들은 평평한 연상 계층을 가진다는, 즉 관심 주제와 간접적으로, 혹은 특이하게 관련된 <가까운 연상물>들을 더 잘 활용한다는, 발견에 대한 과학적 근거를 강조한다.

창의성에 대해 체계적으로 생각하려는 초기의 노력들 중 일부는 컴퓨터 과학자들로부터 나왔는데, 그들은 창의성을 만족스러운 해결책이 발견될 때까지 경험 법칙이 상태 공간(가능한 해결책들의 집합) 내에서 다른 상태들에 대한 점검을 이끄는 경험적 탐색의 과정으로 보았다. 경험적 탐색에서, 문제나 과제의 관련 변수들은 전면에 정의된다. 따라서, 상태 공간은 일반적으로 고정되어 있다. 경험적 탐색의 예로는 문제를 하위 문제로 세분화하고, 목표 상태에서 초기 상태를 향해 역방향으로 작업하는 것을 들 수 있다. 이후 창의성은 사전 정의된 상태 공간에서의 새로운 가능성뿐만 아니라 새로운 상태 공간 그 자체에 대한 탐색을 안내하는 경험적 탐색을 수반한다고 제안되었다.

---

imagery n. 형상화
metaphor n. 은유
expertise n. 전문성
entrenchment n. 확고함
fixedness n. 고착
confirmation bias 확증편향
ideation n. 관념화
ill-defined a. 불분명한
actualization n. 구체화
association n. 연상
hierarchy n. 계층구조
heuristic a. 체험적인(스스로 발견하게 하는)
rule of thumb 경험 법칙, 어림짐작
inspection n. 점검, 검토

01 ▶ 전문성 이론가들은 주어진 분야에 대한 어떤 특별하거나 무의식적인 사고 과정은 창의성에 의해 요구되지 않는다고 했으므로 (A)가 정답이다. 둘째 단락에서 '직관'을 강조하는 이들은 '창의성을 전문성이나 우연의 문제라기보다는'이라고 하였으므로 (B)는 잘못된 진술이다. '창의성에 대해 체계적으로 생각하려는 초기의 노력들 중 일부는 컴퓨터 과학자들에서 나왔다'는 진술을 바탕으로 '오늘날 대부분의 컴퓨터 과학자들이 창의성이 heuristics를 따른다'고 보는 것은 과도하므로 (D)는 잘못된 진술이다.

02 ▶ '관심 주제와 간접적으로, 혹은 특이하게 관련된', '평평한 연상 계층구조'라는 진술에 비추어 볼 때 창의적인 사람들은 '가까운' 연상물들을 더 잘 활용하는 것이 아니라 '멀리 떨어진(remote, distant)' 연상물들을 더 잘 활용하는 사람들이다.

» 정답 01 (A) 02 (C)

영화 "Proof"에서 주인공 마틴(Martin)은 시각장애인으로서, 사물의 존재를 검증하기 위해 사물의 사진을 찍는다. 영화는 마틴과 그의 가정부인 실리아(Celia)의 관계에 초점을 맞추고 있다. 그는 그녀가 그로부터 갈망하는 사랑과 애정을 보류하고, 실리아는 사디즘적인 소소한 행동들로 반응한다. 실리아는 그가 걸려 넘어지도록 물건들을 배치하고, 안내견을 꾀어내고, 그를 계속 관찰하며, 결국 그의 한 친구를 유혹한다. "Proof"에서 분명히 드러나는 악의와 유머는 실리아에 대한 마틴의 거절과 그녀의 사소한 잔혹 행위들을 중심으로 전개되지만, 이 모든 것을 뒷받침하는 것은 신뢰라는 주제이며, 사진술이 이 문제의 핵심이 된다. 마틴은 정상 시력을 가진 사람들을 믿지 않는데, 그들의 설명을 확인할 길이 없기 때문이다. 그에 관한 한, 정상 시력을 가진 사람들은 엉터리로 혹은 부정확하게 겉모습을 설명함으로써 그를 속일 수 있다. 그는 자신의 어머니가 자신을 부끄럽게 여긴다고 믿고, 어머니는 그곳에 존재하지 않는 물건들에 대해 묘사함으로써 그녀 나름의 복수를 했다고 의심한다(그는 심지어 어머니가 그에게서 도망치기 위해 그녀 자신의 죽음을 조작했다고 주장하기도 한다). 마틴은 사물들과 사건들의 사진을 찍고, 그 후에 독립적인 증인들, 즉 처음엔 실리아, 나중에는 그의 친구 앤디(Andy)가 그 사진들을 묘사하게 한다. 그들은 사진 속에 표현된 사물들을 증언한 것이 아니라 그가 알고 있는 사건과 사람들이 그에게 한 말을 확증하는 한, 그는 자신이 경험한 상황들을 검증할 수 있었다. 물론 그는 사진을 해설하는 사람들도 검증하고 있다. (줄거리가 전개될수록, 앤디와 실리아는 점점 더 마틴에게 비밀에 부치기를 원하기 때문에, 상황은 복잡해진다). "Proof"에서 사진술이 이러한 검증의 역할을 수행하는데, 사진은 사물의 외관을 정확하게 재생하는, 자동적이며 기계적인 기록의 기술로 간주되기 때문이다. 이 영화에서 카메라는 사진을 찍는 사람과 그의 욕망(그는 카메라가 보는 것을 볼 수 없다.)으로부터 독립해 작동하는, 객관적이고 독립적인 증인으로 제시된다. 결국, 낡은 흑백 이미지의 매체를 통해, 마틴은 어머니의 서술적 기만의 핵심 예로 삼기 위해 자신이 택한 것이 사실 정확한 설명이었다는 것을 알게 된다.

---

housekeeper n. 가정부
withhold v. ~을 주지 않다, 억누르다
affection n. 애정
crave v. 갈망하다
sadism n. 가학증
stumble v. 발이 걸리다
entice away 꾀어내다
seduce v. 유혹하다
malice n. 악의
revolve around ~를 중심으로 돌다
cruelty n. 잔학 행위
underpin v. 뒷받침하다
sighted a. 앞을 볼 수 있는, 시력이 정상인
verify v. 확인하다
take revenge 복수하다
deceit n. 속임수, 기만

01 ▶ (A)와 (C)는 잘못된 진술이며, (D)에 대해 확인할 수 있는 정보는 본문에 나와 있지 않다. 마틴에게는 점점 더 비밀에 부치기를 원한다고 했으므로 (B)는 사실이다.

02 ▶ '사진은 사물의 외관을 정확하게 재생하는, 자동적이며 기계적인 기록의 기술로 간주된다'고 하였으므로 (B)는 잘못된 진술이다. (D)와 관련하여 '낡은 흑백 이미지의 매체를 통해, 마틴은 어머니의 서술적 기만의 핵심 예로 삼기 위해 자신이 택한 것이 사실 정확한 설명이었다는 것을 알게 된다'고 하였는데, 여기서 '어머니의 서술적 기만의 핵심 예로 삼기 위해 자신이 택한 것'이란 앞서 나왔던 '어머니가 그에게서 도망치기 위해 그녀 자신의 죽음을 조작했다는 주장'을 가리킨다.

03 ▶ '이 영화에서 카메라는 사진을 찍는 사람과 그의 욕망으로부터 독립해 작동하는, 객관적이고 독립적인 증인으로 제시된다'고 하였으므로 (D)는 잘못된 추론이다.

» 정답 01 (B) 02 (B) 03 (D)

지구 온난화에 대해 우리가 알고 있는 거의 모든 것이 1979년에 이해되었다. 1957년 이후 그 해까지 수집된 데이터는 20세기에 접어들기 이전부터 알려져 있던 것, 즉 인류가 화석연료의 무분별한 연소를 통해 지구의 대기를 변화시켰다는 것을 확인시켜 주었다. 주요한 과학적 문제는 논쟁의 여지를 넘어 확실해졌고, 1980년대가 시작되면서 관심은 문제의 진단에서 예측되는 결과를 정교하게 파악하는 것으로 바뀌었다. 끈 이론과 유전공학과 비교해 1900년대 초까지 거슬러 올라가는 "온실효과"의 비유는 "생물학 입문" 교과서에도 기술되어 있는 오래된 역사다. 토대가 되는 과학도 특별히 복잡하지 않았다. 그것은 단순하고 자명한 이치, 즉 대기 중에 이산화탄소가 많을수록 지구는 더워진다는 것으로 요약할 수 있다. 그리고 매년 석탄, 석유, 가스를 태움으로써 인류는 점점 더 터무니없을 정도로 많은 양의 이산화탄소를 대기 중으로 뿜어냈다.

우리는 왜 행동에 나서지 않았을까? 오늘날 사악한 존재로 비난받는 존재는 화석연료 산업인데, 최근 몇 십 년 동안 화석연료 산업은 만화책에나 나올법한 허세를 부리며 악당 역할을 자임했다. 기후관련 문헌의 한 하위 분야는 산업 로비스트들의 술책, 과학자들의 부패, 그리고 최대 석유 가스 회사들이 부인으로 일관하는 팬터마임을 포기한 지 오래인 지금까지도 정치적 논쟁을 계속 저하시키고 있는 선전 캠페인들을 온통 열거해왔다. 그러나 대중을 혼란에 빠뜨리기 위한 조직화된 노력은 1989년 말에야 비로소 본격적으로 시작되었다. 그보다 앞선 10년 동안은, 엑슨과 셸을 포함한 일부 대형 석유회사들은 위기의 범위를 이해하고 가능한 해결책을 찾기 위해 선의의 노력을 기울였다.

공화당을 탓할 수도 없다. 오늘날 공화당원의 42%만이 "대부분의 과학자들이 지구 온난화가 일어나고 있다고 믿는다."는 것을 알고 있고, 그 비율도 감소하고 있다. 그러나 1980년대 동안에는, 많은 저명한 공화당원들은 기후 문제는 당파적일 수 없고, 가능한 가장 중대한 이해관계가 얽힌 거의 보기 드문 최고의 정치적 이슈라는 데 민주당원들과 의견이 다르지 않았다. 이 문제는 은퇴군인들이나 중소기업에 대한 지원 이슈처럼, 비난받을 여지가 전혀 없었다. 기후는 지구상의 모든 인간들로 구성된, 훨씬 더 폭넓은 유권자들을 가지고 있다는 점만 제외한다면 말이다.

---

indiscriminate a. 무분별한
axiom n. 자명한 이치, 공리
belch v. 트림하다, 내뿜다
obscene a. 터무니없는
boogeyman n. 사악한 존재
villain n. 악당
bravado n. 허세, 객기
chronicle v. 연대순으로 기록하다
machination n. 간계, 술책, 음모
debase v. 저하시키다
dumb show 무언극, 팬터마임
in earnest 본격적으로, 진지하게
good-faith a. 선의의
high stakes 중대한 이해관계
unimpeachable a. 의심할 여지없는
constituency n. 유권자들

01 ▶ 둘째 단락 끝 문장에서 '1989년보다 앞선 10년 동안은, 엑슨과 셸을 포함한 일부 대형 석유회사들은 위기의 범위를 이해하고 가능한 해결책을 찾기 위해 선의의 노력을 기울였다'고 하였으므로 (A)가 정답이다.

02 ▶ 밑줄 친 부분을 주어로 한 술부의 내용으로 보아 이것은 기후변화, 즉 지구온난화의 진실과 심각성을 무시하는 산업관련 로비스트들과 과학자들의 왜곡된 글들을 말하므로 (B)가 정답이다. 한편, (A)와 관련하여 '대중을 혼란에 빠뜨리기 위한 조직화된 노력은 1989년 말에야 비로소 본격적으로 시작되었다'지만, 그 후 나온 글들이 모두 그렇다고 추론할 수는 없으므로 잘못된 추론이다.

03 ▶ 첫 문장에서 '지구 온난화에 대해 우리가 알고 있는 거의 모든 것이 1979년에 이해되었다'고 하였으므로 (E)는 타당한 진술이다.

▶ 정답 01 (A) 02 (B) 03 (E)

세상에서 가장 많은 생물은 곤충이며, 알려져 있는 곤충의 종(種)은 다른 모든 동물과 식물을 합친 것보다도 수가 더 많다. 곤충은 생존을 위한 싸움에서 매우 성공적이었기 때문에, 때때로 지구를 지배하는 데 있어서 인류의 강력한 라이벌로 묘사되고 있다. 크기가 작고 상대적으로 먹을 것이 적게 필요하며 또한 빨리 증식하는 덕분에, 수많은 곤충 종들은 영속할 수 있게 되었다. 곤충학자들은 거의 1백만 종의 곤충에 이름을 붙였는데, 이것은 전체 곤충 숫자의 3분의 1에도 미치지 못할 것이다.

곤충은 생물이 살 수 있는 곳이라면 그 어떤 서식지에서도 번성하고 있다. 어떤 것들은 북극 지방에서만 발견되고 있으며, 어떤 것들은 사막에서만 산다. 다른 것들은 오직 민물이나 소금기 있는 물에서만 잘 자란다. 수많은 곤충 종들은 몹시 춥고 더운 기온을 모두 견딜 수 있다. 그런 튼튼한 종(種)은 종종 지구 전체에 걸쳐 광범위하게 분포하는 것으로 알려져 있다. 그러나, 해양과 같은 환경에서는 극소수의 곤충만이 살고 있다.

어떤 기생 곤충들은 음식, 습도, 온기, 그리고 적들로부터의 방어와 같이 살아가는 데 있어서 필수적인 것들이 최적의 조건을 갖추고 있는 숙주 동물의 몸에 또는 몸 안에서 삶의 상당 부분을 보낸다. 다른 종류의 곤충들은 생의 전부 혹은 일부를 양식이 되는 식물에 둘러싸인 채 보낸다.

어떤 종은 변화하는 환경의 요구를 충족시키기 위해 적응하는 데 있어 매우 능숙하게 되었다. 가령, 다양한 수중 벌레들과 수중 딱정벌레들은 기는 것만큼이나 헤엄을 잘 치고 잘 날 수 있다. 벌, 개미, 말벌과 같은 수많은 종류의 곤충들은 복잡한 사회구조와 방어적인 행동에 의지하고 있다. 다른 종을 잡아먹지 않는 종은 종종 불쾌한 맛이나 냄새, 독이 있는 가시, 그리고 위장술과 같은 방어수단을 가지고 있는데, 이런 것들은 적들로부터 자신을 보호해준다.

집단으로서는 적응력이 강하고 융통성이 있지만, 곤충은 가끔씩 비가 아주 많이 오거나, 서리가 일찍 내리거나, 가뭄이 길어지는 것과 같이 날씨가 극단적으로 되는 경우에는 적응을 하지 못하며, 이런 것들은 한 지역에 있는 곤충의 개체군의 수를 급속히 파괴하거나 급격하게 감소시킬 수 있다. 곤충은 동물들 ― 수많은 동물들뿐만 아니라 새, 파충류, 양서류, 그리고 물고기 ― 이 섭취하는 음식물에서 중요한 부분을 이루고 있기 때문에 그 숫자는 항상 억제되고 있다.

개개의 곤충의 생존에 있어 불리한 요인의 수는 엄청나다. 따라서, 어떤 종의 경우, 하나의 암컷이 낳은 수백 개의 알 가운데 겨우 몇 개만이 성충이 된다. 어떤 종에 있어서 생존율은 많은 수의 낳는 알에 의해 높여지고 있다.

---

species n. 종(種), 종류
outnumber v. ~보다 수가 많다
perpetuate v. 영속시키다
brackish a. 소금기 있는
parasitic a. 기생하는
wasp n. 장수말벌
venomous a. 독이 있는; 유해한
spine n. 등뼈; <식물> 가시
camouflage n. 위장(僞裝)
drastically ad. 맹렬한; 과감한, 철저한
reptile n. 파충류 동물
amphibian n. 양서류 동물
overwhelming a. 압도적인, 저항할 수 없는

01 ▶ entomologist n. 곤충학자 nutritionist n. 영양학자 archaeologist n. 고고학자 meteorologist n. 기상학자

02 ▶ 이 글에 의하면 '곤충의 가장 큰 장점은 생물이 살 수 있는 곳이라면 그 어느 곳에서도 번성하는 적응력(adaptability)'이라고 할 수 있다.

03 ▶ 글의 마지막 문장에서 '어떤 종에 있어서 생존율은 많은 수의 알을 낳음으로써 높여지고 있다'고 했다.

04 ▶ '곤충이 번성하고 있는 까닭은 각각의 곤충들이 환경에 맞게 잘 적응을 해왔기 때문'이라 할 수 있다. 따라서 '더 나은 생존 기술을 발전시켜 왔다'한 (D)가 결론으로 가장 적절하다.

» **정답** 01 (A) 02 (C) 03 (B) 04 (D)

에너지만으로는 생명을 유지시키는 데 충분하지 않다. 가령, 조류(藻類)와 같은 몇 포기의 식물을 맑은 물이 가득 찬 살균 소독한 항아리에 넣어 밀폐시키고 햇빛에 충분히 노출시킨 상황을 상상해 보라. 식물들은 광합성 과정에서 이산화탄소를 소모하고 산소를 배출한다. 곧, 이산화탄소는 고갈되어 식물들은 죽게 될 것이다. 실험자가 이산화탄소를 추가로 공급해도 이 식물들은 살지 못할 것이다. 이 식물들은 생명유지에 필요한 다른 화학물질이 부족하여 시들게 될 것이다. 그러나 달팽이와 같이 식물을 먹는 생물을 항아리에 넣고 맑은 물을 연못물로 대체하여 영양소와 미생물을 공급하면 항아리 속의 생명은 유지될 것이다. 적당한 수의 달팽이를 항아리에 추가로 공급하면 항아리는 균형 잡히고 안정된 생태계가 될 것이다. 영양소는 순환을 계속하게 될 것이다.

조류는 물, 이산화탄소, 햇빛, 분해된 영양소를 이용하여 생명을 유지시키고 조직을 만든다. 달팽이는 이 식물들을 먹는다. 산소는 조류의 한 가지 주요 배설물인 동시에 달팽이가 살아가는 데 필수적이다. 반대로, 달팽이는 조류가 필요로 하는 이산화탄소를 배출한다. 식물과 달팽이가 죽으면, 이들은 미생물에 의해 분해되고 분해된 영양소는 순환한다. 밀폐된 항아리의 영양소들은 식물, 동물, 미생물 순으로 순환하고 식물로 재순환되어 사용된다. 따라서 생태계는 무한히 존재할 수 있다. 사실, 생명 활동이 10년 이상 유지된 밀폐된 수조를 일부 생물 실험실에서 찾아 볼 수 있다.

algae n. 조류(藻類), 말무리
seal v. 봉인하다
sterilize v. 살균하다, 소독하다
photosynthesis n. 광합성
starve v. 굶주리다, 굶어죽다
chemical n. 화학제품, 화학물질
pond n. 연못, 늪
nutrient n. 영양분
decay n. 부패, 부식
organism n. 유기체
ecosystem n. 생태계
dissolve v. 분해시키다
indefinitely ad. 무기한으로, 언제까지나

01 ▶ 이 글은 '에너지만으로는 생명을 지탱할 수 없으며, 영양소가 식물, 동물, 미생물, 다시 식물로 순환되어 생명이 유지된다'는 내용이다.

02 ▶ 에너지만으로는 생명 유지가 불가능하고 영양소의 순환이 필요하다는 사실을 설명하기 위해 살균된 항아리 속의 식물을 예로 들고 있다.

03 ▶ 맑은 물을 연못물로 대체하여 영양소와 미생물을 공급하면 항아리 속의 생명은 유지될 것이라고 했다. 즉, 맑은 물만으로는 식물에 충분한 영양소가 될 수 없다고 할 수 있다.

04 ▶ 여러 영양소가 식물, 동물, 미생물, 식물 순으로 반복 순환하여 생태계의 생명이 유지된다는 내용이다.

≫ 정답   01 (A)   02 (B)   03 (D)   04 (B)

라이프니츠가 훌륭하게 설계된 유기조직 속에서 각 구성원이 적소(適所)를 차지하고 "미리 설정된 조화"에 힘입어 신이 부여한 기능을 실행하는 것을 보았을 때 그는 우리가 알고 있는 세상을 "가장 가능성이 있는 세계"라고 일컬었다. 한편, 쇼펜하우어는 이 세상의 선과 악의 실제 양을 달아보고 인생은 "이득이 손실을 거의 메우지 못하는 사업"이기 때문에 우리 인간 세상은 "가장 가능성이 없는 세계"라는 비관적인 결론에 도달했다. 그에게 가장 명백한 사실은 악이 만연해 있다는 것이었고, 우주에 이성이 있는 것으로 보는 것을 가설로 생각했으며 사변 철학가들의 부질없는 기대가 만들어낸 산물로 보았다.

쇼펜하우어는 단치히에서 태어났다. 그는 얼마 동안 프랑스, 영국, 이태리를 여행하면서 세계주의적 안목을 습득하고 타고난 외국어 구사력을 완성시켰다. 그는 조지 고든 바이런 경(卿)의 열렬한 숭배자였지만 이 영국 시인의 여복(女福)을 부러워해 개인적인 교제를 거부했다. 철학을 전공했던 그는 베를린에서 피히테와 슐라이어마허를 청강하고 매우 부정적인 인상을 받게 되어 관념철학의 모든 사상가들에게 일생 동안 적대감을 키웠다.

쇼펜하우어가 '객원강사'로 베를린에 잠시 정착했을 당시, 헤겔과 슐라이어마허는 학계에서 가장 명성이 높았지만 쇼펜하우어의 강의와 저술은 호응을 얻지 못했다. 그는 일반 철학교수들의 전문 철학, 특히 헤겔을 신랄하게 비판하여 자신의 실망을 나타냈다. 그는 헤겔을 허풍선이, 사기꾼, 프러시아 정부의 천한 노예라고 불렀다. 1831년에 콜레라가 유행하여 헤겔이 사망하고, 쇼펜하우어는 프랑크푸르트로 옮겨가 그곳에서 유일한 동료인 충성스런 검은 색 푸들과 "고독한" 여생을 보냈다.

---

armchair a. 이론뿐인, 탁상공론의
cosmopolitan a. 세계주의의
command n. (언어의) 구사력
antagonism n. 적대, 대립, 반감
privatdozent n. 객원 강사(= privatdocent)
give vent to (노여움 따위를) 터뜨리다
dub v. ~라고 칭하다
quack n. 돌팔이 의사
charlatan n. 협잡꾼, 돌팔이 의사
servile a. 비굴한, 천한
epidemic n. 유행병
claim v. (병 등이 인명을) 빼앗다
companion n. 동료

01 ▶ 본문 첫 문장이 라이프니츠에 관한 내용임에 착안한다.
02 ▶ 쇼펜하우어의 강의와 저술이 학계에서 호응을 얻지 못했으므로, (D)의 academic acceptance and recognition이 본문의 내용과 다르다.
03 ▶ 쇼펜하우어는 관념철학자들에게 일생 동안 적대감을 키웠다고 둘째 문단 마지막 부분에 언급되어 있다.
04 ▶ 쇼펜하우어는 비관적 사상을 갖고 있고 바이런의 여복을 시기했으며 여러 언어에 능숙했다.

》 정답 01 (A) 02 (D) 03 (C) 04 (C)

우리는 인생의 많은 시간을 말을 하며 보낸다. 아침부터 밤까지, 심지어 더러는 밤새도록, 사무실에서, 교실에서, 집에서, 회의에서, 파티에서, 가족 간의 식사에서 말들이 쏟아져 나온다. 이러한 모든 말 중 일정량은 정보를 전하거나 지시를 내리거나 설명을 하거나 등, 실제적인 목적을 갖고 있다. 그러나 명확한 목적이 있을 때조차도 대개는 그 주제에 필요한 이상으로 더 많은 말이 행해진다. 사실은, 엄청나게 많은 양의 이야기가 그저 말하는 것을 즐기려고 하는 말로 이루어져 있다.

사람들은 무엇에 대한 이야기를 가장 즐겨 하는가? 그것은 다른 무엇보다 그들 자신에 대한 이야기이다. 그들이 좋아하는 것과 싫어하는 것, 그들의 견해와 희망사항들. 화제가 무엇이든, 음식, 영화, 자동차, 직장, 그리고 이 세상의 그 어떤 것이든, 사람들은 자신의 생각과 경험에 대해 이야기하고 싶어 한다. 야구 같은 인기 있는 주제가 논의되고 있을 때는, 가끔은 마치 모든 사람이 말을 하고 한 사람도 듣지 않고 있는 것 같이 여겨질 수도 있다. 그 시끄러운 소음은 점점 더 커질 수도 있는데 그러면 마침내 누군가가 "잠깐만, 내 말 좀 다 끝내고 보자."라고 외칠 것이다.

이와 같은 경우에서 우리는 말하는 것이 말을 듣는 것보다 더 중요하다는 결론을 내릴지도 모른다. 하지만, 전반적으로 보면, 사람들은 자신이 말하고 싶어 하면 다른 사람의 말도 들어주어야 한다는 불문율을 지킨다. 우리들 대부분은 어려서부터 말을 잘 한다. 그리고 성장하면서 남의 말을 잘 듣는 것도 배워간다. 대화는 말하기와 듣기 모두의 문제이다. 대화는 우리 자신의 인상과 생각이 남들에게 어떻게 여겨지는가를 알아봄으로써 그 인상과 생각을 검토해보는 좋은 방법이다. 따라서 대화는 하나의 사회적 행위이며 기본적인 인간 행위이다. 그리고 보면, 대화가 우리 생활의 너무나 많은 부분을 채우고 있는 것은 당연한 일이다.

instruction n. 훈련, 교육, 가르침
definite a. 확실한; 한정된
consist of ~로 구성돼 있다
impression n. 인상, 생각
conclude v. 결론 내리다
conversation n. 대화, 대담

01 ▶ 엄청나게 많은 양의 이야기가 실제적인 목적이 있어서가 아니라 그저 말하는 것을 즐기려고 하는 말로 이루어져 있다고 했다.

02 ▶ 사람들이 자신에 대한 이야기를 즐긴다는 것은 결국 다른 사람들의 주목을 받길 원한다는 것이다.

03 ▶ 자신이 말하고 싶어 하면 다른 사람의 말도 들어주어야 한다는 불문율을 지키긴 하지만 사람들은 대체로 말하는 것을 우선으로 하는 경향이 있다.

04 ▶ '대화는 우리 자신의 인상과 생각이 남들에게 어떻게 여겨지는가를 알아봄으로써 그 인상과 생각을 검토해보는 좋은 방법이다.'가 (A)와 같은 의미의 진술이다.

≫ 정답 01 (C) 02 (B) 03 (D) 04 (A)

281

수면은 생물학적으로 불가피한 것이지만, 사람들은 과연 수면을 먹고 마실 것처럼 생명유지에 반드시 필요한 것으로 여기고 있는가? 24시간 쉬지 않고 록음악이 울려대는 오늘날의 미국에서는 그렇지 않다. 상점은 문을 닫지 않고, 조립생산라인은 멈추지 않으며, TV가 하루 종일 유혹하고 주식 거래인이 도쿄의 주식 동향을 계속 지켜봐야 하는 그런 사회에서는 그렇지 않다. 너무나 많은 미국인들에게, 수면은 희생시켜도 좋은 사치품이나 참아내야 하는 성가신 것이 되었다.

그러나, 점점 더 많은 과학자들이 휴식을 보류하는 것은 어리석고 종종 위험하기도 한 거래라고 주장하고 있다. 사실, 수면 부족이 가장 널리 만연한 건강 위협 요소 중 하나가 되었다는 증거는 늘어나고 있다. 미국의 학자들은 밤마다 수면을 취하지 못하는 것이 직접 질병을 일으킨다는 것을 아직은 결론적으로 증명하지 못했지만, 여러 연구 결과, 정신적 각성과 업무 수행이 크게 방해받을 수 있는 것으로 드러났다.

전형적인 성인이 효과적으로 활동하기 위해서는 하룻밤에 약 8시간 숙면을 취해야 한다. 그런 기준으로 볼 때, 수백만 명의 미국인들은 예닐곱 시간, 혹은 그보다 훨씬 더 적은 잠으로 때우려는 만성적인 수면 부족 상태에 있다. 많은 가정에서, 잠을 제대로 자지 않는 것이 하나의 무의식적이고 해로운 습관이 되었다. 극단적인 경우에는, 사람들이 잠을 얼마나 적게 자고도 생활을 해나갈 수 있는지 알아보려고 밤을 거의 꼬박 새우기도 한다. 그들은 주말에 낮잠을 자서 보충하려 하지만, 그것은 수면 부족의 일부만을 보충해줄 뿐이다.

잠을 제대로 자지 않는 데서 오는 가장 방심할 수 없는 결과는 아마도 미국 사회에 점점 더 만연해 가는 조급한 흥분일 것이다. 그러나 훨씬 더 험악한 결과도 있다. 병원의 인턴과 레지던트들에게서 끔찍한 이야기들을 듣게 되는데, 그들 중에는 한번에 36시간을 일하는 것을 포함해서 한 주에 120시간을 늘 일하는 사람이 많다. 이들 중에 더러는 실수가 무서우리만치 흔하다고 인정한다. 캘리포니아의 한 레지던트는 한 여성의 자궁을 봉합하다가 잠이 들었고 그리고는 환자 위로 쓰러졌다. 캘리포니아의 또 다른 한 사례에서는, 한 레지던트가 졸려서 당뇨병 환자에게 밤에 인슐린 주사를 놓도록 지시할 것을 잊어버리고 다른 약물을 처방했다. 그래서 그 환자는 혼수상태에 빠졌다.

미국 교통부 보고에 의하면, 매년 최대 20만 건의 교통사고가 졸음과 관련이 있으며, 모든 운전자 중 20%가 적어도 한번은 졸음운전을 한 경험이 있다고 한다. 트럭 운전기사들이 특히 취약하다. 7일 내지 10일 만에 최대 6,500 킬로미터를 달리는 장거리 운전자는 종종 하룻밤에 평균 2시간 내지 4시간만 자기도 한다.

---

imperative n. 명령, 불가피한 것
beckon v. 손짓으로 부르다; 유인하다
nuisance n. 불쾌; 난처한 것
forgo v. ~없이 때우다
deprivation n. 박탈; 결핍
chronically ad. 만성적으로
pernicious a. 유해한
snooze v. 꾸벅꾸벅 졸다
shortfall n. 부족
insidious a. (병이) 모르는 사이에 진행하는, 잠행성의
skimp v. 절약하다, 바싹 줄이다
irritability n. 성미가 급함; 민감
harrowing a. 마음 아픈, 비참한

01 ▶ 현대 미국인들이 전반적으로 수면 부족의 상태에 있다는 사실과 수면 부족이 초래하는 위험한 결과들에 대해 주로 이야기하고 있다.

02 ▶ 두 번째 문단 마지막 문장 참고. 업무 수행에 지장을 받는 것은 신체적인 측면으로 볼 수도 있다.

03 ▶ 주말에 낮잠을 자서 보충하려고 한다고 했다.

04 ▶ 수면 부족이 육체적 정신적으로 부정적 영향을 미치며, 그 결과 실수나 사고를 초래할 수도 있음을 이야기하는 내용이므로, (D)가 정답으로 적절하다.

 ▶ 정답 01 (D) 02 (B) 03 (C) 04 (D)

우주는 수십억 년 전에 태고의 대폭발로 갑자기 생겨났는가? 아니면 명확하게 시작도 끝도 없는 창조의 과정에 있는 것인가? "빅뱅 이론"이라는 첫 번째 이론을 주장하는 과학자들은 옛날 우주의 모든 물질은 학자들이 모종의 거대한 "원자"에 비유해 온 하나의 빽빽한 덩어리를 형성하고 있었다고 믿었다. 그러다가 이 덩어리가 폭발해서 엄청난 불덩어리를 만들었다. 아마도 물질은 순식간에 방대한 우주로 흩어졌을 것이다. 오늘날 이 물질로부터 형성된 별과 은하, 그리고 행성들이 아직도 그 폭발의 결과로 생긴 운동을 하고 있고 엄청난 속도로 서로로부터 균일하게 멀어지고 있다. 여러 가지 화학원소들이 태곳적에 폭발한 물질에서 만들어졌다.

이러한 우주 모형에서는 팽창이 과거의 한 순간 즉, 소위 빅뱅에서 시작되었다는 것이다. 다른 한편으로 지속적인 창조, 즉 "정상(定常) 우주론"을 믿는 사람들은 우주는 오랜 기간 동안 동일한 상태였으며 수소라는 물질이 무(無)에서 계속 생성되고 있다고 말한다. 이 물질이 별과 은하를 만들며 우주 전역에 다소 일률적으로 나타난다. 그러나 이 이론에 의하면 물질의 양은 매우 천천히 증가하고 있다. 즉, 수십억 년마다 텔레비전 한 대의 부피와 같은 우주의 부피 속에 하나의 원자가 증가할 뿐이다.

정상 우주론은 빅뱅이론과 정면으로 배치된다. 후자의 이론에서는 우주는 은하가 서로 멀어지면서 점점 더 비게 된다. 정상 우주론에서는 새로운 물질이 은하 사이의 공간에 계속 창조됨으로써 새로운 은하가 멀어져 간 은하의 자리를 대신 차지한다고 가정해야 한다. 그 새로운 물질이 수소이고, 그리고 그것이 별과 은하를 만드는 근원이라고 믿는다.

originate v. 생기다
primeval a. 초기의, 원시시대의
definite a. 확실한; 일정한
exponent n. (학설 등의) 설명자, 주창자; 옹호자
liken v. 비유하다, 견주다
scatter v. 뿔뿔이 흩어버리다
immense a. 막대한, 광대한
galaxy n. 은하
primitive a. 원시의, 원시시대의
steady a. 고정된, 확고한
hydrogen n. 수소
recede v. 물러나다; 멀어지다; 수축하다
postulate v. 가정하다, 전제로 하다
take the place of ~을 대신하다

01 ▶ 정상 우주론에서는 별과 은하의 근원을 수소로 여기고 있음이 언급돼 있다.

02 ▶ (D)는 정상 우주론에 해당한다.

03 ▶ 정상 우주론에서는 우주에 새로이 생겨나는 물질이 극도로 천천히 증가하는 것으로 본다. 따라서 사실상 측정이 불가능할 것이며, 이로 인해 정상 우주론을 반증하거나 이 이론이 잘못된 것을 증명하는 것은 매우 힘든 일이 될 것이다.

04 ▶ 빅뱅이론에서는 태곳적에 작은 덩어리가 폭발하여 뻗어나가면서 온 우주를 형성했다고 보고 있는데, 이는 풍선이 터지면서 그 풍선 속에 들어있는 것들이 흩어지는 것과 유사하다고 할 수 있다.

≫ 정답   01 (C)   02 (D)   03 (D)   04 (B)

283   미국 초창기 시절에는 우편 요금을 우편물 수취인이 지불했으며, 요금은 배달되는 거리에 따라 달랐다. 1825년, 미국 의회는 각 지역의 우체국장이 우편물 운송인에게 편지를 주어 가정에까지 배달하도록 했으나, 이 운송인들은 정부로부터 급료를 전혀 받지 않았으며, 그들의 보수는 전적으로 편지를 수령하는 사람들이 지급하는 돈에 의존하고 있었다.

　　1847년에 미국 우정국에서는 우표 제도를 채택했는데, 이로 인해 우편 서비스에 대한 지불 방법이 간소화되긴 했지만, 돈을 미리 지불하는 게 달갑지 않은 사람들의 불만을 사게 되었다. 뿐만 아니라, 우표를 사더라도 우체국까지만 배달할 수 있었고 개개인의 주소지로 전해주는 비용은 포함돼 있지 않았다. 가령, 인구가 15만 명인 필라델피아의 경우에도 사람들은 여전히 자신들에게 온 편지를 가지러 우체국에 가야 했다. 각자가 자신들의 편지를 찾으려는 데서 오는 혼잡스러움과 혼란스러움은 편지의 이용을 방해하기에 충분했다. 이런 성가신 제도가 존속하던 때에 사설 편지 배달업과 속달 운송회사가 생겨난 건 전혀 이상할 것이 없는 일이다. 이들 업체의 활동은 불법적인 면도 적지 않았지만, 사업은 점차 번성했고, 보스턴과 필라델피아 사이를 국영 우편을 이용할 때보다 반나절이나 빠르다고 광고를 하기에 이르렀다. 정부의 우편 서비스는 취급하는 우편물의 상당량을 사설 경쟁업체에 내줬고 사업 자체를 효율적으로 관리하지 못하는 데 이르렀다.

　　마침내, 1863년에 의회는 우편물을 개개인의 주소지로 배달해왔던 업자들이 정부로부터 급여를 받으며 우체국에서 개개인의 주소지까지 배달하는 것에 대해 추가 요금을 받지 않도록 하는 규정을 만들었다. 하지만 이러한 배달 서비스는 처음에는 도시에 한정돼 있었고, 그러했기에 무료로 집까지 배달을 해준다는 것은 도시화를 나타내는 일종의 표시가 되었다. 1887년에도, 무료 배달의 혜택을 입으려면 도시의 인구가 1만 명은 넘어야 했다. 1890년에는 미국에 살던 7,500만 명 가운데 2,000만 명이 못 되는 사람들이 집까지 우편물을 배달해 주는 서비스를 받을 수 있었다. 전체 인구가 가운데 거의 4분의 3에 이르는 나머지 사람들은 여전히 우체국에 직접 가지 않으면 우편물을 받을 수 없었다.

recipient n. 수납자, 수령인
compensation n. 배상, 보상; 보수, 급료
congestion n. 혼잡; 과잉, 밀집
cumbersome a. 성가신, 귀찮은
eligible a. 적격의

01 ▶ '돈을 미리 지불하는 게 달갑지 않은 사람들의 불만을 사게 되었다'고 했다.
02 ▶ 앞서 언급한 우편제도가 인구수가 많은 곳에서는 다소 부적절하다는 것을 말하기 위해 필라델피아를 예로 들었다.
03 ▶ 국영우편보다 빠르다는 점을 광고했다.
04 ▶ 나라에서 급료를 준다고 했다.

》 **정답** 01 (A) 02 (B) 03 (C) 04 (A)

비교할 수 없을 정도로 많은 라이브 연주 기회, 뛰어난 음악가들의 집중 지도와 정규 교육을 모두 무료로 제공하는 음악 학교를 상상해 보라. 메리 루이즈 커티스 복(Mary Louise Curtis Bok)은 1924년 필라델피아(Philadelphia)의 커티스(Curtis) 음악원을 처음으로 착상할 때 바로 이러한 것을 상상했었다. 80년이 지난 후에도 커티스 음악원이 지속적으로 지향하고 있는 그녀의 목표는 '비범한 재능이 있는 젊은 음악가들이 가장 뛰어난 전문 연주가들이 될 수 있도록 이들을 훈련시키는 것'이었다.

현재 세계적인 명성의 우수한 중심지인 커티스 음악원은 학생들이 "연주하면서 가장 많이 배운다"는 신념을 고수한다. 이러한 신념은 오케스트라 연주, 오페라, 독주곡과 실내악 리사이틀을 포함하여 연간 100회 이상의 연주회들로 나타나는데, 이들 중 상당수가 텔레비전과 라디오에 지역별로 방송된다.

입학생 수는 하나의 교향곡 오케스트라, 소규모의 오페라 학과, 피아노, 오르간, 하프시코드, 작곡, 지휘 부문의 선택 프로그램에 필요한 음악가들의 수에 맞추어져 있다. 지원자의 5 퍼센트만이 커티스 음악원의 엄격한 기준을 충족하는데, 이는 전 세계 단과 대학과 종합 대학의 입학률 중 가장 낮은 것으로 알려져 있다. 연간 재학생 수는 평균 165~170명이다. "숫자는 정해져있지 않습니다."라고 커티스의 현 음악원장인 로베르토 디아즈(Roberto Díaz)는 말한다. "우리가 원하거나 지원자들의 재능이 출중할 경우에는 더 뽑을 수 있습니다."

커티스 음악원의 혹독한 선발 방침은 수년에 걸쳐 그 가치를 입증해왔다. 유명한 졸업생들로는 레너드 번스타인(Leonard Bernstein), 지휘자 프리츠 라이너(Fritz Reiner), 작곡가 지안 카를로 메노티(Gian Carlo Menotti)와 사무엘 바버(Samuel Barber)가 있다. 최근의 졸업생들 중에는 후안 디에고 플로레즈(Juan Diego Flórez), 랑랑(Lang Lang)과 1990년 10세에 커티스 음악원에 입학해 12세에 음악사 학위 취득 과정에 입문한 힐러리 한(Hilary Hahn)이 있다. 그녀는 9년 간 커티스 음악원에서 수학하다가 1999년에 졸업했다.

전(前) 커티스 음악원장이자 이사인 개리 그래프만(Gary Graffman)은 7세에 커티스 음악원에 입학해 10년 간 수학했다. 대다수 입학생들의 나이가 17~22세이긴 하지만 신입생들은 나이 제한 없이 커티스에 입학할 수 있다. 수학 연한은 보통 3~10년이며, 전공 교수가 학생이 준비를 다 갖추었다고 판단할 때 졸업이 결정된다.

conservatory n. 음악 학교
unrivalled a. 경쟁자가 없는, 무적의
intensive a. 집중적인
for free 무료로
conceive v. 생각하다
aspire v. 열망하다
exceptionally ad. 예외적으로, 특별히
renowned a. 유명한
intake n. 수용 인원
harpsichord n. 하프시코드(피아노의 전신)
conduct v. 지휘하다
applicant n. 지원자, 신청자
criterion n. 기준
enrollment n. 등록자 수
current a. 현재의
notable a. 주목할 만한, 뛰어난
alumnus n. 졸업생(pl. alumni)
bachelor n. 미혼 남자; 학사
entrant n. 신입생

01 ▶ (D)의 경우, 본문 마지막 문단 두 번째 문장의 Entrants can join Curtis at any age를 통해 커티스 음악원은 입학생들의 나이를 제한하지 않는다는 사실을 알 수 있다.

02 ▶ 본문 첫 번째 단락 마지막 문장의 to train exceptionally gifted young musicians와 세 번째 단락 마지막 문장의 We can take more if we want or if applicants are talented enough을 통해 커티스 음악원의 학생 선발 기준은 음악적 재능, 즉, 예술적 장래성인 것을 알 수 있다.

03 ▶ 커티스 음악원이 세계적인 명성의 우수한 중심지가 된 요인으로 엄격한 선발 기준을 두어 소수의 우수한 학생들만을 입학시킨 후에 많은 라이브 연주 기회, 뛰어난 음악가들의 집중 지도를 통해 뛰어난 졸업생들을 배출해왔다는 것을 들 수 있다. 따라서 나머지 보기를 모두 포괄하는 (E)가 정답이다.

04 ▶ 밑줄 친 부분의 앞뒤 문맥을 살펴보면, 커티스 음악원의 입학률이 세계에서 가장 낮지만 커티스의 음악원장에 따르면 학교 측이 원하거나 지원자들의 재능이 출중할 경우에는 학생 수가 늘어날 수도 있다. 따라서 The numbers are not set in stone은 재학생 수가 고정되어 있는 것은 아니라는 의미로 쓰였다. 밑줄 친 부분을 직역하면 "숫자들이 돌에 새겨져 있는 것은 아니다", 즉, "숫자들이 고정되어 있는 것은 아니다"라는 뜻이다.

» 정답 01 (D) 02 (E) 03 (E) 04 (B)

[II] 증강 현실은 실제 세계의 정보와 디지털 정보를 하나로 합치는 정보 시스템을 만들어내는 것을 목표로 하는 컴퓨터 연구를 가리킨다. 증강 현실은 여전히 태동기에 있지만 많은 미래학자들과 연구자들이 2030년대나 2040년대 정도에 증강 현실이 부흥기를 맞이할 것으로 보고 있다.

[IV] 증강 현실 시스템의 주요 목표는 실시간에 주변 환경으로 합성되는 관련 정보를 보여주는 헤드업 디스플레이를 사용자에게 제공하는 고글이나 망막 프로젝터 같은 것이다. 예를 들어, 증강 현실 고글을 착용한 채 레스토랑을 볼 때 그 레스토랑의 웹사이트에서 음식 평가 리스트나 메뉴를 즉시 불러올 수 있다.

[I] 증강 현실은 현재 초보적인 형태로 존재한다. 예를 들어 스포츠 해설가들은 미식축구장 위에 '그림을 그리고' 시각 보조 기구를 자신들의 해설을 보조하는 데 제공하기 위해 라이트펜을 종종 이용할 수 있다. 또 다른 예로는 컴퓨터가 실시간으로, 그리고 이후 지속적으로 업데이트해서 미식축구장 위에 퍼스트다운 라인을 그리는 것을 들 수 있다. 하지만 이러한 것들은 TV 스크린을 응시할 때만 나타나기 때문에 진정한 증강 현실이 아니다. 그러나 이러한 것들은 개념을 어느 정도 증명해준다.

[III] 증강 현실은 정보 시스템에 접근하는 제1의 수단으로서의 고정식 컴퓨터를 사라지게 할 수 있는 잠재력을 가지고 있다. 랩톱과 모바일 폰 브라우저를 선호하게 되면서 데스크톱이 버림받고 있는 것과 마찬가지로 다음 단계는 이러한 것들을 증강 현실 시스템과 맞바꾸는 것이 될 수 있다. 정교한 증강 현실 시나리오 상에서는 인터넷에 접속하거나 컴퓨터 작업을 하기 위해 '현실 세계'를 떠날 필요가 없다. 이 두 세계는 철저하게 뒤섞일 것이다. 하지만 지금으로서는 컴퓨터 사용자들이 대부분 운동을 충분히 하지 못한 채 게으르게 앉아있으며 LED 스크린을 응시하고 있다. 정말로 불행한 사태다.

---

augment v. 증가시키다
refer to ~을 가리키다
merge v. 융합하다
seamlessly ad. 솔기가 없이, 고르게
futurist n. 미래학자
retinal a. 망막의
projector n. 투사기
call up 불러일으키다, 불러내다
currently ad. 현재
rudimentary a. 초보적인, 원시적인
commentator n. 해설자, 논평자
light pen 라이트펜(스크린 상에 입력할 수 있는 장치)
aid n. 보조 기구
accompany v. ~을 수반하다, 동반하다
first down 퍼스트다운 (4회 연속 공격권의 첫 번째)
stare v. 응시하다

01 ▶ 본문은 증강 현실을 소개하는 글로서, 주로 현재 어느 수준으로 사용되고 있으며 앞으로 어떤 목표 하에 어느 수준으로까지 발전될 수 있는지를 기술하고 있다. 따라서 (A)가 정답이다.

02 ▶ 이 글은 우선 증강 현실의 개념에 대해 간단히 설명하고, 증강 현실이 무엇을 추구하는지를 기술하며, 이에 비추어 현재 증강 현실은 어느 정도 구현되었는지를 살펴본 후, 증강 현실의 미래를 예측하는 순서로 글을 쓰는 것이 자연스럽다. 따라서 (B)가 정답이다.

03 ▶ [I]의 Augmented Reality does currently exist in rudimentary form으로 보아 빈칸 ①에는 infancy가 들어가고, sometime in the 2030s or 2040s는 미래의 시점이므로 빈칸 ②에는 renaissance가 들어가는 것이 문맥상 가장 자연스럽다.

04 ▶ (A) [III]의 Augmented Reality has the potential to eliminate the stationary computer as the primary means of accessing information systems를 통해 사용자가 증강 현실상에서는 자유롭게 움직일 수 있음을 추론할 수 있다. (B) 가상의 공간과 사물만을 대상으로 하는 기존의 가상 현실과 달리 증강 현실은 현실 세계의 기반 위에 가상의 사물을 합성하는 것이기 때문에 사용자들은 현실감을 느낄 수 있다. (C) [I]의 Augmented Reality does currently exist in rudimentary form을 통해 추론할 수 있다. (D) [III]의 첫 문장과 셋째 문장을 통해 앞으로 더욱 발전된 증강 현실은 '고정된 컴퓨터 세계'가 아니라 사용자가 자유로이 움직일 수 있는 '현실세계'가 가장 자연스러운 장소임을 추론할 수 있다.

≫ 정답 01 (A) 02 (B) 03 (C) 04 (D)

바비(Brbie)는 그 인형을 최초로 제작한 제조업체이자 바비로 인해 세계에서 가장 큰 장난감 제조업체가 된 마텔(Mattel)사가 장난감 가게 선반을 다시 채우기도 전에 선반에서 사라지는 그런 장난감으로 출발했다. 바비의 인기는 전 세계 사람들에게 패스트푸드, 가전제품, 코카콜라, 여성의 경우는 금발 머리, 큰 가슴, 불가능할 정도로 긴 다리, 최신 썬글라스와 스포츠 자동차를 가지고 싶게 만든 전후(戰後) 미국의 패권과 더불어 올라갔다. 바비는 임신을 하지도 않고 뚱뚱해지지도 않고 늙지도 않는다. 바비는 아름다움뿐만 아니라 라이프 스타일에 대한 무언의 번지르르한 표준으로서 상점 안에 자리를 잡았다.

전 세계적으로 바비는 엄마들과 딸들 모두가 사랑하는 아이콘이 되었다. 이 엄마들과 딸들은 키, 몸매, 피부색, 언어, 문화와는 상관없이 부유한 금발의 나라에서 온 부유하고 금발인 바비와 매우 일체감을 가졌다. 이들은 구매력을 가지고 자신들이 혐오스럽다고 생각하는 몸매, 피부색과 문화적인 정체성에 반대표를 던졌다. 바비가 머리가 텅 빈 헤픈 여성 이미지를 가졌느냐 의식이 깨인 여성 이미지를 가졌느냐는 중요하지 않았다. 바비는 문화를 선도하는 특수한 위치에 있었던 것이다.

미국이 세계 강대국으로 처음 나서기 시작한 이래 "양키는 집으로 가라"는 봉기들, 해방 전쟁과 온갖 종류의 반제국주의적인 반감이 대규모로 빈번하게 미국을 향해 쏟아지는 동안 이에 필적할만한 대중 운동이 바비 문화에 반대해서는 일어나지 않았다. 양키를 영원히 집으로 돌려보내기 위해 서적과 국기가 불에 타고, 인질이 잡히고 폭탄 테러와 공중 납치 사건들이 발생했다. 그러나 바비는 주도권을 유지했다. 바비는 불길에서 살아남았을 뿐만 아니라 바비처럼 자유롭고 아름다우며 세계적인 여성이 되기를 갈망하는 세계 곳곳의 여성들로 인해 구조되었다.

---

whisk off 휙 채가다
restock v. 재고를 다시 채우다
hegemony n. 패권, 주도권
appliance n. 기구, 장치
pregnant a. 임신한
brassy a. 뻔뻔스러운; 싸구려의; 겉만 번지르르한
aspire v. 열망하다, 포부를 갖다
identify with 일체감을 갖다, 공감하다
desperately ad. 필사적으로; 자포자기하여
perceive v. 지각하다, 인식하다
repulsive a. 싫은, 불쾌한
identity n. 정체성
liberate v. 해방하다, 자유롭게 하다
uprising n. 반란, 폭동
spew v. 토해내다
spit v. 뱉다, 토해내다; (폭언 따위를) 내뱉듯 말하다
assert v. 단언하다
corresponding a. 상응하는; 부합하는
hostage n. 인질

---

01 ▶ 본문 두 번째 단락을 보면, 바비가 "bimbo"이든 "liberated woman"이든 간에 바비는 문화를 선도하는 위치에 이르게 되었다고 기술되어 있다. 따라서 바비가 "liberated woman"을 상징한다고 단정 지을 수는 없다. 오히려 바비는 여성의 볼륨있는 몸매와 각선미를 강조하여 외모지상주의를 부추겼다.

02 ▶ 바비의 인기 요인은 바비가 미국의 이상적인 여성의 모습을 재현한 데 있다. (A)는 바비의 신체적인 특징이며, (B)와 (D)는 캐릭터로서의 바비의 특징이다. (C)의 "bimbo"는 "매력적이지만 머리가 텅 빈 여자"라는 뜻을 가지고 있으며, 바비의 부정적인 이미지와 연관되어 쓰이는 말이다.

03 ▶ 바비는 아이들이 가지고 노는 인형의 차원을 넘어서서 하나의 문화적인 아이콘이 되었다. "bizarre"는 이러한 바비의 '특수한' 위치를 표현한 단어이다. (A)의 "peculiar"가 "bizarre"와 가장 유사한 뜻을 가지고 있다.

04 ▶ (A)의 경우, 전 세계의 많은 여성들이 바비를 옹호해왔다고 해서 그 사실만으로 미국의 패권 자체를 인정한 것이라고는 볼 수 없다. 이들이 미국보다는 바비라는 하나의 문화적 아이콘을 옹호한 것이기 때문이다. (B)의 경우, 바비가 인종차별을 야기할 수 있는 근거로 첫 번째 단락의 "With their purchasing power they voted against their own perceived repulsive shapes, colors, and cultural identity" 구문을 들 수 있다. 미국 이외의 다른 나라 여성들은 바비를 구입함으로써 "blonde"인 백인 바비만을 이상적인 미의 표준으로 여기게 되고 상대적으로 자신들의 피부색이나 문화적인 정체성을 부정적으로 보게 된다. 따라서 (B)가 정답이다. (C)의 경우, 바비는 "ordinary woman"이 아닌 "ideal woman"을 구현했으며, (D)의 경우는 바비가 "each country"의 이상적인 미인을 구현한 것이 아니라 미국의 이상적인 미인을 구현한 것이기에 정답이 아니다.

» 정답 01 (D) 02 (C) 03 (A) 04 (B)

얼마 전에 나는 어느 외과 의사가 까다로운 뇌수술을 하는 것을 관찰할 기회가 있었다. 그의 손이 약간만 실수를 했더라면, 그것은 환자에게 마비나 죽음을 의미했었을 것이다. 그 의사에 관해 내가 감동을 받은 것은 그의 기술이 아니라 그의 놀라운 침착함이었다. 수술하기 불과 몇 분전만 하더라도 그가 신경이 예민해져 있다는 것을 나는 알고 있었다. <그러나 일단 그가 수술대 곁에 서자 그는 내가 깜짝 놀랄 정도로 기계와 같은 정확성을 가지고 일을 했던 것이다.> 물론 집중이 가져다주는 이러한 놀랄만한 업적은 각계각층의 뛰어난 사람들에게 흔히 있다. 어떤 순간에라도 지도자적인 훌륭한 인물들은 자신이 해야 할 일에 자신의 모든 것을 집중한다. 그러나 우리들 대부분의 사람들은 신경질이나, 선입견 혹은 상충하는 이해관계 때문에 우리의 주의가 흐트러지도록 내버려둔다. 우리는 종종 한 전문 분야에서 성공한 사람들이 그림도 약간 그릴 줄 알고 시도 쓰며 테니스를 치거나, 브리지게임도 잘하고, 만찬 후 즉흥연설도 할 줄 아는 즉, 한 마디로 말해 다재다능한 그런 사람들에 관해 읽는다. 우리는 그들의 그러한 다재다능한 그런 재주를 부러워한다. 그것은 우리가 그것을 특별한 재능이라고 생각하기 때문이다. 그것은 부분적으로는 그럴지 모르나, 대부분 이 사람들은 집중하는 데 후천적인 재능을 갖고 있다. 그들은 하루 종일 계속되는 매 일과에 산만한 주의를 쏟는 것이 아니라 부드러우면서도 집중적으로 자신들의 모든 재능을 쏟는다. 오늘날은 그 어느 때보다도 효과적인 업무수행뿐만 아니라 기쁨을 최대한으로 만끽하기 위해서도 집중이 필수 불가결하다. 지금은 전화, 친구, 소음, 공포, 그리고 우리 자신의 변덕스러움의 간섭을 받아 주의 집중이 잘 안 되는 시대이다. 점점 더 주의를 집중하기에 부적합한 환경에서 일을 하여야 하는데 ― 그러나 오늘날과 같이 전문화된 세계에선 한 사람의 성공은 더욱더 얼마나 잘 집중하는가에 달려있다. 그것은 일에만 중요한 것이 아니라, 우리의 내적 생활을 풍부하게 하는 데도 중요하다.

---

surgeon n. 외과의사
delicate a. 까다로운
slip n. 과실, 잘못
paralysis n. 마비
outstanding a. 걸출한, 현저한
distract v. (주의 등을) 집중이 안 되게 하다
preoccupation n. 몰두, 열중
impromptu a. 즉흥적인
aptitude n. 재능, 수완
acquired a. 후천적인
facility n. 재능, 솜씨

01 ▶ 바로 앞 문장에서 '전화, 친구, 소음이나 공포 등의 방해로 인해 집중하기 어렵다'고 한 것에 유의하면, (C)가 정답으로 적절함을 알 수 있다.

02 ▶ But 다음에 수술대에서 깜짝 놀랄만한 기계 같은 정확성을 가지고 일을 했다는 내용으로 미루어 제시된 문장은 수술하기 이전의 상황을 묘사하는 내용 다음에 와야 한다. 따라서 위의 문장은 [Ⅲ]의 자리에 있어야 한다.

03 ▶ '집중의 중요성'에 관한 글이다.

» 정답   01 (C)   02 (C)   03 (B)

글을 쓰는 데 있어서 시간과 공간을 절약하고자 이용하는 줄여 쓴 형태의 단어나 어구를 축약어라고 한다. 일부 축약어는 말을 할 때에도 쓰인다.

축약어는 종종 단어의 첫 글자 혹은 어구의 중요 단어로 이루어지며, 대문자로 쓴다. 때때로 축약어 끝에는 마침표(생략점)를 찍는다. 예를 들어, *P.O.*는 우체국(post office)을 나타내며 *C.O.D.*는 대금상환인도(cash on delivery)를 나타낸다.

때로는 축약어를 소문자로도 쓰며, 이 때 마침표를 찍을 경우도 있고 그렇지 않을 경우도 있다. born을 나타내는 *b.*와 died를 나타내는 *d.*가 그 예라 할 수 있다. 서로 다른 말에 같은 축약어를 쓸 수도 있다. 예를 들어, *m.*은 married, masculine, meter를 나타낼 수 있다. 같은 축약어가 2개 이상의 단어에 쓰일 수 있는 경우에는, 글을 읽는 사람이 문맥을 이용하여 그 의미를 판단할 수 있다.

때때로 한 단어에서 두 글자 이상을 이용해 축약어를 만드는 경우도 있다. manuscript의 축약어인 *ms.*와 foot의 축약어인 *ft.*가 그 예이다. 축약어 가운데는 하나의 새로운 단어로 굳어지는 경우도 있는데, *NATO*와 *OPEC*이 이에 해당한다. 이런 축약어를 두문자어(頭文字語)라고 한다. 복수형태를 나타낼 때, 축약어 속의 글자를 두 번 쓰기도 하는데, lines를 나타내는 *ll.*과 pages를 나타내는 *pp.*가 그러한 경우이다. 자주 쓰이는 특정 축약어에는, *A.D.*, *B.C.*, *A.M.*, *P.M.*에서처럼 작은 글씨로 쓴 대문자가 종종 쓰인다.

축약어는 종종 요일, 달, 주(州)의 이름과 같은 일반적인 단어에도 종종 쓰인다. 축약어는 긴 단어나 구절에도 쓰이는데, Lieutenant의 줄임말인 *Lieut*, Rural Free Delivery의 줄임말인 *R.F.D.*를 예로 들 수 있다. 신학박사(Doctor of Divinity)를 줄여 쓴 *D.D.*, 박사(doctor)를 줄여 쓴 *Dr.*에서처럼 학위와 직함도 종종 축약해서 쓴다. 비즈니스에서는 Company를 줄여서 *Co.*, Incorporated를 줄여서 *Inc.*, Limited를 줄여 *Ltd.*로 쓴다.

흔히 쓰이는 여러 라틴어구의 축약어는 각 단어의 첫 글자로 이루어져 있다. nota bene("note well")은 줄여서 *n.b.*로, id est("that is")는 줄여서 *i.e.*로 쓴다. et cetera("and others")의 축약어인 *etc.*는 예외에 해당한다.

고대의 비석들과 사본들을 살펴보면, 알파벳을 이용한 글쓰기가 일반화된 직후부터 사람들이 글자를 줄여서 쓰기 시작했음을 알 수 있다. 미국에서는 축약어가 오랫동안 받아들여져 왔다. *OK*와 *C.O.D.*는 19세기부터 쓰이기 시작했다. 오늘날에는 심지어 연방정부 기관조차도 흔히 머릿글자를 가지고 부른다. 예를 들어, Federal Housing Administration을 줄여 쓴 *FHA*, National Aeronautics and Space Administration을 줄여 쓴 *NASA*는 이미 귀에 익은 단어가 되었다.

abbreviation n. 생략, 생략형; 약어(略語)
period n. 마침표, 생략점
masculine a. 남성의, 남자다운
consist of ~로 구성되어 있다(= be made up of)
context n. 전후 관계, 문맥
manuscript n. 원고
acronym n. 두문자어
household a. 가사의; 귀에 익은

01 ▶ 세 번째 문단 끝에서, 다른 단어에 대해 똑같은 약어가 사용되는 경우에는 그 의미를 '문맥'에 의해 판단할 수 있다'고 했다.

02 ▶ 첫 번째 문단에서 '시간과 공간을 절약하기 위해서'라고 했다.

03 ▶ 긴 단어들을 줄여서 부르는 것이 점점 더 잦아진 것은 그렇게 하는 것이 더 편리하기 때문일 것이다.

04 ▶ 약어를 쓰게 된 근본적인 이유를 상기하면, 답은 (A)이다.

05 ▶ 첫 빈칸의 경우, '각 단어의 머릿글자를 모아서 만든 말'에 해당하는 표현이 필요하므로 acronym이 적절하며, 흔히 쓰이는 라틴어구의 축약어는 각 단어의 첫 글자로 이루어져 있는 반면, et cetera의 축약어인 etc.는 이 규칙에 벗어나 있으므로 예외(exception)에 해당할 것이다.

06 ▶ '~을 부르다, 칭하다'는 표현은 refer to이다. 따라서 ④는 '~ commonly referred to by ~'로 써야 한다.

》 정답 01 (B) 02 (D) 03 (B) 04 (A) 05 (D) 06 (D)

문학사학자들에 의한 분류는 다소 위험한 시도가 될 수 있다. 예를 들어, 흑인 시인들을 집단으로서 개별적으로 논의할 때는 일반적으로 그들의 작품이 시(詩) 발전에 기여한 정도가 잊혀져서는 안 되며, 만약 그렇지 않으면 문학사의 왜곡이 일어날지 모른다. 이런 주의는 세기의 전환기(1900-1909)의 흑인 시인들과 1920년대의 흑인 시인들 사이의 상이점을 평가할 때에 특히 필요해진다. 이 상이점들은 이후 세대의 좀 더 대담하고 더 솔직한 표현과 표현의 기술적인 창의성을 포함한다. 하지만 비교할 수 있는 상이점들이 비슷한 세대의 백인 시인들에게도 존재했다는 사실을 기억해야 한다.

그러나 1910년대와 1920년대의 시인들을 함께 생각해 볼 때는 문학사학자들이 만들었을지도 모르는 '보수적인' 것과 '실험적'이라는 구분은 비록 그것들이 동시대의 백인 시인들에 대한 유용한 분류일지라도 흑인 시인들을 논의하는 데 있어서는 별 중요성이 없을 것이다. 확실히 카운티 컬린(Countee Cullen)과 클라우드 멕케이(Claude Mckay)와 같은 '보수적인' 흑인 시인들과 진 투머(Jean Toomer)와 랭스턴 휴즈(Langston Hughes)와 같은 '실험적인' 흑인 시인들 사이에는 상이점을 확실히 지적할 수 있다. 그러나 흑인 시인들은 구문체와 신문체에 대해서 논쟁하고 있지 않았다. 오히려 한쪽을 성취한 흑인 시인들에게 있어서 중요한 것은 인종적 자부심이었기 때문에 다른 사람의 문체가 무엇이든지 간에 다른 하나를 기꺼이 환영했다.

그러나 1920년대의 흑인 시인들은 그들이 특별히 인종문제를 다루어야 하는지에 대해 토론을 했다. 그들은 흑인 독자를 위해 단지 흑인 경험만을 써야 하는지 또는 그러한 요구들이 제한되어야 하는지에 의문을 제기했다. 제임스 웰던 존슨(James Weldon Johnson)이 올바로 말했듯이 '필연적으로 흑인 시인들이 가장 잘 아는 사실'인 인종적 감정, 인종에 대해 이런 시인들이 말할 때 사실상 그들이 가장 훌륭한 시를 썼다고 할 수 있을지도 모른다.

그와는 대조적으로, 세기의 전환기에는 대부분의 흑인 시인들이 대체로 그 시대의 전통적인 방법으로 글을 썼고, 모호하긴 해도 그들 사이의 고상한 감정을 표현했다. 로스코 제이미슨(Roscoe Jamison)과 G.M. 맥 셀런(McCellen)은 예외로 언급되지만 이런 시인들은 특별한 재능을 부여받지 못했다. 스털링 브라운(Sterling Brown)이 지적했듯이 그들은 방언을 쓰지 않는 것을 택했고 이것이 '흑인생활에 대한 고정관념을 거부한다'는 것을 의미했다. 또한 그들은 인종 문제에 관해서만 쓰는 것을 거부했다. 이러한 거부는 긍정적, 부정적 결과를 동시에 가져왔다. 브라운(Brown)이 말한 바와 같이 "흑인 시인들은 인종 문제에 국한되지 않아야 한다고 가치 있게 주장하는 이런 시인들은 자신들 마음 속을 들여다보고 글을 쓰는 것을 거절한 실수를 저질렀다." 이런 것들은 중요한 간과이지만 이런 내면 관찰의 거절은 당시 미국의 대부분의 백인 시인들에게도 또한 전형적이었다는 것을 강조해야 한다. 또한 그들은 종종 그들 자신의 경험에서 벗어났고 결과적으로 자연의 평화 같은 모호한 주제에 관해서 매우 기억에 남을만한 시를 창작하지 못했다.

distortion n. 왜곡
assessment n. 평가
distinction n. 구별, 차별; 차이, 대조
conservative a. 보수적인
restrictive a. 제한하는, 구속하는
perforce ad. 필연적으로, 강제로
dialect n. 방언
forthright a. 솔직한
stereotype n. 고정관념

01 ▶ '세기의 전환기에는 대부분의 흑인 시인들이 대체로 그 시대의 전통적인 방법으로 글을 썼다'라고 돼 있다.

02 ▶ 두 번째 문단 끝에서 '흑인 시인들에게 있어서 중요한 것은 인종적 자부심이었다'고 했다.

03 ▶ '흑인 독자를 위해 단지 흑인 경험만을 써야 하는 지 또는 그러한 요구들이 제한되어야 하는 지에 의문을 제기했다.'고 했다.

04 ▶ 인종 문제에 관해서만 쓰는 것을 거부한 흑인 작가들의 결과를 스털링 브라운의 말을 인용하면서 이야기하고 있다.

05 ▶ 자신의 경험에서 벗어난 글을 쓴 사람들이 성공적이지 못했다는 언급으로부터 정답을 선택할 수 있다.

» 정답 01 (A) 02 (B) 03 (B) 04 (D) 05 (D)

광신적 행위는 미국정치에서 새롭게 부상하고 있는 것이 아니다. 만일 누군가가 빌 클린턴이 오클라호마에 개인적으로 폭탄을 던지게 했다고 비난을 했다면, 그것은 프랭클린 루스벨트, 해리 트루먼, 린든 존슨, 리처드 닉슨 혹은 조지 워싱턴에 대해 말해진 것보다 훨씬 더 나쁜 것은 아닐 것이다. 시민의 예절에 대한 우리의 기준은 평온한 1950년대인데, 이것은 "오늘날의 미국인들이 느끼는 것보다, 당시 미국에 사는 사람들이 자신들이 보다 더 공통점을 갖고 있다"라고 느꼈던 시기로서 미국인들, 특히 백인들에 의해 가장 일반적으로 언급되는 십년이다. 그러나 뒤이은 35년간의 혼란은 미국인들에게 사실상 대변동과 소란이 미국의 정상적인 상태라는 생각을 주었어야 했다. 1950년대는 우리가 상기하고 싶은 갈등이 없었던 것은 아니다. 올해의 반역자들은 — 정부관리가 자신들에게 소들이 머물 수 있는 장소를 말하는 것을 허용하지 않을 서부의 목장주들 — 만일 더글라스 맥아더 장군이 북한에 대해 사용할 핵무기를 받지 못하면, 모병을 보류할 것이라고 45년 전에 결정했던 몬타나 징병위원회에 자신들과 견줄 수 있는 사람들이 있었다. 50년대 말에 미국 남부에서는 초등학교에 가는 도중에 자신들을 보호하기 위해 연방군대를 필요로 했던 흑인 아동들에게 미국은 특히 평화로운 곳은 아닌 것처럼 보였다. 아마, 놀랄 일은 아니지만, 뉴스위크 여론조사에서 대다수의 흑인들은 1960년대를 미국의 평화로운 시기로 택했다. 그러나 중남미계 미국인뿐 아니라, 흑백인 모두 큰 폭의 차이로 미국의 국민성이 20년 전부터 나빠졌다는 것에는 동의했다.

수세기에 걸쳐 다양한 기관들은 규모와 다양성이라는 원심력에 맞서 미국을 결속시켰다. 뒤이은 세대에서는 이것들이 개신교, 영어, 헌법, 공유된 전쟁경험, 3대 방송사, 디즈니월드였는데, 이 중에서 마지막 것(디즈니월드)만이 미국의 정체성을 나타내는 보편적이고, 도전받지 않은 시금석으로 남아있다. 물론, 헌법은 여전히 유효하다. 그러나 연임제한을 철폐한 5월 판결에서, 미(美) 연방대법원의 힘 있는 소수는 헌법을 전체 국민보다는 독립국가의 협정이라고 급진적으로 재해석하는 데 열중하는 것 같았다. — 이것은, 적어도 북부가 남북전쟁에서 승리한 이후에는 지지를 받지 못했던, 본질적으로 분리주의자들의 견해였다.

---

fanaticism n. 광신, 열광, 광신적 행위
comity n. 예의, 예절
placid a. 조용한, 평온한
upheaval n. 대변동, 격변
turmoil n. 소란, 혼란
bureaucrat n. 관료적인 사람, 관료
counterpart n. 상대물, 대응물
withhold v. 보류하다
induction n. 유도, 귀납법; 모병, 입대식
draft board 징병위원회
plurality n. 대다수, 과반수
halcyon a. 평화로운, 풍요한
centrifugal a. 원심성의, 중심에서 떠나는
tug n. 세게 잡아당기기; 노력, 분투
sovereign states 독립국가
inherently ad. 본질적으로, 타고나서

01 ▶ take it upon itself to do '~하기를 스스로 정하다'는 뜻이다.

02 ▶ 미국의 정체성을 나타내는 보편적이고, 도전받지 않은 시금석으로 남아있는 것은 디즈니 월드이다.

03 ▶ 첫 단락의 "Nor was the 1950's as empty of conflict as we like to recall."을 참고할 것.

04 ▶ 미 연방대법원의 힘 있는 소수는 헌법을 독립국가의 협정이라고 재해석하는 데 열중하였다는 말에 비추어 (A)가 정답이다. 5월 판결로 인해 연임제한이 없어졌으므로 연임제한이 가능해졌다는 (B)는 틀린 말이며, 연방대법원의 힘 있는 소수가 헌법을 재해석했다고 했으므로 5월 판결이 헌법의 원래 목적을 반영한 것으로 받아들여졌다는 (C)는 틀린 진술이 되며, (D)의 약자를 위한 판결이라는 말은 원문에서 찾을 수 없다.

》 정답 01 (C) 02 (E) 03 (B) 04 (A)

매일 미국의 우편함은 수백만 개의 다이렉트 마케팅 업계에서 보낸 유인물들로 가득 차 있다. 대부분의 경우 그것(유인물)들은 상품과 서비스에 관한 노골적인 광고들이다. 미국의 이런 광고의 범람에 대한 반응은 이상하게도 엇갈려왔다. 부정적인 면에서 보면 잘못 실행된 다이렉트 마케팅은 '정크 메일'이라고도 알려져 있는 받길 원하지 않고 성가시고 낭비적인 유인물들을 생산한다.

더욱 심각한 것은 공격적인 다이렉트 마케팅 방법이 사생활 정보에 대한 심각한 위협을 의미한다는 것이다. 과학 기술이 빠르게 발전하면서 다이렉트 마케터들은 사실상 거의 모든 사람들의 개인적인 특성에 접근할 수 있게 되었다. 게다가, 정교한 컴퓨터 매칭 프로그램은 그 자체로는 개인의 사생활을 위협하지는 않는 정보로부터 사생활을 침해하는 개인에 대한 분석을 할 수 있다. 다이렉트 메일을 보내는 사람들은 본래는 프라이버시가 보장된다는 기대 하에 공개되는 이 개인 정보를 퍼트린다. 이 정보는 본인의 동의 없이 유출되고 당사자는 일반적으로 정보가 유출된 것에 대해 아무런 통보를 받지 못한다.

1991년의 Harris-Equifax Consumer Privacy Survey는 다이렉트 메일링 관행에 대한 대중들의 태도와 그것이 정보의 프라이버시에 미치는 영향에 대해 다루었다. 다이렉트 메일을 일반적으로 어떻게 생각하는지 물어보았을 때 46%는 '성가신 것'이라고 대답했고, 9%는 '사생활 침해'로 본다고 답했으며, 6%만이 '유용한 것'이라고 답했다. 그러나 미국인들이 다이렉트 마케팅 업계에 대해 이렇게 부정적인 의견을 가지고 있음에도 불구하고 이런 의견을 이상한 방식으로 보여주고 있다.

다이렉트 마케팅은 영향력이 커지고 있는 효과적인 기법이다. 다이렉트 메일 광고 지출이 1980년 76억 달러에서 1990년 234억 달러로 증가했다. 시장의 법칙에 따르면 회사들은 성공할 가능성이 없었다면 이러한 노력을 기울이지 않았을 것이다.

게다가, 위에 언급된 Equifax 조사에서 보면 다이렉트 메일이 '사생활 침해'라고 여기는 시민들 중 거의 절반이 작년에 다이렉트 메일 광고를 받아 보고 자신들 스스로 물건을 구매했다. 그러면 왜 그들 중 더 많은 사람들이 다이렉트 마케팅에 대해서 더 긍정적인 의견을 표출하지 않았을까?

그럼에도 다이렉트 마케팅은 다른 쇼핑 수단에 비해 실제적인 이득을 가져다준다. 심지어 다이렉트 메일 업계가 일반적으로 부정적인 사회적 영향을 미쳤다고 믿는 사람들도 메일 명부에 남아있고 싶어 할 것이다. 우리는 메일로 쇼핑하는 것을 좋아하고 좋은 점을 나쁜 점과 함께 던져버리고 싶지는 않다.

---

solicitation n. 간청, 권유, 유도
straightforward a. 똑바른; 솔직한
deluge n. 범람, 호우; (편지·방문객 등의) 쇄도
sophisticated a. 정교한; 고도로 세련된
disseminate v. 퍼뜨리다
disclose v. 드러내다; 폭로하다
nuisance n. 성가심; 난처한 것
invasion n. 침입; 침해

01 ▶ 이 글은 대중들의 반대에도 불구하고 다이렉트 마케팅이 성공을 거두고 있는 것은 이를 통해 실제적인 이득을 취할 수 있어 계속 이용하려고 하는 소비자들의 성향 때문이라는 내용이므로 (D)가 정답이다.

02 ▶ 6퍼센트의 사람들이 유용하다고 생각한다고 했는데, 실제로 상품을 구매했는지는 알 수 없으므로 (B)가 정답이다.

03 ▶ 시장의 법칙에 따르면 회사는 성공할 가능성이 없었다면 광고비 지출을 늘리지 않았을 것이므로, 광고비 지출을 늘린 것은 회사의 성공에 대한 '기대감'을 나타낸다고 볼 수 있다.

04 ▶ 다이렉트 메일에 대해 부정적인 시각을 가지고 있으면서도 실제로는 이를 통해 물건을 구매하므로, 의견과 실제 행동이 '모순된다'고 볼 수 있다.

05 ▶ 다이렉트 마케팅이 소비자들에게 실제적인 이득을 주기 때문에 사회적으로 부정적인 면이 있기는 하지만 계속 광고 메일을 받아보고 좋은 상품을 구매하고 싶어 하므로 (D)가 가장 적절하다.

06 ▶ (A)는 다이렉트 마케팅이 사회에 부정적인 영향을 미치고 있고, (B)는 메일을 받아 보기 원하는 모든 사람이 부정적으로 생각하는 것은 아니며, (D)에 대한 언급은 없으므로 정답이 될 수 없다.

≫ 정답 01 (D) 02 (B) 03 (A) 04 (D) 05 (D) 06 (C)

효율성은 일정한 투입으로부터 가장 많이 얻는 것을 의미한다. 생산에 들어가는 투입물들에는 인간의 노력, 기계류와 건물과 같은 물리적 자본에 의한 서비스, 토지나 광물 자원 같은 자연의 산물들이 있다. 생산물들은 수천여 가지의 다양한 상품과 서비스들이다. 사회가 동일한 투입물로 어떤 상품을 더 많이 생산하는 방법을 발견한다면, 그 사회는 효율성을 증가시키는 기록을 올린 셈이다. 시장이 소득을 결정하도록 하는 경제 제도는 시민들 간의 생활수준과 물질적 복지의 상당한 격차를 낳았다. 한편, 소득 차이는 보상과 불이익이라는 동기로서 작동하여 자원 활용의 효율성을 증진시키고 국가의 생산을 크게 증진시키는 역할을 한다.

평등은 지속가능한 생활수준의 측면에서 가족들 간의 격차가 적어지는 것을 의미하며, 이는 다시 다양한 규모의 가족들의 필요에 비례하여 소득과 부의 분배 격차가 줄어드는 것을 의미한다. 그러나 평등한 생활수준이 곧 사람들이 자신의 소득을 소비하고 자신들의 부를 똑같이 할당하는 것까지 같아야 한다는 의미는 아니다. 평등은 모든 시민들의 생활수준을 보장할 것이다. 존 스튜어트 밀(John Stuart Mill)은 경제적 빈곤과 박탈이 자본주의 경제에 내재된 것이라고 생각했다면 자신은 공산주의자가 되었을 것이라고 주장했다. 국가의 주된 역할 중의 하나는 모든 시민들의 평등을 선포하는 보편적으로 분배된 권리와 특권들을 제공하는 것이다. 권리의 영역에 의지하는 정치 제도들은 평등을 촉진하고 인간 존엄을 향상하기 위해 모든 시민들의 지속가능한 생활수준을 보장해왔다.

사회는 그 길을 따라 나아가는 와중에 효율성을 희생하며 더 많은 평등을 제공하거나, 평등을 희생하며 더 많은 효율성을 제공해야 하는 선택에 직면하게 된다. 경제학자의 표현을 빌리자면 평등과 효율성 사이에 교환 관계가 발생한다. 평등한 권리와 불평등한 소득이 뒤섞여 생기는 결과는 민주주의라는 정치 원리와 자본주의라는 경제 원리 간에 긴장을 낳는다. 시장의 보상에서 큰 승리를 거둔 어떤 이들은 돈을 이용하여 평등하게 분배되어야 할 권리들을 가외로 더 얻어가려고 한다. 그렇게 하여 그들은 기회를 불평등하게 만드는 유리함을 얻게 된다. 시장에서 불이익을 당하고 있는 이들에게 이것은 인간 존엄과 상호존중의 민주적 가치와 상충하는 박탈을 초래한다. 권리의 영역에서 평등과 상호존중을 강조하는 사회는 경제의 영역에서 벌어지는 이러한 원리들이 갖는 함의에 직면할 수밖에 없다.

그러나 불평등의 범위와 규모를 감소시키기 위한 경제 정책들이 생산하려는 동기를 약화시키거나 경제적 효율성을 손상시킬 수 있다. 시장에서 획득한 보상은 노력과 생산적 기여에 대한 동기를 제공한다. 시장의 보상이 없다면 사회는 대안적 보상을 찾아 동요할 수밖에 없다. 나라 전체가 성취에 대한 관심, 노력의 동기에 대한 관심을 중단하게 될 것이라고 생각할 수 있다. 그럴 경우, 힘 있는 자들은 물론 낮은 계층 사람들의 생활수준도 낮아지게 된다. 민주적 자본주의 사회는 권리의 영역과 경제의 영역 간에 경계선을 정하는 더 나은 방법을 모색해야 할 것이다. 그럴 때 민주적 자본주의는 발전할 수 있다. 분명한 것은, 평등과 경제적 효율성 간의 갈등은 불가피하기 때문에 그 문제를 결코 풀 수는 없을 것이라는 점이다.

endowment n. 기부; (천부적) 자질, 재능
disparity n. 차이, 격차
differential n. 차이, 격차
incentive n. 동기, 격려, 유인, 자극
relative to ~에 관하여; ~에 비례하여
inherent a. 내재하는, 고유한, 본래부터의
communist n. 공산주의자
privilege n. 특권
proclaim v. 선언[선포]하다, 분명히 보여주다
tradeoff n. (타협을 위한) 거래, 교환, 맞바꾸기
helping n. (한 사람 몫으로 덜어 주는 음식의) 양[그릇]
head start n. (남보다 일찍 시작해서 갖게 되는) 유리함
incur v. 초래하다
penalty n. 처벌, 형벌; 불이익
magnitude n. 규모
thrash v. 몸부림치다, 허우적거리다, 요동치다(about)
mighty a. 강력한, 힘센

01 ▶ 세 번째 단락 첫째 문장에 글 전체의 요지가 함축되어 있다. 효율성과 평등은 그 중 어느 하나를 추구하면 다른 하나를 희생해야 하는 어려운 교환관계에 놓여 있다고 하였다.

02 ▶ 빈칸 Ⓐ 다음 문장에 있는 'the differentials in income'에 주목한다면 그것이 '격차' 또는 '차이'라는 의미의 표현이어야 함을 알 수 있다.

03 ▶ 첫 번째 단락 끝부분에서 "소득 차이는 보상과 불이익이라는 동기로서 작동하여 자원 활용의 효율성을 증진시키고 국가의 생산을 크게 증진시킨다."라고 하였으므로 (A)는 옳지 않은 진술이다.

04 ▶ 두 번째 단락 끝부분에서 '국가의 주된 역할 중의 하나는 모든 시민들의 평등을 선포하는 보편적으로 분배된 권리와 특권들을 제공하는 것'이며, '권리의 영역에 의지하는 정치 제도들은 평등을 촉진한다.'고 하였으므로 (C)는 올바른 진술이다. 한편, 맨 마지막 문장에서 '분명한 것은, 평등과 경제적 효율성 간의 갈등은 불가피하기 때문에 그 문제를 결코 풀 수는 없을 것이다.'고 하였으므로, (E)는 잘못된 진술이다.

》 정답 01 (B) 02 (D) 03 (A) 04 (C)

A 존 롤스(John Rawls)는 다음과 같이 추론한다. 우리가 집단의 삶을 지배할 원칙을 정하기 위해, 즉 사회계약을 작성하기 위해 현재 우리의 모습 그대로 한곳에 모였다고 가정하자. 어떤 원칙들을 고를까? 우리는 아마 그것이 쉽지 않은 일이라고 느낄 것이다. 사람들은 개개인의 다양한 흥미, 도덕적·종교적 신념, 그리고 사회적 지위를 반영하는 원칙들을 고려하여 저마다 다른 원칙들을 선호할 것이다. 몇몇은 부유하고, 몇몇은 가난하다. 몇몇은 권력이 있고 인맥이 화려하지만, 몇몇은 그렇지 못하다. 몇몇은 인종, 민족, 종교적인 면에서 소수 집단에 속하고, 몇몇은 그렇지 않다. 우리는 어쩌면 타협점을 찾을지도 모른다. 하지만 그 타협점조차도 일부 사람들이 다른 이들에 대해 갖는 더 우월한 교섭력을 반영할 수도 있다. 이런 방식으로 만들어진 사회계약을 공정한 합의라고 말할 근거는 없다.

B 이제 한 가지 사고실험을 생각해보자. 원칙을 정하려고 모인 사람들이 자기가 사회에서 어떤 위치에 속할지 모른다고 가정해보자. 우리가 정확히 어떤 사람인지 일시적으로 모르는 상태인 "무지의 장막" 뒤에서 선택한다고 상상하자. 우리의 계층과 성별, 인종과 민족, 정치적 견해나 종교적 신념도 모른다. 내가 건강한지 허약한지, 고등교육을 받았는지, 고등학교를 중퇴했는지, 든든한 집안에서 태어났는지 결손 가정에서 태어났는지 같은 우리의 강점과 약점을 전혀 모른다. 만약 아무도 이러한 것들을 모른다면, 그야말로 원초적으로 평등한 위치에서 선택하게 된다. 이러한 협상에서 어느 누구도 우월한 위치에 놓이지 않는다면, 우리가 합의한 원칙은 공정하다.

C 롤스가 생각하는 사회의 계약은 이처럼 원초적으로 평등한 위치에서 이루어지는 가언합의(가설적 합의)다. 그는 만약 그런 위치에 놓인다면, 합리적이고 자기 이익을 챙기는 우리 같은 사람들이 어떤 원칙을 선택할지 자문해 보라고 한다. 그는 모든 사람이 현실에서 자기 이익에 따라 움직인다고 생각하지 않는다. 다만 사고실험을 위해, 도덕적, 종교적 신념을 고려하지 않는다고 가정할 뿐이다. 그렇다면 우리는 어떤 원칙을 택하겠는가?

D 먼저, 그는 우리가 공리주의를 택하지 않을 거라고 논증한다. 무지의 장막 뒤에서, 우리는 '어쩌면 나는 억압받는 소수에 속할지도 몰라'라고 생각할 수도 있다. 그리고 어느 누구도 군중의 쾌락을 위해 사자 우리에 던져지는 그리스도인이 되고 싶어 하지 않을 것이다. 사람들이 시장 경제에서 벌어들인 돈을 모두 소유할 권리를 인정하는 자유주의의 원칙, 즉 완전한 자유방임을 선택하지도 않을 것이다. 사람들은 이렇게 추론한다. "나는 빌 게이츠(Bill Gates)일 수도 있지만, 어쩌면 노숙자일지도 몰라. 그러니 무일푼에 도움조차 받지 못하는 상태로 살아가게 놔둘지도 모르는 제도는 피하는 게 좋겠어."

E 롤스는 이 가언계약에서 정의의 원칙 두 가지가 나온다고 생각한다. 첫째 원칙은 언론과 종교의 자유와 같은 기본적인 자유를 모든 시민에게 평등하게 제공한다. 이 원칙은 사회적 효용에 대한 고려나 공공복지보다 우선권을 갖는다. 나머지 하나는 사회적, 경제적 평등에 관한 원칙이다. 이 원칙은 동등하게 배분된 소득과 부를 요구하지는 않지만, 오직 사회 구성원 중 가장 어려운 사람들에게 이익이 돌아가는데 이바지하는 사회적, 경제적 불평등만 허용한다.

bargain v. 협상[흥정]하다
bargaining power 교섭력
arrangement n. 합의; 처리
thought experiment 사고실험
frail a. 노쇠한, 허약한
dropout n. 중퇴자
set ~ aside ~을 고려하지 않다
utilitarianism n. 공리주의
for all I know 아마도; 의외로 ~일지도 모른다
laissez-faire n. 자유방임, 무간섭주의
libertarian n. 자유주의, 자유의지론
destitute a. 빈곤한, 가난한
take priority over ~에 대해 우선권을 갖다
general welfare 공공복지
well off 부유한

01 ▶ 이 글은 사회계약의 원칙들을 어떻게 결정한 것인지에 관한 롤스의 견해를 소개하고 있다.

02 ▶ B 단락에서 '자기 자신이 누구인지 모른다'는 가정 하에서 사회계약의 원리들을 선택하자는 사고실험을 하고 있으므로 이러한 상황을 '무지의 베일 뒤에서 선택하는 것'이라고 부를 수 있을 것이다.

03 ▶ D 단락에 따르면 공리주의를 선택하지 않는 이유는 '우리가 억압받는 소수가 될 가능성이 있기 때문이고', 자유방임주의를 선택하지 않는 이유는 '경제적 불평등이 시정되지 않는 체제 속에서 살 가능성이 있기 때문이다'라고 하였다.

04 ▶ E 단락에서 '첫째 원칙은 언론과 종교의 자유와 같은 기본적인 자유를 모든 시민에게 평등하게 제공한다.'고 하였으므로 (D)가 롤스의 주장에 가장 부합한다.

» 정답 01 (B) 02 (D) 03 (E) 04 (D)

A 냄새는 문화권마다 다른 다양한 의미, 상징적 연관성, 가치를 부여받는 사회문화적 현상이다. 좋든 싫든 간에, 우리의 모든 청소 시스템에도 불구하고 우리는 냄새를 풍기는 존재이며, 이러한 냄새는 미각적 소비, 개인위생, 가정, 도시, 계급, 성별, 그리고 사회 생활의 인종 차원에 이르기까지 사실상 우리의 일상 사회 경험의 모든 영역에서 중요한 역할을 한다. 아마도 냄새만이 우리가 꺼버릴 수 없는 유일한 감각일 것이다. 우리는 눈을 감을 수도 있고, 귀를 막을 수도 있고, 만지거나 맛보는 것을 피할 수도 있다. 하지만 우리는 끊임없이 숨 쉴 때마다 냄새를 맡는다. 그러나 냄새는 매우 이해하기 어려운 현상으로, 무언의 감각, 형언할 말이 존재하지 '않는' 감각으로 간주된다. 냄새는 우리를 감싸고, 우리의 몸으로 들어가고, 우리에게서 내뿜어진다. 그러나 우리가 냄새를 묘사하려고 할 때, 후각적 형용어구들은 정확한 묘사를 제공하지 못한다. 예를 들어, 밀러(Miller)는 다음과 같이 지적한다. "냄새 어휘는 매우 제한적이고, 보통 냄새를 풍기는 그 사물을 형용사로 만들어야만 한다. 똥은 똥 같은 냄새가 나고, 장미꽃은 장미꽃 같은 냄새가 난다 … 물렁물렁한, 질벅질벅한, 끈적끈적한 … 눅눅한 그리고 축축한처럼 우리가 풍성하게 구별할 수 있는 촉감과 달리, 냄새에는 특별히 전유되는 질적 표현법이 없다." 심멜(Simmel)도 비슷한 의견이다. "냄새는 시각과 청각처럼 스스로 어떤 대상을 형성하는 것이 아니라, 말 그대로 인간 주체 속에 붙들려 있는데, 이는 미세한 구별을 할 수 있는 독립적이고 객관적인 특징적 표현이 존재하지 않는다는 점 속에 상징적으로 드러난다. 만약 우리가 '시큼한 냄새가 난다'라고 말한다면, 이것은 단지 시큼한 맛이 나는 어떤 사물이 냄새나는 것처럼 냄새가 난다는 것을 의미할 뿐이다." 즉, 냄새는 종종 그 원인이나 결과, 또는 풍미에 근거해 설명된다.

B 더욱이 다른 감각에 대해서는 존재하는 것과는 달리, 후각에 대해서는 과학적인 분류체계조차 없다. 우리의 미각은 단맛, 신맛, 짠맛, 쓴맛의 네 가지 패러다임에 의해 좌우된다. 빛과 파장의 변화는 시각을 확인시켜 준다. 소리는 다양한 진동에 의해 결정되며, 촉각은 압력, 통증 역치 및 기타 다양한 요인에 의해 결정된다. 그러나 후각에 대한 합의는 없다. 냄새 분류 수치에 대한 공감대도 없다. <후각의 부재를 표기하는 측면에서 볼 때도, 다른 감각에 비해 후각에 대해서는 합당한 용어가 부족하다.> 애커먼(Ackerman)이 지적하듯이, "청각이 없는 자는 '귀가 먹은', 시력이 없는 자는 '장님의', 말이 없는 자는 '벙어리의'라는 꼬리표가 붙지만, 냄새 없는 자에 대한 어휘는 무엇인가?" 그녀는 냄새 없는 것에 대해 과학자들이 부르는 '후각 상실'이라는 단어를 소개한다. 이 단어는 "없다"와 "냄새"를 의미하는 라틴어/그리스어의 간단한 조합이다. 그러나 우리들 중 얼마나 많은 이들이 이 용어에 대해 익숙할까?

C 냄새가 우리의 일상생활 경험에서 구별되기는 하였어도 포착하기 어려운 요소였으므로, 사회학자들은 후각에 대해 거의 연구하지 않았다. 아마도 그러한 태만은 신노트(Synnott)와 밀러(Miller)가 주장하는 것처럼 감각 위계에서 후각의 지위가 낮은 탓일 것이다. 예를 들어, 신노트는 후각의 지위가 낮은 것은 후각과 관련된 전문 어휘가 부족한 것에서 잘 드러난다고 주장한다. 앞서 논의한 바와 같이 냄새는 단맛이나 신맛(미각), 강함이나 약함(촉각)의 다른 감각의 단계적 차이를 통해 정의되는 경우가 많다. 신노트는 독립적인 어휘가 없이는 그 주제를 끄집어내기가 어렵다는 것을 인정한다. 냄새와 관련된 내용을 생산하는 일과 관련된 요점은 냄새는 독립적인 실체라기보다는 "문화적으로 새겨진 맥락"을 통해 그 의미가 이해되어야 하는 "고도로 맥락적인 개념"이라는 사실을 관찰하는 데 있다.

gamut n. 범위
gustatory a. 미각의
eschew v. 피하다
sans prep. ~이 없는
emanate v. 발산하다, 뿜다
epithet n. 형용어구
excrement n. 배설물
tactile a. 촉각의
squishy a. 물렁물렁한
oozy a. 질벅질벅한
gooey a. 끈적거리는
threshold n. 한계점, 역치
anosmia n. 후각 상실

01 ▶ 주어진 문장은 '후각의 부재를 표기하는 어휘가 부족하다'는 내용인데, "청각이 없는 자는 '귀가 먹은', 시력이 없는 자는 '장님의', 말이 없는 자는 '벙어리의'라는 꼬리표가 붙지만, 냄새 없는 자에 대한 어휘는 무엇인가?"는 진술이 뒤따라오는 [Ⅲ]에 들어가기에 가장 적절한 내용이다.

02 ▶ '감각 위계에서 후각의 지위가 낮다'고 하였으므로 "후각은 시각, 청각, 촉각과 같은 다른 감각에 비해 중요도 계층에서 상대적으로 중요한 것으로 여겨진다."라고 한 (D)는 잘못된 진술이다.

03 ▶ broach v. (주제를) 꺼내다(= moot)

》 정답 01 (C) 02 (D) 03 (E)

죽은 사람에 대한 유전적 사실을 결정할 때 직면하게 되는 윤리적 문제를 부각시키는 역사적으로 흥미로운 사례 중 하나에는 에이브러햄 링컨이 그 중심에 있다. 의학 유전학자들과 마르판 증후군 환자들을 옹호하는 사람들은 오래전부터 링컨 대통령이 이 특별한 유전병을 가지고 있는지 궁금해 했다. 어쨌든 링컨의 비쩍 마르고 키 큰 체격은 종종 마르판 증후군과 관련되는데, 이 질환은 신체의 결합조직과 연골에 영향을 미친다. 많은 사람들이 우리의 가장 위대한 대통령이라고 여기는 이 남자에 대한 전기 작가들과 연구자들은 링컨이 평생 겪었던 우울증이 마르판 증후군의 고통스러운 관절염 비슷한 증상과 관련이 있었는지 알고 싶어 한다.

링컨은 1865년 4월 14일에 암살당했고 다음날 아침 일찍 사망했다. 부검이 실시되었고, 그의 머리카락, 뼈, 혈액 샘플은 국립 보건의학 박물관에 보존되어 보관되었다. 그것들은 여전히 그곳에 있다. 최근에 발견된 유전자 표지의 존재는 어떤 이가 마르판 증후군을 가지고 있는지 여부를 알려준다. 이러한 발전으로, 에이브 링컨의 보관된 유골 중 일부를 이용해서 그가 이 질환을 가지고 있는지 확인할 수 있을 것이다. 하지만, 이 검사를 수행하는 것이 윤리적일까? 그리고, 허가 없이 검사해서는 안 된다면, 문제의 사람이 사망한 경우에 어떻게 허가를 얻을 수 있을까? 어니스트 에이브의 경우 "환자"가 사망해 직계 유족이 없어 동의할 사람이 없다. 그러나 동의 없이 검사를 허용하는 것은 위험한 선례를 남긴다.

고인에게 프라이버시와 동의의 개념을 적용하는 것은 좀 이상하게 보일 수도 있다. 그러나 오늘날 대부분의 사람들이 이러한 검사가 시행되기 전에 동의를 얻어야 한다는 데 의견이 같다는 점을 고려하면, 단지 그렇게 해서는 안 된다고 말해줄 링컨과 그의 후손들이 주위에 없다는 이유로 인해, 링컨의 DNA를 캐낼 권리가 연구자들에게 있는 것일까? 어떤 사람의 생물학적 구성에 관한 흥미로운 사실을 우리에게 말해줄 수 있는 어떤 유전자 검사가 가능할 때마다 언제든지 그 사람의 신체는 검사해도 된다고 말할 수 있을까? 과거의 많은 저명한 사람들은 그들의 일기, 논문, 편지에 대한 접근을 제한하기 위해 특별한 사전조치를 취했다. 예를 들어, 지그문트 프로이트는 100년 동안 그의 개인 기록을 봉인하였다. 미래의 링컨과 프로이트 같은 저명한 인사들은 원치 않는 유전적 염탐을 다음 세대가 하는 것을 막기 위해 그들의 유해에 대한 접근을 영원히 금지해야 할까?

그리고, 요점을 말하자면, 링컨이 마르판 증후군을 가지고 있었는지를 규명하는 것은 무슨 의미가 있는가? 결국, 우리는 그가 대통령감이었는지 아닌지를 판단하기 위해 그의 유전자를 검사할 필요는 없다. 마르판 증후군을 앓았건, 아니건 간에 그는 분명히 대통령감이었다. 그가 대통령으로서 무엇을 했고 무엇을 믿었는지를 우리가 제대로 이해하고 있는가? 그의 행동은 우리나라를 어떻게 만들었고, 그의 행동들로부터 오늘날 우리에게 도움이 될 만한 무엇을 배울 수 있을까? 하는 것들이 우리가 진짜 던져야 할 질문들이다. 결국 링컨의 행동 및 리더십에 대한 유전적 근거는 아무런 관련성이 없는 것으로 비추어질 수도 있다. 어떤 사람들은 유전자 검사가 링컨의 활동, 글, 생각, 행동으로부터 우리의 관심을 다른 곳으로 돌리게 하고 그를 DNA의 산물들이 뒤섞인 잡동사니쯤으로 보게끔 할 것이라고 말한다. 아마도 링컨의 DNA를 재구성하고 분석하는 것보다 그의 활동을 통해 링컨의 유산을 이해하고 올바르게 인식하는 노력을 장려하는 것이 더 이치에 맞는 것 같다.

gangly a. 키가 크고 여윈, 흐느적거리는
cartilage n. 연골
arthritis n. 관절염
assassinate v. 암살하다
autopsy n. 부검, 시체 해부
precedent n. 선례
pry into ~을 캐내다
precaution n. 주의
embargo v. 금지시키다
mortal remains 시체, 유해
inspect v. 검사하다
divert v. (딴 데로) 돌리다
jumble n. 뒤죽박죽 뒤섞인 것
legacy n. 유산

01 ▶ 필자는 링컨의 유해에 대해 유전자 검사를 하자는 일부 유전학자들의 주장에 대해 회의적이며, 링컨의 유전자를 조사하는 것은 큰 의미가 없다고 보고 있다.

02 ▶ snoop은 '염탐하다'는 의미이므로 '훔쳐보다'는 의미를 가지는 peep, peek 등이 동의어에 해당한다. sneeze는 '재채기하다'는 의미이다.

03 ▶ ①에는 문맥상 과거사실에 대한 추측을 표현하면서 주어가 the depression이므로 수동태가 되는 것이 적절하다. ②에는 문맥상 '~의 여지가 있다', '~을 순순히 받아들이다'는 의미가 들어가는 것이 적절하다. be open to에서 to는 전치사로서 다음에 명사에 해당하는 어구가 와야 한다.

04 ▶ '100년 동안 그의 개인 기록을 봉인하였다', '원치 않는 유전적 염탐', '유해에 대한 접근 금지' 등의 진술을 고려할 때 저명한 인사들은 '그들의 연구물에 대한 접근을 제한하려 하였다'는 것을 알 수 있다.

》 **정답**   01 (C)   02 (D)   03 (B)   04 (D)

철학자들은 오래전부터 동물에 대한 우리의 인식의 모순을 지적해 왔지만, 인간과 동물의 관계에 대한 체계적인 고려가 정말로 융성하며 공공영역에 들어오기 시작한 것은 최근 수십 년 동안이다. 인간과 동물과의 관계는 "종(種) 차별주의"라고 불리는데, 이 용어는 1970년대에 도입되고 대중화되었으며, 인종차별이나 성차별과 같이 다른 부당한 차별들과 나란히 비치도록 하기 위한 특별한 의도가 있는 용어이다. 종 차별주의는 철학 문헌에서 어떤 개체가 속한 종의 자격만을 근거로 서로 다른 고유한 도덕적 지위를 할당하는 것을 말한다.

종 차별주의의 정의와 바로 그 이름에 내포되어 있듯이 종 차별주의는 기술적 의미와 규범적 의미 모두에서 이해될 수 있다. 기술적으로 종 차별주의는 사람들이 어떻게 행동하는지 설명하는 개념이다. 즉, 속한 종의 자격에 기초하여 개체에게 도덕적 가치를 할당하므로, 어떤 사람이 종 차별적 태도를 가졌는지 정확하게 기술될 수 있다. 규범적으로, 종 차별주의에 대한 많은 연구는 사람들이 인종(인종차별주의)이나 성별(성차별주의)에 의해서만 사람들을 다르게 대우하는 것과 유사하게, 오로지 속한 종의 자격에만 근거하여 개체에게 다른 도덕적 가치를 부여해서는 안 된다는 주장에 뿌리를 두고 있다.

종 차별주의는 인간이 본질적으로 다른 종의 개체들보다 더 가치 있다는 거의 보편적인 믿음에서 나타난다. 돼지와 개처럼 정신적, 정서적 역량이 비슷한 종에 대한 차별적 처우가 도덕적으로 정당하다는 믿음에서도 종 차별주의는 드러난다. 이러한 종 차별주의의 발현들은 어디서나 볼 수 있으며, 식량을 위한 동물의 대량 공장형 사육, 서커스에서 인간 오락을 위한 동물의 이용, 동물을 재산으로 간주하고 신체 완전성 권리와 같은 기본적인 권리들을 동물들에게서 부정하는 법적 제도 등을 뒷받침하고 있다. 예를 들어, 개와 돼지는 비슷한 정신적, 정서적 능력을 가지고 있음에도 불구하고, 우리는 개들은 특별한 도덕적 지위를 가진 것처럼 취급하는 반면, 돼지들은 공장에서 사육해서 잡아먹는다. 비록 규범적으로는 어떤 잘못된 것이 있다는 것을 부인할지라도, 이러한 종 차별주의의 발현들은 기술적으로 볼 때 모든 사람들에게 친숙하다. 인종차별주의나 성차별주의와 마찬가지로 종 차별주의는 역사와 문화 전반에 걸쳐 관찰된다.

모든 사회에서 민족적 편견이 관찰되지만 지역 전통과 역사에 따라 다양한 집단들에 대해 그러한 편견이 가해지는 것처럼, 종 차별주의는 문화 전반에 걸쳐 뚜렷하게 나타나지만, 세계적으로 다르게 표현된다. 개와 고양이를 생각해보자. 중국에서 그들은 먹거리로 여겨지고 돼지 같은 다른 동물들과 비슷하지만, 서구 사회에서는 그들이 '가족의 일원'으로 간주되고, 따라서 돼지보다 훨씬 높은 지위를 가진다. 또는 소를 생각해보자. 많은 서구 국가들의 저녁식사에서 일상적인 음식이지만 힌두교 사회에서는 신성한 동물로서, 먹히는 것은 금지되고 숭배를 받는다. 이처럼 문화적으로 결정된 종 차별주의의 발현들은 문화뿐만 아니라 시대를 걸쳐 일어나기도 한다. 말은 수세기 동안 서구 국가에서 일상적으로 소비되었지만, 지금은 말고기 소비가 상당히 감소하고 말의 도덕적 지위가 높아졌다.

speciesism n. 종 차별; 종 차별주의
parallel a. 평행한, 유사한
assignment n. 배정
implicit a. 암시된, 내포된
normative a. 규범적인
analogy n. 비유; 유사
manifest v. 나타내다
ubiquitous a. 어디에나 있는
underpin v. ~을 뒷받침하다
bodily integrity 신체 완전성
fare n. 식사, 음식

01 ▶ 이 글은 종 차별주의의 정의를 소개하고, 그것이 인류의 역사와 문화 속에 인종차별주의, 성차별주의만큼 뿌리 깊게 내재해 있다는 것을 말하고 있다.

02 ▶ 문맥상 cows를 수식하는 어구이므로 '먹는' 주체가 아닌 대상이다. 따라서 eating이 아니라 being eaten의 수동적 표현이 와야 한다. 그리고 forbid는 '목적어+to부정사' 구문을 취하는 5형식 동사이므로 (e)는 forbidden to be eaten and revered as sacred animals가 되어야 한다.

03 ▶ 종 차별주의에 대한 기술적 이해는 '종 차별과 관련해 사람들이 어떻게 행동하는지 설명하는 것'이다. (C)에서 설명하고 있는 것은 종 차별에 대한 '규범적 이해'에 해당한다.

》 정답   01 (D)   02 (E)   03 (C)

다수에게는 기본 기술을, 소수에게는 더 발전된 기술을 갖추게 한 뒤, 경제성장 지향 교육은, 처음부터 초등 교육을 통과하고 상대적으로 소수의 엘리트로 판명될 수 있는 사람들에게는 역사와 경제 사실에 대한 아주 기초적인 지식을 갖추도록 할 필요가 있다. 그러나 역사적, 경제적 서사가 계층, 인종과 성별에 대한, 외국인 투자가 농촌 빈민들에게 정말로 좋은지에 대한, 기본적인 삶의 기회의 큰 불평등이 존재할 때 민주주의가 존속할 수 있는지에 대한, 진지한 비판적 사고로 이어지지 않도록 주의해야 한다. 그래서 비판적 사고는 경제성장 지향 교육에 있어서 그다지 중요한 부분이 아닐 것이며, 기술적 정교함을 유순함 및 집단사고와 결합한 것으로 유명한 인도 서부 구자라트주와 같이 이 목표를 집요하게 추구해 온 국가들에서는 존재한 적이 없었다. 외국인 투자와 기술개발을 목표로 하는 엘리트들의 계획을 수행하기 위해 기술적으로 훈련된 순종적인 노동자들의 집단을 필요로 한다면, 학생 정신의 자유는 위험하다. 오랫동안 구자라트의 공립학교들에서 그랬던 것처럼 비판적 사고는 좌절당할 것이다.

역사 학습은 거의 필수적인 것이라고 나는 말했다. 그러나 경제성장 지향 교육자들은 계급, 카스트제도, 성별, 그리고 민족-종교적 소속의 불의에 초점을 맞추는 역사 학습을 원하지 않을 것이다. 왜냐하면 이것은 현재에 대한 비판적 사고를 촉발할 것이기 때문이다. 또한 그러한 교육자들은 민족주의의 발흥, 민족주의적 이상에 의한 피해, 기술적 숙달이 지배할 때 너무나 자주 무뎌지는 도덕적 상상력의 방식 등에 대한 진지한 사고를 원하지 않을 것이다. 이 모든 주제들은 라빈드라나트 타고르(Rabindranath Tagore)의 민족주의에 대한 통렬한 비관론과 함께 제기되었으며, 제1차 세계대전 동안 행해진 그의 강연들 속에서 전달된 주제였지만, 노벨상 수상자로서의 보편적 명성에도 불구하고 그의 이러한 비판은 오늘날 인도에서 무시되고 있다. 그렇게 제시되는 역사의 버전은 국가적 야망, 특히 부에 대한 야망을 위대한 선으로 제시하고 빈곤과 세계적 책임의 문제를 경시할 것이다. 다시 한번 말하지만, 이런 종류의 교육의 실제 예는 찾기 쉽다.

이러한 역사 접근법의 두드러진 예는 인도의 힌두 민족주의 정당인 BJP가 만든 교과서에서 찾아볼 수 있는데, BJP는 또한 경제성장 기반 개발 의제를 공격적으로 추구하고 있다. 이 책들은 (다행히, 2004년 BJP가 권력을 잃은 이후 지금은 철회되었다) 비판적 사고를 완전히 좌절시켰고, 함께 연구할 자료조차 주지 않았다. 그들은 모든 문제는 외부인과 내부의 '외국적 요소'에 의해 야기되었을 뿐이라며, 인도의 역사에 대해 물질적이고 문화적인 승리에 대한 무비판적인 이야기만 제시했다. 인도의 과거 불의에 대한 비판은 자료의 내용으로 보나, 제시된 교육학(예를 들어 각 장 끝마다 제시된 질문들)으로 보나 사실상 불가능하였는데 이는 진지한 질문을 좌절시키고 동화 및 역류만을 촉구했다. 학생들은 단지 카스트, 성별, 종교의 모든 불평등을 무시하여 오점 하나 없는 지선(至善)의 이야기만 받아들이도록 요구받았다.

rudimentary a. 가장 기초적인
narrative n. 서술, 서사
docility n. 유순
prompt v. 촉발하다
numb v. 마비시키다
under the sway of ~의 지배하에
scathing a. 통렬한
downplay v. 경시하다
salient a. 두드러진
agenda n. 의제
pedagogy n. 교육학
regurgitation n. 역류
unblemished a. 오점 하나 없는

01 ▶ 이 글은 민주주의를 위해서는 비판적 의식을 함양할 수 있는 역사 교육이 반드시 필요하다는 주장을, 경제성장만을 지상 목표로 삼는 잘못된 교육 사례를 통해 부각하고 있다.

02 ▶ '노벨상 수상자로서의 보편적 명성에도 불구하고 그의 이러한 비판은 오늘날 인도에서 무시되고 있다'라고 하였으므로 (E)는 잘못된 진술이다.

03 ▶ 문맥상 '현재에 대한 비판적 사고'는 계급차별, 성차별, 민족-종교적 소속 차별 등 일체의 차별에 대해 문제의식을 갖고 이를 시정하려는 태도와 노력을 총칭한다.

▶ 정답 01 (C) 02 (E) 03 (D)

운동과 건강한 신체가 운동선수, 군인, 소방관, 그리고 고도의 육체활동을 요하는 직업에 종사하는 사람들 모두에게 필요한 것은 명백하다. 그렇다면 안락한 산업사회에서 앉아서 일하는 사람들이 운동을 해야 하는 이유는 무엇인가?

의료진들은 심각한 퇴화를 예방하기 위해 반드시 유지되어야 하는 최소 수준의 육체활동이 각자의 신진대사에 따라 모든 사람에게 존재한다는 사실을 밝혀냈다. 인체와 그 기관들은 살아있는 모든 생물체와 마찬가지로 사용되지 않으면 반드시 쇠약해진다. 부러진 팔을 깁스로 고정시켰을 때 구조와 기능을 상실하게 되는 것은 신체 기관이 운동으로 단련되거나 사용되지 않을 때 나타나는 결과를 명백히 보여준다.

과거에 사회 각층의 사람들은 기본적인 생존을 위해 막대한 육체에너지를 생산해야 했다. 현대의 기술로 인해 생활에 필요한 육체활동은 다양한 형태로 단순화되었다. 세탁기, 자동차, 정교한 산업설비 등 기계의 등장으로 인간에게 필요한 노동량은 줄어들었다. 원시시대에 대다수의 사람들은 섭취한 음식에서 얻은 칼로리를 매일 격렬하게 몸을 움직여서 소모했다. 이 사실은 대다수의 사람들, 특히 산업국가에 살기 때문에 힘든 노동을 하지 않는 사람들에게 더 이상 해당되지 않는다.

많은 사람들이 보유하고 있는 육체 노동력은 사라지지 않는다. 오랫동안 육체활동을 하지 않은 사람들도 한두 달만 매일 운동하면 상실된 체력을 회복할 수 있다. 운동을 해서 체력의 한계에 접근하는 사람들은 격일마다 격렬한 운동을 함으로써 체력을 유지할 수 있다.

건강한 신체와 운동은 체중조절뿐만 아니라 신체건강과 정신건강에도 중요하다. 운동은 강한 자아상과 정서의 안정감을 발전, 유지하는 데 도움이 된다. 30세 이후에 심장이 혈액을 밀어내는 힘은 매 10년 정도마다 약 8퍼센트의 비율로 감소하기 때문에 노령화의 과정을 겪는 우리에게 운동의 중요성은 커진다.

자전거 타기, 수영 등과 같은 가장 흔한 운동이 심한 부상을 일으키는 경우는 아주 드물다. 그러나 축구, 유도 등 신체의 접촉을 수반하는 스포츠는 관절을 마모시켜 관절질환, 즉 관절이상을 일으킨다. 운동을 처음 시작하는 사람들 대다수의 문제는 운동과다이다. 많은 사람들이 운동을 시작한 다음날 몸이 뻣뻣하게 굳어 있는 증상을 경험하지만 이 증상은 신체에 무해하고 오래 지속되지 않는다. 과체중이거나 중년이 지난 사람들 또는 심장질환을 앓고 있는 사람들은 운동을 시작하기 전에 의사와 상담해야 한다.

physical a. 육체의, 신체의
fitness n. 적합; 양호함, 건강함
sedentary a. 앉아 있는, 앉아서 일하는
metabolism n. 신진대사
deterioration n. 악화, 퇴보
organism n. 유기체
atrophy v. 위축하다, 쇠약해지다
immobilize v. 움직이지 못하게 하다
elaborate a. 정교한, 복잡한
consume v. 소비하다, 소모하다
vigorously ad. 정력적으로, 원기왕성하게
strenuous a. 정력적인; 격렬한
retain v. 유지하다, 보류하다
consult v. 상담하다, 의견을 묻다

01 ▶ '원시시대에 대다수의 사람들은 섭취한 음식의 칼로리를 매일 격렬하게 몸을 움직여서 소모했으나 이 사실은 대다수의 사람들, 특히 산업국가에 살기 때문에 힘든 노동을 하지 않는 사람들에게 더 이상 해당되지 않는다'고 돼 있다. 따라서 오늘날의 사람들은 대체로 매일 신체 에너지를 덜 소비한다고 말할 수 있다.

02 ▶ '오랫동안 육체활동을 하지 않은 사람들도 한두 달만 매일 운동하면 상실된 체력을 회복할 수 있다'고 했다.

03 ▶ '현대기술로 인해 생겨난 세탁기, 자동차 등이 인간의 해야 할 일들을 대신하여 노동량이 줄어들었다'고 돼 있다.

04 ▶ '건강한 신체와 운동은 체중조절뿐만 아니라 신체건강과 정신건강에도 중요하며, 운동은 강한 자아상과 정서의 안정감을 발전·유지하는데 도움이 된다'고 돼 있다.

05 ▶ 마지막 문장에서 운동으로 인해 발생하는 문제들을 언급하고 있으나, 그것 때문에 운동 자체를 비판하거나 금하고 있지는 않다. 따라서 운동으로 인해 발생하는 문제들보다 운동으로 인해 얻는 혜택이 더 많음을 알 수 있다.

》 **정답** 01 (A) 02 (C) 03 (B) 04 (B) 05 (A)

미국인이라면 동양에 관해 유럽인들과는 똑같이 느끼지는 않을 것이며, 아마도 그들에게 동양은 매우 다른 극동(주로 중국과 일본)이 연상될 것이다. 미국인과 달리, 프랑스인이나 영국인은 — 또 그들(프랑스인과 영국인) 정도는 아니라고 해도 독일인, 러시아인, 스페인인, 포르투갈인, 이탈리아인, 스위스인도 — 내가 이 책에서 오리엔탈리즘이라고 부르는 것의 오랜 전통을 가지고 있다. 이 오리엔탈리즘이란 서구 유럽인의 경험 속에 동양이 갖는 특별한 위치에 입각해서 동양을 받아들이는 방식을 말한다. 동양은 유럽에 단지 인접되어 있다는 것만이 아니라, 유럽의 식민지 중에서도 가장 광대하고 풍요롭고 오래된 식민지이자, 또 유럽이 갖고 있는 가장 심오하고 반복되어 나타나는 타자(他者)의 이미지(images of the Other)이기도 했다.

게다가, 동양은 유럽(곧 서양)을 대조가 되는 이미지, 관념, 성격, 경험으로 정의하는 데 도움을 주었다. 그러나 이러한 동양의 어떤 것도 그저 상상의 것만은 아니다. 동양은 유럽 물질문명과 문화의 불가결한 부분이다. 오리엔탈리즘은 그 부분을 문화적으로 그리고 심지어는 이데올로기적으로 하나의 담론 방식으로 표현하고 나타내는데, 그러한 담론 방식은 제도, 낱말, 학문, 이미지, 학설, 나아가 식민지의 관료제도나 식민지적 스타일로써 구성된다. 이와 대조적으로, 비록 일본, 한국 및 인도차이나에서 미국인들이 행한 전후의 군사적 행동으로 인하여 어느 정도는 냉정하고 현실적인 '동양' 인식이 생겼다고 할 수 있지만, 미국의 동양 인식이란 유럽의 그것보다는 훨씬 단순하게 보일 것이다. 더구나, 근동(중동)에서 광범위하게 확대된 미국의 정치적, 경제적 역할은 근동에 대한 이해의 확대를 요구하고 있다.

내가 오리엔탈리즘이라는 말에 부여하는 여러 가지 의미는, 내 생각으로는, 그것들 모두는 상호의존 관계에 있는데, 이것은 독자들에게 분명하게 인식될 것이며 그리고 (뒤에 이어질 지면에서 더욱 명확하게 될 것이다). 오리엔탈리즘이 가진 여러 가지 의미 가운데 가장 널리 인정되고 있는 것은 학문적인 것이다. 그리고 사실상 오리엔탈리즘이라고 하는 꼬리표는 여전히 다수의 연구기관에서 쓰이고 있다. 동양에 대해 강의하거나 집필하거나 연구하는 사람은 — 이것은 그가 인류학자이든, 사회학자이든, 역사학자이든 또는 문헌학자이든 간에 적용된다. — 구체적인 분야이든, 일반적인 분야든 오리엔탈리스트이며, 그리고 오리엔탈리스트가 하는 일이 바로 오리엔탈리즘이다. 오늘날의 전문가들은 '오리엔탈리즘'이란 말보다는 동양연구나 동양지역연구라는 말을 더욱 많이 선호하는 것이 사실이다. 그것은 오리엔탈리즘이라는 말이 너무나도 애매하고 일반적인 것이기 때문이며, 그리고 19세기부터 20세기 초까지 유럽식민지주의 위압적인 통치자들의 태도를 암시하는 것이기 때문이다. 그럼에도 불구하고, 동양에 초점을 맞추고, 겉이 새롭든, 낡은 것이든 오리엔탈리스트를 주권위자로 해서, 책이 쓰여지고 학회가 개최되어 왔다. 요컨대 오리엔탈리즘은 과거처럼 존속하고 있다고까지는 말할 수 없어도, 여전히 학문으로 살아있다고 볼 수 있다.

be associated with ~와 관련되다; ~이 연상되다
come to terms with ~와 타협하다, 타협이 이루어지다
adjacent a. 인접한, 부근의
recur v. 재발하다, 회귀하다, 되풀이하다
integral a. 없어서는 안 될, 절대 필요한
discourse n. 강연, 설교
doctrine n. 교의, 교리
bureaucracy n. 관료주의, 관료식의 절차
sober a. 냉정한, 감정적이 아닌
designation n. 지시, 지정; 지명
anthropologist n. 인류학자
philologist n. 언어학자, 문헌학자
specific a. 특수한, 독특한; 특정한
aspect n. 양상; 국면
vague a. 막연한, 애매한
connote v. 암시하다, 내포하다
guise n. 외관

01 ▶ 오리엔탈리즘이란 말이 학문적으로는 쓰이고 있지만, 오리엔탈리즘은 식민지적 관료제도나 식민지적 스타일로 구성된다고 했으며, 오늘날 전문가들은 '오리엔탈리즘'이란 말보다 동양 연구나 동양지역 연구란 말을 더욱 많이 선호하는 것이 사실이라고 했다. 따라서 (B)가 정답이다.

02 ▶ 미국의 동양 인식은 유럽의 것과 비교해서 단순하다고 언급돼 있다.

03 ▶ (가)의 빈칸에는 call의 목적어가 들어가야 하며, call은 여기서 5형식으로 쓰여서 Orientalism이란 단어를 보어로 받았다. 따라서 (가)에는 선행사를 수반하며 목적어 역할을 할 수 있는 관계대명사 what이 들어가야 한다. (나)의 빈칸에는 '오리엔탈리즘을 통해' 다음과 같은 것을 의미한다는 말이 되어야 하므로 by가 적절하다. 따라서 (A)가 정답이다.

04 ▶ 두 번째 단락의 끝 부분을 참고할 것

05 ▶ philologist는 언어학자나 문헌학자를 의미한다.

》 정답 01 (B) 02 (D) 03 (A) 04 (B) 05 (A)

체계적인 인간사고(思考)의 역사는 다음과 같은 두 가지 범주 중의 하나로 질문들이 나뉘는 방식으로 인간사에서 일어나는 모든 질문을 명확히 나타내려는 지속된 노력이다. 즉, 경험적인 질문, 다시 말해, 해답이 결국에는 관찰의 자료에 의존하는 질문과 그리고 형식적인 질문, 다시 말해, 해답이 사실적인 지식에 구애받지 않고 순수한 계산에만 의존하는 질문을 말한다.

그러나 이 두 가지 범주에 쉽게 들어맞지 않는 질문들이 일부 있다. "오카피는 무엇입니까?"라는 질문은 경험적인 관찰행위로 아주 쉽게 답할 수 있다. 마찬가지로, "729의 세제곱근은 무엇입니까?"라는 질문은 용인된 규칙에 따라 한 번의 계산으로 해결된다. 그러나 만일 내가 "수(數)란 무엇입니까?", "지상에서 인생의 목적은 무엇입니까?", "당신은 모든 사람이 형제라고 확신합니까?"라고 묻는다면 어떻게 이런 질문에 대한 답을 찾을까?

이러한 모든 질문에는 수나, 형제애, 혹은 인생의 목적에 관한 질문만큼이나 아주 동떨어진 이상한 것이 존재하는 것 같다. 그 질문들은, 질문 그 자체가 질문에 대한 답변을 찾을 수 있는 방식에 대한 암시를 갖고 있지 않다는 점에서, 다른 범주에 있는 질문과는 다르다. 보다 일반적인 다른 질문들은, 이러한 암시, 즉 질문에 대한 답변을 찾을 수 있는 고유의 기술을 갖고 있다. 수(數) 등에 관한 질문은 질문하는 사람을 매우 당황하게 하고 실용적인 사람을 화나게 한다. 그 이유는 그러한 질문들이 분명한 해답이나 유용한 지식이 되지 못하는 것이기 때문이다.

이것은 원래의 두 개 범주, 경험적인 범주와 형식적인 범주 사이에, 다른 두 가지 범위에 들어맞지 않는 그러한 모든 질문들이 살아있는, 중간의 범주가 있다는 것을 보여준다. 이러한 질문들은 아주 다양하다. 일부는 사실의 질문으로 보이고, 또 일부는 가치의 문제로 보인다. 일부는 단어에 관한 질문이고, 또 일부는 일상적인 생활에서 과학자, 예술가, 비평가, 일반사람이 추구하는 방식에 관한 질문이다. 또 다른 것들은 지식의 다양한 영역사이의 관계에 대한 것이다. 일부는 사고(思考)의 가정을 다루고, 또 일부는 도덕적 혹은 사회적, 혹은 정치적 행위의 정확한 목적을 다룬다.

이러한 모든 질문들이 갖고 있는 것으로 보이는 유일한 공통의 특징은, 이러한 질문들이 관찰이나 계산 혹은 귀납적 방법이나 연역적 방법으로 풀 수 없고 그래서 이것의 결정적인 결과로 생기는 일은 그러한 질문을 하는 사람은 애초부터 당황하게 된다는 것이다. ― 그들은 그 해답을 어디에서 찾아야 할지를 알지 못한다. 이러한 문제에 대해 의심할 바 없는 권위나 지식을 갖고 있다고 자신 있게 언급할 수 있는 사전, 백과사전, 지식의 해설 같은 것도 없고, 전문가나 정설도 없다. 이러한 질문은 철학적이라고 불리는 경향이 있다.

---

sustained a. 지속된
formulate v. ~을 공식화하다, 공식으로 나타내다
empirical a. 경험의, 경험적인
calculation n. 계산; 추정
untrammeled a. 방해[구속] 받지 않은; 자유로운
factual a. 사실의, 사실에 입각한
queer a. 이상한, 이상야릇한
built-in a. 고유한, 붙박이의, 본래 갖추어진
reduce v. (어떤 상태로) 떨어뜨리다, 몰아넣다
perplexity n. 당혹; 난처한 일
crollary n. 필연적인 결과, 직접적인 결과
encyclopedia n. 백과사전

01 ▶ 'reduce+목적어+전치사+명사'는 '~을 …하게 하다'는 의미로 질문하는 사람을 당황하게 했다는 뜻이다. 따라서 perplexity와 비슷한 의미의 단어 puzzled가 포함된 (D)가 적절하다.
02 ▶ 마지막 단락에서 전문가도 철학적인 문제를 해결할 수 없다고 언급되어 있다.
03 ▶ 이 글은 철학의 주제 문제를 다루고 있다.
04 ▶ 빈칸 바로 다음에 '다양한' 예가 나와 있음에 유의한다.
05 ▶ Ordinary questions는 암시(pointer)를 갖고 있다.

▶ 정답 01 (D) 02 (E) 03 (A) 04 (B) 05 (E)

www.kimyoung.co.kr

해독제 Vol.1 초·중급 난이도 300개 독해지문 수록
해독제 Vol.2 중·고급 난이도 300개 독해지문 수록

정가 30,000원

ISBN 978-89-6512-153-4